T0330666

# BUSINESS IN THE AGE OF DEPRESSION AND WAR

Companion volume:

# CAPITAL, ENTREPRENEURS AND PROFITS

edited by R.P.T. Davenport-Hines

## CONTENTS

# BUSINESS IN THE AGE OF DEPRESSION AND WAR

*Edited by*
R.P.T. DAVENPORT-HINES
(With an Introduction by Theo Barker)

FRANK CASS

*First published 1990 in Great Britain by*
FRANK CASS AND COMPANY LIMITED
Gainsborough House, 11 Gainsborough Road,
London E11 1RS, England

*and in the United States of America by*
FRANK CASS
c/o Rowman & Littlefield Publishers Inc.
8705 Bollman Place, Savage, MD 20763

British Library Cataloguing in Publication Data

Business in the age of depression and war.
1. Business enterprise, history
I. Davenport-Hines, R.P.T. (Richard Peter Treadwell),
*1953*– II. Business history
338.6'09

ISBN 0-7146-3387-9


Library of Congress Cataloging-in-Publication Data

Business in the age of depression and war / edited by R.P.T. Davenport-
Hines; with an introduction by Theo Barker.
p.    cm.
Essays published in the first 30 years of the journal, Business
history.
ISBN 0-7146-3387-9
1. Great Britain—Industries—History—20th century.  2. Business—
History—20th century.  I. Davenport-Hines, R.P.T. (Richard
Peter Treadwell), 1953–
HC256.B87  1990
338.0941'09'04—dc20                                          90-1302
                                                              CIP

Printed and bound in Great Britain by
BPCC Wheatons Ltd, Exeter

# CONTENTS

# FRANCIS HYDE, HARVARD, LIVERPOOL AND THE FIRST 30 YEARS OF BUSINESS HISTORY

## By THEO BARKER

The scholarly writing of business history in Britain can be traced back at least to Professor George Unwin's *Samuel Oldknow and the Arkwrights*, published by Manchester University Press in 1924. The subject in its modern form in this country, however, really dates from 1954 and the appearance of Charles Wilson's first two most impressive volumes on Unilever, the Anglo-Dutch giant which then already controlled more than 500 companies world-wide. Although this was a commissioned work, it was written with 'full and free investigation of all the material which the author might consider relevant'.[1] This included much business correspondence, including William Lever's 30,000 files each containing up to 100 letters. These Unilever volumes did not hesitate to pass judgements, by no means favourable, on the sponsoring company. They raised to a higher plane the writing of company history which had previously consisted mainly of short, superficial public relations exercises, often hastily assembled at the last minute for an anniversary by people untrained in historical writing. *Unilever*, on the other hand, was a public relations exercise in the best sense of the term. The volumes carried conviction, were widely reviewed and sold (it is said) 10,000 copies. They certainly brought great credit to their promoters. Other leading businesses started to follow suit.

The later 1950s were a good time for the launching of a British journal to cater for this growing interest in the subject. It was hoped that business men would be among the subscribers as well as supporters of the Business Archives Council, a body started in 1934 as the result of the earlier initiative of Eileen Power, Professor of Economic History at the London School of Economics, supported by William Beveridge, then the School's Director. (The original idea had been to alert London businesses to the importance of preserving their older records; but the geographical scope was widened and the influential support obtained of the Master of the Rolls, a former (and future) Prime Minister (Stanley Baldwin), business men and other academics.)[2] The increasing numbers of young economic historians who were now becoming interested in this branch of the subject were also among the potential readers of the new journal.

Francis E. Hyde, Chaddock Professor of Economics at Liverpool, saw the opportunity and seized it. He himself had, with the assistance of J.R. Harris (then just embarking upon an academic career but in due course to become Professor of Economic History at Birmingham) published *Blue Funnel: A History of Alfred Holt and Company from 1865 to 1914* (Liverpool University Press, 1956), the first of a distinguished series of histories about Liverpool shipping companies to be written by members of his Department at Liverpool. The authors of the later volumes, Dr Peter Davies and Dr Sheila Marriner, as well as Professor Hyde himself, together with J.R. Harris and S.B. Saul (later to move to the Chair of Economic History in Edinburgh and, later still, to become Vice-Chancellor of York University) were to form the editorial backing for the new journal.

Francis Hyde had already learned during the early 1930s much about the complexitites of business history and the difficulty in defining it. By training an historian, he had already come under the influence of G.S. Veitch, Professor of History at Liverpool. Veitch was an old friend of the Hyde family even before Francis had gone to Liverpool in the mid-1920s to take a degree course in the subject. Veitch impressed upon him that the economic aspects were those upon which he should specialise for there lay the most promising future. After obtaining a First in 1929, he was awarded a Gladstone Memorial Fellowship. Veitch recommended a spell at Oxford for seminars with Lipson (whom he found frightening because of Lipson's sarcastic manner) and the acquaintance of Clapham at Cambridge (whose 'unsmiling face' and 'mouth's straight line, turned down at the corners'[3] were to remain the most abiding memory) before doing doctoral research with H.L. Beales at the London School of Economics. It was Clapham who, having strongly recommended Herbert Feis's *Europe, the World's Banker* which had just appeared, in 1930, suggested a detailed investigation of European investment in the United States, particularly in railways, when Dr Hyde, having been awarded a three-year Commonwealth Fellowship, went there to do further research from 1931 to 1933. Harvard was the obvious place for this, for the first Chair of Economic History in the English-speaking world had been created there and an impressive tradition in the subject already built up. Edwin F. Gay, who already enjoyed a world reputation, was in charge.

Gay, a native American of long-established English stock, had been trained as an economic historian largely in Europe, and particularly in Germany, where he had been a graduate student at various universities. He had also studied on his own from 1890 to 1902. Although originally hired by Harvard as Instructor in Economic History in the latter year (at the age of 35), he was appointed the first Dean of the Graduate School of Business Administration in 1908. This was a strange choice, for the new creation required a knowledge of twentieth-century business and some fund-raising ability, neither of which he possessed; but he surrounded himself with influential business men and, as an able workaholic, he was soon in great demand outside the university as well as within, especially during and immediately after the war when he left Harvard altogether.[4] He made valuable new contacts and, soon after his return, in 1924, a donation of 50,000 books and 20,000 pamphlets from a single benefactor enabled a few of his friends to form the Business Historical Society Inc. 'to encourage and aid the study of business in all periods and in all countries'.[5] With Gay among the founders were Herbert Hoover, then Secretary of Commerce, Gordon Selfridge, the American-born London department store owner, and Thomas Lamont of J.P. Morgan, a particularly close supporter whose ailing *New York Evening Post* Gay had edited between 1919 and 1924.[6] The new Society began to collect more historical material and to issue a *Bulletin* (the forerunner of the *Business History Review*) in June 1926. It was soon housed in new quarters at the Baker Library and claimed support from 'business men all over the country and representatives of 30 different colleges'.[7] In 1927 N.S.B. Gras, not a founder member, was brought from the University of Minnesota as Professor of Business History.

When Francis Hyde arrived at Harvard in 1931 he found himself at the very world heart of business history. He was also pitchforked into a debate between Gay and Gras about the nature of the subject. As he later recalled:

> Gay was a very, very powerful man at Harvard at that time and he did control the teaching of economic history in a very authoritarian way ... he had a very German approach to the teaching of economic history. He had spent a great deal of his early life in Germany and had been influenced very largely by German historians and German philosophers, and he brought to the teaching of economic history a great many of the principles of economics which Germans had for long incorporated into their idea of history ... Gras at that time was in a very difficult position because he had to obtain money to build up his business history school, and he found that the only way of doing this was to obtain large grants of cash from firms in return for writing up their histories. Gay, who was a very honest man in the purest sense of the term, believed this to be anathema. He believed that business history should be constructed by the application of economic and social principles to the progress of a firm in as scholarly a manner as possible. He didn't believe that by writing house histories you could get very far ....[8]

At the outset of his academic career then, Hyde was obliged to define business history. Was it company history *à la* Gras? Or was it part of something wider as Gay believed? On balance, Hyde sided with Gay.

After his return to England he became, in 1934, an Assistant Lecturer in Economic History at Liverpool. This was located in the School of Economics there headed by (Sir) George Allen, historian of Birmingham and the Black country who was also to have considerable influence upon Hyde. It was to the Chair of of Economics that he was eventually appointed in 1948. Later, as chairman of the Liverpool

University Press committee and with his interest in business history revived by *Blue Funnel*, he was well placed to launch the new journal, the first number of which appeared in December 1958. The subscription, for two issues a year post free, was 30s. (£1.50) in Great Britain and $5 in the United States. According to an advanced prospectus, by special arrangement with the Business Archives Council (represented by its secretary, Miss Irene Shrigley, and Dr Max Hartwell), those who contributed three guineas or more a year to that body were to receive the new journal free. (The B.A.C. concession was dropped from the title page in 1967). Professor Hyde was the first editor, with J.R. Harris and S.B. Saul as his assistants, and Sheila Marriner as secretary, an editorial team which lasted until 1964 when Saul, having gone to the Edinburgh Chair, joined the impressive list of editorial advisers: Asa Briggs, W.H. Chaloner, S.G. Checkland, W.H.B. Court, J. Simmons, T.S. Willan and Charles Wilson. Max Hartwell was formally added when the B.A.C. link was broken. So was J.R. Harris on his appointment to the Birmingham Chair. The subscription was held at 30s. ($5) a year until publication was moved to Frank Cass in 1972, when – still only two issues a year – it was raised to £3.50 ($9.50).

Dr Marriner became one of the Assistant Editors in 1964 in place of Professor Saul and, in due course other members of the Department – Economic History was hived off from Economics in 1970 – were also involved, notably Dr Peter Davis, later to become Head of the Department. The name of Valerie Dodd, the loyal, long-serving departmental secretary should also be added. Professor Hyde suffered from severe eyesight problems and an increasing reponsibility for the journal fell upon Dr Marriner's shoulders. She succeeded him as editor in 1976, until 1982 when the editorial office also moved to London *pro tem* to the recently-formed Business History Unit at the London School of Economics where the new editors were located. The articles reprinted here, from the first 25 years of *Business History* (two issues a year of roughly 100 pages an issue, until 1981 when it was increased to three, 100-page issues a year for £12.50) cover its pioneer Liverpool phase.

No statement of editorial policy was to be found in the first issue of December 1958 but the prospectus showed clearly that, as well as carrying information about the activities of the Business Archives Council and 'in particular the listing of accessions of business records and other source material of interest to economists, economic historians and business men', the aim was to follow E.F. Gay's broader approach to the subject:

> It is intended to publish articles of academic standing covering a wide range of business activities. Contributions will be welcomed relating not only to the development and policies of particular firms but to the wider implications of industrial and commercial

change. The Editors also invite articles involving the application of statistical and accountancy techniques to business history.

As the contributions reprinted here show, the interpretation of business history has been very wide: indeed many of them could have appeared in more general journals such as the *Economic History Review* or the *Journal of Economic History*. The only distinguishing feature is that, as in the American *Business History Review*, there was a dependence upon business records, particularly British business records, though many of these concerned companies with foreign connections. There was surprisingly little discussion of the nature of the subject and this is reflected in the editor's selection here.

Problems of definition and methodology were, however, raised from time to time. The young Barry Supple, fresh from the heady atmosphere of the Harvard Business School and writing in the June 1962 issue from McGill, reflected upon 'The Uses of Business History'. In that article he considered nine substantial, recently-published company histories, four American and five British. He drew attention to the paucity of research material upon which they were based. Financial records and committee minutes, he rightly insisted, were not enough: correspondence and internal memoranda were needed to discover what went on behind the scenes. The volumes, too, made insufficient use of economic theory. 'It would sometimes appear', Supple concluded, 'that having finished writing their prefaces, business historians forget that Schumpeter even lived – at least until they come to write their last paragraph'. This prompted Professor Hyde to respond in the next issue with 'Economic Theory and Business History. A Comment on the Theory of Profit Maximisation' in which he pointed out that a number of recently-published company histories showed clearly that, whether business men knew about the trade cycle or not, there were those who pursued conservative policies in times of boom, not maximising profit, and benefited when the ensuing slump arrived.

A decade later, an equally young and enterprising scholar, the New Zealander K.A. Tucker (who now occupies a senior post at the Australian National University), having written a Master's thesis at Auckland in 1967 about a local department store there, boldly urged (*Business History*, January 1972), on the basis of that study, that business historians should collect sufficient statistical material to be able to develop counterfactual arguments in order to judge managerial quality. This brought a sharp and swift response from none other than Charles Wilson himself, in the course of a valuable paper 'Twenty Years After: Some Reflections on Having Written a Business History':

> Mr. Tucker evidently has no use for historians whose aim is to provide some illumination of the business scene for non-analysts. Narrative is to be clipped off, written down as merely a public relations exercise and consigned to the dustbin of the general public. He appears to assume that the non-analytical and inexpert

reader will gain nothing from statistics while the experts who know it all will be able to dispense with anything other than the new analytical techniques. People and even things will be of no concern to them .... I believe that this kind of approach to the problems of business, especially business on a large scale, is wholly impracticable. The scale of the operations, the cost of financing the research, writing and publishing of a large scale business history, the patchiness, the imperfection and in places total absence of reliable data are only a few of the considerations which render Mr. Tucker's reflections fruitless ....[10]

Ken Tucker, however, lived to fight another day, though not to enlarge on his original ideas or to try to answer his critic. He reprinted his article in a series of readings, together with those by others which had been printed in American as well as British journals (*Business History*, Cass 1977). This volume provides a valuable complement to the present one. Included is Arthur Cole's clear warning that company history is to business history as political biography is to political history. Perhaps; but the quality, range and usefulness of company history are changing as their authors become more experienced and relate their particular companies to the changing economic background, to competition within the particular branch of business, to changing credit and labour circumstances, to market entrepreneurship and to a clear distinction between the entrepreneur and the manager.

The list of more searching and analytical, and therefore more satisfying and instructive, histories of British companies from which lessons can certainly be learned is growing apace. At least 45 scholarly studies have been published since 1970 compared to just under 40 during the previous half century – and many of those appeared in the 1960s.[11] (The reviews in *Business History*, a most valuable part of the journal, testify to this.) Dr W.J. Reader, in particular, who served his apprenticeship with Charles Wilson when he was writing *Unilever* has gone on to write other notable studies, including *I.C.I.* (2 vols. 1970, 1975), *Metal Box* (1976) and *Bowater* (1981). Professor D.C. Coleman's *Courtaulds* (1969, 1980) has also, and rightly, been highly praised, especially the outspoken third volume (1980), dealing with the years 1940–65, to which those who believe that business historians are merely paid hacks should be immediately directed. All these works analyse and comment as well as tell a story. Now a new generation of business historians is growing up, building upon this earlier work. Many of them are to be found associated with the Business History Unit, formed at the London School of Economics in 1978 and ably led during its first phase by Leslie Hannah who was created the first Professor of Business History at an English university in 1982.

The Business History Unit holds regular seminars at which business men and academics meet to read papers. It is also responsible for courses at graduate and undergraduate level. At Glasgow, a large benefaction will make it possible for a long-standing interest in the subject to be considerably developed. Other universities are also increasing the business history element in their teaching. In London an annual Business History seminar has been held since 1974. It met at first at Ealing College of Technology; and then, when Professor D.J. Oddy, who had started it, moved to the Polytechnic of Central London, it moved with him. Supported by the Economic and Social Research Council, it has become an important annual event, on the lines of the Business History Conference in the United States. As more business archivists have been appointed, a significant sign of the times, the Business Archives Council, under the Presidency of Professor Peter Mathias, has gained renewed vigour. Its annual conference is another important date in the archivists' and historians' calendar, and its publications, particularly its journal *Business Archives* and its listings of records in various branches of business are essential works of reference for anyone seriously interested in British business history.

Harvard set a significant example from which Francis Hyde and a number of other British scholars who studied there in their earlier years derived ideas and enthusiasms which contributed to the post-war rise of British business history and have been reflected in the pages of *Business History*. The subject now flourishes here as much as in the United States; and there is demanding work ahead. Much needs to be done to generalise from existing company histories; and there are still branches of the economy – banking, distribution or catering, for instance – which have not been studied with the same archives access or freedom of comment as have a number of manufacturing concerns. Further forthright studies will increase our understanding of business as well as improve the standing of history.

### NOTES

1. Charles Wilson, *The History of Unilever* 2 vols. (1954), Vol.I, p.v.
2. Peter Mathias, 'The First Half Century: Business History, Business Archives and the B.A.C.', *Business Archives*, No.50 (Nov. 1984), pp.1–4.
3. Interview with Professor Hyde; videotape in the Library of the University of Kent, Canterbury.
4. Herbert Heaton, *A Scholar in Action, Edwin F. Gay* (Harvard, 1952), Chs.1–4.
5. *Bulletin of the Business Historical Society*, Vol.I, No.1 (June 1926).
6. Ibid.
7. *Bulletin of the Business Historical Society*, Vol.I, No.7 (May–June 1927).
8. Interview with Professor Hyde (see note 3).
9. Prospectus (copy in the author's copy of Vol.I, No.1.)
10. *Journal of European Economic History* (Fall 1972), p.454.
11. T.C. Barker, R.H. Campbell, P. Mathias, and B.S. Yamey, *Business History* (Debrett Business History Research Ltd., 1984), pp.22, 26–9.

# THE LARGE MANUFACTURING EMPLOYERS
# OF 1907*

By CHRISTINE SHAW

I

Professor Peter Payne's listing of the largest 52 British industrial companies of 1905, published in 1967,[1] has been widely quoted. An alternative listing is presented here, based on enterprise employment rather than size of capital, confined to manufacturing industry strictly defined, and referring to the nearest possible year to 1907 for which data was available. Appendix 1 presents the new listing of more than 100 large employers; Professor Payne's original listing is reproduced in Appendix 2 to facilitate comparison.

It soon became clear that it would not be possible to compile a definitive list of *the* 100 largest manufacturing employers.[2] The only systematic attempt to compile statistical information about the workforce (but primarily the output) of all British manufacturing enterprises was the 1907 Census of Production, and the returns for that census are not available for consultation.[3] Great care was taken in publishing the statistics of the Census not to reveal any information which would give a clear indication of the contribution of any individual firm to the output or total employment of a particular industry. No information about the number of individual establishments within each firm, or even industry, were published either.[4]

Some statistics were collected by other enquiries, public and private, about the time of the 1907 Census of Production. Detailed statistics for the workforce of individual firms in the mining and quarrying industry can be compiled from the Lists of Mines and Quarries, published annually by the Government Inspectors and this made it possible to separate out mining from manufacturing employment in the statistics for various firms.[5] The Tariff Commission collected a wealth of information (mostly relating to 1903) on a wide range of industries.[6] Many forms filled in by companies for the Commission have been lost, some firms who responded did not reveal the numbers they employed, but still the surviving papers of the Tariff Commission provide a great deal of valuable information about the workforce of individual firms. Partial, but still useful, figures for the engineering industry are to be found among the papers of the Engineering Employers' Federation. The Federation made a survey of the numbers of skilled men and apprentices their members employed in March 1910; and recorded details of those employed on day and night shifts by their members in the 'North West' region of Scotland (that is, around Glasgow) in October 1908, May 1910, and February 1911.[7]

An unexpectedly rich source of information was the *Red Book of Commerce,* a commercial directory which first appeared in 1906.[8] This contains information about thousands of manufacturers, retailers and merchants in the United Kingdom, on the nature of their business, their directors, their premises and their staff. It is clear from the composition of the entries that they were compiled from information supplied by the firms themselves, on forms provided by the editors, which evidently included a heading 'Staff'. Some firms ignored this, others responded only by describing their staff as 'highly efficient', or 'large', or (more modestly) 'adequate'; some merely gave an indication of the size of their workforce, replying that they employed 'several hundreds' or 'several thousands', but many firms supplied more exact information — enough, indeed, to make the *Red Book of Commerce* the single most valuable source for this list.

Leslie Hannah's unpublished list of the 200 largest companies in 1919, measured by market value of capital, was consulted, as well as Payne's list, to establish which firms were likely candidates for inclusion. Additional information was gleaned from industrial and business histories, from companies, and from individual experts on particular businesses or industries, as well as from archivists and librarians.

## II

It should be noted that Appendix 1 comprises 104 firms. Several firms at the foot of the list had the same size workforce (3,000 being the cut-off point) and there seemed little point in including some and not others in the printed list.

In compiling his list of the 52 largest industrial companies in Britain in 1905, ranked by their capitalisation, Professor Payne used information from the *Stock Exchange Year-Book* for 1905. Obviously, there is not one particular index of company size at any date inherently preferable to all other such indexes. Rankings by issued capital, market value, employment or output and so on all have their advantages and their drawbacks. Professor Payne's chosen index appears to offer the possibility of certainty that *the* N largest firms have been identified. However, to use the *Stock Exchange Year-Book* as the only source of information excludes any private limited liablity companies with a high enough capitalisation to come within the top 50.[9] Choosing capitalisation as the index of measurement at a comparatively early stage in the development of the limited company in the United Kingdom has other disadvantages, too. Some of the companies in his list, as he points out, were overcapitalised.[10] Breweries comprise an unrealistically large part of his group of companies, quite disproportionate to their true manufacturing capital, because their capital is inflated by the value of the tied houses they had competed to acquire.[11]

Just as Payne's list of large firms ranked by capital favours capital-intensive industries, so a list of enterprises ranked by employment favours labour-intensive ones. A number of clothing firms, for example, appear in Appendix 1, but would be unlikely to appear in a list of the 100 largest firms compiled using any other basis of measurement. But a major drawback of the new list, given the sources of information available, is, of course, that it is impossible to be sure that the 100 largest firms have been identified. Indeed, it is most probable that they have not all been identified, for it has not been possible to obtain even an estimate of the size of the workforce for some companies, such as English Sewing Cotton, the Linen Thread Company or British Cotton and Wool Dyers (all among Professor Payne's leading companies) which might qualify for inclusion if the data were available. Moreover, reservations have to be expressed about the figures given for many of the firms which *are* on the list: not all the figures found are for the same year (although the great majority are within four years of the target year 1907); while some figures are quite precise, others are estimates; some figures are for only part of the workforce, others may include distributive staff. There are particular problems with those industries, such as shipbuilding, where the workforce could vary considerably from year to year. Some firms took this into account when estimating the size of their workforce;[12] others did not. However, in other industries when figures are available for the same company for two or more years around 1907 the changes in the order of magnitude of the workforce are not usually such that their ranking in this list would be affected greatly.[13]

Where a range of employment was given in the source, the mid-point has been taken. Bearing all these reservations and discrepancies in mind, enough sufficiently reliable information has been found to make the list of interest — so long as too much emphasis is not put on the exact ranking of any firm within the table.

## III

The list is confined to firms with 3,000 or more employees *in manufacturing,* the latter defined to include all the industries in the modern Standard Industrial Classification Orders III-XIX. Professor Payne's list was primarily of manufacturing firms, but also included United Collieries and the Wigan Coal and Iron Company, which were wholly or primarily mining and quarrying companies.[15] Maples, and Waring & Gillow, also in Payne's list, were decorators and furniture retailers on a large scale, as well as furniture manufacturers. On the other hand, some manufacturing employers in Appendix 1 would not have fallen within the categories of the *Stock Exchange Year-Book* from which Professor Payne compiled his tables.[16] Thus he excluded the major railway companies although on the basis of their *manufacturing* workforce alone several of them rank among the largest manufacturing employers.[17] Government enterprises like the Royal Dockyards also did not come within Payne's terms of reference, nor could the cooperative wholesale societies. Private companies were also excluded,[18] although at least one, Platt Brothers, the textile machinery manufacturers, had a capital large enough to bring them within the top 30 of Payne's list.[19] The Yorkshire Wool Combers' Association (48th on Payne's list) does not appear in

Appendix 1 because it was in receivership in 1905. There are also two unaccountable omissions from Payne's list: the electrical engineering firm, British Westinghouse, and Rylands, the textile firm. Both were public companies, with sufficiently large capital to qualify for inclusion on Payne's list, both appear in one of the sections (Miscellaneous Companies) of the *Stock Exchange Year-Book* for 1905 used in its compilation, but they appear to have been missed.

Once these divergences in approach have been taken into account, some real and striking differences between the substance of the two lists remain. There are 17 brewery companies in Payne's list of the largest 52 companies: nearly a third of his total. Of those 17, only two — Bass, Ratcliff, Gretton and Arthur Guinness — were among the top 100 employers, and neither of those fall within the top half. It has been quite difficult to track down figures for the workforces of the leading brewery companies before 1914. Barclay, Perkins, 17th on Payne's list, employed only 800 in 1907,[20] the City of London Brewery (43rd)[21] around 325.[22] The three firms that later amalgamated to form Watney, Combe, Reid (ranked second by Payne)[23] employed a combined total of around 1,170 around 1890; Samuel Allsopp & Sons (12th) employed just over 1,600.[24] It appears, then, that brewery companies, despite the size of their capital, were not large manufacturing employers.

Professor Payne included no companies engaged in the manufacture of clothing, while Appendix 1 includes several such companies. The Cooperative Wholesale Society and the Scottish Cooperative Wholesale Society (the latter's total may well include some distribution staff) both manufactured food and other products as well as clothing. The other two clothing manufacturers were the hosiery firm I & R Morley (which was not incorporated, even as a private company, until 1933) and a corset manufacturer, Charles Bayer & Company. This firm was founded by Charles Bayer in 1870, and does not seem to have been incorporated by 1908.[25] Its presence among the 50 largest manufacturing employers in the United Kingdom is a striking testimony to the importance of the corset in the maintenance of the dignity of the British Empire.[26] There are also two Irish lace manufacturers, the Hibernian Lace Company and the Irish Lace Depot, whose employees were largely outworkers.

Beyond that the two lists show remarkable similarities in what they reveal of the nature of large scale industry before the First World War. There are no firms primarily engaged in motor manufacture in either list (Humber, which employed 5,000 when it opened its new Coventry factory in 1908, was probably still below our cut-off point of 3,000 employees in 1907). Among the other new industries, both lists contain the predictable scatter of chemical and electrical engineering firms, though, apart from the United Alkali Company, their employment levels are relatively low. The textile trades are prominent in both lists, particularly the textile finishing combines, while the other staples — the iron and steel, shipbuilding, and engineering industries — appear on both but are significantly more numerous in Table 1 than in Payne's original list.

IV

Most of the enterprises in Appendix 1, as in Payne's list, were public companies, quoted on the London Stock Exchange. However, a considerable proportion of them were not. Two were government enterprises, two were cooperative societies. At least three firms had yet to be incorporated, even as private companies: I & R Morley, James Williamson & Son, and McIntyre, Hogg. (The latter was incorporated as a public company in 1908.) One other, Charles Bayer, may also not have been a company; its exact legal status is unclear. A further 21 companies were not listed in the official Stock Exchange directory of publicly-quoted companies, the *Stock Exchange Official Intelligence*.[27] However, six of these companies — Horrockses Crewdson, Pilkingtons, North British Rubber, Titus Salt, Asa Lees and Huntley & Palmers were included in the other widely-used directory, the *Stock Exchange Year-Book*. For all six the *Year-Book* notes that reports are not obtainable or had not been received, the entry for Pilkingtons adding, 'the company being regarded as a private concern.'[28] A price is quoted for the stock of only one of the six companies, for the debentures of North British Rubber. Two more companies, Frys and Richard Haworth were included in the *Official Intelligence* for 1907 (as well as the *Year-Book*) but with significant reservations. Frys was said to be a private company,[29] Richard Haworth 'practically a private' company,[30] although £150,000 of debentures had been allocated to the public. Neither firm published its accounts. Another firm, J. & J. Colman had apeared in the *Official Intelligence* for 1906, but had been dropped from the 1907 edition. In the 1906 edition it had been noted that J. & J. Colman was 'stated to be a private company',[31] and the 1907 *Year-Book,* while giving details of the company's capital, noted that 'This being a private company, reports are not published'.[32] Furthermore Gallaher, said in modern editions of the *Stock Exchange Official Year-Book* to have been a public company from 1896 until April 1908, and then to have become a private company,[33] is included in neither of the directories for 1907. Given this ambiguity on the part of the authoritative guides as to what was or was not a private company, a definite figure for the number of private companies among the largest employers cannot be given. Nevertheless, it can be said that about one-third of the enterprises in Appendix 1 were not, or were not regarded as, public companies.

V

The definition of a firm employed in compiling Appendix 1 was that conventionally adopted in concentration studies: any subsidiary firm or plant in which a parent holds more than 50 per cent of the voting capital or other title to control is counted as part of the parent firm. Thus the figure of 3,200 for one of the largest car manufacturers, Wolseley, is included with the total for Vickers, of which it was a subsidiary; while William Beardmore (ranked 52nd) is counted as an independent firm since its capital was equally divided between Vickers (ranked 4th) and John Brown (ranked 8th), and no firm held more than 50 per cent of the capital. Moreover, we cannot be certain that all subsidiaries have been captured. The figures thus do not fully reflect the concentration of financial control in the economy.

By the same token, the figure represents the concentration of employment within firms *not* plants, and the level of plant concentration would have been significantly lower. In some firms, manufacturing employment was heavily concentrated on one site. The largest manufacturing plant in Britain, for example, in terms of the size of its workforce, was probably the Great Western Railway's works at Swindon, with 13,000 employed in its locomotive carriage and wagon shops in 1905,[34] as well as several thousand in other manufacturing establishments. A close second was probably Armstrong Whitworth's Elswick works with over 12,000 employees in 1907.[35]

An attempt has been made to establish how many separate plants each of the firms had and this is shown in Appendix 1. Reasonably certain figures have been traced for 68 of the top 100 firms, and another firm, Hibernian Lace, possibly could not be said to have had any 'factory' at all, only a central warehouse and office. Of the remaining 31, it has been established that 21 had more than one plant, but it is difficult to say exactly how many more. In some cases, it has only been possible to count the number of separate locations where the firms are known to have had works, and to record that number of plants. Thus Rylands, for example, have been counted as having seven plants, because at this period they are known to have had mills and factories at Manchester, London, Gorton, Wigan, Swinton, Heapey and Chorley, though they had 17 mills and factories in the 1880s.[36] Complex plants producing more than one kind of product, such as shipbuilding and engineering yards, have been counted as one, if only one location is mentioned by the firm.

Composite plants, where one factory had been added to another on adjacent sites over a number of years, are another problem. Frys, for example, had eight factories all linked together at Bristol,[37] which arguably form only one plant. Since it is impossible from the information currently available to adopt a uniform system of reckoning for such plants, the firms' own description of their factories has been followed. For a few of the largest firms, the results of the amalgamation of several businesses, resort has had to be had to the dubious expedient of counting the number of firms involved in the original amalgamation, assuming at least one plant per firm, and then taking into account any known closures of works or acquisitions between their incorporations and 1907.

Despite the reservations that must be expressed about some of the figures in Appendix 1 for the number of plants operated by the enterprises on this list, there is still enough information available to indicate a clear answer to the question raised by Prais in his study of the role of giant firms in the British economy: whether multi-plant enterprises are 'a recent innovation'.[38] He noted that already by the end of the last century public flotations of companies often brought together many small firms in great mergers, though it could not be assumed that the merged firms kept all the plants belonging to these companies in operation. The evidence gathered for this study confirms his argument that multi-plant firms were already a recognised feature of the economic scene at the turn of the century. Given the importance that has been attached to the companies formed by such mergers of a large number of smaller firms in discussions of the role of large firms in the economy,[39] it is not surprising that the firms with the largest number of plants in Appendix 1 are the results of multi-firm mergers. Even leaving such companies aside, it is clear that if one should think of the typical giant enterprise of today 'as owning a host of plants', the 'typical' giant enterprise of c.1907 probably owned four or less.[40] In 1972 the 100 largest manufacturing enterprises employed an average of 31,000 workers, spread over an average of 72 plants per firm, while in 1958 the average for the 100 largest enterprises were 20,300 workers, spread over 27 plants, with 750 employees in each plant. The 100 largest employers in Appendix 1 employed an average of 6,820 workers, spread over six plants. The average number of employees per plant for all 100 firms in 1907 was 1,107. Though these figures for 1907 are highly conjectural, and perhaps underestimate the number of plants per firm, they give an idea of the likely order of magnitude.

## VI

The modern multi-plant firm is largely an extrapolation of a phenomenon already established before the First World War, but there is nonetheless a strong indication in Appendix 1 that the largest firms differed from those of today in other ways. In particular, they remained provincially rather than London-orientated. The dominance of the basic industries of the Celtic fringe and the industrial north is evident, and this impression is confirmed by a study of the location of their head offices. It was possible to determine the head office address in 1907 for 98 of the 100 largest firms in Appendix 1.[41] Of these 98, 26 had their main offices in London, and 72 in the provinces. Those with their main offices in London include the special cases of the Royal Ordnance Factories and Royal Dockyards, and five of the major railway companies with lines running from London. Of the rest, 14 had works in or near London, and only five did not. These five were Beardmores of Glasgow, British Westinghouse of Manchester, Dick, Kerr of Preston and Kilmarnock, and Dunlop and Singer. Dunlop was the manufacturing subsidiary of an agency company, and Singer the subsidiary of a large retail organisaton (itself the subsidiary of an American firm). For other firms, it would seem that the attractions of London as the site for head offices had yet to make themselves felt. Nine firms which had a plant in London had their headquarters in the provinces. Of these, three — Armstrongs, Vickers and Rylands — had a London office as well, while six — Brunner Mond, Colmans, Imperial Tobacco, Kynoch, the Midland Railway and Gallaher — had none.

Using the Standard Regions introduced in 1974[42], the location of the plants of the firms on the list has been analysed.[43] Sixty-one firms had all their plants situated in one standard region, and 22 in two. The four firms whose plants were most widely dispersed were the Cooperative Wholesale Society, which had factories in seven standard regions, Imperial Tobbacco and United Alkali, whose plants were scattered among six, and the clothing firm McIntyre, Hogg, Marsh & Company, which had factories in London, Manchester, Taunton, Barrhead in Scotland and Londonderry.

Thirty-six per cent of the firms had at least one plant in the Northwest region, 29 per cent in the Southeast, 22 per cent in Scotland and 21 per cent in the West Midlands.[57] No particular combination of regions was favoured among the 38 firms who had plants in more than one region. Eight firms altogether had plants in the Southeast and the West Midlands (five also having plants elsewhere), eight in the Southeast and Northwest (six with other plants elsewhere), six in the Northwest and the West Midlands (five with other plants elsewhere) and eight in the Northwest and Scotland (six with other plants elsewhere). An analysis of the regions most favoured by those enterprises with plants in more than one region shows that 18 of the 39 firms concerned had plants in the Southeast, 16 in the Northwest, 13 in the West Midlands, 10 in Scotland and 10 in Yorkshire and Humberside.[44]

## VII

The primary purpose of this article has been descriptive, but these lists clearly raise many questions about the analysis of Britain's nascent corporate economy prior to 1914. Generalisations based on an inadequate understanding of the scale and nature of large British enterprise in this period may need to be revised. It is hoped to return to a more analytical treatment of these issues in a future article to be published in this journal.

*Business History Unit*
*London School of Economics*

### NOTES

* This research was funded by the Business History Unit of London University. It is a by-product of my work in compiling representative listings of firms for the *Dictionary of Business Biography* project, financed by the UK Social Science Research Council. The study was originally suggested by Professor Leslie Hannah, who also advised on problems of analysis and statistical technique. Many scholars helped with information on specific firms: they are identified in the footnotes to Table 1, but I would particularly like to thank Dr Bernard Alford, Mr J.H.E. Allison, of Carrington Viyella Ltd., Professor Theo Barker, Dr Michael Bonavia, Dr Geoffrey Channon, Professor Roy Church, Dr Martin Daunton, Dr Richard Davenport-Hines, G.B. de Marsh of the Engineering Employers' Federation, Dr Douglas Farnie, Professor C.H. Feinstein, Mr J. Mathieson of Courtaulds Ltd., Dr R.J. Irving, Dr W. Kennedy, Dr Wayne Lewchuk, Mr Michael Moss, Mr Basil Murray, Mr Trevor Parkhill, Public Record Office of Northern Ireland, Dr W.J. Reader, Mr Clifford, Reckitt & Colman Ltd., Mr C.J. Schmitz, Professor Eric Sigsworth, Mr R.H. Storey, Dr Jennifer Tann, Mr Clive Trebilcock, Mr Geoffrey Tweedale, Professor Charles Wilson, and Mr Jonathan Zeitlin.

1. P.L. Payne, 'The Emergence of the Large-Scale Company in Great Britain, 1870-1914', *Economic History Review*, 2nd. series, xx, December 1967, pp. 519-542.
2. Any reference below to this list as a list of *the* 100 largest manufacturing employers should be read with this reservation in mind.

3. The original papers of the Census of Production are among that class of records which is permanently withheld from consultation by researchers, althought the Wilson Committee on Modern Public Records in its *Report* published in March 1981 (Cmnd. 8204), recommended that access arrangements to the Census of Production records (and others giving valuable information on social and economic history) should be reconsidered. However, it is rumoured that the Census papers are in such bad condition that they are unusable.

4. Information about the number of individual establishments was first published in the 1930 Census of Production.

5. *List of Mines in the United Kingdom of Great Britain and Ireland, and the Isle of Man.* Prepared by His Majesty's Inspectors of Mines, by direction of the Secretary of State for the Home Department. *List of Quarries (under the Quarries Act, 1894) in the United Kingdom of Great Britain and Ireland, and the Isle of Man.* Prepared by His Majesty's Inspectors of Mines, by direction of the Secretary of State for the Home Department.

6. The papers of the Tariff Commission are now held by the Manuscript department of the British Library of Political and Economic Science.

7. These are to be found in the file 'Numbers Employed: From 1910'. Many of the older records of the Engineering Employers' Federation have been transferred to the Modern Records Centre at Warwick University.

8. *Whitaker's Red Book of Commerce, or Who's Who in Business.*

9. See Appendix 2.

10. Payne, 'Large-Scale Company', p. 529.

11. Payne, 'Large-Scale Company', p. 531.

12. See, for example, note 27 to Appendix 1.

13. See the footnotes to Appendix 1 for discussion of the accuracy and reliability of the for individual firms.

14. See Central Statistical Office, *Standard Industrial Classification* (HMSO, 1968). A key to the SIC categories used is given at the end of Appendix 1.

15. The Wigan Coal and Iron Company employed 9,600 in 1903, but only 700 of these were employed at their iron and steel works. (Tariff Commission, TC4 16/13, 34/2, 35/2). I have classified the Salt Union as a mining and quarrying company, rather than following Professor Payne's classification of it as a chemical firm. It employed 3,500 in 1911 (*Red Book of Commerce*, 1912, p. 811). Other large 'coal and iron' companies employing too few ironworkers to qualify for inclusion in the present list, included the Pearson & Knowles Coal & Iron Co., who in 1903 employed a total of 7,150 men, with only 1,600 of them in the ironworks (Tariff Commission, TC4 16/15), the Stanton Iron Works Co., who employed 2,500 in their ironworks and 3,500 ironstone and coalminers in 1908 (Stanley Chapman, *Stanton & Staveley: a Business History* (Cambridge, 1981), p. 119), and the Staveley Coal and Iron Co., who employed 6,768 in the 'coal trade' and 1,970 in the 'iron trade' in 1903 (Tariff Commission,TC4 7/19).

16. It was based on the categories 'Rolling Stock Companies', 'Brewery, Hotel and Kindred Companies', 'Iron, Coal and Steel Companies', and 'Miscellaneous Companies'. (Payne, op. cit., p. 540).

17. The *total* workforces of these railway companies (the GWR, for example, employed 76,480 in 1913) made them the largest private employers in the country, though public bodies such as the Army (239,000 in 1907) and the Post Office (113,921) in 1907 were larger employers.

18. But see above, p.46 for the problems involved in identifying which companies were 'private', and which 'public'.

19. Platt Brothers, when reincorporated in 1898 (the company was originally incorporated in 1868) had an issued capital of £3,091,800, D.A Farnie, 'Samuel Redcliffe Platt', in D.J. Jeremy (ed.), *Dictionary of Business Biography* (forthcoming). Platt Brothers' directors claimed their company was 'the largest textile machine manufacturing concern in the world'. (*Red Book of Commerce*, 1908, p. 662).

20. *Red Book of Commerce*, 1908, pp. 67-8.

21. All the figures in brackets in this section refer to the ranking of the firms concerned in Payne's list.

22. *Red Book of Commerce,* 1908, p. 181.
23. In early 1906 the nominal and paid-up capital of Watney, Combe, Reid was reduced by £2,389, 057 by writing off as lost that amount of Deferred Ordinary Stock to meet a loss ascertained on valuation of assets and goodwill. (*Stock Exchange Official Intelligence,* 1906, pp. 584-5).
24. Alfred Barnard, *The Noted Breweries of Great Britain and Ireland,* 4 vols. (London, 1889-91). Watney & Co. employed 420 hands (this does not include their clerks and managers) (Barnard, Vol I., p. 367), Combe & Co. employed 450 (Vol. 1, p. 296), and Reid & Co. 300 (Vol. II, p. 93); the figure for Samuel Allsopp & Sons does not include clerks and managers. (Vol. 1, p. 161). I have not been able to trace figures for the workforce of Bovril, and the Distillers Co. However, it is possible that most of Bovril's workers were employed abroad, as those of Liebig's Extract of Meat Co. were: Liebig's employed 5,000 in 1907 but their factories were in Argentina and Uruguay, not the United Kingdom *(Red Book of Commerce,* 1908, p. 506).
25. *Red Book of Commerce,* 1909, p. 83.
26. Chappell, Allen & Co. Ltd., another corset manufacturer, of the 'Patriotic Corset Works', in Bristol, employed about 2,000 staff in 1907. *(Red Book of Commerce,* 1908, p. 175).
27. Platt Brothers, Harland & Wolff, Workman Clark, Scott's Shipbuilding, Horrockses Crewdson, Hibernian Lace Co., Irish Lace Depot, Birtwistle & Fielding, Pilkington Brothers, Cadburys, Dobson & Barlow, Cox Brothers, Baxter Brothers, Marshalls, North British Rubber Co., North-Eastern Marine, Robert McBride, Titus Salt, Asa Lees, Gallahers, Huntley & Palmers.
28. *Stock Exchange Year-Book,* 1907, p. 1980.
29. *Stock Exchange Official Intelligence,* 1907, pp. 777-8.
30. *Stock Exchange Official Intelligence,* 1907, p. 807.
31. *Stock Exchange Official Intelligence,* 1906, p. 731.
32. *Stock Exchange Year-Book,* 1907, p. 1835.
33. *Stock Exchange Official Year-Book,* 1978-9, p. 1250.
34. *Victoria County History of Wiltshire,* Vol. iv, p. 217. S.B. Saul, 'The Engineering Industry' in D.H. Aldcroft (ed.), *The Development of British Industry and Foreign Competition, 1875-1914: Studies in Industrial Enterprise* (London, 1968), p. 196, describes this plant as 'certainly the largest single engineering establishment in Britain' in 1914, when 14,000 men were employed there.
35. H.W. Macrosty, *The Trust Movement in British Industry: a Study of Business Organisation* (London, 1907), p. 40. See also Cmnd. 3626, Murray Committee, QQ2227-8.
36. D.H. Farnie, 'John Rylands', in D.J. Jeremy (ed.), *Dictionary of Business Biography* (forthcoming).
37. *Red Book of Commerce,* 1910, pp. 357-8.
38. S.J. Prais, *The Evolution of Giant Firms in Britain* (Cambridge, 1976), p. 64.
39. For example, in L. Hannah and J.A. Kay, *Concentration in Modern Industry* (London, 1977). Particular interest has been shown in such firms partly because of the ready availability of some financial information (given that they were quoted on the Stock Exchange), and because of the attention and disquiet aroused by such mergers at the time, as well as the continued controversy surrounding the growth of giant corporations and multinational companies.
40. Forty-six of the 68 firms for which the number of plants has been established with reasonable certainty had four or less plants.
41. The two exceptions are the Cooperative Wholesale Society, which does not seem to have had a head office as such, though Manchester had the best claim to be considered the centre of the Society's activities, and I. & R. Morley, whose company history, published in 1900, does not make it clear whether the head office of the firm was at their Golden Lane warehouse and factory in London, or at the main factory in Nottingham, Frederick Moy Thomas, *I. & R. Morley, A Record of a Hundred Years* (London, 1900). For those firms listed in the *Stock Exchange Official Intelligence,* the address given immediately below the name of the company has been taken as the address of the head office, though the firms themselves do not always explicitly state that this is the case. In a

few instances, companies distinguished between their 'Registered Office' and their 'office' or 'head office'. When firms distinguished between an 'office' and a 'Registered Office', the former had been taken as the head office.

42. For the definition of these regions see *Regional Trends 1981* (HMSO), Appendix B.
43. It has not been possible to establish whether the Irish plants of five firms were situated in Northern Ireland or in the present-day Republic. In these cases, the Irish plants have been counted as being in one Standard Region.
44. Compare C.H. Lee, *Regional Economic Growth in the United Kingdom since the 1880s* (London, 1971), p. 225, table C1 'Employment by Industrial Order, 1881'. At that date the four regions with the largest total number employed were the Southeast (by a considerable margin), the Northwest, Scotland, Yorkshire and Humberside. The situation was the same in 1921 (pp. 230-1, table C5). Only 10 per cent of the firms on the list had plants in Yorkshire and Humberside.

## APPENDIX 1

104 LARGE MANUFACTURING EMPLOYERS CIRCA 1907

| RANK BY EMPLOYMENT | FIRM | SIC CATEGORY (1968) | ESTIMATED NO. OF EMPLOYEES | YEAR | ESTIMATED NO. OF UK PLANTS | LOCATION OF HEAD OFFICE |
|---|---|---|---|---|---|---|
| 1. | Fine Cotton Spinners' & Doublers' Association | XIII | 30,000 | 1908 | 50 | Manchester |
| 2. | Royal Dockyards | X | 25,580 | 1907 | 5 | London |
| 3. | Sir W.G. Armstrong, Whitworth & Co. | VI, VII, X | 25,000 | 1906 | 4 | Newcastle |
| 4. | Vickers, Sons & Maxim | VI, VII, X | 22,500 | 1907 | 8 | Sheffield |
| 5. | Calico Printers' Association | XIII | 20,495 | 1903 | 26 | Manchester |
| 6. | Great Western Railway Co. | XI | 17,770 | 1913 | 4 | London |
| 7. | John Brown & Co. | VI, VII, X | 16,205 | 1907 | 3 | Sheffield |
| 8. | Royal Ordnance Factories | VII | 15,651 | 1907 | 5 | London |
| 9. | Metropolitan Amalgamated Railway Carriage & Wagon Co. | XI | 13,868 | 1907 | 6 | Birmingham |
| 10. | London & North Western Railway Co. | XI | 13,500 | 1910 | 3 | London |
| 11. | Cooperative Wholesale Society | III, XV | 13,203 | 1907 | 36 | ? |
| 12. | J. & P. Coats | XIII | 12,700 | 1907 | 4 | Paisley |
| 13. | Guest, Keen & Nettlefolds | VI, XII | 12,451 | 1903 | 7 | Birmingham |
| 14. | Bleachers' Association | XIII | 11,280 | 1904 | 50 | Manchester |
| 15. | Platt Brothers | VII | 10,708 | 1907 | 5 | Oldham |
| 16. | Stewarts & Lloyds | VI | 10,600 | 1910 | 11 | Glasgow |
| 17. | North-Eastern Railway Co. | XI | 10,000 | 1900 | 7 | York |
| 18. | United Alkali Co. | V | 9,049 | 1903 | 48 | Liverpool |
| 19. | Pilkington Brothers | XVI | 9,000 | 1913 | 3 | St Helens |
| 20. | I & R Morley | XV | 9,000 | 1907 | 7 | Nottingham? |
| 21. | Midland Railway Co. | XI | 8,500 | 1901 | 4 | Derby |
| 22. | Harland & Wolff | X | 8,500 | 1907 | 2 | Belfast |
| 23. | Workman, Clark & Co. | X | 8,000 | 1907 | 4 | Belfast |
| 24. | Rylands & Sons | XIII | 8,000 | 1907 | 7 | Manchester |
| 25. | North British Locomotive Co. | XI | 8,000 | 1907 | 1 | Glasgow |
| 26. | G. Kynoch & Co. | V, VI, VII, XI | 8,000 | 1907 | 11 | Birmingham |
| 27. | Palmers' Shipbuilding & Iron Co. | X | 7,500 | 1908 | 7 | Jarrow |
| 28. | Bradford Dyers | XIII | 7,500 | 1898 | 40 | Bradford |
| 29. | Lancashire & Yorkshire Railway Co. | XI | 7,250 | 1907 | 3 | Manchester |
| 30. | Scottish Cooperative Wholesale Society | III, XV | 7,000 | 1907 | 1 | Glasgow |
| 31. | Singer Sewing Machine Co. | VII | 7,000 | 1900 | 1 | London |
| 32. | Great Eastern Railway Co. | XI | 7,000 | 1914 | 1 | London |
| 33. | Huntley & Palmers | III | 6,500 | 1907 | 2 | Reading |
| 34. | Associated Portland Cement Manufacturers (1900) | XVI | 6,147 | 1903 | 20 | London |
| 35. | Horrockses, Crewdson & Co. | XIII | 6,000 | 1907 | 3 | Manchester |
| 36. | General Electric Co. | IX | 6,000 | 1907 | 6 | London |
| 37. | Imperial Tobacco Co. | III | 6,000 | 1905 | 3 | Bristol |
| 38. | Fairfield Shipbuilding & Engineering Co. | X | 6,000 | 1903 | 1 | Glasgow |

| | | | | | | |
|---|---|---|---|---|---|---|
| 39. | Steel Co. of Scotland | VI | 5,694 | 1907 | 2 | Glasgow |
| 40. | Bolckow, Vaughan & Co. | VI | 5,487 | 1910 | 6 | Middlesbrough |
| 41. | Fairbairn, Lawson, Combe, Barbour | VII | 5,050 | 1910 | 3 | Leeds |
| 42. | Waterlow & Sons | XVIII | 5,000 | 1907 | 11 | London |
| 43. | Scotts' Shipbuilding & Engineering Co. | X | 5,000 | 1907 | 1 | Greenock |
| 44. | Irish Lace Depot | XIII | 5,000 | 1907 | 1 | Dublin |
| 45. | Howard & Bullough | VII | 5,000 | 1907 | 1 | Accrington |
| 46. | Hibernian Lace Co. | XIII | 5,000 | 1907 | 1 | Dublin |
| 47. | British Westinghouse Electrical Co. | IX | 5,000 | 1907 | 1 | London |
| 48. | Birtwistle & Fielding | XIII | 5,000 | 1911 | 9 | Manchester |
| 49. | Charles Bayer & Co. | XV | 5,000 | 1908 | 10 | London |
| 50. | Lister & Co. | XIII | 5,000 | 1908 | 1 | Bradford |
| 51. | J S Fry & Sons | III | 4,600 | 1907 | 8 | Bristol |
| 52. | Swan, Hunter & Wigham Richardson | X | 4,600 | 1903 | 3 | Wallsend |
| 53. | York Street Flax Spinning Co. | XIII | 4,500 | 1907 | 3 | Belfast |
| 54. | Dobson & Barlow | VII | 4,500 | 1907 | 2 | Bolton |
| 55. | Cox Bros | XIII | 4,500 | 1913 | 1 | Dundee |
| 56. | William Beardmore & Co. | VI,X | 4,500 | 1903 | 2 | London |
| 57. | Cadburys | III | 4,485 | 1907 | 1 | Birmingham |
| 58. | Dorman, Long & Co. | VI | 4,361 | 1907 | 6 | Middlesbrough |
| 59. | Doulton & Co. | XVI | 4,319 | 1907 | 6 | London |
| 60. | John Hetherington & Sons | VII | 4,200 | 1907 | 3 | Manchester |
| 61. | Siemens Bros & Co. | IX | 4,150 | 1911 | 3 | London |
| 62. | Birmingham Small Arms Co. | VII | 4,150 | 1907 | 4 | Birmingham |
| 63. | Hawthorn, Leslie & Co. | X,XI | 4,127 | 1905 | 3 | Newcastle |
| 64. | Great Central Railway Co. | XI | 4,070 | 1903 | 1 | London |
| 65. | James Williamson & Son | XIX | 4,000 | 1911 | 1 | Lancaster |
| 66. | Great Northern Railway Co. | XI | 4,000 | 1914 | 1 | London |
| 67. | Tootal, Broadhurst, Lee & Co. | XIII | 4,000 | 1907 | 3 | Manchester |
| 68. | Thames Ironworks, Shipbuilding & Engineering Co. | X | 4,000 | 1907 | 1 | London |
| 69. | Mather & Platt | VII | 4,000 | 1907 | 1 | Manchester |
| 70. | Hadfield's Steel Foundry Co. | VI | 4,000 | 1905 | 2 | Sheffield |
| 71. | Bass, Ratcliff & Gretton | III | 4,000 | 1907 | 1 | Burton-on-Trent |
| 72. | Dunlop Pneumatic Tyre Co. | XIX | 4,000 | 1913 | 1 | London |
| 73. | Brunner Mond | V | 4,000 | 1909 | 5 | Northwich |
| 74. | Nobel Explosives Co. | V | 4,000 | 1914 | 5 | Glasgow |
| 75. | Cammell, Laird & Co. | VI,X | 3,950 | 1910 | 5 | Sheffield |
| 76. | McIntyre, Hogg, Marsh & Co. | XV | 3,905 | 1903 | 5 | London |
| 77. | Dick, Kerr & Co. | VII,IX | 3,850 | 1903 | 2 | London |
| 78. | J Crossley & Sons | XIII | 3,770 | 1903 | 1 | Halifax |
| 79. | Baxter Bros & Co. | XIII | 3,608 | 1903 | 1 | Dundee |
| 80. | Rowntree & Co. | III | 3,560 | 1904 | 1 | York |
| 81. | Arthur Guinness | III | 3,550 | 1907 | 1 | London |
| 82. | Richard Hornsby & Sons | VII | 3,500 | 1911 | 2 | Grantham |
| 83. | Marshall, Sons & Co. | VII | 3,500 | 1903 | 2 | Gainsborough |
| 84. | Richardsons, Westgarth & Co. | VII,IX,X | 3,500 | 1911 | 3 | Hartlepool |
| 85. | North British Rubber Co. | XIX | 3,500 | 1908 | 1 | Edinburgh |
| 86. | North-Eastern Marine Engineering Co. | X | 3,500 | 1913 | 3 | Wallsend |
| 87. | Robert McBride & Co. | XIII | 3,500 | 1907 | 4 | Belfast |
| 88. | Wallpaper Manufacturers | XVIII | 3,421 | 1903 | 21 | London |
| 89. | Samuel Courtauld & Co. | XIII | 3,270 | 1900 | 6 | London |
| 90. | Sir Titus Salt, Bart, Sons & Co. | XIII | 3,200 | 1908 | 1 | Saltaire |
| 91. | J & J Colman | III | 3,200 | 1907 | 2 | Norwich |
| 92. | John Dickinson & Co. | XVIII | 3,180 | 1904 | 6 | London |
| 93. | John Lysaght | VI | 3,070 | 1903 | 3 | Bristol |
| 94. | Peek, Frean & Co. | III | 3,000 | 1907 | 1 | London |
| 95. | Lever Bros | V | 3,000 | 1903 | 2 | Port Sunlight |
| 96. | India Rubber, Gutta Percha, and Telegraph Works Co. | XIX | 3,000 | 1907 | 1 | London |
| 97. | Asa Lees | VII | 3,000 | 1907 | 1 | Oldham |
| 98. | Richard Haworth & Co. | XIII | 3,000 | 1907 | 4 | Manchester |
| 99. | Gallaher | III | 3,000 | 1907 | 2 | Belfast |
| 100. | W & T Avery | VIII | 3,000 | 1907 | 1 | Birmingham |
| 101. | John Wood & Bros | XIII | 3,000 | 1907 | | |
| 102. | Tangyes | VII | 3,000 | 1912 | | |
| 103. | Seydoux & Co. | XIII | 3,000 | 1911 | | |
| 104. | Gourock Ropework Co. | XIII | 3,000 | 1909 | | |

## NOTES AND SOURCES FOR APPENDIX 1

1. *The Fine Cotton Spinners' and Doublers' Association Ltd.*, (privately printed, 1909), p. 13.
2. *Final Report*, Census of Production, 1907, p. 94.
3. Parliamentary Papers (1907, xi, Report of the Government Factories and Workshops Committee (Murray Committee), QQ 2227-8. In 1903, Armstrong Whitworth employed 22,395 (Tariff Commission, TC4 16/20); in 1908, about 30,000 were employed *(Red Book of Commerce*, 1909, p. 36).
4. Contemporary estimates put Vickers' workforce at about 20,000 (Alex Richardson, *Messrs Vickers. The Works and Manufactures* 1902); *Bradford Daily Argus*, 1 January 1906, (quoting Sir Vincent Caillard). However, Clive Trebilcock considers the estimate too low, and thinks that by 1907, the workforce could have been nearer 24-25,000. The entry for Vickers in the *Red Book of Commerce* does not give any figure for staff employed. Wolseley, the Vickers' subsidiary manufacturing motor cars and boats, had a separate entry in the *Red Book of Commerce* for 1908, giving the number of staff as about 3,200, believed to the largest number employed by any motor manufacturing firm. (*Red Book of Commerce*, 1908, p. 903).
5. Tariff commission, TC4 35/1, TC4 34/7. Four men employed in a sandstone quarry in Buckton Vale, Cheshire, (*List of Quarries*, 1903) have been subtracted from the total given there.
6. *Great Western Railway. General Statistics. 1913-1927* (published by GWR, 1928).
7. *Red Book of Commerce*, 1908, p. 136, gives a total of 20,000 staff, from which 5,795 miners have been subtracted (*List of Mines*, 1907). Sir Allan Grant, in his *Steel and Ships, the History of John Browns* (London, 1950), p. 62, claims that Browns employed 55,000 in 1914, but the entry in the *Red Book of Commerce* for that year still puts Brown's workforce at 20,000. *Red Book of Commerce*, 1908, p. 306 gives Firths (7/8ths owned by Browns) a workforce of 2,000+ and this figure has been added to the total.
8. *Final Report*, Census of Production, 1907, p. 94. I have included the 1,118 workers of the Naval Ordnance Department in this total. See also Murray Committee (Parliamentary Papers (1907) x) for a detailed breakdown of the 16,385 workers employed by the Royal Ordnance in November 1906.
9. *The Times*, 3 June 1907. A subsidiary, the Patent Shaft and Axle-tree Company, employed 132 miners and two quarrymen in Staffordshire in 1907 (*List of Mines*, 1907, *List of Quarries*, 1907) which have been subtracted from the 14,000 quoted in *The Times*.
10. W.J. Gordon, *Our Home Railways: How They Began and How They Are Worked*, 2 vols., (London, 1910), ii, p. 20.
11. Percy Redfern, *The New History of the C.W.S.* (London, 1938), p. 541. This was the total number of employees engaged in 'Productive Works and Services'; another 2,400 were employed in 'Distributive Departments' and the Bank. The figure given may include a few agricultural workers on two C.W.S. estates.
12. Matthew Blair, *The Paisley Thread Industry*, (Paisley, 1907), p. 75 gives a figure of 10,000 for their main Paisley factories. Their works at Bolton and Meltham probably accounted for a further 2,200 and other interests a further 500 (private information). Outside the United Kingdom they had mills in the United States, Canada and Russia. The total number of Coats' employees throughout the world was 30,000.
13. Tariff Commission, TC4 16/23, 34/4, 35/1, 35/2. The various branches of GKN made separate returns to the Tariff Commission, hence the several separate references. 9,259 miners were also specified in these returns.
14. S.J. Sykes, *Concerning the Bleach Industry*, (1925), p. 38. This figure excludes administrative staff for which 500 employees have been arbitrarily added. The same source gives a figure of 10,780 for 1904.
15. *Red Book of Commerce*, 1908, p. 662, gives a figure of 12,000 for the staff, from which 1,292 miners have been subtracted (*List of Mines*, 1907).

16. *Red Book of Commerce,* 1911, p. 843. 2 men employed in a quarry in Worcestershire (*List of Quarries,* 1910) have been subtracted.

17. R.J. Irving, *The North Eastern Railway Company 1870-1914: An Economic History,* (Leicester University Press, 1976), p. 108.

18. Tariff Commission, TC4 34/4, 35/1. 196 rock salt miners and 56 limestone and clay quarrymen have been subtracted from the total given in the Tariff Commission papers. (*List of Mines,* 1903, *List of Quarries,* 1903).According to H.W. Macrosty, United Alkali employed 12,000 men in 1907. (*The Trust Movement in British Industry: a Study of Business Organisation,* London, 1907, p. 193). L.F. Haber in *The Chemical Industry 1900-1930* (Oxford, 1971), p. 141, gives a figure of 8,000-8,500 for their workforce in 1914.

19. T.C. Barker, *The Glassmakers: Pilkington. 1826-1976,* (London, 1977), p. 241. Pilkingtons also employed about 200 in a factory in Northern France, and 30 in agencies in the USA and Canada.

20. *Red Book of Commerce,* 1908, p. 590. About 4,000 of these employees were outworkers. Frederick Moy Thomas gave details about the composition of Morley's workforce in 1900 in *I. & R. Morley. A Record of a Hundred Years,* (London, 1900), p. 100.

21. S.B. Saul, ' The Market and the Development of Mechanical Engineering Industries in Britain, 1860-1914', *Economic History Review,* 2nd series, xx (April 1967), p. 115. This figure relates only to the locomotive works at Derby, not to the carriage and wagon building staff. In 1895 the Locomotive Department employed 4,089 workmen and 257 foremen, clerks etc at the Derby works. (Public Record Office, Kew, RAIL 491/863).

22. This figure is an estimate by W. Johnstone and F. Geary of the Department of Economics in the New University of Ulster who are researching Harland & Wolff's role as a source of growth in the Ulster economy in 1860-1914. In 1892 Harland & Wolff employed 4,589 in their yards, and 2,475 in their engine works. (Information from Jonathan Zeitlin.) In the *Red Book of Commerce* 1908, (p. 380), the firm simply stated that they employed 'several thousands of hands'.

23. *Red Book of Commerce,* 1908, p. 908. In 1903, Workman, Clark employed 7,000 men (Tariff Commission, TC4 34/3, 35/2); by 1913 they employed 9,000 (*Red Book of Commerce,* 1914, p. 1033).

24. *Red Book of Commerce,* 1908, p. 711.

25. S.B. Saul in 'Development of the Mechanical Engineering Industries in Britain', p. 115 estimates their workforce in 1907 at 8,000, a similar figure to that for 1903 in Tariff Commission, TC4 7/61. By 1911, their workforce had dropped to about 7,000 (*Red Book of Commerce,* 1912, p. 689).

26. *Red Book of Commerce,* 1908, p. 479. By 1913 after a series of bad years from 1906-1910, the workforce had dropped to about 5,000. (*Red Book of Commerce,* 1914, p. 569; *Under Five Flags, the story of the Kynoch Works, Witton, Birmingham* (1962).

27. *Red Book of Commerce,* 1909, p. 695. Palmers said they employed 5-10,000 workmen and officials 'according to requirements'.

28. Macrosty, *Trust Movement,* p. 156. Bradford Dyers might well have employed considerably more than 7,500 by 1907, in the opinion of a former member of the board of this company, Mr. H.E. Allison. In 1898 there were 23 operating branches, but there were 40 by 1907.

29. This figure is an estimate based on the fact that the Lancashire and Yorkshire Carriage and Wagon Department employed about 3,000-3500 during 1903 (the total fluctuated throughout the year) at the Newton Heath works and out-stations (Public Record Office, Kew, RAIL 343/805), and 4,000 in the Horwich locomotive works (Saul, 'Development of Mechanical Engineering Industries', p. 115.)

30. *Red Book of Commerce,* 1908, p. 727. This total probably includes some distributive staff. If the Scottish C.W.S. employed the same proportion of distributive staff to 'production' staff as the English C.W.S. (c.18-20 per cent) it would have employed about 5,700 manufacturing staff.

31. S.B. Saul, 'Development of Mechanical Engineering Industries', p. 124.

32. S.B. Saul, 'Development of Mechanical Engineering Industries', p. 115. This figure relates to the locomotive works at Stratford, I have been unable to establish whether the GER also had their own carriage and wagon works.
33. *Red Book of Commerce*, 1908, p. 432. Huntley & Palmers employed 6,200 in 1903 (Tariff Commission, TC4 35/2). Using data from wages-books, T.A.B. Corley gives a figure of 5,409 for the workforce in 1899-1900, and 4,857 for 1909-10. (T.A.B. Corley, *Quaker Enterprise in Biscuits, Huntley & Palmers of Reading 1822-1972* (London, 1972) p. 304.
34. Tariff Commission, TC4 34/6, 35/2. 475 men employed in quarries have been subtracted from the total given there (*List of Quarries*, 1903).
35. *Red Book of Commerce*, 1908, p. 421. Macrosty writing in 1907 put their workforce at 5,300 (*Trust Movement*, p. 125); Dr Douglas Farnie of Manchester University puts it at 5,400.
36. *Red Book of Commerce*, 1908, pp. 333-4. General Electric was growing steadily, during the period before the war, employing 4,485 in 1903 (Tariff Commission, TC4 7/36) and over 8,000 by 1913 (*Red Book of Commerce*, 1914, pp. 386-7.)
37. Estimate by Dr Bernard Alford, of the University of Bristol.
38. Tariff Commission, TC4 34/4, 35/1, 7/60.
39. *Red Book of Commerce*, 1908, p. 771. 306 miners (*List of Mines*, 1907) have been subtracted from this total. In 1903 the company employed 2,450 men and boys (Tariff Commission, TC4 16/10).
40. *Red Book of Commerce*, 1911, p. 113 gives a total of 18,000 for the entire workforce, but 9,931 of those were coal miners, 2,433 ironstone miners and 149 worked in a limestone quarry(*List of Mines*, 1910, *List of Quarries* 1910). In 1903 Bolckow Vaughan had employed a total of 14,700 men and boys of whom 9,595 were miners, and 129 quarrymen. (Tariff Commission TC4 16/21; *List of Mines*, 1903, *List of Quarries*, 1903).
41. Engineering Employers' Federation, *List of Journeymen and Apprentices*, March 1910. This figure relates to journeymen and apprentices only. The proportion of journeymen and apprentices in the workforce of those firms for which figures are available from this EEF document and other sources varies considerably. Apart from differences in the organisation of different plants and engineering trades, not all the separate establishments of an engineering firm necessarily belonged to the local EEF district organisation, nor would all the employees of those establishments that were registered come within the purview of the EEF. The membership subscription of the member firms of the EEF was calculated according to the wages bill for the relevant classes of their workforce, which is one reason why the EEF took so much interest in the number of the members' employees. The firm most closely comparable to Fairbairn Lawson among this group is Platts, another textile machine manufacturer who employed 10,314 apprentices and journeymen in March 1910, practically their entire manufacturing workforce. Platts is exceptional in this, however, most firms registering less than 50 per cent of their workforce on the EEF list, but such firms were engaged in very different activities, such as shipbuilding and in metal manufacture. Consequently, Platts may well be the best guide for estimating the total workforce of Fairbairn Lawson, that is, it may not have been much larger than the total given here, 5,050.
42. *Red Book of Commerce*, 1908, pp. 860-1. This total possibly includes some distributive staff, for among the detailed list of factories and establishments is a Retail Department in London Wall.
43. *Red Book of Commerce*, 1908, pp. 726-7.
44. *Red Book of Commerce*, 1908, p. 441. This figure possibly includes some distributive staff, as the factory in Molesworth Street, Dublin, included 'salesrooms'. The total includes 'assistants and workers in the country'.
45. Information from Dr Douglas Farnie of Manchester University. Howard and Bullough employed 6,000 men by 1914, (S.B. Saul, 'The Engineering Industry' in D.H. Aldcroft, (ed.) *The Development of British Industry and Foreign Competition, 1875-1914: Studies in Industrial Enterprise* (London, 1968), p. 192).

46. *Red Book of Commerce,* 1908, p. 404. No factory is mentioned in this entry — the staff were said to be employed 'throughout Ireland', and were probably very largely outworkers.
47. *Red Book of Commerce,* 1908, pp. 131-.2. 4,500 of the staff were employed in the works and 500 in the offices; by 1914, British Westinghouse employed about 7,000 in the works, and 300 in the offices.
48. *Red Book of Commerce,* 1912, p. 102.
49. *Red Book of Commerce,* 1909, p. 83. This figure may include some distributive staff in several warehouses in England and Ireland.
50. *Red Book of Commerce,* 1909, p. 585. In 1903, 4,380 workers (1,216 men, 3,164 women and children) were employed (Tariff Commission, TC4 26/9, 34/9, 35/1); in 1904 4,900-5,000 (TC3 1/93), by 1913, over 6,000 *(Red Book of Commerce,* 1914, p. 602).
51. *Red Book of Commerce,* 1908, pp. 322-3. By 1913, Frys employed nearly 6,000 *(Red Book of Commerce,* 1914, pp. 372-3).
52. Tariff Commission, TC4 34/2, TC4 35/1. In 1912, Swan Hunter employed 6-7,000 *(Red Book of Commerce,* 1913, p. 886).
53. *Red Book of Commerce,* 1908, p. 913. In 1903, the company employed 4,385 (1,104 men, and 3,281 women and children), and in addition, 'a large number of persons who work for us at their homes in the country', (Tariff Commission, TC4 19/5, 34/7, 35/1). The figure given in the *Red Book* for 1908, therefore, may not include outworkers employed by the company.
54. Information from Dr Douglas Farnie. Saul in 'Development of Mechanical Engineering Industries', p. 112, gives a figure of 4,000 for 1908. Dobson & Barlow's entry in the *Red Book of Commerce,* 1912, p. 286, said that the firm employed 5,000, 4,000 in their Bolton works and 1,000 in their works at Bradley Fold.
55. *Red Book of Commerce,* 1914, p. 238.
56. Tariff Commission, TC4 7/45. The Company was evidently growing rapidly. By 1911 it employed 12-15,000 men *(Red Book of Commerce,* 1912, p. 79) and so the 1907 total should probably be rather higher than that for 1903. A short entry in the *Red Book of Commerce* for 1908 mentions the same works as the 1912 entry, but does not give a figure for staff.
57. Edward Cadbury, *Experiments in Industrial Organisation* (London, 1912). See also the graph in Iolo A. Williams *The Firm of Cadbury 1831-1931* (London, 1931), pp. 276-7. In 1899, Cadburys employed 2,685, and 6,800 at their main factory at Bournville in 1914. (Williams, *Cadburys,* pp. 68-9, p. 100).
58. This figure is an estimate. Dorman Long & Co employed about 3,000 in 1907 (Macrosty, *Trust Movement,* p. 28), and their major subsidiary, Bell Brothers, employed 5,500 men in 1905 (ibid., p. 31), but this included 3,930 miners and 209 quarrymen (*List of Mines,* 1905, *List of Quarries,* 1905). Dorman Long also had another, smaller subsidiary, North-Eastern Steel, for which I have not been able to trace any employment statistics. Judging by the apparent scale of their activities (*The Statist,* 5 December, 1908, pp. 1193-5), North-Eastern Steel, at a guess, employed no more than 1,000-1,500 men.
59. *Red Book of Commerce,* 1908, pp. 263-4. 181 miners and quarryworkers have been subtracted from the figure given there. (*List of Mines,* 1907, *List of Quarries,* 1907).
60. *Red Book of Commerce,* 1908, p. 402. Dr Douglas Farnie puts their 1907 workforce at 3,500. In 1895, Hetheringtons employed 3,500 men in factories, and a further 1,500 at work put out (Saul, in Aldcroft (ed.), *Development of British Industry,* p. 192).
61. *Red Book of Commerce,* 1912, pp. 836-7.
62. *Red Book of Commerce,* 1908, p. 104. This total includes 150 clerks. By 1909, the company employed an average of 5,000 workmen and 150 clerks. (*Red Book of Commerce,* , 1910, p. 102). In 1903 only 2,571 had been employed — (2,158 men, 413 women and children) (Tariff Commission TC4 35/1) — but in 1905 Birmingham Small Arms had bought the Royal Small Arms Factory in Birmingham from the government. In 1903 this factory had employed 754 staff (Murray Committtee, Parliamentary Papers, (1907) x).

63. J.F. Clarke, *Power on Land and Sea. 160 Years of Industrial Enterprise on Tyneside: a history of R & W Hawthorn Leslie & Co. Ltd. Engineers and Shipbuilders* (Newcastle, 1979), p. 73. In 1898, about 10,000 had apparently been employed (information from Jonathan Zeitlin). By 1901, the work force had fallen to 4,513, and in 1903 to 3,697; by 1914 the total had risen again to 5,250. (Clarke, *Power on Land and Sea,* p.73).

64. Tariff Commission TC4 35/2, 34/3. This figure relates only to the locomotive works at Gorton, Manchester.

65. P.J. Gooderson, 'James Williamson', in D.J. Jeremy (ed.), *Dictionary of Business Biography* (forthcoming). This total represented the peak of James Williamson's staff. The factory at Lune Mills, Lancaster, was the largest oil-cloth factory in the world.

66. Saul, 'Development of Mechanical Engineering Industries', p. 196. This figure relates to the locomotive engineering works at Doncaster only.

67. Information from Dr Douglas Farnie.

68. *Red Book of Commerce,* 1908, p. 800.

69. Information from Dr Douglas Farnie. In 1911, the firm's workforce was about 3,000 (*Red Book of Commerce,* 1912, pp. 635-6).

70. Information from Geoffrey Tweedale, Ph.D. student, Economic History Department, London School of Economics.

71. *Red Book of Commerce,* 1908, p. 76. In 1903, Bass employed 3,500 (Tariff Commission TC4 35/1).

72. Saul, in Aldcroft (ed.), *Development of British Industry,* p. 223. It is possible, considering the expansion of the motor industry in the previous several years, that the workforce of the tyre works had expanded since 1907.

73. Entry on Ludwig Mond in *Concise Dictionary of National Biography 1901-1970* (Oxford, 1982), p. 477.

74. Estimate by Dr W.J. Reader.

75. Engineering Employers' Federation, List of Journeymen and Apprentices, March 1910. See above, note no. 41 for the problems involved in expanding these figures to calculate the total workforce. The Cammell Laird plants at Workington and Penistone do not seem to have belonged to the Engineering Employers' Federation. If Cammell Laird had registered about the same proportion of their workforce with the EEF as did other shipbuilding and engineering companies who were members, the figure given here should be doubled, at least, to arrive at an estimate of the total workforce.

76. Tariff Commission, TC4 34/6, 35/1. The firm's entry in the *Red Book of Commerce,* 1909, p. 611, stated that the firm 'employed several thousands of hands at different factories, warehouses etc'. Their Londonderry premises were described there as 'One of the largest shirt factories in the North of Ireland'. This firm of shirt, collar and pyjama manufacturers said that they had 'made a point always of moving with the times, and have adopted every improvement in this branch of business'.

77. Tariff Commission, TC4 7/36.

78. Tariff Commission, TC4 35/2. The anonymous Halifax carpet manufacturers mentioned in this document have been identified as J. Crossley & Sons, because this firm was then, and had been for some years, the largest carpet manufacturers. J. Crossley employed 5,000 in 1912 (J.M. Bartlett, *Carpeting the Millions* (Edinburgh, 1977), p. 211).

79. Tariff Commission, TC4 19/9.

80. C.H. Feinstein, *York 1831-1981* (York, 1981) pp. 124, 154.

81. *Red Book of Commerce,* 1908, p. 368. By 1913 Guinness employed about 4,000 (*Red Book of Commerce,* 1914, p. 427).

82. *Red Book of Commerce,* 1912, p. 478.

83. Tariff Commission, TC4 7/33, 34/2, 35/2. By 1911 the firm employed over 5,000 (*Red Book of Commerce,* 1912, p. 632).

84. *Red Book of Commerce,* 1912, p. 778.

85. *Red Book of Commerce,* 1909, pp. 678-9. By 1910, the firm's workforce had increased to 4-5,000 (*Red Book of Commerce,* 1911, p. 675).

86. *Red Book of Commerce,* 1914, p. 719.

87. *Red Book of Commerce*, 1908, p. 536. In 1903 the firm employed 200 men and 3,000 women and children. (Tariff Commission TC4 19/6).
88. Tariff Commission, TC4 34/8, 35/1.
89. D.C. Coleman, *Courtaulds, An Economic and Social History*, 3 vols. (Oxford, 1969-1980), vol. i, pp. 230-1. By 1907, the Coventry rayon factory, which had not been open in 1900, employed 332 (C.H. Ward-Jackson, *A History of Courtaulds* (London, 1941), p. 92.
90. *Red Book of Commerce*, 1909, p. 789.
91. *Red Book of Commerce*, 1908, pp. 196-7. A detailed analysis of the workforce of J & J Colman, provided by the company, shows that Colman's employed a total of 3,177 in 1905, 1722 men, 400 boys, 630 women and 425 girls. 2,607 were employed at the Carrow Works.
92. Tariff Commission, TC3 1/84.
93. Tariff Commission, TC4 16/4. John Lysaght's workforce had probably grown considerably by 1914, for in 1903 they had not yet built their large Normanby Park Works.
94. *Red Book of Commerce*, 1908, p. 648.
95. Tariff Commission, TC4 34/4, 35/1.
96. *Red Book of Commerce*, 1908, pp. 438-9. See also Tariff Commission, TC4 7/65: in 1903 the Silvertown factory employed 2,985 (2,500 men and boys, 485 women and girls), and a further 437 men and 213 women and children were employed at their factory at Persan (Seine-et-Oise).
97. Information from Dr Douglas Farnie. See also *Red Book of Commerce*, 1912, pp. 567-8, where again the total 3.000 is given.
98. *Red Book of Commerce*, 1908, p. 388.
99. *Red Book of Commerce*, 1908, p. 325.
100. *Red Book of Commerce*, 1908, p. 53; L.H. Broadbent, *The Avery Business (1730-1918)* (privately published, 1949), p. 61.
101. Information from Dr Douglas Farnie.
102. *Red Book of Commerce*, 1913, p. 888.
103. *Red Book of Commerce*, 1912, p. 828. This woollen dress goods manufacturer was based in Watling Street, London.
104. *Red Book of Commerce*, 1910, p. 391.

## KEY TO SIC CATEGORIES

| II | Mining | X | Shipbuilding and Marine Engineering |
|----|--------|---|--------|
| III | Food, Drink and Tobacco | XI | Vehicles |
| V | Chemicals and Allied Industries | XIII | Textiles (including textile finishing) |
| VI | Metal Manufacture | XV | Clothing and Footwear |
| VII | Mechanical Engineering | XVI | Bricks, Pottery and Glass |
| VIII | Instrument Engineering | XVIII | Paper, Printing and Publishing |
| IX | Electrical Engineering | XIX | Other Manufacturing Industries |

## APPENDIX 2

Professor Payne's Listing of the largest 52 Industrial
Companies of 1905

| Name of Firm | SIC Category (see key to Table 1) | Capital in 1905 (to nearest £1,000) |
|---|---|---|
| 1.  Imperial Tobacco Co. | III | 17,545 |
| 2.  Watney, combe, Reid | III | 14,950 |
| 3.  J & P Coats | XIII | 11,181 |
| 4.  United Alkali | V | 8,490 |
| 5.  Calico Printers' Association | XIII | 8,227 |
| 6.  Vickers, Sons & Maxim | VI, VIII, X | 7,440 |
| 7.  Fine Cotton Spinners' & Doublers Assoc. | XIII | 7,290 |
| 8.  Associated Portland Cement Mfrs. | XVI | 7,061 |
| 9.  Bleachers' Association | XIII | 6,820 |
| 10. Arthur Guinness | III | 6,000 |
| 11. Sir W. G. Armstrong, Whitworth & Co. | VI, VII, X | 5,316 |
| 12. Samuel Allsopp & Sons | III | 5,095 |
| 13. Whitbread | III | 4,767 |
| 14. Bass, Ratcliff & Gretton | III | 4,640 |
| 15. Guest, Keen & Nettlefolds | VI, XII | 4,536 |
| 16. Dunlop Pneumatic Tyre Co. | XIX | 4,396 |
| 17. Bradford Dyers' Association | XIII | 4,310 |
| 18. Barclay, Perkins | III | 4,270 |
| 19. Bolckow, Vaughan | VI, II | 4,246 |
| 20. Cannon Brewery | III | 4,200 |
| 21. Wall Paper Manufacturers | XXIII | 4,141 |
| 22. Charrington | III | 4,025 |
| 23. Lever Brothers | V | 4,000 |
| 24. Ind, Coope | III | 3,698 |
| 25. Truman, Hanbury, Buxton | III | 3,515 |
| 26. Mann, Crossman & Paulin | III | 3,250 |
| 27. English Sewing Cotton | XIII | 3,101 |
| 28. Peter Walker & Son | III | 3,000 |
| 29. John Brown | VI, VII, X | 2,947 |
| 30. United Collieries | II | 2,843 |
| 31. Linen Thread | XIII | 2,726 |
| 32. Cammell, Laird | VI, X | 2,623 |
| 33. Maple | XVII | 2,620 |
| 34. Salt Union | II | 2,600 |
| 35. Courage | III | 2,500 |
| 35. Bovril | III | 2,500 |
| 35. William Beardmore | VI, X | 2,500 |
| 38. Huntley & Palmers | III | 2,400 |
| 39. Hoare | III | 2,354 |
| 40. Brunner Mond | V | 2,299 |
| 41. Waring and Gillow | XVII | 2,205 |
| 42. Wigan Coal & Iron | II, VI | 2,193 |
| 43. City of London Brewery | III | 2,127 |
| 44. British Cotton and Wool Dyers' Assoc. | XIII | 2,070 |
| 45. Distillers' Company | III | 2,049 |
| 46. Threlfalls | III | 1,997 |
| 47. Wilson's Brewery | III | 1,992 |
| 48. Yorkshire Wool Combers' Association | XIII | 1,966 |
| 49. Reckitt & Sons | V | 1,950 |
| 50. Lister | XIII | 1,950 |
| 51. J & J Colman | III | 1,916 |
| 52. Dorman, Long | VI | 1,910 |

From: P. L. Payne, 'The Emergence of the Large-Scale Company in
Great Britain, 1870-1914', Economic History Review, 2nd series, xx
(December 1967) pp. 539-40.

# THE LARGE MANUFACTURING COMPANIES OF 1935

By LEWIS JOHNMAN

This list follows that of Christine Shaw[1] who attempted to establish the 100 largest manufacturing employers in the United Kingdom in 1907 and seeks to establish the same for 1935. As Shaw's list counterpointed P.L. Payne's list of the largest British industrial companies in 1905[2] – a list based on the nominal value of the issued capital of the companies (including debentures, mortgages, loans and deposits) so the present listing attempts to counterpoint to a similar degree Leslie Hannah's list of the 50 largest companies of 1930,[3] based on their estimated market value.

Christine Shaw applied a number of reservations and strictures to her work and some would bear reiteration here. It became obvious early in the project that *the* largest 100 manufacturing employers would not be identified. The difficulty of arriving at figures for Unilever, Guest, Keen and Nettlefold and the absence of figures for companies such as Associated Portland Cement Manufacturers (APCM) and the major newspaper publishing houses, attest to this. As with 1907, 1935 was a Census of Production year and this represents the only systematic attempt to compile statistical information about the workforce and output of British manufacturing industry. The Census returns are not available (nor does it seem likely that they ever will be)[4] and the Final Report was published in such a way as to obscure the contribution of any single firm to either total employment or output of any particular industry.[5] Whilst it does provide a wealth of background material (and does give figures for government workshops) it was on the whole little help in the compilation of this list.

As with 1907, detailed statistics do appear for mining and quarrying in the annually published *Lists of Mines and Quarries*.[6] This publication has the merit of listing the owning company and the individual colliery and/or quarrying operations. As we were concerned only with manufacturing firms, the main interest in the *List of Mines* was in allowing accurate details of how many individuals should be subtracted from multi-interest firms.[7]

The single best source of published information on the employment of individual manufacturing firms proved to be the commercial directory, *The Red Book of Commerce*.[8] This work is well described in Shaw,[9] but one point will stand repetition. The entries were compiled on the basis of information provided by the firms themselves in answer to the *Red Book's* standard form. The question on 'staff' seems to have been widely interpreted: ignored at one end of the scale and answered numerically at the other with a range of more impressionistic replies in-between. The notes to the list will indicate just how important the *Red Book of Commerce* has been. One final point concerns the reliability of the directory as far as its figures go. Where other sources have been used they almost without exception confirm the *Red Book's* figures and a cursory check against later figures for rapidly growing firms – such as GEC – indicate that the directory was methodically up-dated.[10]

Government publications were useful in some aspects. As already stated, the *Final Report on the Fifth Census of Production* provided the figures for government manufacture in the ordnance works and dockyards. The *Railway Companies (Staff) Returns*[11] gives figures for the major railway companies (although a fair degree of caution should be applied to these figures) and the *Royal Commission on the Private Manufacture of and Trading in Arms* (1935–36)[12] gives figures for the major private armaments companies. Other information was gleaned from economic, business and company histories, companies themselves, and from individual experts on particular companies and/or industries. As with Shaw's work this list restricts itself to manufacturing employment – those sections which are listed in the Standard Industrial Categories which follow the notes – and therefore excludes all discussion of the public utility or service sectors.

The major drawback to any enterprise of this type is being reasonably sure that *the* largest 100 manufacturing firms have been identified and if such definition is not possible to at least reduce the margin of error to as small a degree as possible. Intuitively one may suspect certain firms should be included in the list: here quite simply the task of gleaning any measure to base even an estimate on may have proved too difficult. APCM, for example, does not appear on the list and in spite of strenuous efforts by certain of their management to calculate a figure none could be realised. Complete absence of data usually explains the absence of any given firm. Other problems bedevil some of the figures: a number are estimates – 'guesstimates' would perhaps be a better description – some may be for part of the workforce and some may include categories which should not be included. Not all of the figures are specific to the target date, although nearly all are within four years. Particular problems apply to industries such as shipbuilding where figures could vary considerably from month to month and season to season. Thus rather weighty reservations must be borne in mind about the list. No systematic attempt was made to collect information about non-manufacturing employers. The railway companies – as in 1907 – remain the largest single employers. The London Midland and Scottish employed 222,220, the London North Eastern 171,339, the Great Western 95,729 and the Southern 65,008. The London Passenger Transport Board had a staff of 14,382.[13] The local authorities employed 191,052, gas undertakings 121,249, electricity undertakings 102,945, Water Boards 31,974, and the General Post Office 37,387 (although this figure seems dubious).[14] J. Lyons employed over 30,000,[15] the Pearl Life Assurance 14,200,[16] and the department store, Harrods, over 6,000.[17] It may be that although much of the discussion of this article will concern itself with a new-old industry divide that the real emphasis of the importance of economic change had already, by 1935, tilted in favour of the service sector and that far more attention should be paid to this sector than it has hitherto had.

Enough sufficiently accurate information has been obtained to make the list useful, without wishing to place any stress on exact numerical ranking: (if ten firms all have 5,000 employees, who is to say which firm should be above or below any other?), and it certainly serves as an indicator of what had happened to the composition of the manufacturing sector and the labour force therein involved. It turns the debate on concentration of industry in Britain[18] away from an emphasis on capital towards that of labour. It may also serve to make one or two points with respect to the dominant inter-war debate around 'new' and 'old' industries.

Visual illustration of both debates – the rising 'newer' industries and declining 'older' industries and of the concentration of both – can be clearly seen from a cursory look at the 1907 and 1935 lists. Of the 104 firms in the 1907 list, only 43 (44.7 per cent) remain in 1935. Of the 61 (55.3 per cent) which have dropped out, 34 are accounted for by amalgamation and merger (35.36 per cent), ten are accounted for but have fewer employees than the 4,000 cut-off point of the 1935 list (10.4 per cent), five are bankrupt and/or closed (the most noted being Palmer's Shipbuilding and Iron Co.). One (Guinness) has its manufacturing basis in the Irish Free State and two could not be accounted for.

Perhaps more surprisingly, of Hannah's 50 companies in 1930 only 29 appear in the 1935 list. Even allowing for the in-built bias of Hannah's list to reflect capital intensive and over-capitalised industries,[19] and the attendant difficulty of determining what capital is being measured (that is, whether the calculation should be based upon historical costs or those appearing in the balance sheet of an attempted independent assessment of the actual value at the time of examination), it seems surprising that 21 (42 per cent) of the 1930 list are missing from that of 1935. Of these 21 firms, six have fewer than 4,000 employees (capital intensity being no indication of the size of the labour force). One is accounted for by amalgamation, three are publishers for which no figures could be found, eight are involved in food and drink (Guinness again, and J. Lyons who employed 30,000, the vast bulk of whom however must have been in services),[20] one asbestos firm, one pharmaceutical chemicals, and one building materials. This last, APCM, being the only company included in the 1907 and 1930 lists which is absent from that of 1935. Perhaps the most significant feature is the percentage – 35.36 per cent – of the 1907 list accounted for by merger by 1935. A more obvious indication of the strength of merger-induced concentration could hardly be found.

A similar situation is revealed when the 'new' 'staple' debate is addressed. Some of the difficulty surrounding this issue has been in deciding exactly what constitutes 'new' industry and what a 'staple'.[21] If the Food, Drink and Tobacco sector and the Co-operative Wholesale Societies are included among the 'new' industries (and there are arguments for and against this) the 1935 list divided between 'old' and 'new'; 54 to 47. From the 1930 list ten are classified as old and 40 as new: a reflection of the capital-intensive nature of some of the 'new' industries although perhaps no less a reflection of the number of food and drink companies in the 1930 list. The earlier strength of the staple sector is immediately apparent in the 1907 list with 76 firms (79.04 per cent) being classified as 'staple' and 28 (29.12 per cent) as new. This is more clearly apparent if one observes that of the first ten companies in the 1907 list all are from the staple sector and of the first 20 only two are classified as new; the first being the Co-operative Wholesale Society and the second the United Alkali Co. Significantly, between categories of ten the only positions where the 'new' industries are as numerically strong as the old are between 30 and 40, and 70 and 80 and where stronger between 90 and 100. There is no such clear-cut disparity in the 1935 list.

Perhaps the most obvious single fact about the 1935 list is its domination by large firms which have undergone substantial recent merger activity, bearing out Hannah and Kay's point that 'growth in concentration . . . in modern manufacturing industry . . . [is] . . . almost wholly due to merger'.[22] It is certainly clear that the share of the 100 largest firms in the total manufacturing workforce of the UK was increasing. In 1907 the 100 firms employed 682,084 people or 12.9 per cent of all manufacturing workers.[23] In 1935 manufacturing industry employed 5,955,300[24] whilst the companies listed employed 1,243,922 or 20.9 per cent of the manufacturing workforce. In terms of output the 100 largest manufacturing companies had 14.3 per cent of net manufacturing output in 1907,[25] and 24 per cent in 1935.

Merger is in fact the dominant force in the 1935 list. One has only to look back at the 1907 list to see how the transformation has been worked. In 1907, Lever Bros. stands 95th in the list with 3,000 employees. By 1935 Unilever leads the list as the result of a series of amalgamations in two main areas of production: margarine and soap manufacture. In 1929 merger between the Dutch Margarine Union and Lever Bros. established Unilever as the largest margarine producer in Britain.[26] Until 1906 the growth of the soap trade was largely a reflection of the growth of Lever Bros. In 1906 the idea of a 'soap-trust' was advanced in which the 11 leading firms responsible for two-thirds of the output would combine. Press and public reaction was so hostile that the measure was scrapped.[27] By 1911, however, Lever Bros. had acquired all but two of the ten concerns of the proposed trust, and by 1921 held more than 70 per cent of the trade.[28] Similarly, ICI formed in 1926 was a consolidation of four of the largest 50 firms of 1919: Nobel Industries, Brunner Mond, the British Dyestuffs Corporation and the United Alkali Co.[29] Of these four – Nobel was a merger of 30 explosives companies in 1918 (it ranked 74th with 4,000 employees in 1907). Brunner Mond had acquired competitors and integrated backwards during the First World War and British Dyestuffs was the result of a government-backed merger during the war and controlled some 75 per cent of British dyestuffs output.[30]

It is not only in the 'newer' industries that increasing concentration is marked. Again a cursory look at the 1935 list will show the continuing strength of much of the old-style sector. Vickers, for example, has retained its numerical listing from 1907 whilst the Fine Cotton Spinners and Doublers Association has retained its total labour force, if not its listing. The strength of the railway companies – a somewhat surprising feature given the date (although this may be more a reflection of inadequate disaggregation of the figures than anything else) – mirrors the mergers which brought about the 'big four'. Interestingly enough, the North British Locomotive Co. does not share in the seeming continuing health of the railway companies, its workforce having slumped to 1,954 from around 8,000 in 1907 and the total value of output having declined from £4,245,533 in 1920 to £502,673.[31] The NBLC is probably a more accurate indicator of the condition of the railway companies than their own figures might suggest.

In the 'staple' sector – particularly iron and steel, heavy engineering and shipbuilding – the spur to amalgamation was the heavy indebtedness of the sector in the 1920s, the so-called 'Black Decade'.[32] In many cases the reconstruction undertaken broke up the elaborate vertical combines of earlier decades and sought horizontal amalgamation instead. A case in point is the breaking-up of the heterogeneous integrations of three of the great pre-war heavy industrial concerns: Vickers, Armstrongs and Cammell Laird. The high-grade heavy steel concerns were formed into the English Steel Corporation (controlled by Vickers) and Armstrong's common-grade steel concerns were also merged into the Lancashire Steel Corporation. Vickers-Armstrong consolidated the shipbuilding interests – again under Vickers control – as were the steel and railway carriage works of the Metropolitan-Cammell Co. Cammell Laird became solely a shipbuilding company[33] and Vickers sold their other interests in electrical engineering (Metrovick) to A.E.I. and motor vehicles (Wolseley) to Morris.[34]

The influence of the banking sector in the steel rationalisation of the 1920s and 1930s attests to the main impetus being financial. Indeed a cursory inspection of the BIDC and SMT papers in the Bank of England[35] bears out Duncan Burn's statement that 'bankers had been concerned in the negotiations and in many if not in all had had a determining influence'. The English and Lancashire Steel Corporations both owed their existence to the Bank of England.[36] Dorman Long's absorption of Bolckow Vaughan in 1929 went ahead because Barclays refused to allow the renewal of Bolckow's £1 million overdraft unless the merger went through.[37] The Bank of England also had the task of dismembering the former giant Armstrong-Whitworth and, later, Beardmores, and also played a leading role in the rationalisation of the Scottish Steel industry around Colville's, a process which was completed in 1936.[38]

Mergers, however, took many forms. ICI, for example, had initially been highly centralised around the Nobel structure. This had brought ICI the benefit of lower costs for a number of reasons: rationalised production and improved buying ability, joint distribution and selling. ICI had reaped substantial economies of scale from this through substantially improving cash flow, the rationalisation of production and vastly increased buying ability as well as the benefits of joint distribution and selling. Between 1928 and 1931, however, manufacturing production was decentralised to eight groups with inter-group policy being controlled by a Central Administration Committee. Thus ICI seemed to have developed into a model of modern corporatism. A centralised and specialised head office now exercised overall financial and managerial control over the groups concerned with efficient plant management.[39]

This was by no means the only form of company organisation to emerge during the 1920s merger wave. Associated Electrical Industries, formed in 1928, served as a holding company until its own merger with General Electric. Its major constituent companies, British Thompson Houston, Metropolitan Vickers, Ferguson Pailin and Edison Swan enjoyed high degrees of autonomy to the extent of competing with each other. There was little central financial or managerial control.[40] Other companies which reflected this looser confederated style of organisation include Tube Investments, EMI and Guest, Keen and Nettlefold. The benefits of this form of organisation are the offsetting of the potential dangers of diseconomies of scale and, although not allowing all of the benefits of rationalisation, they could still gain through collusive pricing, co-ordinated investment, overhead pooling and the general spreading of risk.

Merger, however, was not a simple key to success in the inter-war economy. As already stated, the vast rationalisation of the iron and steel, engineering and shipbuilding sectors proceeded from fears of worse, rather than expectation of better things to come. In the other main branch of the staple industries – cotton – the major merger was centred on the creation of the Lancashire Cotton Corporation. The LCC was a Bank of England-inspired merger of some 100 firms in cotton spinning, the main aim being to substantially reduce the number of operating spindles in the industry. The Corporation managed to carry out its major task, reducing its spindleage from nine million in 1929 to 4.5 million in 1939 and disposing of all of its 20,000 looms.[41] The process, however, was particularly painful – the merger had seen the integration of a mass of small independent cotton firms, mostly of similar size with no obvious dominant company to impose form and structure on the others – the task was of too gargantuan a scale for the resources marshalled to tackle it. The inherent dangers in large multi-firm mergers served as a constant reminder that merger alone was not the easy answer to the economic problems of the 1920s and 1930s.

Some spectacular cases of indigenous growth do stand out. In rayon production Courtaulds gained an early dominance of the market and expanded substantially throughout the 1920s. This expansion required far lower prices to allow viscose to compete with cheaper fibres and British producers to compete with foreign manufacturers. Thus the need to achieve large-scale, low-cost production was the main stimulus to technical innovation and expansion in the 1920s. Courtaulds was in effect able to stave off much of its competition by relying on technical superiority and low costs. Relatively low prices and profit rates were normal for Courtaulds in the 1930s, the company having recognised the need to keep prices down in order to avoid the creation of competition.[42]

Another example of self-generating growth is the motor vehicle industry. Here, too, inexpensive production was stressed and mass production methods early adopted. Output rose from 73,000 vehicles in 1922 to 239,000 in 1929, whilst the average factory price of cars fell from £308 in 1912 to £259 in 1924, £206 in 1930 and reached £130 by 1935–36. After a slight recession in 1931–32 output was more than double its 1929 figure by 1937. Morris were able, through economies of scale, to expand their share of the market from five per cent in 1919 to 41 per cent by 1925. By 1938 six firms accounted for 90 per cent of the total number of cars produced and for 80 per cent of the total number of commercial vehicles.

It seems irrefutable that the industries and companies showing the highest degree of concentration by the 1930s were those which had expanded most rapidly in the 1920s. The steadily increasing concentration in manufacturing – measured by the share of the largest 100 companies in output and employment – and of the role played by the growth of new, inherently more concentrated industries and of increasing concentration within industries is clearly visible in the changing composition of the dominant companies within the economy. It is further support for the analysis of Leak and Maizels which showed that eight per cent of total employment in 1935 was accounted for by industries within which the share of the top three firms in employment was 70 per cent or more.[44] All of the evidence would seem to point to the conclusion that by 1935 concentration amongst manufacturing firms in Britain was as high as it had ever been. It also adds weight to the view of Hannah and Kay that the growth in concentration was almost wholly due to merger. Hannah's analysis of merger activity shows that no fewer than 1884 firms had disappeared through mergers between 1920 and 1929. And the scale of this was something entirely new: 'The average annual level of 188 firms disappearances is over three times the average of the preceding four decades.' It is difficult to disagree with his conclusion: 'that the period from the closing years of the First World War to the early 1930s saw a significant change in the structure of British manufacturing industry'.[45]

Much of the debate concerning the structure of industry between the wars has centred on the role of the 'new industries' during the period generally, and on the 1930s recovery in particular. This debate has spawned a vast literature,[46] and it is not the purpose of this paper to systematically analyse this material: some observations however, are unavoidable. Some of the debate has become heavily obscured in the semantics of trying to establish what is meant by 'new'. Criticising D.H. Aldcroft's article 'Economic Growth in Britain in the Inter-War Years: A Reassessment',[47] J.A. Dowie wrote:

> Apart from the empirical weakness of the 'new-old' division and the difficulty of defining an 'industry' the time may also be ripe for drawing attention to the danger of circularity which the use of the

'new industry' argument creates at the analytical level. The assertion that a structural shift from 'old' towards 'new' was a prominent source of growth can easily degenerate into a tautology . . . . There is . . . probably a tendency to define 'new' in terms of 'expanding' and certainly a failure to recognise the importance of distinguishing clearly between the two.[48]

Indeed the whole area is fraught with a range of methodological problems.

Nevertheless discussion continues and various attempts have been made to explain the changes in the structure of the economy between the wars. Much of the debate has been taken up with the examination of growth and investment.[49] No full-scale study has attempted to analyse inter-war data purely in terms of employment shifts between the two divisions 'old' and 'new' – and as already stated – agreement about what constitutes each is unclear.

This article is concerned only with manufacturing industry and divides the industries as follows: (a) 'new': chemicals and allied trades, non-ferrous metals and other metal goods, electrical engineering, vehicles, precision instruments, rayon, food, drink and tobacco and paper printing and publishing; (b) 'old': brick, china and glass, iron and steel, shipbuilding, naval dockyards and ordnance factories, mechanical engineering, railway workshops, textiles (excluding rayon, nylon and silk) leather, clothing trades (including boots, shoes, slippers and clogs, but excluding rubber) and timber trades.[50] Those anonymous groups defined as 'other manufacturing industries' were divided equally between old and new. The following tables illustrate the results.

Table 1 shows the proportion of the manufacturing workforce in the staple and new industries. It shows quite clearly the gradual shift in proportions between 1920 and 1935. Overall the series is remarkable only for its steadiness – large shifts occurring between 1920 and 1921 in a period of general recession and between 1929 and 1930 at the outset of the crisis of the 1930s. It also bears out the view that the 1920s were more important for the development of the 'new' industries than the 1930s.[51] It would certainly seem, on the basis of these figures, difficult to argue that a 'development bloc' of industries existed in employment terms given the rate of expansion between 1931 and 1935.[52]

Table 2 is an index of manufacturing employment and of employment in the 'staple' and 'new' industries. These indices tend to support earlier conclusions. It is in the 'new' industries that growth is most prominent in the 1920s. The 1929–31 slump is far more pronounced in the staple sector than in the new and recovery at least until re-armament much slower. The recovery in the 'new' industries is considerably stronger with the high point of 1929 almost being regained by 1933. It may be that Buxton's assertion that 'there is little evidence of any significant change in the structure of British industry over the remainder of the 1930s'[53] is partly correct. Although Table 1 would support his conclusion that resource transfer in the 1930s was no more significant than in the 1920s – in fact it was less –

TABLE 1

PROPORTION OF MANUFACTURING WORKFORCE IN 'STAPLE' AND 'NEW'
INDUSTRIES

| Date | Staple | New |
|------|--------|-----|
| 1920 | 67.22 | 32.78 |
| 1921 | 63.50 | 36.50 |
| 1922 | 63.88 | 36.12 |
| 1923 | 63.01 | 36.99 |
| 1924 | 62.93 | 37.07 |
| 1925 | 61.85 | 38.15 |
| 1926 | 60.37 | 38.63 |
| 1927 | 61.49 | 38.51 |
| 1928 | 60.60 | 39.40 |
| 1929 | 59.50 | 40.10 |
| 1930 | 57.89 | 42.11 |
| 1931 | 56.73 | 43.27 |
| 1932 | 56.36 | 43.64 |
| 1933 | 56.64 | 43.36 |
| 1934 | 56.44 | 43.56 |
| 1935 | 56.23 | 43.77 |

*Source:* Calculated from A.L. Chapman and R. Knight *Wages and Salaries in the United Kingdom 1920–1938* (Cambridge 1958)

Table 2 would suggest that at least in employment terms the 'new' industries were more important during the pre-rearmament period than were the staples. It does also seem that the shared conclusion of Richardson (Buxton's main target) and Buxton's that during the 1929–32 depression there was little resource movement, is challenged by the figures in Table 1.

This is by no means an acceptance of either the traditional or revisionist case about the inter-war period. Nor is it a blasé attempt to dismiss an unemployment rate of 16.4 per cent for 1935. The issue under discussion is manufacturing industry alone – not industry, still less the economy. What seems very clear from the list, however, is that in spite of the healthy position of a number of the staple firms the structure of the manufacturing sector was changing steadily to reflect the growing importance of the 'new' industries as was the structure of employment.

Population tended to move towards areas with expanding industries (the

TABLE 2

INDEX OF MANUFACTURING EMPLOYMENT AND OF EMPLOYMENT IN
THE 'STAPLE' AND 'NEW' INDUSTRIES

| Date | Manufacturing | Staple | New |
|------|--------------|--------|-----|
| 1920 | 177 | 125 | 103 |
| 1921 | 90  | 91  | 88  |
| 1922 | 94  | 96  | 92  |
| 1923 | 98  | 98  | 97  |
| 1924 | 100 | 100 | 100 |
| 1925 | 101 | 99  | 104 |
| 1926 | 98  | 94  | 104 |
| 1927 | 105 | 102 | 109 |
| 1928 | 105 | 101 | 110 |
| 1929 | 106 | 101 | 115 |
| 1930 | 98  | 91  | 112 |
| 1931 | 91  | 82  | 107 |
| 1932 | 93  | 83  | 109 |
| 1933 | 97  | 87  | 114 |
| 1934 | 102 | 91  | 120 |
| 1935 | 105 | 93  | 123 |

*Source:* Calculated from A.L. Chapman and R. Knight, *Wages and Salaries in the United Kingdom 1920–1938* (Cambridge 1958).

vast increase in services is once again being ignored) – the main areas to gain being Greater London, the South East and West Midlands, whilst the areas losing population tended to be the centres of the 'staple' industries, the North East of England and South Wales. The proportions of insured employed individuals in the northern and southern counties of the UK were almost exactly reversed between 1923 and 1937.[54] There can be little doubt that the South-East and Midlands absorbed considerable numbers of migrant labour between the wars. In the South-East the areas of highest growth were Dagenham 28.7 per cent, Dover 19.5 per cent, Slough 15.6 per cent, Welwyn 13.9 per cent, Canterbury 12.8 per cent, Harrow 13.0 per cent, Hendon 13.1 per cent, Southall 11.4 per cent, Hounslow 10.5 per cent, St. Albans 10.5 per cent, and Letchworth 9.7 per cent. The main products of these towns and areas were, of course, those of the new industries – although the growth centred on Canterbury and Dover must reflect the absorption of miners from South Wales and the North-East into the Kent coalfield – Ford's at Dagenham, Kodak at Harrow plus a whole range of expanding industries and services, electrical wiring, and contracting, electric cables, food production, printing and publishing, paper and paper board, tobacco, tramway and omnibus services and the growth of local government services.

Of those migrating, 24 per cent came from the North-East; 19 per cent from the South-West; 18 per cent from Wales; 15.5 per cent from the Midlands; 15 per cent from the North-West and eight per cent from Scotland. Two main factors seem to have contributed to the urge to migrate: the extent of the depression in the home area and the proximity to more prosperous areas. Hence the dramatic outflow from Wales – 40 per 1,000 or one out of every 25 insured individuals moved to the south-east of England. The figures for the North-West and Scotland reflect immobility as well as indigenous conditions – the large scope for female employment in the textile trades, for example, had the effect of mitigating family unemployment as well as the traditional roles of short time and underemployment – the Midlands figure reflects the relative prosperity of the region although the mobility here seems very surprising. The South-West has for long been a traditional exporter of population along the coast to London and the south-eastern counties whilst the high number from the North East reflects the depression in the staple trades.[55]

Much the same picture emerges from analysing labour influx into the Midlands. An important caveat needs to be observed here, however. There is a very direct two-way correspondence between population moving from the Midlands to the South-East and vice-versa. It is unfortunately impossible to say whether this represents migrants from depressed areas moving a second time or movement of the indigenous population. In all probability it was a combination of both. The areas showing the greatest rates of absorption in the Midlands are Coventry and North Warwickshire, the Eastern Midlands centred on Peterborough, Huntingdon and Corby and Birmingham and the West Midlands. Of those migrating 20 per cent came from the North-East; 19 per cent from the North-West; 18 per cent from Wales; 17 per cent from London and the South East; Scotland nine per cent and the South-West seven per cent. The predominance of the depressed areas in this migration is clear.[56]

No matter how the issue is construed the list provides clear evidence of structural change taking place in manufacturing industry. It may well be correct that the improved manufacturing growth performance of the 1930s cannot be attributed solely to the new industries and it is doubtful if anyone would take such a position. It may also be that the new industries account for only an annual average of five per cent of total investment undertaken between 1924 and 1937,[57] although this refers only to net investment and thus neglects the possibility of a relatively high rate of replacement in the 'new' industries. On the other side of the coin during the period 1920 to 1930 one-third of gross capital formation was directed to five major growth industries: motor vehicles, chemicals, electricals, rayon and paper.[58] What remains as irrefutable is that as far as the composition of the dominant enterprises within the economy goes the massive pre-war dominance of the staple trades had been broken irretrievably. In a period when the hold of large firms on the economy was becoming consolidated and concentration reaching an all-time high – the emergent giants are chemical firms, electrical firms and motor car producers. The structure of employment had been remarkably transformed.

## NOTES

This research was funded by the Business History Unit of the London School of Economics and Political Science. The study was originally suggested by Professor Leslie Hannah to whom I am grateful for considerate and considerable help. I am also grateful to other members of the Business History Unit, Dr Christine Shaw, whose article on 1907 this study succeeds, Dr R.P.T. Davenport-Hines and Dr David Jeremy. Many scholars helped with information on specific firms and are identified in the footnotes to the listing but I would particularly like to thank Professor Bernard Alford, Mr T.A.B. Corley, Dr D.A. Farnie, Mr Michael Moss, Dr C.W. Munn, Dr S. Tolliday, Dr J. Shorter and Professor A.J. Slaven. I am also indebted to the large number of company chairmen, personnel officers, secretaries and librarians who took time to answer written enquiries. Professor R.H Campbell and Dr M.W. Kirby kindly read an earlier draft of the manuscript and made helpful suggestions and comments. All errors are my own.

1. C. Shaw, 'The Largest Manufacturing Employers of 1907', *Business History*, Vol.25 (1983).
2. P.L. Payne, 'The Emergence of the Large-Scale Company in Great Britain, 1870-1914' *Economic History Review*, 2nd Series, Vol.20 (1967), pp.539–40.
3. L. Hannah, *The Rise of the Corporate Economy* (London, 1976), pp.118–9.
4. From inquiries made concerning the Census material it appears that the Confederation of British Industry is intractably opposed to any alteration of the regulations governing the use (non-use) by researchers of Census of Production material.
5. *Final Report on the Fifth Census of Production, 1935* (HMSO, 1938).
6. *List of Mines and Quarries in the U.K.* (HMSO, 1936).
7. Within the definition manufacturing, mineworkers and quarrymen are specifically excluded, they have therefore, where possible, been subtracted from the totals of companies' figures.
8. *Whitaker's Red Book of Commerce, or Who's Who in Business 1936* (London, 1936).
9. Shaw, op. cit., pp.42–3.
10. Hannah, op. cit., p.125; *The Red Book of Commerce, 1939*, p.304.
11. *Railway Companies (Staff) Returns* (Board of Trade/Ministry of Transport 1935).
12. *Royal Commission on the Private Manufacture of and Trading in Arms 1935–36.*
13. *Railway Companies (Staff) Return*, p.5
14. *Census of Production* Part IV, Section IV Public Utility Services and Government Departments, pp.2 and 92.
15. *Red Book of Commerce*, p.467.
16. Ibid., p.567.
17. Ibid., p.344.
18. S.J. Prais, *The Evolution of Giant Firms in Britain, a Study of the Growth of Concentration in Manufacturing Industry in Britain 1909-1970* (Cambridge, 1976); L. Hannah and J.A. Kay, *Concentration in Modern Industry* (London, 1977).
19. The most notable example of overcapitalisation is probably brewery companies. These are disproportionate to their true manufacturing capital because of the value of tied houses.
20. Cf. note 16.

21. Cf. J.A. Dowie, 'Growth in the Inter-War Period: Some More Arithmetic', *Economic History Review*. 2nd Series, Vol.21 (1968).
22. Hannah and Kay, op. cit., p.1. For the purposes of this list one should be aware of the problem of interlocking or overlapping companies and of being certain that units which appear legally distinct are so in fact.
23. Calculated from Shaw, op. cit.
24. A.L. Chapman and R. Knight, *Wages and Salaries in the United Kingdom 1920-1938* (Cambridge, 1958), p.100.
25. Calculated from Shaw, op. cit.
26. C. Wilson, *The History of Unilever*, Vol.2 (London, 1954) pp.301-99; R. Evely and I.M.D. Little, *Concentration in British Industry: An Empirical Study of the Structure of Industrial Production 1935-1951* (Cambridge, 1960), pp.121, 128 and 137.
27. Ibid, p.122.
28. Ibid.
29. W.J. Reader, *Imperial Chemical Industries: A History*, Vol.1 (Oxford, 1975), pp.300-16.
30. Ibid.
31. R.H. Campbell 'The North British Locomotive Company Between the Wars', *Business History*, Vol.2. (1978), p.231.
32. D.L. Burn, *The Economic History of Steelmaking 1867-1939* (Cambridge, 1940), pp.393-448.
33. Ibid.
34. Ibid.
35. Bankers Industrial Development Corporation and Securities Management Trust Papers, Bank of England.
36. Burn, op. cit, p.439.
37. Ibid.
38. P.L. Payne, *Colvilles and the Scottish Steel Industry* (Oxford, 1979), pp.190-222.
39. Hannah, *Rise of the Corporate Economy*, op. cit., pp.93-5.
40. D.L. Burn (ed.), *The Structure of British Industry Vol.II* (Cambridge, 1958), p.151.
41. Ibid., pp.157-8.
42. Ibid., pp.282-3.
43. Ibid., p.3.
44. H. Leak and A. Maizels, 'The Structure of British Industry', *Journal of the Royal Statistical Society*, Series A, Vol. 108 (1945), p.157.
45. Hannah, *Rise*,op. cit., p.111.
46. Indicative of this is the collection of essays in D.H. Aldcroft & H.W. Richardson *The British Economy 1870-1937* (London, 1967) and the articles by N.K. Buxton, 'The Role of the "New" Industries in Britain during the 1930s: A Reinterpretation', *Business History Review*, Vol.XLIX, No.2 (1975) and J.A. Dowie, 'Growth in Inter War Britain', op. cit.
47. D.H. Aldcroft, 'Economic Growth in Britain in the Inter-War Years: A Reassessment', *Economic History Review*, 2nd Series, Vol.20 (1967).
48. Dowie, op. cit., p.104.
49. A common feature of Aldcroft, Richardson, Buxton and Dowie.
50. Chapman and Knight, op. cit., pp.100-3.
51. Hannah and Kay, op. cit., p.2.
52. Cf. Buxton op. cit., p.222.
53. Ibid.
54. C.L. Mowat, *Britain Between the Wars 1918-1940* (London, 1968).
55. B. Thomas, 'Movements of Labour into South East 1920-1932', *Economica*, Vol.1 (1934).
56. B. Thomas, 'The Influx of Labour into the Midlands 1920-1937', *Economica*, Vol.5 (1938).
57. Buxton, op. cit., p.218.
58. Hannah, op. cit., p.122.

APPENDIX

LIST OF LARGEST EMPLOYERS IN 1935

| FIRM | NO. OF EMPLOYEES | SIC CATEGORY |
|---|---|---|
| 1. UNILEVER | 60,000 | III V |
| 2. GUEST, KEEN & NETTLEFOLD | 50,000 | VI |
| 3. IMPERIAL CHEMICAL INDUSTRIES | 49,706 | V |
| 4. VICKERS | 44,162 | VI VII X |
| 5. LONDON, MIDLAND & SCOTTISH RAILWAY | 41,301 | XI |
| 6. COOPERATIVE WHOLESALE SOCIETY | 36,831 | III XV |
| 7. LONDON , NORTH EASTERN RAILWAY | 36,789 | XI |
| 8. NAVAL DOCKYARDS | 31,680 | X |
| 9. IMPERIAL TOBACCO | 30,000 | III |
| 10. FINE COTTON SPINNERS & DOUBLERS ASSOCIATION | 30,000 | XIII |
| 11. ASSOCIATED ELECTRICAL INDUSTRIES | 30,000 | IX |
| 12. HARLAND & WOLFF | 30,000 | X |
| 13. DUNLOP | 28,000 | XIX XIII |
| 14. TEXTILE MACHINERY MANUFACTURERS | 24,300 | VII |
| 15. GENERAL ELECTRIC | 24,000 | IX |
| 16. COURTAULDS | 22,506 | XIII |
| 17. LUCAS | 20,000 | IX |
| 18. UNITED STEEL | 19,229 | VI |
| 19. AUSTIN MOTOR | 19,000 | XI |
| 20. GREAT WESTERN RAILWAY | 18,766 | XI |
| 21. DORMAN LONG | 18,028 | VI |
| 22. LANCASHIRE COTTON | 15,000 | XIII |
| 23. TUBE INVESTMENTS | 15,000 | VI VII XII |
| 24. ORDNANCE FACTORIES & ORDNANCE DEPT. WORKSHOPS | 14,231 | VII |
| 25. JOSEPH FOSTER & SON | 14,000 | XIII |
| 26. CALLENDERS CABLES | 14,000 | IX |
| 27. SOUTHERN RAILWAY | 13,714 | XI |
| 28. METAL BOX | 12,813 | XII |
| 29. BRITISH COCOA & CHOCOLATE (CADBURY-FRY) | 11,685 | III |
| 30. STEWARTS & LLOYDS | 11,009 | VI |
| 31. M. BURTON | 11,000 | XV XIII |
| 32. COMBINED EGYPTIAN MILLS | 10,500 | XIII |
| 33. MORRIS MOTORS | 10,200 | XI |
| 34. PILKINGTONS | 10,000 | XVI |
| 35. J. & P. COATS | 10,000 | XIII |
| 36. EMI (The Gramophone Co.) | 10,000 | IX |
| 37. JOHN BROWN | 9,381 | X VI |
| 38. RICHARD THOMAS | 9,000 | VI |
| 39. BABCOCK & WILCOX | 8,700 | VII |
| 40. BLEACHERS' ASSOCIATION | 8,500 | XIII |
| 41. LANCASHIRE STEEL | 8,399 | VI |
| 42. BRITISH INSULATED & HELSBY CABLES | 8,200 | IX |

| | | |
|---|---|---|
| 43. SINGER (Sewing Machines) | 8,103 | VII |
| 44. RECKITT'S | 8,100 | V |
| 45. RYLAND & SONS | 8,000 | XIII |
| 46. NATIONAL CASH REGISTER | 8,000 | VII |
| 47. BEARDMORE | 8,000 | VI X VII |
| 48. SINGER(Cars) | 8,000 | XI |
| 49. AMALGAMATED COTTON MILLS TRUST | 8,000 | XIII |
| 50. SCOTTISH CO-OPERATIVE WHOLESALE SOCIETY | 8,000 | III XV |
| 51. BRITISH ROPES | 8,000 | XIX |
| 52. STANDARD TELEPHONE AND CABLE | 7,911 | IX |
| 53. J. HOYLE | 7,500 | XIII |
| 54. ASSOCIATED BISCUITS | 7,245 | III |
| 55. FORD | 7,128 | XI |
| 56. BOOTS | 7,000 | V |
| 57. PATONS & BALDWINS | 7,000 | XIII |
| 58. FERRANTI | 7,000 | IX |
| 59. TATE & LYLE | 7,000 | III |
| 60. ROLLS ROYCE | 6,900 | XI |
| 61. BRITISH IRON & STEEL (Guest, Keen & Baldwins) | 6,855 | VI |
| 62. NAVAL ORDNANCE DEPOTS | 6,837 | VII |
| 63. BRADFORD DYERS ASSOCIATION | 6,750 | XIII |
| 64. VAUXHALL | 6,726 | VII |
| 65. HORROCKSES, CREWSDON & CO. | 6,500 | XIII |
| 66. SIEMENS BROS. | 6,245 | IX |
| 67. ENGLISH ELECTRIC | 6,091 | IX |
| 68. W. & T. AVERY | 6,000 | VIII |
| 69. LEYLAND MOTORS | 6,000 | XI |
| 70. WALLPAPER MANUFACTURERS | 5,500 | XVIII |
| 71. ROWNTREE | 5,500 | III |
| 72. LONDON BRICK CO. | 5,500 | XVI |
| 73. CARRON | 5,325 | VI |
| 74. DE HAVILLAND | 5,191 | XI VII |
| 75. I. & R. MORLEY | 5,000 | XV |
| 76. SCOTT'S SHIPBUILDING & ENGINEERING | 5,000 | X |
| 77. MITCHELLS & BUTLERS | 5,000 | III |
| 78. W. BARBOUR & SONS | 5,000 | XIII |
| 79. CAMMELL LAIRD | 5,000 | X |
| 80. BRIGGS BODIES | 5,000 | VII |
| 81. WATNEY, COOMBE REID | 5,000 | III |
| 82. D. & W. HENDERSON | 5,000 | X |
| 83. J. BIBBY | 5,000 | V |
| 84. SWAN HUNTER & WIGHAM RICHARDSON | 5,000 | X |
| 85. BIRMINGHAM SMALL ARMS | 4,907 | XI VII |
| 86. NORTH BRITISH RUBBER | 4,500 | XIX |
| 87. CROSSES & WINKWORTH | 4,500 | XII |
| 88. WATERLOW | 4,500 | XVIII |
| 89. YORK STREET FLAX SPINNING | 4,500 | XIII |
| 90. BOWATER | 4,400 | V |
| 91. KODAK | 4,400 | V |
| 92. COLVILLES | 4,366 | VI |
| 93. BRISTOL AEROPLANE | 4,200 | XI VII |
| 94. RALEIGH CYCLE HOLDINGS | 4,060 | XI |

| | | |
|---|---|---|
| 95. HADFIELDS | 4,052 | VI |
| 96. BASS, RATCLIFFE & GRETTON | 4,000 | III |
| 97. J.B. LEWIS | 4,000 | XV |
| 98. STEEL COMPANY OF SCOTLAND | 4,000 | VI |
| 99. J. TEMPLETON | 4,000 | XV |
| 100. TOOTAL, BROADHURST & LEE | 4,000 | XIII |
| 101. FAIRBAIRN, LAWSON & COMBE BARBOUR | 4,000 | XIII |

## NOTES TO APPENDIX

1. An accurate figure for Unilever has been very difficult to ascertain. *The Times* of 7 May 1936 gives the total number of UK employees in the Unilever Pension Fund as 30,000 but this figure applies only to all male office employees. *The Times* of 14 May 1938 reports the Chairman's speech in which he gives a worldwide employment figure of 200,000. The estimate of 60,000 is a very rough approximation.

2. As with Unilever, accurate information for GKN has been difficult to ascertain. *The Times* of 27 June 1935 reports the Chairman's speech in the course of which he refers to 'our shareholders who number 33,000 and to our employees who vastly exceed the shareholders in number'. Information from the company gives the number of employees in the pension scheme at 25,000 in 1935 but similar strictures may apply to GKN as apply to Unilever cf. above. The figure is again a rough approximation.

3. Reader, *I.C.I.,* Vol.2 (Oxford 1975), p.497, cites a figure of 50,000 for 1935. The Board of Trade *List of Mines 1935* (HMSO, 1935) p.95, cites a figure of 294 miners employed by ICI. Thus the final figure is 49,703. Reader also gives figures for the following years: 1927 – 47,000; 1929 – 57,000; and 1932 – 36,000

4. *The Royal Commission on the Private Manufacture of and trading in Arms 1935-1936.* Minutes of Evidence, pp.434-5, cites the following figures: Vickers Group 4,733; Vickers-Armstrong 25,426; English Steel Co. 9,370; Metropolitan Cammell 4,633. Vickers have majority control of Vickers Armstrong and Metropolitan Cammell and almost total control of the English Steel Corp.

5. *Railway Companies (Staff) Returns 1935* (Ministry of Transport/Board of Trade) pp.8-9. All of the railway estimates here are almost certainly high, as it has been impossible to separate those engaged in straightforward manufacture and those engaged in repair and maintenance work. The figure given includes the Locomotive, Carriage and Wagon Department; Civil Engineer's Department (Permanent Way); Signal and Telegraph; Electrical Engineer's Department; General Stores; Stationery and Sheet and other departments. A detailed breakdown within these categories is given in the Returns.

6. P. Redfern, *The New History of the C.W.S.* (London, 1938), p.541, cites figures of 42,207 – comprising 33,980 in Productive Works and Services and 8,221 in Distribution and Banks – for 1932; and of 57,049 – comprising 48,194 in Productive Works and Services and 8,855 in Distributive and Banks for 1937. *The Red Book of Commerce 1936* (London, 1936), p.185 cites a figure of 46,107. On the basis of Redfern's figures it seems reasonable to expect that some 8,500 of the Red Book return are engaged in Distribution and Banking. Accordingly the estimate is 36,831, a figure which also excludes 776 miners. *List of Mines* (1935), p.81.

7. *Railway Companies (Staff) Returns 1935,* op. cit., pp.8-9; cf. note 5.

8. *Final Report on the Fifth Census of Production, 1935,* Vol.4, p.92.

9. On the basis that the total employment in tobacco was 42,859 *(Final Report on the Fifth Census of Production, 1936,* Vol.3, p.236), and that Imperial Tobacco held something in the region of 80% of this market, an estimate of 30,000 is not unreasonable. In 1932 Imperial acquired a controlling interest in Gallaher and also controlled WD and HO Wills who employed 8,500; B.W.E. Alford, *WD & HO Wills and the Development of the UK Tobacco Industry, 1786-1965* (London, 1975), p.383. Imperial also controlled Franklyn Davey, Edwards, Ringer and Bigg, Lambert & Butler, Hignetts, Adkins and Sons, Hignett Brothers, W. Clarke & Sons, Richard Cavendish, Stephen Mitchell, Ford

J. Smith, D. & J. MacDonald, John Player & Sons and Ardath. In their turn, Gallaher acquired B. Jackson, International Tobacco Co. and National Tobacco in 1934. Carreras, which was not part of the Imperial Group, employed 3,000 in 1928 at their newly opened Arcadia Works in Northern Ireland.

10. *Red Book of Commerce, 1936*, p.273. Figure confirmed by Dr. D.A. Farnie in a private communication.

11. *The Times* 5 April 1935, reports the chairman's speech in which he states that 'employment in the factories of our group is on a substantially higher level than it has been during the past two or three years . . . over thirty thousand . . . twelve months ago . . .twenty six thousand'.

12. Information from Mr Michael Moss in a private communication.

13. A figure for Dunlop has been difficult to ascertain. Sir Charles Tennyson, *Stars and Markets* (London, 1957), p.174 cites the Dunlop workforce as 55,000 in 1928 and 'well over' 80,000 in 1948. These figures almost certainly include Dunlop's overseas holdings. 28,000 therefore is a very rough estimate.

14. Textile Machinery Manufacturers comprised the following companies and workforces: Platt Brothers – 12,000; J. Hetherington & Sons – 4,000; Brooks & Doxey – 1,000 and Dobson and Barlow –300. *Red Book of Commerce*, pp.581, 358, 120 and 225. No figures were given for the other constituent firms, Asa Lees and Howard and Bullough, but on the basis of the 1907 figures and known 1935 figures these were estimated at 2,500 and 4,500 respectively. This gives a total for the company of 24,300. Dr D.A. Farnie in a private communication estimates T.M.M's workforce as 23,300, a figure which excludes 1,300 machine tool makers.

15. *The Red Book of Commerce*, 1936; p.298; L. Hannah, *The Rise of the Corporate Economy* (London, 1976), p.125, gives a figure of 40,000 for 1939. Such a growth rate is confirmed by *The Red Book of Commerce* which quotes 40,000 in its 1940 edition.

16. D.C. Coleman, *Courtaulds*, Vol.2 (Oxford, 1968), p.430.

17. *Red Book of Commerce, 1936*, p.464.

18. *Red Book of Commerce, 1936*, p.741, cites a figure of 25,000 from which 5,771 miners have been subtracted: *(List of Mines*, pp.51–2 and 113), *The Sunday Express*, 13 Sept. 1936, gives a daily figure of 21,000, a figure which appears to exclude miners. *The Daily Independent* (Sheffield), 9 Jan. 1937, cites a figure of 28,000 employees in all.

19. R.A. Church, *The British Motor Car Industry to 1941* (London, 1979), p.149.

20. *Railway Companies (Staff) Returns 1935*, op. cit., pp.8–9 cf. note 5.

21. Information from Dorman Long.

22. Information from Dr D.A. Farnie in a private communication.

23. Information from T.I. Industries.

24. *The Final Report on the Fifth Census of Production 1935*, Vol.4, p.114.

25. *Red Book of Commerce*, 1936, p.282.

26. *Survey of Industrial Development, Lancashire (I)*, Board of Trade 1934, p.156. Although the survey does not mention the firm by name it does state that the works are 'extensive' and situated at Leigh where Callenders main plant was. The figure given is 9.575. Callenders also had a plant in Kent. The figure is again a rough estimate.

27. *Railway Companies (Staff) Returns 1935*, op. cit., pp.8–9, cf. note 5.

28. W.J. Reader, *Metal Box* (London, 1976), p.241, cites a figure of 16,505 for the company in 1948 when employment in the industry as a whole was 26,505. Employment in the industry as a whole in 1935 was 20,577 *(Final Report the Fifth Census of Production 1935*, Vol.2, p.87): therefore on constant ratios an estimated figure of 12,813 seems reasonable.

29. Information from Cadbury-Schweppes.

30. *Red Book of Commerce*, 1936, p.691, cites a figure of 12,000 from which 991 miners have been subtracted (*List of Mines*, pp.112 and 149).

31. *Red Book of Commerce*, 1936, p.135, *Ideals of Industry* (Burton Ltd., 1950), p.107, cites a contemporary report on the extension of its Hudson Road Works in 1935, 'It . . . [Burton's] . . . now possesses the largest tailoring workshops in the world, employing 10,000 people'.

32. Information from Dr D.A. Farnie in a private communication.

33. Information from company sources. The estimate includes Morris Cowley, Radiators and Pressed Steel.
34. T.C. Barker, *The Glassmakers* (London, 1971), p.396.
35. C.A. Oakley, *Scottish Industry Today* (Edinburgh, 1937), p.161.
36. *Red Book of Commerce*, p.314, gives a figure of 7,000 for EMI but does not appear to include HMV in this figure. The total is again an estimate.
37. A definite picture for Brown's has been difficult to ascertain. A.J. Slaven, 'A Shipyard in Depression: John Brown's of Clydebank, 1919-1939', *Business History*, Vol.19 (1977), p.204, cites a figure for the Clydebank yard of 5,381. *The Red Book of Commerce*, p.275 gives a figure of 4,000 for the subsidiary Thomas Firth and John Brown. It is unclear as to whether or not this excludes the Aldworks and Rotherham Main Collieries which employed between them 2,132. *List of Mines*, p.103.
38. An accurate figure for Richard Thomas has been difficult to ascertain. *The Times*, 19 July 1935, reports the decision to transfer the works to Lincolnshire and states that: 'The removal of the industry would throw out of work in South Wales no fewer than ten thousand men – namely four thousand who were engaged in the tin plate trade and six thousand who were working in steel and coal.' The figure is a rough estimate.
39. Information from Babcock International.
40. *The Red Book of Commerce*, 1936, p.85. Information from Dr D.A. Farnie in a private communication corroborates this figure.
41. The Lancashire Steel Corporation was formed in 1930 from Pearson & Knowles Iron and Steel Company, Partington Steel & Iron Company, the Wigan Coal & Iron Company, Rylands, Whitecross and W. Robertson. *The Red Book of Commerce* cites figures of 1,600 for Whitecross, 1,850 for Rylands and 14,500 for the Wigan Coal & Iron Co. *The Red Book of Commerce*, pp.781, 631 and 248; from this total 11,051 miners employed by the Wigan Coal & Iron Co. have been subtracted. *List of Mines*, pp.154 and 182-4. Estimates for Pearson & Knowles and Partington have been added.
42. *Economist*, 24 March 1938, p.604. The figure is for 1928.
43. Information from Dr C.W. Munn derived from a Glasgow University dissertation by M.C. McDermott using company sources.
44. Information from Reckitts.
45. *Red Book of Commerce*, p.631.
46. *Red Book of Commerce*, p.527.
47. Information from Mr Michael Moss using company sources. The firm was 'technically' bankrupt.
48. David J. Jeremy and Christine Shaw (eds.), *Dictionary of Business Biography* (hereafter *DBB*), Vol.5 (London, 1986). Entry on Singer. In 1929 the company had 7 factories and produced 28,000 cars, but by 1938 was only producing 9,000 cars.
49. Information from Dr D.A. Farnie in a private communication.
50. *Red Book of Commerce*, p.643, gives a figure of 11,563. Allowing for a percentage based on the C.W.S. Figures (see note 6) – to be engaged in retailing, services, distribution and banking, a figure of 8,000 does not seem unreasonable. C.A. Oakley, *Scottish Industry Today*, op. cit., p.276, states that 'the SCWS may become within the next few years the largest employer of Scottish industrial labour . . . [with] . . . 8,000 workers employed in their various factories'.
51. British Rope was an amalgamation of 26 rope making companies. The *Red Book of Commerce* cites figures for the Edinburgh Roperie and Sailcloth Co. of 1,000, Doncaster wire 500 and Cradock 600, pp.245, 226 and 192. The 23 other companies are listed on p.115. The figure is a rough estimate.
52. Information from S.T.C. cf. also P. Young, *Power of Speech: A History of Standard Telephones and Cables 1883-1983* (London, 1983), p.213, where the same figure is given.
53. Information from Dr D.A. Farnie in a private communication.
54. *Red Book of Commerce*, p.569, gives a figure of 4,000 for Peek Freen. Information from Mr T.A.B. Corley suggests a figure of 3,245 for Huntley & Palmers.
55. Information from Dr S. Tolliday based on data from Dagenham Labour Exchange.
56. *Boots Annual Report 1936*. The figure is for manufacturing and wholesale. S.D.

Chapman, *Jesse Boot of Boots the Chemist* (London, 1976), p.102, cites a total
employment figure of 12, 339 for 1917. Of this total 6,603 are described as retail and
4,801 as manufacturing and wholesale.

57. *Red Book of Commerce*, p.564.
58. *Red Book of Commerce*, p.271.
59. *Red Book of Commerce*, p.706.
60. Information from Rolls Royce.
61. The Company was incorporated in March 1930 to effect an amalgamation of the heavy
    iron and steel business of GKN and Baldwins. The Company own the entire share capital
    of Briton Ferry Works, Dowlais Collieries and Cribbwr Fawr Collieries. *Red Book of
    Commerce*, p.110. Elsewhere the *RBC* gives figures of 8,000 for Baldwins, p.46, and
    1,100 for Briton Ferry. 2,205 miners have been subtracted from this total, *List of Mines*,
    pp.248–9.
62. *Final Report on the Fifth Census of Production*, 1935, Vol.4, p.92.
63. Information from Dr. D.A. Farnie in a private communication. The *Red Book of
    Commerce*, p.97 gives the same figure.
64. Official Vauxhall figure. Information from Dr S. Tolliday in a private communication.
65. Information by Dr D.A. Farnie in a private communication. The *Red Book of
    Commerce*, pp.375–6, gives the same figure.
66. According to J.D. Scott, *Siemens Bros., 1858–1958* (London, 1958), pp.252 and 266,
    Siemens employed 9,500 people in April 1939. In 1935 they employed 5,576 at their main
    works in Woolwich. They did have other smaller plants and I have estimated the total
    taking 8,831 as the 1939 Woolwich total from the combined works total of 9,500 and
    added the difference to the 1935 Woolwich total.
67. *DBB*, Vol.4, p.420, entry on F.H. Nelson states that English Electric employed 4,000 in
    1932 and 35,000 in 1949. Using the formula: $r = \left(\sqrt[m]{\left(\frac{xn}{xt}\right)} - 1\right)100$ to calculate the growth
    rate, a figure of 5,865 is derived.
68. *Red Book of Commerce*, p.39.
69. *Red Book of Commerce*, p.444.
70. On the basis that there were 6,096 employed in wallpaper as a whole in 1935 – *Final
    Report on the Fifth Census of Production*, Vol.4, p.29, and that the Wallpaper
    Manufacturers had approximately 90% of the market, a figure of 5,500 seems
    reasonable.
71. Information from Rowntree-Mackintosh.
72. R. Hillier, *Clay that Burns: A History of the Fletton Brick Industry* (LBC 1981),
    pp.70–74, states that '5,500 employees were eligible for the firms' bonus scheme in 1934
    ... [but that] ... in 1947 the company urgently needed its full complement of 8,000
    men.'
73. *Red Book of Commerce*, p.149, gives a figure of 6,000 from which 675 miners have been
    subtracted. *List of Mines, 1935*, pp.38, 42 and 47.
74. *DBB*, Vol.2, p.51, entry on De Havilland, The figure is for 1937.
75. *Red Book of Commerce*, p.514.
76. *Red Book of Commerce*, p.643.
77. *Red Book of Commerce*, p.507.
78. *Red Book of Commerce*, p.50.
79. *The Shipbuilder and Marine Engineer*, July 1935, p.475.
80. *Red Book of Commerce*, p.102.
81. Estimate based on a report in *The Times* of 1 August 1935, p.19, which states that
    Watney Coombe Reid are 'The largest brewing company in the country'. Bass employed
    4,000, cf. note 96.
82. *Red Book of Commerce*, p.355.
83. *DBB*, Vol.1, p.326, entry on Bibby. The figure given is for 1940.
84. *The Shipbuilder & Marine Engineer*, Sept. 1933, p.430: 'with this work in hand we
    expect in a few months to be employing in our shipyards and engine works on the Tyne
    about 4,000 to 5,000 men which is about half our workers in busy times'.
85. *Royal Commission on the Private Manufacture of and Trading in Arms*, Minutes of
    Evidence, 1935–1936, p.492. The figure is for 1934 and probably includes Daimler and
    Lanchester.

86. *Red Book of Commerce*, p.541.
87. Information from Dr D.A. Farnie in a private communication.
88. *Red Book of Commerce*, pp.764–5.
89. *Red Book of Commerce*, p.811.
90. W.J. Reader, *Bowater* (Cambridge, 1981), p.367. From Annual Reports; Bowater internal statistics. The figure is for 1936.
91. *DBB*, Vol.3, p.195, entry on Mattison. The figure is for 1938.
92. P.L. Payne, *Colvilles and the Scottish Steel Industry* (Oxford, 1979), p.221.
93. C.H. Barnes, *Bristol Aircraft Since 1910* (London, 1964), p.34.
94. *Red Book of Commerce*, p.598.
95. *Royal Commission on the Private Manufacture of and Trading in Arms*, Minutes of Evidence, 1935–36, p.483.
96. *Red Book of Commerce*, p.57.
97. *Red Book of Commerce*, p.443.
98. *Red Book of Commerce*, p.685.
99. *Red Book of Commerce*, p.712.
100. Information from Dr D.A. Farnie in a private communication.
101. *Red Book of Commerce*, p.264.

# TAKEOVER BIDS IN BRITAIN
# BEFORE 1950: AN EXERCISE
# IN BUSINESS 'PRE-HISTORY'[1]

by LES HANNAH

IN the course of the present century many British industries which were once characterized by a competitive structure of small, privately-owned firms have been transformed into monopolies and oligopolies dominated by large publicly-quoted companies. Together with the rapid expansion in the size of firms, there has been a significant change in the structure of ownership of these enterprises. Whereas the small firms of the nineteenth century were normally closely held by managing families and partnerships, by the mid-twentieth century the divorce of ownership and control in large corporations was already well-developed.[2] Yet the takeover bid, which has been seen by economists as one of the most important corollaries of this development, emerged only after a considerable time lag. The present article analyses some of the reasons for the virtual absence of the technique of takeover bidding in the United Kingdom before mid-century.

I

Already by the interwar years the quoted sector extended over a considerable portion of the economy. In addition to the numerous companies with quotations on the still lively provincial stock exchanges, there were, in 1924, 726 companies quoted on the London Stock Exchange Official List in the manufacturing and distribution sectors and by 1939 this had risen to 1,712 in the Official and Supplementary Lists combined.[3] W. H. Coates, in evidence to the Colwyn Committee estimated that by the early 1920's about 57 per cent of profits originated in public companies,[4] and by 1951 quoted companies alone accounted for some 71 per cent of profits generated by the corporate sector.[5] Yet it was not until the second half of the twentieth century that the takeover bid really emerged in Britain as a

---

[1] A study of mergers noticed in the *Investor's Chronicle* between 1919 and 1939, on which the present study draws, was financed by the Nuffield Foundation and the Social Science Research Council and carried out by Mrs P. D. Wright. M. R. Freedland, R. M. Hartwell, J. A. Kay, W. J. Reader and J. Wright commented helpfully on earlier drafts. They are not, of course, responsible for any errors or omissions. I have been asked to point out that reference in subsequent footnotes to the private archives of companies does not imply the existence of general access to those archives.
[2] P. Sargant Florence, *Ownership, Control and Success of Large Companies, 1936–1951* (1961).
[3] P. E. Hart and S. J. Prais, 'The Analysis of Business Concentration: A Statistical Approach', *Journal of the Royal Statistical Society*, series A, CXIX, (1956), 153; see also E. V. Morgan and W. A. Thomas, *The Stock Exchange* (1962), 280–1.
[4] [Colwyn] Committee on National Debt and Taxation, *Minutes of Evidence*, (1927), QQ, 8550–1. Of course, not all public companies were quoted.
[5] National Institute of Economic and Social Research, *Company Income and Finance* (1949–1953), (privately printed, 1956), 7–8.

significant force in industrial life. When the bid did become established, however, it was an important part of the mechanism of adjustment by which assets in a modern economy are transferred to their most profitable use.[1] This important role is reflected in the quantitative significance of takeover bidding and the attention which it attracts: in the year ending 31 March 1971, for example, the City Panel on Takeovers and Mergers examined 249 takeover bids, many of which were opposed by directors or by rival bidders.[2]

It is at first sight surprising, in view of the already important role of the quoted sector three decades earlier, that the takeover bid was for so long dormant, for one would expect bids to be a feature of any capitalist economy in which ownership is divorced from control, and the stock market provides a fluid market in corporate control. In these circumstances bids can be made directly to the general body of shareholders, contesting the views of their own directors, and there is the possibility of a struggle for control between the existing directors and one or more take-over raiders. Moreover firms in which ownership is divorced from control may have a greater propensity to accept merger proposals than owner-controlled enterprises. The stereotypes here are well known. On the one hand the family firm is said to shun merger proposals, valuing its traditional character and independence, whilst, on the other, the publicly quoted company, its shares being freely transferable, may change ownership through merger or acquisition without such personal factors entering into consideration.

There is, of course, some truth in these stereotypes. A confidential government enquiry into the reasons for the slowness of the merger movement in the 1930's, for example, found that the personal feelings of aged family proprietors were often the major reason for the rejection of merger proposals.[3] However, in one sense the procedure for acquiring private companies was easier than that for quoted companies. The take-over of the Melyn Works in Neath by Baldwins Ltd, may serve as an example. The private owner of this tinplate works was Mr F. W. Gibbins: 'At last after thirty-one years in the business he decided to sell out in 1921. He put up to J. C. Davies, the managing director of Baldwins, a memorandum running to about six lines. There were 144 shares at a paid up price of £250. Gibbins asked Davies for £1,000 per share, making £144,000. After visiting the works, Davies suggested knocking off £10,000. Gibbins agreed and sold each share for £900 odd.'[4] This was, perhaps, typical in all except its simplicity, for often the procedure was complicated by at least an accountant's investigation into the profit record of the company.[5] The crucial factor was, of course, the willingness of the private owner to sell, and many private owners did, of course, for a variety of reasons, refuse to sell.[6]

1 B. Hindley, 'Separation of Ownership and Control in the Modern Corporation', *Journal of Law and Economics*, XIII, (1970); R. Marris, *The Economic Theory of 'Managerial' Capitalism* (1964).
2 The Panel on Take-overs and Mergers, *Report on the Year Ended 31 March 1971*, (1971), 5.
3 P.R.O. Board of Trade Papers, BT/56/37, 'Industrial Reorganization', 1, 3, 37.
4 T. Jones, *Welsh Broth* (1950), 130.
5 For more sophisticated methods of valuation see e.g. A. E. Cutforth, *Methods of Amalgamation* (1926); D. Finnie and S. Berlanny, *Business Investigations* (1938), ch. 2.
6 J. L. Carvel, *The Alloa Glass Works* (1953), 53.

It cannot, however, be assumed that the acquisition of a publicly quoted company is necessarily less dependent on such personal factors and private negotiations. It is true that with the dispersal of the ownership of shares the *locus* of decision-making changes, but parallel factors could come into play on quoted company boards, and their directors were indeed often tarred by rationalizers with the same brush as family firms. They too were accused of being irrationally averse to merger. Complaints that there was 'a national bias on the part of industry to regard its troubles as merely temporary',[1] and that many industrialists did not realize 'the precarious position in which the industry now is'[2] could apply to public as well as to private firms. Moreover, public company directors could be as averse as owner-managers to losing their positions on the board. The directors of Tweedales and Smalley, for example, who found that other textile machinery manufacturers were acquiring their company's shares on the open market after they had refused a merger, resisted it with all the tenacity usually ascribed to family firms.[3]

The statistics of the relative incidence of disappearance by merger of quoted companies in the interwar and postwar periods are illuminating here. Between 1948 and 1961, some 25 per cent of the companies quoted on the London Stock Exchange were taken over by other quoted companies, a proportion which by the 1957–68 period had risen to 38 per cent.[4] In the interwar period, by contrast, the population of quoted firms was much less exposed to this danger. A study of 726 firms quoted on the London Stock Exchange in 1924, for example, found that only thirty-three of them – less than 5 per cent – disappeared by merger in the next fifteen years.[5] It is possible that this lower level can be accounted for by the more abundant supply of unquoted companies available for acquisition, or by a generally lower motivation for merger in the depressed interwar years; but an alternative explanation – that the directors of quoted companies could more easily resist takeovers in the period – also merits attention.

II

The ease with which a takeover bid is resisted is a function both of the spread of shareownership and of the general institutional arrangements of the stock market. Many of the companies quoted on the stock exchange in the interwar period, especially those in which the founding families still maintained a managerial interest plus board representation were still closely controlled by large share-

---

[1] [Macmillan] *Committee on Finance and Industry, Minutes of Evidence*, 1931 (hereafter *Macmillan Evidence*) II Q.5995.
[2] M. Webster Jenkinson, 'Memorandum on the Steel Trade' in P.R.O. BT 56/2; see also *Macmillan Evidence* QQ, 859, 2800, 7497; P. W. S. Andrews and E. Brunner, *Capital Development in Steel* (Oxford, 1951), 123.
[3] Though their attempt to change their articles to limit the bidders' powers failed, they succeeded in maintaining their independence, see *Investors' Chronicle*, (1933), 8 April, 754, 772.
[4] R. L. Marris, 'Incomes Policy and the Rate of Profit in Industry', *Trans. Manchester Stat. Soc.* (1964–5), 18; Department of Trade and Industry, *Survey of Mergers 1958–68* (1970), 19.
[5] P. E. Hart and S. J. Prais, op. cit., 169. The contrast in unsuccessful bids is even more marked. Between 1948 and 1961, Marris, loc. cit., estimated that there were two to three hundred unsuccessful bids. In the interwar period, such bids were, for reasons which will now be discussed, extremely rare.

holding blocs. Effective voting control by the large holders – usually directors – of such companies (which might in some cases be achieved by the ownership of as little as 20 per cent of the shares) only gradually declined. [1] For such companies, of course, as for private companies, bids would naturally be made to the directors and it is unnecessary to distinguish director-agreed bids from bids direct to shareholders: the support of the directors would normally be necessary to secure the assent of the majority of the shareholders. [2]

There remained, however, a large number of quoted firms with more widely dispersed shareholdings and largely non-owning directors, which formed a population of potential takeover victims but yet did not in general attract direct bids. In the case of these firms, also, an approach through the directors, followed by controlled stock transfers on the recommendation of the directors (rather than contested takeover raids) remained the norm in these years. The purchase by Stewarts and Lloyds of Alfred Hickman Ltd, in 1920 to secure their supplies of iron may be taken as a typical example. [3] When Hickman's chairman was approached he agreed to recommend an offer equivalent to £4 for each Hickman's £1 fully paid share. In the next few months Stewarts and Lloyds' technical adviser reported on Hickman's works and the two companies' auditors made a joint report. On the 24 June, some three months after the discussion with Hickman's chairman, a Stewart and Lloyds' board committee authorized the purchase at the Hickman's suggested price, to be paid partly in cash and partly in deferred shares. After further correspondence and meetings, there was a provisional agreement by which the Hickman directors accepted on their own behalf and the Stewarts and Lloyds' directors formalized the offer making it conditional on acceptance by 80 per cent of the shareholders. Meanwhile rumours had reached the market and the two companies' share prices fluctuated considerably. Despite such fluctuations the directors of both companies were confident enough of their judgement to go ahead. A meeting of shareholders at the end of September formally approved the terms and by 30 October the purchase was complete.

This was the usual form of merger between two quoted companies and it therefore seemed quite natural for an accountant to insist in 1926 that 'the negotiations must obviously be conducted by the Directors. In order to preserve proper secrecy, it is not possible for the Directors to acquaint the shareholders of the matter.' [4] Almost invariably, the shareholders were passive agents in the decision making process, and the history of their attempts to thwart the decisions of directors and achieve a better bid price is largely a study in failure. [5]

This was partly because some directors felt a responsibility to recommend

[1] W. H. Coates, 'Administration and Capital', *British Management Review*, III, (1938), 62; 'Shareholders and Control', *Economist*, (1929), 30 Mar., 691; C. Erickson, *British Industrialists: Steel and Hosiery 1850–1950* (Cambridge, 1959), 51–2; P. S. Florence, op. cit. (1961), 70–73, 109–39, 186–7.

[2] *Investors' Chronicle*, (1924), 13 Dec., 1056; (1925), 5 Dec., 1112.

[3] Sir Frederick Scopes, *The Development of Corby Works* (1968), 37–9; *Investors' Chronicle*, (1920), Apr.–Oct., *passim*.

[4] A. E. Cutforth, op. cit., 37.

[5] For examples of the failure of shareholders to achieve better terms, see *Stock Exchange Gazette*, (1927), 25 Jan., 162; *Investors' Chronicle*, (1933), 21 Oct., 835.

offers to their shareholders when the bid price was pitched reasonably. There was therefore some opportunity for financiers and industrialists to contemplate an agreed takeover of quoted firms for the purpose of restructuring industry. E. R. Lewis, for example, a stockbroker who had floated the Decca company, suggested to its directors that they buy another record company, Duophone. When they refused, he bought Duophone himself, and then, in 1929, suggested that they sell him the Decca company. Though not personally wishing to sell, the Decca directors realized the financial attractiveness of the offer and agreed to pass it on to the shareholders. It was accepted by over 95 per cent of them.[1] Similarly, Lord Leverhulme's offer of £13 10s. od. per share for the deferred shares of Knights in 1920 was so attractive that the company's directors, whilst seeing no logic in the merger, advised their shareholders to accept on purely financial grounds.[2] Yet not all such offers were passed on by directors. Sir Herbert Dixon, responding to rumours of bids for his company, insisted that it was the duty[3] of the board to pass on suitable offers to shareholders, however averse the directors might personally be to the bid; but, as the *Investors' Chronicle* pointed out, the view of directors as to 'suitability' did not necessarily mean that the bids received were not above the market price.[4]

## III

One tentative explanation[5] of the failure of contested direct bidding to emerge in its modern form is the quality of information available to shareholders and potential bidders in the interwar years. That this was poor is evident from the accountancy literature of the period.[6] Neither balance sheets nor profit and loss accounts gave adequate indications either of assets and liabilities or of trading profits. For a variety of reasons – commercial secrecy, preservation of credit status, reduction of trade union wage pressure, discouragement of new entry – directors sometimes published figures which understated or overstated the true position of their company. The imperfect state of the law relating to company accounts, and in particular to secret reserves and holding company accounts, allowed common resort to such malpractice. Business historians have revealed many examples of

---

[1] E. R. Lewis, *No C in C* (1956), 15–19.

[2] C. Wilson, *The History of Unilever* (1954), I, 247; *Investors' Chronicle*, (1920), 27 Mar., 196, 306.

[3] This must be taken as a moral, not a legal, statement. According to the law, directors have a duty only to the company not to its shareholders.

[4] *Investors' Chronicle*, (1920), 29 May, 508.

[5] J. B. Tabb 'Accountancy Aspects of Takeover Bids in Britain 1945–1965', (Ph.D. Thesis), Sheffield, 1968, ch. 2 has advanced the alternative explanation that the law provided no means for a successful bidder to remove an incumbent board except at specified times; but, since the Stock Exchange normally required a clause to the effect of the voluntary clause 80 of Table A of 1929 Companies Act empowering the removal of directors at short notice this explanation must be viewed with reservation (see D. G. Hemmant, *The Companies Act 1929*, (1930), 363.)

[6] Sir Gilbert Garnsey, *Holding Companies and Their Accounts* (1931); F. R. M. De Paula, *Developments in Accounting* (1948); Lord Plender, *Some Observations on Balance Sheets* (1932); A. J. Simon, *Holding Companies* (1927); see also Committee on Company Law Reform, *Report*, Cmd. 2657, 1926; and *Minutes of Evidence*, (1925–6); N. A. H. Stacey, *English Accountancy* (1954).

untrue statements being made [1] and contemporary accountancy scandals, including the *cause célèbre* of Lord Kylsant in the Royal Mail Case, revealed the existence of significant, yet legally permitted, deception by directors. [2] The governments of the day were deeply committed to the right of privacy of enterprise and the minor improvements in the law incorporated in the Companies Act of 1929 effected no decisive change. The voluntary attempts at amelioration by accountants like F. R. M. de Paula at Dunlops in the 1930's were equally ineffective except in the case of a few large companies which were in any case not vulnerable to bids. The chairman who remarked that: 'We bring into our accounts just as much . . . as will enable us to pay dividends we recommend and to place to general reserve or add to carry forward just as much as will make a pretty balance sheet' [3] was perhaps more honest than most, but he was accurately describing the large area of discretion which directors could exercise in providing the stock market with information. The sheer absence of information not only reduced the number of *known*[4] profitable acquisition situations but also weighted the advantage in favour of negotiating through the directors those which *were* perceived. A normal part of such negotiations was for the victim firm to make available more information to the bidding firm (either directly, or if secrecy were desired, through neutral accountants) than was in fact available to their own shareholders.

There remained, in principle, the possibility of a direct bid to shareholders, where the desired merger partner's directors refused to impart information or refused to recommend the offered price. Whilst, without the co-operation of the intended victim's directors, a potential bidder could not gain access to reliable accounting information, the bidder might be able to determine a bid price for its own purposes on the basis of 'capitalized nuisance value' [5] or on physical plant values. One should remember, however, that contested takeover bidding is a difficult and risky business (even today only a minority of bids are contested) and this was especially so between the wars when the loyalty of shareholders to directors was strong, and directors of other companies had a natural aversion to challenging it. [6] Even if a direct bid were to be made, the directors of the victim firm remained in a strong position relative to their own shareholders. In practice the shareholders would recognize the superiority of the directors' information

---

1 P. W. S. Andrews and E. Brunner, *Capital Development in Steel*, 131–3; E. J. Cocks and B. Walters, *A History of Zinc Smelting* (1968), 68; J. D. Scott, *Vickers, A History* (1962), 155; 'William Hollins & Co.', *Economist*, (1924), 22 Mar., 628.

2 C. Brooks, ed., *The Royal Mail Case* (1933); P. N. Davies and A. M. Bourn, 'Lord Kylsant and the Royal Mail', *Business History*, XIV (1972), 103–23.

3 Quoted in A. G. H. Dent, 'The Administrator's Responsibility', *British Management Review*, III (1938), 29.

4 Though, by distorting share prices it may have *created* some profitable acquisition situations (see A. J. Simon, op. cit., 23), it tended to keep the *knowledge* of such situations in board circles. Furthermore the accountancy defects may have produced a negative valuation discrepancy (i.e. too high rather than too low a market price) thus discouraging bids, in contrast to the postwar situation where conservative accountancy during inflation may have worked to produce positive discrepances. Directors could of course try to keep their company's share price at what they considered a reasonable level by controlling the flow of information to the market; see e.g. I.C.I. *Archives*, Managing Director's reports to NIL Board, (1921–5), *passim*.

5 R. Jones and O. Marriott, *Anatomy of a Merger: A History of GEC, AEI and English Electric* (1970), 124; W. J. Reader, *Imperial Chemical Industries, A History*, I (1970), 400.

6 H. B. Samuel, *Shareholders' Money* (1933), 7.

and tend to take their advice on the true value of the company in relation to the
bid price. Thus when bids were recommended by directors, the incidence of shareholder opposition was low.[1] The need for the bidding company to secure the
support of the directors was intensified by the absence of power to enforce the
purchase of minority holdings when it had succeeded in purchasing more than
50 per cent of the shares. They were more likely to achieve something approaching
total ownership (which might be desirable for reasons of management and finance)
if they had the directors' support.[2]

IV

Nevertheless the stock market could in the interwar years be used to transfer
resources to more profitable uses, and firms which were obviously undervalued,
were, of course, more clearly open to approach by bidders. As the Board of
Inland Revenue commented, 'concerns of which the market capitalization is low
as compared with the proper value may be more likely than others to be selected
for purchase' and a number of companies showing such 'unrevealed value' were
said to 'have changed hands at a price clearly and markedly in excess of the market
capitalization of their assets'.[3] These adjustments to stock exchange prices through
merger and acquisition would, however, normally take place under the close
surveillance and control of directors rather than of outside bidders. The bidder's
weapons were persuasion and bribery, rather than the takeover bid as we know it.
Boards generally preferred to negotiate mergers secretly in order to fix up
deals before market rumours created large and often inconvenient fluctuations in
share prices. If the relative share prices were not right they could either call off the
deal or attempt to force the share prices to a level which they considered appropriate. Often it was possible to arrange deals on the basis of eve-of-merger prices
or slight premiums[4] but in some cases the deal had to be called off because the
news got out and the victim's share price rocketed.[5] Yet the power of incumbent
directors is shown in stark form in those occasional acquisitions in which the
price paid was actually below the pre-merger market price of the acquired
company's shares. In the Stewarts and Lloyds-Hickman merger of 1920 instanced

---

[1] For an exception see *Investors' Chronicle*, (1935), 2 Nov., 955. 959; (1935), 16 Nov., 1077; (1935), 30 Nov.,
1203. Easiphit made a bid for Lennards, another shoe company, with the blessing of the Lennards' board, but,
to the surprise of the *Chronicle* commentator, local shareholders successfully organized opposition, and Easiphit
failed to gain the required 75 per cent acceptances.
[2] The position of an acquiring firm was improved significantly by the Companies Act 1928 (clause 50,
consolidated as clause 155 of the Companies Act, 1929) which provided for compulsory acquisition of the
shares of a dissentient minority where 90 per cent of the shares had already been acquired, thus facilitating
the achievement of complete ownership; see A. F. Lucas, *Industrial Reconstruction and the Control of Competition*
(1937), 184; *Economist*, (1929), 13 July, 83. The same effect could be achieved by the difficult and somewhat
unethical expedient of juggling the subsidiary's accounts in order to oppress the minority, see Sir Josiah Stamp
and C. H. Nelson, *Business Statistics and Financial Statements* (1924), 267. Nevertheless bids were sometimes
withdrawn even when acceptances were as high as 74 per cent, see e.g. *Investors' Chronicle*, (1920), 4 Sep., 257.
[3] *Suggested Taxation of Wartime Increases in Wealth. Memoranda submitted by the Board of Inland Revenue to
the Select Committee of the House of Commons on Increases in Wealth (War)*, Cmd. 594, (1920), 43, 45.
[4] *Economist*, (1939), 10 June, 612-3.
[5] *Investors' Chronicle*, (1920), 17 July, 95.

above, the final bid price of 7s. 6d. plus one Stewarts and Lloyds' deferred share was some 12s. 6d. below the market price, yet the directors of the two companies forced the deal through at that price. Again, when Alpha Cement bid for the Central Portland Cement Company it offered its own shares to a total market value of £380,000, though the market capitalization of Central's shares on the eve of the offer was some £63,750 higher. Press criticism notwithstanding, the directors of both companies justified the terms on the grounds that the market undervalued Alpha and overvalued Central. With this announcement, the negative valuation discrepancy disappeared and the merger went through.[1] As the *Investors Chronicle* commentator advised when Ranks later made a board-approved bid for the John Greenwood Millers, 'if the directors decide that the business should be sold it is difficult to make any other suggestion',[2] and attempts by shareholders to organize opposition to mergers were almost invariably unsuccessful.[3]

The returns to directors in the prevailing conditions of imperfect information could naturally be considerable. There were not only the profits of inside dealing[4] but it was also widely recognized that the failure to offer suitable 'compensation' to the incumbent directors could jeopardize merger discussions.[5] Often a place on the new board was offered, or alternatively a cash payment for loss of office was made which could sometimes amount to as much as one-tenth of the purchase price,[6] a practice condemned by shareholders and the more ethical businessmen,[7] but still extremely common. Middlemen with the ears of several boards could earn high returns from their knowledge. Thus Dudley Docker suggested various mergers to the Vickers Board and made considerable profits from this intermediation: £10,000 for the Docker Brothers-Pinchin Johnson merger, and £50,000 for the transfer of Vickers' electrical interests to Associated Electrical Industries.[8]

## V

However, despite all the difficulties which the powers of directors created, it is not inconceivable that a direct bid to shareholders contesting the view of their own directors, would be considered by rejected suitors, and, indeed, there are a number of exceptions to the generalization that contested bidding did not occur in the interwar years. Cobbold and Company, for example, in 1936 made a bid

1 *Economist*, (1935), 28 Dec., 1321-2. In fact, there was some justification for the directors' view. Alpha profits showed an increase from £47,478 to £79,422, cf. ibid., (1936), 22 Feb., 445.

2 *Investors' Chronicle*, (1938), 6, 13, 27 Aug., 338, 373, 464.

3 *Investors' Chronicle*, (1929), 28 Sep., 595.

4 H. B. Samuel, op. cit., 168-70; cf. *Investors' Chronicle*, (1920), 31 July, 136.

5 *Macmillan Evidence*, QQ, 859, 7947; Sir Adam Nimmo, 'The Control of Industry', *The Times*, (1934), 10 May, 16; M. W. Jenkinson, 'The Steel Industry' in P.R.O. BT/56/2.

6 *Investors' Chronicle*, (1927), 20 Aug., 411; Monopolies Commission, *Report on the Supply of Chemical ertilisers*, (1959), 66; R.Wilson, *Scotch, The Formative Years* (1970), 436.

7 H. O. O'Hagan, *Leaves from My Life* (1929), I, 407; *Investors' Chronicle*, (1927), 30 Apr., 1001; (1927), 7 May, 1056; (1927), 14 May, 1120.

8 R. Jones and O. Marriott, op. cit., 108-9; J. D. Scott, op. cit., 140-1, 156; *Vickers Archives*, Board Minutes for 1926-28. £50,000 was at the time more than most chairmen of large corporations would expect to earn in a year.

in cash and shares for Daniell and Sons Breweries directly to the shareholders after the Daniell's Board had refused a merger. However, a circular from the Board advising refusal had the desired effect: the holders of over two-thirds of the Daniell's capital refused the offer and the bid thus failed.[1]

Other kinds of exceptions also tend to confirm the general hypothesis. Debenture holders, for example, were sometimes in a stronger position than ordinary shareholders, especially if the Debenture Trust Deed specified that a large proportion of the votes, or court sanction, was needed to change the deed.[2] Where they had a specific mortgage on a particular works, a minority of debenture holders could sometimes effectively block a merger by refusing to allow post merger integration, thus destroying the rationale of the exercise. Also where new capital had to be raised to finance post merger integration and development, existing debenture holders could refuse to allow the new capital to take precedence over their own claims. Thus even after directors and shareholders had agreed to mergers, debenture holders could object, or at least jockey for a better position. This happened, for example, in the projected fusion of two Newport breweries in 1926[3] and in the attempts by Dorman Longs to consolidate under its control the steel companies of north-east England.[4]

Debenture holders were also more frequently in a position to delay mergers because of the prevalence of 'overcapitalization', a term with many, sometimes inconsistent, meanings. It often referred merely to the exaggerated share values with which promoters endowed the companies they floated,[5] but its effect was particularly crucial to merger negotiations when there was a high proportion of fixed interest stock (in modern parlance high 'gearing' or 'leverage'), for in the deflationary conditions of the time some companies could not maintain the payment of gross interest and redemption obligations which they had contracted.[6] The directors of these companies naturally found it difficult to raise funds for investment in modernization and reorganization either by new issue or by seeking an acquirer.[7] A reconstruction of the company's capital – a process which required the co-operation of loan holders in the recognition of their losses – normally had to precede new issue or acquisition, but an acceptable formula was often difficult to devise where control was very finely balanced by high gearing.[8] The delay

---

[1] *Investors' Chronicle*, (1936), 27 June, 1649; (1936), 4 July, 25; (1936), 11 July, 84; *Economist*, (1936), 27 June, 788.

[2] Sir Gilbert Garnsay and T. B. Robson, *Holding Companies* (1936), 13–14; D. G. Hemmant, op. cit., 154–5; *Macmillan Evidence*, Q 1499; P. F. Simonson, *A Treatise on the Law Relating to Debentures and Debenture Stock*, (4th ed., 1913), 23–4.

[3] *Investors' Chronicle*, (1926), 23 Jan., 174.

[4] J. C. Carr and W. Taplin, *A History of the British Steel Industry* (Oxford 1962), 531; *Economist*, (1933), 1 Apr., 696–8; (1933), 5 Aug., 286; (1933), 16 Dec., 1135, 1186; (1934), 24 Nov., 991–2.

[5] *Committee on Industry and Trade, Further Factors in Commercial and Industrial Efficiency*, ch. 3; P. Fitzgerald *Industrial Combination in England* (1927), 191; A. F. Lucas, op. cit. 199; H. A. Marquand, *The Dynamics of Industrial Combination* (1931), 88–92.

[6] J. C. Carr and W. Taplin, op. cit. 359–61, 447; [Colwyn] *Committee on National Debt and Taxation, Report*, Cmd. 2800, (1927), para 55; A. T. K. Grant, *A Study of the Postwar Capital Market*, (1937), 166.

[7] P. W. S. Andrews and E. Brunner, op. cit. 349–60; *Macmillan Evidence* QQ 7976–9.

[8] J. C. Carr and W. Taplin, op. cit. 446–50; 'The Position of Debenture Holders in Steel Reconstruction Schemes', *Economist*, (1928), 10 Nov., 851–2; 'Financial Problems of the Iron and Steel Industry', ibid, (1928), 8 Dec., 1056–7.

which the debenture holders could cause in merger negotiations and the uncertainty about control which this introduced could be sufficient to discourage merger negotiations altogether. As the experienced accountant, Sir Mark Webster Jenkinson, explained to the Macmillan Committee, 'Some have got financial millstones round their necks, and they do not know how to bring about fusion. Nobody will take them in'.[1]

The danger for a bidder in the situation to which he refers was forcibly illustrated in Eastwoods attempt to acquire its overcapitalized rival, Allied Cement, which had encountered financial difficulties in the slump of 1929. Although Eastwoods gained control of the ordinary shares of Allied and placed some of their own directors on the Allied Board, they were unable to raise adequate finance to cover the company's fixed obligations. The debenture holders of Allied therefore appointed a receiver and the Eastwoods directors were removed. In April 1931 the receiver accepted a bid from a rival group, Associated Portland Cement Manufacturers (which had earlier refused to accept the company as a subsidiary because of the complexity of its financial ramifications) and they thus gained control. The wisdom of their earlier caution had in the event been amply confirmed.[2]

The capacity to unseat the directors and realize the asset of value of a company by forced sale also attached to other creditors. Here again, therefore, direct competitive bids emerged when the receiver put such companies up for auction. This, for example, was how Rolls Royce acquired Bentley in 1931.[3] In some cases, however, the creditors' interest was too large and the breakup value of the companies too low for such *ad hoc* procedures to be used. The banks in particular, with many fixed interest advances frozen in unprofitable companies, were in this position and were in some cases able to make a concerted initiative to overcome the financial difficulties by drastic reorganization. Though they frequently disclaimed responsibility for forcing bank debtors to merge and officially ruled out joint action as a breach of the confidential customer-client relationship,[4] they were in fact already participating in some enforced reconstruction and amalgamation schemes. In the steel industry, for example, Barclays forced the unwilling directors of Bolckow Vaughan to accept a bid from Dorman Long by the simple expedient of making the renewal of the company's million pound overdraft conditional on the consummation of the merger.[5]

Action by the banks was given a more formal structure with the creation, on Bank of England initiative, of the Bankers' Industrial Development Company

1 *Macmillan Evidence*, Q.3700.
2 P. L. Cook and R. Cohen, *The Effects of Mergers* (1958), 87–8. *Economist*, (1931), 31 Jan., 32; for a further example of acquisition from the receiver for debenture holders, see J. D. Scott, op. cit. 167; St. John C. Nixon, *Wolseley* (1949), 105; P. W. S. Andrews and E. Brunner, *The Life of Lord Nuffield* (Oxford, 1955), 155.
3 H. Nockolds, *The Magic of a Name* (1938), 178, 264; W. J. Reader and C. H. Wilson, *Men and Machines* (1958), 138–9; *Economist*, (1931), 5 Dec., 1086.
4 *Macmillan Evidence*, QQ, 1869–74, 1950, 1977, 2203, though cf. QQ, 2388–9. For a complaint by Steel-Maitland of the timidity of bankers and particularly of McKenna of the Midland see Baldwin Papers, v. 29, 54–63. Of course, bankers did regularly put defaulting creditors into liquidation and invite bids for their assets, see Lord Chandos, *Memoirs* (1962), 130.
5 J. C. Carr and W. Taplin, op. cit., 449.

(BIDC) in 1929.[1] This was intended to devise schemes to re-equip and, where necessary, to amalgamate, companies in the staple industries; and appears to have been primarily an attempt to head off possible government intervention in the financing and reorganization of industry.[2] With financial backing from the Bank of England and other City institutions, and with a high-powered staff, it aimed discreetly to catalyse the banks into action which was felt to be in their long term interests.[3] The most spectacular example of BIDC's work was the formation of the Lancashire Cotton Corporation which between 1929 and 1932 absorbed almost a hundred firms.[4] The majority of these were forced by their bankers, on the threat of withdrawal of overdraft and loan facilities, to accept the terms offered by the Corporation, though the bankers in fact delayed the process, ever hopeful that by dilatory quibbling they would gain better terms.[5] Though it is conceivable that mergers would have occurred in the industry in the absence of BIDC (as they did in the fine spinning section of the industry[6]), the Corporation was undoubtedly larger and the operation more swiftly executed than would have been the case if the matter had been left to the directors of the individual companies. Smaller scale mergers were also encouraged by BIDC in the steel industry, though they were, as the historians of the industry comment, 'in large part due to the initiative of individual companies and only partly to Montagu Norman's promptings'.[7]

## VI

The market in titles to control of assets was, then, still, by postwar standards, underdeveloped. Significantly it was not until the 1950's, when the informational constraints had been removed by the more stringent 1948 Companies Act, when overcapitalization was being supplanted by underdevaluation, when share ownership was more widely dispersed and the market in shares was more active, and when the rewards were sufficiently high to justify the risks of direct bids, that they began to appear in large numbers.[8] The effects on economic welfare of these institutional developments are, however, by no means easily assessed, though it is clear that they were not wholly beneficial. One corollary of the development of

---

[1] Sir Henry Clay, *Lord Norman* (1957), ch. 8; A. F. Lucas, 'The Bankers' Industrial Development Company', *Harvard Business Review*, (1930), Apr., 270–9.
[2] Sir Henry Clay, op. cit., 358: P.R.O. BT/56/14.
[3] It was seen in the City as an essentially temporary expedient and it was hoped that the financial burden which the banks had shouldered, would eventually be floated off to the public when conditions were favourable, see *Macmillan Evidence*, QQ, 828–59, 9146. The company was known in the City as 'B.I.D. – Brought in Dead'.
[4] *Lancashire Cotton Corporation Archives*, *Annual Reports* and *Reports of Extraordinary General Meetings*, 1929–1933. The more generally quoted figure of 140 is incorrect; it refers to projected acquisitions and to *mills* not firms.
[5] *Macmillan Evidence*, QQ, 1511–25; *The Times*, (1930), 30 Feb., 13; Lancashire Cotton Corporation Board Minutes (1929–30), *passim*.
[6] R. Robson, *The Cotton Industry in Britain* (1957), 158–9.
[7] J. C. Carr and W. Taplin, op. cit., 441, 44–7, 536.
[8] G. Bull and A. Vice, *Bid for Power* (1958); R. W. Moon, *Business Mergers and Takeover Bids* (1959); J. F. Wright, 'The Capital Market and the Finance of Industry', in G. D. N. Worsick and P. H. Ady, eds., *The British Economy in the Nineteen-Fifties* (Oxford, 1962), 464–473.

takeover bidding, for example, is the inadequately prepared and often hurriedly consummated merger which provides its share of the 'lame ducks' of the current industrial scene.[1] The mergers in the first half of the century, by contrast, were voluntarily consummated by both parties and they were in general preceded by intensive discussions on the existence and nature of the real benefits of the combination, or, in modern parlance, of the 'synergy' expected to flow from merger. The managerial strains of postmerger integration were correspondingly smaller and, since both parties knew their position, the prospects of a post merger boardroom struggle (an eventuality which is normally detrimental to the prosperity of a company) were reduced. The industrial logic of agreed mergers was then likely in these circumstances to be more swiftly and surely worked out.[2] A further point is that the higher levels of industrial concentration created by takeover bids are not necessarily in the social interest: there may be heavy social costs of redundancies and of monopoly powers, which, in ill-conceived bids, may not be redeemed by any managerial synergy or economies of scale. The judgement of an interwar analyst of the stock market will serve to remind us that the rise of takeover bids may not have been an unmixed blessing: 'From the standpoint of general utility', he wrote, 'there is all the difference between the promoter of a real new enterprise and the promoter of a combination or amalgamation. The former is calculated to increase wealth; the latter is rather likely to diminish it. The former is good for employment, the latter is likely to reduce it. The former increases the good things of the world and multiplies the conveniences of life. The latter aims at restricting them and so increasing their cost. One is addition, the other subtraction. One enlarges the world's resources and enriches the consumer by giving him something new; the other exploits him by establishing a monopoly and so forcing him to pay higher prices or to pay the old prices for inferior articles.'[3] This is, of course, the extreme view of a liberal free-marketeer, but it highlights the point that a cost benefit analysis of the rise of the takeover bid would have to take into account a wider range of effects than we are able to discuss here.[4]

In one respect, however, the rise of takeover bids has had beneficial results of a kind which could not have been achieved by merger activity of the type experienced in earlier years. This is in the reinforcement of the disciplinary function of the stock market, a reinforcement which, arguably, was much needed. Today, the board of a public company which fails to put its assets to profitable use, or which fails to exploit favourable opportunities open to the

---

[1] For the incidence of failure in modern merger waves, see G. D. Newbould, *Management and Merger Activity* (1970); A. Singh, *Takeovers, their relevance to the Stock Market and the Theory of the Firm* (Cambridge, 1971), ch. 7.

[2] Of course, the earlier merger waves were not without their failures but these can generally be attributed to an over-rapid rate of expansion or to financial manipulation by company promoters, see L. Hannah, 'Managerial Innovation and the Rise of the Large Scale Company in Twentieth Century Britain', *Econ. Hist. Rev.* (forthcoming, 1974) and ibid., 'The Political Economy of Mergers in Manufacturing Industry in Britain between the Wars', D.Phil. thesis, (Oxford 1972), 90–3.

[3] F. W. Hirst, *The Stock Exchange* (1932), 222.

[4] For a fuller analysis see L. Hannah *The Rise of the Corporate Economy* (Methuen, forthcoming, 1974).

company, risks being displaced by aggressive take-over bidders able and willing to pay to shareholders a premium price, reflecting the more efficient use of the company's assets which they believe to be possible under reformed management. The carrot of private profit for the bidder thus provides an admonitory stick for a sleepy management.[1] In the earlier decades of this century by contrast, managers were in general able, if they so wished, to reject perfectly rational bids which, though they might result in a less quiet life for themselves, were economically advantageous. The full implications of the divorce of ownership and control in the modern capitalist economy thus went unrealized. Only the banks, operating through BIDC on a limited number of companies, came close to determining industrial policy through operations designed to override board decisions and gain effective control of assets for the purpose of managerial reorganization. For the majority of companies, however, the first five decades of this century were a golden age of directorial power, an age of transition from the disaggregated Victorian economy of self-financing owner-entrepreneurs disciplined by competition in the product market to the present generation of 'managerial' capitalists operating in an economic system whose logic is still being developed and is still only imperfectly understood.

*University of Essex*

---

[1] For a more sophisticated statement of the role of the takeover bid in stock market discipline, see H. G. Manne, 'Mergers and the Market for Corporate Control', *Journal of Political Economy*, LXXIII (1965), R. Marris, *Economic Theory of 'Managerial' Capitalism*; D. A. Kuehn, 'Stock Market Valuation and Acquisition: An Empirical Test of One Component of Managerial Utility', *Journal of Industrial Economics*, (1969), 132–44.

# CASH AND CONCRETE

## Liquidity Problems in the Mass-Production of 'Homes for Heroes'[1]

### by SHEILA MARRINER

I

The misfortunes of the crusade to build 'homes fit for heroes' feature in most general histories of building and housing;[2] its failures have been attributed to many factors, although a good deal of emphasis has rightly been placed on the competing demands for and absolute shortages of real resources, especially of building materials and skilled labour. Much less attention has been paid to the problems experienced in raising adequate supplies of money at central and local government levels and to finance the operations of the contractors who actually built most of the houses. The difficulties contractors encountered resulted in waste and dislocation, in abortive or uncompleted contracts and in a mounting refuse heap of defunct companies, as building firms were overwhelmed by liquidity crises. Sometimes these were aggravated by mismanagement, extravagance and miscalculations, but basically they stemmed from the failure of fund-raising issues to attract sufficient response from the investing public. The government recognised that there was a general shortage of capital for house-building and, indeed, for all local and central government activities and, to try to prevent a scramble for the available funds, the Financial Facilities Committee was created in the closing stages of the war to determine some order of priorities. No steps at all, however, were taken to help private enterprise to raise the necessary capital for building or for producing building materials. In fact, as we shall see, every request for such assistance from private firms was categorically rejected.

The target for the crusade was set up primarily by the Tudor Walters Committee:[3] it was for the completion of half a million houses. In 1919, the *Interim Report of the Treasury Committee on Housing Finance* estimated that it should be possible to complete 100,000 houses by September 1920, and 200,000 a year in each of the next two years, at a total cost of four hundred million pounds. As early as the end of 1919, idealistic optimism and euphoria were fading. Despite generous subsidies, the anticipated mass production of houses failed to materialise, costs escalated and bottle-necks and shortages bedevilled building programmes. The tide of criticism mounted and, in July 1921, after only two years, the government decided that no more contracts should be approved. Instead of building half a million houses, local authorities eventually completed 170,090, and a further 39,186 were built by subsidised

private enterprise. The crusade had fizzled out after achieving
only just over two-fifths of its target.

The government had seriously underestimated the magnitude
of the difficulties. During and immediately after the war, it was
realised that, without adequate planning, 'there will be an unholy
scramble . . . with the usual results of extravagance and inefficiency'.[4] In an effort to foresee and forestall obstacles, there was a
great proliferation of committees, investigations, recommendations
and counter-recommendations. Disagreements led to confusion and
inefficiency, vividly highlighted by Dr. Christopher Addison. In
1917, he commented critically upon the utter inadequacy of existing
administrative agencies for a task of this magnitude: 'the Local
Government Board', he wrote, 'apparently think they can do a job
sixty times greater than before with three men and a boy'.[5] He
records how, in 1918, a committee presided over by Eric Geddes
threw overboard all the arrangements painstakingly made by Sir
James Carmichael to try to ensure a rapid expansion in the output
of building materials after the war.[6] 'I have scarcely known anything
which created more widespread disgust than this reckless scrapping
of all the arrangements Carmichael had made for fostering local
production all over the country.' Carmichael, himself a building
contractor, 'prophesied with literal accuracy what would happen'.
In November 1918 and January 1919, Dr. Addison was 'aghast' at
the 'appalling backwardness' of the Local Government Board's
preparations, and regarded it as 'the most shocking revelation of
incompetence that I have ever experienced.'[7]

The government did, however, produce a battery of devices
to try to implement the housing programme. The major piece of
legislation was, of course, Addison's Act.[8] In addition, attempts were
made to restrict luxury building, and a committee was set up to
report on the feasibility of postponing government departments'
building programmes in order to prevent them competing with
house-building for scarce resources, especially for skilled labour.[9]
The Local Government Board set up an Advisory Council. Eleven
Regional Housing Commissioners assisted and supervised local
authorities in the preparation and implementation of their schemes.
The Ministry of Reconstruction's Department of Building Materials
Supply bought materials for resale to local authorities at controlled
prices. Restrictive and monopolistic practices were to be investigated
by the Profiteering Section of the Board of Trade. In 1918, the
British Standards Association, was incorporated under licence by
the Board of Trade. The Board of Building Research was founded in
1920 in the Department of Scientific and Industrial Research and,
in 1921, the Building Research Station came into being. The
functions of these bodies were to look for and test new and substitute materials and methods. A Standardisation and New Construction Committee of the Housing Department of the Local
Government Board aimed to encourage standardisation of components and the use of new methods. Schemes were mooted for

re-training ex-servicemen and adopting building techniques that required less skilled labour. Bye-laws were modified to allow the wider use of non-traditional methods and materials. The Office of Works staff was expanded to act as architect and builder for up to ten thousand houses, for authorities who failed to obtain tenders. The Ministry of Health instituted a national propaganda campaign to advertise these facilities and to cajole or coerce authorities to act with greater speed.

Of key importance, of course, was the question of how the bills were to be paid. Prices escalated: there were regional variations, but the cost per house was usually around a thousand pounds, and many exceeded this. For central and local government agencies, there were two basic financial problems: to raise loans to cover the building costs, and to ensure that, despite paying interest and redemption charges for these loans, the working-class families for whom the houses were built could afford to pay the rents. Addison's Act dealt with the latter problem. Rents were to be fixed at a reasonable level, ratepayers subsidised the building up to the proceeds of a one penny rate per annum, and the whole of the cost over and above this fell on the taxpayer. To recommend ways of raising the actual cash to finance the building, a Treasury Committee on Housing Finance was set up on 31 October, 1919, under the Chairmanship of W. H. N. Goschen. Its task was to 'consider the steps that should be taken by Local Authorities to facilitate the raising of capital to defray the cost of housing schemes and in particular to make suggestions for a model long-term security for this purpose'.

This committee reported on 27 November, 1919.[10] It recommended that local authorities with a rateable value of under £200,000 p.a. should have access to the Local Loans Fund of the Public Works Loans Board if they could not find other sources of finance. Other authorities should continue to raise mortgage loans (which should rank as Trustee Securities), they should issue stock and borrow abroad. The Committee rejected the raising of large sums in the form of short-term loans from banks, because of the adverse effect on interest rates. Equally, it was of the opinion that the central government could not intervene, because of the pressing post-war demands on capital generally, and the heavy funding operations with which it was faced—'the effect upon the credit of the country would be very serious if the State were to enter the market for the purpose of financing the whole of the housing scheme'. The proposed new model securities were to be called 'Local Bonds'. These could be of varying denominations and duration, secured on the rates, revenues and properties of the issuing local authority, and bondholders could use them to buy houses from local authorities. They were to rank as Trustee Securities.

Grave difficulty was anticipated in raising enough money. In November 1919, some local authorities were unable to raise sufficient cash; in February 1920, fifty of the larger local authorities conferred with the Government; in March, Liverpool was in danger of having to suspend contracts because of lack of finance.[11] Meanwhile, the Ministry was pushing ahead with plans to launch a campaign to sell Local Bonds, as recommended by the Goschen Committee, and in this Mr. J. Ferguson, Managing Director of Lloyds Bank, played an active role.[12] It had been hoped that interest rates could be limited to 5½ per cent, but Mr. Ferguson convinced Dr. Addison that 'nothing short of 6 per cent will give us the unqualified success the great importance of the scheme demands'.[13] In the event, even six per cent was not sufficiently attractive. The prospects were bad and local authorities were deplorably slow in arranging to issue bonds.[14]

The national campaign was, however, launched publicly on 12 April, 1920, by appeals to patriotism and resort to all sorts of propaganda gimmicks involving ex-servicemen and boy scouts, and assisted by newspapers, banks and chambers of commerce. The bonds were in denominations of £5 and upwards, and carried interest at six per cent. By late April, it was clear that the campaign needed 'much more steam'.[15] Certainly, it had very mixed results. Liverpool's first issue fell flat, as only two-thirds were taken up; the county of Hertford's issue fell even flatter—only five per cent was taken up.[16] Others were more successful: by the end of May 1920, Bolton had raised £465,000, Bradford £400,000 and Birmingham £250,000.[17] For the whole country, it had been hoped that it would be possible to collect ten million pounds a month in this way, but in the first two months, only £4,100,000 was raised.[18] Because of the failure to reach the hoped-for target, local authorities were allowed to borrow half the proceeds from the sale of National Savings Certificates in their own area, to supplement their resources from October 1920.[19] Meanwhile, the financial stringency continued. In May 1920, the Ministry of Health's Housing Committee reported that some twenty schemes, including 1,912 houses, were held up for lack of funds and, in June, a Ministry of Health memo to the Cabinet's Housing Committee attributed delays primarily to the difficulties involved in obtaining finance.[20]

In an attempt to overcome some of these difficulties, the Housing Finance Advisory Committee was set up by the Treasury, under the chairmanship of W. H. N. Goschen. This Goschen committee operated from 3 May, 1920 to 31 July, 1921.[21] It estimated that the amounts raised for housing by local authorities in England and Wales from all sources, to 31 March, 1921, were approximately as follows:

| | |
|---|---|
| By the issue of Stock | £35,000,000 |
| By the issue of Local Bonds | £17,000,000 |
| By the issue of Mortgage Loans | £15,000,000 |
| Loans by the Public Works Loans Commissioners | £60,000,000 |
| Total | £127,000,000 |

In addition, issues totalling some £11,000,000 were ready to be floated. Of these various sources of finance, the Goschen Committee was particularly concerned with issues of stock and with mortgage loans. It worked in conjunction with the Governor of the Bank of England, the Chairman and Committee of the Stock Exchange, the Ministry of Health and the group of brokers who normally handled municipal loans. The aim was to plan the timing of issues (to avoid flooding the market with securities and so unduly raising interest rates), and to look for alternative sources of finance. The committee even investigated the possibility of raising loans in the U.S.A., but concluded that it would be expensive and would involve the risk of exchange losses.

It proved difficult to keep interest rates on mortgage loans below seven per cent. The main sources for such loans were institutional investors, especially insurance companies and the Ecclesiastical Commissioners. One insurance company lent five million pounds at an interest rate of six and three quarters per cent, but many mortgage loans were at seven per cent. In some cases, there was strong prejudice against corporation house-building, and loans were only forthcoming if local authorities agreed not to use them for housing. On stock issues, interest rates were kept to six per cent, although most of the stocks were issued at only ninety five and a half per cent of their nominal value. On two loans of three million pounds, and three and a half million pounds for Birmingham and Liverpool, the interest rate was down to five and a half per cent, but the issue price was only ninety per cent of nominal value. The great difficulty in stock issues, however, was the general lack of public response. Table 1 vividly illustrates the fact that, in the majority of cases, the initial response of investors was such that well over two-thirds of each issue was left on the underwriters' hands. It was then necessary for the underwriters to feed stock slowly on to the market to dispose of it and, according to the Goschen Committee, this method proved relatively satisfactory.

Despite all the Goschen Committee's efforts, however, and despite the sixty million pounds lent by the Public Works Loans Commissioners (mostly to the smaller local authorities), by the beginning of 1921, several local authorities were in serious difficulties. Birmingham's Finance Committee reported that the 'programme of housing construction . . . is proving a great strain'. The Corporation had been compelled to borrow abroad, 'where loans can only be raised at prices which the Corporation would not think of considering if it had not housing expenditure to meet'. In fact, 'at the present time nearly every proposal requiring new capital where new contracts have not been entered into is being held up'. Nottingham had to postpone further schemes, having 'authorised expenditure of £1,400,000 for housing but so far only about £500,000 had been raised', and York had insufficient money for its schemes.[22]

The central government could not raise funds directly, and local authorities were getting out of their depth, and yet it does not

Table 1: Stock Issues arranged by the Housing Finance Advisory Committee to 31 March, 1921

| Local Authority | Nominal Amount £000s | Proportion Subscribed Per cent |
|---|---|---|
| Lincoln | 750 | 100 |
| Newcastle | 1,000 | 100 |
| Nottingham | 1,000 | 100 |
| Brighton | 500 | 56 |
| Birkenhead | 1,000 | 47·5 |
| London | 3,500 | 37 |
| Bournemouth | 650 | 33 |
| Bristol | 1,500 | 33 |
| Salford | 750 | 31·5 |
| Bradford | 2,000 | 31 |
| Portsmouth | 1,000 | 28 |
| Birmingham | 3,000 | 26·5 |
| Liverpool | 3,500 | 25·5 |
| Coventry | 1,000 | 25 |
| Croydon | 1,000 | 23 |
| Middlesborough | 1,250 | 20 |
| South Shields | 1,000 | 20 |
| Plymouth | 1,000 | 18 |
| Cardiff | 1,500 | 16 |
| Northampton | 400 | 9 |
| Swansea | 1,000 | 9 |
| Bootle | 500 | 6·5 |
| Wolverhampton | 500 | 6 |
| Ipswich | 300 | 5 |
| Stoke-on-Trent | 900 | 4 |
| Rotherham | 750 | 1 |
| Total | 31,250 | |

Source: Report of the Goschen Committee, 26 April, 1921. P.R.O., HLG 48 698/92038/1/230.

seem to have occurred to them to try to help the firms on which they relied to build the houses. The government could not plead ignorance of the grave difficulties besetting building firms: these were spelled out by at least one company, in February 1920, as we shall see below. In 1921, builders giving evidence before the Departmental Committee on the High Cost of Building Working-class Dwellings complained of the increased amounts of capital needed for building, of high interest rates, lack of credit and a slower turnover of capital than pre-war.[23] This committee discovered that many contractors and brick manufacturers had experienced great difficulty in getting the necessary financial support.[24] In 1919 and 1920, however, the government assumed that private enterprise would build sufficient houses with marginal intervention by the Office of Works and with some use of direct labour by local authorities.[25]

## II

How, then, did building firms respond to the opportunities, challenges and problems of this housing campaign? Initially, it was welcomed as an attractive field for enterprise. This attitude is typified in a prospectus issued by the firm of Henry Boots in November 1919, which refers to the 'immense field for commercial enterprise' opened up by this 'enormous volume of construction', and anticipates that 'there will be hardly any sphere of operations to compare in the same degree either in volume or importance with the development of constructional and building undertakings'. Quantitatively, however, progress was very slow. Building tended to proceed on the basis of very small contracts. By the beginning of 1922, some 4,400 local authority housing schemes had been approved.[26] The number of local authority houses eventually built under Addison's Act was 170,090, so the average size of the schemes was under 40 houses, and the average size of contracts was even smaller. *The Builder* published details of contracts week by week, and one has to comb through carefully to find examples of contracts for even one hundred houses at a time. A breakdown of Birmingham's housing contracts (Table 2), as at July 1920, shows a fairly typical picture.

*Table 2: Birmingham Corporation's Housing Contracts, July 1920*

| No. of houses per Contractor | No. of Contractors | Houses in Contracts of this size Number | Percentage |
|---|---|---|---|
| Less than 99 | 13 | 555 | 32·9 |
| 100–199 | 6 | 804 | 47·7 |
| 200–299 | 1 | 257 | 15·3 |
| Direct Labour | — | 68 | 4·1 |
| | | 1,684 | 100·0 |

*Source: The Builder, 16 July, 1920.*

Most authorities split large estates into small lots: in May 1920. for example, Sheffield wanted to build 496 houses on one estate, It employed twenty-one contractors, the smallest contract being for six houses, the largest for forty-nine.[27]

On the whole, traditional building methods and organisation favoured such small contracts, but it is also possible to find a few larger ones. In April 1919, Sheffield had two contracts for 184 houses and 263 houses and, in November 1919, it negotiated one for 694 houses. In January 1920, Leeds had two contracts for 800 and 500 houses.[28] Liverpool tended to operate for most of its building on the basis of relatively large contracts (Table 3).

There were a few contractors who had had experience of large contracts before and during the war. Henry Boot & Sons, for example, was established in the late nineteenth century and incorporated as a private company in 1910. During the war it built houses, factories, colliery buildings, an aerodrome, a power station for a naval base, an army hospital etc. In November 1919, it was taken over, at a cost of £154,680, by a new company, Henry Boot & Sons (London) Ltd., with a nominal capital of £500,000. It was claimed that 'work is now rapidly proceeding in connection with the erection of houses. . . . Provisional arrangements have been made

Table 3: *Liverpool Corporation's Housing Contracts, July 1920*

| No. of houses per Contractor | No. of Contractors | Houses in Contracts of this size Number | Percentage |
|---|---|---|---|
| Less than 99 | 4[1] | 61 | 1·1 |
| 100–199 | 1 | 100 | 1·8 |
| 200–299 | — | — | — |
| 300–399 | — | — | — |
| 400–499 | 1 | 400 | 7·2 |
| 500 | 5[2] | 2,500 | 44·9 |
| 2,000 | 1 | 2,000 | 36·0 |
| Direct Labour | | 500 | 9·0 |
| | | 5,561 | 100·0 |

*Source:* Compiled from the Proceedings of Liverpool City Council.

NOTES

1. One of these contracts was simply for the purpose of demonstrating building by the Doric System by the Modern Building Co. of Brighton.

2. Although four of these contracts were subsequently reduced to between 400 and 499 houses, they were still relatively large compared with those signed by most authorities.

to proceed at once with several large housing contracts involving the building of some thousands of houses under the Ministry of Health Scheme . . . *the Directors propose to employ a large proportion of the new working capital upon this important national work*' [my italics].[29] Boots did become important house-builders, but despite their optimism and long experience, one large contract for a thousand houses for Birmingham Corporation, signed in February 1920, had been abandoned by July of that year.[30]

For the government to have even a sporting chance of hitting the target of half a million houses in three years, mass-production methods were essential, and for the first time a section of the building industry developed for this purpose. Before and during the war, sporadic experiments had occurred, but now intensive, sustained and more widespread efforts were made to devise building technology amenable to mass-producing small houses. Some of the firms concerned were newly created, some were incorporated to take over existing one-man or family businesses, a few were large concerns of long-standing. What they all had in common was their own building system to mass produce houses. These building systems used non-traditional building materials, especially concrete blocks, slabs and sections (though some also used wood or metal), and they aimed to economise in skilled labour.

The government encouraged such efforts. The Ministry of Health scrutinised them, modified its standard specifications to suit each approved system, and allowed local authorities to use them for building under the subsidised scheme. By 4 May, 1921, two hundred and sixty-five systems and methods of construction had been submitted and, of these, one hundred and forty-one had been approved.[31] A few well-publicised ones were:

| | |
|---|---|
| Unit Construction Co. Ltd. | Unit system |
| Dorman Long & Co. Ltd. | Dorlonco |
| Modern Building Co. Ltd. | Doric |
| Wm. Airey & Co. Ltd. | Duo-Slab |
| Adams Housing Syndicate | Adams |
| National Improved Housing Co. Ltd. | Condual later called Jefferies |
| Hill, Richards & Co. Ltd. | Waller |
| Winget Ltd. | Winget |
| Walter Jones & Sons | Interloc |
| John Laing & Son Ltd. | Easiform |
| British Léan Co. | Léan cavity block |

These and other building systems needed large contracts to be commercially viable, and the firms operating them advertised their willingness to build on a large scale. The National Improved Housing Co. Ltd. told the Ministry of Health that its system needed a minimum contract for a hundred houses, and offered to build in lots of between a hundred and a thousand at a time.[32] The Waller system was said to need minimum contracts for five hundred houses, although Hill, Richards advertised that they could build four thousand a year in lots of two hundred and fifty.[33] Walter Jones and Unit Construction both offered to build three thousand houses a year.[34]

Building in this way, however, necessitated the provision of financial resources on a scale familiar to only a handful of the largest building firms before the war. Firms needed resources to cover costs until they had developed their building systems and received the Ministry's approval, which might take some months, if modifications were suggested. Then they had to advertise, or to tender for schemes, or to finance an entry to a building exhibition, which could cost as much as £1,000. When a local authority offered to negotiate a contract, it could take months to finalise the arrangements with the local authority itself, with the regional housing commissioner and with the Ministry's officials. After the contract was signed the firm had, in addition to its head office and works, to build and equip depots, offices, stores for materials, canteens and other working buildings on each site.

Most building systems also needed fairly heavy investment in equipment. If bricks were used, it was the brick manufacturers who had to find the capital to manufacture the bricks. Systems using concrete required equipment to manufacture blocks, slabs or sections on or near the site. This called for expenditure on concrete grinders and mixers and block-making machinery. The weight and awkwardness of concrete blocks and slabs also necessitated more mechanical handling. On large new housing estates, transport of bulky goods around the site could call for the provision of fleets of lorries or light railways. Some of this equipment could be bought on hire purchase, in fact, Winget Ltd, a major supplier of concrete block-making machinery and related equipment such as elevators, mixers etc. had increased its own share capital in 1915, partly in order to provide more working capital to develop its hire purchase

department.[35] Of the four companies examined below, three used
Winget equipment, but there is no evidence that they took advantage
of the hire-purchase facility.[36]

The provision of building materials for large contracts also
presented considerable problems. Prices were high and rising through
1919 and most of 1920, and many materials were in short supply.
A good deal of cement had to be imported. Some suppliers might
allow builders credit, but in a sellers' market, the suppliers could
usually dictate their own terms, and many of them were desperately
short of capital themselves. Some building systems, for example,
although making extensive use of concrete, needed bricks for some
purposes, such as chimneys. Evidence in 1921, before the Committee
on the High Cost of Building Working-Class Dwellings, considered
the problems involved in extending existing brick works and
opening new ones, and concluded 'The main obstacles to extension
are financial . . . generally investors are shy of putting their money
into brick works. *Numerous requests are received for capital assistance from
the Government* [my italics] and in a recent case the maker offered
the whole of his output pending repayment of the government
mortgage'.[37] Far from receiving financial assistance from materials
suppliers, in fact, builders found that they were more often faced
with shortages and late deliveries which caused costly delays.
Labour was scarce, skilled labour was very difficult to hold and
wages had to be paid even if building was suspended for lack of
materials.

The Office of Works was under no illusions about the need for
adequate finance for its contracts. When the Office agreed to build
houses for a local authority, it demanded payment *in advance*. Before
work could start, a local authority had to advance as much as
five per cent of the estimated cost and then make regular monthly
payments in advance for the duration of the work.[38] It appears,
however, that although some authorities dutifully paid up, others
did not: 'there were cases where work could not be put in hand
because the local authorities were not advancing the money . . . It
was the function of the Ministry . . . to see that the Local Authorities
were kept up to the mark on this point . . . by impressing on them
the fact that they must take up loan sanctions immediately and
authorise advances being made payable to the Office of Works, as
and when required'.[39]

No such concessions were made to private enterprise. In 1921,
it was admitted[40] that contractors using new methods of construction had 'expended considerable time and thought in developing their systems but many have had great difficulty . . . in getting
the necessary financial support to carry out their proposals'. They
certainly could not look for financial assistance from the Ministry
of Health's standard contracts. There were long debates about the
form and content of contracts for subsidised housing schemes, and
about the rate of profit contractors should be allowed to earn.
Eventually, it was decided that profits should be of the order of

five per cent of the *initial estimated cost*, and that there should be seven types of contract:[41]

A. A lump-sum payment to contractors allowing, in some cases, variations for increases or decreases in wages and materials.
B. Cost plus fixed profit.
C. Cost contracts but with maximum prices.
D. Contracts for builders who sold to local authorities houses they built on their own land.
E. Contracts for local authorities building by direct labour.
F. Contracts for Building Guilds.
G. Office of Works contracts.

Of contracts for 160,000 houses signed by 29 April, 1921, those for 108,700 houses came under A and a further 29,650 under B.[42] The contracts won by the firms considered in this article were all, as far as can be ascertained, of the lump-sum type. The basic terms usually provided that no payment at all would be made until the contractor had expended a minimum sum (usually several thousands of pounds). Thereafter, the contractor could claim ninety per cent of the value of work done each month until the retention money was built up. As from May 1920, the retention money had to be a minimum of five per cent of expected cost,[43] a heavy burden on large contracts (although some interest might be paid). Until the retention money was built up, the contractor had to deposit with the local authority securities to the amount of the retention money. The retention money was held until the building was complete—perhaps as long as two years on a large contract—then half was repaid; the other half was repaid six months later, if the architect certified that all defects had been made good.

Some contracts were fixed-priced ones, others included provision for varying prices of materials and/or wage rates. In the latter case, contractors' profits were calculated on the estimated initial cost— they received no percentage profit on increased expenditure, and this caused grave discontent. Unit Construction Co. sent a strongly-worded letter of complaint to Sir James Carmichael pointing out that on one of their contracts for eighty houses, increased wages and prices were going to add £10,000 to the cost, but they received no percentage on this.[44]

Payments for plant and equipment seem to have varied somewhat. Long discussions took place, and no very clear picture emerges, except that once equipment was on the site it became the property of the local authority until the architect released it. Frequently, though not invariably, the payment seems to have been of the order of one and a half or two per cent of the value of the equipment per month until one third of its value had been paid; thereafter, payment fell to half of one per cent per month.

Contractors were strongly criticised for insisting on variable-price contracts, which forced local authorities to take the risk of price and wage variations;[45] the *Report of the Departmental Committee on the High Cost of Working-Class Dwellings* (p. 8) included the general criticism that contractors took advantage of the situation to insist on variable-cost contracts, and this statement was avidly seized on by newspapers and journals. The media, however, completely failed to report the general conclusion (p. 55), in which the Committee was forced to admit that cases in which builders earned excessive profits (i.e. over five per cent) were exceptional, and the Committee itself omitted to take any account of the high failure rate amongst contractors. It also failed to note that some contractors signed fixed-price contracts, as we shall see below.

How, then, did contractors raise the cash to cover their heavy financial outlay on large contracts? Potential sources of cash were issues of shares and debentures and the raising of mortgages, loans and overdrafts. The *upper* limit to the amount of cash that could be raised from share issues was fixed by the size of the company's nominal capital. On the whole, 'building and contracting' firms floated between 1919 and 1921 set their sights very low when fixing their nominal capital. Of two hundred such firms chosen at random from amongst the companies floated between February 1919 and November 1921, one hundred and twenty limited their nominal capital to £5,000 or less. Thirty-nine fixed theirs at between £5,000 and £10,000, and only twenty-one aimed over £10,000. Of these, the largest issue was by Henry Boot & Sons (London) Ltd., for £500,000; the National Improved Housing Co. Ltd. and the Waller Housing Corporation Ltd. both aimed for £250,000; Sir James Carmichael (Director-General of Housing) aimed for £130,000 for his contracting business in Wandsworth; William Moss's of Loughborough for £100,000 and John Laing & Son Ltd. of Lancaster for £60,000.

A large nominal capital, however, need not necessarily produce much cash. As we shall see below, the Waller Corporation's £250,000 yielded no cash at all. Shares may be allotted in payment for goodwill, patent rights or contracts; shares allotted may not be fully paid-up, and there may be an unenthusiastic response from the investing public, so that issues may fail to reach their targets by a very large margin.

In order to illustrate some of the problems, it is proposed in the rest of this article to draw on the experiences of four firms. It is often possible to learn more from failure than from success and, in any event, in an industry with such a notoriously high failure rate as building, it is not necessary to justify choosing as examples three firms which had short effective lives, and only one which has survived to the present day. The firms that failed were the National Improved Housing Co. Ltd., the Waller Housing Corporation Ltd. and the Economic Building Corporation Ltd. The fourth example, Unit Construction Co. Ltd., overcame the difficulties to become a major contractor which still thrives today.

Initially, these four firms had a good deal in common: all were incorporated in 1919; they were primarily concerned with house-building, especially with local authority contracts; each had its own building system which involved the extensive use of concrete. The major contributory factor in the three failures was lack of liquid capital, aggravated in two cases by mismanagement and extravagance. Unit Construction was fortunate in becoming the junior member of a large group of companies, so that its capital requirements appeared small in relation to those of the group. Within the confines of an article, it is not possible to give a detailed history of each firm; only the salient factors that contributed to failure or success can be isolated and highlighted.

## III

The promoter of the National Improved Housing Co. Ltd. was the Concrete Construction Co. Ltd., which had been incorporated on 26 June, 1918, with a nominal capital of £1,000, raised to £20,000 in March 1919, of which £18,152 had been paid up by 31 December, 1919.[46] Its offspring, the National Improved Housing Co., was incorporated on 27 May, 1919, to build local authority houses and to buy the assets of the Concrete Construction Co. Ltd.[47] The two companies shared many of the same personnel and, in fact, a shareholder who later petitioned for the compulsory winding up of the Concrete Construction Co. made the point in his Affidavit that 'the affairs of the two companies are much interwoven'; so much so that he claimed that there should be an investigation.[48]

With regard to personalities, the managing director of the new company, Frederick King, was a director of the Concrete Co.; Sir Valentine R. Grace was Chairman of both companies and Mabel Simons was Secretary of both. The director of works of the new company was F. W. Fryer, who, together with his family, held a quarter of the shares in the Concrete Company. Some £7,250 of the Concrete Company's shares were held in South Wales, and the National Improved Housing Company had a moderate body of shareholders in the same area.

The new company was liberally provided with technical expertise in its directors. Colonel H. V. Kent was a consulting engineer who had formerly been Assistant Director of Fortifications and Works; Francis Bateman and C. E. Wilkinson were both contractors; T. G. Jones was a newspaper proprietor and member of Glamorgan County Council; Arthur F. Jefferies, the contracts manager, was a designer and builder of concrete houses.

From its parent company, the new firm acquired a building system, the Condual System of Economic Concrete Construction; an agreement with Winget Ltd. for preferential terms for concrete block-making machines and mixers; a fully equipped building works; and the lease of administrative offices.[49] In theory, it should have been equipped to start building operations fairly quickly.

The company's nominal capital was set at £250,000, and at the end of July, 1919, the public were invited to subscribe for £185,000 shares. The prospectus painted a rosy picture. The building industries were faced with 'opportunities for vast and profitable undertakings', especially in house-building. There was 'plenty of work to do; plenty of men and materials to do it with, and the highest expert advice obtainable'. 'The demand for houses is very great, and large *Cash Contracts* [my italics] are assured'. 'With its complete organisation and the large number of CASH CONTRACTS [*sic*] immediately available to the Company, the Directors estimate that, if only 2,500 houses per year are erected, a net profit of £125,000 per annum' would be earned.

The issue could hardly be regarded as a shattering success. Only £50,000 of shares were allotted; of these, £14,006 10s. went to the Concrete Construction Co. Ltd.; £10,000 were allotted to the Omnium Trust Co.; £11,000 went to the directors and two of the founder members; the remaining £15,000 was subscribed by the public.[50] Of this, £7,000 was subscribed in holdings of £250 or over, and £8,000 in very small holdings (some as low as £5) by nearly five hundred shareholders. The shareholders were drawn from a very wide range of occupations—doctors, accountants, bankers, architects, civil servants, teachers, ministers of the Church, hotel keepers, licensed victuallers, clerks, engineers, retailers, traders, manufacturers, members of the armed services, artists and theatrical agents, carpenters, joiners, foremen, 'gentlemen', 'wives' and 'widows'. These small subscriptions were drawn from a wide geographical area, with one moderate block of shareholders concentrated in South Wales, perhaps linked with Mr. T. G. Jones, one of the directors.

Despite casting its net so widely, the actual amount of cash raised was small. Of the £50,000 of shares allotted, only £34,000 was paid in cash and, of this, £20,000 had to be handed over to the Concrete Company under the terms of the contract.[51] It was estimated that the company's preliminary expenses amounted to £12,000.[52] After these commitments were met, there was only £2,000 left in cash, and the directors had to be paid £200 a year each, the chairman £250 a year.[53]

Furthermore, the company could not start to earn quickly, so running costs had to be covered for several months with no incoming revenue. Although the company had bought the Condual system, this system had not yet received Ministry of Health approval. F. W. Fryer, the company's chief director of works, carried on a lengthy correspondence trying to persuade the Ministry that the system was cheap, hygienic, cool in summer and warm in winter and that at least fifteen per cent of its labour force would consist of demobbed or disabled men.[54] He offered to build houses at a fixed price, £1,470 a pair for contracts of a hundred or more houses, a very low price at the end of 1919. 'The company will be prepared to build and sell to the authorities *at a fixed price, taking all risks of fluctuation of labour and material markets*, [my italics] and guarantee delivery at fixed dates'. He offered to build not less than five thousand houses a year on these terms.

The specifications for the Condual system were not, however, approved by the Ministry until 21 February, 1920,[55] although they are listed amongst Ministry of Health approvals in *The Builder* on 30 January, 1920. The company could not, therefore, even start to build for the first eight months of its life. Its contracts manager had meanwhile been busy, and by February 1920, he had won firm contracts with eight local authorities for 1,232 houses worth £1,150,952. Eight other contracts were under consideration for a further 2,493 houses, worth £2,150,742.[56]

Ironically, just as all the preparatory work was completed and the company could have started operations, it was overwhelmed by its failure to raise the required amount of liquid capital. It had its building system, its technical experts and eight firm contracts, but no cash. In a desperate bid to avert disaster, the Chairman and Managing Director sent three identical letters on 16 February, 1920: one to the Rt. Hon. David Lloyd George, then Prime Minister, one to Dr. Addison, Minister of Health and one to Sir James Carmichael, Director-General of Housing.[57] The letters are extensively quoted because of the light they throw on the nature and magnitude of such contractors' financial difficulties.

After opening with the words 'We approach you to prevent a National Scandal', the letters go on to outline the progress of the firm to date and its success in winning contracts but 'it is regretted that these offers of contracts will have to be thrown back on the Authorities unless the Government can immediately see their way to financially assist by loaning to this Company on reasonable terms, say, one hundred thousand pounds (£100,000) which will make it possible to turn over work to the extent of one million pounds in housing construction'. The company had tried to raise capital by public issue 'but with absolute [*sic*] negligible results, although the Press have given every encouragement to the issues'. The letters attribute the lack of response by investors to uncertainty, labour unrest, 'paralysed transport and the very obvious "rings" in building materials' which 'create a prejudice fatal to potential investors'. The company was willing and able to build, but 'finds itself crippled for working capital'. Local authorities are 'pressing us daily to commence building, which we are only too anxious to do, given the necessary capital'. In these circumstances, 'we ask for your immediate assistance to enable us to make every effort to assist the housing shortage . . . and otherwise prevent what can only be summarised as a lamentable and avoidable scandal by being compelled to abandon the schemes'.

On 24 February, P. Barter, private secretary to the Ministry of Health, replied[58] 'I am desired by Dr. Addison . . . to say that he has given careful consideration to the request . . . for assistance in the provision of the necessary capital for the National Improved Housing Company.

'The Minister desires me to point out that the Ministry have no funds from which to assist companies with working capital and *the Government could not contemplate the financing of private firms* [my italics].

'In these circumstances he much regrets that he is unable to assist your company in the manner suggested.'

Sir Valentine Grace tried again. Could not the Government 'take the lead in arranging some concession to proposed contractors, to enable them to cope with the heavy initial expense'? During the war, contractors were allowed a deposit of ten per cent on signing contracts. He suggested that the Ministry should allow local authorities to pay contractors five per cent in advance. 'This would go some little way towards the initial outlay of providing the enormous amount of plant and materials required in commencing the building schemes'.[59]

Sir James Carmichael took advice from Ministry Officials and replied, on 2 March, 'I have placed your suggestions with regard to an advance on signing of contracts, before the Accountant General, and it is regretted that the Ministry cannot entertain the proposals put forward.'[60] No reasons are given either in this letter or in the extant correspondence within the Ministry.

No information is available about any other attempts by the company to raise loans or overdrafts. No mortgages, overdrafts or debentures are listed in its register of mortgages and charges.[61] The company was doomed. On 20 April, 1920, Mr. Justice Astbury ordered that it should be wound up, and on 8 June, 1920, he also ordered that the Concrete Construction Co. should be wound up.[62]

A. F. Jefferies, the contracts manager, tried to salvage something from the ruins. He went into partnership with an employee of Unit Construction Co. Ltd., formed the Jefferies Construction Co., took over the Condual System and renamed it the Jefferies system, although again he failed to raise sufficient finance to operate it.[63] The Ministry kept him under close surveillance. He actually won a contract for seventy-eight houses for Willington Urban District Council,[64] but J. Wightman Douglas of the Ministry of Health deliberately intervened to prevent the signing of the contract on the grounds that 'it was quite evident that they had no capital and are only endeavouring to obtain contracts with the hope of forming a company afterwards'.[65] The Regional Housing Director for Region A, in which Willington was located, was told that '*We have had several cases recently where new companies, after having accepted contracts, have been badly handicapped in carrying out the work or have had to stop entirely because they had not the money to pay for the material*' [my italics].[66]

The National Improved Housing Company's experience illustrates vividly the paralysing effects of failure to acquire sufficient liquid capital. It also provides irrefutable evidence from the Ministry of Health's own files that both the government and the Ministry were fully aware of the capital requirements for this type of contract, especially in its initial stages, and of the difficulty of meeting those requirements. It further suggests that, by the end of 1920, the Ministry was beginning to be aware of the need to scrutinise firms more carefully before approving contracts. The close watch kept on the activities of the Jefferies Construction Co. is indicative of the fact that the Ministry was taking this responsibility upon itself instead of relying on local authorities, although its attitude was still wholly negative; no positive assistance was forthcoming to help firms to surmount the cash barrier.

## IV

The second company, the Waller Housing Corporation Ltd., registered on 13 December, 1919, was promoted by Hill, Richards & Co. Ltd., a private company engaged in building and public works.[67] The new company was to take over the Waller building system which belonged to Philip E. Hill and Major James Hardress de Warenne Waller (Hill, Richards' engineer).[68] Hill, Richards were also in the process of negotiating three contracts for eleven hundred houses, and the new company paid for the privilege of these, too, although, in the event, they did not fully materialise.[69]

The Ministry of Health approved the Waller system at the end of 1919.[70] The system used concrete, but not in the form of blocks. Factories had to be built to precast walls in two large sections—an inner and outer section. These had to be taken on to the site and assembled by special cranes. The roofs were concrete, too. This method almost completely dispensed with bricklayers, slaters, plasterers and joiners and approached nearer to modern ideas of prefabrication than any other contemporary system. When investigating concrete systems in 1924, Sir Ernest Moir adjudged the Waller system to be the most ingenious to date, although Major Wightman Douglas, who had special responsibility in the Ministry of Health for new building methods, reported in 1920 that the Waller system was disappointing because it was difficult to get contracts for it.[71]

It certainly appears that the system was a costly one. The Waller Corporation had a contract with Liverpool City Council for five hundred houses, but only ninety-four were completed, at a cost of over £2,000 each, nearly twice as much as the next most expensive houses Liverpool built at this time.[72] Probably this was due to the smallness of the contract, and certainly the company tendered too low. Its losses on contracts amounted to at least £34,000.[73]

It seems, then, that this company had a technically advanced building system of considerable merit, but its commercial viability was suspect except for large contracts. The company was well-equipped with technical advice. Major Waller could supply engineering skill, one of Hill, Richards' directors, C. W. Maplesden, was an architect and Philip Hill was an estate agent.[74] The financial arrangements for the new company were, however, extremely complex and completely failed to produce the cash necessary to keep the company operational. In the first place, Hill, Richards' own finances were limited. This company had been registered on

1 March, 1916; its nominal capital was £80,000; only £5,000 of this was paid up although, by 1919, the company had raised a further £52,316 by mortgages and debentures.[75] The Waller Corporation's nominal capital was originally fixed at £250,000. Under an agreement between Hill, Richards and the Waller Corporation, the latter was to pay the former £200,000 in shares and £15,000 in cash for the Waller system and for promoting the company.[76] Hill, Richards kept £149,993 shares and allotted £50,000 to their nominees Messrs. Garsia, Bingley, Metcalfe and the Hon. Edward Coke. They were given these shares as a reward for raising £46,000 in cash for the company in the form of debentures, and they all became directors, with E. J. Metcalfe as Chairman and Philip Hill as Managing Director. The other £50,000 of shares were not issued initially, but a further £3,000 was raised from debentures. The company therefore started out with £34,000 in cash.

By the time the Waller Corporation became operational, five contracts had been secured for building 1,850 houses.[77] Of these, Liverpool, Manchester and Leeds each signed contracts for five hundred houses, Cardiff for two hundred and fifty and Poole for a hundred. Under the Poole contract, payment was not to be in cash but in interest-bearing mortgages issued by Poole Corporation and repayable in five years: the company subsequently lost £5,000 on these.[78] The Waller system necessitated the building of factories on each site to manufacture the large concrete sections—the Liverpool factory cost nearly £16,000 so, for five sites, factory-building could absorb as much as £80,000; vehicles and cranes were needed to move and assemble the sections; depots had to be provided for storing materials; wages had to be paid and materials bought; Hill, Richards charged the new company £42,000 for plant and machinery.[79] The retention money for the five contracts totalled £72,000.[80] Clearly, £34,000 in cash was totally inadequate to meet such commitments.

In an effort to improve liquidity, it was decided, in November 1920, that £70,000 of preference shares should be issued and that a further £60,000 should be raised in the form of credit notes. The parent company, Hill, Richards (whose own paid-up capital was only £5,000) agreed to underwrite £50,000 of the credit notes and £50,000 of the preference shares for a further cash payment of £15,000.[81] The large number of ordinary shares held by Hill, Richards and the directors was an embarrassment when asking for public subscriptions, so £153,000 ordinary shares were transferred from Hill, Richards and from Messrs. Coke and Metcalfe to a Trustee (Edward E. Robb, the company's solicitor), and these shares now carried neither voting rights nor dividends. Investors did not, however, rush to take up these issues. Less than £4,700 was subscribed by the public.[82] Some £37,501 were exchanged for existing debentures and so produced no new cash, and £13,789 were allotted to directors. According to the firm's books, the amount of cash raised was £42,000, but some of this was not paid up. Hill,

Richards, as underwriters, had to take £12,000, but never paid for
them and Hill, Richards allotted £9,329 preference shares to
another company, the Holborn Trust Ltd., registered in April
1920.[83] Nearly £7,000 due from this company was not paid up,
and the Official Liquidator subsequently ordered an investigation
into the circumstances under which this allotment was made.[84]
This time Hill, Richards failed to collect the underwriting commission of £15,000 in cash—instead, they received a further £10,000
in ordinary shares (which proved worthless), only £787 in cash and
the remainder was not paid at all.[85]

The subscriptions to both ordinary and preference shares
from the 'public' were limited to a very narrow social and geographical circle, mostly London-based.[86] The ordinary shares
must have been either sold or given away by the directors, who had
received the allocation of £50,000 from Hill, Richards, so it is not
surprising that their families were drawn into the circle: there were
six members of the Garsia family in addition to the director, Lieu-
tenant-Colonel Clive Garsia and there were three Cokes in addition
to the Hon. Edward Coke. Excluding the directors themselves,
there was a liberal sprinkling of Honourables (4), Ladies (3),
Brigadier-Generals (2), Lieutenant-Colonels (4), one Colonel, one
Commander and two Majors. Less than £1,000 of the ordinary
share capital and just over £6,000 of preference shares were held
outside London.

The Waller Corporation did not try to issue any further
capital. It raised an overdraft of £25,000 from its banker, the
London County and Westminster and Parrs Bank, under which
£8,645 had been drawn by the time the firm was liquidated.[87]
Cash was also raised on the security of the Borough of Poole mortgage bonds: £9,000 from the Bank of Liverpool, £18,000 from the
London County and Westminster Bank and £9,000 from the
Manchester and Liverpool District Banking Co. Ltd.[88] Losses on
contracts were, however, mounting and the company's debts were
escalating, too. In May 1921, five creditors, led by Mr. V. G.
Crittall of the Crittall Manufacturing Co. Ltd., forced the Waller
company into liquidation, against the wishes of the rest of the
creditors.[89] A receiver was appointed on 19 May, 1921, and a
compulsory winding-up order made on 3 August, 1921.[90] On 7 June,
1921, a meeting of Hill, Richards resolved that this company, too,
should go into liquidation, because it could not meet its liabilities.[91]

In his affidavit petitioning for the winding up of the Waller
Corporation, Mr. V. G. Crittall claimed that 'the business of the
Company has been carried on with disastrous results and the
Company is wholly insolvent. It also appears that the object for
which the Company was formed *viz.* to effect and carry out contracts with various Corporations for the construction of houses has
entirely failed inasmuch as all the said Contracts have been
repudiated or rescinded or terminated.'[92] A Cardiff accountant,
Sydney E. Clutterbuck, who was a member of the committee of

Trade Creditors and Credit Note-holders, was asked by the unsecured creditors to make an independent investigation into the
company's affairs and he reported that, in his judgment, 'the failure
of the company is wholly due to the fact that from the outset its
capital was inadequate'.[93] This verdict was largely substantiated
by the Official Receiver, who reported that in his opinion, too, 'the
capital at the disposal of the Company from its inception was
entirely inadequate to carry out the contracts entered into'.[94]

Certainly, the results were financially disastrous.[95] As at
25 October, 1921, there was a deficiency in the company's finances
of some £220,000, of which some major items were the cost of
formation of the company (nearly £19,000), depreciation of its
property (over £83,000), losses on contracts (£34,000), salaries
(nearly £20,000). An entry in the Olympia Ideal Home Exhibition
had cost nearly £1,000. The company had paid Hill, Richards
£42,000 for plant and machinery, but this was now written down as
worth only £1,673, and the £200,000 paid in shares for the Waller
system yielded no contribution at all to the company's assets in
liquidation because, under the terms of the agreement with Hill,
Richards, the latter could 'determine the licence' if the Waller
Corporation went into liquidation.

There were other minor factors which apparently contributed
to the company's failure as well as lack of capital: the Official
Receiver criticised the extravagant expenditure on the Head Office;
Hill, Richards' handling of the company and its affairs was subjected to considerable criticism. In fact, the Official Receiver declared that Philip E. Hill was guilty of 'misfeasance and breach
of trust in that he has misapplied and retained for his own use and
benefit out of the assets of the Company the sum of £6,726-0-5 in
respect of remuneration for his services as a Director to which he was
not entitled'.[96] These were, however, only additional factors aggra-
vating the basic cause of failure—inadequate capital for a building
system that was technically ahead of its competitors but too expensive
to be commercially viable at this time.

V

At the very time that the National Improved Housing Company
was issuing abortive threats of a national scandal if the government
did not provide financial assistance, the Economic Building Corporation Ltd. was negotiating with Liverpool City Council a
mammoth contract for two thousand houses. This contract blazed a
trail of glory for a short time, being heralded in the press and
technical journals as *the* great break-through in the mass-production
of working-class houses, before exploding into a public scandal of
national proportions—and, according to the Ministry of Health's
Inspector of Audits, it should have been abundantly clear to everyone from the outset that the company's financial resources were
totally inadequate for such large-scale operations.[97]

The Economic Building Corporation Ltd. was incorporated on 5 June, 1919.[98] It was promoted by T. Arthur Locan and David E. Landale. David Landale, proprietor of John Watson & Co., a London East India Merchant, seems to have been a passive, if not actually sleeping partner, primarily concerned with financing the company in its early stages. By October 1920, he had sold his shares and resigned his directorship.[99] T. Arthur Locan was a highly active partner who promoted several other companies too, including the National Standardised Joinery Co. (which supplied standardised doors and window frames for the Economic Building Corporation), the Monument Trading Company for importing Belgian glass and Jenbird Production Co., which was concerned with theatres, opera houses and cinemas and reputedly linked with the stage-career ambitions of Locan's mistress, Mildred Baker.[100]

Locan's experience of building stemmed from his father, a builder and plasterer of Lower Broughton, Salford.[101] Initially, he was trained as a decorator, but he and his father floated several small building-materials supply companies (which did not survive for long) in the Manchester and Liverpool areas before Locan moved south, during the First World War. He built small numbers of houses in London and Byfleet, before recognising the potential for mass-producing working-class houses at the end of the war. His search for financial support led him to approach David Landale through one of the latter's clients, and together they floated the Economic Building Corporation Ltd., in June 1919.

According to the Memorandum of Association, this company was to take over Locan's existing business, although the relevant agreement was not signed until May 1920.[102] The first directors were Locan, Landale and Malcolm McNeil McBride, a captain in the Highland Light Infantry, later described as 'engineer'.[103] The technical expertise at the company's disposal was decidedly limited, and there is no evidence of any previous experience of large-scale building operations. The supply of capital was equally limited. Of the nominal capital of £10,000, initially Landale held £2,500 shares and C. C. Bracebride ('gentleman') held £500. Locan paid £1 for one share, but he was later accredited with £5,000 shares in payment for his existing business.[104] So, for the expenditure of only £1, he retained control of his existing business operations and gained control of the new company (although he subsequently bought Landale's shares).

Locan and Landale developed a building system using concrete blocks which was approved by the Ministry of Health and patented.[105] Just before signing the contract with Liverpool, the Economic Building Corporation's bank turnover was at the rate of £33,000 a year and its capital was fully employed in some small operations involving the building of a handful of bungalows, cottages and garages at Ealing, Gerrard's Cross, Egham, Sunningdale, Burton, Kingswood and Sutton in Ashfield.[106] Its aspirations were out of all proportion to its achievements. On 5 March, 1920, it was claimed that the company was buying lands adjacent to large towns to develop middle-class housing estates, and that it had 'contracts for housing work on the Continent which will be available when rates of exchange are more favourable'.[107] There is no evidence that exchange rates ever became sufficiently favourable, although a printed brochure lists offices in Brighton, Birmingham and Blackburn and a 'Continental Office' in Antwerp.

In February 1920, *the Daily Mail's* Ideal Home Exhibition at Olympia, designed particularly to demonstrate non-traditional methods for building working-class houses, included a demonstration cottage by the Economic Building Corporation (as well as exhibits by the Waller Corporation and Unit Construction).[108] Liverpool Corporation had already signed several moderately large contracts but, because progress was severely inhibited by a chronic shortage of skilled labour and traditional materials,[109] a deputation of its Housing Committee visited the Exhibition on 7 February, and was so impressed by the Economic Building Corporation's exhibit, that negotiations started immediately. On 13 February, the company offered to build two thousand concrete houses.[110] On 1 March, the proposal was submitted to the Ministry of Health. On 11 March, the Ministry gave provisional approval,[111] and on 11 May, 1920, the contract, initially worth one and three quarter million pounds, was signed.

Sir E. D. Simon, Chairman of Manchester's Housing Committee, said later that one of the Ministry's 'high officials' agreed that twenty weeks was the minimum time necessary for approving a housing scheme.[112] The Ministry approved this, probably the largest housing contract to date, in just half that minimum time. It is perhaps not irrelevant to note that Liverpool and Manchester were both located in the Ministry's Region C. The first housing commissioner for Region C was Brigadier-General G. Kyffin Taylor, member of Liverpool City Council since 1904, Chairman of its Housing Committee from 1907 to 1919, and a member of the Dwellings Sub-Committee.[113] Liverpool may, therefore, have been advantageously placed in learning how to operate quickly under the system.

The negotiations and discussions are highly illuminating. The Economic Building Corporation wanted payment after the expenditure of £2,500 and for ninety-five per cent of the value of certified expenditure on both work and plant. The Ministry of Health's Inspector of Audits later called this an 'extraordinary demand;[114] although in fact the National Improved Housing Corporation was, at this very time, pointing out that contractors urgently needed a five per cent *advance* payment on signing the contract and the Office of Works *demanded* a five per cent advance.[115] The Ministry insisted that this contract[116] must conform to the standard specifications and terms. No payment at all could be claimed until £5,000 of expenditure was certified. Over and above this, the company was to be paid ninety per cent of the value of the work certified until the retention money of £10,000 had been built up. This may have been either a concession or good luck. Nowhere is there any discussion of the reason for setting the amount so low. In May 1920, the month in which the contract was signed, it was ruled that retention money must equal five per cent of expected cost,[117] which would have been of the order of £85,000. The contract may have escaped this ruling, as it was provisionally approved in the previous March.

Until the retention money had been built up, the company had to deposit with Liverpool Corporation securities valued at £10,000. The retention money was to be held until the contract was complete (which should have been in two years); then half the money would be repaid, and the other half would be repaid six months later, if the architect certified that all defects had been made good.

After the retention money was built up, payment was to be at the rate of ninety-five per cent until fifty per cent of the value of plant had been recouped—this contract providing an initial payment of fifty per cent for plant and equipment. In the event, on 27 May, 1921, certified valuers estimated that the value of the equipment on this site was £242,163 2s. 4d., but that Liverpool had only paid £69,000, so the company had £170,000 tied up in this way.[118] It had to erect working buildings—a block-making factory equipped with Winget machines, a wood-working shop and stores for materials, the canteen alone cost £16,000; living accommodation was provided for about four hundred workmen (approximately a quarter of the labour force) because of the difficulties involved in commuting daily to the site, which was farm-land on the city boundaries. The company also had to cover the cost of wages and materials. Salaries to its own staff on the site cost £8,000 a year plus bonuses and Locan, the managing director, was due to receive £5,000 a year plus one per cent of the turnover, which he claimed as royalty on the building patents.[119] On 30 November, 1920, an additional director was appointed: Richard Fletcher was a slater and tiler and proprietor of Richard Fletcher Ltd. of Blackburn; as we shall see later, he, too, received a handsome commission.[120] In addition, the company had to pay the expenses of its head office in London.

Clearly, the demands on its financial resources were considerable. Its existing small resources were already fully committed. The Ministry approved the contract with the vague proviso that Liverpool Council should take 'steps to satisfy themselves as to the ability of the Company to carry out the work'.[121] No indication is given by the Ministry of any reason for doubting the company's ability, there is no mention of capital and no specific proposals for investigating or correcting any weaknesses in the company. In fact, the Ministry ensured that it was much more difficult for the company to cope, by refusing to make the concessions in the contract terms that the company had requested.

In the light of this, some of the *retrospective* comments by the Inspector of Audits make fascinating reading, especially if taken in conjunction with the Ministry's simultaneous correspondence with the National Improved Housing Corporation. '*There was some doubt in the minds of the Ministry's officials*' [my italics] as to the company's viability. There was no doubt in the Inspector's mind: 'It was impossible for the Economic with its meagre capital to carry out the contract'. In fact, 'nothing but a very large increase in their capital could have enabled them to perform the contract'.[122] That was the verdict in 1923. In 1920, neither the Ministry nor Liverpool Corporation seriously inquired into the company's finances.

In February 1920, the company's Secretary said that an additional million pounds of capital was to be raised.[123] Neither Liverpool nor the Ministry checked if this had materialised. In June 1920, an unsuccessful attempt was, in fact, made to float yet another company to take over the Economic Building Corporation, and £450,000 of the million pounds of capital was underwritten, but the issue was withdrawn and not revived[124] and, in fact, on 4 September, 1920, the company's Secretary actually certified to the Registrar of Joint Stock Companies that 'no invitation has been issued to the public to subscribe for any shares or debentures'. He did this in order to claim 'private company' status.[125] This could easily have been discovered, by checking the company's file in the Board of Trade, but this was not done and this letter was not even mentioned in the public inquiry.

What, then, were the company's financial resources? An additional £2,000 of shares were allotted for cash; a bank overdraft of £10,000 was obtained on the directors' personal security; Landale definitely lent the firm £10,000, and claims that he lent a further £7,000, although this is open to some doubt. A friend of Landale lent the £10,000 of securities that had to be deposited until the retention money was built up.[126] At most, at the time the contract was signed, in May 1920, there was £29,000 cash and of this, Landale's £10,000 had been repaid as early as 17 September, 1920.[127] How, therefore, did the company cover its expenditure?

Lack of space prevents a detailed account of all the practices divulged at the public inquiry,[128] but the most important ones included departing from the terms of the contract, over-charging and charging for work not done and materials not delivered. From the beginning, Liverpool's housing director and the Chairman of the Housing Committee had agreed to assist the company by certifying payment on *outlay* on wages, materials and plant, although the contract specified payment on *work done* and *materials on the site*. The company took advantage of this to charge excessive prices for materials and plant. In addition, workmen later described how loads of materials were charged twice over, claims were made for materials never brought to the site, and materials on the site that had already been charged were subsequently removed for use on other contracts.

These practices were facilitated by the fact that Colonel Hodge, the Liverpool Corporation surveyor responsible for checking invoices before payment was certified, became a director of the

National Standardised Joinery Co., the subsidiary company that supplied doors and window frames for the contract. He quickly resigned from Liverpool's employment in January 1921, when Mr. F. E. G. Badger, Liverpool's Housing Director realised that the company had been over-paid. Liverpool Corporation and the Economic Building Corporation disputed the over-payment issue from January to August 1921; valuers and arbitrators were brought in, but the company even challenged the arbitrators' decision in court.[129] Eventually, in August 1921, it was established that the company had been overpaid £338,000, and the arbitrators certified 'lack of diligence' on the company's part. Work ground to a halt, and Liverpool took possession of the site.

The company had clearly made up for its lack of financial resources by devious practices, but a good deal of the money so obtained was also syphoned off for the directors' personal gain.[130] Locan, for example, personally acquired furniture, plate, jewellery and £5,000 of shares in other firms at the company's expense. He charged to the company £2,000 of his own hotel and entertaining bills, he over-drew his salary by £6,300 and paid a £400 rate bill for his brother and, in addition to paying his mistress £1,500 in cash, he passed £11,500 of the Economic Building Corporation's money through her bank account. He also entered into various arrangements, some kept secret from the other members of the firm, with Richard Fletcher.[131] In December 1919, the company agreed to reserve the whole of Fletcher's output of slates from March 1920. In April 1920, an agency agreement was signed whereby Fletcher received a commission of two and a half per cent of the contract price of all contracts signed by the Economic Building Corporation in Lancashire, Cheshire and Yorkshire—under this agreement, Fletcher received £16,234 2s. 6d. in January 1921, and he refunded half of this to Locan.

When the Economic Building Corporation was wound up, it had 'no tangible assets' apart from the lease of a wharf in London worth a few hundred pounds,[132] and £40,000 paid by Unit Construction for the Liverpool contract.[133] Under the terms of the original contract all the plant, materials etc. on the site became the property of Liverpool Corporation. The company's debts amounted to some £100,000; Locan became bankrupt; the National Standardised Joinery Company went into voluntary liquidation; Jenbird was first reorganised and then liquidated and Richard Fletcher Ltd. was also liquidated.[134]

Work had stopped on the site in the autumn of 1921, and at this time only the equivalent of 567 houses had been completed out of the 2,000. The contract was still a very valuable one. It was a fixed-price contract, for materials and prices had fallen dramatically, although the contractor had to accept decreases in price due to reductions in wage rates. As far as Liverpool Corporation was concerned, it was vital that the contract should not be allowed to lapse because, after July 1921, new contracts did not attract any subsidies under Addison's Act, even if they were to complete schemes started under the Act. Both the Economic Building Corporation's creditors and Liverpool Corporation therefore wanted to keep the contract alive, so that it could be taken over by another contractor. Negotiations with Richard Costain, William Moss and Parkinsons of Blackpool fell through,[135] but eventually, on 27 June, 1922, the supplemental contract was signed under which the Unit Construction Company Ltd. agreed to pay the Economic Building Corporation £40,000 and to complete the contract in two years at a cost of £678,000.

A week before the supplemental contract was signed, the Ministry of Health's Inspector of Audits opened a public inquiry into the whole affair. One might, with some justification, ask why government inspection of the accounts was delayed so long. The answer is that, although the government housing programme involved expenditure on a hitherto unprecedented scale, there was, in fact, no adequate machinery for supervising and checking contractors' accounts. Each local authority dealt with its own contractors. This in itself raised problems of lack of experience amongst local authority staff, and of lack of any standardised procedure. It was, however, not until towards the end of 1921 that serious discussions even started between the Treasury and the Ministry of Health about the possibility of government supervision of accounts presented to local authorities by contractors. The outcome of these discussions seems to have been that it was decided that the task of checking even all the *final* accounts was so daunting that inspection should be limited to a sample, in order to get an approximate idea of the validity of contractors' claims.[136] Apart from the fact that it was not comprehensive, this procedure could not stop contractors over-charging; it could only ensure that, in the cases examined, such practices would come to light after the event.

The Economic Building Corporation's claims for payment would not, therefore, have been subjected to any scrutiny at all by Ministry of Health officials, until the time when the contract was investigated in the public inquiry.[137] Reports of the inquiry's findings received extensive coverage in the local and national press, and shocked ratepayers and taxpayers all over the country. There were bitter quarrels on Merseyside, and equally bitter recriminations. The Minister of Health's Inspector of Audits blamed Locan; he also criticised both the incompetence and the actions of Liverpool's Housing Director and of the Housing Committee, especially its chairman. Strangely, he did not recommend surcharging anyone and, although the papers went to the Director of Public Prosecutions, Locan was not prosecuted, despite threats from Liverpool councillors and ratepayers that they would institute proceedings against him if no-one else did. In the event, the only prosecution was that of a clerk of works, George Washington Snooks, who was sentenced to three months imprisonment for embezzling £20 of materials and equipment.

As nobody was sufficiently guilty to be prosecuted or sur-
charged, the £338,000 over-payment had to be met either by
Liverpool ratepayers or by the Ministry. Liverpool said the Ministry
was responsible under Addison's Act, which limited local authority
commitment to the annual proceeds of a penny rate over the whole
of its building under the Act. The Ministry blamed Liverpool for
failing to investigate the company's financial viability, and for
departing from the contract terms in making payments. The battle
(including legal proceedings) continued until the end of 1934.
Then the Ministry capitulated, accepted responsibility under
Addison's Act and agreed to pay £345,000.[138]

VI

In its capacity as a creditor, the Crittall Manufacturing Co. Ltd.
successfully forced the Waller Housing Corporation Ltd. into
liquidation.[139] As company promoter, Crittalls were equally successful
in launching the only survivor of this quartet, Unit Construction Co.
Ltd., although Unit's long-term success was due to Alfred Booth
& Co. Ltd., not to Crittalls.

Crittalls had already been in business in Braintree since the
middle of the nineteenth century when, at the end of the century,
Mr. F. H. Crittall began to develop window manufacture. During
the First World War, their experience of shell production convinced
them of the economic advantages of standardisation, and they
proceeded to apply this experience to manufacturing building
components.[140] Towards the end of the war, at the government's
request, Crittalls and nineteen other firms formed the Steel Window
Association to produce standardised metal window frames, to
counter the desperate shortage and high cost of seasoned wood.[141]
Mr. F. H. Crittall, the firm's managing director, served on one of
the Ministry of Reconstruction's Committees, and was asked to
give evidence before the Tudor Walters Committee and, in July
1918, Crittalls offered to build two demonstration houses for Dr.
Addison in order to prove that satisfactory homes could be built by
'modern production' methods.

The houses were built of concrete blocks made on special
Winget machines, the floors and roofs were of reinforced concrete,
doors and windows were of steel. No timber or bricks were used.
The method adopted was the so-called 'Unit' system:[142] every part
of the building was designed in multiples of the 'unit', so that every
component could be standardised. Crittalls were convinced (cor-
rectly though prematurely) that British building would be converted
to the metric system, so their original unit was the metre, but they
reverted to the 'yard' in 1920. The two houses, finished in May 1919,
aroused great public interest, for it was claimed that they were the
first houses completed in Britain after the war. They became the
first instalment on an estate designed for a hundred houses for

Braintree Co-operative Homes Ltd., a public utility society created by Crittalls' employees.

Crittalls embarked on the building themselves but, on 6 February, 1919, the Unit Construction Co. Ltd. was incorporated, with a nominal capital of £100—it was to act as contractor for the workers' housing estate. The directors were F. H. Crittall and W. F. Crittall and the manager A. Dale Harris, an engineer.[143] By the summer of 1919, Crittalls' window manufacture was so successful that they needed to concentrate all their capital resources in this business, so they sold Unit to Alfred Booth & Co. Ltd., and agreed, on 6 September, 1920, not to engage in any more housebuilding for five years.[144] In the nineteenth century, Alfred Booths were merchants and shipowners who engaged extensively in trade in hides and skins between Liverpool, Brazil and the U.S.A.[145] When the firm was converted into a limited company, in 1914, it already controlled a group of companies—its special interests were in shipping, merchanting and leather, but it was diversifying into other businesses as well. In 1917, J. G. White & Co., an English branch of an American civil engineering and finance company, was brought into the group. In 1919, Booths had very large cash reserves and, having lost many ships during the war, were looking for suitable new investment outlets: one such outlet was Unit Construction Co. Ltd. J. D. Fleming, one of J. G. White's directors, became a director of Unit as well. A. Dale Harris, Unit's manager, was also made a director, together with G. M. Booth and two of Booth's close associates, W. V. Foulis and T. G. Randolph.[146]

Unit's original nominal capital was £100. Booths quickly increased it. By September 1919, it was £20,000 and, in April 1920, it was raised to £50,000. F. H. and W. F. Crittall retained seven hundred preference shares each, A. Booth & Co. Ltd. now owned £14,850 preference shares and £20,000 ordinary shares, and the rest were credited to members of the Booth organisation. Of the £50,000 nominal capital, £48,600 was paid up.[147]

To give additional support to their construction companies, The Rom River Sand and Gravel Co. Ltd. was incorporated on 25 August, 1920, with a nominal capital of £15,000 (all paid up), to manufacture and deal in builders' supplies, and it was especially important in supplying gravel to Unit and Whites; and the North Essex Portland Cement Co. was created to supply them with cement.[148]

Unit's main, though not exclusive, business was house-building. The 'Unit' system was formally approved by the Ministry for local authority building in November 1919 and, in February 1920, Unit entered an exhibit in the Ideal Home Exhibition.[149] Its first major local authority contract was for two hundred houses for Southport, then it acquired one for three hundred and fifty for Edinburgh, a hundred for Newport and contracts varying from twenty-five to seventy for Birmingham, Wellington, Welwyn Garden City, Risca and Rugby.[150] Before taking over the Liverpool contract, it had completed or was in process of building some one thousand houses; it had also built two factories and several sewerage schemes.[151] The Unit system, like other building systems, involved some outlay for machinery for mixing concrete, making blocks, transporting the blocks etc., and because of this, lower prices were quoted for contracts of a hundred houses or more,[152] although the firm did not now restrict itself to the use of concrete blocks. Some houses were built by pouring concrete between metal shutters, and others by the use of traditional materials and methods.

Unit's first experience of a very large contract came when it took over from the Economic Building Corporation. There were still nearly 1,500 houses to be built—half as many again as Unit's house-building total to date—and this called for considerable resources. Under the terms of the agreement, Unit had to pay £40,000 to the Economic Building Corporation.[153] The contract was for two years, and Unit was to receive £678,000 for its completion. The rate of payment was ninety per cent of the value of work done and eighty per cent of the value of materials until the £10,000 retention money was built up. Booths acted as guarantors.

The contract was satisfactorily completed by mid-1924, and at more than £100,000 below the original contract price in 1920. Liverpool was delighted by this outcome and Unit quickly won another contract for 1,000 houses, with the option of increasing it to 2,000.[154] This inaugurated a fruitful partnership between Liverpool Corporation and Unit, which resulted in the latter becoming the largest single contractor for Liverpool Corporation housing during the inter-war years, and Unit has continued to play a major role in Liverpool's building programme since the Second World War.

Of recent years, Unit has become the largest member of the Booth organisation, but its position in the early 1920s as the smallest member was probably a major factor assisting in its successful survival at a time when so many similar firms were foundering. The surviving documentary evidence is slight, but it gives some fascinating glimpses of Unit's position within the Booth organisation in the early 1920s.[155] Compared with traditional building methods, building systems and large contracts required large amounts of capital which, as we have seen, many firms could not raise. Compared with Alfred Booths' shipping and leather interests, Unit's demands for fixed capital were insignificant. Early in 1920, the value of the group's capital was £1,766,626 at balance sheet values, of which Unit's share was £1,100 and £2,272,300 at market values, of which Unit accounted for £1,000. The group's anticipated income for 1920 was £201,400, of which Unit was expected to contribute only £3,000.[156]

By the end of October 1920, Unit's plant was worth £15,000 of the group's total of £1,379,188, and it was estimated that after 30 April, 1921, the group would need a further £360,000 in cash, of which Unit's requirement would be a mere £7,500.[157] Unit's main need was for working capital and, by March 1920, Booths were planning to 'transfer our free cash to Unit Construction Company within a very short period probably £40,000'.[158] In fact, Booths regarded Unit as 'a business in which the fixed capital is probably going to be not more than one-eighth of the turnover, and therefore the rate of profit, in comparison with the fixed capital is liable to be high'.[159] Unit was also able to gain access to large overdraft facilities through Booths acting as guarantors, and Booths could do this with a fair degree of certainty that the overdrafts would not have to be repaid at short notice and so would not strain their own resources.[160] By the end of October 1920, Unit had an overdraft facility with Glyns for £75,000 and by the end of 1924 for £100,000.[161] In addition, by the end of 1922, Booths had loaned Unit £56,032[162] and, on 11 March, 1924, Booths advanced £150,000 covered by a debenture.[163] Clearly, financial facilities of this order of magnitude were a basic requirement for firms undertaking these large housing contracts.

## VII

Is it possible to draw general conclusions from the experiences of these four firms in the years immediately following the First World War? These were the formative years for the section of the building industry that was eventually to handle the large local authority housing schemes in the inter-war years and after. It was a period of experimentation in new building technology, in the organisation and operation of large contracting firms, and in the relationships that were to evolve between private enterprise and the central and local government agencies responsible for mass-producing working-class accommodation. It was unfortunate that the preliminary experiments had to take place in a particularly difficult environment with dire shortages of materials, skilled labour and financial capital. The very high failure rate bears witness to the inability of inexperienced, and even of some experienced, firms to overcome the problems.

We have seen that, in the case of the companies that failed, lack of adequate finance was the over-riding factor. Whatever other causes contributed to the liquidations, each of the three companies was doomed to failure from the start because its maximum financial resources could not possibly have met its minimum commitments. The only survivor, Unit Construction, had an adequate supply of fixed capital and generous overdraft facilities but, in this case too, it must be noted that, by 1924, even a substantial organisation such as Booths was feeling the strain of supporting two contractors. Early in 1924, it was decided that Unit and J. G. Whites must be reorganised to share some facilities, in order to reduce their financial requirements.[164] For some years they were to share one London office, to have one head accountant and to share a contract costs accountancy department and, in fact, it was said that without some measure of consolidation of the two concerns, Booths could not afford to meet their capital requirements.[165] Little wonder that the firms examined above failed to keep their heads above water with their pitifully inadequate financial backing.

The government, strangely, was totally unsympathetic and utterly intrinsigent in its refusal to make any concessions of any sort. Not only did it refuse any financial assistance, but it also refused to allow any concessions in the terms on which contracts were granted, as requested by the Economic Building Corporation; it would not countenance the idea of local authorities making advances to contractors as requested by the National Improved Housing Company, despite the Office of Works' insistence that it could not attempt to start any contract without an advance payment and, in fact, without regular payments in advance throughout the entire operation. Liverpool Corporation tried to help a contractor by relaxing its terms of payment, and was severely reprimanded for so doing. True, the privilege was abused in this case, but it was reprimanded as a matter of principle, not because of the outcome of this particular contract.

Until late in 1920, the Ministry did not even institute adequate procedures to check the financial viability of contractors before approving large contracts and, despite the statement after the event by the Ministry's own Inspector of Audits that it should have been abundantly clear to everyone from the outset that the Economic Building Corporation's financial resources were inadequate, the Ministry itself gave approval to the contract without seeing that the proviso about ensuring that the company could manage was carried out.

One might, perhaps, say that the £345,000 that the Ministry had to produce to cover the over-payment on this contract was the price of failing to heed the very sensible appraisal of the plight of such companies given by the National Improved Housing Company. In short, despite the government's public protestations of willingness to take all the steps necessary to ensure that the campaign for building 'Homes fit for Heroes' reached its target, the government was not prepared to adopt any measures at all to assist contractors to overcome what was, for many firms, the most intractable problem of all. Failure to raise sufficient cash meant insolvency for contractors and contributed materially to the serious shortfall in the supply of houses.

*University of Liverpool*

## NOTES

1. I have made extensive use of material in the Public Record Office, London, and I should like to express my sincere gratitude to the staff of the P.R.O. for their advice, assistance and patience. I am especially indebted to Mr. E. W. Denham, Mr M. Roper and Dr C. J. Kitching.

2. See especially, Marion Bowley, *Housing and the State 1919–1945* (1945). Also J. B. Cullingworth *Housing and Local Government*, (1966); G. D. H. Cole, *Building and Planning*, (1945); J. Parry Lewis, *Building Cycles and Britain's Growth*, (1965); H. W. Richardson and D. H. Aldcroft, *Building in the British Economy Between the Wars*, (1968); B. S. Townroe, *A Handbook of Housing*, (1924); ed. John A. Rosevear—A. Sayle, *The Houses of the Workers*, (1924); P. Wilding, 'The Administrative Aspects of the 1919 Housing Scheme,' *Public Administration*, 51 (1973).

3. *Report of the Committee appointed to Consider Questions of Building Construction in Connection with the Provision of Dwellings for the Working Classes*, Cd. 9191 (1918).

4. C. Addison, *Four and a Half Years*, II (1934) 525.

5. C. Addison *Politics from Within, 1911–1918*, II (1925) 216.

6. *Ibid.*, 219

7. *Four and a Half Years*, II, 586.

8. *Housing and Town Planning, etc. Act*, 9 and 10 Geo. V, cap. 35 (1919), supplemented by the *Housing (Additional Powers) Act*, 9 and 10 Geo. V, cap. 99 (1919).

9. Report of the Committee on the Building Programme of Government Departments, 25–6–20, P.R.O., CAB 27 86, Paper CP1531.

10. *Interim Report of the Treasury Committee on Housing Finance*, Cmd. 444, (1919). It should be noted that there were two committees concerned with housing finance that were under the chairmanship of W. H. N. Goschen, and one can find references to both as the 'Goschen Committee'. The other one was a standing committee set up in May 1920 and dissolved at the end of July 1921. Its most useful papers are referred to in note 21 below.

11. Minutes of the 1st Meeting of the Housing Committee, Ministry of Health, 16 December 1919, P.R.O., HLG 52/881 92053/8/313; *The Builder* 21 November, 1919, 519 and 2 February, 1920, 228; *Liverpool Housing Committee Minutes*, 24 March, 1920, Liverpool Record Office.

12. 'Loans, Rate of Interest, Housing Finance, Local Bonds Regulations.' P.R.O., HLG 52/209 91032/4/5A.

13. J. Ferguson to Dr. Addison, 27 January, 1920, *ibid.*

14. E. J. Strohmenger to F. Ogden Whiteley, 26 March, 1920, *ibid.* Also Minutes of the 9th, 11th and 12th Meetings of the Housing Committee, *loc. cit.* See also P. Wilding, *op. cit.*, 315–6.

15. Minutes of the 16th Meeting of the Housing Committee, *loc. cit.*

16. *The Builder*, 23 April, 1920, 481.

17. *Ibid.*, 28 May, 1920, 638.

18. Minutes of the 19th Meeting of the Housing Committee, *loc. cit.* In March 1922, it was reported that the whole campaign had only raised £20 million: E. J. Strohmenger to O. E. Niemeyer, 20 March, 1920, 'Loans, Rate of Interest etc.', *loc. cit.*

19. *The Builder*, 8 October, 1920, 408.

20. Minutes of the 19th Meeting of the Housing Committee, *loc. cit.* and Memo. by the Ministry of Health, 'Distribution of Building Progress', 19 June, 1920, Housing Committee Report, Proceedings and Memoranda, P.R.O., CAB 27/89, HC13.

21. The following account of the committee's work is based primarily on the Report of the Housing Finance Advisory Committee (Goschen Committee) to the Lords Commissioners of His Majesty's Treasury and the Minister of Health, 26 April, 1921, P.R.O., HLG 48/698 92038/1/230. See note 10 above.

22. *The Builder*, 7 January, 1921, 43; 14 January, 1921, 74; and 5 August, 1921, 168.

23. *Report of the Departmental Committee on the High Cost of Building Working-Class Dwellings*, Cmd. 1447 (1921) 19–23.

24. Some of the evidence collected for this committee has been retained amongst the Ministry of Health's files: Cost of Building Committee, Miscellaneous Papers, 1921, P.R.O., HLG 49/6 92022/7/2.

25. 'Erection of Houses by Direct Labour', Memorandum to Housing Commissioners, No. 34, 21 August, 1919, P.R.O., HLG 31/1.

26. E. J. Strohmenger to F. Phillips, 16 January, 1922. 'Examination of Final Housing Accounts (England)', P.R.O., T161 S14960 Box 162.

27. *The Builder*, 21 May, 1920.

28. For Sheffield's contracts see *The Builder*, 11 April, 1919 and 14 November, 1919. For Leeds', see *ibid.*, 16 January, 1920.

29. Prospectus, Henry Boot & Sons (London) Ltd., File of Returns to the Registrar of Joint Stock Companies, Companies House.

30. *The Builder*, 6 February and 16 July, 1920. By July, this scheme had been reduced to fifty houses.

31. 'Special Methods of Construction', 24 May, 1921, Cost of Building Committee, Miscellaneous Papers, 1921, *loc. cit.* Housing Commissioners were instructed to look favourably on new methods 'with a view to encouraging mass production': Minutes of a meeting of the Housing Commissioners at the Ministry of Health, 28 November, 1919, in 'Model Contract, Standard Terms of Tenders and Contracts' P.R.O., HLG 52/61 91007/2/3. Also Minutes of the Meeting of the Ministry of Health's Housing Committee, 2 March, 1920, *loc. cit.*
Lists of new methods approved by the Ministry were published in the Ministry's *Housing* from October 1919 to August 1921, and reports appear in technical journals such as *The Builder* and *Concrete and Constructional Engineering*. Those approved to April 1920 are included in *Standardisation and New Methods of Construction Committee. Report on the First Year's Work of the Committee*, April 1919 to April 1920.

32. F. W. Fryer to S. B. Russell, Chief Architect, Ministry of Health, P.R.O., HLG 52/893 92053/8/374.

33. R. B. White, *Prefabrication* (National Building Studies Special Report 36, Ministry of Technology Building Research Station, 1965) 54 and *Concrete and Constructional Engineering*, December 1919, 718.

34. *Concrete and Constructional Engineering*, December 1919, 717–8.

35. Prospectus, 10 February, 1915, Winget Ltd., File of Returns to the Registrar of Joint Stock Companies, P.R.O., BT 31 Box 18,399. The (U.K.) Winget Concrete Machine Co. Ltd. had been formed in 1908 by Mr. J. Faulder Burn, who, on a visit to the U.S.A., had been impressed by the potential of the Winget concrete block-making machine. He acquired patent rights from Mr J. M. McDowell. By 1920, the company (now called Winget Ltd.) was the largest U.K. producer of concrete block-making machinery. It also supplied a range of supplementary machinery and produced houses on the Winget system. I am grateful to Mr. R. V. Still of Winget Ltd. for information about the formation of the company.

36. The National Improved Housing Co. Ltd. acquired from the Concrete Construction Co. Ltd. an agreement with Winget Ltd. for preferential terms for block-making machines and concrete mixers, but there is no information to show whether this related to hire purchase, see below, p. 164.

37. P.R.O., HLG 49/6 92022/7/2.

38. 'Employment of the Office of Works to carry out Housing Schemes', Memorandum to the Housing Commissioners, No. 113, 26 October, 1920, P.R.O., HLG 31/2.

39. Minutes of the 7th Meeting of the Housing Council, 8 November, 1920, P.R.O., HLG 52/880 92053/8/312. At the 12th meeting of the Council, serious delays were reported in the receipt of advance payments for eight schemes. For examples of authorities that did pay, see P.R.O., Works 6, 135/3, 136/6, 136/8 and 136/11.

40. 'Special Methods of Construction', *loc. cit.*

41. *First Report of the Treasury Standing Committee on the Coordination of Depart-*

*mental Action in regard to Contracts* (Colwyn Committee), Cd. 9179 (1918). There are several files amongst Health and Local Government records containing relevant material, especially P.R.O., HLG 52/61 91007/2/3; HLG 52/62 91007/2/7A; HLG 52/63 91007/2/7B; HLG 52/64 91007/2/9. Further information is available in 'Contracts', Memorandum to the Housing Commissioners, No. 85, 26 February, 1920, P.R.O., HLG 31/1. H.M. Stationery Office published a *Model Form of Tender and Agreement*, August 1919, Form D88, and a revised version, May 1920, D88a.

42. *Report on the High Cost of Building Working-Class Dwellings*, 45.

43. *Model Form of Tender and Contract*, May 1920, D88a, p. 10.

44. W. Foulis to Sir James Carmichael, 17 February, 1920: Model Form of Contracts, P.R.O., HLG 52/64 91007/2/9.

45. See, for example, Marion Bowley, *Housing and the State 1919–1945*, (1945) 29–30.

46. The Concrete Construction Co. Ltd., File of Returns to the Registrar of Joint Stock Companies, P.R.O., BT 31 Box 24,101.

47. The National Improved Housing Co. Ltd., File of Returns to the Registrar of Joint Stock Companies, P.R.O., BT 31 Box 24,663.

48. Affidavit of T. G. Ackland, 17 May, 1920, P.R.O., J13, File 8428, No. 00165 of 1920.

49. Prospectus of the National Improved Housing Co. Ltd., 25 July, 1919, P.R.O., HLG 52/893 92053/8/374.

50. Return of Allotments, National Improved Housing Co. Ltd., 14 August, 1919, P.R.O., BT 31 Box 24,663.

51. Prospectus, 25 July, 1919, *loc. cit.*

52. The prospectus estimated expenses at £9,000, but it was subsequently claimed that the cost was £12,000: Sir Valentine R. Grace and F. King to the Rt. Hon. David Lloyd George, 16 February, 1920, P.R.O., HLG 52/893 92053/8/374.

53. Prospectus, *loc. cit.*

54. Correspondence between F. W. Fryer and Dr. Addison, G. Illsley and S. B. Russell, September 1919 to February 1920. P.R.O., HLG 52/893 92053/8/374.

55. E. Tudor Owen to F. W. Fryer, 21 February, 1920, *ibid.*

56. Sir Valentine R. Grace to Sir James Carmichael, 25 February, 1920, *ibid.*

57. P.R.O., HLG 52/893 92053/8/374.

58. *Ibid.*

59. *Ibid.* The Office of Works demanded a 5 per cent advance and *The Report of the Committee on the High Cost of Building Working-Class Dwellings* (p. 22) also emphasised that contractors experienced special difficulties 'during the early stages of the contract, when expenses and overcharges are heavy in proportion to actual output of houses'.

60. P.R.O., HLG 52/893 92053/8/374.

61. File of Returns to the Registrar of Joint Stock Companies, *loc. cit.*

62. *Ibid.* See, also, P.R.O., J13 File 8611 No. 00121 of 1920; J14 Files 828 and 837; BT 34 Box 4,366. For the Concrete Construction Co. Ltd. see P.R.O., BT 31 Box 24,101 and J13 File 8,428 No. 00165 of 1920.

63. A. F. Jefferies to Captain Sharp, Housing Dept., Ministry of Health, 15 May, 1920, P.R.O., HLG 52/893 92053/8/374. Also *The Builder*, 16 April, 1920 and the *Evening Standard*, 11 May, 1920.

64. *Concrete and Constructional Engineering*, December 1920, 849.

65. J. Wightman Douglas to C. J. Maslin, 21 January, 1921, P.R.O., HLG 52/893 92053/8/374.

66. J. Wightman Douglas to the Housing Commissioner of Region A, 30 October, 1920, *ibid.*

67. Official Receiver's Report, 4 April, 1922, 2, P.R.O., J13 File 9327 No. 00295 of 1921.

68. *Ibid.*

69. *Ibid.*

70. *Concrete and Constructional Engineering*, December 1919, 718. The system is described in *The Builder*, 20 February, 1920, and in R. B. White, *Prefabrication* (1965) 53–4.

71. Sir Ernest Moir, 'Statement to be made at the Meeting of the Housing Committee Today' 21 November, 1924, in 'Housing, New Methods of Construction, Concrete Systems 1924' and 'Moir Committee on New Methods of House Construction 1924–5', P.R.O. HLG 52/771 92020/10/6. Also, Minutes of the 19th Meeting of the Housing Committee, 8 June, 1920, P.R.O., HLG 52/881 92053/8/313.

72. F. E. G. Badger, Director of Housing, *City of Liverpool, Housing, State-aided Schemes, Schedule of Particulars as to Cost of Erection of Houses*, 14 December, 1923. Sir Ernest Moir commented on the high cost of the system, *loc. cit.*

73. Official Receiver's Report, *loc. cit.*

74. Hill, Richards & Co. Ltd., File of Returns to the Registrar of Joint Stock Companies, P.R.O., BT31 Box 23,184.

75. *Ibid.* Also Waller Housing Corporation, Official Receiver's Report, *loc. cit.* and P.R.O., J13 File 8983 No. 00351 of 1921.

76. Official Receiver's Report, *loc. cit.*

77. *Ibid.*

78. *Ibid.*

79. *Ibid.* For the cost of the Liverpool depot, see *Minutes of Liverpool Housing Committee*, 2 January, 1920, Liverpool Record Office.

80. Official Receiver's Report, *loc. cit.*

81. *Ibid.*

82. Lists of Shareholders and Debentures, P.R.O., J13, File 9327 No. 00295 of 1921.

83. *Ibid.*

84. Official Receiver's Report, *loc. cit.*

85. *Ibid.*

86. Lists of Shareholders and Debentures, *loc. cit.*

87. Statement of Affairs by J. J. Sneddon, 24 October, 1921, P.R.O., J13 File 9327 No. 00295 of 1921. Also P.R.O., J14 File 948.

88. *Ibid.*

89. Affidavit by V. G. Crittall, Petition for Winding-Up, 6 May, 1921, P.R.O., J13 File 9326 No. 00295 of 1921.

90. Official Receiver's Report, *loc. cit.*

91. Hill, Richards & Co. Ltd., File of Returns to the Registrar of Joint Stock Companies, *loc. cit.*; also Liquidator's Accounts, P.R.O., BT34 Box 4,151.

92. Affidavit, *loc. cit.* Certainly, the contract with Liverpool had been abruptly terminated on receipt of a letter from the Waller Corporation. No reason for Waller's decision is minuted. *Minutes of Liverpool Housing Committee*, 14 March, 1921, Liverpool Record Office.

93. Affidavit, *loc. cit.*

94. Official Receiver's Report, *loc. cit.*

95. *Ibid.* Also Statement of Affairs by J. J. Sneddon, *loc. cit.*

96. Official Receiver's Report, *loc. cit.*

97. *Interim Report of Mr. J. Orchard, Inspector of Audits, Ministry of Health on the Local Inquiry at Liverpool in reference to the Garston Housing Contract*, 31 March, 1923, 9 (hereafter cited *Interim Report*), Liverpool Record Office, Gladstone Bequest (hereafter L.R.O., GB) VIII. I should like to thank Miss Janet Smith and the staff of the Liverpool Record Office for their assistance in finding material.

98. Economic Building Corporation Ltd., File of Returns to the Registrar of Joint Stock Companies, P.R.O., BT31 Box 24,691.

99. *Ibid.* Also *Second Report of Mr. J. Orchard, Inspector of Audits, Ministry of Health on the Local Inquiry at Liverpool in reference to the Garston Housing Contract*, 2 February, 1924, 5 (hereafter cited *Second Report*), L.R.O., GB, VIII.

100. 'T. Arthur Locan, Managing Director of the Economic', L.R.O., GB, IX.

101. *Ibid.*

102. File of Returns to the Registrar of Joint Stock Companies, *loc. cit.*

103. *Ibid.*
104. *Ibid.*
105. The patent specifications were 153,102 of 1920 and 172,800 of 1921.
106. *Second Report*, 6.
107. *The Builder*, 5 March, 1920, 292.
108. Cost of Building Committee, Misc. Papers, P.R.O., HLG 49/6 92022/7/2. Also *The Builder*, 13 February, 1920, 198–9.
109. See above p. 189 for Liverpool's contracts. The Department of Building Materials Supply admitted that it had failed to carry out promised deliveries of bricks to Liverpool: Minutes of the 11th Meeting of the Housing Committee, P.R.O., HLG 52/881 92053/8/313.
110. *Interim Report*, 8. Also *Liverpool Housing Committee Minutes*, 13 February, 1920, Liverpool Record Office.
111. E. R. Forber, Assistant Secretary, Ministry of Health to Liverpool's Town Clerk, 11 March, 1920. Copy in L.R.O., GB, V.
112. E. D. Simon, *A City Council from Within* (1926) 35.
113. 'Appointment of Housing Commissioners', *The Builder*, 4 April, 1919, 330. For such a large contract, it seems unlikely that the Commissioner would have sole responsibility for making the final decision. For contracts of 500 houses or more, the Ministry took an active part in deciding whether or not to give approval: 'Contracts', Memorandum to the Housing Commissioners, No. 85, 26 February, 1920, P.R.O., HLG 31/1. Commissioners were, however, instructed to pay regular visits to inspect work in progress to ensure efficiency because the Ministry had 'a strong financial interest' although technical responsibility for efficiency lay with the local authority. 'Inspection of Work in Progress', *ibid.*, No. 56, 10 November, 1919, *loc. cit.*
114. *Interim Report*, 8.
115. See above, p. 161.
116. E. R. Forber to Liverpool's Town Clerk, 11 March, 1920, *loc. cit.* 'Articles of Agreement between the Lord Mayor, Aldermen and Citizens of the City of Liverpool and the Economic Building Corporation Ltd.', 11 May, 1920, LRO, GB, XA.
117. *Model Form of Tender and Contract*, May 1920, D88a, 10.
118. 'Report of Speeches delivered at a Meeting of the City Council held on Wednesday, 6 February, 1924 in reference to the Garston Housing Contract', L.R.O., GB, VIII.
119. *Second Report*, 17. Also report of T. Arthur Locan's public examination by the Official Receiver during his own bankruptcy proceedings, *Liverpool Echo*, 13 November, 1924.
120. Richard Fletcher Ltd., File of Returns to the Registrar of Joint Stock Companies, P.R.O., BT 31 Box 24,113. Also *Second Report*, 41–3.
121. E. R. Forber to Liverpool's Town Clerk, 11 March, 1920, *loc. cit.*
122. *Interim Report*, 8.
123. *Ibid.* An entry in 'Trade News', *The Builder*, 5 March, 1920, reported that the company was going to raise 'at least' a further million pounds.
124. *Second Report*, 7.
125. Economic Building Corporation Ltd., File of Returns to the Registrar of Joint Stock Companies, *loc. cit.*
126. The friend was Mr. Creighton of Messrs. Sinclair & Co., provision merchants of Liverpool, L.R.O., GB, IX, 41.
127. *Second Report*, 7.
128. *Interim Report*, 12–18 and *Second Report*, 8–13.
129. Economic Building Corporation Ltd. *v.* Lord Mayor, Aldermen and Citizens of the City of Liverpool and John Leaning & Sons, 25 August, 1921, P.R.O., J15/3584/2720.
130. *Second Report*, 14–20 and 41–3.
131. *Ibid.*, 21–30 and 41–3.
132. Order in the High Court of Justice, Chancery Division, Sanctioning the Scheme of Arrangement, 20 June, 1922, P.R.O., J13 File 9534, No. 00273 of 1922.
133. An Agreement between the Lord Mayor, Aldermen and Citizens

of the City of Liverpool, the Economic Building Corporation Ltd., the Unit Construction Co. Ltd. and Alfred Booth & Co. Ltd., 27 June, 1922, L.R.O., GB, XA, 64.

134. Scheme of Arrangement, *loc. cit.* Richard Fletcher Ltd., File of Returns to the Registrar of Joint Stock Companies, *loc. cit.*

135. Scheme of Arrangement, *loc. cit.*

136. Some of the correspondence has survived between the Treasury and the Ministry of Health about the feasibility of checking accounts in 'Examination of Final Housing Accounts (England)', P.R.O., T161 S14960 Box 162.

137. The inquiry by the Ministry of Health's Inspector of Audits opened on 19 June, 1922 and continued until 14 July. The *Interim Report* was published on 31 March, 1923. The inquiry was re-opened on 24 April, 1923, and the *Second Report* was published on 2 February, 1924.

138. The prolonged negotiations were reported intermittently in newspapers and in the proceedings of the City Council. The Town Clerk was authorised in 1932 to take legal action against the Minister of Health: *City of Liverpool Proceedings of the Council*, 6 July, 1932. The final settlement was recorded in the *Proceedings*, 2 January, 1935. I am indebted to Mr. D. Chalmers of the P.R.O. for trying to find the Ministry's records of these negotiations. Unfortunately, no records at all of this contract have survived amongst Ministry of Health papers.

139. See above, p. 170.

140. Crittall Manufacturing Company Ltd., *An Example of Unit-building carried out by the Crittall Manufacturing Company at Braintree, Essex* (1919) 7.

141. Steel Window Association, *A Detail of Reconstruction*, (1919). I am indebted to Mr. A. F. Garland of Crittall Windows Ltd. for information about Crittalls and about the Steel Window Association.

142. Crittall Manufacturing Co. Ltd., *op. cit.*

143. Unit Construction Co. Ltd., File of returns to the Registrar of Joint Stock Companies, Companies House.

144. *Ibid.*

145. For a history of the Booth organisation see A. H. John, *A Liverpool Merchant House. Being the History of Alfred Booth and Company 1863–1958* (1959).

146. Unit Construction Co. Ltd., File of Returns, Companies House.

147. *Ibid.*

148. L.R.O., GB, XII, 27–37.

149. 'Housing Exhibition at Olympia', *The Builder*, 13 February, 1920, 198–9.

150. L.R.O., GB, *loc. cit.*

151. *Ibid.*

152. 'A Concrete Housing Scheme at Braintree', *Concrete and Constructional Engineering*, November 1919, XIV, 658–61.

153. An Agreement between the Lord Mayor, Aldermen and Citizens of the City of Liverpool, the Economic Building Corporation Ltd., The Unit Construction Co. Ltd., and Alfred Booth & Co. Ltd., 27 June, 1922, L.R.O., GB, XA, 64.

154. *City of Liverpool, Proceedings of the Council 1923–4*, 30 July, 1924, 404 and *ibid.* 1924–5, 4 December, 1924, 177.

155. I am deeply indebted to Mr. R. H. Amis, Chairman of Alfred Booth & Co. Ltd., for allowing me to read through the Booth Partners Letter Books and to Mr. J. W. Booth, former Chairman of Alfred Booth & Co. Ltd., for reading through the section on Unit, for advice in interpreting the surviving evidence and for remedying deficiencies in the documentary evidence from his personal knowledge of Unit's history. I am also grateful to Mr. C. P. Morley, Deputy Chairman of Unit Construction Co. Ltd., and to Miss D. Kershaw of Alfred Booth & Co. Ltd. for their assistance in my researches into Unit's early history.

156. G. M. Booth to E. E. Fletcher, 23 February, 1920, Booth Partners Letter Books (hereafter cited B.P.L.B.).

157. 'Liverpool Cash Requirements 31 October 1920 to 31 October 1921' and 'Supplementing Statement of Liverpool Cash Requirements 11 November 1920', B.P.L.B., England to America, 1920.

158. W. Harold Tregonning to E. E. Fletcher, 25 March, 1920, B.P.L.B., England to America, 1920.

159. *Ibid.*

160. 'Liverpool Cash Requirements 31 October 1920 to 31 October 1921' *loc. cit.*

161. *Ibid.*, and W. Harold Tregonning to W. C. Burton, 31 December, 1925, B.P.L.B., England to America, 1924.

162. A. A. Booth to G. M. Booth, 8 December, 1922, B.P.L.B., England to America, 1922.

163. Statement of Mortgage, 26 March, 1924, Unit Construction Co. Ltd., File of Returns to the Registrar of Joint Stock Companies, Companies House.

164. G. M. Booth to D. H. Crompton, 29 February, 1924, B.P.L.B., England to America, 1924.

165. *Ibid.*

# BUSINESSMEN, INDUSTRIES AND TARIFF REFORM IN GREAT BRITAIN, 1903–1930

## By A.J. MARRISON

There is a long-established tradition amongst historians that business-men's support for free trade or protectionist policies can be analysed according to determinist considerations. We are used to dividing indus-tries into two camps, a 'free trade interest' and a 'protectionist interest', and to making the assumption that, historically, they have acted accord-ing to a 'given' interest, an interest at once real, obvious and unambi-guous. 'Cosmopolitan' business groups, such as bankers, financiers, mer-chants, and manufacturers with a high degree of export orientation, traditionally supported free trade whilst 'nationalist' groups, mostly manufacturers without large export markets and perhaps with home markets vulnerable to foreign competition, were more open to protec-tionist influences. As Michael S. Smith observes of France after 1860:

> ...one could say that the conflict on the tariff was part of a struggle between two mutually exclusive capitalist communities seeking to project French economic development in opposite directions ... between cosmopolitan commercial capitalists, striving to integrate France into the world economy, and nationalistic industrial capital-ists, striving to make France economically self-sufficient.[1]

Such explanations are widespread and familiar, and other examples need not be documented here. But their application to the British Tariff Reform campaign of 1903-13 and its aftermath needs to be handled with care. If we follow Schumpeter, we can agree that pre-war Britain saw less close an alliance between 'high finance and the cartel magnates' than did other advanced countries;[2] certainly the merger movement was relatively slow and limited, and does not appear to have involved finance capital on the American or German scale.[3] Hence the confusing tendency for finance capital to espouse protectionist causes because of its links with manufacturing industry, acting 'in the actual interest of only a *small* proportion [of capitalists] and, indeed, ... sometimes not even in the interests of capital as such at all', becomes less important in the British case, and the 'typical and fundamental' conflict between capitalists and entrepreneurs is maintained.[4] But even if this is historically true, there is still the difficulty of which industries are to be labelled free trade and which protectionist. Here Schumpeter's 'typical and fundamental' con-flict does not help, for it implies that all manufacturing industries should be protectionist by interest and instinct.[5] Mid-nineteenth-century history often supports this. Taussig's classic study of the antebellum US tariff finds no industrial support for the powerful free trade lobby of merchants and raw cotton exporters, even non-cotton farmers being protectionist, whilst List's *National System* was a broadly based appeal to a whole nation.[6] Even in the hegemonic Britain of the 1830s and 1840s, less prey to infant industry sentiment, we must be careful of the textbook view of manufacturers joining the political economists in the vanguard of the free trade movement. Ship-owning and agriculture may have been entrenched defenders of protection, but it does not appear that their stance was as isolated as is often assumed. McGregor and the Select Committee on the Export of Machinery had to admit that, in certain other industries also, opinion was predominantly hostile to a change in system. Generally, the Committee gave a 'misleading impression of the extent of the support which they actually enjoyed'. Apathy, sometimes hostility, was the order of the day. 'In formulating a general criticism of the tariff it would seem that the Board of Trade was leading a new movement of opinion, rather than expressing one which was already there.'[7]

This is not to suggest that, in the conditions of the early 1900s, we should expect a general predisposition towards protection among British manufacturers. The mere occurrence of free trade gave the question a historical dimension. But two of the most widely-read writers on fiscal alignment have gone to the other extreme. Bernard Semmel, in his influential *Imperialism and Social Reform*, has postulated what virtually amounts to a 'conspiracy' thesis. Evidently sympathetic to Churchill's fear that if the Tariff Reformers were successful the Conservatives would become 'a party of great vested interests',[8] Semmel analyses the economic interests of the Tariff Commission, an unofficial commission of businessmen established by Chamberlain early in 1904 to construct a 'scientific' tariff.[9] He particularly mentions four representatives of the iron and steel industry upon the Commission,[10] and then goes on to list a heterogeneous group of representatives of meat-packing, armaments, glass manufacturing, electrical engineering, building and contracting, and chemicals.[11] These ten, selected from the list of 59 Commission members, lead Semmel to conclude that: 'Iron and steel, tin, building materials, glass and chemicals, all midlands products hard hit by German and American competition. These interests constituted the heart of the Commission and of the [Tariff Reform] League itself.'[12]

In some senses, Richard Rempel is even more bold than Semmel. Concentrating on the opposition to Tariff Reform rather than the support for it, he slightly confuses the issue by discussing the views of the work-force as well. Nevertheless, his overall message is clear enough:

> The major reason for the failure of Chamberlain's campaign was that, apart from iron and steel, the major industries in the country still prospered under free trade ... Even in the iron industry itself there was no solidarity behind Chamberlain ... Indeed, the only groups completely supporting Chamberlain were the clearly declin-

ing industries, such as silk [and linen], badly hit by competition at home and badly desiring simple protection.[13]

Cotton remained 'particularly strong in its commitment to free trade', whilst coal 'remained unshaken in its attachment'. The interests of shipping and shipbuilding 'remained largely bound up with free trade', as did those of their 'kindred' industry, engineering. Rempel thus musters a formidable Free Trade support. It is therefore curious that, citing Semmel approvingly, he should conclude that 'The Tariff Reformers had most of the heavy industry interests'.[14]

Thus, we can compile a composite view of the 'interests' in the Tariff Reform controversy. On the Free Trade side Rempel includes cotton, coal, shipping and shipbuilding, and engineering. Semmel would apparently add woollen manufacture to this list.[15] On the protectionist side we have iron and steel, tin, building materials, glass and chemicals, as well as meat-packing, armaments and electrical engineering. We are told that these industries not only supported Tariff Reform, but also that they lay at the *centre* of it.[16]

Our concern here is not with the working man's vote. There was a Liberal 'landslide' in 1906, though it should never be forgotten that some 43 per cent of the electors voted Unionist.[17] Rather, we seek to examine the validity of claims that, in the British Tariff Reform controversy, industrial interest and business opinion can be classified with such broad and bold strokes. Can industries always be marshalled into huge, cohesive *blocs*? Already, in the above, armaments and electrical engineering have been separated from the rest of the engineering trades and placed in the protectionist camp. It would seem that industries need to be examined for internal divisions along product or market lines.[18] Secondly, even within the more narrowly defined industry-group, how far should we expect unanimity of opinion? When examining smaller groups such as the Unionist Free Traders or the members of the House of Commons, Rempel freely acknowledges many exceptions. Is deviation from economic determinism merely the prerogative of the politically *active*? In any case economic determinism cannot simply imply that men act out of their own self-interest: rather, it must mean that they act according to their own *perceptions* of what their particular economic interest *is*. Often, no doubt, the two coincide clearly. But the Tariff Reform debate was not simply a controversy over short-term economic interests and objectives: occurring in the context of Britain's industrial retardation, it involved fundamentally different perceptions and interpretations of the desirable and the likely path of Britain's long-term development over the next 50 or even 100 years.[19] Under such conditions even partners in the same firm might have had different conceptions and made different predictions. And thirdly, closely related to this point but analytically separable from it, the existence of an imperial element in Chamberlain's scheme, with its surrounding political motives and objectives, may have tended both to confuse and to modify a simple determinist stance. There are infinite variations, from complete incongruity to perfect complementarity, in which profit and patriotism can be combined. It was in such a context that even fiscally orthodox Sir Robert Giffen was prompted to observe, in a weighty letter to *The Times*, that the partly political and partly economic objectives of imperial preference might render 'something we may not quite approve ... expedient'.[20]

Any discussion of economic interest in the Tariff Reform campaign needs to distinguish between two issues: the role of economic interest in explaining the allegiance of individuals and parties actively participating in it, and the stance of particular industries on the fiscal question generally. We shall start by discussing industrial representation on the Tariff Commission in the light of Semmel's analysis of it.

I

A systematic examination of the business representation on the Tariff Commission illustrates certain difficulties that stand in the way of precise categorisation, notably those of sources of income and overlapping interests. Certainly businessmen were heavily represented.[21] If we classify the members into four groups – agricultural, industrial and commercial, imperial, and miscellaneous – we find the second to be by far the largest, comprising 47 out of the 59 original members. It is necessary to point out that some members overlapped even these large categories. Thus, to the two representatives of the agricultural interest, W.H. Grenfell[22] and Henry Chaplin,[23] might be added John Dennis, who in addition to interests in the wholesale provisions trade farmed 4,000 acres in partnership. More importantly, six of the eight 'imperial' members had (discovered) interests in industry or commerce, whilst several 'industrial-commercial' members had some kind of interest in colonial enterprise.

Ideally, an analysis of economic interest needs to take account of source(s) of income and proportion of income from each source. Since we are denied access to Inland Revenue information, our data are far from perfect and often impressionistic.[24] Obviously this is unimportant for 'single-interest' Commissioners: those who derived their income from only one source. But only 13 of the 47 industrial-commercial members seem to fit this category clearly.[25] Even within this group, we are obliged to assume, probably fairly safely in most cases, that income from their primary interest was not overshadowed by investment or property income from accumulated family wealth.[26]

The remaining 34 industrial-commercial members are less clear-cut cases in that they possessed dual or multiple interests (sometimes within the same firm or group of associated firms), but with 13 of them it seems fairly clear that those interests can be readily divided into major and minor components.[27] Such interests as railway directorships (W. Goulding and R.H. Reade) and involvement in shipping lines (T. Gallaher and C. Lyle) can be regarded as subsidiary. Sometimes minor interests were internal to the firm, as with both Gallaher and Lyle,[28] whilst at others they were external, for it was common for businessmen to become involved in local and even national transport concerns by accepting directorships which imparted prestige to both sides of the compact. Two iron and steel representatives, Allen and Keen, held bank directorships, but they were essentially local and it is likely that they saw them as complementary to, and not in conflict with, their other industrial interests. Thus, though railways, shipping and banking might appear on the cosmopolitan, free trade side of the fiscal balance, such directorships would have been unlikely to constitute a significant economic interest for industrialists of the stature of most Commission members.[29] Furthermore, it seems clear that in many other cases additional interests were even more directly subordinate to the main one, as with Maconochie's tinning and tinplate concern, Joseph Rank's involvement in oil milling,[30] Charles Eckersley's very marginal and Henry Marshall's somewhat stronger connection with coal-mining, and Howard Colls' minor interest in interior-decorating inherited from the Trollope side of the merger of 1903.[31] Alfred Jones' multifarious activities in West Africa and the Caribbean were virtually all through wholly or partly-owned subsidiaries of Elder, Dempster.[32]

The remaining 21 industrial-commercial Commissioners were interested in two or more distinctly different branches of activity. Even where such distinctions existed within the same firm, we cannot be sure of the proportion of direct personal income which arose from each branch. In some cases it seems fairly safe to divide such interests into primary and secondary interests. Frederick Baynes' partnership in a cotton merchant business may have developed merely as a device for placing the products of his own mills with export merchants. Sir Samuel Boulton's timber-importing business was presumably subsidiary to his chemicals business, which was largely tar-distilling. Though GKN's engineering activities were growing in 1904 they were still minor compared with iron and steel,[33] Arthur Keen's main interest. Sir William Lewis's many interests in local South Wales railways, docks, water and electric utilities, insurance, iron and steel and tinplate all seem to have been consequent on the development of his coal-mining interests, first as agent for the Bute estates and then as an independent colliery proprietor.[34] Directorships held by Sir Andrew Noble in oil, nickel, copper and silver companies were minor compared with the chairmanship of Armstrong-Whitworth, which employed 22,400 in 1904. Alfred Gilbey's interest in the production of wines and spirits had developed considerably since the 1880s, but our impression is that dealing in wines and spirits was still the main element in his firm's profits.[35]

But in other cases, even where different activities were carried on within the same firm, we can be less sure of the accuracy of such assessments. Though the late Professor John's study of Alfred Booth & Co. shows clearly the decline of leather merchant business, it gives no very clear indication of the relative importance of steam shipping and (US) leather manufacturing for Charles Booth's personal income, though the general impression created is that the two were relatively equal in importance.[36] The very extent and variety of the trading, mining and manufacturing interests of merchants and bankers Antony Gibbs & Sons in Latin America and Australia is sufficient to make an assessment of the precise origins of the components of Vicary Gibbs' income bewildering, except to say that they were channelled through one of the great mercantile houses of the nineteenth century.[37]

Those with dual or multiple interests in unconnected firms cause no less problems. Henry Birchenough's family silk firm suffered badly in the late nineteenth century,[38] but even at its peak it would have been a small concern compared with the Imperial Continental Gas Association (capitalised at nearly £6m in 1900), of which he was also a director.[39] Leverton Harris's links with the family firm of shipowners, Harris & Dixon Ltd., seem to have been fairly slight by 1904, on an administrative level at least, but it seems to have been this rather than his other interests in Indian coal-mining, the London discount market and electricity supply that was the basis of his 'considerable fortune'.[40] Sir Alexander Henderson, in addition to being the head of an important stockbroking firm, had not surprisingly acquired significant investments in railway and canal companies.[41] Even Sir Charles Tennant, head of the huge St Rollox complex and president of United Alkali, may not be as straightforward as he appears. An adept speculator and company promoter, he had large interests in railways, oil companies and insurance as well as in hugely profitable gold, sulphur and copper extraction companies (though many of his mining ventures were tied to his chemicals business, they did not exist to supply St Rollox alone). Given the recent findings of Rubinstein, which suggest that great wealth more readily accrued from trade and finance than from manufacturing in the nineteenth century, it may be wondered just how central was the ailing St Rollox to Tennant's personal fortune.[42] In a similar vein, Sir Vincent Caillard's long involvement in international finance and financial diplomacy should make us wary of identifying his personal economic interests too closely with those of Vickers, Sons and Maxim. It is likely that the period 1903–5 was one of transition in Caillard's economic interests as he rose to prominence within the firm, and no arbitrary division (such as that made in Table 1 below) can adequately reflect his position.[43]

This catalogue of imprecision is not offered by way of apology. Rather, it demonstrates the difficulty of making accurate assessments of direct personal economic interest. Very often, 20 years' experience in a given trade must have 'conditioned' belief,[44] but in 1904 there must have been many retired or semi-retired rentiers whose direct present economic interest contrasted strongly with their experience of a working lifetime. But inherited and accumulated wealth *versus* industrial income is not the only problem. Table 1 highlights the more marked examples of Tariff Commissioners with dual or multiple interests. The *expected* affiliation of the trade (according to the determinist considerations discussed above) is given in brackets. Clearly, this table shows a considerable presence of expected Free Trade interests (a feature, it should be emphasised, not

TABLE 1

TARIFF COMMISSION MEMBERS WITH SIGNIFICANT DUAL INTERESTS (1904-5)

| | Primary | Secondary |
|---|---|---|
| F Baynes | cotton manufacturing (FT) | cotton shipping (FT) railways (FT) |
| J H Birchenough | silk manufacturing (P) | fgn. gas utilities (FT) misc. colonial (IP) |
| C Booth | steam shipping (FT) | fgn. leather prodn. (FT) leather merchant (FT) |
| Sir S B Boulton | chemicals (P?) | timber importing (FT) |
| R Burbidge | retail trading (FT) | colonial trading (IP) |
| Sir V Caillard | international finance (or) (FT) arms, engineering and shipbuilding (FT) | public utilities (FT) motor cars (P) explosives (?) |
| J J Candlish | glass bottles (P) | newspapers (FT) |
| J Dennis | wholesale produce (FT) | farming (P) |
| G Flett | electrical engineering and traction (P) | coachbuilding (?) rolling stock (FT) motor cars (P) electricity supply (FT) |
| Hon. V Gibbs | merchanting and banking (FT) | insurance and finance (FT with some IP) nitrates and other minerals extraction (FT) fgn. land development (FT) misc. fgn. manufacturing (FT) |
| W A Gilbey | wines and spirits merchant (qual. FT) | wines and spirits producer (qualified FT) |
| F L Harris | shipowning (FT) | electric utilities (FT) finance (FT) impl. coalmining (IP) |
| Sir A Henderson | stockbroking (FT) | railways (FT) canals (FT) foreign investment (FT) |
| A Keen | iron and steel (FT) | engineering (subsid) (FT) fgn. iron ore (subsid) (FT) banking (FT) |

TABLE 1 (continued)

| | Primary | Secondary |
|---|---|---|
| Sir W T Lewis | coalmining (FT) | iron, steel, tinplate (P) railways, docks, public utilities, insurance (FT) |
| R Littlejohn | impl. banking (IP?) | distribution & storage (IP?) tramways & property (IP?) mineral extraction (IP?) |
| Sir A Noble | arms, engineering and shipbuilding (FT) | oil, nickel, silver, copper extraction (FT) water utilities (FT) |
| Hon. C A Parsons | electricity generating equipment (P) marine engineering (FT) | electric utilities (FT) optical lenses (P?) |
| Sir C Tennant | chemicals (P?) | oil, gold, sulpher & copper extraction (FT) railways, insurance, banking, company promotion (FT) explosives (?) iron and steel (P) |
| Sir J Turney | leather production (P) | light engineering (FT) |
| S J Waring | furniture making (P) | furniture retailing (FT) interior decorating (FT) |

Notes:   (i)   FT = Free Trade, P = Protectionist, IP = Imperial Preference. It should be mentioned that IP is a difficult category: the mere fact that a business-man had, say banking or merchant or mineral extraction interests in the Empire does not necessarily give him determinist interests in a policy of imperial preference.

(ii)   The categories FT, P and IP are not meant to signify that the trade concerned, or even the individual Commission member, necessarily exhibited those sympathies. Rather, they are categories which a narrow determinist approach might lead us to expect.

(iii)   W A Gilbey. The position of the liquor trade was complex. Though, on the surface, it would have had an interest in maintaining cheap grain imports, the heavy liquor duty already in existence made possible the prospect of a compensating reduction of this in any overall fiscal package.

absent from the 'single interest' members discussed earlier). It also shows some members, for instance, Birchenough, Boulton, Burbidge, Dennis, Keen, Lewis, Parsons and Waring, whose business activities were a mixture of expected Free Trade and Tariff Reform interests.

The present writer is aware that Rubinstein suggests that 'the vast majority of Britain's wealth-holders earned their fortunes overwhelmingly in one trade or line of business, and held other interests only as a clear sideline to their main field', and that, 'For the majority, the family firm was enough'.[45] Indeed, we have attempted above (pp.151-6) to sort out those dual interests of obviously minor importance. However, the examples Rubinstein tabulates are for millionaires and half-millionaires, a complete sample for his purposes but one which numbers only 101 for millionaires in 1900–19 and 78 for half-millionaires in 1900–06. Furthermore, the proportion of those holding multiple directorships is pushed down by the high proportion who held *none*. If we remove this group from Rubinstein's figures, we find 71.4 per cent of millionaires *with* directorships who died in 1900–19 held two or more, and an identical proportion of half-millionaires with directorships who died in 1900–06.[46] Furthermore, some may have shed directorships before their deaths, and partnerships are not included. Rubinstein's purpose is to separate the family firm interest from outside interests. Mine, in addition, is to point out that, from the point of view of fiscal stance, there may be dual and even contradictory interests within the same firm.

Nevertheless, we must be wary of not exaggerating the importance of secondary interests. Table 2 summarises our information on the *primary* economic interests of the 47 industrial-commercial Commissioners.[47] Representation was quite heavily weighted towards manufacturing industry, though those representing primary production, food processing (including tobacco) and the tertiary sector did comprise 22 out of the 47. The biggest industry *blocs* were engineering and food processing (seven Commissioners each) and textiles (six Commissioners).[48] Chemicals and distribution could count four members each, and iron and steel and shipping three each.[49]

Semmel's analysis of the Commission, mentioned above, is easily dispensed with. Table 3 shows the number of Commissioners who represented the 'heart'[50] of the Commission. These 13 separate industry representations were held by 11 individual members. Since no one had primary interests in tin,[51] and since any (small) interest Colls had in building materials was in producing them for his building firm's own use, there is strong ground for reducing the number of Commissioners representing these trades to ten or even nine. It is to be conceded that the heart is a relatively small part of the body, but if it is Semmel's supposition that this group exercised a functional importance within the Commission greater than its size would indicate, there is no basis for this. Arthur Keen was if anything a disruptive force whilst Sir William Lewis and Sir Charles Tennant were infrequent attenders.[52]

Indeed, the wide range of industry representation suggests that a thesis

TABLE 2

Tariff Commission: Industrial-Commercial Members

| Primary* | Food Processing | Secondary (*Textiles*) | Tertiary (*Distribution*) |
|---|---|---|---|
| Sir W.T. Lewis | T. Gallaher | F. Baynes | R. Burbidge |
| | J.M. Harris | J.H. Birchenough | W. Cooper |
| | C. Lyle | J.A. Corah | J.W. Dennis |
| | A.W. Maconochie | C. Eckersley | A. Gilbey |
| | C.J. Phillips | W.H. Mitchell | A. Mosely |
| | J. Rank | R.H. Reade | W.B. Webb |
| | F. Tonsely | | |
| | | (*Iron & Steel*) | (*Shipping*) |
| | | C. Allen | C. Booth |
| | | Sir A. Hickman | F.L. Harris |
| | | A. Keen | Sir A.L. Jones |
| | | (*Engineering*) | (*Other*) |
| | | Sir V. Caillard | J.H. Colls |
| | | F. Elgar | V. Gibbs |
| | | G. Flett | Sir A. Henderson |
| | | W. Harrison | R. Littlejohn |
| | | H. Marshall | C.A. Pearson |
| | | Sir A. Noble | |
| | | C.A. Parsons | |
| | | (*Chemicals*) | |
| | | S.B. Boulton | |
| | | Sir W.J. Goulding | |
| | | I. Levinstein | |
| | | Sir C. Tennant | |
| | | (*Other*) | |
| | | H. Bostock | |
| | | J.J. Candlish | |
| | | L. Evans | |
| | | Sir J. Turney | |
| | | S.J. Waring | |

* Does not include Agriculture.

postulating a conspiracy originating in a narrow group of distinct trades unique in experiencing the blast of foreign competition is incorrect. Foreign competition was felt more widely than this,[53] and it was felt unevenly, not only between different branches of the same industry, but also between different firms within the same branch. In fact, the objective pursued in selecting members of the Tariff Commission was to secure as wide a range of industry representation as possible, consistent at least with securing men willing to assist in the drafting of a 'scientific' tariff and with keeping the Commission down to a manageable size.[54]

That examination of industrial-commercial representation on the Tariff Commission offers little support to the variant of economic deter-

TABLE 3

Representation of Iron and Steel, Coal, Tin, Building Materials, Glass and Chemicals on
the Tariff Commission (1904–5)

| | Primary Interest | Secondary Interest | |
|---|---|---|---|
| Iron and Steel ⎫ Coal ⎭ | 4 | - | { *Allen,*[1] *Hickman, Keen* *Lewis* |
| Tin or Tinplate | - | 2 | Lewis, Maconochie |
| Building Materials | 1 | 1 | *Colls,*[2] Boulton[3] |
| Glass | 1 | - | *Candlish* |
| Chemicals[4] | 4 | - | { *Tennant, Levinstein* *Goulding, Boulton* |

Notes:
1. Those members holding primary interests are underlined.
2. Colls, though included as holding a pirmary interest in building materials, would, as a builder and ocntractor, have had a buyer's rather than a seller's interest in such products.
3. Boulton has been included, in building materials, as a timber importer. It is unknown, however, how much of the timber he imported was used in building.
4. Chemicals interests are here defined to exclude explosives.

minism invoked by Semmel to explain it does not necessarily negate the importance of economic motivation. Of course it is possible that some Commission members held strong 'political' views which led them to advance a cause against their own economic interest. Most exhibited a considerable personal loyalty to Chamberlain and several can be identi-fied with the Germanophobia of Maxse and the *National Review* or the militarist imperialism of the territorial movement.[55] But most did not support Tariff Reform out of altruism: they expected that their industries would gain from a policy of economic nationalism. Because many of them came from industries which have traditionally been classified as 'Free Trade' interests, this does not mean they were economically irrational. This, for two reasons. Firstly, their prediction of the likely effects of a Tariff Reform policy may have *differed* from that of others within their trade (and the impossibility of the counterfactual proposition means that the historian cannot know which prediction was correct). And secondly, the traditional location of 'Free Trade' interests rests heavily on the presumption that an industry's experience of export-orientation or im-port competition was not only homogeneous but also relevant, a pre-sumption which is buttressed by a *belief* (seldom proven) that the great majority of businessmen in that industry were of one mind. To put the issue baldly, since we can never know whether Tariff Reform was right or wrong, we cannot question the rationality of a minority view in an industry without also similarly questioning the majority view, especially when we have *assumed* rather than *proven* that the minority was a minority and the majority was a majority.

## II

The Tariff Commission example also exposes weaknesses in a wider use of the conventional model of industry alignment in the fiscal controversy. Many of those interests labelled 'Free Trade' (FT) in Table 1 may only remain so at a very superficial level. Furthermore, under the Semmel-Rempel scheme at least 30 of the 47 industrial-commercial Commissioners would have come from 'Free Trade' industries (coal, food processing,[56] textiles, engineering, distribution and shipping).[57] Since the Commission was a specially picked body of businessmen prepared to help in the construction of a tariff scheme, it is perfectly possible that this was so. But it is unlikely that all these industries were in fact so heavily inclined towards Free Trade as has been implied, and important areas of distinction need to be made within them.

Engineering was far from a uniform or a unified industry. In 1906, when trying to collate the information received in answer to the Commission's questionnaires, its secretary, W. A. S. Hewins,[58] found it 'an entirely disgusting business. I thought cotton was sufficiently complicated, Wool made Cotton seem quite simple, but Engineering seems to me more complicated than all the others put together'.[59] He found some 500 groups of engineering products in which foreign imports were complained of, so that engineering 'is not one industry, but is really a large group of industries'.[60] Much earlier he had noticed differences in the difficulty of persuading businessmen from the different sectors of the industry to join the Commission. Whilst there was no shortage of electrical or agricultural engineers, he knew that the textile machinery makers had such a large export trade that 'I gather they are not likely to make any move at present for representation on the Commission'.[61] Thus, at the very least, it seems necessary to apply a product market analysis to the main sectors of engineering. Intuitively we might expect those branches in which British firms still retained some of their mid-nineteenth-century glory – textile machinery,[62] shipbuilding,[63] marine engineering, etc. – to incline towards Free Trade, whilst expecting those branches under threat from the 'American System' or German applied science – light machine tools,[64] some branches of agricultural machinery,[65] electrical engineering,[66] and perhaps motor cars[67] – to exhibit a protectionist posture. Of course, some British firms were remarkably successful even in the teeth of strong American competition,[68] but this would not preclude protectionist sentiment, sometimes along *quasi*-'infant industry' lines.

Chemicals presents further difficulties for the Semmel-Rempel case. Haber has noted that in the late nineteenth century English industrial chemists 'were often Free Traders and Liberals'.[69] The dominant alkali section of the industry, though its export growth was decelerating through foreign competition and tariffs, was heavily dependent on exports. Furthermore, Brunner, Mond, the self-styled and rather pompous mouthpiece of the progressive Solvay branch of the alkali trades, was largely dominated by Free Traders and Liberals.[70] Protectionist Ivan

Levinstein admitted that cheap raw materials and high transport costs kept the home market relatively immune from foreign competition.[71] Even the ponderous and technically backward United Alkali Co.. of which Tariff Commissioner Sir Charles Tennant was president, would not co-operate with the Commission.[72]

In dyestuffs, however, we might expect a different stance. Here British failure was more obvious, with output 20-30 times less than that of Germany, and with 90 per cent of home consumption imported. Furthermore, in this branch the industry 'spokesman' was a protectionist. Ivan Levinstein was a long-time campaigner against foreign tariffs and abuses of the patent system.

It is true that the three largest British dyestuffs manufacturers did agree to give evidence before the Tariff Commission, though only two did so.[73] Further than this, however, it is difficult to sustain the thesis of a split between Free Trade alkali producers and protectionist dyestuffs manufacturers. The Tariff Commission's investigation into chemicals did not begin until June 1905, when trade recovery was already well under way, but even so it found the search for willing witnesses a terrible struggle. As a last resort, Levinstein supplied the Commission with a complete list of members of the Society of Chemical Industry, marking 500 or so who he thought might give information, but he stressed that 'I cannot warrant however that all, or how many are favourable to a tariff reform'.[74] Even though the Commission apparently acted on his advice to invite them all,[75] it appears that only four chemicals witnesses were examined, and two of these were Tariff Commission members.

It may be, as Haber has suggested, that even the dyestuffs firms had nothing to gain from protection,[76] but it is nevertheless hard to understand how so few open supporters of fiscal change could be found amongst the Society of Chemical Industry's 2,400 members, especially given widespread dissatisfaction over the related area of patents legislation and the bleak positions of both the Leblanc and dyestuffs interests. It is hard to imagine these interests so firmly united behind Free Trade, but the Tariff Commission's experience certainly suggests an alignment of the industry very different from that postulated by Semmel.

The woollen industry seems an equally problematic case. Bradford has a good claim to be regarded as the 'cradle' of the Fair Trade movement of the 1880s, and included amongst its leading citizens several influential manufacturers who paved the way for Chamberlain's later campaign.[77] In pre-war Leeds, Huddersfield and Dewsbury manufacturers were also questioning economic liberalism.[78] Whilst admitting variations in the different sections of the industry, Jenkins and Ponting conclude that on the whole it was 'more adversely affected by tariffs than almost any other British industry'.[79] B.H. Brown, working impressionistically, counts woollens and worsteds as less enthusiastic for Fair Trade only than iron and steel, hardware, cutlery, implements and tools.[80] By 1904 protectionist feeling in Bradford at least had grown stronger. A rare glimpse of the voting behaviour of the Bradford Chamber of Commerce in that year gives a clear indication of fiscal division in an important worsted centre. Piece merchants, spinner manufacturers, manufacturers, and wool merchants and top makers were predominantly in favour of Tariff Reform (84 to 55) whilst spinners, yarn merchants, piece and yarn merchants, dyers and combers were predominantly hostile (52 to 17). As Sigsworth notes, the division reflected the difference in experience of the piece-goods and yarns sections except for the unexpected allegiance of the dyers for Free Trade (9 to 3) and the wool merchants and top makers for Tariff Reform (18 to 10).[81] Certainly, the Bradford chamber had 'departed a long way' from its Free Trade posture of the early 1880s.[82] The evidence we have at present,therefore, suggests a divided industry, but one in which, rather surprisingly, producers and merchants in a given line were more united than might have been expected.

We might also question the protectionist stance of the armaments industry in the Semmel-Rempel scheme. Certainly the iron and steel industry was heavily in favour of Tariff Reform,[83] and the bigger, integrated armaments concerns had interests in this field. But they were by their nature more closely related to Free Trade shipbuilding and to engineering, which was at the least *less* committed than iron and steel. Furthermore, in a market situation where arms producers sought a special relationship with the British government and where a large export business depended on delicate negotiations with foreign governments,[84] Tariff Reform may simply have been irrelevant. This was certainly the view of Douglas Vickers when invited to give evidence before the Tariff Commission.[85] Even Commissioner Sir Andrew Noble, of Armstrong Whitworth, admitted being in a 'special position', having 'neither the competition nor the same difficulties... that other manufacturers have'.[86] Francis Elgar of Fairfields echoed his view: 'The battleship industry is really a protected industry as far as the British admiralty is concerned'.[87] Producers of smaller weapons systems or certain components may have been more vulnerable to foreign competition abroad or even at home, but there was little emphasis on these trades in the Commission's report on engineering.[88] Of course, considerations of small-group sociology *may* have meant that most of the industry's leaders, with strong determinist reasons for being Unionist in politics, supported Tariff Reform, but their interest in a tariff *in itself* was probably small and even negative.[89]

Similar considerations apply to the later period, c.1909–18, when many of the leaders of the industry are known to have advocated Tariff Reform.[90] Even if it is shown that a substantial majority in this concentrated industry supported the movement during the War, it is hard to explain this on the determinist basis of self-interest in a tariff *per se*, given the industry's insulated and favoured market position. More important would be the appendicular elements of Tariff Reform (for example, patents legislation, tied loans and proposals for a Ministry of Commerce), and the broader political implications that underlay the movement (business-government relations, state assistance, post-war economic relations

with Germany, etc.). It is feasible that the leaders of a highly concentrated industry might well have a more homogeneous view of the future,
based on commonly perceived 'political' and 'extra-tariff' determinist
considerations, than businessmen in less concentrated industries.
Whether the armaments manufacturers were united in support of Tariff
Reform or not, their case offers little support for a narrow view of
market-led tariff determinism.

### III

A determinist scheme based on Schumpeterian principles possesses considerable strength. There is no doubt that the financial sector retained its
loyalty to Free Trade with the exception of some firms closely associated
with colonial finance. The Tariff Commission met with a wall of silence
when it tried to extend its enquiries into banking,[91] in spite of the strong
conservative sympathies of many in the City. There is no evidence,
either, of substantial merchant support for Tariff Reform.[92] Levinstein,
who resigned the presidency of the Manchester Chamber of Commerce
to join the Tariff Commission, even blamed the cotton merchants alone
for Manchester's hostility to the cause. It was 'the game of many of our
merchants to set the foreign producer against the British in order to
squeeze down prices', he commented. 'They don't care whether the working classes are employed.'[93] Whether or not a merchant-manufacturer
conflict in the cotton trade is historically tenable, it is clear at least that the
merchants were Free Traders.[94]

We can also agree with much of the Semmel-Rempel composite. Iron
and steel, coal, shipbuilding, and probably electrical engineering seem to
require no modification. Furthermore, criticisms of Semmel and Rempel
do not necessarily imply criticisms of the underlying principles on which
their analyses are based. The chemical industry, for instance, could
simply be moved into the Free Trade camp on the basis of acceptable
economic considerations.

But further difficulties arise when trades were obviously heavily divided. Of course, no trade was 100 per cent solid. Even in banking, Sir
Ernest Cassel made heavy contributions to the TRL and Tariff
Commission.[95] Where division was more marked, we are still left with the
question of whether it simply reflected the different market experience of
different products and branches, or whether there were more random and
personal divisions reflecting differences in politics and perceptions.

Detailed study of chambers of commerce and trade associations offers
little hope of clarifying even the simple issue of business alignment, let
alone the more complex one of its motivation.[96] But the very difficulties
involved carry with them a lesson. Such organisations frequently left poor
records of their members' views precisely because fiscal reform was so
contentious, and the organisations' leaders were reluctant even to find
out themselves what the balance of opinion was. Often, perhaps, the
somewhat 'closed' nature of trade associations was more due to fear of

publicising differences among members than to the reluctance of attracting wider public attention to businessmen's supposed 'hawkishness'. On labour relations, employer consensus may have been relatively easy,[97] but those associations dealing with trade matters were on less certain ground.

Thus it was that the Tariff Commission, which warmly encouraged trade associations to give evidence before it, met with little success. Unlike local chambers of agriculture, only a handful of trade associations responded to its invitations. James Hamilton, secretary of the Scottish Iron Manufacturers' Association, spoke for the majority: 'I had the matter brought before a meeting of this Association and it was agreed not to ask any member to give evidence before the Commission, but to leave individual firms to act on their own account, as they thought best.'[98] But even in the rare case of the secretary of a trade assocation being delegated to give evidence, his position was still not necessarily straightforward. As J. S. Jeans of the British Iron Trade Association explained, he was 'not instructed (sic) to put forward any views or to express any leanings ... on the fiscal question'. Even when he had, in 1903, been authorised to elicit views on the tariff question, only just over 70 out of 225 member firms had replied, though of these 95 per cent had favoured 'some reform of the existing situation ... although hardly any suggestions were made as to ... the precise character of that reform'.[99]

Thus, with BITA as with SIMA, a certain shyness obscures the historical record. In certainty, only 67 or so of 225 BITA firms acknowledged dissatisfaction with the existing fiscal system: whether through apathy, hostility to Tariff Reform or reluctance to make their views known, some 70 per cent did not reply. Things were little different in the Association of British Chambers of Commerce. In 1908 a joint resolution on Tariff Reform and Imperial Preference 'found only forty supporters. There were thirty against ... and thirty-one who were described as neutral'.[100] Individual chambers were scarcely more decisive. In spite of the growth in strength of those advocating retaliation in the Leeds Chamber in the 1890s, it was agreed on several occasions not to put resolutions so as to avoid a split. Eventually, a special general meeting passed a Chamberlainite resolution by 76 to 65, with over 150 abstentions. In 1910 a similar resolution attracted 164 votes, with 71 against, 91 abstentions and no reply from 66.[101]

The cautious approach of many leaders and secretaries of such bodies is understandable. Tariff Reform was, in all its complexity, a 'political' as much as an 'economic' question. Political alignments in the previous generation had been largely decided on very different issues: in any real sense, the politics of Home Rule were remote from factory floor and counting house. Many businessmen found it uncomfortable that their own position had become a primary issue of party conflict. Though many were, defensively and half-ashamedly, to claim the mantle of 'true free trader', others kept their own counsel, inhibited by the fact that the very word 'protection' invoked contempt.[102] Furthermore, in the early period of Tariff Reform, with the Unionists divided and with Chamberlain's proposals unformulated and uncertain, there was relatively little concrete policy upon which to decide.[103] As Arthur Pearson of the *Daily Express* commented when trying to select businessmen to serve on the Tariff Commission, 'Really the difficulty of getting accurate information on how people think is appalling'.[104]

There is also a temporal aspect to business opinion, a dimension which has no close relation with the traditional analysis of 'cosmopolitan' versus 'nationalist' economic interest. P.F. Clarke has presented a strong case for arguing that even the cotton industry was heavily divided, and that after 1906, as the Liberals departed from laissez-faire in their welfare reforms, the cotton bosses were forced to re-order their priorities, so that by the 1910 elections they were even less united behind Free Trade than they had been in 1903.[105] Such a change cannot be related to tariff-orientated determinism in view of the rapid growth of exports between 1900 and 1913.[106] Rather, defence of Free Trade was not worth its price in terms of continued support of the Liberal Party. Similar examples can be found amongst Tariff Reform businessmen. There were those who, after the election defeats of 1906 and 1910, thought that the wider aspects of Tariff Reform, especially food taxes, were preventing realisation of their more immediate objective of industrial protection,[107] whilst, on the wider issue, it cannot be too readily assumed that there was negligible business support for the fight against food taxes within the Unionist Party because they delayed the return of a Unionist government needed to counter Irish Home Rule and the Liberal attack on the House of Lords.[108] We are unable to investigate the dynamics of changes in business opinion during these years here, but clearly the period 1906–14 was one in which prosperous trade probably lessened the tariff-based determinist support for Tariff Reform in most industries, whilst at the same time being a period in which businessmen's fears of socialism and liberal collectivism led to a wider reassessment of political priorities on grounds which, though not being 'non-economic', were much less immediately related to the specific issue of tariffs. At least until the immediate pre-war period, therefore (when a growth of nationalist and anti-German feeling may have influenced the picture), we have an almost paradoxical pattern where the determinist support for a tariff was probably lessening but the determinist support for the Unionists was probably increasing amongst busnessmen in general. In the present state of research it is impossible to assess the net quantitative effect of these movements, except to point to a poor proxy, the difficulty experienced by the Tariff Commission in raising financial contributions from industry during these years.[109]

Whatever the trend of business opinion in the period 1906–14, there can be little doubt that the War itself both encouraged protectionists sympathies amongst businessmen and allowed them to crystallise. Tariff Reformers took great comfort from the introduction of the McKenna Duties, much more, in retrospect, than they should have done. The increased acceptability of state intervention had as its counterpoise a

revitalisation of existing businessmen's organisations and the formation
of new ones: the 'business interest' in British politics was coming of
age.[110] Also, the War and wartime jingoism gave respectability to 'beg-
gar-my-neighbour' policies, in the form of planned post-war retaliation
against Germany. At last trade sanctions could be equated unequivocally
with patriotism: this was the legacy of the Paris Economic Conference of
1916.[111] The appointment of the Balfour of Burleigh Committee seemed
to give institutional approval to at least *discussion* of the fiscal issue,
especially when resolutions it had passed favourable to imperial preference were leaked to the press.[112] It is perhaps significant that the business
members of the Committee became more united on 'key' duties and an
anti-dumping tariff as it proceeded,[113] though they remained divided on
the basic issue of a post-war general tariff.[114] Where the Committee did
cast a dim light on wider business opinion, there was evidence of considerable interventionist feeling. Of the 12 known replies to a circular sent to
chambers of commerce on 1 August 1916, several suggested subsidies or
government-sponsored financial facilities, whilst the London Chamber
went so far as to provide a 'tentative *ad valorem* tariff' for use 'pending the
elaboration of a scientific Tariff of specific duties'. The Wolverhampton
and Nottingham Chambers urged 'key' industry status for motor cars,
dyestuffs and chemicals, enamelling and holloware, rubber and leather.
Much of this related specifically to the wartime rather than the post-war
situation, but only the Plymouth Chamber set its face clearly against
post-war prohibitions and tariffs. Even the Manchester Chamber urged
the government to consider a diluted form of reciprocal preference after
the War, though only 932 members supported this, 234 being opposed
and 1,311 abstaining.[115] If the War influenced pre-war economic liberals
like Alfred Mond and F. Smith,[116] it certainly provided ideal conditions
for latent protectionists to come out into the open.

  This being said, however, the uncertain political currents of the Lloyd
George coalition and its aftermath still left businessmen in an awkward
position. After the War, there were more trade associations prepared to
come out openly for protection than before it, but divisions between and
within trades again acted to conceal the overall direction in which business opinion was headed. Just as, before the War, division between and
within branches produced a level of abstention which has allowed later
historians to exaggerate the support which Free Trade probably enjoyed,
so the attempt to *hide* division in the 1920s has, paradoxically, created the
impression that the main British employers' association, the Federation
of British Industries, was deeply divided over tariff policy.[117] But it is
overwhelmingly likely that the division was unequal, and that a substantial majority of members supported protection in the 1920s. This notwithstanding, however, the public face of the FBI kept a strict neutrality until
the crisis conditions of 1930.[118]

IV

The Tariff Reform objectives of FBI founder Dudley Docker were thwarted by the absorption of the Employers' Parliamentary Association, based largely on the Manchester cotton trade, into the Federation. In the early years Docker, helped by Tariff Commissioner Sir Vincent Caillard,[119] attempted to push the FBI towards alliances with protection-ist associations, a policy endorsed by many members since it was felt that government endorsement of the principle of imperial preference in the Finance Act of 1919 removed the issue from the sphere of party politics. Negotiations with the British Empire Producers' Organisation, which encompassed 31 trade associations[120] and many British agricultural asso-ciations, depended on the FBI's willingness to commit itself to imperial preference. In spite of the confusing element of preference and its im-plication of food taxes, the issue did in the main encapsulate the free trade-protectionist split in the FBI. There is a hollow ring to the statement made at a meeting of the Manchester district branch, where one of the speakers 'said that he would have taken the same line if the Federation had been going to amalgamate with a Free Trade Union, and the whole meeting applauded this'.[121]

Caillard was not alone in thinking that 'a very big majority' of FBI members favoured amalgamation with BEPO, but when FBI Director Roland Nugent put the issue squarely before the industrial groups, the Textile Group refused to answer and the Chemicals group equivo-cated.[122] In spite of this, Nugent at first thought it best to amalgamate:

> ... whilst there very likely may be a campaign run against us in the North on the ground that we have gone 'protectionist' ..., and while the Association which is at present being run by Sir Robert Priestley in Bradford (and which has long being trying to get our Wool Trade Members) may no doubt profit by this campaign, a campaign in the other sense run by Mr Terrell's National Union of Manufacturers on the ground that by turning down the amalgama-tion we had definitely gone Free Trade would probably do us more harm still.[123]

Even the Manchester branch was not entirely united, with Peter Rylands of the Warrington wire-making concern, Sir Herbert Dixon of the Fine Cotton Spinners' and Doublers' Association and a Mr Davies of the Bleachers' Association in favour of amalgamation. But, with the weighty support of the Federation of Master Cotton Spinners' Associations and the Cotton Spinners' and Manufacturers' Association, the district passed a resolution against amalgamation by 31 votes to four, with about 12 abstentions. Rylands admitted that amalgamation might result in the loss of virtually the whole of the Manchester membership. Armitage, the Bradford district secretary, discerned a similar threat from his members.

Intelligence from other districts was less clear. The *leaders* of the Leeds district were solid against amalgamation, and Liverpool members were probably mostly opposed as well. From Nottingham, London, Swansea, Newcastle and the Scottish districts came reports of indifference. Only Birmingham and Sheffield, according to the intelligence on which the FBI central staff acted, seemed very keen.[124] But this should not be taken to demonstrate strong Free Trade alignment in the FBI as a whole. Nugent had sufficient proxies to carry the day. He also knew that he had tactical advantage: '... it has been possible to beat up a considerable number of individual supporters from the engineering and similar trades who can get to London easily, and it will be difficult for Northern manufacturers to get here ...'[125]

So Nugent certainly had an effective majority for amalgamation. In all probability, he had more than this. But he feared the after-effects. Mass defections in Lancashire and parts of Yorkshire might lose several hundred members, a clear minority but an important one. Significantly, what Nugent feared most was a 'multiplier' contraction of membership. Given the precarious finances of the FBI and the high membership contribution, even marginal losses in members might force a reduction in FBI services to members in certain fields. These members also then might resign, and necessitate a further round of economies.[126] Indeed, similar considerations ensured that FBI leaders, as well as members, were for years vexed by the taunts of the Birmingham-based, protectionist National Union of Manufacturers that the FBI was a 'Free Trade body'.[127] As Docker, who had himself founded the NUM, observed wryly, 'If I had to describe [the FBI] as anything I should say that it probably would like to be a Protectionist party (sic) but dare not'.[128] And, as Nugent confided to his Leicester district secretary, 'We are being blocked in the matter [of amalgamation with BEPO] chiefly by two big trades, the cotton trade and certain sections of the chemical trade'.[129] Aggregate figures for main industrial groups were not split up in the FBI survey of members compiled in 1926. Textiles were the biggest group, contributing 18.7 per cent of FBI funds in 1921 and 20.7 per cent in 1926, but the group included protectionist silk, hosiery and carpets, and wool, where protectionist feeling was considerably stronger than in cotton. Chemicals contributed 5.2 per cent of total funds in 1921 and 4.8 per cent in 1926. Even if these two groups had opposed Tariff Reform in their entirety, they still would have represented less than 25 per cent of the membership. Indeed, it may well be that the hard core of support for Free Trade came from as little as (say) 15 per cent of the membership.[130]

A further indication that the FBI was largely inclined towards protectionism in the 1920s is that remarkably little opposition was voiced towards its assisting individual trades in their applications for key industry status or safeguarding under the legislation of the early 1920s. Certain members of the Manchester district were 'very sore over the action the Federation took with regard to the Dyestuffs Act', of 1920,[131] but it seems that such complainants were well aware that objection was futile. Though the FBI had declined to give evidence before the Balfour of Burleigh Committee in 1917 because of the 'divergence' of members' opinions on trade policy,[132] by 1919-20 the Federation was keeping the government informed 'of the considered arguments of a number of trades which felt themselves entitled to the protection afforded by the Key Industry Legislation proposed'.[133] Immediately after the War, the FBI sought to promote discussion in the case of conflict between producers and users of products potentially subject to import restrictions,[134] but as the 1920s wore on the emphasis shifted to assisting trades in preparing their cases to put before the Board of Trade.[135]

What are the lessons to be learned from the FBI's experience in the 1920s? Certainly cotton remained true to Free Trade. It may be that Clarke's estimate of a pre-war majority of 60:40 is too low, but in any case that majority still seems to have been basically intact in the 1920s. Though Lancashire's fortunes may have plunged, cotton's problems were of collapsing export markets rather than mounting imports.[136] The coal-exporting districts too, though now more vulnerable to foreign competition in a weak market, seem to have maintained their support for Free Trade.[137] Iron and steel, though scarcely mentioned in the FBI controversy, remained heavily protectionist in spite of some division between producers and users of semi-products.[138]

But woollens and worsteds, chemicals and engineering are again found to be problem areas. Woollens and worsteds may or may not have been a significant component of the Textile Group's opposition to the proposed BEPO and NUM amalgamations, depending on the typicality of events in Bradford. But in any case it is worth remembering that if cotton stood on the brink of the abyss in 1918, woollen manufactures had turned the corner, at least in terms of the threat from abroad. The ratio of imports to exports, peaking at 63.3 per cent in 1895–99 and still 59.7 per cent in 1900–04, fell hugely thereafter, and climbed only gradually from 12.2 per cent in 1921 to 27.5 per cent in 1927. Unlike in cotton, the War retarded the growth of capacity abroad, and by and large foreign tariff increases fell below the trend established before 1914.[139] A modified determinist explanation might recognise that this industry would be *less* protectionist after the War than before it.

Explaining the split in chemicals is as difficult as accounting for the industry's apparent unanimity before 1914. Dyestuffs manufacturers were not reticent in their demands: there was indeed considerable public suspicion that 'unfair methods' had been used to induce Sir Albert Stanley to introduce the prohibition on aniline dyes in February 1919, and Lloyd George would hardly have included dyestuffs in his first attempt at safeguarding if the manufacturers had not been pretty solid in advocating them.[140] Of course, desiring protection for one's own trade was not the same as desiring protection all round, but it would be over-cynical to imagine that this group, having climbed the ladder, now kicked it down to obstruct would-be followers. Protection in Britain was too new and fragile: its maintenance needed a broader base and all the support it could muster. It thus seems more likely that the alkali producers, and perhaps the soap-makers, were still the backbone of the opposition. Though these faced a weak and stagnating demand in the 1920s,[141] it may be significant that market leaders Brunner, Mond were expanding output and, largely on the basis of determined export development in the Far East, exporting about 40 per cent of their alkali output.[142] Of course, Brunner, Mond were deeply enmeshed in global agreements with foreign combines, and it is unsatisfactory to account for the attitudes of many smaller and weaker firms with reference to an untypical market leader which, even after 1926, controlled only one-third of the chemical industry.[143] But it is significant that Brunner, Mond and its satellites did produce over 75 per cent of UK alkali output in the mid-1920s, and was still weak in dyestuffs and organic chemicals generally.[144] Clearly, the substantial retention of Free Trade support amongst chemicals producers deserves further study, and chemicals cannot be left in the position it occupies in the Semmel-Rempel scheme.

FBI experience of engineering suggests that pre-war divisions had become less equal, the scales being tipped towards protectionism. In the Manchester district the cotton interests still received some support from textile machinery-makers dependent on their domestic consumers and on foreign markets. But the position of shipbuilding and marine engineering had deteriorated markedly,[145] and Nugent's opinion that even some shipping lines were favourable to the proposed BEPO amalgamation suggests that the opposition of the shipbuilders to Tariff Reform may also have lessened.[146] According to Nugent, strong support for the amalgamation came from London and Midlands engineering works,[147] and we know that the Association of British Motor and Allied Manufacturers[148] and the British Electrical and Allied Manufacturers' Association[149] were strongly protectionist. It is not safe to characterise engineering in the 1920s as even a moderately Free Trade industry.[150]

## V

This essay has questioned the narrowly deterministic view of industry alignment that some historians have seen as operating in the Tariff Reform campaign of 1903–13. We could, of course, criticise determinist explanations on fundamental grounds. Party allegiance seldom stems from one overriding issue: often it involves a compromise choice between different packages of policy, each of which contains a mixture of (more or less) concrete proposals and less tangible ideological approaches. Given also a historical dimension, it was often the case that, as Clarke has observed, 'Far from fiscal attitudes dictating party allegiance, it would be truer to say that party allegiance dictated fiscal attitudes'.[151] We might need to recognise a determinist element in the historical origins of allegiance,[152] which might prevent businessmen splitting on the tariff issue in a completely random way, but there would be little reason to expect the 'broad economic biases' proposed by Rempel.[153] Indeed, given the long-term shift of employers to the Unionists after 1880, as that party emerged more clearly as the counterpoise to organised labour and as the Liberals emerged as the party of progressive taxation,[154] Clarke's explanation is consistent with his claim that even in cotton support for Tariff Reform has been too easily overlooked.

A different criticism of a determinist model may dwell less on its inapplicability than on its lack of depth and subtlety. Simple determinist approaches may not allow for the complications stemming from the fact that some businessmen have dual interests, and that some of those dual interests may exist *within the same firm*, or for the complex differences in the market situations of different branches within an industry, or even of different firms within the same branch. Even then, we might find that, acting on the basis of perceived self-interest, partners or managers *in the same firm* might evaluate best policy differently.[155]

In fact, the empirical historian need not regard the anti-determinist and modified-determinist approaches as completely antagonistic. For some businessmen, politics determined fiscal views, for others fiscal views determined politics. The main casualty is the expectation that all, or even a majority, of industries can be classified neatly. The basic Schumpeterian divide may hold up well in explaining the allegiance of banking and finance (where politics did not determine fiscal views, nor did fiscal views determine politics), most merchants, coal-owners, and the majority of cotton bosses. But in the main the attempt to use Schumpeterian criteria for the division of industries into two camps is less satisfactory. Before 1913 industrialists were more divided, and more evenly divided within industries, than has generally been recognised. After 1918 they were less divided than has commonly been thought. But the underlying reason for these two misconceptions is the same. Most protectionist businessmen shrank from a clear expression of views: they were reluctant to be stigmatised within the odious label of 'protectionist'. Free Traders could display their self-interest in more open, more 'moral' terms. The Cobden Club had done its job well.

*University of Manchester*

## NOTES

I would like to thank the Confederation of British Industries for permission to consult their records, and Deborah Jenkins, CBI archivist at the Modern Records Centre, University of Warwick, for help in using them. My thanks are also due to T. Balderston, R. Davenport-Hines and A.E. Musson for their comments on earlier drafts of this article.

1. M.S. Smith, *Tariff Reform in France 1860–1900: The Politics of Economic Interest* (Ithaca, N.Y., 1980), 148. Smith adds that businessmen were 'little concerned with the French economy as a whole ... [but] concerned mostly with maximizing their own net incomes'. Export-orientated manufacturers are included with cosmpolitan commercial capitalists in Smith's classification of free trade interests (see p. 149).
2. J.A. Schumpeter, *Imperialism and Social Classes* (Oxford, 1951), 106.
3. L. Davis, 'The Capital Markets and Industrial Concentration: The US and UK, a Comparative Study', *Economic History Review*, XIX (1966), pp. 255-72; Leslie Hannah, *The Rise of the Corporate Economy* (London, 1976), 24-5.

4. Schumpeter, op. cit., 106-7 (original emphasis).
5. Schumpeter underlines this. Entrepreneurs

   are benefited only by the tariff that happens to be levied on their own product. But this advantage is substantially reduced by the countermeasures adopted by other countries ... and by the effect of the tariff on the prices of other articles, especially those which they require for their own productive process. Why, then, are entrepreneurs so strongly in favour of protective tariffs? The answer is simple. Each industry hopes to score *special* gains in the struggle of political intrigue, thus enabling it to realize a net gain. Ibid., 103 (original emphasis).

6. F. W. Taussig, *Tariff History of the United States* (1st edn., New York, 1888), *passim* but especially 70-6; F. List, *The National System of Political Economy* (London, 1904 edn.), *passim* but especially 156 and Chs. 26-27.
7. L. Brown, *The Board of Trade and the Free Trade Movement 1830-42* (Oxford, 1958), 181-3. See also A. E. Musson, 'The "Manchester School" and Exportation of Machinery', *Business History*, XIV (1972), 17-50.
8. Quoted in B. Semmel, *Imperialism and Social Reform* (London, 1960), 100.
9. The Commission was publicised as an attempt to bring the business mind to bear on the controversy and thus cut through party political wrangling. This stress on a new business expertism to set against the old sterility of party politics was an approach similar to that of the 'National Efficiency' movement. See A. J. Marrison, 'The Development of a Tariff Reform Policy during Joseph Chamberlain's First Campaign', in W. H. Chaloner and B. M. Ratcliffe (eds), *Trade and Transport* (Manchester, 1977), 214-41; cf. G. R. Searle, *The Quest for National Efficiency* (Oxford, 1971), 80-3, 86-95.
10. Charles Allen of Sir Henry Bessemer and Co., Sir Alfred Hickman, Arthur Keen of GKN, and Sir William T. Lewis. It must be observed that Lewis had far greater interests in coal than in iron and steel.
12. Respectively, A. W. Maconochie, Sir Vincent Caillard of Vickers, Sons and Maxim, J. J. Candlish, Charles Parsons, Howard Colls and Sir Charles Tennant.
12. Op. cit., 102. Semmel further notes (p. 103) that 'Woollen goods and cotton goods had, it ought to be noted, no representation upon the Commission'. In fact there were two cotton men (Frederick Baynes and Charles Eckersley) and one worsted spinner and manufacturer (W. H. Mitchell), in addition to members of the Commission's later established Textile Committee.
13. R. A. Rempel, *Unionists Divided: Arthur Balfour, Joseph Chamberlain and the Unionist Free Traders* (Newton Abbot, 1972), 97.
14. Ibid., 97, 98, 101, 104.
15. Semmel, op. cit., p. 103.
16. To the objection that this 'composite' is artificial, it can be answered that, at least when talking in aggregate terms, Rempel accepts and endorses Semmel's earlier work. See P. F. Clarke's review of *Unionists Divided* in *English Historical Review*, 89 (1974), 688-89.
17. A. K. Russell, *Liberal Landslide* (Newton Abbot, 1973), Table 26, 166. This percentage varies very slightly between different authorities.
18. See M. S. Smith, op. cit., as a model in this respect, and my review of it in *Business History*, XXIV (1982), 121-3.
19. For three of the best pro-Tariff Reform treatments of the long-term context, see W. J. Ashley, *The Tariff Problem* (London, 1903); V. H. P. Caillard, *Imperial Fiscal Reform* (London, 1903); and W. A. S. Hewins' sixteen articles in *The Times* between June and September 1903, all entitled 'The Fiscal Policy of the Empire'.
20. Sir Robert Giffen to Ed., *The Times* (28 May 1903), 5.
21. That Chamberlain's portrayal of the Commission as 'the most wonderful representation of British industry that has ever been brought together' was not mere hyperbole is perhaps endorsed by the fact that it suited the purposes of the Free Trade *Leeds Mercury* to concede the inclusion of 'many able businessmen ... the majority of them the heads of great industrial concerns'. See Chamberlain to Lady Jeune, quoted in J.

Amery. *Life of Joseph Chamberlain*, VI (London, 1969), 532; *Leeds Mercury* 18 December 1903, 4.

22. Grenfell owned 12,000 acres. It might be noted, however, that his family had important banking and financial interests, as well as some connections with imperial enterprise.

23. Chaplin's Lincolnshire estate had slipped from his impecunious grasp by 1903. His continuing political advocacy for the agricultural interest and his dependency on the Duke of Sutherland justify his continued inclusion, however. See Marchioness of Londonderry. *Henry Chaplin: A Memoir* (London, 1926).

24. The main sources for this examination are 'Members of the Commission', in *Report of the Tariff Commission*, vol. 1, *The Iron and Steel Trades*, (London, 1904), para. 1; 'Members of the Tariff Commission', B-272, Tariff Commission Papers (hereinafter TCP); *Who Was Who*. Vols. I-IV, H. H. Bassett (ed), *Men of Business at Home and Abroad, 1912–1913* (London, n.d.); T. Skinner, *Directory of Directors* (London, 1904 and 1905 edns.).

25. J. M. Harris (bacon curing, Wiltshire); C. J. Phillips (brewing, London); F. Tonsley (baking and confectionery, London); W. H. Mitchell (worsted spinning and manufacturing, Yorkshire); J. A. Corah (hosiery, Leicester); F. Elgar (shipbuilding, Glasgow); W. Harrison (agricultural engineering, Lancashire); H. Bostock (boots and shoes, Stafford); L. Evans (paper making, Herts.); W. Cooper (meat wholesaler, London); C. A. Pearson (newspapers, London and provincial); A. Mosely (diamond merchant, London); I. Levinstein (dyestuffs, Manchester). It must be stressed that inclusion in this single-interest group necessarily rests on a negative proof, that is, that no further interests *have been discovered*.

26. A rare glimpse is furnished by our knowledge of Andrew Bonar Law. On entering Parliament in 1900 he gave up active business in his iron merchants' partnership, William Jacks & Co. Thereafter, of his income of £6,000 p.a., 75% came from investment income and 25% from director's fees. See R. Blake, *The Unknown Prime Minister* (London, 1955), 37.

27. (Major interests are emphasised) C. Lyle (*sugar refining*, steam shipping); A. W. Maconochie (*meat-packing*, tinplating); J. Rank (*flour milling*, oil milling); T. Gallaher (*tobacco*, steam shipping); C. Allen (*steel*, iron and coal, banking); A. Hickman (*iron and steel*, coal, property development); C. Eckersley (*cotton spinning*, coal); R. H. Reade (*flax spinning*, railways); H. D. Marshall (*argicultural engineering*, coal); A. Jones (*shipowning*, banking, importing, oil milling, cotton growing, coal, mining and quarrying, railways, etc); W. B. Webb (*grain importing*, insurance); H. Colls (*building*, interior decorating, cabinet making); W. H. Goulding (*agricultural chemicals*, railways, docks).

28. Even though Abraham Lyle and Sons had developed from a shipowning firm. See G. Fairrie. *The Sugar Refining Families of Great Britain* (priv. publ., London and Liverpool, 1951).

29. For a generalised support, see M. Robbins, *The Railway Age* (Harmondsworth, 1965), 76-9.

30. Rank regarded oil milling as a 'diversion' and 'little more than a challenge to his business abilities'. See H. Janes, *The Master Millers* (priv. publ., London 1955), 37.

31. Anon., *History of Trollope and Colls* (priv. publ., n.d. but 1978); see also A. Tough's article on J. H. Colls in *Dictionary of Business Biography* (forthcoming).

32. P. N. Davies. *Alfred Jones* (London, 1978); P. N. Davies, *The Trade Makers* (London, 1973); A. H. Milne, *Sir Alfred Lewis Jones* (Liverpool, 1914).

33. D. Burn, *An Economic History of Steelmaking 1867–1939* (Cambridge, 1940), 224; J. C. Carr and W. Taplin, *A History of the British Steel Industry* (Oxford, 1962), 268.

34. *DNB*; C. Wilkins. *History of the Iron, Steel, Tinplate and Other Trades of Wales* (Merthyr Tydfil, 1903); J. H. Morris and L. J. Williams, *The South Wales Coal Industry 1841–1875* (Cardiff, 1958), 128; W. E. Minchinton, *The British Tinplate Industry* (Oxford, 1957), 96-7

35. This is the impression gained from Sir Herbert Maxwell. *Half-A-Century of Successful Trade* (priv. publ., London, 1907).

36. A. H. John, *A Liverpool Merchant House* (London, 1959).
37. J. A. Gibbs, *History of Antony and Dorothea Gibbs* (London, 1922); D. C. M. Platt, *Latin America and British Trade 1806–1914* (London, 1972), 138-9; R. Greenhill, 'Merchants and the Latin American Trades' and 'The Nitrate and Iodine Trades 1880–1914', in D. C. M. Platt (ed.), *Business Imperialism 1840–1930* (Oxford, 1977), pp. 159-97, 231-83.
38. *Report of the Tariff Commission*, Vol. 2, Part 6, *Evidence on the Silk Industry* (London, 1905), paras. 3258-73.
39. N. K. Hill, 'Accountancy Developments in a Public Utility Company in the Nineteenth Century', *Accounting Research*, V (1955), 328-90.
40. In later years, Harris's active concern with the wider aspects of the maritime trade was shown in his campaign against the Declaration of London in 1909–10 and in his work in the Trade Division of the Admiralty, the Department of Restriction of Enemy Supplies at the Foreign Office, and the Ministry of Blockades, in the Great War. See *DNB*.
41. *Sheffield Daily Telegraph* (18 December 1903); D. A. Farnie, *The Manchester Ship Canal and the Rise of the Port of Manchester* (Manchester, 1980), 12-14. Around 1890 Henderson had an interest in the Shelton Iron and Steel Company of North Staffordshire, but I have no evidence that he still possessed this interest in 1903–6.
42. N. Crathorne, *Tennant's Stalk* (London, 1973), 131-47; see also W. D. Rubinstein, 'The Victorian Middle Classes: Wealth, Occupation, and Geography', *Economic History Review*, XXX (1977), 602-23.
43. Though becoming a director of Vickers on leaving the Ottoman Public Debt Council in 1898, his role in the company was probably relatively small until the death of Sigmund Loewe (effectively the company's financial controller) in 1903, but increased thereafter until he was made financial controller in 1906. But he remained a director of the National Bank of Egypt until 1908, and banking and finance may well have been his dominant interest in 1903-5. See *The Times* (20 and 29 March 1930); *DNB*; C. Trebilcock, *The Vickers Brothers* (London, 1977), 45,·51; J. D. Scott, *Vickers: A History* (London, 1962), 77-8, 92.
44. Here we come near to the issue of 'economic determinism' *versus* 'economic interpretation'. For the classic discussion, in the context of the debate over the forces behind the American Constitution, see Lee Benson, *Turner and Beard* (Glencoe Ill., 1960), pt. III.
45. W. D. Rubinstein, *Men of Property* (London, 1981), 58, 178.
46. Ibid., 178-82, especially Tables 6.1 and 6.2.
47. Caillard's primary interest has, rather arbitrarily in view of the remarks on p. 153 above, been given as engineering.
48. There was also a Textiles Committee on which, in addition to Commission members, sat one flax and jute spinner and manufacturer (J. B. Don, Dundee); one worsted manufacturer (J. H. Kaye, Huddersfield); one woollen manufacturer (J. Peate, Guiseley); one tweed, worsted and flannel manufacturer (A. J. Sanderson, Galashiels); and two carpet manufacturers (G. Marchetti of Crossley's, Halifax, and M. Tomkinson, Kidderminster).
49. Of course, many in related trades would have indirect knowledge of the trade or *bloc* concerned.
50. Semmel, op. cit., 102.
51. Semmel, op. cit., 102n, points out that Maconochie was chairman of the Solderless Tin Co. Ltd., but misses Lewis's chairmanship of the much more important Mellingriffith Tinplate Works. Of course, the tinplate trade had close relations with the iron and steel industry, and so other Commissioners may have had indirect knowledge (Minchinton, op. cit., 95-7).
52. Semmel's stress on the regional element in support for Tariff Reform, his specific mention of the Midlands, is presumably meant to imply that Midlands industrialists fell within Chamberlain's sphere of political influence, through personal acquaintance and the influence of the Birmingham Liberal Unionist Association which he dominated. Whilst this probably holds some general truth, it scarcely fits the Tariff

Commission's membership or several of the industries that he mentions. Only three Commissioners had West Midlands addresses (Sir Alfred Hickman, Arthur Keen and Henry Bostock, the Stafford boot and shoe manufacturer), though to this group we should probably add Unionist MPs (Henry Chaplin, W. H. Grenfell, Leverton Harris, Sir Alexander Henderson and A. W. Maconochie), two of whom represented agriculture and none of whom represented Midlands industry as such. Likewise, to regard iron and steel as a 'Midlands industry' is to deny the great variety of the 10 or so main UK producing regions, some of which fared better under foreign competition than the admittedly hard hit South Staffordshire region. Chemicals, too, was scarcely a Birmingham-centred industry. In 1901 the industry employed less than 7,000 in the West Midlands compared with, for example, nearly 23,000 in the North West. See C. H. Lee, *Regional Employment Statistics 1841–1971* (Cambridge, 1979).
53. This is not to say that it was not frequently exaggerated by those who felt it.
54. For more detail, see A. J. Marrison, 'British Businessmen and the "Scientific" Tariff: A Study of Joseph Chamberlain's Tariff Commission, 1903–1921' (unpublished Ph.D thesis, University of Hull, 1980), 91-6.
55. Colonel Charles Allen, Henry Birchenough and Sir Vincent Caillard are examples.
56. Except for brewing and distilling, historically and with reason anti-Liberal, and sugar refining, hit by export bounties on European beet sugar, this would seem the logical alignment for food processing, even though the industry is not mentioned (except for meat packing) by Semmel or Rempel. Chamberlain encapsulated the issue nicely: 'Sugar has gone. Let us not weep for it – jam and pickles remain'. See Chamberlain at Greenock, 7 October 1903, reprinted in J. M. Robertson, *The Collapse of 'Tariff Reform'* (London, 1911), 100.
57. This assumes that, in Table 2, both 'other secondary' and 'other tertiary' are not classified as 'Free Trade' interests. If, as seems plausible, 'other tertiary' were included as 'Free Trade' interests, the figure would rise to 35 out of 47. However, the removal of those exceptions admitted by Semmel or Rempel (silk, linen and electrical engineering) would reduce the figure to 31 out of 47.
58. First Director of the LSE and a well-known Historical Economist. See his autobiography, *The Apologia of an Imperialist* (London, 2 vols., 1929).
59. Hewins to P. Hurd (6 September 1906); C-174.1, TCP.
60. Tariff Commission Minutes (typescript) (23 May 1907), 28; TCP.
61. Hewins to Arthur Pearson (24 December 1903); C-176, TCP.
62. S. B. Saul, 'The Market and the Development of the Mechanical Engineering Industries in Britain, 1860–1914', *Economic History Review*, XX (1967), 111-30.
63. S. Pollard, 'British and World Shipbuilding, 1890–1914: A Study in Comparative Costs', *Journal of Economic History*, XVII (1957), 426-44.
64. Saul, loc. cit.; also S. B. Saul, 'The Machine Tool Industry in Britain to 1914', *Business History*, X (1968), 22-43.
65. For the two branches of the industry, see Saul, 'Market', loc. cit., and R. J. Munting, 'Ransome's in Russia: An English Agricultural Engineering Company's Trade with Russia to 1917', *Economic History Review*, XXXI (1978), 257-269.
66. I. C. R. Byatt, *The British Electrical Industry 1875–1914* (Oxford, 1979), Ch. 9; I. C. R. Byatt, 'Electrical Products', in D. H. Aldcroft (ed.). *The Development of British Industry and Foreign Competition 1875–1914* (London, 1968). Ch. 8.
67. S. B. Saul, 'The Motor Industry in Britain to 1914', *Business History*, V (1962-3), 22-44.
68. As would be Saul's general presumption for the industry. See also A. E. Harrison 'The Competitiveness of the British Cycle Industry, 1890–1914', *Economic History Review*, XXII (1969), 287-303. It should not be forgotten, however, that in those branches of light engineering where this was so, the more dynamic firms were frequently critically dependent on the adoption of American methods and, sometimes, of American machinery and machine tools.
69. L. F. Haber, *The Chemical Industry during the Nineteenth Century* (Oxford, 1958), 196.
70. A partial exception was conservatively-minded Ludwig Mond. See J. M. Cohen, *Life*

*of Ludwig Mond* (London. 1956), 168; S. E. Koss, *Sir John Brunner* (Cambridge. 1970), 193-9; A. Mond, 'The Alkali Industry', in H. Cox (ed.), *British Industries under Free Trade* (London. 1903), 214-26. On Brunner, Mond's strong position in Empire markets, almost *de facto* imperial preference secured by market sharing agreements, see W. J. Reader, *Imperial Chemical Industries* (London. 1970), 169-72.

71. Printed proof copy of Levinstein's evidence before the Tariff Commission; TCP.
72. Both John Brock and F. Davidson (chairman and joint managing director of UAC respectively) refused to give evidence. According to Levinstein, this reflected division on the Board over the fiscal issue. See Levinstein to Hewins (29 October 1905); C-599, TCP.
73. Ivan Levinstein and L. B. Holliday. Martin Dreyfus of the Clayton Aniline Co. Ltd. has left no trace of having given evidence.
74. Levinstein to Hewins (25 October 1905); C-599, TCP.
75. P. Hurd to Levinstein (26 October 1905); C-599, TCP.
76. L. F. Haber, *The Chemical Industry 1900-1930* (Oxford, 1971), 148.
77. *The Economist* (19 November 1881), quoted in B. H. Brown, *The Tariff Reform Movement in Great Britain 1881-95* (New York, 1943), 11-12. Woollen and worsted manufacturers involved in the early campaign in Bradford included Farrer Eckroyd and J. H. Mitchell.
78. Brown, op. cit., 10, 130, 141.
79. D. T. Jenkins and K. G. Ponting, *The British Wool Textile Industry 1770-1914* (London, 1982), 293.
80. Op. cit., 139-40.
81. E. Sigsworth, *Black Dyke Mills* (Liverpool, 1958), 107.
82. Ibid.
83. Rempel (op. cit., 97) cites the inevitable Hugh Bell, progressive Cleveland ironmaster, to show that 'Even in the iron industry itself there was no solidarity behind Chamberlain'. But Bell may not have been typical even of North Eastern producers. According to Arthur Keen, himself a director of Bolckow Vaughan, the 'largest Companies in [the Middlesbrough] district are very divided' over the issue. Based on numbers employed in the UK industry as a whole, those iron and steel firms replying to the Tariff Commission's questionnaires constituted 87.2%. See Keen to Ponsonby (1 March 1904); C-512, TCP, and *Report of the Tariff Commission*, Vol. I, *The Iron and Steel Trades*, (London, 1904), para. 10.
84. See especially C. Trebilcock, *The Vickers Brothers* (London, 1977), 11, 22.
85. Albert Vickers, on the other hand, was a Tariff Reformer. See Hewins to D. Vickers (2 March 1904), D. Vickers to Charles Allen (15 March 1904), C-286, TCP, and J. D. Scott, *Vickers: A History* (London, 1962), 76.
86. Evidence of Sir Andrew Noble, *Report of the Tariff Commission*, Vol. IV, *The Engineering Industries* (London, 1909), para. 509. Noble claimed to speak on behalf of engineering generally, both as president of the Engineering Employers' Federation (1898-1915) and as one who had considerable knowledge of engineering in continental Europe.
87. Ibid., para. 501.
88. John Thorneycroft recorded that foreign competition in torpedo boats had led his firm to diversify over the previous 25 years, but most of his evidence concentrated on motor cars. Ibid., paras. 528-38.
89. An industry with little or no import competition in the home market is unlikely to be aided by a policy which raises its input costs. In this case a negative rate of effective protection on the final products would, given the semi-monopolistic position at home and the large element of non-tariff protection, be less important than the effect on the competitiveness of the industry's exports.
90. Arms makers such as Caillard, Francis Barker, Sir Trevor Dawson and F. Orr-Lewis of Vickers were prominent in the establishment of the pro-Tariff Reform British Commonwealth Union in December 1916, whilst Dudley Docker, a director of BSA in addition to many less defence-orientated industries, founded the protectionist National Union of Manufacturers and was a slightly offstage supporter of Caillard's efforts to

commit the Federation of British Industries to Tariff Reform and imperial preference in its early years. On the BCU, see J. A. Turner, 'The British Commonwealth Union and the General Election of 1918', *English Historical Review*, 93 (1978), especially p. 532.

91. See Marrison, thesis, 465-73.
92. Ibid., 464-5.
93. Levinstein to Hewins (8 February 1904); C-599, TCP.
94. Even P. F. Clarke, who argues the case for very deep division within the cotton industry, agrees with this point. See 'The End of Laissez-Faire and the Politics of Cotton', *Historical Journal*, XV (1972), especially p. 510.
95. 'Tariff Commission Account, 1910–1922', TCP, and J. Amery, *Life of Joseph Chamberlain*, Vol. V (London, 1969), 288, 301.
96. The record of a local chamber's debates, whilst illuminating the views of that minority who spoke, only counts (if it counts at all) the votes of those present, generally only a small sample of total membership. Given that votes recorded are seldom identifiable to individuals and thereby to the industries they represented, and since chambers recruited members from more than one industry and usually from a heterogeneous mixture of small tertiary occupations as well, such records provide a very incomplete picture.
97. E. Wigham, *The Power to Manage* (London, 1973), 1.
98. Hamilton to Hewins (27 February 1904); C-618, TCP. Those associations appointing delegates or representatives included the British Tube Trade Association, the Paper Makers' Association, the India Rubber Manufacturers' Association, the Institute of British Carriage Manufacturers, the Timber Trades Federation, the Musical Instrument Traders' Protection Association, the Warwickshire Felt Hat Manufacturers' Association and the National Glass Bottle Manufacturers' Association. The biggest association represented was the British Iron Trades Association.
99. *Report of the Tariff Commission*, Vol. 1, *The Iron and Steel Trades* (London, 1904), para. 929.
100. A. R. Ilersic and P. F. B. Liddle, *Parliament of Commerce* (London, 1960), 154-6.
101. M. W. Beresford, *The Leeds Chamber of Commerce* (Leeds, 1951), 115-9.
102. W. E. Dowding, *The Tariff Reform Mirage* (London, 1913), 4-7.
103. Marrison, 'The Development of a Tariff Reform Policy', loc. cit.
104. Quoted in S. Dark, *Life of Sir Arthur Pearson* (London, n.d.).
105. Clarke argues convincingly that, even in 1903–6, cotton bosses may have had only a 2:1 majority in favour of Free Trade, compared with the 9:1 that Free Traders often claimed. See 'The End of Laissez-Faire and the Politics of Cotton', *Historical Journal*, XV (1972), especially pp. 499, 511.
106. By volume, British yarn exports grew 34.1% and piece-goods exports 22.3% between 1900–04 and 1909–13. Figures derived from *Annual Statement of Trade of the United Kingdom* (1900–13).
107. For instance, Tariff Commissioner and ex-Unionist M. P. Sir Alfred Hickman. See Hickman to W. A. S. Hewins (26 April 1906), Hewins Papers.
108. On this reaction, see A. Sykes, *Tariff Reform in British Politics 1903–1913* (Oxford, 1979), Ch. 10-12.
109. Marrison, thesis, 174-80, 519-20.
110. J. A. Turner, loc. cit., especially pp. 528-33. Turner maintains that 'For most of the organisations which looked beyond the immediate problems of businessmen [that is, employers' associations], Tariff Reform was the foundation of a political platform, and for many it was the whole of it'. His evidence rests on a rather narrow range of examples – the British Empire Producers' Organisation, the British Manufacturers' Association and the National Union of Manufacturers (which were actually the same organisation) and the British Commonwealth Union – but I suspect it is largely correct.
111. Some internationalist Free Traders saw this clearly. See J. A. Hobson, *The New Protectionism* (London, 1916), and J. M. Robertson, *The New Tariffism* (London, 1918).

112. Committee on Commercial and Industrial Policy after the War, 17th meeting (15 February 1917); BT 55/8/107-8, PRO.
113. W. K. Hancock, *Survey of British Commonwealth Affairs*. Vol. II, Part I, *Problems of Economic Policy 1918–1939* (London, 1940), 97.
114. Committee on Commercial and Industrial Policy, *Final Report*, Cd. 9035 (1918), Vol. xiii.
115. BT 55/8/357, PRO.
116. Lord Melchett, *Imperial Economic Unity* (London, 1930), 12. Balfour of Burleigh Committee, 12th meeting (18 January 1917); BT 55/8/91, PRO.
117. Holland has argued that 'considerable differences existed as to the extent of [FBI members'] dependence on overseas markets. There was consequently no obvious consensus on the desirability of a tariff'. Blank writes of the FBI leaders' inability 'to take any stand in favour of Protection because of the opposition of many groups within it'. See R. F. Holland, 'The Federation of British Industries and the International Economy, 1929-39'. *Economic History Review*, 34 (1981), 228; S. Blank, *Industry and Government in Britain* (Farnborough, 1973), 27.
118. In general terms, Forrest Capie agrees with the need to reject the view that business men turned to protection only as a 'crisis policy' in or around 1930. For his analysis, which concentrates heavily on the steel industry, see 'The Pressure for Tariff Protection in Britain, 1917-31', *Journal of European Economic History*, 9 (1980), 431-47.
119. President of the FBI in 1918-19.
120. Mostly based in the Empire or on trade in Empire foodstuffs.
121. Nugent to Caillard (5 November 1919); FBI 200/F/3/D1/2/2. (Modern Record Centre, University of Warwick).
122. 'Report of a Meeting held between Representatives of the British Empire Producers' Organisation and the Federation of British Industries, 13 June 1919'; FBI 200/F/3/D1/3/8.
123. Nugent to Caillard (20 October 1919); FBI 200/F/3/D1/2/2.
124. Nugent to Caillard (6 November 1919); FBI 200/F/3/D1/2/2.
125. Ibid.
126. Nugent to C. Cookson (28 April 1927); FBI 200/F/3/D1/6/10.
127. Copy of NUM pro-forma letter (5 October 1923); FBI/S/Walker/100/2.
128. Docker to Sir David Brooks (25 October 1923); FBI/S/Walker/100/2.
129. Nugent to Allard (17 June 1919); FBI/S/Walker/100/2.
130. FBI Analysis of Membership, 1921-6; FBI/S/Walker/70/1. In 1921 Manchester firms comprised only 13.2% of the numerical strength of the FBI, and Manchester, Leeds, Bradford and Liverpool combined only 26.9%.
131. J. J. Butler (Manchester district secretary) to G. Locock (8 April 1931); FBI/S/Walker/93/4.
132. FBI, *First Annual Report* (to 30 June 1917), 6.
133. FBI, *Fourth Annual Report* (1919–20), 15-16.
134. FBI, *Fifth Annual Report* (1920–1), 17.
135. FBI, *Tenth Annual Report* (1925–6), 17. It is true that the FBI backed away from giving wholesale support to those of its members who feared the government might remove the McKenna Duties in 1924, but the withdrawal had a large tactical element and was in any case endorsed (and even anticipated) by the interested trades them selves. Such a resolution was passed later, in the crisis conditions of 1930. See 'Minutes of Meeting of Trades Affected by the McKenna Duties' (25 June 1924), FBI 200/F/1/1/138, 79-81 and *Grand Council Minutes* (12 March 1930), 248-56, FBI 200/F/1/1/1 (Vol. II).
136. Imports are scarcely mentioned in Committee on Industry and Trade, *Survey of the Textile Industries* (Board of Trade, 1928). Even that most trenchant critic of Manchester's liberalism, Bowker, saw a control board rather than protection as the answer to Lancashire's problems. See *Lancashire Under the Hammer* (London, 1928), 116-26.
137. W. A. Lee, chairman of the Mining Association of Great Britain, noted that prior to the turbulent events of 1930 'the export coal districts had been against making any change'. See *Grand Council Minutes*, (13 October 1930), 269; FBI 200/F/1/1/1 (Vol.

II). Lee apparently excluded those coalfields working mainly to supply the domestic market.
138. F. Capie, loc. cit., 435-7.
139. Raw figures in Committee on Industry and Trade, *Survey of Textile Industries*, loc. cit., Table 6, 276 and 223-4.
140. R. K. Snyder, *The Tariff Problem in Great Britain 1918–1923* (California, 1944), 21, 30.
141. A. E. Musson, *The Growth of British Industry* (London, 1978), 338-9.
142. W. J. Reader, *Imperial Chemical Industries*, Vol. I (London, 1970), Ch. 16 especially p. 345.
143. Musson, op. cit., 340.
144. L. F. Haber, *The Chemical Industry 1900–1930*, (Oxford, 1971), 292-3.
145. D. Dougan, *The History of North East Shipbuilding* (London, 1968), Ch. 5.
146. Nugent to Caillard 6 November 1919; FBI 200/F/3/D1/2/2.
147. Ibid.
148. R. K. Snyder, op. cit., 31-2.
149. BEAMA, *The Electrical Industry of Great Britain* (priv. publ., London, 1919), especially p. 70.
150. Indeed, the reverse is suggested by a poll of 1,894 iron and steel, shipbuilding, engineering and electrical engineering firms by the British Engineers' Association in 1923. 81.8% of the respondents declared themselves in favour of Baldwin's policy (which excluded agricultural protection) and 15.4% against. Of course, the response rate is not known. See *Electrical Review* (7 December 1923) 863.
151. P. F. Clarke, *Lancashire and the New Liberalism* (Cambridge, 1971), 274.
152. As with the brewers or the cotton trade.
153. R. A. Rempel, op. cit., 104.
154. H. V. Emy, 'The Impact of Financial Policy on English Party Politics before 1914', *Historical Journal*, XV (1972), 103-31.
155. It is to be stressed that Rempel's discussion of individual deviations, though conducted in terms of economic representation in the House of Commons, does separate him from Semmel's more straightforward view to some extent.

# A SHIPYARD IN DEPRESSION: JOHN BROWNS OF CLYDEBANK 1919-1938[1]

## by A. SLAVEN

Few companies are entirely representative of the industry of which they are a part, but in British shipbuilding, John Browns of Clyde-bank was important enough to reflect major areas of change in the industry between the wars. With a capacity of between 90,000 and 100,000 tons it was one of the largest single establishments in the country. Over 723,000 tons came off its slipways between 1919 and 1938, taking the yard to third place on the Clyde behind Lithgow and Harland and Wolff. Two-thirds of this was passenger and passenger cargo tonnage, seventeen per cent was naval and seventeen per cent mixed cargo. The yard was involved in all the main types of shipbuilding, though passenger and naval construction were most important. It was not equally representative of all types of construc-tion, but the balance and diversity of its output make it a fair indicator of the problems of the industry and of the adjustment which companies attempted in response.

*The Industry Problem*

Sharp fluctuations in output have been a characteristic feature of the shipbuilding industry. In large part this instability has been inherent in the nature of the product and its market. Such large capital goods as ships take many months to build and the orders for their construction fluctuate with the derived demand of ship-owners whose policies for new and replacement tonnage ebb and flow with the volume of world trade. Owners' decisions to order new tonnage may also be influenced by a range of considerations includ-ing the course of freight rates, the price of scrap tonnage, the elasticity in lifespan of vessels in relation to earning power vis-à-vis new tonnage at any point in time.

Given these conditions it is not surprising to find that ship-builders' order books were subject to dramatic contraction at irregular intervals. Yet, with the knowledge that orders could recover quickly, shipbuilders felt obliged to instal capacity sufficient to cater for peak demand. Moreover, builders frequently found that occasional orders for large or specialised tonnage necessitated investment in enlarged facilities. Consequently, even without the influence of abnormal conditions, shipbuilding suffered from an inherent tendency to develop excess capacity.[2]

These familiar problems were much aggravated between the wars by three related circumstances. After a brief post-war replace-ment boom the potential demand for new tonnage barely grew.

Wartime extensions had created a world shipbuilding industry of great size and productive capacity which drove world mercantile tonnage from 51 million tons in 1919 to 62 million in 1921, and 65 million by 1923. For the remainder of the years between the wars the industry had to work within a context of generally weak demand. A second circumstance emerged from this. Shipbuilders experienced unprecedented competition domestically and internationally for scarce new orders. The combination of weak demand and fierce competition induced, in Britain, a third feature, a tendency to sectoral decline in Britain's share of world ship construction.[3] (Table I).

TABLE I

Merchant Tonnage Launched 1919–38
(vessels of 100 gross register tons and over)
(thousand tons)

| Year | Clyde | UK | World | Clyde as a percentage of UK | UK as a percentage of World |
|---|---|---|---|---|---|
| 1919 | 518 | 1,620 | 7,144 | 31·9 | 22·7 |
| 1920 | 671 | 2,056 | 5,862 | 32·6 | 35·1 |
| 1921 | 510 | 1,538 | 4,357 | 33·2 | 35·3 |
| 1922 | 387 | 1,031 | 2,467 | 37·5 | 41·8 |
| 1923 | 175 | 646 | 1,643 | 27·1 | 39·3 |
| 1924 | 537 | 1,440 | 2,248 | 37·3 | 64·0 |
| 1925 | 522 | 1,085 | 2,193 | 48·1 | 49·5 |
| 1926 | 275 | 640 | 1,675 | 42·9 | 38·2 |
| 1927 | 440 | 1,226 | 2,286 | 35·9 | 53·6 |
| 1928 | 581 | 1,446 | 2,699 | 40·2 | 53·6 |
| 1929 | 557 | 1,523 | 2,793 | 36·9 | 54·5 |
| 1930 | 525 | 1,479 | 2,889 | 35·5 | 51·2 |
| 1931 | 149 | 502 | 1,617 | 29·7 | 31·0 |
| 1932 | 62 | 179 | 727 | 34·6 | 25·8 |
| 1933 | 49 | 133 | 489 | 36·8 | 27·2 |
| 1934 | 238 | 460 | 967 | 51·7 | 47·5 |
| 1935 | 161 | 499 | 1,302 | 32·3 | 38·3 |
| 1936 | 282 | 856 | 2,118 | 32·9 | 40·4 |
| 1937 | 337 | 921 | 2,691 | 36·6 | 34·2 |
| 1938 | 412 | 1,030 | 3,034 | 40·0 | 33·9 |
| 1919–23 | 2,261 | 6,891 | 21,464 | 32·8 | 32·1 |
| 1924–28 | 2,355 | 5,837 | 11,101 | 40·3 | 52·6 |
| 1929–33 | 1,342 | 3,816 | 8,515 | 35·2 | 44·8 |
| 1934–38 | 1,430 | 3,766 | 10,112 | 37·9 | 37·2 |

Sources: Lloyds Annual Summary; Glasgow Herald Annual Trade Review

This crippling combination of weak demand, fierce competition and slow sectoral decline plunged the industry into a more unstable condition which strongly favoured the buyer over the producer of ships. For most of the period between the wars, British shipbuilders faced an intractable market problem and had to grapple with it from a weak and deteriorating operating position. The root of their problem was overcapacity in relation to potential demand. Overcapacity burdened the builders in a number of ways. The need to deliver orders on time, and sooner than competitors, encouraged individual yards to retain more labour than could usefully be employed at all stages of construction, thus leading to at least periodic overmanning. The unpredictability of orders also persuaded yards to retain a whole range of berth sizes keeping in existence tonnage capacities far beyond available orders. Further, the low load factors in relation to existing capacity meant a heavy burden of capital investment in relation to earnings.

The inevitable consequences were high costs and poor profitability. The cost problem impinged immediately on the shipbuilder's ability to obtain new orders, and completed a cycle of linked circumstances which debilitated the industry between the wars. Weak demand made for a poor order book which meant a low level of capacity utilisation. Low load factors increased overheads and raised production costs. High levels of costs contributed to high prices and poor competitiveness, which made it even more difficult for a company to obtain a share of the few orders available in the market place. In the medium and longer terms the weakening flow of orders was reflected in declining earnings and failing profits. The serious long term implication was the threat to investment programmes and the ability of the industry to plan for its own future. This was particularly worrying, for the industry's survival demanded investment in the development of new technologies; the diesel engine, and welding. A failure to invest at these points clearly carried with it the penalty of falling far behind foreign competitors, especially in the provision of new types of ships.

The industry problem therefore rested unevenly on three legs. The market problem of falling orders and persistently weak demand exacerbated by a slippage in the British share of world ship construction. The second leg was the production problem arising from excess capacity and expressed in the equation of high cost, weak competitiveness and poor profitability leading to investment difficulties. The third strand was the technology problem; the conflict of balancing claims on scarce capital in conditions of excess capacity, claims as between simple replacement investment through obsolescence and wear and tear, and new and uncertain investment to accommodate diesel and welding innovations. Such was the quicksand business environment of the shipbuilder between the wars: the Clydebank experience gives some clue to the reactions of the industry and to that of individual companies.

## John Browns and the Market

A highly volatile market was the everyday problem for the shipbuilder who sought to keep his workmen and his berths fully occupied. Building up the order book was of critical importance and most builders took steps to attempt some control over their own market situation. Consequently, well before the end of the first world war the Clydebank management was planning its post-war construction strategy in terms of alliances with buyers and associations with suppliers; the latter was an attempt to ensure that construction would proceed without delay.

By early 1919, John Browns had formed links with five groups in an attempt to secure a regular flow of work. As early as November 1916, they had joined with Fairfields and Harland and Wolff in a ten-year arrangement to build steamers for the Canadian Pacific Railway Company.[4] Two years later the Board concluded a trio of berth allocation arrangements with Lord Pirrie, the Orient Steam Navigation Company[5] and the Cunard Steamship Company.[6] The following year, 1919, together with Fairfield and Cammell Laird, Browns agreed to extend their existing links in the Coventry Syndicate[7] into a joint marketing and sales agency for foreign naval and merchant work.[8] These were all arrangements made in anticipation of a boom in merchant work at the end of hostilities. In addition, Browns clearly hoped that their lucrative links with the Admiralty would be continued, though they were not optimistic on this count.

This cultivation of 'builders' friends' was the favoured device for ensuring a flow of orders, and the arrangements appeared to work very well at the end of the war. The most productive of these friends was Lord Pirrie, chairman of six companies including Harland and Wolff, and director of 27 others including John Brown and Co.[9] This link derived from 1907 when John Browns interchanged a substantial shareholding with Harland and Wolff, by which Lord Pirrie held 61,111 ordinary and 4,000 preference shares in John Brown and Company.[10] The influence of this connection was remarkable. Clydebank laid down twelve merchant vessels between December 1918 and December 1920: seven were for the Royal Mail[11] Group of companies and were directly attributable to the berth booking agreement with Lord Pirrie.[12] In addition the Cunard agreement to book a large and an intermediate berth for ten and five years respectively yielded two large passenger liners, the *Franconia* and the *Alaunia*.

Although these agreements were formally negotiated and signed, they carried few penalties if the conditions were not fulfilled. The Cunard agreement was typical in that it obliged the steamship company to 'place or procure to be placed . . . orders for the building of such numbers of steamships as shall be required to keep the said berths continuously occupied'.[13] But if Cunard failed in this undertaking, Brown's only recourse was to 'be at liberty to take orders for other vessels and proceed with their construction on these reserved berths as if this agreement had not been entered into'.[14] The Clydebank managing director, Sir Thomas Bell, appreciated the weakness but considered it 'unwise to take up too legal an

attitude with Mr. Booth, in view of the fact that he has got both
Vickers and Swan Hunter to accept similar agreements'.[15] This
type of arrangement was clearly an advantage to builder and ship-
owner alike in buoyant conditions; but in the downswing the attempt
to manipulate the market to protect the order book proved to be
beyond the strength of the contracts and the ability of 'friends' to
make effective. Shipowners miscalculated the future just as badly
as shipbuilders, pouring orders on to slipways in 1919, but already
sensing the misjudgment by early 1920. Even as the keel was being
laid for the second Cunarder, the *Alaunia*, in April 1920, the Company was sounding out John Browns on the cancellation of the
berth allocation contract, 'in view of the extraordinary high costs of
shipbuilding and the disappointingly slow deliveries of ships'.[16]
Since John Browns felt themselves 'probably one of the worst
offenders' in this respect, it was agreed to relieve Cunard of their
obligation for a period of two years from the date of launch of the
two vessels under construction.[17]

One apparently sound association seemed suddenly insecure and
worse was to follow. In the collapsing conditions of 1921 Cunard
went so far as to suggest the cancellation of the *Alaunia*, deeming it
cheaper to meet the penalty costs involved than to continue construction.[18] In the end however, work was suspended on both
Cunarders. Work suspension was in fact the typical reaction to the
crisis, and was normally at the request of the owner. By mid-1921,
the two Cunarders were suspended, work on two of Lord Pirrie's
vessels was stopped and two proceeding at half pace. One berth was
already vacant, and work proceeded normally on only one contract.[19] The industry had abruptly entered conditions of depressed
demand from which it only emerged twice into what J. M. Reid
described as 'blinks'[20] of sunlight in 1926–8 and 1936–8 in the long
period between the wars.

Although Clydebank was as deeply affected by the sharp contraction of 1921 as other yards, its stocked-up order book protected it
till 1923. But by then its berths were emptying and Sir Thomas Bell
wrote in desperation to Lord Pirrie, seeking an order and reminding
him that he had requisitioned four of Brown's eight berths in 1919
and that Browns were 'given to understand that these might be
required for at least five or six years'.[21] Clydebank was seeking a
contract at 'whatever prices are obtainable' but Pirrie could only
reply that 'you can rely on me to bear you in mind if anything turns
up'. In extreme conditions, even a man of Lord Pirrie's influence
could not offer Clydebank any protection from the forces of the
marketplace. Fortunately the links with the Orient Company and
the Canadian Pacific Railway Company did provide some relief.
The *Oronsay* was laid down for the Orient Company in 1923, and
two Canadian Pacific vessels the following year. But after that the
pipe ran dry. The Clydebank yard did not gain another Orient
vessel throughout the interwar period, and the Canadian Pacific
agreement was terminated in February 1926.[22] By that time, too,

Lord Pirrie's death in 1924 had removed the connection with the Royal Mail Group, the Cunard agreement had been quietly forgotten, and the Coventry Syndicate agency had expired at its full term in 1924 without delivering a single order to Clydebank. To make matters worse, the link with the Admiralty had been abruptly ruptured in 1919 with the cancellation of five destroyers; ten years were to pass before another British naval vessel was to be laid down at Clydebank.

As the links with 'builders' friends' dissolved, John Browns found themselves plunged into an environment of scarce orders and fierce competition. Inevitably this placed pressure on costs and forced the Clydebank management, like others, to seek their orders by other means. As price and early delivery became the determinants, Browns found that the main area of flexibility open to them lay in varying their tendering practices in direct proportion to the urgency with which an order was desired. This was a uniform response in the industry and while participating in the dog-fight, Sir Thomas Bell could only comment regretfully that 'each of the larger firms in turn, when short of work, make a plunge, taking an important contract with practically no charges, and the result of this is that the market price on which owners appear to base estimates of what new construction will cost, is fictitiously low.'[23] In the immediate post-war boom tenders normally included costs of material and labour for hull, machinery and fittings, together with a proportion of yard overhead charges, and a percentage varying from $7\frac{1}{2}$ to 10 per cent of cost for profit. The contract was normally paid for in instalments, either by time or by work stage in the course of construction; some owners, like Cunard, simply paid each instalment in cash. But these conditions did not last. By May 1920 Cunard had changed to payment by bills, and by the end of the year owners were asking for verbal quotes on a fixed price basis.[24] The pattern was quickly set for the next two decades. A buyer's market with fixed price contracts, extended payment facilities by bills, and prices were cut to the bone.

The Clydebank tendering records reveal the extent of the difficulties facing an important shipbuilder in these years. In the entire decade, 1919-28 (Table II), John Browns tendered on 221 occasions for merchant vessels; the yard had 26 accepted, a success rate of under 12 per cent. Twenty-three of these 26 orders were obtained between 1922 and 1928. In contrast to the position before 1921, all were at fixed prices; moreover the tender records show only six of the contracts including any element of charges. Only one had a portion included for profit at a rate of 0·5 per cent. Without exception, the vessels were to be paid for by bills over lengthy periods requiring Clydebank to seek extensive overdraft facilities from its bankers. Even ships begun in the more benign conditions before 1921 were caught up in the changed circumstances; bills on the Elder Dempster vessels laid down in 1920 were not finally paid until 1929, and had been outstanding for nearly eight years.

TABLE II

Record of Tendering, Clydebank Shipyard, 1919–38

| Year ending 31 December | Merchant Vessels | Accepted | *Nos. of Tenders Sent Out* Naval Vessels | Accepted | Total Accepted |
|---|---|---|---|---|---|
| 1919 | 10 | 1 | 19 | 0 | 1 |
| 1920 | 2 | 0 | 2 | 0 | 0 |
| 1921 | 8 | 2 | 6 | 1* | 3* |
| 1922 | 28 | 4 | 6 | 0 | 4 |
| 1923 | 52 | 6 | 0 | 0 | 6 |
| 1924 | 29 | 4 | 6 | 0 | 4 |
| 1925 | 41 | 3 | 3 | 2 | 5 |
| 1926 | 29 | 2 | 9 | 0 | 2 |
| 1927 | 12 | 0 | 3 | 2 | 2 |
| 1928 | 10 | 4 | 4 | 2 | 6 |
| 1929 | 6 | 1 | 1 | 0 | 1 |
| 1930 | 14 | 1 | 3 | 0 | 1 |
| 1931 | 5 | 0 | 0 | 0 | 0 |
| 1932 | 3 | 0 | 10 | 4 | 4 |
| 1933 | 8 | 1 | 7 | 1 | 2 |
| 1934 | 1 | 0 | 7 | 1 | 1 |
| 1935 | 14 | 3 | 13 | 2 | 5 |
| 1936 | 6 | 1 | 4 | 3 | 4 |
| 1937 | 1 | 0 | 11 | 5 | 5 |
| 1938 | 5 | 1 | 7 | 1 | 2 |
|  | 284 | 34 | 121 | 24 | 58 |

1* naval vessel cancelled

| | | | | | |
|---|---|---|---|---|---|
| 1919–28 | 221 | 26 | 58 | 7* | 33 |
| 1929–38 | 63 | 8 | 63 | 17 | 25 |

*Source:* Compiled from John Brown & Co., Clydebank, Tender Books 1919–38, UCS1/74/7–11

Tendering for orders in such conditions was a risky business, the gamble taken by the builder being that on fixed price contracts, containing minimal or no charges, efficient working and possible reductions in labour and material costs would enable him to deliver the vessel at less than the contracted price. Such risk taking was not always successful. In Brown's case, substantial losses were made on eight of the 23 contracts taken on between 1922–8. In another twelve cases the margin of profit was under three per cent, and usually less than half this, while on the remaining three vessels, profits ranged from five to twelve per cent. This was a disastrous six years for the yard, the net loss on the 23 contracts being over £211,000. Indeed on three vessels for the New Zealand Shipping Company, the loss was £280,000, indicating the pressure the yard was under to take orders on any terms, and the mistakes that could ensue. The power of the buyer was well illustrated in this instance, for Browns found themselves having trouble with the owners' consultants 'to whose rapacity there appears to be no limits'.[25] The consultants excelled themselves in applying a specification which Browns found to be an 'extraordinary document, full of subtle phrases and conditions'. Bell commented wryly that 'it would appear that its compiler . . . has acquired an unenviable notoriety in this connection, but unfortunately for us we were not aware of this when entering into the Contract'.[26] The losses here were compounded by a confusion over specifications which resulted in serious alterations in the stability conditions which had to be carried out at Brown's expense;[27] but the basic source of weakness lay in scarce orders, stringent contract conditions, fierce competition and price cutting.

It was this combination of circumstances which drove shipbuilders to a new approach to their problems. Individual action and bilateral agreements appeared powerless. The pressures were growing in favour of co-operative action on an industry basis, the outcome of which was the Shipbuilding Conference in 1928. The Conference aimed at three objectives. To co-operate to remove unfair conditions in contracts; to act as a confidential pool to which firms would supply details of tenders, and, if members requested, to arrange meetings between tenderers on specific contracts to decide on minimal acceptable conditions; third, to develop an information service for the industry, and prepare schemes to assist the members in their adjustment to the commercial situation.[28] The birth pangs of this organisation were protracted and painful, the necessity for group action being only slowly appreciated by a strongly individualistic industry. Brown's correspondence with the steering committee, and with their London agent, clearly reveals the internal conflicts. Browns were committed to the arrangements, but were hesitant concerning entry till their main competitors also agreed to be parties.

The discussions on the idea of a Conference began in April 1927, but the formal constitution of the group came only in April 1928. Even then it was only at the end of 1928 that Browns, Vickers and Cammell Laird agreed to join provisionally, without signature of the covenant, for a trial period to test the scheme in operation. The critical areas of difference surrounded the proposals for pooled tenders, the idea of adding additional sums in tenders to cover the costs of unsuccessful tenderers, and the fear that shipowners would regard such arrangements as collusive price-increasing. Browns were particularly sensitive to this since pressure was being placed on them to agree to a pooled tender on a proposed CPR liner in 1928. The pool arrangement was such as not only to provide for reimbursement of costs on unsuccessful tenders, but to place every tenderer on an equal footing by dissolving any special links between builder and shipping line. As Sir Thomas Bell made plain, 'our rivals are clearly wishing us to come out of our specially entrenched position and to consider them on an equality with ourselves, and this can easily happen if we allow ourselves to be lured out by them.'[29] Browns also felt that once pooling was begun more firms would attempt to be invited to tender for every contract 'in view of the pickings to be made' and 'any pooling will really come out of the pockets of the successful firm'.[30] In the particular case of the CPR Bell did not think he could afford, 'for the sake of good comradeship, tell our rivals how thoroughly we are in with the CPR . . . [a position] which has caused me years and years of scheming and thought.'[31]

How far Clydebank was involved is clear from the construction records. In spite of the fact that the tri-partite arrangement of Browns, Fairfield and Harland and Wolff was discontinued in 1926, Browns obtained no fewer than five contracts from the CPR between 1927 and 1928. Understandably Browns was unwilling to relinquish such an advantageous position. It is clear that other shipbuilders had similar entrenched positions, yet the pressure on contract conditions and costs of multiple tendering progressively drove them toward working in co-ordinating pools. By the end of 1928 these were working effectively on a voluntary job-contract basis, on the pattern of informal co-operation which some builders had adopted on occasion in earlier years. Although the Conference specifically excluded warships from its operation, the naval builders found it convenient to operate a similar scheme informally, adding it to the rota arrangements previously agreed with the aid of the Admiralty in November 1926.[32] Consequently Browns found themselves at 1 January 1931 in the position of being entitled to receive £33,000 in tender reimbursements from successful tenderers party to the pool arrangements, while at the same time being liable to payments of £77,500 for the same purpose.[33] These types of mutual assistance and protection schemes involving tendering conditions and costs were later formally adopted on an industry wide basis. Among the more significant was of course the creation of National Shipbuilders Security Ltd. in 1930, with the aim of tackling the unused capacity in the industry in the hope of spreading work more effectively among a smaller number of yards. Clydebank was a direct beneficiary of this body when its first purchase and closure was Beardmore's Dalmuir yard, one of Brown's main rivals in naval and passenger construction on the Clyde.

The harsh conditions of the 1920s pushed the industry hesitantly toward more co-operative action. In theory this should have been a broad support to the individual firms, protecting them from the worst of the predatory actions of shipowners and the self-destroying, uncontrolled competition of their own number. In practice, the conditions affecting the Clydebank yard show that these hopes were not fully realised in the 1930s.

While the 1920s had been difficult years for shipbuilders, the decade 1929 to 1938 brought unprecedented problems. Tendering for scarce orders had been vigorous in the 1920s; in the 1930s with almost no new orders coming forward, competition became fiercer still. That this should be the case was not surprising. In the year ending March 1931, the Shipbuilders Employers Federation reported that only ten yards in the entire United Kingdom had started on new orders, and 25 had suspended their staffs and closed temporarily.[34] Indeed in the eight years December 1930 to December 1937, the entire production of British yards, allowing for an adjustment to include naval tonnage, averaged only 750,000 tons per year, or 30 per cent of the total plant and berth capacity. Merchant tonnage averaged only 630,000 tons, a mere 25 per cent of capacity.[35]

The threat of widespread yard closures hung over the industry in the early 1930s, and John Browns came to the verge of this in September 1930. Following the launch of a destroyer all eight berths lay empty, and not a single order was on the books. Utter despondency was only avoided because the contract for the giant Cunarder, eventually to be the *Queen Mary*, had been promised since May. But uncertainty over the insurance cover, and the extent of government assistance, delayed the final signing of the contract till 1 December. It is difficult to exaggerate the importance of this contract for Clydebank. Without it the yard would probably have had to close; it had already been without work for three months. Without the £250,000 in advance instalments which Cunard paid John Browns on Boxing Day, the Clydebank overdraft with the Union Bank would have deteriorated to £300,000, 50 per cent beyond the normal limit. Moreover the contract represented between three and four years' work in an industry saturated with unemployment and unused capacity.

Unfortunately the relief was to be temporary. All work ceased on 12 December 1931 when Cunard's chairman had to inform Clydebank that 'the Discount Market is out of action and the Banks will not take its place. Neither the government nor the Bank of England will come to Cunard's aid.'[36] Work was not to be resumed till 3 April 1934, two years and four months later, on the conclusion of the Cunard-White Star merger and the granting of government financial assistance to complete the liner. Throughout the period of idleness it was Cunard who paid for maintenance, inspection and continuous painting of the stranded hull. John Browns, like so many of their neighbours, had to sit idly by and wait for better days. Not that the yard management did not try for other orders; it did, but in the five years 1930–4 Clydebank gained only two merchant contracts, one of which was for the Cunarder. After their bitter experience in the 1920s, Clydebank eschewed orders whose prices covered nothing but material and labour, being convinced that such contracts 'became solely a liability instead of an asset, and the resultant losses can best be avoided by keeping the works empty'.[37] This they did, and this was the response of one yard to the harshness of the conditions in the early 1930s.

Indeed the tendering practice of Clydebank was much more cautious in the 1930s than in the previous decade. Between 1929 and 1938, Browns tendered for merchant vessels on only 63 occasions (Table II) as against 221 in the previous period. They gained only eight contracts as against 26 in the 1920s; but in each case, in contrast to the 1920s, there was a modest inclusion of charges at an

average rate of just under ten per cent of cost, half the rate of the
boom years of 1919–21. This was sufficient to ensure modest profits
on each contract, even though inadequate to keep the entire yard
fully occupied. It is in the context of only eight orders in ten years
that the significance of the Cunard connection is evident. The contract value of the other six vessels was £3·5 million; with the two
Cunarders it was £11·8 million.

Even at this rate, the workload of eight merchant vessels in
eight berths over ten years indicates the weakness of the shipbuilders'
market in the 1930s. Yet John Browns could probably support this
situation more comfortably than many rivals. The long dormant
outlet for Clydebank skills, the Admiralty, revived its naval construction programme in 1932–3. This together with the operation
of the warship builders' rota delivered a regular supply of naval
work to Browns from 1932 onward (Table II). The importance of
this connection, like that with Cunard, is again difficult to over-
estimate. In the 1920s, from 1919 to 1928, Clydebank received only
seven naval contracts, one of which was cancelled within a few
months of commencement. But in stark contrast to merchant orders
at the same time, all the naval orders included an allowance for
charges and profit, averaging 15 to 17 per cent of cost, in comparison
with 23 or 24 per cent during the First World War. All the orders
produced a profit at rates of between three and eleven per cent,
and few as they were, they made the difference between survival and
failure for the yard in the 1920s.

In the 1930s, naval orders once more became a transfusion of
profitable work for the ailing Clydebank yard. Seventeen orders
were obtained between 1932 and 1938. In these, the proportion of
charges and profit included in the cost was 25 per cent, back to the
level common in naval contracts during the First World War. Again,
all registered profits for the yard. Those completed before the war
fell within the range of eight to twelve per cent over cost, while
those extending into the early years of the war attracted profits at
twice these levels. The contract value of these seventeen orders was
£11·1 million. Consequently naval work represented about half the
value of all ship construction at Clydebank in the 1930s.[38]

John Brown's experience in the market place for ships highlights the problems confronting every shipbuilder between the wars.
Sensible arrangements with shipowners to keep berths occupied
dissolved in the weak demand situation that persisted, with only
brief interludes, from 1921 to 1938. The extended capacity of the
industry fostered fierce competition for orders which could only
be obtained on the most stringent of conditions affecting price, construction, delivery and payment. In a buyer's market tendering,
far from being an attempt to plan a steady order book, deteriorated
into a device of procurement for survival. Charges and profit
margins were pruned ruthlessly, to the extent that the viability of
yards was threatened. Clydebank was fortunate: in the end, residual
relationships with Cunard and the Admiralty were resuscitated

and saved the yard from extinction. The attempts at industry wide co-operation were an encouragement, but the short run benefits were slender. In the troubled conditions between the wars, it seems that the external situation of weak demand and fierce foreign pricing was beyond the control of either individual or corporate action by British shipbuilders. Survival for Clydebank, as for most yards, meant coping with unstable and weak order books, operating at low load factors, and somehow withstanding the pressures of occasional losses and regularly low profits.

### The Production Cost Problem

The production problem was essentially one of containing costs within the limits set in the estimate for any vessel. Since contracts were frequently gained at prices which left no margin for error, the problem was particularly severe between the wars. In trying to meet this the management was set the task of controlling costs arising from materials, labour, and charges. If these got out of control they ate into the fourth component in the tender or contract price, the margin left over for profit, where that had been included.

Since the construction of a vessel involved the assembly of a wide variety of components, shipbuilders attempted to internalise the production of as many of the parts as possible. Thus the Clydebank yard, as part of the John Brown-Thomas Firth steel and engineering empire had direct access to special steels, armour plate, forgings, machined parts and other supplies. But by being so linked, the Clydebank yard did not participate directly in the extension of Clyde shipbuilding control over Scottish steelworks in the 1920s.[39] Consequently in two critical periods 1920–1 and 1937–8, the yard had more difficulty than some of its neighbours in obtaining regular supplies of steel. One temporary solution adopted in 1920 was the direct import of over 4,000 tons of American steel to enable contracts to proceed.[40] On the other hand, Clydebank stabilised its position in the supply of rivets, bolts and nuts by exchanging £25,000 of shares with the North West Rivet Bolt and Nut Company in December 1919.[41] In addition, Clydebank possessed its own large engine and boilerworks, ensuring a phased delivery of machinery as the construction of hulls proceeded.

Yet, in spite of such arrangements even a complex organisation like Clydebank had to concede that the costs and deliveries of the bulk of components were largely outside its control. These costs could be calculated but not directly influenced. Clydebank shared this vulnerability, in greater or smaller measure, with every other shipyard. In contrast, wages and charges were more within the manipulation of the management.

Since the direct wages included in the costs of constructing a vessel varied from roughly a quarter to one third of total cost, it is not surprising that in conditions of price competitiveness John Browns should have been concerned to reduce labour costs. By 1920 the average weekly wage at Clydebank was 225 per cent above the

## TABLE III

### John Brown & Co., Clydebank
### Average Employment and Earnings per Week, 1914–38

| Year | Average No of Men per Week | Average Pay Bill | | | Average Wages per Man per Week | | |
|---|---|---|---|---|---|---|---|
| | | £ | s | d | £ | s | d |
| 1914 | 9,260 | 16,947 | 16 | 2 | 1 | 16 | 7 |
| 1915 | 10,088 | 24,050 | 4 | 2 | 2 | 7 | 8 |
| 1916 | 10,031 | 24,166 | 8 | 6 | 2 | 8 | 2 |
| 1917 | 9,444 | 25,868 | 6 | 5 | 2 | 14 | 9 |
| 1918 | 9,209 | 32,894 | 10 | 4 | 3 | 11 | 5 |
| 1919 | 9,049 | 33,520 | 8 | 4 | 3 | 14 | 1 |
| 1920 | 9,297 | 38,072 | 16 | 6 | 4 | 1 | 11 |
| 1921 | 6,322 | 23,274 | 6 | 1 | 3 | 13 | 8 |
| 1922 | 3,653 | 9,883 | 2 | 2 | 2 | 14 | 1 |
| 1923 | 3,404 | 8,219 | 10 | 3 | 2 | 8 | 4 |
| 1924 | 5,181 | 13,686 | 15 | 0 | 2 | 12 | 10 |
| 1925 | 4,353 | 12,341 | 1 | 6 | 2 | 16 | 8 |
| 1926 | 4,150 | 10,724 | 8 | 0 | 2 | 11 | 8 |
| 1927 | 5,372 | 14,566 | 8 | 9 | 2 | 14 | 3 |
| 1928 | 7,626 | 21,743 | 1 | 11 | 2 | 17 | 0 |
| 1929 | 6,675 | 18,428 | 12 | 7 | 2 | 15 | 3 |
| 1930 | 5,085 | 13,430 | 15 | 1 | 2 | 12 | 10 |
| 1931 | 3,556 | 9,484 | 13 | 7 | 2 | 13 | 4 |
| 1932 | 422 | 1,279 | 4 | 7 | 3 | 0 | 7 |
| 1933 | 675 | 1,847 | 10 | 5 | 2 | 14 | 9 |
| 1934 | 3,758 | 10,366 | 13 | 9 | 2 | 15 | 2 |
| 1935 | 5,381 | 14,504 | 8 | 4 | 2 | 13 | 11 |
| 1936 | 5,617 | 16,172 | 2 | 3 | 2 | 17 | 7 |
| 1937 | 6,198 | 18,645 | 2 | 1 | 3 | 0 | 2 |
| 1938 | 8,075 | 25,657 | 5 | 4 | 3 | 3 | 7 |

*Source:* Compiled from Abstract Wages Books, John Brown & Co., Clydebank, 1914–1938. UCS/1/52/1–6

1914 rate (Table III), and since materials prices had escalated proportionately, Browns could not deliver a vessel at less than 3·5 times the 1913 cost.[42] At the outset Browns were resigned to continuing wage increases, but the break of the boom in early 1921 provided the first opportunity for applying wage reductions. Even then Browns were not free agents. Like other yards they negotiated yard rates for different grades of work, but these were minor variations on the base rates established between the Shipbuilding Employers Federation and the trades unions. Moreover shipbuilders felt that they could only enforce wage reductions if those employed in 'protected industries', that is those whose jobs were not substantially affected by the need to export or live with foreign competition, could be similarly reduced. In turn this depended upon a reduction in the costs of living to protect the real value of the shipyard workers' wages.

The shipbuilders felt that their freedom of action in this respect was seriously limited because of 'the manner in which all the necessaries of life . . . are controlled by the network of rings which maintain a marvellous uniformity of prices all over the United Kingdom, and this operates most prejudicially against wage reductions'.[43] This was Bell's view in late 1921, even though substantial wage reductions, together with an easing in materials prices, had cut the cost of their ships to 2·5 times the pre-war price.[44] Two years later he still argued that 'from the way things are going Great Britain does appear to constitute a Shopkeepers "Paradise", and in their own quiet way they constitute a greater hindrance to recovery of trade than the extremist section of the workers.'[45]

This was also the view of the 'Joint Inquiry into Foreign Competition and Conditions in the Shipbuilding Industry' in 1926 which presented tables based on Ministry of Labour data to show the lesser reductions in 'protected' industry wages. The report made the further allegation that prices of many items required by shipbuilders 'were maintained at their unreasonable figure through the operation of rings and price-fixing associations'.[46] This outburst was provoked by the dismay surrounding contracts for Furness Withy vessels going to a German yard at £153,000 per ship compared with the lowest British tender of £213,000, a margin of 28 per cent in favour of Germany. No charges had been included in the British tender forcibly making the point, to Clydebank and other British yards, that even the most stringent reduction and control of wages was unlikely to withstand the challenge of subsidised foreign competition. The average weekly wage at Clydebank had by then been reduced to £2. 11s. 8d., only 63 per cent of the rate prevailing in 1920. Indeed the policy of wage reduction was extraordinarily successful; from 1922 to 1936 Clydebank wages varied only slightly between 60 and 74 per cent of the 1920 figure.

Wages were clearly pulled down and stabilised, but by themselves they were not effective in pulling down the price of a vessel below continental levels. The other element which management could adjust was charges. As the name implies, charges were the costs of paying indirect wages in drawing offices, to management staff, timekeepers, the outlay on repair and maintenance of plant and equipment and so on. If these elements were not covered by earnings in contracts the yard faced losses in the short term, and falling into disrepair in the longer view. Charges were therefore added on strictly proportional terms of up to 45 per cent of the total direct wage bill of each contract, and consequently added substantially to the overall cost of the vessel. Savings could be made by cutting down on staff, closing surplus capacity in drawing offices and the like, but beyond a certain point the reduction of these facilities would seriously impair the efficiency of the yard as a whole. The men on the berths required the support of a whole range of 'indirect' facilities.

Browns did dramatically reduce their annual general charges.

Excluding a £100,000 contribution to Head Office charges and a two-fifths responsibility for Debenture interest and bank overdrafts, Clydebank charges in 1920 were £600,000 per year. Since these were directly related to the general pay bill this meant that the yard had to have a direct wage bill of at least £2·7 million to support these charges. When the average weekly pay bill was reduced by forty per cent between 1920 and 1921, this meant that charges had to be reduced in like proportion. By 1928, Clydebank's general charges were down to £200,000, but as Sir Thomas Bell said, they had to earn that 'or go under'. Charges were indeed the critical element in the creation of profit on a contract. Without the recovery of charges no profit could accrue. As we have seen, the pressure of events in the 1920s was such that Clydebank did tender for many contracts with minimal or no charges element included, with the result that serious losses were made between 1922–28.

The recovery of charges clearly required a high utilisation of capacity to generate a large direct wage bill over which minimum charges could be spread without seriously increasing the cost of individual vessels. In 1930, Bell reported that on full charges, Clydebank would require about £4 million worth of work per year, and even this would only leave a small margin of £15–20,000 for profit and £10,000 for depreciation.[47] But the average value of work done from 1919 to 1938 was barely half that. In fact in tonnage terms the work load in relation to capacity taken at 100,000 tons per year was 38 per cent between 1919 and 1938, a bare 19 per cent from 1929–33, and 48 per cent between 1934 and 1938. The inability to build up the work load clearly nullified the benefits which should have accrued from the control and reduction of wages and charges. This had serious consequences for the prospects of profit and the planning of investment.

### The Clydebank Profit Record

One indicator of the achievement of Clydebank in these years is its profit record, but the assessment of profit is not an easy one to make. No separate Clydebank profit returns appear before 1934 in the available records, the contributions to head office being obscure before that time.

On the other hand we can say something of the profit and loss position on individual contracts, but it is dangerous to attribute figures compiled in this way to individual financial years. Ships take a long time to build, profit and loss is ascribed to each contract in progress in any financial year. Profits made along the way can still be negated by a final loss, and losses can be made during construction due to strikes or other unforeseen circumstances, while the contract in the end might still record a profit.

Bearing these cautions in mind, something meaningful can still be said. From 1919 to 1938 inclusive, Clydebank launched 46 merchant vessels, twelve of which made a loss. The total cost of construction was £31·7 million and the gross profit £965,469, a modest three per cent on cost. In addition, 28 naval vessels were launched at a cost of £9·3 million. These earned profits of £870,789, some 9·3 per cent on cost. The overall position was 74 launches at a cost of £41 million and gross profits of £1·8 million, a margin of just 4·4 per cent.[48] While these figures should be treated only as a general approximation, the pattern is nevertheless clear. Naval work was safer and more profitable than merchant work. While valued at under 23 per cent of total contract costs, the naval construction earned over 47 per cent of profits and undoubtedly kept the yard alive between the wars.

Fragmentary information in the Board papers and minute books also gives some idea of the incidence of profit over the years. In the twelve years from March 1919 to March 1931 Clydebank transferred £1·2 million to Sheffield for profit and loss and depreciation.[49] Unfortunately this cannot be broken down further. No figures exist for 1932 or 1933, but the loss for the year ending March 1934 was £69,000. Since the yard was virtually closed in each of the two previous years the losses could scarcely have been less. Thereafter net profits, after deduction for charges, depreciation etc, are known. A mere £3,372 for the year to March 1935, £99,000 the following year, £187,000 to March 1937, and £148,000 to March 1938. Net profits of over £437,000 in four years. Since about £78,000 was then being deducted for charges, depreciation etc., this places the gross profits in the area of £750,000.

It is in a sense remarkable that any shipyard could earn profits in the conditions existing between the wars: but the level of profit attained reflects the degree of difficulty. Normal expectations were for profits of 7 to 10 per cent on each contract, yet the achievement during the interwar years suggests a rate of only 4 or 4·5 per cent on cost. This is about half the desired rate and is in line with the fact that Clydebank worked at under half capacity, with reduced and sometimes no charges. The price of survival was a real sacrifice, not only in wages and charges, but a low expectation of profit. In turn, this in some measure influenced the investment record.

*The Investment Record*

In the twenty years under review, gross capital outlays at Clydebank totalled £600,450; this compared with £756,000 between 1900–18.[50] Two-thirds of this £600,000 went to machinery for the yard and engine works; a fifth was allocated to shipyard property. In only two of the twenty years, 1923 and 1927, were no capital additions made (Tables IV–VI). Two aspects of this have to be explained: the general timing of the investment, and its allocation.

Two considerations strongly influenced the Clydebank management's investment decisions at the end of the war. The first was the imperative of switching from naval to merchant work; the second was the high cost of labour. Even though the order book was bulging, Browns believed heavy investment to be necessary since 'only those firms equipped with every type of labour-saving appliance and the

TABLE IV

Gross Capital Additions to Shipyard, Boiler Works, Engine Works and Dock,
1919–38; John Brown & Co., Clydebank

| Year | Capital Additions £ |
|---|---|
| 1919 | 25,555 |
| 1920 | 79,325 |
| 1921 | 208,984 |
| 1922 | 42,171 |
| 1923 | Nil |
| 1924 | 4,259 |
| 1925 | 32,012 |
| 1926 | 9,702 |
| 1927 | Nil |
| 1928 | 7,127 |
| 1929 | 20,817 |
| 1930 | 11,790 |
| 1931 | 17,740 |
| 1932 | 5,130 |
| 1933 | 1,972 |
| 1934 | 7,770 |
| 1935 | 20,987 |
| 1936 | 19,052 |
| 1937 | 45,404 |
| 1938 | 40,659 |

*Source:* Compiled from Plant and Property Registers, UCS 1/25/10–12.

TABLE V

Percentage Distribution of Total Capital Additions, Clydebank

| | 1919/23 | 1924/28 | 1929/33 | 1934/38 | 1919/38 |
|---|---|---|---|---|---|
| Total Capital Additions | £356,045 | £53,100 | £57,450 | £133,855 | £600,450 |
| Shipyard machinery | 38·5 | 29·9 | 30·5 | 27·8 | 34·6 |
| Engine Works machinery | 12·9 | 52·9 | 44·2 | 64·9 | 31·1 |
| Boiler Works machinery | 2·3 | 0·0 | 16·8 | 1·4 | 3·3 |
| General machinery | 0·8 | 9·6 | 0·2 | 2·1 | 1·8 |
| Shipyard property | 33·4 | 1·6 | 7·0 | 0·0 | 20·6 |
| Engine Works Property | 6·2 | 0·0 | 1·2 | 0·0 | 3·8 |
| Boiler Works Property | 5·7 | 0·0 | 0·0 | 0·0 | 3·3 |
| General property | 0·2 | 5·9 | 0·0 | 0·0 | 0·5 |
| Dock | 0·0 | 0·0 | 0·0 | 3·7 | 0·8 |
| | 100·00 | 99·9 | 99·9 | 99·9 | 100·0 |
| | (59·3) | (8·8) | (9·6) | (22·3) | |

*Source:* Plant and Property Registers, John Brown & Co., UCS 1/25/10–12.

most advantageous arrangements for transport of materials can hope to hold their own.'[51] In line with this conviction £356,000 was laid out between 1919 and 1923, and all but £40,000 had been taken up by April 1921. A small part of this was necessary on behalf of the merchant work in hand, but most of the outlay was a conscious long term addition to capacity, and an improvement in yard layout, facilities and efficiency. This was an investment in expectation of future expansion, but the failure of demand from 1921 fundamentally altered the prospects. A heavy investment programme, which must have appeared to be a sound management decision, was rapidly transformed into a heavy burden of overheads unsupported by adequate work. In such circumstances the momentum of investment inevitably slackened and longer views gave way to *ad hoc* measures.

The post-war investment boom soaked up sixty per cent of the entire interwar capital outlays at Clydebank. In the next ten years, 1924–33, capital additions totalled only £110,000. The overriding factor in these years was unused capacity, recently installed. New investment in this period was dominantly unavoidable outlays in connection with particular contracts. £56,000 of the £110,000 was directly linked to the contracts for the *Empress of Britain* and the *Queen Mary*, nearly £46,000 being required in berth extensions, new cranage and machinery to cope with the giant Cunarder. Only from 1935 onward, with the recovery of the naval building programme, did broader investment decisions once more prevail, £134,000 being added between 1934 and 1938. The overall pattern of expenditure between the wars must therefore be seen in terms of the anticipation of market trends in relation to existing capacity and costs, allied to demands imposed by particular contracts.

Two main allocations of capital are evident within this broad pattern. In the immediate post-war investment boom over seventy per cent of total outlay was concentrated on shipyard machinery and property. This was the big stake in modernisation and new capacity in constructional facilities which appears to have added about twenty per cent to Clydebank's tonnage capacity. Thereafter, the most persistent investment was in machinery for the engine works. This sector attracted £140,428 between 1924 and 1938, 60 per cent of all outlays on machinery, and 57 per cent of total capital invest-ment in these years. Two purposes were served by this. First the engine work capacity was gradually brought into line with tonnage capability, and secondly, as we shall see, there were important allocations to support the development of new technologies. The low level usage of the new capacity installed by 1923 clearly inhibited further large general capital outlays. Yet within that constraint there is evidence that the management were not unwilling to take the risks of further investment to support new developments.

In an industry like shipbuilding where cyclical fluctuations could encourage capital additions in upswings and then suddenly leave expensive capacity unemployed in the slump, it was important for any yard not to permit its fixed capital to become too heavy an

overhead charge on the business. Vigorous depreciation was therefore to be expected, and Clydebank made regular adjustments in
this light (Table VI). It seems clear from the company papers that
depreciation was real, transferring sums from gross profits to reserves,
throughout the 1920s. But in contrast, the deep difficulties of 1929–35
appear to have made the depreciation allowances a book-keeping
exercise, or as Sir Thomas Bell stated 'purely as a paper figure'.[52]
Real depreciation seems to have been applied again thereafter. In
sum, £383,000 of the £600,000 outlay was written off in real terms
during the period.

The Board papers are unequivocal that the funds for investment
came from profits. Clearly the bulk of the interwar outlays drew on
the profits accumulated during the first world war. It is doubtful
if they could have been entirely drawn from current profits without
extensive resort to bank loans. There may have been an element
of this concealed in Clydebank's relationship to and dependence for
investment approval on Sheffield, but the Clydebank records of
themselves do not indicate any such arrangement. Simply measured
against gross profits at Clydebank, the capital outlay between the
wars appears to have represented about one-third.

### The Technology Problem

The diesel engine and electric welding represented the new challenges in propulsion and construction in shipbuilding between the
wars. Yet it should not be forgotten that the reduction geared
turbine was also a relative newcomer, especially significant to the
builder of large passenger and naval vessels requiring large pro-
pulsive power. Consequently Clydebank attempted to make provision on all three fronts in these years.

Clydebank first entered the turbine business by taking up
licences from Parsons in 1905 and from the American Curtis Turbine
Company in 1909.[53] Parsons applied reduction gearing commercially
in 1910, and Browns developed this on the basis of the Curtis
turbine. By 1913, engines developed under this licence were being
installed as Brown-Curtis turbines. These were to become the main
basis of the Clydebank engine works' output, though Parsons types
were regularly built on licence. The newness of the development
can be seen in that in the whole period from 1905, when Browns
first installed a direct drive turbine in the *Carmania*, to 1918, the
Clydebank yard built 58 sets of turbines. After 1914, only one of
thirty turbines built was not a geared version and Browns had established a sound reputation in this field.

The other innovation was the diesel. In 1914 only 0·5 per cent
of the world's tonnage was powered by the internal combustion
engine, a mere 234,000 tons. By 1920, this had climbed to 938,160
tons, 4·8 per cent of world tonnage. Six years later the diesel powered
tonnage was 4·27 million, 6·5 per cent of the world's fleet. The
signs were unmistakable, and in 1926 the United Kingdom was

## TABLE VI
### Capital Additions and Depreciation, Clydebank, 1919–38
(£ Sterling)

**A MACHINERY**

| Period | Shipyard | | Engine Works | | Boiler Works | | General | | All Machinery | |
|---|---|---|---|---|---|---|---|---|---|---|
| | Additions | Deprec. | Additions | Deprec. | Additions | Deprec. | Additions | Deprec. | Additions | Deprec. |
| 1919–23 | 137,236 | 81,166 | 46,126 | 43,198 | 8,393 | 10,186 | 2,782 | 21,243 | 194,537 | 155,793 |
| 1924–28 | 15,869 | 41,254 | 28,123 | 22,679 | — | 3,982 | 5,110 | 4,024 | 49,102 | 71,941 |
| 1929–33 | 17,505 | 26,730 | 25,382 | 19,032 | 9,673 | 3,179 | 150 | 3,067 | 52,710 | 52,008 |
| 1934–38 | 37,240 | 29,451 | 86,923 | 25,192 | 1,846 | 3,998 | 2,846 | 2,746 | 128,855 | 61,387 |
| | 207,850 | 178,601 | 186,554 | 110,101 | 19,912 | 21,345 | 10,888 | 31,080 | 425,204 | 341,129 |

**B PROPERTY**

| Period | Shipyard | | Engine Works | | Boiler Works | | General | | All Property | |
|---|---|---|---|---|---|---|---|---|---|---|
| | Additions | Deprec. | Additions | Deprec. | Additions | Deprec. | Additions | Deprec. | Additions | Deprec. |
| 1919–23 | 119,101 | 20,705 | 22,020 | 9,105 | 20,173 | 4,626 | 214 | 3,462 | 161,508 | 37,898 |
| 1924–28 | 832 | 12,252 | — | 4,032 | — | 1,638 | 3,166 | 1,215 | 3,998 | 19,137 |
| 1929–33 | 4,040 | 19,140 | 700 | 9,829 | — | 3,460 | — | 2,960 | 4,740 | 35,389 |
| 1934–38 | — | 17,395 | — | 8,897 | — | 3,426 | — | 2,676 | 133,855 | 32,095 |
| | 123,973 | 69,492 | 22,720 | 31,863 | 20,173 | 13,150 | 3,380 | 10,313 | 170,246 | 124,818 |

**C DOCK**

| | Additions | Deprec. |
|---|---|---|
| 1919–23 | — | 7,587 |
| 1924–28 | — | 1,421 |
| 1929–33 | — | — |
| 1934–38 | 5,000 | — |
| | 5,000 | 9,008 |

**D TOTALS**

| | Additions | Deprec. |
|---|---|---|
| 1919–23 | 356,045 | 201,278 |
| 1924–28 | 53,100 | 92,499 |
| 1929–33 | 57,450 | 87,397 |
| 1934–38 | 133,855 | 93,482 |
| | 600,450 | 474,955 |

*Source:* As for Tables IV and V

building 39 per cent of all motor vessel tonnage under construction in the world.[54]

John Brown's management was well aware of the new challenge and launched their first diesel driven vessel, the *Loch Katrine*, in 1921. The engines were supplied by Harland and Wolff, but Browns clearly regarded it as a learning exercise. The Board felt that as 'we have never had to fit up a Diesel Engine boat before, this vessel will supply us . . . with much needed information and experience'.[55] The exercise was expensive; on a vessel costing over half a million pounds, Clydebank finally made a profit of £589.

Brown's first venture into independent diesel construction was on the basis of the Cammell Laird Fullager, for which they paid a licence fee of £6,000 in 1920, and agreed to royalties of £1,000 per engine constructed.[56] This was an unhappy experiment. Two orders for the Kawasaki Dockyard company were plagued with piston ring and lubrication problems, and before the orders were completed at the end of 1923, Browns had already taken out an alternative licence for the French Sulzer Diesel.[57] The Fullager was already in operation in several vessels but ran into problems identical to those experienced on the Clydebank test bays. As Sir Thomas Bell reported 'the unfortunate results on the Brocklebank steamer *Malia* and on the *La Playa* have, I fear, practically sealed the reputation of the Cammell-Laird Fullager Engine as far as the near future is concerned.'[58] Browns decided to leave development work on the Fullager in abeyance and to push on with three different sizes of the Sulzer in the belief that this 'should equip the firm to be competitive in this field'.[59]

This decision to invest in diesel construction was a risk, for as the firm and the industry were aware, considerable costs were involved in the adoption of diesel propulsion. The two basic problems were the high initial cost of diesel engines relative to reciprocating machinery, and the much longer construction time involved. Clydebank could build the hull for a cargo vessel powered by a 3,000 hp reciprocating engine in eight or nine months, but required thirteen to fourteen months for a diesel power unit.[60] Nevertheless the management were certain that the future lay with diesels and were convinced that 'we must to a certain extent take our courage in our hands and proceed with it if we are desirous of obtaining a proper share of Diesel Engine building in the immediate future.'[61] Sulzers remained the basis of the Clydebank investment in diesels from 1923–4, but in 1932 their capacity was once more extended by the purchase of a Doxford licence, that engine having by then proved its economy and reliability.[62]

In the uncertain environment between the wars, the push into diesel construction was to an extent a gamble. The immediate pay-off would appear to be limited. In the entire period 1920 to 1938, Clydebank only built ten vessels of 110,104 tons powered by diesels. Slender as this seems it still represents 21·5 per cent of merchant tonnage delivered by John Browns in these years; this compares with 26 per cent for Britain as a whole. Significantly for the future, Clydebank delivered five merchant vessels between 1930 and 1938. Of these, only the *Queen Mary* was not diesel driven. Clydebank had certainly not neglected a new innovation, though its pattern of building large liners and warships still favoured turbines over all other types of engine.

The other departure from previous practice was electric welding. Some welding was undertaken at Clydebank during the war, but the first real step toward adopting the new technique followed on obtaining the contract for the *Queen Mary*. Increasingly favourable comment in the technical press, and successful application in other yards, particularly in Stephens of Linthouse, convinced the Board that the new technique would be advantageous. In a sense the depth of the depression provided the training ground and training time for the yard. With all work stopped Clydebank negotiated with the English Electric Company in early 1933 for the construction of a welding shop together with the installation of transformers, machines and all equipment.[63] The instruction of apprentices in the new technique was vigorously pushed ahead, and since work was slack the foremen got 'an insight into the details of electric welding which they could not possibly have had under normal circumstances'.[64]

The consequences of adopting welding were far-reaching. It was not simply a matter of purchasing a few machines. Men had to be trained, extensive new electrical installations had to be provided, covered working areas had to be extended. Moreover, welding immediately brought the yard up against the problem of increasing pre-fabrication of sections. Especially in naval construction, welding was producing sections up to ten tons in weight; most of the cranes in the yard had only a five ton lifting capacity. Consequently, by the end of 1934, still in the grip of depression, Browns had taken steps to equip four of their eight berths with ten ton cranes, and had installed welding capacity to cater for half the berths in their establishment.

It is difficult to determine the costs of investing in diesel and welding technology in the yard. Much was accomplished by phasing out obsolete boiler shop capacity and so on, simply converting existing premises to new uses. Equally, much machinery appears in the books simply notated 'for the engine works' and it is not possible to isolate the function of all the machinery and tools purchased. Nevertheless, capital outlays on both diesel and welding can be traced to a minimum of about £100,000, and it seems certain much more was involved. If Clydebank is typical of the larger yards it is doubtful that shipyard management could be criticised for failing to invest in new technology, even though they were hard pressed simply to survive in the conditions between the wars.

*Conclusions*

The Clydebank story highlights many of the major problems confronting the shipbuilding industry between the wars. Brown's

experience clearly shows the abrupt transition from boom conditions to stagnant demand, bringing in its wake the high costs of
unused capacity and the challenge of extraordinary competition.
The problem was how a firm, and an industry, could adjust to the
new situation.

As far as the individual firm is concerned, the areas of positive
response open to it were severely limited. As the Clydebank record
demonstrates, normal associations with shipowners, as stabilisers
of the order book, crumbled as shipowners sought the cheapest
builder in a buyer's market. Brown's experience also indicates that
aggressive cutprice tendering, in response, could fill the order book,
but such action threatened profitability and carried the risk of
serious losses which, if continued, could lead to eventual yard
closure. The attempts to cut costs by rigorous control of wages and
charges helped, but since the work-load remained low, the effect
was still to mortgage the future of the yard through a reduced
ability to earn and invest.

The Clydebank dilemma of heavy charges through expensive
investment in capacity, low work-load through scarce orders, and
exposure to cut-throat competition was symptomatic of the troubles
of the entire industry. Caught in the storm, the urge to retain
individuality struggled with the rationality of giving up some
freedom of action in return for the protection promised by industry
wide co-operation and collectivism. Neither Browns, nor their rivals,
deceived themselves regarding the costs and benefits of collective
measures. Tendering schemes, reductions in capacity, measures to
promote fair pricing and limit internal competition were all brought
into play as aids and supports to the individual company. But while
group action moderated domestic competition, it still left the industry
exposed to external international conditions which neither individual company nor industry based policies could entirely override.
Foreign cost advantages based on state subsidy, credit arrangements
and currency controls were beyond the power of action of Browns,
their neighbours, or their industry conference. Seen in this perspective it is difficult to envisage what response was open to the
industry other than that adopted. The pay-off was half capacity
working and half pre-war profit rates for John Browns. It is likely
that the rest of the industry fared little better. The results might
have been worse but for the bold self-imposed reductions in capacity
and controls on competition.

Judging from the Clydebank papers, shipbuilding management
lived in a world of extreme uncertainty between the wars. Decision-
taking frequently meant a choice of the least harmful course rather
than some optimum. In taking their decisions the Clydebank
management clearly operated on two time horizons. The first was
set by the contract time of ships under construction, and within
that the day-to-day problems of keeping to schedules and costs.
This was the most important level of control and attracted continuous
attention to detail. Yet, pressing as these problems were, they were

overlain by a longer management horizon. One aspect of this forward thinking was the support for a Shipbuilding Conference to cope with longer term projections of market and demand patterns. Another was the continuing debate on the direction to be taken by the firm itself. The Clydebank Board papers clearly reflect awareness of new trends.

If Clydebank is typical, then the future of the industry was not unduly discounted by doubt and uncertainty. Investment provision was made, at considerable risk, to secure the firm's position in a changing world. While it is true that British shipbuilding lost some of its giant share of world construction between the wars, Clydebank's experience suggests that conventional explanations of this trend require revision. That British yards frequently could not compete in price with continental rivals is true. But there is little evidence in the Clydebank papers to suggest that this was significantly due to inferior technology, inefficient working or outdated yard layout. Price advantages were maintained over British producers largely by subsidy and other supports. In large measure the problem of insufficient work, affecting Clydebank and other British yards, lay in depressed world demand arising out of excess tonnage in existence by 1923. Actions by firms individually and collectively could bring some adjustment to this reduced situation, but the regeneration of the industry was largely outside the control of its managers, irrespective of the effort made by them in co-operation with the workforce or with each other.

*University of Glasgow*

## NOTES

1. I would like to thank Professor S. G. Checkland, Dr. John Brown, and Miss Jean M. Verth who read an earlier draft of the paper and made many helpful comments. They are in no way responsible for the opinions expressed in the text.

2. For a discussion of this see K. J. W. Alexander and C. L. Jenkins, *Fairfield, A Study of Industrial Change* (London, 1970), 25–7.

3. For a brief discussion of Scottish shipbuilding problems in relation to the interwar experience generally, see A. Slaven, *The Development of the West of Scotland* 1750–1960 (London, 1975), 186–90.

4. Minutes of Clydebank Committee of the Board, 30 November 1916, UCS 1/1/1.

5. *Ibid.*, 1 August 1918.

6. Berth allocation agreement, John Brown and Company and the Cunard Steamship Company, 17 April 1918, UCS 1/21/138.

7. See W. H. Macrosty, *The Trust Movement in British Industry* (London, 1907), 43–6.

8. Scheme for future Syndicate procedure, 16 May 1919, UCS 1/9/5.

9. Returns of Directors, quoted in David Colville & Sons Ltd., Company Registration file, BT2/2965, West Register House, Edinburgh.

10. Cunard Letter Book No. 1, Sir Thomas Bell to Sir Percy Bates, 26 May 1930, UCS 1/16/1.

11. On the Royal Mail Group holdings see P. N. Davies and A. M. Bourn, 'Lord Kylsant and the Royal Mail', *Business History* 14, 1972.

12. John Brown and Co. (Clydebank), 'Ships Built and Particulars', UCS 1/93/40.

13. Berth Allocation agreement, John Brown and Company and the Cunard Steamship Company, 17 April 1918, UCS 1/21/138.

14. *Loc. cit.*

15. Clydebank Committee of the Board, Papers, 22 April 1918, UCS 1/21/138.

16. *Ibid.*, 25 June 1920, UCS 1/5/19.

17. *Loc. cit.*

18. Clydebank Committee of the Board, Papers, 7 April 1921, UCS 1/5/20.

19. *Ibid.*, 4 May 1921.

20. J. M. Reid: *James Lithgow, Master of Work* (London, 1964), 109–10.

21. Bell to Pirrie, 10 May 1923, UCS 1/5/22.

22. Clydebank Committee of the Board, Papers, 1 December 1926, UCS 1/5/25.

23. *Ibid.*, 1 August 1928, UCS 1/5/27.

24. *Ibid.*, 1 December 1920, UCS 1/5/19.

25. *Ibid.*, 27 April 1928, UCS 1/5/27.

26. *Ibid.*, 21 November 1928.

27. *Ibid.*, April and May 1929, passim, UCS 1/5/28.

28. Rules and Regulations of the Shipbuilding Conference, March 1928, UCS 1/9/35.

29. Bell to Captain T. E. Crease, 15 September 1928, UCS 1/9/35.

30. *Loc. cit.*

31. *Loc. cit.*

32. Bell to Crease, 14 November 1930, UCS 1/9/37.

33. Payments to be made and to be received by John Brown and Co., 1 January 1931, UCS 1/9/38.

34. Reports of the Clydebank Board, 1 May 1931, UCS 1/5/30.

35. Memorandum on Conditions now existing in the Shipbuilding Industry. Confidential report to Members by the Shipbuilding Conference, December 1938, UCS 1/9/79.

36. Sir Percy Bates to Sir Thomas Bell, 1 December 1931, UCS 1/5/30.

37. Clydebank Committee of the Board, Reports, 27 April 1932, UCS 1/5/31.

38. Data on tenders and prices compiled from Tender Books, John Brown and Co., Clydebank, UCS 1/74/7–11. Information on charges and profits prepared from Abstract Cost Books, John Brown's UCS 1/5/19.

39. Clydebank was indirectly involved through the exchange of shares between Harland and Wolff and John Brown & Co. by which Lord Pirrie and Lord Aberconway took directorships on each others boards. Moreover when Harland and Wolff acquired the shares of Colvilles in 1919, John Brown & Co. had a small holding of 4,500 ordinary shares in the steel company.

40. Clydebank Committee of the Board, 29 June 1920, UCS 1/5/19.

41. *Ibid.*, 18 December 1919.

42. *Ibid.*, 23 August 1920, UCS 1/5/19.

43. *Ibid.*, 1 September 1921, UCS 1/5/20.

44. *Loc. cit.*

45. Clydebank Committee of the Board, 26 September 1923, UCS 1/5/22.

46. Shipbuilding Employers' Federation and Shipyard Trade Unions; Report of the Joint Inquiry into Foreign Competition and Conditions in the Shipbuilding Industry (1926), 19.

47. Clydebank Committee of the Board, 22 January 1934, UCS 1/5/29.

48. Figures compiled from Profit and Loss Contract Registers, Abstract Cost Books, Progressive Cost Books, and Instalment Records. The data is not all compiled on the same basis and the figures for profit should be treated only as a rough approximation.

49. Clydebank Committee of the Board, 23 March 1931, UCS 1/2/1.

50. Compiled from Shipyard Valuation Books, 1900–38, UCS 1/25/10–12.

51. Clydebank Committee of the Board, 25 October 1919, UCS 1/15/8.

52. *Ibid.*, 27 March 1935, UCS 1/5/34.

53. Turbine engines manufactured under licence for the Parsons Marine Steam Turbine Co. Ltd., UCS 1/105/2. Record of Curtis Turbines Manufactured by John Brown and Co. Ltd., UCS 1/105/1.

54. Compiled from data in *Survey of the Metal Industries* ch. IV, Shipbuilding, 388–9, 405.

55. Clydebank Committee of the Board, 1 September 1921, UCS 1/5/20.

56. Minutes of the Clydebank Board, 29 April 1920.

57. Clydebank Committee of the Board, 1 March 1923, UCS 1/5/22.

58. *Ibid.*, 29 November 1923, UCS 1/5/22.

59. *Ibid.*, 20 February 1924, UCS 1/5/23.

60. *Ibid.*, 4 February 1924, UCS 1/5/23.

61. *Ibid.*, 1 November 1924, UCS 1/5/23.

62. Minutes of the Clydebank Board, 2 November 1932.

63. Clydebank Committee of the Board, 2 February 1933, UCS 1/5/32.

64. *Ibid.*, 28 April 1933, UCS 1/5/32.

NB. UCS is the notation reference for records of the constituent companies of the former Upper Clyde Shipbuilders. The records, under the care and superintendence of the Keeper of the Records of Scotland, are now deposited in the business record collection of the Economic History Department of the University of Glasgow, and in Strathclyde Regional Archives.

# THE VICISSITUDES OF A BRITISH AIRCRAFT COMPANY: HANDLEY PAGE LTD. BETWEEN THE WARS

by PETER FEARON

The growth of firms which formed the backbone of the British aircraft industry has been virtually ignored by business historians. Responsibility for this neglect must, however, be borne by the companies which have shown such a great reluctance to allow scholars access to their company records. Indeed the only material available for inspection is contained in the archives of Sir Frederick Handley Page whose firm went into liquidation in 1970.[1] These documents, which include correspondence with the Air Ministry in the inter-war years, Minutes of the Board of Directors for 1920–26 and 1937–46, and the company accounts for 1919–37, form the basis of this paper. Unfortunately, as the records are far from complete, a very detailed picture of the business cannot be painted. For example, there is little information on the size of the labour force and, as is often the case, the Board Meetings were not minuted in detail. However, additional material on Handley Page has been gained from the Air Ministry files in the Public Record Office, London, and these go some way towards filling in the gaps in our knowledge.[2]

The pattern of Handley Page's development mirrors that of the British aircraft industry as a whole: a shaky beginning followed by explosive growth in the First World War, a growth which made the post-war contraction particularly acute.[3] There then followed a period of consolidation when those firms chosen by the Air Ministry were guaranteed enough orders to survive, at least as designers if not as vigorous manufacturers. Rearmament in the later 1930s pulled the industry from its manufacturing doldrums and a further period of growth ensued, not as dramatic as that which had taken place some two decades earlier but none the less sufficient to transform the small, often struggling enterprises which comprised the peacetime British aircraft industry. The main part of this paper will look at Handley Page during three very different moments in the firm's life. These were the post-war contraction, the period of low level consolidation and finally rearmament. Firstly, however, we must consider the early history of the company.

## War and Growth

Frederick Handley Page, the son of a Non-Conformist minister, was born in 1885 and at the age of seventeen embarked on a career in electrical engineering. His passion for aeronautics soon led him to set up, in 1909, the first British company to be constituted exclusively for the design and manufacture of aeroplanes.[4] As

Handley Page was not a wealthy man his interest in aviation was partially financed by teaching and partly by persuading acquaintances to put money in his risky business.[5] In 1912 the British government, conscious of development overseas, became interested in the military implications of the aeroplane. At the same time Frederick Handley Page moved from Barking to Cricklewood where the new factory occupied 20,000 sq. ft., roughly double the size of the one it replaced.[6] A new designer, George Volkert, was engaged and immediately made his presence felt by designing the company's first bi-plane.

In 1913 the firm received a contract from the War Office to build five bi-planes and at the same time embarked upon the design of the L.200 with which they hoped to win £10,000 offered by the Daily Mail for the first transatlantic flight. The outbreak of war put paid to this latter venture and the L.200 was never completed but the company's interest in building a large aeroplane had attracted the attention of the Admiralty who wanted a twin-engined bomber. Handley Page accepted the challenge and the design of the 0/100 commenced in January 1915, the prototype flew in the following December and deliveries to the R.N.A.S. began in November 1916. It soon became clear that a more powerful bomber was required and a slightly modified 0/100 with Rolls Royce Eagle engines emerged as the 0/400 to become Britain's standard heavy bomber of the First World War. Over four hundred 0/400s were built forcing the company to introduce large-scale production methods, greatly to expand its plant and equipment and to cope with all the organisational problems which growth on this scale brings.

The public cry for vengeance against Germany plus an increasing faith in (and fear of) the bomber shared now by both politicians and military strategists led to the design of the V/1500. This was a four-engined bomber of prodigious size capable of reaching Berlin from English bases. The design of the V/1500 was begun in October 1917 but only fifteen of these aircraft were built[7] before the armistice made it redundant. By 1918 the company had established itself as one of the world's leading manufacturers of big bombers: indeed, its fame was such that the name Handley Page became synonymous in the English language with that type of aircraft.

It is clear that the war transformed this small company into a manufacturing concern enormous by contemporary aeronautical standards. The really astonishing period of growth came in the closing stages of the war and can be illustrated by the following figures. By December 1917 Handley Page employed 1,120 workers and occupied a floor space of 138,000 sq. ft. but even these figures had swollen by early 1919 into a labour force of about 2,500 employees working in 376,000 sq. ft. of floor space. The company which had produced a mere handful of aeroplanes in the years before 1914 delivered 211 aeroplanes in 1918 and a further 103 in 1919[8] as the Government had agreed to purchase all work in progress when hostilities ceased.

No aircraft firm could finance war-time expansion from its own resources and in 1918 most of the new premises at Cricklewood were owned not by the company but by the Ministry of Munitions. The Ministry charged Handley Page a rental of 7½ per cent on the original cost of the buildings but once the war was over they became an unwilling landlord and in April 1919 sold the premises to the firm. Company records do not disclose the sum paid to the Ministry but it is recorded that a large loan was obtained from Barclays Bank for this purpose. At the same time Frederick Handley Page decided to offer shares in his company to the public for the first time. Although financial pundits regarded the shares as speculative members of the public took up the issue, paying 21s. for each of the 500,000 7 per cent cumulative preference shares of £1. The ordinary shares (150,000 £1 shares) were allotted to shareholders in the original company which meant that the bulk went to Mr Handley Page. The new proprietor, however, faced a number of pressing problems of which his stockholders were blissfully ignorant or only partially aware. These problems would require more than Handley Page's personal ingenuity if they were to be solved and the company remain solvent.

*Post-war Diversification*

The difficulties facing Handley Page Ltd. in the early post-war years were shared by all those firms that endeavoured to remain in this rapidly contracting industry. It was clear that the demand for aircraft would be minimal for many years to come as the surplus aircraft in depots up and down the country hung like a millstone around the necks of those who had produced them so feverishly only a short time before. All the airframe manufacturers had huge areas of land on which there were large assembly shops and hangars, yet once orders in progress for the government were finished, the sheer size of these establishments made the inevitable empty silence all the more ominous. Diversification was of prime importance and Handley Page moved quickly in an attempt to keep plant and equipment fully employed.

One of the most popular methods of diversification in the aircraft industry at the time was to enter the motor trade or at least to ally with an established motor manufacturer.[9] For the majority of pioneer aircraft firms entry into the motor trade was fraught with disaster and perhaps only Short Brothers, who specialised in the production of omnibus bodies, got any lasting benefit from it. The experience of Handley Page confirms this view. In July 1920 an agreement was reached between Handley Page Ltd., and Eric Campbell & Co. Ltd., motor manufacturers, for the assembly of cars.[10] This was to be a shortlived but costly alliance for the airframe makers as the motor trade was about to be rocked by the slump of 1920–21, whilst at the same time aviation was experiencing a depression of its own. By December 1920 Handley Page's Profit and Loss Account shows that debts of £77,273 incurred by Campbells had already been written off and, what is more, so had shares in that company which had cost Handley Page £60,000. Frederick Handley Page had personally provided Campbells with £1,000 to enable them to pay wages for the first two weeks in March 1921[11] but this gesture was not sufficient to save Campbells who succumbed in that year: not however, before their debt to Handley Page had increased by £13,057. This figure raised the aircraft firm's losses on its brief flirtation with the motor industry to £150,330.

Like many others Handley Page were quick to see in 1919 that if sales were doomed at home there could yet be profits to be earned overseas. If markets for the company's products were established in far flung corners of the globe this surely would compensate for any lack of domestic profitability. The idea appealed to Frederick Handley Page and lavishly-equipped missions were soon on their way to India, Burma, South Africa, Brazil, the Argentine and many other places. On this occasion however, Handley Page seems to have taken an almighty leap over the dividing line which separates far-sighted business policy from sheer foolhardiness. By the end of 1920 the company accounts show that the debt incurred by the expedition to India and Burma had been written off at a cost of £79,518 as had the South African expedition at a cost of £52,904. In all the total loss on expeditions by 31 December 1920 was a staggering £286,492. Never again was exporting contemplated on such a grandiose scale; it was to be very limited in the 1920s and even less important in the 1930s. If the losses in the motor trade and on foreign expeditions had been the only disasters to strike Handley Page in 1920 one might be forgiven for thinking that such an enterprise was lucky to survive. There was, however, one further financial shock of major proportions to come.

One form of diversification into which the company could move with relative ease was civil aviation, where large aeroplanes could be used considerably more effectively than any other war-inspired machine. A converted 0/400 could and did carry up to twenty passengers or a great deal of freight. Its two engines gave nervous passengers an extra, if illusionary, feeling of security which they did not have flying in single-engined aircraft. Handley Page, therefore, with some other manufacturers,[12] entered this new, exciting, but very uncertain section of the transportation industry with enthusiasm. The early civil aviation companies were given some very indirect encouragement by the report, in 1918, of a government-appointed Civil Aerial Transport Committee[13] which went so far as to recommend subsidies to ensure the success of civil aviation.

Even if Frederick Handley Page had known that the recommendations of this committee were to be largely ignored, a subsidiary company, Handley Page Transport, would still have been incorporated in June 1919 with George Woods-Humphrey (later to head Imperial Airways) as General Manager. Soon routes were opened to Brussels and Paris[14] but a combination of factors, for example, competition from heavily-subsidised French airlines and

the fact that converted bombers made uneconomic civil aircraft,
led to heavy losses. The Profit and Loss Account for 1920 shows
that there was an estimated loss in Handley Page Transport of
£119,152 and that £50,000 worth of shares in the subsidiary company
had been written off. The misfortunes of Handley Page in this
sphere were also felt by its domestic competitors to such an extent
that by early 1921 all British civil airlines had ceased operations;
these were only resumed after the government had reluctantly
agreed to subsidise services, a move which at least cut down losses in
this sector of Handley Pages' operations.[15]

With subsidies Handley Page Transport could continue in
business but it was soon apparent that this method of fostering civil
aviation was unsatisfactory. In 1923 the Hambling Committee[16]
came to the conclusion that the existing air lines should be amalgamated into a state company, Imperial Airways, which, with
governmental approval, was incorporated in March 1924: not,
however, before Handley Page Transport had received £94,472 as a
subsidy for its operations.[17] Handley Page was paid £51,500 for the
sale of its transport subsidiary, one third of the amount in cash and
the rest in Imperial Airways shares. Thus ended a brave but
unsuccessful venture which had encouraged the firm to build the
first of a long line of civil airliners for which they achieved some fame
over the ensuing decade.

The vital question at this stage is how Handley Page was able to
survive the catastrophic change in its fortunes which came about in
1920. In that year losses on motor cars, foreign expeditions and civil
aviation alone totalled £606,000. And this was not all, for the
company's debts in 1920 included a bank overdraft of over
£272,000[18] whilst further sundry creditors were owed the not
inconsiderable sum of £399,365. Total indebtedness was, therefore,
clearly in excess of the £112,400 owed to the firm. Furthermore the
large profit which had attracted so many investors was considerably
diminished once Treasury claims for unpaid taxes were presented to
the company. The 1919 balance sheet shows that Handley Page had
set aside nearly £217,000 in a Tax Reserve Account but even this
large sum did not include a provision for Excess Profits Duty or
Income Tax for which the firm would be liable in 1919. Fortunately
the company was able to pay the final demand for Excess Profits
Duty which came in 1920. This tax was the final straw for many
pioneer aircraft companies and was instrumental in the collapse of
some of the most famous names in British aviation.[19] The only
reason why Handley Page did not tread the well-worn path to the
bankruptcy courts was because of its tempestuous but fortunate
association with the Aircraft Disposal Company.

### The Financial Battle

In 1920 the Disposals Board set up by the Ministry of Munitions
entered into an agreement with the Imperial and Foreign Corporation
Ltd. whereby the entire surplus aviation stock would be sold to the

Corporation. Almost immediately this contract was transferred to
the Aircraft Disposal Co. (A.D.C.) which took over a mountain of
equipment including 10,000 airframes, 30,000 aero engines and spare
parts.[20] The agreement reached with the Disposals Board was that
A.D.C. would pay £200,000 when the contract was signed in March
1920, a further £300,000 in September 1920 and a lump sum payment of £500,000 in March 1921.[21] In addition A.D.C. agreed to
return to the Government half the difference between gross expenditure and gross receipts on the sale of surplus stock. The Managing
Director of A.D.C. was Charles Godfrey Isaacs of the Marconi
Wireless and Telegraph Co. who was joined on the Board by
Frederick Handley Page.[22] The role of Handley Page in this liaison
was to inspect and to lend the company's good name to the products
of A.D.C.[23] In fact this was a considerable coup for Frederick Handley Page because it was obvious that surplus stocks would exert a
depressing effect upon the market for many years to come and it
seemed that he was to be the only aircraft manufacturer who would
make some profit from this glut.

  A.D.C. began with an ordinary share capital of £600 but also
issued debentures worth £1,200,000. Handley Page purchased £236
of ordinary shares and 1682 debentures of £300 each but secured on
payment of £100. At this time a considerable change both in the
company's fortunes and in its relationship with A.D.C. took place.
An investigation into Handley Page's accounts for 1920 shows that
£55,104 was earned from A.D.C. sales and £9,977 interest from
A.D.C. stock yet at the same time Handley Page had to pay A.D.C.
£10,172 interest on loans advanced. This figure was not far short of
the amount paid on Handley Page's colossal overdraft at Barclays
Bank. The following year, 1921, saw the revenue from A.D.C. sales
fall to £27,338 and interest on A.D.C. stock rise slightly to £10,255
but interest charges were now £27,761, more than two and a half
times the interest paid to Barclays.

  Meanwhile changes were taking place in the management of
Handley Page, for in April 1921, at the instigation of the creditors,
J. Barrett-Lennard of Marconi became General Manager, and four
new directors joined the Board.[24] In November Barrett-Lennard
became a director[25] and in the following month Chairman,[26] with
the daunting task of applying a tourniquet to the Company's
financial haemorrhage. The deposed Frederick Handley Page lost
not only power but also £176,000 which the company had, in happier
times, agreed to pay him for his designs and inventions.[27]

  For the next four years, business decisions were taken largely by
those directors who had been appointed at the insistence of the
creditors. Frederick Handley Page was, however, given the post of
managing director so his considerable technical expertise was at the
disposal of the company, though there was not the opportunity to
use it to the full. Necessity dictated that the men of the moment
should be experienced in the art of finance rather than in the skills of
aircraft design.

By late 1921 the inadequacies of Handley Page were a serious embarrassment to A.D.C. for the more the former company struggled to escape from the quicksands of debt, the deeper it sank. In 1922 Handley Page were compelled to transfer all A.D.C. shares to a trust where the voting rights would be exercised by the Trustees. As interest was still paid, the company received £3,342 from A.D.C. sales and £8,900 interest from A.D.C. stock but at the same time it paid £17,666 interest on loans. It was surely no surprise that when A.D.C. demanded £40,000 as the next instalment on their shares Handley Page could not pay and had to forfeit £120,000 worth of debentures.[28] In May 1922 Barrett-Lennard joined the Board of A.D.C. to cement further the links between the two companies but the effect of this interlocking directorship was to demonstrate that Handley Page was being run by A.D.C. in consultation with the representatives of Barclays Bank. Handley Page could do nothing without consulting their financial overlords though their fortunes were somewhat brightened in 1923 by a bonus issue of A.D.C. debentures worth £172,190 to add to the £3,957 earned from the interest on existing stock. Interest charges, however, still remained high at £12,763.

In 1924 A.D.C. was determined to sort out its tangled relationship with Handley Page and did so by demanding that debts, which now totalled £242,477, be discharged. Fear of bankruptcy concentrated Frederick Handley Page's mind and eventually he was able to effect a compromise[29] which reflected the fact that the company he had founded was so deeply in debt to A.D.C. and Barclays Bank that neither wished to see him liquidated. The first part of the deal was acceptance by A.D.C. of 1402 debentures of £145 each, owned by Handley Page but in the hands of Barclays Bank, as collateral. Once the bank had agreed, Handley Page's debt was reduced by £175,250. Secondly, some £17,000 cash, which had been received for the sale of Handley Page Transport, went straight to A.D.C. and Handley Page renounced 13,260 ordinary shares of 1s. each in A.D.C. which they had the right to apply for and pay at par. Thirdly, Barclays were persuaded to lend Handley Page £60,000 to settle the rest of the debt and this sum was added to the £154,661 which was already owed to the bank. On the completion of these transactions Barrett-Lennard resigned his position at Handley Page[30] but stayed on the Board of A.D.C.

In 1925 Handley Page obtained its last tangible benefits from A.D.C. in the form of a bonus issue of debentures worth £9,375. For their part A.D.C., now interested in designing their own aircraft, purchased the rights of Martinsyde, changed the company's name to A.D.C. Aircraft Ltd., and appointed John Kenworthy as designer.[31] This was not a surprising move because A.D.C. had a very large and competent staff to overhaul thoroughly the aeroplanes they sold. The company was also profitable having paid the government £1,070,489 at the end of 1926,[32] but there are no records to show how much was eventually made. The editor of *The Aeroplane* suggested that '[A.D.C.] paid something like £6,000,000 to the British Government before they shut down'[33] but this seems a gross exaggeration for by 1926, much of the surplus stock had been sold and the remainder must have been depreciating rapidly. The debt Handley Page owed to A.D.C. is difficult to measure. In the narrow accounting sense the Profit and Loss Account shows that a figure of about £340,000 can be calculated. Yet this tells us nothing of the essential loans the firm secured only because of A.D.C. backing. In short A.D.C. was the main reason why Handley Page was able to overcome the disaster of 1920 in which so many other companies perished.

For the Board of Directors at this time, life was a perpetual balancing act, as loans had to be raised, debts paid and working capital provided. The company adopted the sensible practice of calling in their loans where possible and selling their assets. Monies owed to the firm diminished from a total of £112,450 in 1920 to a mere £7,718 in 1924. Investments which had been worth £168,337 in 1920 fell to £5,364 in 1924, and of course, no dividend was paid from December 1919 until 1927. In 1922 cash was in such short supply that the Directors fees could not be paid,[34] and the constant battle for working capital was clearly illustrated in 1923 when the Board negotiated with A.D.C. for permission to retain the sum of £2,600 for a few months.[35] By 1924 the company was in such dire straits that the Gas Light and Coke Co. threatened proceedings if not paid immediately and the Chairman reported gloomily that 'the company's operations must cease if it is unable to obtain financial assistance'.[36] Throughout the early 1920s the Board sold off as much land as they could, obtaining £30,000 for 51½ acres in 1924[37] and £12,500 from Smiths Potato Crisps for a factory site in 1925.[38] Subletting revenue for a variety of purposes including indoor tennis was about £4,000 for 1923 alone.[39]

In 1926 Handley Page at last discharged its indebtedness to Barclays Bank and the 33,334 shares in Imperial Airways which had been deposited as collateral were released.[40] In fact during 1926 Handley Page wiped the slate clean on its debts and began afresh, by using the rare step of capital reduction. The dismal performance of the Company since 1920, its enormous and seemingly irreducible debt, and the low value of its shares meant that the issued capital of £650,000 was totally unrealistic. Consequently the 500,000 preference shares of £1 were revalued at 8s. and the 150,000 ordinary shares of £1 were written down to 1s. giving a new issued capital figure of £206,644. This measure marked the end of post-war financial instability for Handley Page and from this point onwards monetary problems were never so dominant in the company's history.

## The Demand for New Aircraft

Handley Page were in business to make aeroplanes, though this was not easy in the troubled post-war years. The company's first

post-war design was a civil airliner, the W/8, which flew in December
1919 and proved to be far more economic than the converted wartime craft it was to replace.[41] In spite of this aircraft, 1920 was as
depressing a year for Handley Page as it was for other aircraft
producers[42] and contracts from the Air Ministry amounted to a
paltry £1,005.[43] However, in 1920, the Air Ministry decided that a
select 'ring' of manufacturers would be formed and government
orders would only be placed with members of that 'ring'.[44] Furthermore an agreement was reached with the Society of British Aircraft
Constructors that orders would always be placed with the designing
firm if the price was fair and the execution of the work was within
the firm's capacity.[45] The Ministry stood firmly by its decision to
form a 'ring' of some sixteen firms even though there were suggestions
that such a number was excessive: the Ministry's view was that any
diminution of the size of the 'ring' would lessen design competition.[46]
As a producer of heavy bombers and large civil aircraft Handley
Page was dependent upon government orders for survival and its
inclusion in the Ministry's list of select firms assured it some sort of
future[47] even if, in view of that Department's penury, it was not a
rosy one.

Ministerial tutelage offered a number of advantages to a
struggling firm like Handley Page. In the first place, the production of
airframes for the state was divided into stages and eighty per cent
of the cost of each stage was paid promptly when the work was
satisfactorily completed, thus saving substantially on the amount
of working capital an aircraft firm required for a contract. Secondly,
each firm could use government research facilities at the National
Physical Laboratory, whilst the Aerodynamics Department of the
Royal Aircraft Establishment provided information and advice on
current aviation problems.[48] Moreover, the fact that potential new
competitors were excluded from Air Ministry contracts was an
advantage to members of the 'ring' but it also gave the Ministry
substantial powers over the aircraft firms as well as responsibility
for them.[49]

A glance at Table I shows the severity of the post-war depression
for Handley Page. The company's workforce fell dramatically and
the picture was so depressing that Volkert left the company,
fortunately to rejoin it a few years later. In 1921 the Air Ministry
placed a contract with Handley Page for three W/8bs, a more
powerful version of the W/8,[50] and for three Hanley[51] torpedo
aircraft. Even this small contract placed a strain on the firm and the
Board had to struggle to provide the necessary working capital.[52] In
1922 the Air Ministry could offer no aircraft and in response to a
desperate letter from Frederick Handley Page, who claimed he now
employed only thirty men in his workshops, some D.H.9as were sent
to Cricklewood for reconditioning.[53]

The events of 1923 further illustrated the firm's dilemma, for
early in the year a Russian contract neared completion but there was
not sufficient money to pay Napiers £4,860 for the engines.[54]

TABLE I
Handley Page Ltd.

| Year to 31 Dec. | Issued Capital £ | Capital¹ Worth £ | Sales £ | Wages £ | Salaries £ | Net Profit after deduction 'extraordinary items'² £ | Net Profit as reported by company £ | Working Capital £ |
|---|---|---|---|---|---|---|---|---|
| 1918 | 10,000 | 286,439 | n.a. | n.a. | 70,123 | 234,475 | 114,952 | −232,593 |
| 1919 | 650,000 | 699,145 | 1,625,076 | 277,792 | 97,516 | 174,094 | 51,285 | −146,433 |
| 1920 | 650,000 | 71,825 | 411,129 | 133,104 | 97,047 | −273,549 | −645,773 | −286,890 |
| 1921 | 650,000 | −38,324 | 27,349 | 7,913 | 26,029 | −54,923 | −68,149 | −435,009 |
| 1922 | 650,000 | −32,657 | 85,049 | 26,573 | 19,607 | −7,509 | 3,767 | −391,020 |
| 1923 | 650,000 | 144,222 | 105,736 | 40,162 | 22,039 | −1,189 | 146,780 | −321,082 |
| 1924 | 650,000 | 92,212 | 111,676 | 42,022 | 23,523 | −13,858 | −22,010 | −90,465 |
| 1925 | 650,000 | 131,194 | 169,297 | 55,698 | 21,934 | 44,856 | 38,982 | −36,161 |
| 1926 | 206,644 | 206,644 | 192,206 | 54,809 | 21,194 | 47,062 | 53,922 | −9,906 |
| 1927 | 206,644 | 243,325 | 192,672 | 62,729 | 25,687 | 55,317 | 46,638 | 9,189 |
| 1928 | 206,644 | 271,206 | 173,780 | 59,230 | 27,843 | 49,182 | 47,795 | 17,374 |
| 1929 | 206,644 | 311,276 | 189,481 | 80,878 | 35,335 | 24,678 | 40,508 | 32,683 |
| 1930 | 206,644 | 369,740 | 278,705 | 144,506 | 43,825 | 34,456 | 43,147 | 14,172 |
| 1931 | 206,644 | 378,162 | 263,991 | 125,578 | 42,305 | −38,269 | 3,594 | 30,787 |
| 1932 | 206,644 | 380,230 | 88,409 | 35,586 | 37,641 | −22,661 | 8,135 | 9,960 |
| 1933 | 206,644 | 435,658 | 126,462 | 77,730 | 41,470 | −40,877 | 20,441 | 86,804 |
| 1934 | 206,644 | 459,514 | 323,299 | 125,380 | 46,155 | 27,134 | 44,590 | 29,707 |
| 1935 | 206,644 | 520,825 | 436,596 | 163,202 | 60,687 | 66,920 | 77,893 | −22,770 |
| 1936³ | 323,609 | 559,807 | 665,413 | 265,093 | 87,076 | 108,358 | 100,181 | −101,274 |
| 1937⁴ | 448,074 | 703,170 | 1,311,335 | 419,672 | 119,851 | 332,881 | 210,126 | −107,719 |
| 1938⁵ | 572,539 | 815,120 | n.a. | n.a. | n.a. | n.a. | 190,696 | −451,810 |
| 1939 | 572,539 | 959,889 | n.a. | n.a. | n.a. | n.a. | 219,479 | −722,752 |

Source: Company ledgers and balance sheets.

¹ Capital worth = issued capital and reserves ± profit and loss a/c + patent realisation a/c.

² 'Extraordinary items' include depreciation, royalties, dividends, reserves, interest charges and receipts.

³ In 1936 share capital was increased from £206,644 to £323,609 by capitalising £116,965 from Patents Realisation Account.

⁴ In 1937 share capital was raised to £448,074 by capitalising £60,000 from General Reserve and £64,465 from Patents Realisation Account.

⁵ In 1938 share capital was increased to £572,539 by capitalising £124,465 from General Reserve.

Fortunately the aero-engine makers accepted £1,000 deposit with
the final adjustment to be made when the Russian government paid
for the aeroplanes.[55] An out of the blue award from the Royal
Commission on Awards to Inventors enabled the company to set
aside £600 for the development of a small aeroplane[56] and even to
talk of increasing the design staff.[57] Yet at the same time Frederick
Handley Page wrote to the Air Ministry saying that work was so
scarce that he would soon have to discharge 600 men.[58] Whether
this was desperation or duplicity is difficult to say, but the upshot
was that a November order for six Hendon torpedo aircraft and
another almost as valuable for reconditioning D.H.9as was quickly
followed in January 1924 with further contracts for one W/8F and
three Handcross day bombers which considerably reduced anxiety
at Cricklewood.

By now a pattern of Air Ministry orders was emerging which
kept the wolf from the door but never sent it far away. The piecemeal
nature of the orders meant that most firms were never sure about
their future prospects and could not afford to tool-up properly and so
produced their aircraft by hand. Another perpetual problem for any
manufacturer who did not get a long production run was that skilled
labour had to be continually declared redundant then later re-
engaged. Table I shows marked annual fluctuations in the wages bill
but disguises the very short-term fluctuations that took place in less
than twelve months. This hand to mouth existence naturally affected
the quality of research each design department could undertake as
well as undermining productive capacity.

The year 1924 was a crucial one for Handley Page's manufacturing ambitions. By adapting a W/8 the firm produced a night
bomber known as the Hyderabad which found favour in the Air
Ministry. However, the Board were reluctant to accept a contract for
Hyderabads because of the financial uncertainty which surrounded
the Company.[59] Consequently they were in some difficulty in July
1924 when they were offered a contract for 15 Hyderabads. As no
price had yet been negotiated, Handley Page would have to proceed
at its own risk[60] during a period of doubt, uncertainty and financial
chaos. On the other hand the Air Ministry might have looked upon a
rejection of the contract as a clear indication that the firm was no
longer to be seriously considered as an airframe manufacturer and
was undeserving of further orders. The firm tried delaying tactics
and angered the Air Ministry which threatened to withdraw the
contract.[61]

The prospect of losing the firm's largest post-war order was
appalling but the turmoil in Handley Page during 1924 magnified
problems endemic since 1920. The Chairman was certain the works
were being run at a loss,[62] as indeed they were, for the setback in
profit for 1924 was caused solely by a deterioration in the Manufacturing Account. Several Board meetings were called to investigate
the provision of working capital and a scheme to transfer, temporarily,
the manufacturing side of Handley Page to Handley Page Transport

came to naught.[63] The crunch came early in 1925, by which time the firm had spent £2,300 on drawings for the Hyderabad without committing themselves fully to it. Eventually Barclays Bank, A.D.C., Mr Handley Page and an outsider, George Leavey, reached an agreement on the provision of working capital,[64] and the production of the aircraft got underway. Ultimately 79 Hyderabads, and its derivative the Hinaidi, were built but as the maximum order in sight at any one time was fifteen the aircraft were, as usual, made by hand.

By the end of 1925 the manufacturing side of the business was out of the woods and profits on the Manufacturing Account rose until the next crisis in the early 'thirties. Even so, because of the way in which the orders dribbled in, there were periodic panics as each batch neared completion and workers were dismissed before new contracts were awarded.[65] Moreover the firm was very dependent upon Air Ministry work as overseas orders were few and far between.[66] However with the capital re-organisation of 1926, Handley Page achieved stability and was able to share the trials and tribulations of an aircraft industry moving, in Higham's terminology, from demobilisational instability to peacetime equilibrium.[67]

If we look at the financial record of Handley Page from the mid-1920s to the advent of rearmament two main areas of interest are apparent. One is the worsening of the Company's manufacturing performance in the early 1930s for which some explanation is necessary. The second is the extraordinary amount of money which was paid into the Patents Realisation Account which reached over £400,000 between 1926 and 1939 and which bolstered the company's fortunes when they were at a low ebb.

### Trading problems

Throughout this period Handley Page concentrated on large civil and military aircraft though occasionally the firm felt tempted to build a smaller aeroplane.[68] The aircraft which kept the firm's name in the public eye, however, were the Heyford night bomber and the famous Hannibal and Heracles airliners.[69] Some 125 Heyfords were built (though only ordered in small batches of no more than 16) but only eight of the civil airliners. Handley Page, of course, continued to build aeroplanes such as the Hyderabad Hinaidi class which were introduced before the period which immediately concerns us.

Radical technical changes were taking place at this time, as Air Ministry policy was to force the aircraft firms to use metal instead of wood for manufacturing.[70] By the early 1930s the Air Ministry felt that Handley Page was on a par with the rest of the industry in metal work,[71] but it was impossible for any enterprise to be competent in metal aircraft without large orders and these were not forthcoming. Air Ministry ordering was based on the belief that war was not imminent,[72] and on a desire on the part of politicians that Britain should be seen to obey all the current disarmament rules. The result was fewer orders for bombers, which were held to be aggressive rather than defensive, and no attempt to cheat by developing large civil aeroplanes which could be converted into bombers if the need arose.[73] The fact that the two types of aircraft in which Handley Page specialised were at the core of this policy had unfortunate repercussions on the firm in terms of the quality and quantity of its output.

The deterioration in the company's fortunes between 1931 and 1933 was due to a fall off in orders and to losses made on the eight airliners built for Imperial Airways. To some extent the drop in demand for new military airframes was offset by the large amount of reconditioning work given to aircraft manufacturers. For example, when the Hyderabad/Hinaidi bombers were equipped with more powerful engines this necessitated a great number of modifications all done by the parent firm. The aim of the Air Ministry was to keep each aeroplane flying as long as possible so reconditioning was virtually automatic even when it would have been more economic to scrap the airframe. From 1927 to 1931 inclusive the cost of reconditioning aircraft for the Air Ministry was 70 per cent of the cost of new airframes. When some firms were on the brink of extinction reconditioning contracts were placed with them even if they were not the designing firm. Thus in the early 1920s the D.H.9a performed this useful function and later so did the Siskin and the Hart. Income from reconditioning was therefore very important to the aircraft industry and even by 1929 some 28 Hyderabads had been returned to Cricklewood for a thorough overhaul, thus establishing a trend that was to continue through the early 1930s.[74]

The state airline was obliged to buy only British aircraft, thus giving the manufacturers a subsidy, but Imperial Airways was in a very powerful bargaining position *vis-à-vis* the few firms which built large airliners. Indeed so powerful was its position that Handley Page signed a much too optimistic contract which, on their founder's reckoning, lost the company up to £70,000.[75] Imperial Airways could choose the type of aircraft it wanted and get a firm to make it. The implications of this need some explanation. For example, when Imperial Airways decided to concentrate on flying boats this was a boon for Short Bros. but a blow to Handley Page. The Hannibal/Heracles aircraft were comfortable, safe and reliable but when the new all-metal monoplanes built by Douglas and Lockheed emerged they were seen to be incredibly slow.

Handley Page wanted to follow the lead of their American competitors but were prevented from doing so for at least two reasons. Firstly Imperial Airways only ordered small numbers of each type of land plane, in fact never more than eight. Douglas, however, calculated that the break-even point for the DC-2 was 75 aircraft[76] so that Handley Page would have required a large subsidy for jigging and tooling in order to produce small numbers of a similar aeroplane and this was out of the question. Secondly, it is by no means clear that Imperial Airways wanted the British Aircraft industry slavishly to follow the American lead in civil airliners.

In 1935, the state airline asked Handley Page to build an airliner but stipulated that the company must not consider selling the aeroplane to any other airline before 1939. Only a mere handful of these specialised aircraft were to be ordered by Imperial Airways and Handley Page turned down the contract.[77] Frederick Handley Page was deeply resentful of the way in which Imperial Airways exercised its power. He came to the conclusion, which was shared by many other aviation executives, that the aircraft industry subsidised the state airline. Moreover, the policies of the state airline had led to a situation where it was clear that some types of British civil aircraft, most notably large airliners, were inferior to their American counterparts.[78]

Perhaps the influence of Imperial Airways explains why Handley Page airliners were not as popular in the fleets of European airlines during the 1930s as they had been in the preceeding decade.[79] The invasion of American civil airliners had shown that British land planes were technologically inferior and soon pressure from re-armament was to make catching up in this field difficult. Fear of American technology led Frederick Handley Page to suggest a tariff which would exclude American aircraft from Britain and the Empire.[80] If this did not happen the British and Colonial market would be swamped with United States aircraft and, as he put it, 'we have not had enough people trained in gaols to be able to compete with American businessmen'.

Mr Handley Page's xenophobia was a direct response to his firm's unhappy time in the civil aircraft market of the 1930s.[81] It is interesting to speculate what would have happened to the firm if Imperial Airways had decided to use land planes and not sea planes for Empire flights, or if the government had decided to rearm sooner. However, the fact remains that governmental direction of both civil and military markets at this time had unfortunate trading and technological implications for Handley Page.

### The Success of the Slot

Handley Page were able to make some money from non-manu-facturing activities during the inter-war years. For example, as Cricklewood became unsuitable, the company moved to nearby Radlett which had better facilities for flying large aeroplanes. Cricklewood was sold to the Golders Green Development Corpora-tion of which Barrett-Lennard was Chairman, a transaction which ultimately realised a capital gain of some £100,000 when the long drawn out move was completed.[82] A far bigger sum, however, was derived from the slotted wing which was patented by Frederick Handley Page. When fitted to the wing the slot reduced the danger of stalling so that the aircraft with slots was far more stable than the one without. Hence the demand from Governments for permission to incorporate the invention in their aircraft.

Frederick Handley Page was always interested in stability and as a result of wind tunnel tests he was able to satisfy himself that the slot worked.[83] In October 1919 he wrote to Brewer & Son, London Patent Agents, asking them to investigate the possibility of patenting his invention.[84] Eventually Brewer & Son wrote back saying that the only possible complication would be a patent taken out by Dr. Gustav Lachmann in Germany who had independently come across the slot.[85] Mr Handley Page saw that Lachmann's patent could possibly harm his own overseas and suggested that Brewers open negotiations to buy him out.[86] By the end of 1921 Lachmann and Handley Page had made their first formal agreement[87] in which the German surrendered his patents and finally, a few years later, he came to England to work for Handley Page. Mr Handley Page was always confident that the slot would make money and his desperation to get orders from the Air Ministry often reflected his anxieties that the development of the slot could not progress without them.

For the most part the sums to be paid for use of the slot were settled without a battle. Possibly the only challenge Frederick Handley Page had to face on this score was from his own Air Ministry, and the incident is an interesting one because it shows not only the inventor's pertinacity but also the Ministry's view of its own relationship with firms in the industry. Negotiations between the two parties began in 1927 and there is a lot of confusion about the amount Handley Page wanted the government to pay for use of the slot, because his original idea was that his firm would be paid a bounty for each aircraft which incorporated it. The Ministry thought this figure would be in excess of £125,000 but they were determined to pay no more than £80,000. When Handley Page turned down their offer and approached the Royal Commission on Awards to Inventors, officials at the Ministry were furious. They felt very strongly that tests made on the slot at the R.A.E. were vital to its development and had cost the taxpayer around £25,000. Far from being a Handley Page invention they thought it a joint effort between private and state research.[88] The Air Ministry went to a lot of trouble to discover as much as they could of the commercial side of Handley Page's business so that they could show any arbitrator just how important the Ministry was in keeping aircraft firms in business.[89] All this was to no avail and the legal advice to the Ministry was that Handley Page could well get the £125,000 he demanded. In March 1929 the aircraft firm accepted the Ministry's compromise offer of £100,000 to be paid over two years.

The money came at a welcome time for Handley Page, just as aircraft production started to make losses, and its flow was so steady that in 1936 and 1937 a total of £191,430 earned from the slotted wing was capitalised and given as a bonus to stock-holders. There is little doubt that the slot was the most important contribution to aviation in the firm's history.

### Rearmament

On the eve of rearmament, Handley Page had just emerged from a depressing period of three years during which the firm made trading losses. Sales fell to the exceptionally low level of £88,409 in 1932, or only one third of the 1930 figure, and although there was some improvement in 1933 the outlook still seemed bleak. The company's wage bill suggests that dismissals must have forced the firm to such a position in 1931 that the manufacturing side of its business was probably at a virtual standstill. Although by 1934 most of the workers who had been made redundant over the previous few years had been re-engaged management and labour can hardly have been full of confidence about the future.

It would be wrong to assume that other firms in the British aircraft industry did not experience similar belt-tightening. This was a time when public expenditure was reduced to the absolute minimum, and when the hope of a peaceful solution to Europe's economic and political problems was an end towards which low levels of military expenditure were a means. The S.B.A.C. claimed that only one quarter of the companies in the Air Ministry's 'ring' had production experience on even a small scale between 1928 and 1934. Furthermore in 1934, of the fifteen largest airframe contractors, seven had little work and as a result, operated with skeleton staffs, whilst three more were not much better off.[90] It was during this period that Gloster produced car bodies, milk churns, all-metal shopfronts and fishfryers; the firm's empty hangars contained pigs and cultivated mushroom-beds.[91] Short Bros. built omnibus bodies;[92] Westland turned out milk churns, pianos and light engineering assemblies; Saunders continued as power-boat builders and even Bristol manufactured coach bodies for the Bristol Tramways Company.[93]

Many firms, therefore, were forced to turn to work outside aircraft manufacture and it was enterprises such as these, some located far from the centres of skilled labour, which now had to cope with the rapidly increasing demand for aircraft embodying a new and in some ways alien technology. It is not difficult to imagine the strains which this imposed upon managements whose main problems up to 1935 were quite the reverse of those which were shortly to become so dominant.

When Lachmann began to design Handley Page's first monoplane bomber, the Hampden, in 1934, he could not have realised that only two years later it would be ordered in quantity before Air Ministry tests had been completed. Nor would Lachmann have guessed that when he began the Harrow design a year later only lack of productive capacity prevented that aircraft from being ordered on the same scale as its immediate predecessor. In March 1934 Baldwin announced that Britain was to have parity with the German Air Force and a modest expansion of the Air Force was ordered, and this was to be further supplemented in May 1935. The change from near-starvation to plenty for the aircraft industry was rapid. In January 1935 Handley Page learned from the Air Ministry that during the next twelve months the firm could expect orders for four or possibly six new aircraft. Some four months later the firm was asked just how many Heyfords it could produce working flat out.[94] The request was, in a sense, academic since the Heyford was obsolete and of little use for the expansion programme.

Rearmament orders enabled Handley Page to become exclusively a producer of heavy bombers. New life was infused into the company but the concomitant strains were not always easy to overcome. The aeroplane was now a much more complex machine than when expansion last took place (see Table II) and extra design staff and skilled metal-workers had to be recruited. Shortages of the appropriate types of labour plagued the aircraft industry throughout the war. Some idea of the comparative size of the Handley Page enterprise at this time can be seen from Table III which is the only record of labour employed in the industry during the inter-war years which is not shrouded in the anonymity of official government statistics. Handley Page is shown to be a medium-size firm in a very small industry which was clearly going to need the help of the motor car manufacturers if the envisaged expansion was to be completed satisfactorily.

Oddly enough Handley Page seems to be the only firm excluded from the report by the Air Ministry on investigations into airframe producers which took place in 1936.[95] This omission could mean that the Ministry was happy, or at least not desperately unhappy, with the firm. There were, in fact, a number of reasons why the firm should have earned some praise. Firstly, the specification for the Hampden had included weight limitations which were laid down by the Geneva Convention on disarmament. These were studiously ignored by Handley Page and the Hampden emerged far heavier but far more suitable for the changed international conditions when it flew.[96] Secondly, the prolonged move from Cricklewood to Radlett had resulted in the bulk of the firm's manufacturing operations taking place in the older works. Handley Page therefore had to build in components which could be easily transported to Radlett and assembled. This technique, which became known as split construction, was a great advantage. Many small sub-contractors, with no previous experience of aircraft work and only limited factory space, were more easily able to turn over to producing airframe assemblies than with alternative methods.

Unfortunately the Minutes of the Board are very uninformative about the Company's activities at this time but there is sufficient to show the contrast with the depressed years of the early 'thirties. In 1937 Handley Page could consider spending over £5,000 on a wind tunnel,[97] buy a sports ground for their employees and set aside, before war was declared, £20,000 to develop a tail-less plane.[98] At each Board Meeting the purchase of additional plant was discussed and more land was bought including some which had been sold by the company in the early 1920s.[99] As the Air Ministry removed all financial restraints on R.A.F. expansion the firms responded by increasing output but at the same time they were

TABLE II

The Changing Complexity of Handley Page Bombers

| Type | A.U.W. lbs. | Design Begun | Prototype flew | Av. No. of Technical staff | Design Weeks | No. of drawings |
|---|---|---|---|---|---|---|
| O/100 | 14,000 | Jan. 1915 | Dec. 1915 | 6 | 300 | 295 |
| V/1500 | 30,000 | Oct. 1917 | Apr. 1918 | 20 | 600 | 2,025 |
| Hampden | 21,000 | May 1934 | June 1936 | 21 | 2,364 | 8,000 |
| Harrow | 23,500 | Sept. 1935 | Oct. 1936 | 42 | 2,500 | 7,000 |
| Halifax | 65,000 | Aug. 1937 | Oct. 1939 | 71 | 8,320 | 13,000 |

*Source:* Sir F. Handley Page, *op.cit.*, 4.

TABLE III
Labour Employed by British Airframe Manufacturers[1]

| Name of Company | Personnel Employed in April 1935 | | |
|---|---|---|---|
| | Opera-tives[2] | Admini-strative[3] | Total |
| Sir W. G. Armstrong Whitworth Aircraft Ltd. | 837 | 255 | 1,092 |
| Boulton & Paul Aircraft Ltd.[4] | 500 | 100 | 600 |
| Bristol Aeroplane Co. Ltd. | 1,139 | 277 | 1,416 |
| Blackburn Aeroplane Co. Ltd. | 1,100 | 270 | 1,370 |
| De Havilland Aircraft Co. Ltd. | 1,060 | 530 | 1,590 |
| Fairey Aviation Co. Ltd.[4] | 1,500 | 400 | 1,900 |
| Handley Page Ltd. | 970 | 190 | 1,160 |
| Hawker Aircraft Ltd. | 1,523 | 233 | 1,756 |
| Gloster Aircraft Co. Ltd.[5] | 970 | 230 | 1,200 |
| A.V. Roe | 1,207 | 113 | 1,320 |
| Supermarine Aviation Works (Vickers) Ltd. | 621 | 190 | 811 |
| Short Bros. Ltd. | 1,133 | 321 | 1,454 |
| Saunders Roe Ltd. | 480 | 174 | 654 |
| Vickers Aviation Ltd. | 1,560 | 350 | 1,910 |
| Westland Aircraft Works | 242 | 64 | 306 |
| G. Parnall & Co. | 61 | 20 | 81 |
| Totals | 14,903 | 3,717 | 18,620 |

*Source:* P.R.O. Air 8/196 3206.

[1] The firms in this table constitute the 'ring' of government contractors.
[2] Operatives are those directly concerned with the manufacture of airframes on the shop floor and are identical with wage employees as shown in Table I.
[3] Administrative staff are salaried employees and include design staff, sales, research as well as clerical workers.
[4] The rounded totals for Boulton & Paul and Fairey suggest estimates but there is no reason to suggest they were not accurate.
[5] Gloster was a subsidiary of Hawker Aircraft so the two firms should be considered together as a manufacturing unit.

uneasy lest the orders they were fulfilling were not renewed. A majority of firms in the industry became public companies at this time and the sale of their stock helped to provide some of the enormous amount of working capital which the industry swallowed up. Handley Page did not go to the stock market. The increases in the Company's share capital from £206,644 in 1935 to £572,539 in 1939 came about because of capitalisation of reserves or of profits from the slotted wing. As the figures for working capital show, the company's practice was to borrow and this becomes particularly marked after 1934. At the same time the firm's trading profit rocketed.

The culmination of Handley Page's war effort was Volkert's four-engined Halifax, the company's greatest bomber. To produce this aircraft a Group was set up comprising Handley Page, Fairey Aviation, English Electric, Rootes Securities and London Aircraft Production. During the war the Group produced 6,000 Halifaxes and Handley Page was once again firmly embedded in the public's imagination as the producer of big bombers. At the end of the war the company had £1,106,900 in the bank and investments totalling about £776,000.[100] It was taking steps to purchase £250,000 worth of machine tools which had been installed in the works at Air Ministry expense.[101] The reader can be forgiven a feeling of *déja vu* though on this occasion the short-run post-war problems the company faced were not so dramatic as after the previous holocaust. At least on this occasion there was a demand for civil and freight transport aeroplanes.

## Conclusion

Although the history of Handley Page between the wars is unique in detail, in general it illustrates very clearly the problems facing airframe manufacturers at this time and their response to them. Practically every firm in the industry at some time or another felt the cold, and at times severe winds of depression. On the other hand, Handley Page, because of its dependence upon the Air Ministry, was not subject to the same economic forces as firms in other sectors of the economy. Official policy was that firms in the 'ring' be given enough work to ensure their survival but, as we have seen, Handley Page was considered much more as a vehicle for producing aircraft designs than for making aeroplanes in quantity. The small numbers of civil and military aeroplanes ordered between 1920 and 1935 inevitably meant that Handley Page had no experience of mass-production techniques and no opportunity to incorporate some of the latest aviation technology, such as all-metal construction, into its aircraft. This was particularly serious in the early 1930s when the Americans took the lead, producing large civil airliners which could only be commercially justified if produced in large numbers.

Handley Page owed its survival partly to its own determination and partly to the fact that the Air Ministry resuscitated it at intervals. There were, however, other important influences on the company's fortunes. Firms survive both by accident as well as design and the relationship which Handley Page had with A.D.C. enabled it to escape the blunders and misfortunes of 1920. It is hard to believe that a firm which suffered such a great reversal in its fortunes at this time could possibly have ridden out the storm. Mr Handley Page also had the good fortune to patent the slotted wing before Lachmann and this gave the company a steady rate of return not dependent upon their performance as manufacturers at a vital time.

One cannot escape a feeling of regret that more is not known about Frederick Handley Page. He certainly lacked both the genius of de Havilland and the wealth and all-round business ability of Sopwith and yet he possessed a combination of technical skill and business ability that few other pioneers had. His handling of the company's post-war crisis left a lot to be desired but the manner in which he ensured that the slot would be commercially profitable showed business acumen. The appointment of Lachmann and Volkert to the company demonstrated an ability to pick and retain first-rate staff. The freedom of the entrepreneur was circumscribed by the powers of the Air Ministry which, to a large degree, controlled the quality as well as the quantity of British aircraft. It is impossible to say, given the information at our disposal, whether Handley Page did better or worse in their negotiations with the Air Ministry than other companies in the industry. All that can be said is that the Ministry had little to spend on what the firm wanted to produce.

Given the limited use of civil aircraft the only rapid expansion the company could hope for was war or rumour of war. Yet Handley Page was not, in 1935, ready for very rapid expansion. The firm was still recovering from a lean period, it was in the process of moving from Cricklewood to Radlett, of introducing new types of aircraft and above all it was totally lacking in experience of mass-production techniques. Any enterprise which had spent so long in the wilderness as Handley Page was, however, unlikely not to try to maximise its good fortune in this changed state of affairs. The determination which saw it through the lean years was now harnessed to a more productive use and it was this determination which ensured that the name Handley Page was as dominant in the Second World War as it had been in the first.

*University of Leicester*

## NOTES

1. They are located in the Royal Air Force Museum, Hendon.

2. I should like to thank the Research Board of the University of Leicester for a grant towards expenses incurred in undertaking this research and Mr. A. J. Morris for his invaluable help in unravelling the firm's accounts.

3. For an account of this period see: P. Fearon, 'The Formative Years of the British Aircraft Industry, 1913–24', *Business History Review*, XLIII (1969), 476–95.

4. For the early Handley Page aircraft see: P. Lewis, *British Aircraft 1809–1914* (1966), 298–308; H. Penrose, *British Aviation, The Pioneer Years 1903–1914* (1967), *passim* and 'Handley Page's Half Century', supplement to *The Aeroplane and Astronautics* 5 June 1959.

5. H. Penrose, *op. cit.*, 258–9, 327, 354.

6. Sir F. Handley Page, *Development and Organisation of Handley Page Ltd.* L.S.E. Seminar Paper, 165 (1955).

7. The aircraft were built by Harland and Wolff in Belfast as Handley Page were working at full capacity.

8. The statistics showing company growth at this time are few and scattered. These are taken from Frederick Handley Page's correspondence with the Income Tax authorities with whom he was in dispute in the late 1920s. They are part of the Handley Page Archives which can be distinguished from other footnotes by their distinctive classification, this one being AC 70/10/217.

9. As airframes were made of wood and covered with fabric the airframe industry had but a few skilled metalworkers so firms could not readily undertake body-building themselves. Among the first to try their hands at motor vehicles were: The Aircraft Manufacturing Company, Claude Grahame-White, Fairey Aviation, The British and Colonial Aeroplane Co. (later Bristol), Short Bros., and Martinsyde. Sopwiths laid down assembly lines for motorcycles.

10. Minutes of the Board of Directors of Handley Page (hereafter M.B.), July 1920.

11. M.B., May 1921. Mr. Handley Page received four motor cars as collateral.

12. Among these were: Air Transport and Travel, a subsidiary of the Aircraft Manufacturing Company, Blackburn Aircraft which formed North Sea

Aerial Navigation Co. Ltd., British Aerial Transport Co. an offshoot of Waring and Gillow a furniture firm, Supermarine Aviation and A. V. Roe.

13. *Report of the Civil Aerial Transport Committee with Appendices* (P.P. 1918, V).

14. The early growth of civil aviation in Britain has been described by R. Higham, *Britain's Imperial Air Routes 1918–1939* (1960). See also H. J. Dyos and D. H. Aldcroft, *British Transport: An Economic Survey from the Seventeenth Century to the Twentieth* (1969) Chap. 13; and E. Birkhead, 'The Beginnings of British Civil Air Transport 1919–1924' (unpublished M.A. Thesis, University of Leicester 1959). For international comparisons see the masterly work by R. E. G. Davies, *A History of the World's Airlines* (1964).

15. Some information exists about the extent of the loss. In the Handley Page Profit and Loss Account the figure is £6,126 but in the Accounts of Handley Page Transport the net loss for the calendar year of 1921 is given as £32,072.

16. *Civil Air Transport Subsidies Committee Report on Government Financial Assistance to Civil Air Transport Companies* (P.P. 1923, IX, 711).

17. Higham, *op. cit.*, 66.

18. One large item in the overdraft was a sum of nearly £60,000 borrowed in 1920 to acquire the freehold of Cricklewood.

19. Among them The Aircraft Manufacturing Co., Sopwith Aviation and Martinsyde.

20. Marquess of Londonderry, *Wings of Destiny* (1943), 15; *The Aeroplane*, 17 March 1920, 549–50.

21. *136, H.C. Deb. 5.S.*, 2094, 23 March 1920.

22. The few surviving documents relating to A.D.C. are to be found in P.R.O., BT 31 32395/164792.

23. *The Aeroplane*, 24 March 1920, 602.

24. M.B., April 1921.

25. M.B., Nov. 1921.

26. M.B., Dec. 1921.

27. H. Penrose, *British Aviation The Adventuring Years 1920–29* (1973) 96, *The Aeroplane*, 5 July 1922, 12 and 12 July 1922, 42.

28. M.B., April 1922. A.D.C. however did not demand the £6,367 interest due from Handley Page because of the delay in settling this issue.

29. Details in M.B., June and July 1924.

30. At roughly the same time Frederick Handley Page resigned from the Board of A.D.C.

31. A.D.C. were never able to break into the 'ring' of government contractors and were not a success in aircraft design and manufacture. The company was wound up in 1931.

32. *200 H.C. Debates 5.S.* 2097, 8 Dec. 1926; *The Aeroplane*, 25 Nov. 1925, 608–14.

33. *The Aeroplane*, 21 June 1939, 793.

34. M.B., July 1922.

35. M.B., Sept. and Nov. 1923.

36. M.B., June 1923.

37. M.B., Oct. 1924.

38. M.B., April 1925.

39. M.B., Nov. 1923.

40. Minutes of Board of Handley Page Transport Ltd., 21 July 1926.

41. For the characteristics of this and some other early Handley Page airliners, see P. Brooks, *The Modern Airliner* (1961), 50.

42. 1920 was the worst post-war year, see *The Aeroplane*, 30 June 1920, for a survey which sparked off the Air Ministry's own in P.R.O., Air 6, Air Council Precis 479.

43. Only copies of Handley Page Air Ministry contracts for the years 1920–26 survive in P.R.O., Avia 8/63.

44. A list of members can be found in Table III.

45. P.R.O., Air 2/1322, Aircraft Supply Committee Report, Sept. 1931, 75.

46. In 1924 it was suggested within the Ministry that Handley Page should amalgamate with other firms in the industry, P.R.O., Air 2/226 no.S. 23563,

but the idea came to naught. There was so little work for the firms in the early 1920s that work was taken from the more prosperous and given to the others (termed 'ordering out'). P.R.O., Air 2/226 No. 2523447, 30.4.1925.

47. For a fuller account of the relationship between the Air Ministry and the Aircraft Industry see P. Fearon, 'The British Airframe Industry and the State 1918–1935', *Economic History Review* Second Series XXVII (1974), 236–51 and my chapter 'The British Aircraft Industry' in D. H. Aldcroft and N. K. Buxton (eds.) *Instability and Industrial Development 1919–39* (forthcoming).

48. M. M. Postan, D. Hay and J. D. Scott, *Design and Development of Weapons* (1964), 437–8, 445–7, 468–9.

49. See R. Higham, 'Government, Companies and National Defence: British Aeronautical Experience as the Basis for a Broad Hypothesis', *Business History Review*, XXXIX (1965).

50. For the company's civil aircraft see A. Jackson, *British Civil Aircraft 1919–59* (1960).

51. A description of Handley Page British Military aircraft can be found in P. Lewis, *op. cit.* Although the company's speciality was large aircraft they occasionally entered the field of torpedo craft but with no great success.

52. M.B., 1 April, May, June, Sept. 1921.

53. AC 70/10/77, Frederick Handley Page to Air Ministry, 8 June 1922.

54. M.B., 5 Feb. 1923.

55. M.B., 7 Feb. 1923. Even the £1,000 had to be borrowed from Handley Page Transport.

56. M.B., May 1923.

57. M.B., July 1923.

58. AC 70/10/78, Frederick Handley Page to Air Ministry, 12 July 1923.

59. M.B., June 1924.

60. AC 70/10/78, Air Ministry to Frederick Handley Page, 7 July 1924.

61. *Ibid.*, Air Ministry to Frederick Handley Page, 28 Nov. 1924.

62. M.B., 14 Oct. 1924.

63. AC 70/10/78, Frederick Handley Page to Air Ministry, 11 Dec. 1924 and 10 Jan. 1925. This scheme is not reported in M.B.

64. M.B., 2 and 26 March 1925.

65. AC 70/10/78, Frederick Handley Page to Air Ministry, 9 and 22 March 1926. In that month Handley Page discharged 230 from a work force of about 550.

66. In fact the W/8 derivatives provided the only substantial export earnings in the 1920s. By 1929 Sabena flew 14 Handley Page aircraft, all versions of the W/8 which were the only British aeroplanes in service with a foreign country in this period. They were built under licence by the Belgian company *Société Anonyme Belge de Constructions Aéronautiques* and were replaced by Fokkers in 1929. See J. Stroud, *European Transport Aircraft since 1910* (1966) 29; R. E. G. Davies, *op. cit.*, 64, 69, 121.

67. R. Higham, 'Quantity vs. Quality: The Impact of Changing Demand on the British Aircraft Industry 1900–1960', *Business History Review* XLII (1968), 447.

68. The smaller aircraft were never commercially successful. Between 1926 and 1933 seven prototypes were built of which the Harrow, Hamlet, Hare, Gugnunc, HP 46 and HP 47 were all small craft and the HP 43 a large bomber.

69. The HP 42 Hannibal class was for Empire flights while the HP 45 Heracles was fitted for European service though both aircraft were structurally the same.

70. For more details see Fearon, *Economic History Review, op. cit.*

71. P.R.O., Air 2/1208.

72. See the debate between P. Silverman, 'The Ten Year Rule' *Royal United Service Institution Journal*, 116 (March 1971), 42–5 and K. Booth 'The Ten Year Rule: An Unfinished Debate', *Journal of the Royal United Services Institute for Defence Studies*, 116 (Sept. 1971).

73. D. Carlton, 'The Problem of Civil Aviation in British Air Disarmament Policy, 1919–1934', *The Royal United Service Institution Journal*, 111 (1966), 307–16.

74. All the information on reconditioning is taken from P.R.O., Air 2/1322.

75. AC 70/10/53, Frederick Handley Page evidence to the Cadman Committee, 4.

76. J. B. Rae, *Climb to Greatness: The American Aircraft Industry, 1920–1960* (Cambridge, Mass. 1969), 68–71.

77. AC 70/10/53, *op. cit.*, 6–8.

78. AC 70/10/55, *op. cit.*

79. See tables in R. E. G. Davies, *op. cit.*, 69, 121 and note 66.

80. Mr. Handley Page thought that the import duty on imported American motor cars had saved the British automobile industry. A similar tariff to keep United States aeroplanes out of the Empire would, he felt, have the same effect upon the domestic aircraft industry.

81. It could also have been due to the fact that in 1920 the United States Government intervened to prevent A.D.C. and Handley Page selling 2,365 aeroplanes and 34,000 engines in America. *The Times*, 26 March and 11 Dec. 1920.

82. H. Penrose, 'British Aviation 1920–29', *op. cit.*, 632–3.

83. The best account of the development of the slot is in R. Miller and D. Sawers, *The Technical Development of Modern Aviation* (1968), 80–2.

84. AC 70/10/129, Frederick Handley Page to Brewer, 9 Oct. 1919.

85. *Ibid.*, Brewer to Frederick Handley Page, 26 Jan. 1921.

86. *Ibid.*, Frederick Handley Page to Brewer, 27 Jan. 1921.

87. AC 70/10/77. First agreement was dated 18 Nov. 1921 and there were several renewals. Most of the Lachmann correspondence is taken up with complaints that Frederick Handley Page did not pay him promptly. Of course Handley Page had the considerable advantage of being able to pay Lachmann small sums in sterling at a time when the value of the mark was falling daily.

88. P.R.O., Avia 8/60.

89. P.R.O., Avia 8/63. Many Air Ministry officials thought the government and producers were so interdependent that they should have access to the Profit and Loss Account of airframe producers as they had with major aero-engine firms Rolls Royce and Bristol: P.R.O., Air 19/143 Nov. 1935.

90. AC 70/10/55.

91. D. N. James, *Gloster Aircraft since 1917* (1971), 27–8.

92. C. H. Barnes, *Shorts Aircraft since 1900* (1967), 18–19.

93. C. H. Barnes, *Bristol Aircraft since 1910* (1964), 33.

94. AC 70/10/79, letters 23 Jan. and 23 May 1935.

95. P.R.O., Air 2/1790 No. S.38208 and P.R.O., Air 6/23.

96. Postan, Hay and Scott, *op. cit.*, 75–6.

97. M.B., April 1937.

98. Ultimately £35,000 was spent developing the H.P. 75 before the idea was abandoned in 1944.

99. For example the premises occupied by Smiths Potato Crisps were taken over by Handley Page: M.B., Jan. 1939.

100. M.B., Aug. 1946.

101. M.B., 29 Nov. 1946.

# THE NORTH BRITISH LOCOMOTIVE COMPANY BETWEEN THE WARS

by R. H. CAMPBELL

## I

The North British Locomotive Company was formed in 1903 through the merger of three established locomotive builders in Glasgow: Neilson, Reid and Company; Dubs and Company; Sharp, Stewart and Company. All were already large, employing respectively 3,410, 2,423 and 1,737 men and boys in September 1902. The amalgamation dominated British locomotive manufacturers. Before 1914 its labour force was about one-half of all labour in the industry, and about one-third if the workshops of the railway companies are included. For over fifty years, until it delivered its last model to Nyasaland in 1958 the North British was a major manufacturer of steam locomotives, producing about thirty per cent of British output in the later 1920s and an even higher proportion after the Second World War. The major part of production went overseas.

In the 1950s the Company encountered difficulties and was eventually forced into liquidation. The reasons for that failure—technical, financial, or whatever they may be—are not the concern of this article. It has the more limited objective of examining the Company's activities, especially between the wars. Though only a study of one firm, it throws light on some controversial issues in the industrial history of those years: on the extent to which a large firm in a vital British industry was in difficulties before 1914; on the extreme nature of the collapse of demand, especially in overseas markets, and of the unprofitability of the inter-war years; on how war, and the post-war boom, made the need for adaptation and change more necessary than ever, but postponed any immediate need to take action; on how those bred to accept the cyclical disturbances of the heavy industries in the years before 1914 postponed any remedial action in spite of catastrophic depression for the relatively few years from 1922 until the beginning of recovery in 1937, and so to a war which repeated many of the benefits and burdens of that of 1914 to 1918.

No generalisations may be based on one case, but a study of the North British contributes as much as many to that accumulation of detailed case studies from which increasingly reliable generalisations about industrial history may be made.[1]

## II

The North British Locomotive Company was floated with a nominal capital of £2 million, consisting of 100,000 five per cent cumulative preference shares of £10 each and 100,000 ordinary shares of £10 each. The ordinary capital and 75,000 of the preference shares were issued. The ordinary stock and 2,000 of the preference shares were allotted to the three vendor companies as follows: Neilson, Reid and Company, £466,316; Dubs and Company, £313,684; and Sharp, Stewart and Company, £240,000. The omens for the financial success of the new company seemed good, so good indeed that the accountants' certificate in the prospectus assured potential subscribers that the experience of the three manufacturing companies indicated that the profits of the new concern would still leave 'a large surplus', even after meeting all expenditure on maintenance, a full allowance for depreciation, payment of five per cent on the preference stock and ten per cent on the ordinary stock.[2] The profit record of the three companies over the previous five years seemed to confirm the accountants' view that the dividends could easily be met on the initial capital stock.

TABLE I

Profits of the Companies before the Formation of the North British Locomotive Company, 1898–1902

|  | 1898 | 1899 | 1900 | 1901 |
|---|---|---|---|---|
| Neilson, Reid & Co. | 107,429 | 133,293 | 105,930 | 107,899 |
| Dubs & Co. | 53,235 | 77,878 | 82,880 | 89,048 |
| Sharp, Stewart & Co. | 58,644 | 55,104 | 53,461 | 64,790 |
| Total | 219,308 | 266,275 | 242,271 | 261,737 |

|  | 1902 | Average 1898–1902 |
|---|---|---|
| Neilson, Reid & Co. | 204,702 | 131,851 |
| Dubs & Co. | 159,809 | 92,570 |
| Sharp, Stewart & Co. | 68,213 | 60,043 |
| Total | 432,725 | 284,464 |

Source: Deloitte papers. UGA. UGD 109/2/3.

The message of the prospectus was that with a good profit record in the past, the amalgamation would ensure that even better years lay ahead. The three works were

all thoroughly equipped and up to date, and in excellent running order; upwards of £450,000 having been spent in extension and improvement of buildings and plant during the last ten years .... They are designed to produce about 600 locomotives per annum, and additional large and costly extensions are now in progress to meet increasing requirements and to admit of further business developments. At present the works are going full time, with large orders in hand .... The Combination will also, it is believed, aid the efforts now being made to standardise locomotives.

The complexity of some of the accounts complicates comparison of performance with prediction.[3] In particular adjustments were made to the figures for profit and loss for reasons which did not produce consistent patterns and which can introduce random fluctuations into the figures quoted. First, the allowance for additions to plant

varied sharply in the years before 1914, from £8,375 in 1912 to
£124,086 in 1909. The Annual Report for 1906 provides an illustration:

> The expenditure in improving and adding to the Buildings
> and Plant of the Company has been considerably greater than
> in any previous year, mainly owing to the extension of the
> Works at Polmadie (the name of which has been changed to
> the Queen's Park Works), and your Directors have thought it
> judicious to provide for part of that outlay out of the revenue
> of the year.[4]

Second, in some years, perhaps most often in years when profits
might otherwise have been high, as shortly before 1914, an allowance
was made for depreciation of investments. How much was allowed
is not stated, but the amount allowed or not affected the level of
profit or loss. The Annual Report for 1911 referred to the balance
of profit 'after making full provision for the further depreciation of
the Investments in the Company'.[5] The third and fourth adjustments,
for depreciation and allocations to reserves, are stated and so can be
added or subtracted as required. Allowances for both followed
similar practices: larger amounts were put to reserve when funds
were available, so that they tended to rise or fall with profits, and,
while the balance of profit and loss carried forward before the war
was positive, any substantial accumulation was prevented by larger
amounts being placed to reserve and depreciation as in 1907 and
1908. In one respect the two allowances differed significantly: while
it was always possible to reduce that for depreciation, or to stop it
altogether, it could not be transferred back to the cumulative balance
of profit to make good any current shortfall, which was exactly the
ultimate necessity for which the general reserve was held. It seems
reasonable to include the amount placed to reserve in the amount
quoted for profits, and to compare it with the promises of the
prospectus.

When compared with the average of the three amalgamating
companies from 1898 to 1902, the North British Locomotive Company's profit record is not good. Between 1903 and 1914 profits
never reached the average level of the three companies in the five
years before the amalgamation, and in only four years (1906, 1907,
1908 and 1914) were the profits higher than in the worst year between
1898 and 1902. It is not surprising in these circumstances that the
ultimate test to the shareholders of the dividend paid was not one
the Company passed with flying colours. In 1904 the dividend paid
to the ordinary shareholders was cut from the promised ten per cent
to eight per cent (though the deficiency was made good in 1906)
and the promised ten per cent was not paid in four more years to
1914. In the same years earnings on total assets employed topped
ten per cent only twice. The directors could maintain that more
important than paying high dividends was the need to follow a
policy which placed the Company in a strong financial position,

and that they were justified in doing so because of the economic conditions in which the Company operated.

Output, which never reached the capacity of 600 engines annually mentioned in the prospectus, fell sharply in 1909 and had not fully recovered before the war.[6] In these years the annual reports complained about adverse trading conditions. In 1909, 'During the 12 months under review there was a great falling off in the demand for Locomotives, and the Works were not fully employed. This, with the lower basis of prices ruling, accounts for the reduction in the Profit shown': in 1910, 'The reduced demand for Locomotives referred to in the last Report has, unfortunately, continued, and been even more pronounced during the year under review, and, with the lower range of prices consequently obtainable, has caused the material diminution of Profit shown'; in 1911, 'The relatively small demand for Locomotives during the year has prevented the Works of the Company being employed to their best advantage, and this, combined with the continued low level of prices, accounts for the result shown in the Balance Sheet not being more satisfactory'; in 1912, 'While the demand for Locomotives improved during the year the Colliers' Strike, together with other local labour difficulties, seriously interfered with the output from the Works.'[7]

The fall from the more prosperous conditions of 1905 to 1908 was no great surprise to the directors. In the west of Scotland they were accustomed to mixed prosperity and so had no desire to pay more in dividends than had been stated in the prospectus and to cut the dividend with alacrity when necessary to ensure the Company would be able to withstand the next depression. In the Report for 1904, when the ordinary dividend was cut from ten to eight per cent, the directors specifically stated that it was their policy to continue to build up reserves because 'of the probability that some time may elapse before the present depression passes away'.[8] That trade was considered bad in the years before the war is evident in the chairman's remarks at annual general meetings. In 1909 he reported cheerfully that the Company's 'position was better, not worse, than it was a year ago, and that the era of reduced dividends had not yet arrived'. But, even when reporting record profits he reminded shareholders that their trade was largely export and subject to such fluctuations that 'it was not unlikely that they might have been prepared for a bad loss'.[9] At the annual general meeting on 14 March 1911 the chairman recalled the prediction:

> I remember saying to you, I think, two years ago, that the reports we had submitted up till that time disclosed a condition of prosperity so monotonous in its uniformity that I felt I would have but little to say at future meetings until the time came when we had to show you the other side of the shield. That time, unhappily has now come . . . .[10]

After another two years the annual general meeting was given another gloomy speech from the chairman, who lamented:

a much reduced output from the workshops, the result being that this restriction added about £2·10s. per ton to the cost of the work turned out over that of former years. Within the last two years foreign competitors had booked about 212 locomotives for markets which were formerly British exclusively, and all these engines could quite comfortably have been built in British shops in the time required, in addition to the work produced therefrom, if the workmen had only maintained their former output. Markets which had been thus entered by the foreigner would be more difficult to recover and retain in the future.[11]

Even then a new phase of prosperity was beginning, though one which, as for so much else in that year, bore ill omens. By then the reluctance to raise the ordinary dividend above ten per cent when profits rose, and the readiness to cut it whenever profits fell, combined with the failure to transfer adequate funds from the general reserve to maintain the dividend, ensured that reserves were built up. In spite of an indifferent financial performance before the war, substantial sums had been put towards depreciation, and in 1914 the Company had investments standing in its balance sheet at £639,930, a cumulative reserve standing at £500,000, and a carried forward balance of profit of £33,594.

### III

In 1919 the Company was in a stronger financial position than ever and well set for expansion. In the balance sheet investments stood at £1,265,379 after providing for their depreciation; the general reserve fund was £600,000; the cumulative profit carried forward was £338,783; £100,000 was placed to depreciation; though, unfavourably, there were sundry creditors of £1,013,595 against sundry debtors of only £226,797. In 1920 the ordinary stock of the Company was increased from £1 to £2 million and the reserve of £600,000 reduced to £350,000 by issuing one new share for every four held on the old ordinary stock of £1 million. The tone of the report for 1919, when presented in 1920, was understandably congratulatory: 'in view of the difficulties of the situation . . . the result set forth will no doubt be considered satisfactory'.[12] What was not foreseen, and what perhaps could not have been foreseen, was the change in the conditions under which the Company was to operate for the next two decades. Unsatisfactory trading did not appear immediately. In 1920 the Company enjoyed the prosperity of the post-war boom and orders were accepted for 315 locomotives which were built later. Orders fell sharply in the following year, but recovered steadily until 1930. As before 1914 a major part of the orders came from overseas—India, Egypt, China, and particularly from South Africa, but from 1923 the new railway companies at home provided an important demand. Orders remained at a high level, even if not approaching the heights of 1920, until the end of the decade. A catastrophic collapse came only in the 1930s.

TABLE II
Contracts and Locomotives, 1920 to 1938

| Year | Contracts | Total locomotives | LMS | Locomotives ordered by LNER | GWR | SR |
|------|-----------|-------------------|-----|------|-----|-----|
| 1920 | 29 | 315 | — | — | — | — |
| 1921 | 4 | 49 | — | — | — | — |
| 1922 | 8 | 79 | — | — | — | — |
| 1923 | 14 | 116 | 20 | 20 | — | — |
| 1924 | 13 | 142 | 52 | — | — | 20 |
| 1925 | 16 | 117 | — | — | — | 25 |
| 1926 | 14 | 199 | 85 | — | — | — |
| 1927 | 14 | 149 | 80 | — | — | — |
| 1928 | 10 | 145 | 1 | 10 | 50 | — |
| 1929 | 13 | 137 | — | — | 25 | — |
| 1930 | 7 | 60 | — | — | 25 | — |
| 1931 | 4 | 13 | — | — | — | .. |
| 1932 | 3 | 15 | — | — | — | — |
| 1933 | 2 | 51 | 50 | — | — | — |
| 1934 | 4 | 60 | — | — | — | — |
| 1935 | 10 | 155 | 73 | 20 | — | — |
| 1936 | 7 | 7 | — | — | — | — |
| 1937 | 11 | 120 | — | — | — | — |
| 1938 | 7 | 58 | — | — | — | — |

*Source:* NBLC papers: UGA, UGD 11/6/1, 2 and 3 and Mitchell Library, *Engine Orders 1903 to 1961.* (In the financial accounts a small number of contracts (19 out of a total of 190) were amalgamated and so the number of cases considered in the financial analysis below is less than the number of contracts. In the above table one contract for one locomotive for stock in 1924 is excluded because no details are given. In the discussion on material costs one other is excluded because of doubtful information.)

But, even in 1920 while many contracts were still being placed, symptoms of the insecure competitive position of the Company, which were to become evident in the 1930s, may be detected. A change emerged between the contracts accepted in 1920 and in 1921.[13] With one exception, a contract for five engines with South Indian Railways, concluded in October 1920 and completed in November 1920, the other contracts of 1920 were recorded as profitable. The exception made a loss of £1,113 over the contract price of £44,639, but it was swamped by the profitability of the others, though their profitability, covering 310 locomotives, varied: 18 locomotives were in the range of 0 to 9 per cent; 155 between 10 and 19 per cent; 77 between 20 and 29 per cent; 48 between 30 and 39 per cent; and 12 between 40 and 49 per cent.

Variations in the level of profitability of contracts can be explained more by the date of their acceptance than by the date of their completion. The seventeen contracts covering 175 locomotives agreed in the second half of 1920 were distributed in the upper levels of profitability more than the twelve contracts covering 140 locomotives agreed in the first half. By contrast there was no apparently consistent pattern in the profitability of the contracts as they were completed between December 1920 and May 1922.

Throughout 1921, and into May 1922, the Company was completing contracts accepted in 1920 and doing so at levels of

TABLE III
Profitability of Contracts Accepted in 1920

| | Per cent | Contracts (locomotives) | |
| | | January to June | July to December |
| --- | --- | --- | --- |
| Loss | 0–9 | — | 1 (5) |
| Profit | 0–9 | 2 (12) | 1 (6) |
| | 10–19 | 6 (89) | 6 (66) |
| | 20–29 | 4 (39) | 4 (38) |
| | 30–39 | — | 3 (48) |
| | 40–49 | — | 2 (12) |
| | | 12 (140) | 17 (175) |

Date of Completion of Contracts Accepted in 1920, Showing Number of Locomotives and Rate of Profit on Contract

*1920*
December    15 at 17%.

*1921*
January     —
February    7 at 0·2%; 15 at 19%.
March       14 at 12%; 6 at 17%.
April       50 at 17%; 5 at 8%.
May         —
June        2 at 13%; 2 at 17%; 15 at 26%; 15 at 23%; 4 at 25%
July        10 at 15%; 5 at 22%; 2 at 40%; 3 at 33%.
August      10 at 45%.
September   —
October     20 at 17%; 7 at 25%.
November    7 at 16%; 5 at −2%.
December    8 at 11%; 1 at 25%; 25 at 29%; 25 at 36%; 5 at 22%

*1922*
January     —
February    —
March       6 at 12%.
April       6 at 3%.
May         20 at 39%.

*Source:* NBLC papers. UGA, UGD 11/6/1 and Mitchell Library *Engine Orders, 1903–1961.*

profitability which differed, but which showed a marked tendency to earn higher profits on the more recently accepted contracts. That contracts for only 49 locomotives were accepted in 1921 against the 315 of 1920 is in itself not surprising and, in light of the subsequent expansion of demand in the later 1920s, could easily have been interpreted, on the practice of pre-war years, as an inevitable response to the high demand of the previous year. Certainly at the annual general meeting in March 1921 the chairman was optimistic: when, referring to the recent trade depression, 'he thought that in their specific business it would not be so severe nor so prolonged as in many others', and held that the 'supreme necessity' for improvement lay in cheaper coal.[14] That more was at stake was evident in a significant and sharp change in the profitability of contracts accepted in 1921 and completed in 1922. Three contracts of 1920 were completed in that year, and, running true to the form of those accepted in 1920, all were profitable though at different levels. In March one for six locomotives produced a profit of £10,452 on a contract price of £97,304. In April the last contract accepted in 1920, a relatively small one for six locomotives for the Glasgow and South Western Railway Company proved barely profitable, leaving £2,265 on the contract price of £87,840. In May a large contract of twenty locomotives for the New Zealand Government, accepted in November 1920, was highly profitable, at a rate of profit on the contract of 39 per cent. Thereafter disaster struck.

The first contract of 1921, for Bombay Railways, was not accepted until May, when many contracts, which were to prove profitable, had still to be completed, but, when the Bombay contract was completed, in October 1922, it gave only a small profit of 3·7 per cent. Worse followed. All other contracts of 1921 were unprofitable, and so were all contracts until 1925. From 1921 to 1929 inclusive 106 contracts were accepted for 1,133 locomotives and, in 1922, two contracts were accepted to supply mechanical parts for locomotives to the English Electric Company. Of the former 18 supplying 154 locomotives were profitable, but at lower levels than in the post-war boom: 13, supplying 135 locomotives in the range of 0 to 9 per cent; 5, supplying 19 locomotives, in the range of 10 to 19 per cent. Sometimes the profits earned were very low, as in two large contracts with the LMS for 55 locomotives in 1926. On the contract prices of £101,441 and £136,250 profits of only £4,312 and £3,863 respectively were realised. After 1925 until the end of the decade the only contract to give a profit of over 10 per cent was one completed from August 1929 to March 1930 for Sao Paulo Railway. It stood out exceptionally, being along with two others of September 1929 and May 1935 the only profitable contracts accepted between September 1927 and June 1937.

By contrast, contracts accepted from 1921 were often substantially unprofitable: 30, supplying 367 locomotives were in the range of 0 to 9 per cent; 20, supplying 244 locomotives, between 10 and 19 per cent; 24, supplying 331 locomotives, between 20 and 29 per cent; 7, supplying 22 locomotives, between 30 and 39 per cent; 6, supplying 14 locomotives between 40 and 49 per cent and 1, supplying 1 locomotive, between 50 and 59 per cent.

The 1920s saw the establishment of unprofitable contracts. The early years of the 1930s were marked, not by changes in the level of profitability of contracts, but by their sparseness, though the losses on some were appalling. The level of unprofitability changed markedly after June 1935, and from contracts accepted after mid-June 1937 until the outbreak of war, only one, agreed in the summer of 1937, was unprofitable. Appropriately it was a contract for twenty locomotives for Egyptian State Railways, for which on all contracts completed between the wars, covering 225 locomotives, losses were recorded. Though profitable, the number of

TABLE IV
Profitability of Contracts and Locomotives, 1930 to 1938

|  | Per cent | Contracts | Locomotives |
|---|---|---|---|
| Profit | 10–19 | 7 | 56 |
|  | 0–9 | 5 | 57 |
| Loss | 0–9 | 14 | 118 |
|  | 10–19 | 8 | 165 |
|  | 20–29 | 4 | 12 |
|  | 30–39 | 2 | 53 |
|  | 40–49 | 3 | 30 |
|  | 50–59 | 6 | 24 |
|  | 60–69 | 1 | 10 |
|  | 70–79 | — | — |
|  | 80–89 | 1 | 5 |
|  | 90–99 | 1 | 1 |
|  | 100–109 | 2 | 7 |
|  | 110+ | 1 | 1 |

*Source:* NBLC papers. UGA, UGD 11/6/2 and 3, and Mitchell Library *Engine Orders 1903–1961.*

TABLE V

| | | Total contract cost £ | Total ascertained cost £ | Profit £ | Loss £ |
|---|---|---|---|---|---|
| | 1920 | 4,008,199 | 3,313,091 | 695,108 | — |
| | 1 | 446,538 | 498,515 | — | 31,979 |
| (total contracts) | 2 | 488,046 | 544,334 | — | 56,228 |
| (locomotive contracts) | | 395,660 | 421,180 | — | 25,250 |
| | 3 | 665,827 | 960,063 | — | 295,016 |
| | 4 | 931,047 | 1,011,728 | — | 80,618 |
| | 5 | 653,801 | 731,588 | — | 77,787 |
| | 6 | 983,761 | 1,097,429 | — | 113,293 |
| | 7 | 976,286 | 1,027,054 | — | 50,768 |
| | 8 | 726,457 | 879,643 | — | 153,186 |
| | 9 | 865,710 | 947,395 | — | 90,685 |
| | 1930 | 335,620 | 451,056 | — | 115,436 |
| | 1 | 68,099 | 130,416 | — | 62,317 |
| | 2 | 103,433 | 178,987 | — | 75,554 |
| | 3 | 297,899 | 406,522 | — | 108,623 |
| | 4 | 366,660 | 800,692 | — | 434,032 |
| | 5 | 894,862 | 1,009,447 | — | 114,585 |
| | 6 | 38,640 | 39,833 | — | 1,193 |
| | 7 | 922,207 | 1,094,715 | — | 172,508 |
| | 8 | 604,815 | 537,408 | 67,407 | — |

*Source:* NBLC papers in UGA, UGD 11/6/1, 2, 3 and Mitchell Library *Engine Orders, 1903–1961.*

contracts from mid-1937 to the end of 1938 was only sixteen, and none showed the level of profitability of earlier days, none achieving the level of 20 per cent.

The morass into which the contracts for locomotives took the Company in the fifteen years from 1921 to 1937 may be summarised

by taking the total value of contracts accepted each year, and com-
paring it with the total ascertained costs of completion for the years
from 1920 to 1938. The two terminal years stand out from the
similarity of all the others. The losses of the 1930s are worse, not in
total, apart from the enormous loss of 1934, but because the losses
were incurred on a smaller number of contracts or locomotives.

IV

The changed position of the Company was evident in the profits—
and losses—which were earned.[15] Losses in 1923 and 1924, and in
1928 to 1935 (with the exception of 1932) alone demonstrated the
change. Earnings on total assets employed were correspondingly
low. The ten per cent dividend at the end of the war was not maintained long and the dividend to ordinary stock holders fell throughout the 1920s. They received their last dividend of 2½ per cent in
1929 until 3 per cent was paid in 1942. The preference dividend
was reduced in 1933, passed altogether between 1933 and 1939,
and was made up only by 1942.

The immediate reason why the Company was able to survive
was that it was in a strong financial position in 1919 and gained from
the post-war boom. From the experience of the pre-war years a collapse
in trade was not unexpected and was a hazard to be met by the
established procedure of drawing on accumulated reserves. In their
report for 1924, a year when a loss was recorded, the directors held
that 'the trading loss sustained has in some measure been modified
by the strong financial position of the Company', a statement which
could be applied more generally to other years between the wars.
The level of profit and the dividend paid were poor, but they would
have been much worse but for action to support them by drawing on
those items in the accounts which had been used to build up the
Company's financial resources before the war.

First, in 1920 some unstated allowance was made for the
depreciation of investments. Subsequently the report of the annual
general meeting in 1922 showed that such resources were being
consolidated. 'Advantage was taken throughout the year of the rise
in certain securities held, and these have been realised at a profit to
the company. The funds so obtained, not being immediately required for the financing of contracts, have been reinvested in what
are considered marketable securities.'[16] But after 1920 the issue is
not mentioned in the directors' reports until 1932, and in those years
the level of investments was substantial, at around one million
pounds. In 1932, when the ordinary shareholders were receiving
nothing, and when the preference dividend was being halved, the
directors observed in their annual report that 'while there was an
actual trading loss, this was more than offset by substantial gains
which accrued from interest, and from realisation and conversion
of investments. Such favourable financial conditions are exceptional
and cannot be relied upon to recur.'[17] Similarly in 1933, 'while there
was an exceptional loss on trading, this was modified considerably

by gains which accrued from interest and from realisation of investments'.[18] And again, in 1934, '... the loss on manufacture was
partly met from interest on investments and satisfactory realisation
of certain securities'.[19] Investments, which had stood in the balance
sheet at around one million pounds were reduced by almost half in
value in the balance sheets from 1934 until the Second World War.
Second, depreciation allowances had fluctuated before the war but
had averaged over £40,000 annually from 1903. After the war the
amount allowed fell sharply from £100,000 in 1919 and £50,000 in
1920 to nothing from 1933 to 1938 inclusive. Third, the cumulative
balance of reserves, which had stood at £350,000 after the restructuring of the capital of the Company in 1920 rose again to a maximum of £500,000 in 1922. Thereafter it was reduced steadily until
it reached £15,000 in 1933. When transfers from it were no longer
possible the reduced preference dividend had to be cut altogether.
Even these measures were, however, inadequate to prevent the
Company sinking into deeper financial problems in the mid-1930s.
The cumulative balance of profit, which had stood at £338,783 at
the beginning of 1920 and at £404,503 at the beginning of 1921 was
also eaten into and, when depreciation, transfers from the reserve,
and dividends had all ceased, became negative in 1935, and fell to
its record low debit balance of £119,491 in 1936, remaining negative
until wartime profits rendered it positive once more.

Not surprisingly, the attitude of the directors seems to have been
that the only way to deal with the situation between the wars was
to wait till the depression ended, as in the shorter depressions of the
pre-war years. The attitude was soon evident. In the report for 1922,
a year

> of extreme trade depression, during which it has not been
> possible to keep the Works of the Company adequately engaged
> ... As a temporary measure, and in the hope of a revival in
> trade, your Directors have endeavoured to keep all three
> Establishments in operation and to retain the services of as
> many as possible of their skilled staff and workmen, and to this
> end have taken certain contracts of unremunerative prices.[20]

Even the phraseology of the annual reports became standardised:
'difficult trading' in 1926, 1928 and then 'extreme depression' in
1929, 1930, 1931. By the 1930s the possibility of profitable contracts
had almost been abandoned. In 1933 an 'important' contract for
fifty locomotives for the LMS 'at extremely low prices'[21] later produced a loss of almost £100,000; in 1934 'the contracts ... were
mainly secured with the object of giving employment and of maintaining the plant and machinery in the highest state of efficiency',
though they were insufficient to do so;[22] in 1935, 'such contracts as
were available could only be obtained on conditions which left
little hope of remunerative return'.[23]

By the mid-1920s there is some evidence that the Company
considered that it faced conditions different from the short-term

depression of the pre-war years. The statement of the chairman at the annual general meeting in March 1924 contrasts with the less concerned view of depression at the meeting in 1911.[24] Sir Hugh Reid was reported as having

> alluded to the continued depression . . . which was not due as in pre-war times to over-production, but rather to the restricted purchasing powers of the different markets of the world, the aftermath of the war. This country had spent vast sums in the alleviation of distress arising from unemployment, while Continental countries had striven rather to assist their manufacturers to secure employment for their workpeople, particularly those having technical skill in the basic industries, such as the locomotive trade. The dole, even if it could be fairly distributed, would always be a very poor substitute for wages, the recognised reward of productive labour . . . . Imperial and local taxation was now a grievous burden and a very severe handicap to industry, especially when in competition for the export trade, so essential to the well-being and prosperity of this country.[25]

The attribution of blame to a mixture of collapsing overseas markets, especially in the Empire, and to both government action and inaction foreshadowed Sir Hugh Reid's later approach to rationalisation. The worsening depression of the 1930s was explained with increasing emphasis to the shareholders as the consequence of collapsing overseas markets. The report for 1937 is typical:

> The number of orders obtained in the overseas markets on which the Company now so largely depends did not fulfil expectations. This no doubt was due in a large measure to the disturbed international situation which prevailed throughout the year. In particular, the unfortunate conflict in the Far East arrested progress in what appeared to be a promising development in railway enterprise in China. In South America an early promise of increased business from that quarter did not materialise, while, with the notable exception of South Africa, the Dominions provided little or no work.[26]

The Company's analysis was supported by others. *The Glasgow Herald Trade Review* showed an increasing testiness in its comments on overseas customers as the 1920s passed and recovery failed to materialise: in 1922, it noted that the North British had secured an order for 48 engines for India,[27] and continued:

> India, on which the prosperity of our locomotive builders has so largely depended in the past, is now, in furtherance of the policy of 'India for the Indians', desirous of having the work done within her own borders, and is ready to give preference to the native production. Even in the case of contracts which she is prepared to place outside she is advertising her require-

ments and inviting offers for the work from foreign builders, and orders for our Indian Empire have recently been placed with Continental builders.[28]

In 1928: 'The excellence of British workmanship is known the world over, and overseas purchasers, especially those within the borders of the Empire, should be willing to accord British builders a certain preference in price over their foreign competitors';[29] in 1930: 'India remains the industry's best customer, and it is to be deplored that the Mother Country in these times is set aside and denied the work which would go so far to afford employment to her idle men.'[30]

As the markets remained stagnant complaints against government policy led to more direct demands for aid, as in 1934, when it was argued in the annual report that '... the Locomotive Industry, having a definite value which affects the balance of international trade through its exports, calls for Government support equally with that recently accorded to shipping, agriculture, etc. ...'[31] With government aid not forthcoming, possible remedial action lay in the manipulation of costs, but examination of their costs indicates the difficulties of determining any line of action which might have provided a solution and engenders sympathy with the view that the catastrophic collapse of their traditional markets virtually provided a problem beyond their power to solve.

## V

The most consistent breakdown of costs in contracts is for materials. Details of those for 652 locomotives, manufactured under 76 contracts at the Queen's Park works before 1914 are used for comparison with those of the inter-war years.[32]

Though the distribution of the proportions of material to total costs was widespread both before and after the war, the proportion tended to fall afterwards, reversing a tendency which had been evident in 1912, and especially in 1913. Of the sample of the 76 Queen's Park contracts 32 (42·1 per cent) had material costs of over 50 per cent, but their distribution was concentrated towards the immediate pre-war years: two out of 12 in 1909; four out of 13 in 1910; one out of 14 in 1911; but 10 out of 17 in 1912 and 15 out of 20 in 1913.[33] By contrast only seven out of 29 (24·1 per cent) were over 50 per cent in 1920. Thereafter throughout the remainder of the inter-war years none exceeded 50 per cent, except one small contract (L.858) for the LMS, on which the material costs were 61 per cent, but for which the information is so suspect that it has been excluded from the analysis. The next highest, of 50 per cent, was in a very large contract for 50 engines for the New Zealand government, with an invoiced cost of £466,274. The contrast is as striking when the lower proportions of material costs are compared. Of the 76 cases in the sample before the war, 11 (14·5 per cent) had material costs of less than 40 per cent; seven out of 29 (24·1 per cent) in 1920; 62 out of 92 (67·4 per cent) in the subsequent years of the 1920s; 34 out of 49 (69·4 per cent) in the 1930s.

Though the proportion of material costs fell from the years before the war, it remained low in contracts of small total costs and high in the larger contracts. The position before the war may be summarised by examining the material costs of the contracts with the largest and smallest costs in each year. Though the smallest and largest did not always have the lowest and highest material costs, the combination of large contracts with high material costs and small contracts with low material costs is apparent.

TABLE VI
Proportion of Material Costs in Lowest and Highest Total Costs

|      | Lowest (materials cost per cent) | Highest (materials cost per cent) |
|------|------------------|------------------|
| 1909 | £3,636 (42%) | £75,225 (50%)** |
| 1910 | £2,178 (36%)* | £91,129 (46%) |
| 1911 | £2,080 (40%) | £112,995 (43%) |
| 1912 | £2,060 (38%)* | £106,216 (59%)** |
| 1913 | £2,228 (33%)* | £101,047 (57%) |

* Also lowest percentage for the year.
** Also highest percentage for the year.

Source: NBLC papers. UGA, UGD 11/4/1.

The same tendency appeared after the war. Of the 81 cases of total costs of under £50,000 between 1920 and 1938, 47 (58 per cent) had material costs of 33 per cent of total costs and below and only four (5 per cent) had material costs of over 45 per cent, but of the 53 cases of over £100,000 only five (9 per cent) had material costs of 33 per cent and below but 16 (30 per cent) had material costs of over 45 per cent.

Though before and after the war the smaller contracts had smaller material costs, the tendency for the proportion to rise before the war and to fall after it, especially after 1920, cannot be explained by changes in the size of contracts. The increasing proportion of material costs in 1912 and 1913 was evident even in the lower ranges. Of the 22 cases in ranges below £15,000 in 1909 to 1911 only one had a proportion greater than 50 per cent, while in 1912 and 1913, six of the 13 cases in the same range exceeded 50 per cent. Nor can the return to lower material costs after the war be explained by changes in the size of contracts, when judged by the number of locomotives in them. The change before and after the war was in the number of contracts and not in the number of locomotives they covered.[34]

Since the proportion of material costs was lower than before the war, it was easy to subscribe in the 1920s to the popular view that higher wages caused much of the unprofitability of the contracts, especially when there was an apparent association of lower material costs, or high non-material costs—of which labour was always an important element—and decreased profitability. In 1920 the most profitable contracts were those with high material costs. Of the seven above 25 per cent profit, material costs ranged from 40 to 55 per cent

TABLE VII
Contracts and Locomotives, 1903 to 1913

|      | Contracts | Locomotives |
|------|-----------|-------------|
| 1903 | 52*       | 335         |
| 4    | 52        | 377         |
| 5    | 66*       | 620         |
| 6    | 63        | 573         |
| 7    | 57        | 485         |
| 8    | 49        | 431         |
| 9    | 53        | 323         |
| 1910 | 48        | 348         |
| 1    | 47        | 317         |
| 2    | 59        | 471         |
| 3    | 64        | 640         |

* Excludes one cancelled.

Source: NBLC papers in Mitchell Library, Engine Orders, 1903–1961.

with an average of 46 per cent. By contrast from 1921 to 1938 the most unprofitable cases had lower material costs. Of the 32 with losses of over 25 per cent, material costs ranged from 11 to 40 per cent with an average of 28 per cent. Comparison with the experience of 1920 may be misleading because of the year's exceptional characteristics. Comparison is preferable of the material costs of the most unprofitable contracts of 1921 to 1938 with those of all contracts, or with the small, and so unreliable, sample of profitable contracts in the same period. The difference is then less, but not unimportant. The average material cost of 28 per cent for the unprofitable contracts from 1921 to 1938 has to be compared with that of 34 per cent for all 141 contracts, and of 37 per cent for the 27 profitable contracts.

The explanation of differences in profitability does not lie entirely in the size of the contracts. Though the more profitable contracts between the wars had higher material costs, and the larger contracts had higher material costs, there is no automatic link between the size of the contract and profitability. Of the 81 contracts between 1921 and 1938 which had total costs of less than £50,000, 26 (32 per cent) were profitable—seven in 1920 and five in 1938—and 55 (68 per cent) were unprofitable. In the same period, 53 contracts were in ranges over £100,000 and 17 (32 per cent) were profitable—11 in 1920—and 36 (68 per cent) were unprofitable. The peculiar conditions of 1920 and, to a lesser extent, of 1938 affect the conclusion, but the identical proportions prevent any firm distinction being drawn between the profitability of the large and the small contracts to lead to an outright rejection of the possibility, entertained by many in the 1920s at least, of an association of low material costs and profitability in a way which placed responsibility for the lack of profitability of contracts on the higher proportion of non-material costs, and that meant especially on higher labour charges. The possible association warrants further investigation.

Changes in the value of money alone inhibit comparisons of wages over time, but the records of the Company reveal changes both in the inter-war years and in comparison with pre-war in the proportions of wages paid to the value of total output. In the years 1904 to 1913 the average annual percentage was 32·168.[35] The three years with higher percentages, 1909, and especially 1910 and 1911, were also the least profitable of the decade, though the reasons for the changed proportions varied. In 1909 the wages bill fell below £500,000 for the first time, the consequence more of a sharp fall in wages than in the numbers employed. In 1910 the wages bill fell more substantially still, but chiefly because of a fall in the numbers employed, by 18·3 per cent from the previous year, which offset the higher average wages paid. In 1911 a further increase in wages to among the higher levels of the pre-war years, and increased employment, took the wages bill for the year over £500,000 again. But output, while higher than in 1910, was still low by the standards of the decade. A high percentage of wages to output coincided with diminished profitability and low value of output.

After the war the evidence seemed to provide some support for those who attributed the diminished profitability to higher wages. Average wages paid per employee were substantially above the pre-war earnings. The highest average before the war was 31s. 9½d. per week in 1913, while the lowest between the wars was 41s. 0½d. in 1922, itself low by the standards of those years, as the next lowest was 45s. 4d. in 1931. And after the war the percentage of wages to the total value of output was 47·815 per cent compared with 32·168 per cent before the war. The explanation of the increased percentage was not increased wages per employee because, in spite of that increase, a sharp fall in employment led to lower total wages bills. The annual average number of men and boys employed between 1904 and 1913 of 7,169 was never exceeded after 1920; even half the average was exceeded, and that only slightly after 1922, in three years of the 1920s and never in the 1930s. So even with the higher wages per employee, the annual average wages bill between 1904 and 1913 of £513,520 was greater than that between 1922 and 1938, except in 1925 and 1927, and in these years the excess was slight.

The higher proportion of wages to output was, therefore, as dramatically as in the pre-war years, the result of a fall in output, the average value of which between 1904 and 1913 was not exceeded after 1921. The fall in output was particularly sharp in the unprofitable years. After the war, though operating with different magnitudes, the same relationships were evident as before the war: the proportion of total wages to total output was high when output was low and returns were unprofitable. The experience of nine years between the wars, when the proportion of total wages to total output was over 45 per cent provides illustrations. Between 1922 and 1927 the average value of annual output was £1,016,677. Two years, 1923 and 1924, had proportions of total wages to total output of over 45 per cent; they were years with output well below the average; they were years of losses, the only ones of the period. From 1928 to 1938 the average output was £603,983. In the seven years which had a percentage of wages to total output above 45 per cent, only one, 1929, had an output above the average. Of the remaining six all had output below the average and only two made a profit: 1932, when the total collapse of output makes the year exceptional, and 1937, when the fall in output, of 35 per cent from 1936, was accompanied by stable average wages and a fall in employment of only 13 per cent from 1936, reflecting the beginnings of revival in the heavy industries and leading to the unusually high percentage of wages to total output. By contrast 1928 and 1929, before the total collapse of the 1930s, recorded losses, but in both output was still above the average for the period and in 1928 the percentage of wages to total costs was still below 45.

The higher percentage of wages to total output, notably in the less prosperous years before the war, was even more notable after 1921. It was easy to explain the cause as the higher wages being paid, even when their effect was offset by reduced employment, but the critical factor in explaining the higher percentages and the overall losses which so usually accompanied them was the reduction in output.

From 1933 the Company undertook a more detailed analysis of costs which confirms the contribution of stagnant output to unprofitability by revealing the high level of oncost charges in those years.[36] Though details of oncost charges were available earlier they were analysed in the 1930s as had not been done previously. It is therefore possible to show for each contract from 1933 to 1938 a distribution of costs between materials, net wages incurred on that contract, and oncost added to the time wages. Similar figures have been calculated separately for 1920.[37] The problem which clearly worried the compilers of the fuller information on costs in 1931 and 1932 was the high level of oncost. In a contract accepted in June 1931 the proportions were: materials, 17: net wages, 12; oncost, 65; other, 6; eliciting a marginal note from the bookkeeper against the entry for oncosts, 'shops practically empty'. Hence the high level of oncost until the shops were fuller in the later 1930s. The average percentage of oncost was 26 in 1920 and the same again from mid-1937 to the end of 1938. From 1933 to mid-1937 it was 36 per cent. In 1938, when all contracts were profitable, the total oncost was only once above that for net wages, whereas throughout all the other contracts accepted during the 1930s, of which only five (four of which were in 1937) were profitable, oncost was less than net wages in only three—two accepted in 1934 and the last of those accepted in 1937. It was on this element that attention could be concentrated in attempts to reduce costs, but it was one which ceased to be a problem if output was increased. That solution, rather than any reduction in costs, was the solution to its problems to which the Company subscribed strongly in its public statements. Its catastrophic performance between the wars was because its traditional markets had collapsed.

Any study of the experience of one firm does not provide adequate evidence for generalisations, only a demonstration of some problems which had to be tackled. The examination of the experience of the North British Locomotive Company between the wars highlights the gravity of its trading position. Demand collapsed so catastrophically that the possibility of any internal action rectifying the Company's parlous situation was unlikely. In general the principles and practice of the calculation of overhead costs are varied, even confused, and, in the particular case of the North British Locomotive Company, no matter how calculated, overhead costs were inescapably high. The Company began operations claiming a capacity output of 600 locomotives, a level of production it never reached. The nature of locomotives changed much in the years after 1903, and so did the capacity output, but by any standards of capacity, the output of many years between the wars was so abysmally low that the attribution of overheads, even reduced to take account of the extraordinary trading conditions, could only load contracts with such charges that profitable production was virtually impossible. Acceptance of orders at patently unrenumerative rates in order to provide some employment to hold a skilled labour force together exacerbated the unprofitable production. The solution lay in expanding sales. Concentration on the desirability of doing so—by what action or by whom is another matter—reflected a valid appraisal of the problems facing the Company, the analytical validity rendered superficial only by the practical improbability of re-establishing the old level of demand.

So long as such an ultimate solution was expected, concern over the rising proportion of costs which seemed attributable to higher wage rates than before the war was a subsidiary issue, any change in which was likely to contribute only marginally towards profitable production so long as demand was so low. Profitability lay not in the manipulation of costs, not in changes in production, but in an increase in demand. To expect an increase in demand after 1920, and to base policy, however remotely on such an expectation, may have been short-sighted, reflecting an inability to recognise the influence of changing technology on the aggregate demand for steam engines and of changing international production and commercial policy on the demand for the engines produced in Britain, but to have done otherwise required a rapid change in outlook by those reared in the tradition of the production of steam locomotives before 1914, and one which seemed less necessary by the later 1930s in any case. Above all, perhaps, in the case of the North British Locomotive Company, its financially strong position, built up partly as a deliberate policy, born of the experience of the years before 1914, to provide in good years the resources for the lean years, enabled it to survive the years of poor trading conditions until recovery, limited though it was, emerged in the later 1930s. To suggest the Company should have acted otherwise would be to suggest it should have escaped from the limitations of its time and place and have acquired the wisdom of hindsight granted only to latter-day historians.

*University of Stirling*

TABLE VIII

North British Locomotive Company Annual Accounts

| Year | B/f profit/loss £ | Profit/Loss (excl. depreciation) £ | Ordinary Dividend % | Reserves To £ | Reserves From £ | Cumulative Reserve £ | Additions to Plant £ | Investments in balance sheet £ | To Depreciation £ | Fixed Assets £ | Profit Fixed Assets % | Total Assets £ | Profit Total Assets % |
|---|---|---|---|---|---|---|---|---|---|---|---|---|---|
| 1903 | — | 193,065[1] | 10 | 40,000[1] | | 40,000 | 41,845 | 376,752 (+loans) | 40,000 | 965,341 | 20·0 | 2,050,610 | 9·4 |
| 4 | 3,189 | 179,515 | 8 | 40,000 | | 80,000 | 21,194 | 511,991 (+loans) | 50,000 | 908,057 | 19·8 | 2,071,391 | 8·7 |
| 5 | 17,704 | 206,394 | 10 | 70,000 | | 150,000 | 17,225 | 680,905 | 50,000 | 875,283 | 23·6 | 2,153,123 | 9·6 |
| 6 | 16,599 | 225,520 | 12 | 70,000 | | 220,000 | 54,582 | 787,589 | 50,000 | 879,865 | 25·6 | 2,262,568 | 9·1 |
| 7 | 14,620 | 234,790 | 10 | 80,000 | | 300,000 | 20,258 | 732,401 | 60,000 | 840,124 | 27·9 | 2,350,165 | 10·0 |
| 8 | 31,911 | 241,095 | 10 | 100,000 | | 400,000 | 12,128 | 1,068,532 | 60,000 | 792,252 | 30·4 | 2,423,563 | 9·9 |
| 9 | 35,506 | 165,659 | 8 | 50,000 | | 450,000 | 124,086 | 1,057,636 | 50,000 | 866,338 | 19·1 | 2,451,253 | 6·8 |
| 1910 | 33,666 | 9,233 | 5 | | 50,000 | 400,000 | 95,684 | 883,370 | 20,000 | 942,023 | 1·0 | 2,351,986 | 0·4 |
| 11 | 5,399 | 45,554 | 5 | | 40,000 | 360,000 | 20,582 | 672,930 | 20,000 | 942,605 | 4·8 | 2,278,956 | 2·0 |
| 12 | 3,454 | 116,106 | 7½ | — | | 360,000 | 8,375 | 661,168 | 20,000 | 930,980 | 12·5 | 2,449,094 | 4·7 |
| 13 | 7,061 | 180,889 | 10 | 40,000 | | 400,000 | N/A | 567,561 | 25,000 | 923,915 | 19·6 | 2,449,340 | 7·4 |
| 14 | 10,450 | 260,643 | 10 | 100,000 | | 500,000 | 34,193 | 639,930 | 60,000 | 898,108 | 29·0 | 2,535,085 | 10·3 |
| 15 | 33,594 | 174,241 | 8 | — | | 500,000 | 34,594 | 766,789 | 50,000 | 882,703 | 19·7 | 2,666,475 | 6·5 |
| 16 | | | | | | | | | | | | | |
| 17 | | | | | | | | | | | | | |
| 18 | | | | | | | | | | | | | |
| 19 | 306,732 | 289,550 | 10 | 100,000[3] | | 600,000 | 144,824 | 1,265,379 | 100,000 | 869,012 | 33·3 | 3,892,914 | 7·4 |

continued over

TABLE VIII—*continued*
North British Locomotive Company Annual Accounts

| Year | B/f profit/loss £ | Profit/Loss (excl. depreciation) £ | Ordinary Dividend % | Reserves To £ | Reserves From £ | Cumulative Reserve £ | Additions to Plant £ | Investments in balance sheet £ | To Depreciation £ | Fixed Assets £ | Profit Fixed Assets % | Total Assets £ | Profit Total Assets % |
|---|---|---|---|---|---|---|---|---|---|---|---|---|---|
| 1920 | 338,783 | 233,220 | 10 | —[4] | — | 350,000[5] | 126,669 | 957,389 | 50,000 | 945,681 | 24·7 | 3,492,692 | 6·7 |
|  | 404,503 | 367,738 | 10 | 150,000 | — | 500,000 | N/A | 1,710,705 | 50,000 | 949,511 | 38·7 | 3,529,245 | 10·4 |
| 2 | 204,741[6] | 35,751 | 7½ | — | — | 500,000 | 4,879 | 1,611,076 | 20,000 | 934,390 | 3·8 | 3,015,107 | 1·2 |
| 3 | 109,242 | −43,404 | 5 |  | 50,000 | 450,000 | N/A | 1,422,399 | — | 935,979 | −4·6 | 2,810,867 | −1·5 |
| 4 | 15,838 | −13,038 | 5[7] |  | 85,000 | 365,000 | 6,389 | 1,423,399 | 10,000 | 932,368 | −1·4 | 2,804,479 | −0·5 |
| 5 | 6,081 | 37,100 | 5 |  | 50,000 | 315,000 | 8,951 | 1,280,451 | 20,000 | 921,320 | 4·0 | 2,793,587 | 1·3 |
| 6 | 13,807 | 30,480 | 4 |  | 40,000 | 275,000 | N/A | 1,187,701 | 10,000 | 911,320 | 3·3 | 2,606,220 | 1·7 |
| 7 | 14,288 | 38,334 | 4 |  | 25,000 | 250,000 | 16,200 | 1,050,982 | 20,000 | 875,120 | 4·4 | 2,533,864 | 1·5 |
| 8 | 7,622 | −2,305 | 2½ |  | 50,000 | 200,000 | 24,986 | 980,694 | 20,000 | 880,107 | −0·3 | 2,349,449 | −0·1 |
| 9 | 317 | −21,676 | 2½ |  | 80,000 | 120,000 | 5,015 | 931,052 | 25,000 | 880,122 | −2·5 | 2,289,330 | −0·9 |
| 1930 | 3,641 | −2,910 | — |  | 30,000 | 90,000 | 70,973 | 922,932 | 10,000 | 941,095 | −0·3 | 2,262,228 | −0·1 |
| 1 | 1,668 | −18,079 | — |  | 45,000 | 45,000 | 8,305 | 922,741 | 5,000 | 944,400 | −1·9 | 2,157,287 | −0·8 |
| 2 | 463 | 15,556 | — |  | 15,000 | 30,000 | 1,545 | 940,185 | 5,000 | 940,945 | 1·7 | 2,220,551 | 0·7 |
| 3 | 2,895 | −2,661 | —[8] |  | 15,000 | 15,000 | 2,012 | 757,184 | — | 942,957 | −0·3 | 2,073,231 | −0·1 |
| 4 | 1,172 | −34,656 | —[9] |  | — | 15,000 | 33,212 | 552,084 | — | 976,170 | −3·6 | 2,147,823 | −1·6 |
| 5 | −33,483 | −86,007 | —[9] |  | — | 15,000 | 3,091 | 560,903 | — | 979,261 | −8·8 | 2,113,514 | −4·1 |
| 6 | −119,491 | 5,712 | —[9] |  | — | 15,000 | 5,511 | 560,903 | — | 984,773 | 0·6 | 2,069,702 | 0·3 |
| 7 | −113,779 | 1,945 | —[9] |  | — | 15,000 | 2,850 | 560,903 | — | 987,623 | 0·2 | 2,164,581 | 0·1 |
| 8 | −111,833 | 63,136 | —[9] |  | — | 15,000 | 2,073 | 560,903 | — | 989,697 | 6·4 | 2,252,911 | 2·8 |
| 9 | −48,696 | 144,298 | —[9] |  | — | 15,000 | 4,203 | 562,655 | 20,000 | 973,900 | 14·8 | 2,341,932 | 6·2 |

1 Also written off £19,282 preliminary expenses.
2 Also £5,000 to Workmen's Compensation Fund.
3 Also £20,000 to Special Fund for employees.
4 £5,000 to Special Fund for employees.
5 £250,000 of reserve capitalised.
6 Reduction in balance brought forward because of taxation payments.
7 Dividend paid net of tax from 1924.
8 Preference dividend cut from 5 per cent to 2½ per cent.
9 Preference dividend passed.

*Sources:* Annual balance sheets in Deloitte and Company papers in University of Glasgow Archives (UGA) UGD 109/2/5 and 8–27, and in Dissolved Companies files in Scottish Record Office (SRO) BT 2/5278/1–20.

TABLE IX
North British Locomotive Company Output, 1904–13 and 1920–38

| Year | No. of engines completed | Value of engines £ | Value of engines and duplicates £ |
|---|---|---|---|
| 1904 | 485 | 1,508,961 | 1,671,891 |
| 5 | 573 | 1,543,330 | 1,690,725 |
| 6 | 520 | 1,853,062 (?) | 1,984,885 (?) |
| 7 | 539 | 1,958,161 | 2,100,030 |
| 8 | 462 | 1,617,120 | 1,812,678 |
| 9 | 398 | 1,222,341 | 1,336,674 |
| 1910 | 289 | 858,220 | 1,010,006 |
| 1 | 349 | 1,163,935 | 1,343,583 |
| 2 | 335 | 1,269,181 (?) | 1,451,604 |
| 3 | 433 | 1,717,887 | 1,879,032 |
| 1920 | 307 | 3,592,937 | 4,245,533 |
| 1 | 240 | 3,167,729 | 3,864,804 |
| 2 | 97 | 859,059 | 1,179,210 |
| 3 | 143 | 672,464 | 932,435 |
| 4 | 74 | 429,807 | 606,404 |
| 5 | 197 | 1,152,696 | 1,258,907 |
| 6 | 156 | 772,183 | 884,455 |
| 7 | 182 | 1,104,885 | 1,238,648 |
| 8 | 141 | 775,190 | 1,135,193 |
| 9 | 96 | 505,433 | 723,514 |
| 1930 | 130 | 781,678 | 992,852 |
| 1 | 41 | 237,761 | 308,071 |
| 2 | — | — | 40,439 |
| 3 | 16 | 108,680 | 169,691 |
| 4 | 83 | 517,060 | 585,406 |
| 5 | 74 | 400,353 | 502,673 |
| 6 | 106 | 607,824 | 699,143* |
| 7 | 42 | 266,199 | 452,504* |
| 8 | 68 | 632,693 | 1,034,266* |

* including shells: 1936, £11,865; 1937, £31,237; 1938 £26,490.

Source: North British Locomotive Company papers in Mitchell Library, Glasgow. Continuous series from 1904 to March 1948 of *Output, etc. Statistics*. (The earliest volume has been damaged and some figures are slightly doubtful. They are marked '?').

TABLE X

North British Locomotive Company Engine Contracts, 1920–38

| Contract | No. of Engines | Cost | | Profit/Loss £ | Profit/Loss on cost | | Material Total Cost % | Notes |
|---|---|---|---|---|---|---|---|---|
| | | Invoiced £ | Ascertained £ | | Invoiced % | Ascertained % | | |
| 1920 | | | | | | | | |
| L.734 | 50 | 512,500 | 437,748 | 74,751 | 14·6 | 17·1 | 48 | |
| 5 | 7 | 79,218 | 79,058 | 159 | 0·2 | 0·2 | 47 | |
| 6 | 15 | 202,102 | 172,673 | 29,429 | 14·6 | 17·1 | 52 | |
| 7 | 5 | 70,563 | 65,342 | 5,221 | 7·3 | 8·0 | 46 | |
| 8 | 14 | 152,628 | 136,363 | 16,264 | 10·7 | 11·9 | 53 | |
| 9 | 15 | 180,662 | 151,311 | 29,350 | 16·2 | 19·4 | 47 | |
| 740 | 6 | 64,950 | 55,574 | 9,375 | 14·4 | 16·9 | 44 | |
| 1 | 2 | 30,900 | 27,338 | 3,561 | 11·5 | 13·0 | 49 | |
| 2 | 10 | 90,522 | 78,606 | 11,915 | 13·2 | 15·2 | 23 | |
| 3 | 5 | 78,191 | 63,879 | 14,312 | 18·3 | 22·4 | 42 | |
| 4 | 2 | 10,333 | 8,822 | 1,511 | 14·6 | 17·1 | 34 | |
| 5 | 8 | 119,600 | 107,267 | 12,332 | 10·3 | 11·5 | 43 | |
| 6 | 20 | 335,849 | 287,077 | 48,771 | 14·5 | 17·0 | 51 | |
| 7 | 15 | 274,515 | 216,970 | 57,545 | 21·0 | 26·5 | 55 | |
| 8 | 15 | 281,700 | 226,871 | 52,314 | 18·6 | 23·1 | 56 | |
| 9 | 7 | 68,166 | 58,732 | 9,433 | 13·8 | 16·1 | 37 | |
| 750 | 2 | 20,156 | 14,369 | 5,786 | 28·7 | 40·3 | 45 | |
| 1 | 7 | 79,992 | 64,217 | 15,775 | 19·7 | 24·6 | 43 | |
| 2 | 1 | 8,667 | 6,943 | 1,724 | 19·9 | 24·8 | 39 | |
| 3 | 10 | 112,750 | 77,957 | 34,792 | 30·9 | 44·6 | 42 | |
| 4 | 3 | 45,990 | 74,724 | 11,351 | 24·7 | 32·7 | 43 | |
| 5 | 6 | 97,304 | 86,852 | 10,452 | 10·7 | 12·0 | 45 | |
| 6 | 25 | 349,424 | 271,718 | 77,705 | 22·2 | 28·6 | 52 | |
| 7 | 4 | 47,909 | 38,396 | 9,602 | 20·0 | 25·0 | 54 | |

continued over

TABLE X—*continued*
North British Locomotive Company Engine Contracts, 1920–38

| Contract | No. of Engines | Cost Invoiced £ | Cost Ascertained £ | Profit/Loss £ | Profit/Loss on cost Invoiced % | Profit/Loss on cost Ascertained % | Material Total Cost % | Notes |
|---|---|---|---|---|---|---|---|---|
| 8 | 5 | 44,639 | 45,752 | (1,113) | (2·5) | (2·4) | 33 | |
| 9 | 25 | 291,614 | 214,651 | 76,962 | 26·4 | 35·9 | 42 | |
| 760 | 5 | 45,956 | 37,498 | 8,458 | 18·4 | 22·6 | 26 | |
| 1 | 20 | 223,559 | 160,808 | 62,750 | 28·1 | 39·0 | 40 | |
| 2 | 6 | 87,840 | 85,575 | 2,265 | 2·6 | 2·6 | 36 | |
| *1921* | | | | | | | | |
| 763 | 20 | 220,000 | 212,208 | 7,791 | 3·5 | 3·7 | 36 | |
| 4 | 6 | 65,700 | 71,606 | (5,906) | (9·0) | (8·2) | 30 | |
| 5 | 1 | 7,482 | 12,569 | (5,087) | (68·0) | (40·5) | 15 | |
| 6 | 22 | 173,350 | 202,122 | (28,772) | (16·6) | (14·2) | 36 | |
| *1922* | | | | | | | | |
| 767 | 2 | 4,980 | 8,323 | (3,343) | (67·1) | (40·2) | 16 | |
| 8 | 12 | 69,654 | 94,428 | (24,774) | (35·6) | (26·2) | 33 | |
| 9 | 8 | 41,686 | 54,494 | (12,808) | (30·7) | (23·5) | 33 | |
| E.2 | — | 57,200 | 82,977 | (25,696) | (44·9) | (31·0) | — | |
| 770 | 2 | 11,470 | 12,653 | (1,183) | (10·3) | (9·3) | 26 | |
| 1 | 7 | 27,454 | 39,904 | (12,450) | (45·3) | (31·2) | 27 | |
| E.3 | — | 35,186 | 40,177 | (4,991) | (14·2) | (12·4) | — | |
| 727 | 23 | 60,380 | 115,449* | (33,705)* | (41·2) | (29·2) | 30* | *incl. 776. |
| 3 | 16 | 92,080 | 112,096 | (20,016) | (21·7) | (17·9) | 39 | |
| 4 | 15 | 87,956 | 99,282 | (11,326) | (12·9) | (11·4) | 42 | |
| *1923* | | | | | | | | |
| 775 | 13 | 75,487 | 183,142* | (38,449)* | (26·6) | (21·0) | 43* | *incl. 778. |

*continued over*

TABLE X—continued
North British Locomotive Company Engine Contracts, 1920–38

| Contract | No. of Engines | Cost Invoiced £ | Cost Ascertained £ | Profit/Loss £ | Profit/Loss on cost Invoiced % | Profit/Loss on cost Ascertained % | Material Total Cost % | Notes |
|---|---|---|---|---|---|---|---|---|
| 6 | 6 | 21,364 | * | * | | (29·2) | * | *with 772. |
| 7 | 5 | 25,500 | 30,201 | (4,701) | (18·4) | (15·6) | 32 | *with 775. |
| 8 | 12 | 69,205 | * | * | | (21·0) | * | |
| 9 | 1 | 7,289 | 7,746 | (456) | (6·3) | (5·9) | 24 | |
| 780 | 10 | 61,500 | 83,040 | (21,540) | (35·0) | (25·9) | 39 | |
| 1 | 2 | 12,530 | 17,907 | (5,377) | (42·9) | (30·0) | 36 | |
| 2 | 5 | 22,863 | 32,917 | (10,053) | (44·0) | (30·5) | 35 | |
| 3 | 15 | 94,588 | 119,256 | (24,667) | (26·1) | (20·7) | 42 | |
| 4 | 1 | 8,150 | 12,393 | (4,243) | (52·1) | (34·2) | 33 | |
| 5 | 6 | 14,484 | 28,129 | (13,645) | (94·2) | (48·5) | 23 | |
| 6 | 5 | 26,250 | 31,565 | (5,315) | (20·2) | (16·8) | 38† | |
| 7 | 20 | 177,067 | 235,481 | (58,414) | (33·0) | (24·8) | 41† | |
| 8 | 15 | 49,550 | 62,837 | (13,287) | (26·8) | (21·1) | 42† | |
| *1924* | | | | | | | | |
| 789 | 4 | 17,280 | 19,567 | (2,287) | (13·2) | (11·7) | 33 | |
| 790 | 1* | 11,625 | 22,140 | (10,515) | (90·5) | (47·5) | 13 | *Stock locomotive. |
| 1 | | No details | | | | | | |
| 2 | 1 | 2,788 | 5,514 | (2,726) | (97·8) | (49·4) | 21 | |
| 3 | 10 | 76,620 | 97,813 | (21,193) | (27·7) | (21·7) | 34† | |
| 4 | 2 | 4,400 | 5,799 | (1,399) | (31·8) | (24·1) | 20 | |
| 5 | 1 | 2,085 | 2,793 | (708) | (34·0) | (25·3) | 18 | |
| 6 | 15 | 76,415 | 91,863 | (21,980) | (28·8) | (23·9) | 37 | |
| 7 | 2 | 9,690 | 10,313 | (623) | (6·4) | (6·0) | 43 | |
| 8 | 35 | 172,550 | 174,870 | (2,320) | (1·3) | (1·3) | 41† | |

continued over

TABLE X—continued

North British Locomotive Company Engine Contracts, 1920–38

| Contract | No. of Engines | Cost Invoiced £ | Cost Ascertained £ | Profit/Loss £ | Profit/Loss on cost Invoiced % | Profit/Loss on cost Ascertained % | Material Total Cost % | Notes |
|---|---|---|---|---|---|---|---|---|
| 9 | 1 | 2,055 | 2,048 | 6 | 0·3 | 0·3 | 23 | |
| 800 | 20 | 232,699* | 251,107* | (18,408)* | (7·9) | (7·3) | 43*† | *incl. 803. |
| 1 | 25 | 163,307 | 175,365 | (12,057) | (7·4) | (6·9) | 42† | |
| 2 | 25 | 141,125 | 152,536 | (11,411) | (8·1) | (7·5) | 38† | |
| *1925* | | | | | | | | |
| 803 | 10 | * | * | * | (7·9) | (7·3) | * | *with 800. |
| 4 | 1 | 2,340 | 2,327 | 17 | 0·7 | 0·7 | 23 | |
| 5 | 1 | 2,200 | 1,963 | 236 | 10·7 | 12·0 | 27 | |
| 6 | 3 | 17,400* | 15,836* | 1,563* | 9·0 | 9·9 | 23* | *incl. 809. |
| 7 | 4 | 37,380 | 41,875 | 4,495 | 12·0 | 10·7 | 28† | |
| 8 | 2 | 14,000 | 21,674 | (7,674) | (54·8) | (35·4) | 30 | |
| 9 | 5 | * | * | * | 9·0 | 9·9 | * | *with 806. |
| 810 | 4 | 91,210* | 87,062* | 4,147* | 4·5 | 4·8 | 40*† | *incl. 813. |
| 1 | 20 | 224,175* | 261,847* | (37,672)* | (16·8) | (14·4) | 39* | *incl. 812. |
| 2 | 15 | * | * | * | (16·8) | (14·4) | * | *with 811. |
| 3 | 12 | * | * | * | 4·5 | 4·8 | * | *with 810. |
| 4 | 15 | 87,871 | 111,939 | (24,067) | (27·4) | (21·5) | 30† | |
| 5 | 1 | 6,620 | 6,729 | (109) | (1·6) | (1·6) | 26 | |
| 6 | 1 | 2,150 | 2,610 | (460) | (21·4) | (17·6) | 19 | |
| 7 | 20 | 151,610 | 161,995 | (10,385) | (6·8) | (6·4) | 42† | |
| 8 | 3 | 16,845 | 15,731 | 1,113 | 6·6 | 7·1 | 38 | |
| *1926* | | | | | | | | |
| 819 | 30 | 100,185 | 113,564 | (13,378) | (13·4) | (11·8) | 43* | *incl. 820. |
| 820 | 30 | 101,441 | 97,128 | 4,312 | (4·2) | (4·4) | * | *with 819. |

continued over

TABLE X—*continued*
North British Locomotive Company Engine Contracts, 1920–38

| Contract | No. of Engines | Cost Invoiced £ | Cost Ascertained £ | Profit/Loss £ | Profit/Loss on cost Invoiced % | Profit/Loss on cost Ascertained % | Material Total Cost % | Notes |
|---|---|---|---|---|---|---|---|---|
| 821 | 25 | 136,250 | 132,386 | 3,863 | 2·8 | 2·9 | 41† | |
| 2 | 15 | 85,779 | 107,068 | (21,291) | (24·8) | (19·9) | 30† | |
| 3 | 6 | 47,463 | 51,354 | (3,891) | (8·2) | (7·6) | 39† | |
| 4 | 20 | 206,974* | 249,328* | (42,853)* | (20·7) | (17·2) | 37† | *incl. 825. |
| 5 | 20 | * | * | * | (20·7) | (17·2) | * | *with 824. |
| 6 | 2 | 9,307 | 9,946 | (639) | (6·9) | (6·4) | 31 | |
| 7 | 12 | 64,740 | 79,144 | (14,404) | (22·2) | (18·2) | 37† | |
| 8 | 1 | 2,275 | 3,184 | (909) | (40·0) | (28·5) | 22† | |
| 9 | 5 | 27,775 | 32,511 | (4,736) | (17·1) | (14·6) | 35† | |
| 830 | 20 | 118,884 | 132,268 | (13,383) | (11·3) | (10·1) | 42† | |
| 1 | 10 | 59,485 | 64,403 | (4,918) | (8·3) | (7·6) | 39† | |
| 2 | 3 | 23,205 | 25,145 | (1,940) | (8·4) | (7·7) | 43† | |
| *1927* | | | | | | | | |
| 833 | 25 | 386,250* | 398,803* | (12,553)* | (3·2) | (3·1) | 46* | *incl. 834. |
| 4 | 25 | * | * | * | (3·2) | (3·1) | * | *with 833. |
| 5 | 30 | 142,950* | 147,247* | (4,297)* | (3·0) | (2·9) | 46*† | *incl. 836. |
| 6 | * | * | * | * | (3·0) | (2·9) | * | *with 835. |
| 7 | 1 | 5,185 | 5,409 | (244) | (4·3) | (4·1) | 31 | |
| 8 | 2 | 11,880 | 13,502 | (1,622) | (13·7) | (12·0) | 37† | |
| 9 | 1 | 2,350 | 2,239 | 110 | 4·7 | 4·9 | 20 | |
| 840 | 3 | 25,755 | 37,736 | (11,981) | (46·5) | (31·7) | 25† | |
| 1 | 20 | 123,015 | 140,910 | (24,008)* | (9·8) | (8·9) | 42*† | *incl. 842. |
| 2 | 20 | 123,015 | 129,128 | * | (9·8) | (8·9) | * | *with 841. |
| 3 | 1 | 6,360 | 6,104 | 255 | 4·0 | 4·2 | 31 | |

*continued over*

TABLE X—continued
North British Locomotive Company Engine Contracts, 1920–38

| Contract | No. of Engines | Cost Invoiced £ | Cost Ascertained £ | Profit/Loss £ | Profit/Loss on cost Invoiced % | Profit/Loss on cost Ascertained % | Material Total Cost % | Notes |
|---|---|---|---|---|---|---|---|---|
| 4 | 1 | 6,015 | 5,624 | 390 | 6·5 | 6·9 | 31 | |
| 5 | 18 | 133,695 | 130,446 | 3,249 | 2·4 | 2·5 | 48† | |
| 6 | 2 | 9,816 | 9,965 | (89) | (0·9) | (0·9) | 33† | |
| *1928* | | | | | | | | |
| 847 | 30 | 118,500 | 130,245 | (11,745) | (9·9) | (9·0) | 41† | |
| 8 | 2 | 15,690 | 16,510 | (820) | (5·2) | (5·0) | 42† | |
| 9 | 29 | 189,580 | 226,362 | (36,782) | (19·4) | (16·2) | 44 | |
| 850 | 10 | 72,894 | 85,140 | (12,245) | (16·8) | (14·4) | 42† | |
| 1 | 3 | 12,801 | 13,953 | (1,152) | (9·0) | (8·3) | 33† | |
| 2 | 25 | 69,875 | 88,620 | (40,728)* | (29·1) | (22·6) | 32*† | *incl. 853. |
| 3 | 25 | 69,875 | 86,949 | * | (29·1) | (22·6) | † | *with 852. |
| 4 | 18 | 157,500 | 204,978 | (47,478) | (30·1) | (23·2) | 34† | |
| 5 | 2 | 13,900 | 14,722 | (822) | (5·9) | (5·6) | 32* | |
| 6 | 1 | 11,685* | 14,510* | (2,825)* | (24·2) | (19·5) | 25* | *incl. 857. |
| *1929* | | | | | | | | |
| 857 | 1 | * | * | * | (24·2) | (19·5) | * | *with 856. |
| 8 | 1 | 5,576 | 8,125 | (2,741) | (49·2) | (33·7) | ? | |
| 9 | 13 | 102,472 | 110,637 | (8,164) | (7·8) | (7·4) | 43 | |
| 860 | 8 | 65,095 | 69,204 | (4,109) | (6·3) | (5·9) | 36† | |
| 1 | 4 | 28,222 | 40,941 | (12,719) | (45·1) | (31·1) | 37† | |
| 2 | 5 | 36,918 | 49,805 | (12,886) | (34·9) | (25·9) | 40† | |
| 3 | 25 | 76,400 | 88,332 | (11,932) | (15·6) | (13·5) | 35† | |
| 4 | 6 | 46,840 | 41,322 | 5,517 | 11·8 | 13·4 | 46† | |

continued over

TABLE X—continued
North British Locomotive Company Engine Contracts, 1920–38

| Contract | No. of Engines | Invoiced £ | Cost Ascertained £ | Profit/Loss £ | Profit/Loss on cost Invoiced % | Ascertained % | Material Total Cost % | Notes |
|---|---|---|---|---|---|---|---|---|
| 5 | 20 | 98,564 | 123,476 | (24,912) | (25·3) | (20·2) | 42 | |
| 6 | 6 | 44,400 | 49,716 | (5,316) | (12·0) | (10·7) | 38† | |
| 7 | 18 | 126,000 | 118,297 | 7,702 | 6·1 | 6·5 | 47† | |
| 8 | 12 | 85,560 | 97,085 | (11,525) | (13·5) | (11·9) | 42† | |
| 9 | 18 | 134,820 | 143,190 | (8,370) | (6·2) | (5·8) | 46 | |
| *1930* | | | | | | | | |
| 870 | 8 | 69,884 | 89,537 | (20,133) | (28·8) | (22·5) | 38 | |
| 1 | 4 | 17,937 | 26,832 | (8,874) | (49·5) | (33·1) | 25† | |
| 2 | 25 | 75,000 | 85,783 | (10,783) | (14·4) | (12·6) | 33† | |
| 3 | 6 | 33,522 | 52,057 | (18,535) | (55·3) | (35·6) | 31† | |
| 4 | 1 | 5,425 | 6,880 | (1,455) | (26·8) | (21·1) | 25 | |
| 5 | 10 | 71,727 | 115,590 | (43,863) | (61·1) | (37·9) | 29 | |
| 6 | 6 | 62,125 | 74,377 | (12,252) | (19·7) | (16·5) | 36† | |
| *1931* | | | | | | | | |
| 877 | 1 | 5,300 | 6,321 | (1,021) | (19·3) | (16·1) | 27 | |
| 8 | 4 | 21,551 | 65,886* | (24,207)* | (58·1) | (36·7) | 35*† | *incl. 879. |
| 9 | 3 | 20,128 | * | * | (58·1) | (36·7) | * | *with 878. |
| 880 | 5 | 21,120 | 58,209 | (37,089) | (175·6) | (63·7) | 17† | |
| *1932* | | | | | | | | |
| 881 | 5 | 31,139 | 93,658* | (47,025)* | (100·8) | (50·2) | 30* | *incl. 882. |
| 2 | 2 | 15,510 | * | * | (100·8) | (50·2) | * | *with 881. |
| 3 | 8 | 56,800 | 85,329 | (28,529) | (50·2) | (33·4) | 32 | |

*continued over*

TABLE X—continued

North British Locomotive Company Engine Contracts, 1920–38

| Contract | No. of Engines | Cost Invoiced £ | Cost Ascertained £ | Profit/Loss £ | Profit/Loss on cost Invoiced % | Profit/Loss on cost Ascertained % | Material Total Cost % | Notes |
|---|---|---|---|---|---|---|---|---|
| *1933* | | | | | | | | |
| 884 | 1 | 5,399 | 14,539 | (9,140) | (169·3) | (62·9) | 11 | |
| 5 | 50 | 291,500 | 391,983 | (99,598) | (34·1) | (25·4) | 38 | |
| *1934* | | | | | | | | |
| 886 | 3 | 24,400 | 32,168 | (7,768) | (31·8) | (24·1) | 39 | |
| 7 | 50 | 301,992 | 347,072 | (45,079) | (14·9) | (13·0) | 46 | |
| 8 | 1 | 4,568 | 7,150 | (2,581) | (56·5) | (36·1) | 21 | |
| 9 | 6 | 35,700 | 47,642 | (14,342)* | (40·1) | (30·1) | 35 | *Late addition to profit of £2,400. |
| *1935* | | | | | | | | |
| 890 | 20 | 110,300 | 155,787 | (45,487) | (41·2) | (29·2) | 40 | |
| 1 | 1 | 5,400 | 5,753 | (353) | (6·5) | (6·1) | 30 | |
| 2 | 50 | 281,908 | 333,084 | (51,176) | (18·2) | (15·4) | 42 | |
| 3 | 1 | 5,382 | 6,553 | (1,171) | (21·8) | (17·9) | 25 | |
| 4 | 2 | 13,710 | 21,556 | (7,846) | (57·2) | (36·4) | 30 | |
| 5 | 2 | 15,980 | 19,412 | (3,432) | (21·5) | (17·7) | 34 | |
| 6 | 73 | 413,466 | 411,341 | (3,043) | (0·7) | (0·7) | 43 | |
| 7 | 1 | 4,700 | 4,848 | (148) | (3·1) | (3·1) | 34 | |
| 8 | 4 | 29,805 | 28,408 | 1,099* | 3·7 | 3·9 | 46 | *Late deduction from profit of £298. |
| 9 | 1 | 14,211 | 22,692 | (13,487) | (94·9) | (59·4) | 26 | |
| *1936* | | | | | | | | |
| 900 | 1 | 5,608 | 5,767 | (159) | (2·8) | (2·8) | 32 | |
| 1 | 1 | 10,909* | 11,070* | (161)* | (1·5) | (1·5) | 33* | *incl. 902. |
| 2 | 1 | * | * | * | (1·5) | (1·5) | * | *with 901. |
| 3 | 1 | 22,123* | 22,996* | (873)* | (3·9) | (3·8) | 31* | *incl. 904, 905, 906. |
| 4 | 1 | * | * | * | (3·9) | (3·8) | * | *with 903. |
| 5 | 1 | * | * | * | (3·9) | (3·8) | * | *with 903. |
| 6 | 1 | * | * | * | (3·9) | (3·8) | * | *with 903. |

| Contract | No. of Engines | Cost Invoiced £ | Cost Ascertained £ | Profit/Loss £ | Profit/Loss on cost Invoiced % | Profit/Loss on cost Ascertained % | Material Total Cost % | Notes |
|---|---|---|---|---|---|---|---|---|
| *1937* | | | | | | | | |
| 907 | 18 | 161,683 | 191,214 | (29,531) | (18·3) | (15·4) | 42 | |
| 8 | 2 | 25,364 | 25,640 | (276) | (1·1) | (1·1) | 34 | |
| 9 | 1 | 6,475 | 6,593 | (118) | (1·8) | (1·8) | 34 | |
| 910 | 1 | 4,875 | 5,565 | (690) | (14·2) | (12·4) | 20 | |
| 1 | 11 | 104,315 | 104,935 | (620) | (0·6) | (0·6) | 38 | |
| 2 | 6 | 47,355 | 52,236 | (4,880) | (10·3) | (9·3) | 41 | |
| 3 | 1 | 9,600 | 9,158 | 441 | 4·6 | 4·8 | 41 | |
| 4 | 2 | 19,150 | 17,937 | 1,212 | 6·3 | 6·8 | 41 | |
| 5 | 20 | 161,743 | 169,766 | (8,022) | (5·0) | (4·7) | 48 | |
| 6 | 4 | 35,900 | 31,219 | 4,680 | 13·0 | 15·0 | 44 | |
| 7 | 44 | 507,430 | 480,452 | 26,977 | 5·3 | 5·6 | 48 | |
| *1938* | | | | | | | | |
| 918 | 1 | 6,720 | 5,936 | 783 | 11·7 | 13·2 | 36 | |
| 9 | 6 | 62,565 | 52,163 | 10,401 | 16·6 | 19·9 | 43 | |
| 920 | 6 | 52,699 | 48,896 | 3,800 | 7·2 | 7·8 | 38 | |
| 1 | 1 | 6,387 | 5,697 | 689 | 10·8 | 12·1 | 38 | |
| 2 | 2 | 19,960 | 17,336 | 2,623 | 13·1 | 15·1 | 43 | |
| 3 | 30 | 446,274 | 398,678 | 47,395 | 10·7 | 11·9 | 50 | |
| 4 | 1 | 10,210 | 8,702 | 1,508 | 14·8 | 17·3 | 34 | |

Notes: † Based on ascertained costs in UGD 11/4, which differ from those in UGD 11/6. See general note a.

a. The figure given for ascertained cost is from UGD 11/6/1–3, which occasionally differs slightly from that in UGD 11/4/2. To enable comparisons to be made with pre-war years, the figure for the calculation of percentage profit/loss and material cost is from UGD 11/4/2. Any difference is minimal.

b. The practice followed in the calculation of the percentage profit or loss varies in the Company's records. Generally it is calculated on ascertained and very rarely on invoiced costs. Both are given in the table but the discussion follows the Company's usual practice and refers to the percentage calculated on ascertained cost.

*Sources:* North British Locomotive Company Papers in UGA. *Contract Books, 1920 to 1938,* UGD 11/6/1–3 and *Engine Order Costs,* UGD, 11/4/2.
North British Locomotive Company Papers in Mitchell Library, *Engine Orders, 1903–1961.*

TABLE XI
North British Locomotive Company Wages, Employment and Output, 1904–13 and 1920–38

| *Year* | *Average wages per man per week* £ | *Number employed* | *Total wages bill* £ | *Total value of output* £ | *Wages output* % |
|---|---|---|---|---|---|
| 1904 | — | 7,464 | 521,747(?) | 1,671,891 | 31·207 |
| 5 | 27/11 | 7,364 | 534,324 | 1,690,725 | 31·603 |
| 6 | 28/2¼ | 7,763 | 569,007 | 1,984,885(?) | 28·667 |
| 7 | 30/4 | 7,854 | 583,566 | 2,100,030 | 27·788 |
| 8 | 28/2 | 7,534 | 530,541 | 1,812,678 | 29·268 |
| 9 | 25/8¼ | 7,359 | 462,818 | 1,336,674 | 34·625 |
| 1910 | 26/4¾ | 6,012 | 388,887 | 1,010,006 | 38·503 |
| 1 | 29/7¼ | 6,802 | 503,493 | 1,343,583 | 37·473 |
| 2 | 29/7½ | 6,066 | 449,426 | 1,451,604 | 30·960 |
| 3 | 31/9½ | 7,468 | 593,533 | 1,879,032 | 31·587 |
| | | | | | |
| 1920 | 80/10 | 8,033 | 1,656,140 | 4,245,533 | 39·008 |
| 1 | 67/– | 6,894 | 1,154,991 | 3,864,804 | 29·884 |
| 2 | 41/0½ | 4,075 | 418,377 | 1,179,210 | 35·479 |
| 3 | 50/5¾ | 3,690 | 465,634 | 932,435 | 49·937 |
| 4 | 47/9 | 2,433 | 285,821 | 606,404 | 47·132 |
| 5 | 53/7½ | 3,861 | 517,643 | 1,258,907 | 41·118 |
| 6 | 46/8 | 3,087 | 367,391 | 884,455 | 41·539 |
| 7 | 52/11½ | 3,896 | 526,254 | 1,238,648 | 42·486 |
| 8 | 51/5 | 3,474 | 455,292 | 1,135,193 | 40·107 |
| 9 | 50/1 | 2,686 | 336,404 | 723,514 | 46·495 |
| 1930 | 51/8¼ | 3,088 | 398,921 | 992,852 | 40·179 |
| 1 | 45/4 | 1,345 | 152,385 | 308,071 | 49·464 |
| 2 | 45/9 | 389 | 46,319 | 40,439 | 114·540 |
| 3 | 46/1½ | 689 | 81,103 | 169,691 | 47·794 |
| 4 | 50/6 | 2,568 | 337,307 | 585,406 | 57·619 |
| 5 | 49/5¼ | 1,954 | 246,435 | 502,673 | 49·024 |
| 6 | 54/0¾ | 2,166 | 298,891 | 699,143 | 42·751 |
| 7 | 54/9½ | 1,892 | 264,533 | 452,564 | 58·452 |
| 8 | 61/6½ | 2,337 | 366,941 | 1,034,266 | 35·478 |

*Source:* As for Table IX.

TABLE XII
1920 Proportions of Total Ascertained Costs on Contracts

| Contracts | Materials % | Net Wages % | Oncost % |
|---|---|---|---|
| L734 | 48 | 26 | 24 |
| 5 | 47 | 23 | 27 |
| 6 | 52 | 23 | 22 |
| 7 | 46 | 23 | 26 |
| 8 | 53 | 25 | 22 |
| 9 | 47 | 23 | 28 |
| 740 | 44 | 25 | 29 |
| 1 | 49 | 26 | 23 |
| 2 | 23 | 37 | 39 |
| 3 | 42 | 29 | 25 |
| 4 | 34 | 33 | 30 |
| 5 | 43 | 27 | 24 |
| 6 | 51 | 22 | 23 |
| 7 | 55 | 21 | 19 |
| 8 | 56 | 22 | 18 |
| 9 | 37 | 26 | 32 |
| 750 | 45 | 27 | 24 |
| 1 | 43 | 26 | 28 |
| 2 | 39 | 27 | 32 |
| 3 | 42 | 28 | 26 |
| 4 | 43 | 29 | 25 |
| 5 | 45 | 24 | 28 |
| 6 | 52 | 23 | 23 |
| 7 | 54 | 23 | 19 |
| 8 | 33 | 27 | 36 |
| 9 | 42 | 26 | 27 |
| 760 | 26 | 30 | 40 |
| 1 | 40 | 23 | 31 |
| 2 | 36 | 26 | 34 |

*Source:* North British Locomotive Company papers in UGA. *Engine Order Costs,* UGD 11/4/2.

TABLE XIII
1920 Proportions of Total Ascertained Costs on Contracts

|          | Contracts | Materials % | Net Wages % | Oncast % |
|----------|-----------|-------------|-------------|----------|
| 1933     | 884       | 11          | 13          | 73       |
|          | 5         | 38          | 28          | 32       |
| 1934     | 6         | 39          | 30          | 31       |
|          | 7         | 46          | 26          | 25       |
|          | 8         | 21          | 39          | 35       |
|          | 9         | 35          | 25          | 38       |
| 1935     | 890       | 40          | 24          | 34       |
|          | 1         | 30          | 29          | 40       |
|          | 2         | 42          | 21          | 26       |
|          | 3         | 25          | 33          | 40       |
|          | 4         | 30          | 28          | 34       |
|          | 5         | 34          | 28          | 33       |
|          | 6         | 43          | 27          | 29       |
|          | 7         | 34          | 31          | 39       |
|          | 8         | 46          | 25          | 27       |
|          | 9         | 26          | 36          | 51       |
| 1936     | 900       | 32          | 29          | 36       |
|          | 1–2       | 33          | 28          | 36       |
|          | 3–6       | 31          | 25          | 40       |
| 1937     | 907       | 42          | 19          | 26       |
|          | 8         | 34          | 23          | 31       |
|          | 9         | 34          | 25          | 37       |
|          | 910       | 20          | 33          | 41       |
|          | 1         | 38          | 26          | 30       |
|          | 2         | 41          | 25          | 26       |
|          | 3         | 41          | 24          | 31       |
|          | 4         | 41          | 23          | 31       |
|          | 5         | 48          | 18          | 21       |
|          | 6         | 44          | 25          | 26       |
|          | 7         | 48          | 23          | 22       |
| 1938     | 8         | 36          | 29          | 30       |
|          | 9         | 43          | 26          | 25       |
|          | 920       | 38          | 28          | 26       |
|          | 1         | 38          | 29          | 28       |
|          | 2         | 43          | 25          | 25       |
|          | 3         | 50          | 21          | 20       |
|          | 4         | 34          | 31          | 28       |

Source: North British Locomotive Company papers in UGA. *Contract Books 1933 to 1938*, UGD 11/6/3.

## NOTES

1. This article was possible only because the directors of the North British Locomotive Company ensured the preservation of their records in the University of Glasgow Archives and in the Mitchell Library, Glasgow, when the Company went into liquidation. For that action I am particularly grateful. I have received much help from Mr. Michael Moss and Mr. A. Slaven of the University of Glasgow; Mr. M. Nicholson of the Mitchell Library; Dr. M. W. Kirby, Dr. R. Ruffell and Dr. N. L. Tranter of the University of Stirling. I owe a particular debt to Dr. Ruffell, who has ensured that my non-quantitative approach has been tested by more rigorous methods than I am capable of applying unaided.

2. Deloitte papers. University of Glasgow Archives (hereafter UGA) UGD 109/2/2.

3. Summaries of the accounts are in Appendix, Table VIII.

4. Deloitte Papers. UGA. UGD 109/2/11.

5. Deloitte Papers. UGA. UGD 109/2/15.

6. See Appendix, Table IX.

7. Deloitte Papers UGA. UGD. 109/2/13,14,15,16.

8. Deloitte Papers. UGA. UGD 109/2/9.

9. *Glasgow Herald*, 13 March 1909.

10. Deloitte Papers. UGA. UGD 109/2/5.

11. *Glasgow Herald*, 13 March 1914.

12. Deloitte Papers. UGA. UGD 109/2/21.

13. Details of contracts are in Appendix, Table X.

14. *Glasgow Herald*, 25 March 1921.

15. For details of profits and losses, see Appendix, Table VIII.

16. *Glasgow Herald*, 7 March 1923.

17. Deloitte Papers. UGA. UGD 109/2/5.

18. *Ibid.*

19. *Ibid.*

20. *Ibid.*, UGA. UGD 109/2/24.

21. *Ibid.*, UGA. UGD 109/2/5.

22. *Ibid.*

23. *Ibid.*

24. See above p. 204.

25. *Glasgow Herald*, 15 March 1924.

26. Deloitte Papers. UGA. UGD 109/2/5.

27. And was to gain orders for another 38 in the first half of 1923.

28. *Glasgow Herald Trade Review*, 1922, p. 30.

29. *Glasgow Herald Trade Review*, 1928, p. 43.

30. *Glasgow Herald Trade Review*, 1930, p. 45.

31. Deloitte Papers. UGA. UGD 109/2/5.

32. Details of the contracts from 1920 to 1938 are in the Appendix, Table X. Since the financial records of some contracts were combined, the number of cases for which a breakdown of costs is possible is not identical with the number of contracts. Between the wars 19 contracts were combined out of the total of 190 and one is not included because of inadequate information; no details are given of another.

33. NBLC Papers. UGA. UGD 11/4/1.

34. For post-war contracts and locomotives, see Appendix, Table X.

35. See Appendix, Table XI.

36. Even assuming that oncost charges were fully recorded.

37. See Appendix, Tables XII and XIII.

# EMPLOYERS' LABOUR POLICY: A STUDY OF THE MOND-TURNER TALKS 1927-33

## by HOWARD F. GOSPEL

The labour policy of British employers is a curiously neglected subject in economic history. In business history, there is in Great Britain no really good study of the industrial relations experiences and policies of a particular firm or group of firms. Those business histories which touch on the labour activities of the firm do so only briefly and almost as an aside. In labour history, studies of the development of the British system of industrial relations tend to be from the perspective of the trade union and the role of the employer is usually overlooked. Yet it could be argued that it is the employer who plays the main part in shaping the industrial relations system and trade unions basically react to employer initiatives.

This article investigates the labour policy of British employers in one particular context, viz. during the Mond-Turner Talks and their sequel, talks which involved a wide spectrum of British employers and the Trades Union Congress in the years after the General Strike. This episode, important not so much for what it achieved, but for what it signified, is used as a case study to suggest some provisional conclusions about employers' attitudes, the difference between employers, and their relations with organised labour. The main concern therefore is not with the talks themselves but with the employers involved in them.

## I

The background to the Mond-Turner Talks had been documented elsewhere —the factors in the period after the General Strike conducive to co-operation between labour and capital, the initial T.U.C. suggestion for national-level talks, and the unfavourable response from the central employers' body, the National Confederation of Employers' Organisations (N.C.E.O.).[1] In November 1927 Sir Alfred Mond, who had already contacted a number of prominent employers, approached the T.U.C. with proposals for talks to discuss rationalisation of industry, compulsory conciliation, security of employment, disclosure of information to trade unions, and schemes for worker participation. In preliminary talks with the T.U.C. it was agreed that no limit should be placed on what would be discussed and that the chair at subsequent meetings would alternate between Mond and Ben Turner (Textile Workers and T.U.C. President)[2]—hence the popular name of the talks.

The employers who took part in the conferences claimed to act as individuals and not as representatives of employers organisations or their own businesses. However, it is interesting to look in some detail at the composition and business interests of the Mond Employers.[3]

| Name | Industries | Companies[4] |
|---|---|---|
| Lord Aberconway | Coal | John Brown (Ch.) |
| | Shipbuilding | Palmer's Shipbuilding (D) |
| | Iron and Steel | Tredegar Iron & Coal (Ch.) |
| | | Metropolitan Railway (Ch.) |
| | | Industrial Housing Assoc. (Ch.) |
| Lord Ashfield | Railways | Underground Electric Railway |
| | Motor Transport | (Ch. and Man. D.) |
| | Anthracite Coal | British Dye Stuffs (Ch.) |
| | Chemicals | I.C.I. (D) |
| | | Amalgamated Anthracite Collieries (D) |
| | | Associated Daimler (D) |
| | | Midland Bank (D) |
| Sir H. Austin | Automobiles | Austin Motor (Ch. and Man. D) |
| A. Baker | Paper Making | Bowater Paper (Man. D) |
| B. Bacon | Tobacco | Carreras (Ch.) |
| H. Bond | Iron and Steel | Richard Thomas (Ch.) |
| | Tin | S. Wales Tin Plate (D) |
| | Collieries | |
| Sir H. Bowden | Engineering | Raleigh Cycles (Ch. and Gen. Man.) |
| | | Sturmey Archer Motors (Ch. and Gen. Man.) |
| Sir D. Brooke | | Birmingham City Council |
| P. B. Brown | Iron and Steel | Hadfields (Man. D) |
| Sir J. Cadman | Oil | B.P. (D) |
| | | Anglo Persian (Ch.) |
| Lord Colwyn | Cotton and Silk | Joshua Smith (Ch.) |
| | Chemicals | British Dye Stuffs (D) |
| | Railways | Underground Electric (D) |
| | Rubber | Dunlop (D) |
| | | Lancs. & Yorks. Bank (Ch.) |
| S. Courtauld | Artificial Silk | Courtaulds (Ch.) |
| Col. D. Davies | Railways | G.W.R. (D) |
| | Coal | Ocean Coal & Wilson (Ch.) |
| | Printing | Cambrian Press (Ch.) |
| | Banking | Midland Bank (D) |
| Sir A. Dorman | Iron and Steel | Dorman Long (Ch. Man. D) |
| | Coal | Other steel companies and collieries |
| Sir R. Hadfield | Iron and Steel | Hadfields (Man. D) |
| | Engineering | Sheffield Gas (D) |
| | Nickel | Mond Nickel |
| W. J. Hadfield | | Sheffield City Engineer |
| Sir H. Hirst | Elec. Engineering | G.E.C. (Ch. and Man. D) |
| Dr. A. E. Humphries | Flour Milling | Coxes Lock Milling Co. (Ch.) |
| W. H. Hazell | Printing | Hazell Watson & Viney (Ch.) |
| | | Letts Diaries (Ch.) |
| W. Harrison | Agric. Engineering | Harrison McGregor (Ch.) |
| | Brewing | Distillers Co. (D) |
| | | Buchanan Dewar (D) |
| T. B. Johnston | Pottery | Johnston Allen & Co. (D) |
| K. Lee | Cotton | Tootal Broadhurst Lee (Ch.) |
| | Banking | District Bank (D) |
| Lord Londonderry | Coal | Londonderry Collieries (Ch.) |
| Sir H. McGowan | Chemicals | I.C.I. (Deputy Ch. and Pres.) |
| | | Nobel Inds. (Ch. and Man. D) |
| M. Mannaberg | Iron and Steel | Bolcklow Vaughan (D) |
| Sir D. Milne Watson | Gas | Gas Light & Coke Co. (Governor) |

| Name | Industries | Companies |
|------|-----------|-----------|
| Sir E. Manville | Automobiles | Daimler (Ch.) |
| | Civil Engineering | W. Jessop (Ch.) |
| | Elec. Engineering | Baird Television (Ch.) |
| | Insurance | B.S.A. (V. Chairman) |
| | | Phoenix Oil (Ch.) |
| | | Metropolitan Railway (D) |
| | | Car & General Insurance (Ch.) |
| | | Royal Exchange |
| Sir A. Mond | Chemicals | I.C.I. (Ch.) |
| (Lord Melchett) | Coal | Brunner Mond (Ch.) |
| | Banking | Amalgamated Anthracite Collieries (Ch.) |
| | | Westminster Bank (D) |
| Sir F. Mills | Iron and Steel | Ebbw Vale Steel Iron & Coal (Ch.) |
| Sir C. Parsons | Elec. Engineering | C. A. Parsons (Ch.) |
| | | Parsons Optical Glass (Ch.) |
| | | Cleveland Shipbuilding (Ch.) |
| | | Ross Ltd. (Ch.) |
| Sir P. Rylands | Iron and Steel Wire | Rylands (Man. D) |
| | Coal, etc. | |
| Sir J. Stamp | Railways | L.M.S. (Pres.) |
| | Chemicals | I.C.I. (D) |
| | | Nobel Inds. (D) |
| | | Bank of England |
| G. S. Tomkinson | Pottery | Worcester Royal Porcelain Co. |
| | | Kidderminster Gas |
| G. C. Vyle | Engineering | W. & T. Avery (Man. D) |
| | | H. Pooley & Son (Man. D) |
| Lord Weir | Engineering | G. & J. Weir (Man. D) |
| | | I.C.I. (D) |
| | | National Bank of Scotland (D) |
| Col. V. Willey | Wool | Francis Willey (Permanent Governor) |
| (Lord Barnby) | Banking | Lloyds Bank |

In the absence of any other sample of British employers, it is difficult to generalise about the type and size of the Mond Employers. However, it can safely be said that a number of them were connected with some of the very largest U.K. companies—I.C.I., G.E.C., Dunlop, the railway companies, Dorman Long, Courtaulds, John Brown, Bolckow Vaughan, Richard Thomas, Hadfields, Austin Motors, B.P., Bowater Paper, Distillers' Company, the major banks. Certain of these firms held dominant positions in their industries and because of their scale could often afford to make concessions to labour in return for a peaceful settlement of industrial relations. There were few small firms represented. As the Federation of British Industry (F.B.I.) Director pointed out,

There are few, if any, people on the list of signatories . . . who would have any very first hand knowledge or detailed experience of the difficulties of the small firms who are not financially very strong or of the highly competitive industries. . . . They are nearly all men from very big combinations in big industries which are in many cases of a more or less monopolistic character, and schemes which are possible for, . . . say I.C.I., may be complete impossibilities for a small wool firm in the West Riding or a small motor firm in Coventry or even for a big firm in some industry where employment and production are not as regular and continuous as they are in the chemical industry.[5]

The Mond Employers were often big not only in their own industries, but also had diversified interests and directorates in firms in various industries.

Although the staple industries were well represented, there was also a significantly large number of new industries or industries supplying a rapidly expanding consumer market e.g. parts of the chemical industry, motor cars, cycles, rubber, oil, artificial fibres, electricity supply, electrical goods, tobacco and brewing. Of those employers in the engineering industry a large number were connected with the expanding sectors which relied on domestic, not foreign, markets. For example, Sir H. Hirst was chairman and managing director of G.E.C.; Sir H. Austin was chairman of Austin Motors; Sir E. Manville was chairman of Daimler Co., vice-chairman of B.S.A., and a director of Baird Television; Sir H. Bowden was chairman of Raleigh Cycle and Sturmey Archer Motors; C. Parsons was chairman of C.A. Parsons, the electrical engineering firm; and Lord Ashfield was on the board of Daimler. The Engineering Employers' Federation (E.E.F.), the employers' organisation for the engineering industry, certainly felt that Mond had chosen his engineering representatives carefully. He had not approached the Federation itself because he felt it would not fall in with his 'broad' views; Lord Weir (Managing Director of the engineering firm G. & J. Weir) and Sir G. Vyle (managing director of the scale and weighing machine firm of W. & T. Avery) were chosen as prominent engineering employers connected with the Federation, but 'of an advanced turn of mind' and 'not bound by the reactionary policy of the Federation as a whole'.[6]

It is noticeable that a number of the employers were connected with the newly formed I.C.I. and its subsidiary companies. There was Sir A. Mond himself and Sir H. McGowan, the two chiefs of I.C.I.; Lord Ashfield was a director of I.C.I., chairman of British Dye Stuffs, and a personal friend of Mond; Lord Colwyn was on the board of British Dye Stuffs, Sir J. Stamp was on the board of I.C.I. and Nobel Industries; and Sir R. Hadfield was on the board of Mond Nickel.

Several of the groups were closely connected with banking and finance and might therefore be expected to have a general industrial interest and an interest in company finance, amalgamation, and rationalisation. Mond was a director of the Westminster Bank and chairman of the Anglo-American Finance Co., Sir J. Stamp was on the board of the Bank of England; Lord Ashfield was a director of the Midland Bank; Colonel Davies was on the board of the Midland and K. Lee of the District Banks; Weir was a director of the National Bank of Scotland; and Colonel Willey was a director of Lloyds Bank.

Fourteen of the Mond Employers had been active in the F.B.I., the central trade and commercial association, but only three in the N.C.E.O., the industrial relations equivalent. This was in part the result of the different composition of the two organisations, the F.B.I. being composed largely of individual firms, often large firms, whereas the N.C.E.O. membership was restricted to employers' organisations. Mond had chosen his employers from those whom he knew in individual firms and not from employers' organisations. The N.C.E.O. calculated that there were ten industries represented among the Mond Employers whose employers organisation (if one existed) was not a member of the N.C.E.O.[7]

| | |
|---|---|
| Brewing and Distilling | W. Harrison |
| Docks | Lord Colwyn |
| | Lord Londonderry |
| Flour Milling | A. E. Humphries |
| Oil | Sir J. Cadman |
| | Sir E. Manville |
| Paper Making | A. Baker |
| Pottery | T. B. Johnston |
| | G. S. Tomkinson |
| Rubber | Lord Colwyn |
| Artificial Silk | S. Courtauld |
| Tobacco | B. Baron |
| Wire Rope | Sir P. Rylands |

There was particular resentment in the N.C.E.O. that these employers, not members of employers' organisations, should have been connected with the talks.[8]

The Mond Employers were therefore mainly top businessmen many of whom, because of their position, probably had little contact with industrial relations at shopfloor level. They were what might be called the statesmen of industry: as one small printing employer said, they were 'giants in industry' but 'very few of them had ever been in active negotiation with labour'.[9]

A good number of the Mond Group came from firms which were the products of recent amalgamations or which were interested in rationalisation (I.C.I., Dunlop, Distillers Company, G.E.C., Courtaulds, the railway companies, including the Underground Electric, the banks, Raleigh Cycles, Richard Thomas, and S. Wales Tin Plate). Those who were interested in such schemes included Weir who had been connected with an attempt to rationalise the building industry; Milne Watson who was interested in gas rationalisation; and Austin who would have liked a British motor car trust headed by himself. Amalgamation and rationalisation usually involved displacement of labour, dilution, and relaxation of trade union practices. The process of rationalisation could be facilitated by agreement with individual unions and, possibly, with the trade union movement generally. As Mond said in his original letter to the T.U.C., 'We realise that industrial reconstruction can be undertaken only in conjunction with and with the co-operation of those entitled and empowered to speak for organised labour'.[10] Rationalisation and amalgamation always headed Mond's list of subjects for discussion.

There were a number of contemporaries who saw the motives of the Mond Employers in these terms. G. D. H. Cole, for example, argued that Mond and his colleagues wanted T.U.C. support to get through new legislation on rationalisation and to repeal some of the older legislation on trusts; they hoped that in return for certain concessions the trade unions would not oppose their schemes; they wanted T.U.C. support to obtain more state assistance in raising capital, protecting British industry, and securing markets; and Cole concluded, they wanted a friendly T.U.C. in case the Labour Party came to power.[11] A memorandum from an unnamed M.P. in the F.B.I. archives[12] contains a similar argument, though referring primarily to Mond himself. It argued that in July 1926 Mond had tried to amend the Mining Industry Bill so as to enable his company Amalgamated Anthracite Collieries to compel the sale of independent concerns in Wales to his combine. Mond was defeated in this attempt to create a monopoly, but in the process he realised that with the support of trade union M.P.s he would have been successful. Mond had seen the example of his business colleague, Lord Ashfield, who as chairman and general manager of the Underground Electric Railway had combined with the T.G.W.U. to secure the passage of the 1924 London Traffic Act and who intended with union help to build up a passenger monopoly. Mond, it was argued, hoped to do the same thing: he aimed to create an even bigger chemical trust, to raise a protective duty on chemicals, to obtain the renewal of the Dye Industries Act, to secure compulsory powers of amalgamation for competing firms, and to induce a more favourable monetary situation for the implementation of these schemes.

Mond did indeed have a number of irons in the fire. He was trying to introduce a new industrial relations structure at I.C.I. and may have seen the talks as a possible means of furthering this.[13] He probably also had the idea of using the talks to promote further amalgamations. He certainly believed in the benefits of rationalisation and hoped to convince British industry as a whole of the merits of his ideas.[14] The talks were also a good opportunity for him to project himself as the leader of British industry and to cut a figure in the political world. Mond consequently chose his fellow employers carefully. He chose the kind of industrialist he knew and associated with, mainly employers from large companies, industrialists who he thought would fall in with his schemes for industrial reorganisation, progressive employers who would not be restricted by the policies and decision-making of some of the more cautious employers' organisations and more backwoods companies.

## II

An Interim Report was produced by the conference in July 1928. In many ways it was a remarkable statement of progressive employer thought. It made recommendations in five areas. Firstly, it recommended trade union recognition. The T.U.C. was acknowledged to be 'the most effective organisation' on the trade union side and the only body which possessed the authority to 'discuss and negotiate' on all questions relating to industrial relations and industrial reorganisation. In individual industries it recommended that co-operation could best be obtained by 'negotiations with the accredited representatives of affiliated unions or of unions recognised by the General Council of the T.U.C. as *bona fide* trade unions'. Such negotiations should not be confined to wages and conditions, but should go beyond this and cover 'other matters of common interest to the trade and industry concerned'.[15] The trade union side greatly valued this section on recognition,[16] and the employers' side also believed that it was important.[17] Secondly, the Interim Report condemned victimisation of workers for being members of unions or union representatives for acting in pursuit of 'legitimate trade union activities'. Those dismissed because of their activities in the General Strike were to be reinstated and appeals procedure established to hear complaints of unfair dismissal.[18] There had been widespread victimisation by some employers after the General Strike, especially in the road transport, railway and printing industries.

Thirdly, the Report recommended the establishment of a National Industrial Council (N.I.C.), to be made up of an equal number of representatives from the T.U.C. on the one side and the N.C.E.O. and F.B.I. on the other. The Council, once established, was to hold regular quarterly meetings and to investigate and discuss general industrial relations questions. At the request of either side to a dispute the N.I.C. could appoint a Joint Conciliation Committee (composed of ten T.U.C. and ten N.C.E.O. representatives). Once such a Committee had been appointed neither side was to stop work or alter the conditions of employment in any way; and the Committee would try by investigation and pressure to arrange a peaceful settlement. There was to be no compulsion, and it was stressed that the intention was not to interfere with already existing machinery—though it was added that 'during the last few years the existing machinery has failed to deal with certain disputes of a serious magnitude.'[19] Mond said later that the proposed N.I.C. and Conciliation Committee was the most vital part of the Report.[20] The T.U.C. for its part saw the N.I.C. as an important means of influencing economic policy.[21]

Fourthly, the Report welcomed the rationalisation of industry, including the relaxation of union restrictive practices. Amalgamations and general reorganisation were to be encouraged where they brought about efficiency and higher real wages. Such rationalisation, it was stated, was best achieved by the co-operation of unions and employers. At the same time the Report recognised that the interests of workers displaced by rationalisation would have to be safeguarded.[22] Mond and the other employers undoubtedly also saw this emphasis on rationalisation as important.

Finally, the Report expressed doubts about the Gold Standard to which Britain had returned in 1925. It argued that this restricted the supply of money and credit available to industry, held back economic expansion, and that an overvalued pound handicapped Britain's export trades. The Mond Employers had already persuaded the trade union side of the committee to join them in addressing a memorandum on this subject to the Chancellor of the Exchequer, Winston Churchill, in April 1928. At a later stage the F.B.I. was to try again to use T.U.C. support to pressurise the government and monetary authorities into changing their financial and credit policy. From the employers' point of view there was, moreover, always the prospect of the Labour Party coming to power, in which case the T.U.C. was expected to have more direct influence on economic and financial policy.

A further Report, on unemployment, was adopted by the Conference in March 1919. Among other things this recommended government financial assistance to promote amalgamations; joint management and union discussions on rationalisation in the coal, iron and steel, and shipbuilding industries and in certain branches of the engineering and textile trades; a state development fund large enough to stimulate the economy during depression; an increase in old age pensions to encourage older workers to retire and to make place for younger unemployed workers; the raising of the school leaving age from 14 to 15 to withdraw an estimated half million young people from industry; and finally a full enquiry, on which employers and unions would be represented, into how Bank of England and Treasury monetary policy might be adapted to encourage industrial expansion.[23]

## III

There was some opposition to the talks within the trade union movement, but this was never very powerful and failed to win over the General Council or the 1928 Conference which passed a large vote in favour of the talks. Leaders such as Turner, Bevin, Thorne, Thomas and Pugh felt that the union movement had something to gain from these discussions with employers in terms of union recognition, the status of unions, and the protection of their members.

The main opposition came from the employers' side, in particular from the employers' organisations. It was obvious that the two central organisations, the N.C.E.O. and F.B.I., had to react to the Interim Report, in particular to the proposed N.I.C. and conciliation machinery. At a special meeting of the employers' organisations convened to consider the Report, Mond, Willey, Muspratt and Hazell as members of the F.B.I. and Weir and Milne Watson of the N.C.E.O. urged the organisations to accept the proposals. It was clear at this meeting that the N.C.E.O. was more reluctant than the F.B.I. to have discussions with the T.U.C.[24] Both, however, decided to consult their members. The replies they received, extremely full and informative, offer a valuable and unique insight into employers' attitudes on a wide range of subjects. In general the members of the two organisations rejected the proposed N.I.C. and conciliation machinery, but favoured exploratory talks with the T.U.C. The members of the F.B.I., made up of trade associations and individual firms, were, however, generally more favourable than the members of the N.C.E.O. which was made up solely of employers' organisations.[25]

Some respondents argued against the whole of the Mond-Turner Talks and Interim Report. They saw the talks as an attempt by the T.U.C. to re-establish its position after the debacle of the General Strike. They pointed to the connection the T.U.C. had with the Labour Party and expressed a fear that the T.U.C. would use the N.I.C. to advance socialism. Industrial and political matters they held should be kept separate.[26] They argued that the Mond-Turner proposals were contrary to the system of collective bargaining as it had developed in the U.K. and that the Interim Report was a destabilising influence on industrial relations generally: the Mond Employers acted as individuals, binding neither themselves nor their firms, and they could therefore make concessions on paper, thereby raising hopes which more practical employers could not fulfil. More particularly the proposed N.I.C. and conciliation machinery met with strong opposition. It was argued that the best place to secure industrial peace was at the industry or workshop level. For this adequate machinery already existed. The proposed machinery would merely provide a court of appeal for the prolongation of disputes, unions would hold out for better settlements, and the existing procedures would be undermined.[27] Moreover, it would represent undue interference in the affairs of individual employers and constitute a diminution of their managerial autonomy.

One of the main arguments levelled against the N.I.C. was that the N.C.E.O., F.B.I., and their respective members had separate functions: the former were employers' organisations, the latter trade associations; the former could not discuss trade matters, the latter could not deal with labour questions. The benefits of bringing the different bodies together were uncertain, members might secede, and the outcome might be the disintegration of the central employers' organisations. Some N.C.E.O. members saw this as related to the managerial prerogatives issue: trade and labour matters should be kept separate and the former should not be discussed with the trade unions.[28]

Some argued against other specific parts of the Interim Report. Many objected to the clause on the recognition of T.U.C. unions. Prominent among these were the Shipping Federation (which had a close relationship with Havelock Wilson's National Union of Seamen, recently expelled from the T.U.C.), the Mineowners' Association (which objected to the T.U.C.'s role during the coal stoppage and which was involved in the creation of Spencer's Non-Political Miners' Union),[29] the Glass Manufacturers' Federation (an industry in which union organisation was weak), and the Engineering Employers' Federation (which, though it recognised trade unions, opposed the recognition of white collar sections of manual unions and the unionisation of foremen and which was prepared to make no concessions in the area of managerial prerogative).[30] A number of large firms in the F.B.I. also expressed doubts about trade union recognition: Lever Bros., Brown and Polson, the United Glass Bottle Co. Ltd., the Bristol Carriage and Tramway Co. Ltd. and the Bristol Aeroplane Co. Ltd.[31] These firms claimed that they did not oppose the talks as such, but preferred to decide their own recognition policies.

Finally the Report's views on rationalisation displeased some. The Wool Textile Employers' Association, representing an industry made up largely of small family firms, questioned the need for rationalisation and said that they were sceptical of the value of the mass production of standardised goods.[32] The British Engineers' Association and the E.E.F. particularly disliked the idea of recognising that labour had a right to be consulted at all in this area which would infringe managerial prerogative.[33]

Supporters and opponents among N.C.E.O. and F.B.I. members do not fall into any clearly defined industrial categories such as expanding/contracting, sheltered/unsheltered, capital/labour intensive. The N.C.E.O. analysed the replies it received from member organisations according to their employing capacity and classified them according to their attitude towards the Mond-

Turner Report, Of the thirty-seven member organisations, thirty-five produced definite replies.[34] Of these thirty-five, seven organisations, representing roughly six per cent of the total labour-employing capacity of the Confederation, supported the proposals:

Association of Bleachers, Dyers, Printers and Finishers
Chemical and Allied Employers' Federation
National Federation of Dyers and Cleaners
Federation of Gas Employers
Association of Jute Spinners and Manufacturers
Lead Employers' Council
Sheffield Lighter Trades Employers' Association

Four organisations, representing roughly seventeen per cent of the total employing capacity of the Confederation, accepted the proposals, but subject to various limitations:

Federation of Civil Engineering Contractors
Leather Producers' Association
Railway Companies' Association
National Federation of Vehicle Trades

Nineteen organisations, representing about sixty-two per cent of the Confederation, rejected the proposals, but at the same time favoured or did not actually oppose some kind of meeting with the T.U.C.:

British Tin Box Manufacturers' Federation
Employers' National Council for the Clay Industries
National Association of Coke and By-Product Plant Owners
Wholesale Clothing Manufacturers' Federation
Federation of Master Cotton Spinners Associations
Employers' Federation of Envelope Makers and Manufacturing Stationers
National Federation of Iron and Steel Manufacturers
London Employers' Association (Clothing)
Mining Association
Employers' Association of the Port of Liverpool
Federation of Master Printers and Allied Trades
Federated Quarry Owners
Shipbuilding Employers' Federation
Shirt, Collar and Tie Manufacturers' Federation
Scottish Tube Makers Wages Association
Wool (and Allied) Employers' Council
Cotton Spinners' and Manufacturers' Association
Newspaper Society
Shipping Federation

Five organisations, representing fourteen per cent of the N.C.E.O., did, according to this analysis, reject the proposals completely:

Engineering Employers' Federation
Glass Manufacturers' Federation
National Federation of Launderers
Crucible Steel Makers' Association
National Light Castings Ironfounders' Federation

In these classifications there was obviously a certain amount of overlap and it was difficult to make definite distinctions. To the final list of opponents could, for example, be added the Shipping Federation, the Mineowners' Association, and possibly the Shipbuilding Employers' Federation. The two organisations which expressed some of the strongest views in opposition were the Engineers' Federation and the Shipping Federation. The firmest supporters of talks and of the Interim Report were the Chemical Employers' Federation and the Gas Employers' Federation.

While rejecting the proposed N.I.C. and conciliation machinery, the majority of employers felt that something positive had to be done. Press and public opinion were in favour of talks and the employers were reluctant to disappoint expectations and to appear in an unfavourable light.[35] Some argued that total rejection would have a detrimental effect on industrial relations generally and that, if the T.U.C. was moving from a political to an industrial strategy, it should be encouraged for fear that left extremists would once again seize power in the union movement.[36] The approach of a General Election in 1929 was a consideration which weighed with many employers: to refuse to talk to the T.U.C. would be to present the Labour Party with an excellent electoral advantage. A further consideration with some employers was that 'the existence of a conference on these lines would provide a most valuable means of contact with the Government in the event of a Labour Government coming to power'.[37] Furthermore, there was a feeling that if industry did not work out its own problems voluntarily, government might intervene with a compulsory national council and arbitration machinery. Throughout, most of the employers showed that they wanted a voluntary system of industrial relations without government intervention. However, despite these pressures, the Engineering and Shipping Employers still opposed talks with the T.U.C. and at one point threatened secession from the N.C.E.O. if the talks went ahead. As a compromise, it was decided therefore to invite the T.U.C., not to talks, but to see if talks were feasible.[38]


IV


The T.U.C. accepted the employers' invitation, and the first official talks between the N.C.E.O., F.B.I. and T.U.C. were held in April 1929. It was agreed that, since the organisations on both sides were national, they could not discuss the problems of particular industries; it was the two employers' organisations, however, which laid most stress on their inability in this respect. It soon became clear that one of the main difficulties was the constitutional and functional limitations of the two employers' organisations—the N.C.E.O. being able to discuss only labour questions and not commercial matters, while the reverse held for the F.B.I. The T.U.C. objected that this would result in much more limited talks than those they had with the Mond Employers and pointed out that the T.U.C. could cover the whole field of labour and economic affairs. The T.U.C. expected the employers' organisations to be in a similar position.[39]

The Labour victory at the General Election in May 1929 made the employers more favourably inclined to talks: they saw advantages in having contacts with the T.U.C. in order to moderate any disagreeable Labour measures, to forestall the imposition of a compulsory N.I.C., and to apply pressure for more favourable trade and monetary policy.[40] They therefore produced a form of procedure whereby the N.C.E.O., F.B.I. and T.U.C. could propose for discussion any subject within their respective provinces which did not encroach on any of their constituent members; the two employers' bodies would set up an allocation committee to assign subjects between themselves; any of the three organisations could refuse to discuss a subject, but a reason for refusal had to be given. The T.U.C. replied that the employers' organisations were offering them much less than the Mond Employers, but agreed to the procedure.[41]

In the early 1930s a series of talks was held in which the F.B.I. and T.U.C. took the initiative, while the N.C.E.O. played a passive, even obstructive, role. The F.B.I. hoped through the talks to woo the T.U.C. from its traditional commitment to free trade and to obtain its support for protection and cheaper money.[42] Joint evidence would have been given to the Macmillan Committee on Finance and Industry, had the T.U.C.'s own report not been leaked to the press.[43] Between 1930 and 1933 a number of conferences were held on imperial trade and preference, a series of joint memoranda were produced, largely on F.B.I. lines, and joint representation was made to the Government.[44] The F.B.I. would have liked to have discussed Japanese competition with the T.U.C. Their intention was to obtain T.U.C. support in order to persuade the Government to abrogate the Anglo-Japanese Trade Treaty. However, at the allocation committee meeting the N.C.E.O. argued that consideration of this would touch on wages and conditions of employment, which the N.C.E.O. was not particularly desirous of discussing with the T.U.C.[45] This effectively stopped the F.B.I. initiative. The T.U.C., for their part, initiated talks with the F.B.I. on the promotion of Anglo-Russian trade, a subject in which the T.U.C. had always shown an interest.[46]

The T.U.C. invited the N.C.E.O. to discuss rationalisation, displacement, and unemployment. The Mond-Turner Talks had helped the T.U.C. to see this problem more clearly and some union leaders hoped through joint talks to devise some national guidelines or policy. However, no joint policy emerged from the talks. The Confederation was reluctant and half-hearted. It had never been enthusiastic about joint talks, and its attitude at this point may have been influenced by a deepening depression and a shift of bargaining power back further towards the employers. It argued that rationalisation and its industrial relations effects were best dealt with at industry or plant level. It also pointed out the difficulty of distinguishing between unemployment caused by rationalisation and unemployment caused by other factors.[47] The Engineering Employers came out in opposition to the talks and sent a special memorandum to the Confederation reiterating that the discussion of labour displacement due to rationalisation and the introduction of new techniques would constitute an invasion of managerial prerogatives. Engineering Employers could not accept that changes should only occur with union consent: 'in 1897 and again in 1922', it said, referring to the two major engineering disputes of the nineteenth and twentieth centuries, 'the Federation was compelled to take action of a very serious nature for the purpose of securing the retention of the employers' freedom in this respect.'[48]

A pamphlet issued at this time by the N.C.E.O. and sent to the leaders of the political parties and the T.U.C. shows just how far apart the N.C.E.O. and T.U.C. were on economic policy and planning.[49] This document argued that the solution to the economic crisis was to reduce wages, to let export industries, not sheltered industries, set the wage pattern, to cut unemployment benefit and to reduce government expenditure. The T.U.C., on the other hand, in part influenced by the Mond-Turner Talks,[50] was at this time developing its own under-consumptionist and proto-Keynesian demand theories.[51] In reply to the N.C.E.O. document the T.U.C. stated:

> Reduction in social services, restrictions on wage fixing machinery, the cutting down of unemployment benefit, the reduction of wages in the public services, these are apparently the only remedies this organisation (N.C.E.O.) can offer in the present emergency. From beginning to end of the manifesto there appears to be nothing of a constructive character. There is no recognition of the fundamentals of the problem, and indeed nothing to indicate that the writers are living in 1931 and not 1881. Such a policy is merely a confession of intellectual and moral bankruptcy.[52]

It was under these circumstances that the last N.C.E.O.-T.U.C. meeting was held in May 1931. In 1933 there was talk of a joint N.C.E.O.-T.U.C. meeting under Ministry of Labour auspices on hours and unemployment. Once again, however, the E.E.F. expressed its opposition and threatened to disassociate itself from any talks on Mond-Turner lines.[53] Nothing therefore materialised.

### V

As set out in the Interim Report the intention of the Mond-Turner Talks was to restructure the British system of industrial relations by introducing a National Industrial Council and new conciliation machinery; to promote rationalisation and to secure greater flexibility and higher productivity in industry; and finally to re-examine Britain's monetary and trade policy. Taking these objectives in reverse order, it may be said that indirectly the Mond-Turner Talks and their sequel may have helped prepare the way for the abandonment of free trade and the gold standard in the 1930s.[54] However any influence was indirect and limited. The series of talks may have helped secure a better understanding on both sides of the relationship between rationalisation, productivity, and union-management relations. But once again any influence was limited and there was no wholesale reorganisation of British industry on Mond-Turner lines. Finally, the proposed National Industrial Council and conciliation machinery were not established. The most that was achieved in this respect was a recognition by the Mond Employers of the unions' right to be consulted on, and the value of joint discussion of, general industrial policy.[55] The significance of this, however, should not be exaggerated. Mond felt it was important: 'If someone had told you 25 years ago,' he said 'that a body of employers and workers' leaders were going to sit round a table and discuss the question of what the national credit system of this country ought to be, you would have looked on him as a lunatic. Yet that is the stage to which we have now advanced'.[56] But the fact remains that no permanent procedural relationship was established and there was no reform of the British system of industrial relations.

There were a number of reasons for this failure—a deterioration in the economic situation, trade union fear of industrial reorganisation which might lead to further unemployment, and lack of government encouragement.[57] The main reason, however, was probably the fact that the central employers' organisations and their members were *unable* and *unwilling* to establish a permanent relationship with the unions and to enter into co-operation on Mond-Turner lines. They were unable in that the N.C.E.O. was a federal organisation in which authority was highly decentralised; it had no power to bind its constituents; and it could not exercise leadership over them. The F.B.I. and T.U.C. had only slightly more discretionary authority as bargaining agents and would themselves probably have faced problems had the talks ever got round to implementing policies. The fact was that the constituent employers' organisations and trade unions were jealous of their independence and were not prepared to give their central organisations any greater authority. Moreover on the employers' side, the situation was complicated by the existence of two organisations each with their separate spheres of interest. But even had the institutional arrangements been more favourable, the desire to co-operate on Mond-Turner lines was lacking on the part of the main employer groupings. These were more influenced than the Mond Group by relationships and traditions at the industry and workplace level. They were not prepared to see these relationships complicated and their position prejudiced by national talks. They were influenced in particular by considerations of managerial rights and prerogatives. As a result they were not prepared to recognise the unions as equal partners and insisted that labour matters should be treated separately from general industrial and economic matters.

It is difficult to say whether the two central employers' organisations were more representative of British management thought and practice than were the Mond Employers. The latter group certainly contained some very important industrialists. On the one hand they were very much in line with a traditional element among British employers which favoured co-operation with the trade unions.[58] On the other hand it might be argued that they represented a new element among British employers who favoured a more enlightened and sophisticated labour policy commensurate with the development of corporate capitalism. It should be remembered, however, that they tended to reflect the views of certain very large firms in certain industries—in particular those which were expanding or which were based on consumer or domestic markets. It is also important that they acted as individuals, without committing either themselves or their firms to anything. They were talking about what *ought* to be done rather than about what *could* be done. Even in the case of Mond there was a disparity between his position and attitudes in the talks and the labour policy he pursued as Chairman of I.C.I., a paternalistic policy which was not aimed at encouraging trade unionism or collective bargaining.[59]

The F.B.I. and N.C.E.O. represented a much broader cross-section of British industry than did the Mond Employers. The N.C.E.O. itself claimed to represent over fifty per cent of the working population of Great Britain (including public employees) and nearly ninety per cent of the organised employers in the country.[60] It certainly represented the vast majority of small and medium sized firms in the old and basic industries. A study of the records of the two central employers' organisations and in particular of the detailed views of their constituent firms and organisations on the Mond-Turner Interim Report shows that the N.C.E.O. and F.B.I. policies (though in themselves somewhat different) did for the most part reflect the views of the vast majority of their members.

The question of managerial rights and prerogatives was an important issue throughout the official talks. It affected the employers' attitude towards trade union recognition; it affected their attitude towards procedural machinery in the form of opposition to outside interference and arbitration; above all it affected the employers' attitude towards the scope of negotiations and the range of subjects they were prepared to discuss with the trade unions. The N.C.E.O., largely influenced by the Engineers, the Mineowners, and the Shipowners, was not prepared to discuss production or commercial matters with the T.U.C. or recommend that its members discuss such matters with individual unions.

However, though managerial prerogatives emerged as important, nevertheless, along with other industrial relations attitudes and policies, the defence of managerial prerogatives was always subservient to broader economic ends. All the groups of employers saw industrial relations objectives as very much means to other ends. Industrial relations policies were therefore seen as instruments for accomplishing the firm's primary commercial purposes. The main objective among the Mond Employers seems to have been industrial reorganisation through rationalisation and the improvement of the international competitiveness of British capital. Trade union co-operation was seen as necessary for the success of this. Among the Mineowners, Engineers, and other basic industry employers in the N.C.E.O. the main emphasis was on reducing labour costs and improving the export potential of British goods. A firm line on management authority and wage bargaining was seen as being essential in this. For all the employers therefore industrial relations objectives were very much secondary to other commercial objectives.

Finally, the Mond-Turner Talks and their sequel show that British employers were not a monolithic group, but rather a number of groups with different economic interests, favouring different strategies and embodying different traditions and attitudes towards labour relations. Differences existed not only between the two central employers' organisations and the Mond Employers, but within the various groupings. The variations in orientation may in part have been the result of differences in the economic position of industries; in part they may have reflected differences in the size of firms between and within industries; and in part variations may have been due to differences between functional groups and between levels of authority (e.g. directors and senior executives, managers with direct labour responsibilities, and officials of employers' organisations). British employers were not therefore a homogeneous group when it came to industrial relations: there were considerable differences among them over the best strategy for coping with the problems posed by labour relations.

*University of Kent*

## NOTES

1. G. W. McDonald and H. F. Gospel, 'The Mond-Turner Talks 1927–33: A Study in Industrial Co-operation', *Historical Journal*, XVI, 1973, 807–29.
2. Federation of British Industry (hereafter F.B.I.) kept at C.B.I. in London/330K2(A)/I, Report on Meeting of 12 Jan. 1928; T.U.C., *T.U.C. Report 1928*, 211.
3. Included in the list are those who signed the letter to the T.U.C. and those who were present at the joint meetings on 12 January 1928 and 4 July 1928. The list is compiled from information in National Confederation of Employers' Organisations (hereafter N.C.E.O.) kept at C.B.I. in London /C66/I and from *The Director of Directors, 1927*. It does not contain all the companies and directorships of the Mond Group. The T.U.C. Research Department calculated that the Mond Employers represented directorships in 189 companies and included 98 chairmen of these companies, T.U.C., *T.U.C. Report 1928*, 407–8.
4. Ch. = Chairman; D = Director; Man. D = Managing Director.
5. F.B.I./330K2(A)/I, Letter, R. Nugent to Lord Gainford, 21 Nov. 1927.
6. Engineering Employers' Federation (hereafter E.E.F.) kept at E.E.F. in London, Parcel 29, Memorandum entitled Industrial Peace, 7–9. This was the Federation's view of Mond's rationale.
7. The fourteen employers in the Mond Goup who were connected with the F.B.I. were Aberconway, Baker, Bowden, Colwyn, R. Hadfield, Hazell, Lee, Mannaberg, Manville, Mond, Mills, Milne Watson, Rylands, Willey: the three connected with the N.C.E.O. were Weir, Milne Watson, and Hazell; Stamp had a tenuous connection with the N.C.E.O.
8. Sir J. Lithgow of the Shipbuilding Employers' Federation referred to them as 'blackleg employers', N.C.E.O./C66/I, G.P.C., 11 July 1928, 7.
9. N.C.E.O./C66/III, Supplementary Minutes of Council Meeting of Federation of Master Printers, 10 July 1928, 2.
10. Conference on Industrial Reorganization and Industrial Relations (henceforward C.I.R.I.R.), *Interim Report*, adopted 4 July 1928. Letter Sir A. Mond to the T.U.C., 23 Nov. 1927, 4.
11. *Yorkshire Post*, 25 Feb. 1929; *The Highway*, Oct. 1928, 7–10.
12. F.B.I./330K2(A)/III, Memorandum on Mond-Turner Conferences in letter to F. King (on behalf of L. B. Lee) to R. Nugent, 18 March 1929. The M.P. was probably Austen Hopkinson, Independent M.P. for Mossley, a strong critic of trusts who had fought Mond's coal amendments in 1926 on behalf of the coal owners.
13. This was certainly seen as one of his objectives by the E.E.F., E.E.F., Parcel 29, Memo entitled 'Industrial Peace', 1–2, 4–8.
14. He considered that the ideas in the Interim Report reflected in large part what he was doing at I.C.I. See F.B.I./330K(A)/II, Summary of Statement by Lord Melchett, President, to the Annual Meeting of the Chemical and Allied Employers' Federation, 5 Dec. 1928.
15. C.I.R.I.R., *Interim Report*, 9.
16. See Bevin's opinion in T.U.C., *Industrial Conference Report*, 68.
17. N.C.E.O./C66/I, Notes on Discussion of G.P.C., 11 July 1928, 2–3, 9–10.
18. C.I.R.I.R., *Interim Report*, 10.
19. C.I.R.I.R., *Interim Report*, 10.

20. F.B.I./330K2(A)/II, Summary of Statement by Lord Melchett, President, to Annual Meeting of the Chemical and Allied Employers' Federation, 5 Dec. 1928, 8–13.
21. Lord Citrine, *Men and Work* (London, 1964), 246.
22. C.I.R.I.R., *Interim Report*, 13.
23. C.I.R.I.R., *Interim Joint Report on Unemployment*, adopted 12 March 1929, 1–15.
24. N.C.E.O./C66/I, Council of N.C.E.O. and Grand Council of F.B.I., 11 July 1928. The main opposition was expressed by Wedgwood, Gregorson (Federation of Iron and Steel Manufacturers), Ross and Williams of the N.C.E.O. and Gainford, Geddes (Dunlop) and Nimmo (Mining Association) of the F.B.I.
25. F.B.I./330K2(A)/II, Members' Attitudes to the Proposed N.I.C., 13 Dec. 1928; N.C.E.O./C66/VI, G.P.C. Sub-Committee on Mond-Turner Talks, 28 Dec. 1928.
26. For various expressions of these arguments see N.C.E.O./C66/II-VII, Replies from Members: F.B.I./330K2(A)/1–11; N.C.E.O./C66/VII/G.P.C., 8 Feb. 1929.
27. N.C.E.O./C66/I, G.P.C., 4 July 1928, 8; F.B.I./330K2(A)/I, Statement of the views of the National Association of Coke and Bye Product Plant Owners, Sept. 1928, 6–8.
28. N.C.E.O./C66/I, Draft Report of Special Committee appointed to consider the invitation to participate in the proposed N.J.I.C., Undated. See N.C.E.O./C66/V, Reply of E.E.F., 30 Nov. 1928; *Ibid.*, Reply of Shipping Fed., 7 Dec. 1928; *Ibid.*, Reply of National Fed. of Clay Industries, 12 Dec. 1928.
29. After the General Strike G. A. Spencer established the Notts. and District Miners' Industrial Union. This was financially assisted for pension purposes by mine owners.
30. The replies from these organisations are to be found in N.C.E.O./C66/V–VII.
31. The replies from these firms are to be found in F.B.I./330K2(A)/I and II.
32. N.C.E.O./C66/V, Wool (and Allied) Textile Employers' Council Examination of Interim Report, 7.
33. F.B.I./330K2(A)/I, Letter, D. Bremner (British Engineers' Association) to D. Walker (F.B.I. Secretary), 3 Oct. 1928 and E.E.F. Reply in N.C.E.O./C66/V.
34. N.C.E.O./C66/VI/N.C.2575; N.C.E.O./C66/VII/N.C.2587. The two organisations which did not produce definite replies were the National Federated Electrical Association and the Hotels' and Restaurants' Association.
35. N.C.E.O./C66/III and IV, Letter, Sir A. Ross to J. Forbes Watson, 13 Nov. 1928.
36. N.C.E.O./C66/VII, Letter, Sir J. Lithgow to J. Forbes Watson, 4 Feb. 1929.
37. F.B.I./330K2(A)/I, Mond-Turner Conference Memo, 5 Sept. 1928, 5.
38. N.C.E.O./C66/VII/G.P.C., 8 Feb. 1929; N.C.E.O./C66/VII, Letter, N.C.E.O. and F.B.I. to T.U.C., 13 Feb. 1929.
39. N.C.E.O./C66/VIII Conference between N.C.E.O., F.B.I. and T.U.C./N.C.2678 23 April 1929.
40. N.C.E.O./C66/IX, Joint F.B.I.–N.C.E.O. Meeting, 18 July 1929, 5.
41. N.C.E.O./C66/X, Joint Conference, 19 Dec. 1929. The agenda covered unemployment, industry and finance; taxation of industry; social services—co-ordination; education and industry; delegated powers to government departments; inter-Empire trade; international trade; trade facilities; insurance and export credit; general international labour questions; industrial and commercial statistics.
42. F.B.I./330K2(A)/IV, Committee on Finance and Industry, 14 May 1930, 7–8.
43. F.B.I./330K2(A)/IV, Minutes of T.U.C. Economic Committee of 18 June 1930.
44. See F.B.I./330K2(A), IV.
45. F.B.I./330 W. 28, Allocation Committee, 19 July 1933.
46. F.B.I./330K2(A)/IV, Joint Meeting between Representatives of the General Council of T.U.C. and F.B.I., 22 Nov. 1932.
47. N.C.E.O./C530/I, Notes on Meeting with T.U.C., 4 Nov. 1930.
48. N.C.E.O./C530/I, Letter, E.E.F. to N.C.E.O., 1 Sept. 1930.
49. N.C.E.O., *The Industrial Situation* (1931).
50. Both A. Bullock, *The Life and Times of Ernest Bevin*, Vol. I, (London, 1960) 403, 426, and R. Skidelsky, *Politicians and the Slump* (London, 1970), 61, say that the talks were of educational value to some members of the General Council.
51. See S. Pollard, 'Trade Union Reaction to the Economic Crisis', *Journal of Contemporary History*, IV, 1969.
52. F.B.I./330K2(A)/IV, T.U.C. General Council Economic Committee, *Short Statement on Economic Policy*, 2–3.

53. E.E.F./XXXI/M.B., 9 March 1933; E.E.F./XXXI/M.B., 11 April 1933.
54. See, for example, R. Skidelsky, *op. cit.*, 61, 406.
55. This was also the conclusion of Milne Bailey, *Trade Unions and the State* (London, 1934), 149, and of a foreign observer, R. Cassirer, *Die Beziehungen Zwischen Kapital und Arbeit in England: Die Mond-Turner Konferenze 1928-1930* (Heidelberg, 1933).
56. F.B.I./330K2(A)/II, Summary of Statement by Lord Melchett, President, to Annual Meeting of the Chemical and Allied Employers' Federation, 5 Dec. 1928, 11.
57. For a more detailed discussion of these factors see G. W. McDonald and H. F. Gospel, *loc. cit.*
58. One might cite examples going back to Robert Owen, A. J. Mundella, and David Dale in the nineteenth century. See also R. Charles, *The Development of Industrial Relations in Britain 1911-39*, (London, 1973), *passim.* which deals extensively with this element among British employers.
59. See W. J. Reader, *Imperial Chemical Industries*, I, (London, 1975), 61-70, for a detailed account of the industrial relations policy of I.C.I.
60. N.C.E.O./C66/VII, Notes 28 Feb. 1929. See also N.C.E.O., Annual Report 1924, N.C.1215, 12.

# UNEMPLOYMENT IN THE THIRD REICH

## By RICHARD OVERY

Whatever its social and economic implications, the problem of unemployment in Germany in the recession and recovery years from 1929 to 1936 was closely bound up with German politics. It was against a background of rapidly rising unemployment that the Nazi Party became a major electoral force. Although it was by no means clear quite how a National Socialist government would tackle unemployment when it came to power in January 1933, there was no doubt in the minds of Germany's new leaders that their own political survival was bound up with the success or otherwise of the 'Battle for Work'. Economic recovery would only occur, Hitler argued, 'if measures are taken again and again with energetic attacks and fanatical tenacity against unemployment'.[1] From 1930 Nazi leaders saw unemployment as a key political issue, to be solved by 'general labour service' and 'general conscription' or by public works; and they feared the effects on Nazi electoral prospects if unemployment were solved by the other parties.[2] The crisis of unemployment was a key plank in the Nazis' growing attacks on the Weimar governments in 1931 and 1932. But having made much of the failure of the 'party state' to solve the question, the Nazis put themselves in the position in January 1933 of having to make good their promise to provide bread and work.

By early 1933 this task was less daunting than it might have been, for the economy was showing the first slender signs of recovery from the autumn of 1932 onwards. The new government was able to make much propaganda on its own behalf riding on the back of an autonomous upswing in the business cycle, and on the legacy of policies already begun in 1932. Indeed a strategy for work-creation was only introduced in the middle of 1933, so that the initial Nazi claims to be solving unemployment were largely spurious. Nevertheless the desire to tackle unemployment was real enough. Hitler wanted economic recovery to be identified in the eyes of the population with the claims for national renewal and a new beginning heralded in January 1933.[3] He recognised that it was a precondition for achieving other goals as well: 'If there is success in solving this question, we have created for the new system such a situation that the government can realise step by step its other tasks. Work! Work!'[4]

I

The employment situation inherited by the Nazi government was an extraordinary one. The number of Germans in full-time employment fell from 20 million in the middle of 1929 to 11.4 million in January 1933, a fall of almost nine million. The total number of registered unemployed rose over the same period from 1.25 million to six million (see Table 1). The fall in employment was greater than the rise in unemployment because large

TABLE 1
REGISTERED UNEMPLOYMENT IN GERMANY, 1929–40* ('000s)

|         | 1929    | 1930    | 1931    | 1932    | 1933    | 1934    | 1935    | 1936    | 1937    | 1938    | 1939  | 1940  |
|---------|---------|---------|---------|---------|---------|---------|---------|---------|---------|---------|-------|-------|
| Jan     | 2,850.2 | 3,217.6 | 4,886.9 | 6,041.9 | 6,013.6 | 3,772.7 | 2,973.5 | 2,520.4 | 1,853.4 | 1,051.7 | 301.8 | 159.7 |
| Feb     | 3,069.7 | 3,365.8 | 4,971.8 | 6,128.4 | 6,000.9 | 3,372.6 | 2,764.1 | 2,514.8 | 1,610.9 | 946.3   | 196.3 | 123.8 |
| Mar     | 2,483.9 | 3,040.7 | 4,743.9 | 6,034.1 | 5,598.8 | 2,798.3 | 2,401.8 | 1,937.1 | 1,245.3 | 507.6   | 134.0 | 66.2  |
| Apr     | 1,711.6 | 2,786.9 | 4,358.1 | 5,739.0 | 5,331.2 | 2,608.6 | 2,233.2 | 1,762.7 | 960.7   | 422.5   | 93.9  | 39.9  |
| May     | 1,349.8 | 2,634.7 | 4,052.6 | 5,582.6 | 5,038.6 | 2,528.9 | 2,019.2 | 1,491.2 | 776.3   | 338.3   | 69.5  | 31.7  |
| Jun     | 1,260.0 | 2,640.6 | 3,953.9 | 5,475.7 | 4,856.9 | 2,480.8 | 1,876.5 | 1,314.7 | 648.4   | 292.2   | 48.8  | 26.3  |
| Jul     | 1,251.4 | 2,765.2 | 3,989.6 | 5,392.2 | 4,463.8 | 2,426.0 | 1,754.1 | 1,169.8 | 562.8   | 218.3   | 38.3  | 25.0  |
| Aug     | 1,271.9 | 2,882.5 | 4,214.7 | 5,223.8 | 4,124.2 | 2,397.5 | 1,706.2 | 1,098.4 | 509.2   | 178.7   | 33.9  | 23.1  |
| Sep     | 1,323.6 | 3,004.2 | 4,354.9 | 5,102.7 | 3,849.2 | 2,281.8 | 1,713.9 | 1,035.2 | 469.0   | 155.9   | 77.5  | 21.9  |
| Oct     | 1,557.1 | 3,252.0 | 4,623.4 | 5,109.1 | 3,744.8 | 2,226.6 | 1,828.7 | 1,177.4 | 501.8   | 163.9   | 79.4  | –     |
| Nov     | 2,035.6 | 3,698.9 | 5,059.7 | 5,355.4 | 3,714.6 | 2,352.6 | 1,984.4 | 1,197.1 | 572.6   | 152.4   | 72.5  | –     |
| Dec     | 2,850.8 | 4,383.8 | 5,668.1 | 5,772.9 | 4,059.0 | 2,604.7 | 2,507.9 | 1,478.8 | 994.7   | 455.6   | 104.4 | –     |
| Average | 1,898.6 | 3,075.5 | 4,519.7 | 5,575.4 | 4,804.4 | 2,718.3 | 2,151.0 | 1,592.6 | 912.3   | 429.4   | 104.2 | 43.1  |

* from March 1935, including Saar; from March 1939 including Sudetenland, from June including Memel.

Source: Statistisches Jahrbuch für das Deutsche Reich (Berlin, 1940), p. 389.

numbers of workers, particularly women and the long-term unemployed were removed from the register by 1933. The dimensions of the economic and political crisis in 1932 are easier to understand once it is recognised that the problem was not six but nine million unemployed. Two out of every five Germans employed in 1929 were without work in the winter of 1932–33.

There are a number of special factors in the German case which help to explain the exceptionally high levels of registered unemployment compared with other European economies. Seasonal unemployment was high in Germany because of the large agricultural sector and the harsher winters, which affected the construction industry in particular. Throughout the 1920s there were always 1.5 to two million unemployed in the winter months.[5] The age-structure of the population was also unfavourable. The high pre-war birth rate meant that higher numbers of young Germans were seeking work in the late 1920s and early 1930s. In the summer of 1932 over a quarter of those unemployed were aged 14–25.[6] Women, too, formed a larger proportion of the work-force in Germany than in other industrial countries, and could legally register as unemployed. Women comprised about 20 per cent of German unemployment in 1932, where in other countries female unemployment tended to be under-recorded or unacknowledged.[7]

But the real cause of Germany's high level of unemployment lay in the weaknesses of the German economy in the 1920s. Shortages of capital after the inflation of 1923 meant high interest rates and a heavy dependence on foreign funds. The sluggish revival of world trade hit the German economy more than others because of its high export dependence. Agriculture and small businesses were hit by falling prices and high interest charges and taxes. The overall performance of the German economy stagnated between 1913 and 1929, in marked contrast to other industrial economies.[8] The effect of these problems on employment was very different from the British experience. There was far less of the structural and regional unemployment brought about by the collapse of Britain's geographically concentrated export industries. Unemployment in Germany both during the 1920s and during the recession was spread much more evenly across the German provinces and between different economic sectors. Although industrial regions had higher unemployment rates than rural areas, and producer goods suffered a higher loss of manpower than the consumer sectors, these were the conventional features of the industrial business cycle. There is some evidence to suggest that there was growing technological unemployment in the 1920s as firms modernised factory methods and shed labour, although it would be wrong to exaggerate the effects or scope of rationalisation. Small and medium-sized firms were discouraged from rationalising because of the high cost of capital, while some of the rationalised sectors actually expanded their work-force in the 1920s as demand for their products rose, cars and chemicals, for example.

It has also been argued that German unemployment was made worse by high wages and the political strength of the trade unions. Again this argument should be treated cautiously. Wages in Germany had barely reached the real levels of 1913 by the late 1920s, and were considerably lower than wage costs in other industrialised countries. What hampered Germany's competitive position was not high wage costs, but poor productivity and the failure to invest sufficiently in modernised equipment, the high cost of capital, and the sluggishness of home and foreign demand. It is certainly true that once the recession began to bite in 1930 prices fell faster than wages, so that real hourly wage-rates reached an inter-war peak in the following two years. But real wage rates actually fell faster in Germany during the recession than in any of the major competitor economies. It seems unlikely that sharper wage cuts would have persuaded businessmen to keep going, since the major part of the crisis was a fall in demand and a slump in prices caused by credit restrictions and the collapse of world trade.[9]

Once the German economy turned down in 1928–29 (and it began to do so well before the Wall Street Crash in October 1929), employment fell continuously until 1932. Unemployment was higher in the winter months than the summer because of seasonal unemployment, although in 1930–32 the gap between winter and summer employment was only 600–700,000, where it had averaged approximately two million in the period 1925–29.[10] Nor do the global employment figures show the full picture. Hours of work declined during the recession from an average of 7.67 hours per day in 1929 to 6.91 in 1932. Many workers found themselves on short-time during the depression (an estimated 60 per cent of trade union members in 1931–32), so that real earnings fell much faster than real wage rates. To cope with the recession businessmen preferred to employ women because they were cheaper, so that male employment declined faster than female. In 1928 women made up 33 per cent of the work-force, but 36 per cent in 1932. Female wages in the metal industry in 1931 were 59 per cent of the wages of skilled male workers.[11]

The exceptionally high levels of unemployment in 1930–33 were produced by the near collapse of the German credit system in 1931 and the decline in foreign trade. The withdrawal of loans created a major liquidity crisis, while the value of German exports fell by almost two-thirds between 1929 and 1932. There was little the government could do under the circumstances, although what it did do made the employment situation worse rather than better. Taxes were raised and incomes reduced by decree, and the additional taxation used for unemployment relief. Government spending was cut back and every effort made to avoid fiscal policies that might be construed as inflationary because of fears of the political repercussions. Local government was forced to lay off workers because of their worsening credit position, and in the end depended on central government for additional funds to meet emergency relief for the long-term unemployed. Government policies in general had the effect of further depressing demand, reducing prices and squeezing profits. Business confidence ebbed away.[12]

Although there is strong disagreement on exactly when the economy began to turn up again, there is general acceptance that the trough of the

recession was reached in the course of 1932. Industrial production reached
its lowest level in July 1932 and then moved continuously upwards, spurred
on by the demand for re-stocking and helped by lower costs. But the
aggregate figure of hours worked in industry was lower in each month
between March 1932 and February 1933 than in the preceding year, reaching
its lowest point of the depression in January 1933. The number of registered
unemployed was higher in December 1932 than in December 1931, but lower
from January 1933 onwards.[13] Some level of recovery was assured from
the late months of 1932, although the economy was still deep in recession.
Some part of the credit for this lies at the door of the government and the
Reichsbank for initiating relief schemes of paid work from mid-1932
onwards, and for easing credit conditions while maintaining confidence
in the currency, although the effects of both on employment were slight in
the short term.[14] And it was only on employment that the Nazi Party had
anything very positive to say; their economic plans had a 'work' priority,
and Nazi publicists were less inhibited than either Brüning or von Papen
by the hostility of orthodox financial and business circles to economic experiments. Unemployment was the most conspicuous and socially damaging
consequence of the depression, and the slowest of the economic indicators
to respond to government initiatives.

## II

The course of unemployment under the Nazi government reflected the
priority that Hitler gave to policies that directly promoted work at all costs.
Unemployment declined steadily until by 1938 Germany enjoyed a position
of full employment. But it is important not to exaggerate the speed and
scope of the decline. It is tempting with hindsight to see the elimination
of unemployment as an irreversible process set in train with the coming
of Hitler's government, but it was by no means a foregone conclusion and
was certainly not regarded as such either by politicians or businessmen at
the time. Unemployment on a large scale did not disappear in 1933 but
averaged 4.5 million over the year, and was 3.7 million at its lowest point
in November, helped by the mild winter which permitted building work
to continue for longer than usual.[15] Throughout 1934 unemployment
remained close to three million and was over two million for six of the 12
months of 1935. Only in June 1936 did unemployment fall below the level
of 1928–29, and in 1937 unemployment was lower in every month than
in 1927, the year of lowest unemployment before the slump. The decisive
change came in the course of the winter of 1933–34, when unemployment
fell by 1.25 million between September and April against the seasonal trend.
During the period from summer 1934 to May of 1935 unemployment remained stable and without the introduction of general military conscription
and increases in arms expenditure in 1935 might well have remained high
throughout the year. Unemployment then declined steadily during 1936,
reaching full employment during 1938–39.[16]

Unemployment was thus a major economic and social problem for at
least the first three years of the regime, and was historically very high until

TABLE 2
UNEMPLOYMENT RELIEF EXPENDITURE AND INCOME, CENTRAL AND LOCAL GOVERNMENT IN
GERMANY 1932/3–37/8 (BILL. RM)

| | A | B | C | D | E |
|---|---|---|---|---|---|
| Fiscal Year | Total Reich Expenditure | Total Local Expenditure | Total Income Reich Insurance Fund | Total Income Local Relief Income * | Excess of Expenditure over Income (A+B–C+D) |
| 1932/3 | 3.15 | 1.39 | 1.32 | 1.02 | 2.20 |
| 1933/4 | 2.76 | 1.23 | 1.54 | 0.94 | 1.51 |
| 1934/5 | 2.06 | 0.79 | 1.48 | 0.46 | 0.91 |
| 1935/6 | 1.63 | 0.51 | 1.37 | 0.31 | 0.46 |
| 1936/7 | 1.30 | 0.30 | 1.54 | 0.36 | -0.20 |
| 1937/8 | 0.72 | 0.16 | 1.71 | 0.24 | -1.07 |

* includes funds for other forms of public relief. Figures for 1932/3 and 1933/4 include special payments from central government.

*Source: Wirtschaft und Statistik, Vol. 16 (1936), pp. 86–7, 852; Statistisches Jahrbuch für das Deutsche Reich, 1937–40.*

at least the spring of 1936, although it never returned to the exceptional levels of 1932. Unemployment relief was a large item of expenditure for the local communes and the government until the same year (see Table 2 for details). Local authorities paid out three billion (1 billion = 1,000 million) RM in relief in the financial year 1932–33 and were still paying 2.25 billion in 1934–35, although the proportion of payments going to the relief of unemployment declined more rapidly than general relief expenditure. The unemployed as a proportion of those in receipt of relief declined from 66 per cent in March 1933 to 38 per cent in June 1935.[17] This left a substantial financial burden to be borne each year by the Reich government after deduction of local welfare contributions: 1.7 billion RM in 1932–33 and 1.6 in 1933–34. Total central funds expended on unemployment relief reached 3.1 billion and 2.8 billion in the same years.

The aggregate figures on unemployment tell only part of the story. The increase in employment during the period was higher than the decrease in unemployment, a result of labour not on the register returning to full-time work, and the higher take-up of school leavers each year after 1933. The number of young unemployed declined faster than unemployment among older workers, or unemployment in general.[18] Total employment increased from an average of 12.5 million in 1932 to an average of 18.3 million in 1937, although unemployment fell by only 4.6 million over the same period. Nevertheless unemployment was lower than the 1929 figure by 1936, whereas the employment peak in 1929 was not exceeded until 1938. The figures for total hours worked and the average length of day reveal the same lag. Total hours worked in industry did not reach the level of 1929 until 1937, a reflection of the slow revival of consumer goods production and trade after 1933.[19] The average hours worked per day developed slowly too, and actually fell in 1935 against the figure for 1934 because of the slower expansion of consumer goods. Again the figure for 1929 was not exceeded until 1937 (see Table 3), and then only for producer goods rather than consumer production. Although employment expanded rapidly during the 1930s this was due to some extent to a shorter working day and working week. It took longer for the economy to return to the employment position of 1929 than it did to reach the unemployment levels of that year.

This pattern was partly the result of the government's determination to reduce the statistical unemployed as quickly as possible for political reasons, either by encouraging people to leave the unemployment register or by offering so-called 'substitute employment'. The government also sponsored a campaign to reduce the length of the working week in order to spread the available work more widely. These policies were related to but distinct from the general economic policies for the recovery and the direct work-creation projects. They were aimed at removing substantial numbers from the unemployment figures as an end in itself, or, in the case of military conscription, as a fortuitous by-product of other policies.

Changes in registration procedures had the effect of removing some of the long-term and female unemployed from the registers, although this practice had served to disguise the true level of unemployment throughout

TABLE 3

TOTAL EMPLOYMENT AND HOURS WORKED IN GERMAN INDUSTRY 1929–37

| | Total Employment* | Total Hours Worked (1936=100) | Average Hours per Day | | |
| | | | All Ind | P | C |
| --- | --- | --- | --- | --- | --- |
| 1929 | 20,750,000 | 103.6 | 7.76 | 7.77 | 7.75 |
| 1930 | 16,843,000 | - | - | .- | - |
| 1931 | 15,020,000 | - | - | - | - |
| 1932 | 12,756,000 | 54.8 | 7.10 | 7.03 | 7.19 |
| 1933 | 13,436,000 | 63.0 | 7.16 | 7.16 | 7.15 |
| 1934 | 15,533,000 | 82.5 | 7.43 | 7.53 | 7.30 |
| 1935 | 16,640,000 | 90.1 | 7.41 | 7.64 | 7.10 |
| 1936 | 17,839,000 | 100.0 | 7.59 | 7.77 | 7.37 |
| 1937 | 19,095,000 | 110.2 | - | - | - |
| 1939 | 20,170,000 | 119.2 | - | - | - |

* figure for July    P=Producer Goods    C=Consumer Goods

*Source: Statistisches Jahrbuch für das Deutsche Reich, 1930–40.*

the recession, and was not a specifically Nazi device. Much more important for removing workers from the register were the schemes of substitute employment or work-camps for young people, and in particular the Labour Service scheme. This, too, was no novelty in Germany, and had been practised elsewhere in Europe before 1933. Its roots went back to the First World War and proposals for community service to sustain a spirit of solidarity and comradeship among young Germans once military service was over. It was taken up in the recession by the Brüning government as part of the battle against unemployment, the Freiwillige Arbeitsdienst (Voluntary Labour Service) providing youths with some limited work-experience in land reclamation, road-building and general construction.[20] The Nazi Party was also keen on such schemes and the introduction of some form of compulsory labour service became a stock electoral pledge before 1933.[21] In 1931 Konstantin Hierl was appointed Hitler's special commissioner for labour service. He advocated service not simply as an economic necessity, but because it was seen to have educational and propaganda possibilities as well. Labour Service was seen as a means of cementing bonds of loyalty to the racial community by bringing together young men and women from very different walks of life and forcing them to share a common work environment. Once in power the Nazis maintained the existing Labour Service, linking it with Hitler Youth activity, and finally in June 1935 introduced a law compelling 'all young Germans of both sexes to serve their Volk in the Labour Service'.[22]

Before 1935 voluntary labour service became for all intents and purposes compulsory, while a number of additional schemes were introduced. The first was a special project to provide cheap labour for agriculture, the *Landhilfe*, which was established in the middle of 1933. Under its provisions 16–21-year-olds had to spend six months in agricultural work and were given board, lodging and pocket money in return. The scheme was 'voluntary', although those who turned it down without good cause lost their entitlement to unemployment pay. Between July 1933 and March 1934 the numbers engaged in *Landhilfe* averaged 159,000 (36,000 of whom were girls) and a fixed quota of 160,000 was established for the scheme. It was an unpopular system, both with the farmers who had to take the new work-force on and with the mainly urban youth who took part. When the job market improved in 1936 the scheme declined rapidly and by 1938 involved only 40,000 workers, who were employed on a more regular wage-labour basis.[23] The Hitler Youth ran a similar scheme for 14–26-year-olds, the *Landdienst* (land service). Most of those involved were under 16 and were sent in large groups to help with agricultural work in the summer months, with the day divided between work and political education and military-style training. In Prussia a rather different plan was introduced through which 14-year-olds had to spend nine months on the land, organised into camps of 60 to 150 children. This 'year on the land' (*Landjahr*) was confined to selected candidates from the cities who were also given political education. *Landjahr* service entitled them to special access to jobs when they left school.[24] Between them these schemes involved around 400,000 young people (see Table 4 for details). The main occupation was land reclamation.

TABLE 4
SUBSTITUTE EMPLOYMENT IN GERMANY 1932–36*

| | Labour Service Men | Women | Land-hilfe | Land-jahr | Land-dienst | House-service** | Total |
|---|---|---|---|---|---|---|---|
| 1932 | 285,494 | - | - | - | - | - | 285,494 |
| 1933 | 252,780 | 10,212 | 155,939 | - | - | - | 418,931 |
| 1934 | 237,451 | 11,556 | 123,551 | 22,000 | 500 | 5,000 | 398,058 |
| 1935 | 230,195 | 12,659 | 139,232 | 31,000 | 3,500 | 5,000 | 421,586 |
| 1936 | 265,214 | | 49,441 | 35,000 | 14,388 | 25,000 | 389,543 |

* yearly peak
** additional female labour service

*Source:* F. Petrick, 'Eine Untersuchung zur Beseitigung der Arbeitslosigkeit unter der deutschen Jugend in den Jahren 1933 bis 1935', *Jahrbuch für Wirtschaftsgeschichte*, 1967, Part I, p. 299: F. Wunderlich, *Farm Labor in Germany 1810–1945* (Princeton University Press, 1961), pp. 321–2: *Wirtschaft und Statistik*, Vol. 16 (1936), pp. 134–7.

By 1936 work was under way or completed on 530,000 hectares of land, with projects in all the major Reich provinces.[25]

It is usually argued that these various forms of labour service were primarily designed to reduce overall unemployment figures quickly. While there is no doubt that they did contribute to keeping down unemployment among school-leavers, it is important not to forget that some form of Reich or community labour service was already in existence before 1933. Indeed the numbers in voluntary labour service before January 1933 were higher than at any point thereafter. In November 1932 some 285,000 Germans were on the scheme, while the highest number during the Third Reich was 252,000 in the middle of 1933 (both figures excluding women). The Labour Service was used to depress unemployment figures both before and after the seizure of power and did not amount in 1933 to an additional net reduction in numbers. Nor were the other schemes as important as the peak annual figures suggest. Many of those involved were still at school and would not have been counted as unemployed anyway, while outside harvest time the numbers involved were very much smaller. In December 1934 there were 69,000 on *Landhilfe*, in December 1935 82,000,[26] just over half the level in the harvest period. Moreover, *Landhilfe* gave harvest and casual work to young workers which would otherwise have been done by teams of urban or rural workers (mainly women and children) as a way of supplementing income during the summer and autumn, and was thus not new but transferred employment. And until the late 1930s female labour service remained largely optional. Only a few thousand girls took up voluntary labour service, or the 'year of household service' during 1933–35, leaving a large pool of cheap female labour seeking work at just the time that the government was looking for ways of reducing the number of women in the work-force.[27] The impact on the economy of all these schemes should not be exaggerated; they removed a certain number of young workers and school-leavers for a few months at a time from the job market over and above the level of substitute employment already reached in late 1932 and did little to boost demand since payments were small and partly in kind.

The efforts to remove women from the unemployment registers were equally mixed in their success. The Nazi government from the outset worked to remove women from the labour force and give their jobs to unemployed men, and married men first of all. The criterion used to judge the success of the employment drive was the increase in full-time male employment, and had been so even before 1933. In order to ensure that displaced women workers did not swell the ranks of the unemployed after 1933, efforts were also made to keep women off the unemployment registers or to keep them out of the job market altogether. Fritz Reinhardt, state secretary in the Finance Ministry, announced in February 1934 that it was the government's intention to cut the number of women in full-time employment in industry and services from six to three million.[28] The first major piece of legislation on work-creation in June 1933 was directed at female labour; and the Göring-Plan for employment for married males continued the policy in 1934.[29]

The major device for reducing female employment was the marriage loan. The state offered loans of 1,000 RM free of interest to racially and politically acceptable newly-weds on the condition that the woman gave up her job and undertook not to seek employment again unless her husband's pay dropped below 125 marks a month, or until the loan was paid off (at the rate of ten marks a month, or eight years). The loan was in the form of certificates to be redeemed at shops selling furniture and household goods so that the scheme would also directly stimulate particular sectors of industry as well. The scheme initially proved very popular, so much so that the average value of each loan had to be reduced. By the end of 1934 some 365,000 loans were paid out, 183,000 in the first five months of the scheme.[30] Special forms of labour service were also devised that did not pose a threat to male employment. Young girls could volunteer for work as low-paid domestic servants, with a special subsidy paid to employers who took on the additional help. The campaign against two-income families was directed mainly at women, and the propaganda in the Battle for Work played up the place of women in the home and denigrated the growth of female industrial employment.[31]

The overall effect on female employment was mixed. The employment of women was exceptionally high during the depression because female labour was cheap and could protect businesses against the profit-squeeze. Contemporary surveys discovered that a high percentage of women in work in industry was there because their husbands were unemployed.[32] As the economy revived it was likely that some of these women would leave employment as their husbands found work. But although the proportion of women at work in industry declined from 30 per cent at the beginning of 1933 to 24 per cent by mid-1936, the absolute number of women in commercial and industrial employment increased steadily to the outbreak of war, from 5.1 million in 1933 to 6.5 million in 1938.[33] Most women who were registered as unemployed in 1932 found their way back into the work-force after 1933, not into the kitchen. Indeed the numbers of women in employment was high by comparison with other industrial economies. The total number of women in the active work-force, including services, agriculture and small businesses increased throughout the period, from 11.4 million in 1933 to 14.8 million by 1939.[34] Although Nazi promises may well have appealed to the clerks and skilled workers who were displaced by women in the recession, the effect of the government's efforts to reduce female employment was slight. By 1938 the policy was fully reversed as the government tried to encourage women to take up work to cope with the labour shortages created by rearmament.[35]

Although the attempt to reduce the unemployment statistics by substitute employment and campaigns to remove workers from the register had a limited success between 1933 and 1935, it explains only a small part of the decline. Many of the schemes proved unpopular after a while. Those on labour service or *Landhilfe* worked sometimes for only a few months and then returned to look for regular paid work, so that there was always a gap between official establishment figures and the actual number on the projects.[36] Since unemployment declined much faster for younger workers (aged 16–25) than for other groups it was tempting to get back into full-time employment.[37] In 1935 this situation was changed with the introduction of military conscription. This was a form of national service which was impossible to avoid, and it took over a million out of the regular job market over the next two years, accelerating the trend towards full employment and selective labour shortages which set in during 1937 and 1938.

### III

By 1938 Germany was faced with labour shortages rather than unemployment. During 1938 the number of foreign workers in Germany increased to 381,000, and by March 1939 to 435,000. In June 1938 there were only 292,000 registered German unemployed, of which 43 per cent were classified as unemployable through disability, illness or psychological disorder. By the eve of war in August 1939 there were only 33,000 unemployed, so that even those classed as unemployable had been found jobs of some description during 1939.[38] The creation of substitute employment and the attack on female labour were no longer necessary, and was now an impediment to higher levels of productive employment as the demand for higher-paid factory labour increased.

There are a number of ways to explain this fall in unemployment. As we have seen, the opportunities to reduce statistical unemployment were limited, and were only introduced from mid-1933 when the downward movement of unemployment was already well under way. The early reduction in unemployment was brought about by a conventional upswing in the business cycle, helped by the changed economic climate in the second half of 1932, and the stimulus of low prices and wages. Although the recovery may have stabilised at a point well short of full employment if left to take its own course, as it did in Britain, Germany did not have Britain's structural problems; any recovery would be spread fairly evenly across the country and between different sectors. Since the main reason for Germany's exceptional unemployment was the credit crisis, the most severe in Germany's history, it was certain that re-employment would occur extensively once the crisis was past.

There is no effective way of measuring how much of the increase in employment was a result of the autonomous working of the business cycle, but most government schemes only began to take effect during late 1933 and 1934, while the more general controls over trade and the capital market were also introduced too slowly to explain the sharp fall in unemployment during the first half of 1933. Nevertheless the direct and indirect policies of the government were important in maintaining the momentum of re-employment when at certain times during 1933 and 1934 it looked as though recovery might come to a halt. Government intervention was the major reason why the economy moved so rapidly and thoroughly to a position of full employment in contrast to all the other major industrial states.

The government response to unemployment can be divided between direct and indirect measures. The most important direct measures were the various work-creation schemes introduced during 1932 and 1933. Since the schemes provoked much academic discussion at the time and made much useful propaganda for the Battle for Work they are worth looking at in some detail. The main object of the work-creation programmes was to provide temporary employment for the long-term unemployed who were no longer covered by insurance, and to promote schemes that would act as a stimulus to private economic activity. The idea of the 'initial spark' (*Initialzündung*), first popularised by the Brauns Kommission investigating the depression in Germany in 1931, was taken up during 1932 and 1933 as the justification for embarking on state-financed programmes which might otherwise have alarmed orthodox financial circles.[39]

Work-creation, like the Labour Service, was not a Nazi invention. The idea of using relief funds for public works went back to the brief recession of 1926, and was maintained every year thereafter, although the sums involved never exceeded 40 million RM a year before 1933.[40] But during 1932 the government supplemented direct relief work with federal work programmes funded directly by the state, primarily through short-term bills which were to be repaid out of future tax revenues when the economy recovered. The first scheme was initiated by Brüning shortly before his fall from office in June 1932, at a total cost of 165 million RM. On 4 September von Papen, his successor, introduced a second programme worth 182 millions and in December and January 1932/33 an emergency programme (*Sofortprogramm*) was brought in by the Reich Commissar for Labour, Günter Gereke, worth 500 million RM, increased to 600 millions in July. The most important of all was the Reinhardt-Programm authorised by the Law for Reducing Unemployment on 1 June 1933, which made 1,000 million RM immediately available for public works.[41] The schemes were aimed at public services and construction, watei ways, road-building, bridge repair and general maintenance left undone during the depression because of declining local government income. The funds were distributed by four main Reich agencies, the most important of which was the Deutsche Gesellschaft für öffentliche Arbeiten (Offa), which administered 60 per cent of the funds released by the government.[42] Details of the finance made available under the work-creation programmes are set out in Table 5.

The employment effects of these direct schemes are difficult to ascertain precisely because there was considerable overlap between work-creation, Labour Service and additional work-creation schemes funded by the German railways (991 million RM) and the Post Office (111 millions), all of which used the same sort of suppliers and drew on a common pool of unskilled and semi-skilled labour. The figures of those working directly on the project sites are set out in Table 5. The peak was reached in March 1934 with 630,000 workers, but as the funds were gradually used up during 1934 the numbers employed on the projects dropped away to reach less than 200,000 by 1935.[43] To encourage higher levels of employment all work-creation contractors were compelled to operate a 40-hour week, as were other public services, and overtime was banned.[44]

The work-creation employment contributed an estimated 20 per cent to

TABLE 5
WORK-CREATION FUNDS AND EMPLOYMENT IN GERMANY 1932–35

|  | Funds Expended (Mill. RM) | Employment | |
|---|---|---|---|
| 1932–33 | 1,455 | Jan 1933 | 23,665 |
|  |  | Jul 1933 | 140,126 |
| 1934 | 1,985 | Nov 1933 | 400,847 |
| 1935 | 593 | Jan 1934 | 385,275 |
|  |  | Mar 1934 | 630,163 |
|  |  | Jun 1934 | 392,433 |

*Source:* L. Grebler, 'Work Creation Policy in Germany 1932–1935', Part II, *International Labour Review*, Vol. 35 (1937), p. 513; F. Baerwald, 'How Germany Reduced Unemployment', *American Economic Review*, Vol. 24 (1934), p. 263.

the increase of 2.8 million in employment in 1933–34, although most of it was concentrated in the winter and spring of 1933–34. Like the Labour Service programme work-creation took time to get going. Initially there was some distrust of the schemes in business circles, based on a fear of their long-term fiscal effects and on the evidence that the Papen programmes in particular had no real impact on the rising unemployment levels, although they may well have prevented even higher levels during the winter of 1932–33.[45] There was also a considerable gap between the sums authorised for expenditure and the actual sums taken up. Even by December 1933 only 77 per cent of the Papen programme had been taken up, and 55 per cent of the Sofort-Programm. The Reinhardt-Programm launched in mid-1933 had allocated only 47 per cent of its funds by December but had only paid out 38 million RM, or four per cent. Almost 50 per cent of the payments for work-creation were made during 1934 so that there was something like a nine-month or a year lag between establishing a programme and turning it into actual projects employing labour.[46] Some of the major cities where unemployment was highest did not even apply for funds from the Sofort-Programm because of the poor state of municipal finances.[47] In addition, most of the projects were fairly short term, which may well explain the slowing down of the decline in unemployment during the summer of 1934 and early 1935 as the projects petered out and men looked for long-term employment again; and although they were intended to be labour-intensive, the balance swung towards material costs away from wages in 1933. The Papen-Programm funds went 44 per cent to wages, 56 per cent to materials, but the Sofort-Programm was divided 38 per cent and 62 per cent respectively.[48]

There is some case for saying that work-creation was a cheap substitute for straight employment relief and did not constitute 'real' jobs. Pay was in the form of certificates which could be exchanged at certain shops for goods and services. Contractors were obliged to provide one warm meal a day.[49] The value of the work certificates was less than the level of minimum relief, which saved the government money, and the certificates did not have to be redeemed immediately, which again helped to cut the government's short-term obligations. But the certificate system also reduced the secondary employment effects which higher wages paid in cash might have produced. It was these secondary effects of work-creation which had provided one of the main arguments for launching them in the first place. Although there is no doubt that the construction industry was stimulated significantly by the schemes, the secondary employment effects elsewhere in the economy were much more muted. The government was forced to rely more on indirect ways of stimulating employment, which not only proved more effective but were less alarming in appearance for those who disliked economic experiments.

IV

Work-creation was only one weapon in the attack on unemployment after 1933 and was effective only to the extent that there was substantial improvement in the general conditions governing business activity in Germany. Without general signs of business revival and a slow restoration of business confidence it is unlikely that contractors would have been willing to take up government funds for work projects on the same scale. Part of this revival in business confidence can be attributed to the 'stabilisation' of politics promised by the Nazis after January 1933, although it would be wrong to ignore the deep distrust with which many businessmen approached the new government and its economic policies, except, of course, for wage controls. Part can be attributed to the government propaganda on employment. After January 1933 the government openly promoted work at every opportunity: exhorting businesses to take on extra workers and subsidising their wage bills; bringing political pressure to bear to get firms to restrict hours of work and overtime; and making noisy propaganda on the importance of re-employment for Germany's political and economic future.[50] During 1933 public opinion was quite prepared to support these initiatives so that there was little political resistance to the employment campaign, in contrast to the difficulties met by both Brüning and von Papen in 1932. In 1933 political conditions were quite different. The Trade Unions were disbanded in May, and labour's bargaining position emasculated. The other political parties were wound up and all political resistance to government policies in the economy overturned by an assertive and increasingly *dirigiste* administration.

It was in the area of general interventionist economic policies that the government proved most successful, building on the initial efforts made under the last Weimar governments to tackle the major problems of the economy. General policies on trade, finance and investment helped to sustain and promote the upswing from early 1933 onwards more than did the specific policies on work-creation. The credit structure which had ground almost to a standstill in 1931 was stabilised during 1932 and over the following two years credit was generally eased through careful initiatives taken by the government and the Reichsbank in lowering interest rates, consolidating and securing local government debts and exercising greater control over the banking system. The balance of payments and external debt were also stabilised to avoid any repetition of the crisis of 1930–32. The government not only tackled the problem of public finance, but also eased the capital position of private business. Agriculture was given tax relief and a reduction in the burden of debt, while industry gained subsidies and tax relief for new investment and employment. In September 1932 a system of tax remission was introduced designed to stimulate the productive sectors of the economy through government rebates on taxes paid during 1932/33. The rebates came in the form of tax certificates which could be used to pay off taxes in future years or could be used to acquire liquid funds directly from the banking system. In practice many firms used the new liquidity to pay off existing bank loans, but this in itself helped to unblock the arteries of the credit structure. The quantity of tax certificates in circulation reached a peak of 1,135 million RM in March 1934 and declined thereafter as they were paid off by the government (at the rate of one-fifth per year for five years) out of the revenues acquired from expanding business and employment.[51]

The government combined a policy of cautious credit creation with the promise that all 'wild experiments' would be avoided. 'The economy', Hitler told a Party gathering in July 1933, 'must be treated with extraordinary cautiousness'.[52] In June 1933 the Reichsbank president, Hjalmar Schacht, was put at the head of a special commission charged with supervising and regulating everything to do with the capital markets to ensure that work-creation and other short-term credit schemes did not undermine public credit or confidence in the currency.[53] The effect of the appointment was as much psychological as anything, for the commission never met, and Schacht continued to regulate capital markets as head of the Reichsbank. Although confidence could hardly be described as bouyant during 1933–35, his presence was sufficient evidence of a public determination to promote sensible credit policies and allay fears of inflation. Direct and indirect taxation was kept at the high depression levels and it proved necessary to introduce price and wage controls in order to avoid any risk of the recovery petering out on rising costs and inflationary crisis. Profits were also controlled by limiting their distribution and encouraging re-investment and the expansion of employment. The government also extended controls over foreign trade. The object was to avoid too rapid an expansion of imports in response to the state-created credit and the overvalued mark, which might well have depressed domestic employment or brought on balance-of-payments problems. Work-creation and government investment were concentrated in sectors like construction with a low import content for the same reason. When consumer demand began to expand in 1934, sucking in further imports, even more stringent controls had to be introduced, and the government began to think seriously about programmes of import-substitution. The government's increasingly autarkic views reflected a desire both to promote the rapid expansion of domestic output and employment, and to avoid too great a reliance on the world economy after the bruising experiences of the previous decade.[54] Without this wider range of controls and regulations, higher levels of employment would have been postponed, work-creation or not.

The introduction of wage controls in particular helped to reduce wage costs in both public and private employment, continuing the wage reduction policies of the Brüning and von Papen administrations. Wage rates were fixed at the lowest level reached during the recession, and were held steady at depression rates until the late 1930s, declining in real terms between 1932 and 1938 by six per cent. Figures for the changes in real rates, money rates and real earnings are set out in Table 6. During the recovery period

TABLE 6
STATISTICS ON GERMAN WAGES 1929–38

|  | Money Hourly Wage Rates (1913/14 = 100) | Real Hourly Wage Rates | Real Weekly Earnings (1932 = 100)* | Wages as % of National Income |
|---|---|---|---|---|
| 1929 | 177 | 115 | 118 | 62 (1928) |
| 1930 | 180 | 122 | – | – |
| 1931 | 171 | 125 | – | – |
| 1932 | 144 | 120 | 100 | 64 |
| 1933 | 140 | 119 | 104 | 63 |
| 1934 | 140 | 116 | 109 | 62 |
| 1935 | 140 | 114 | 110 | 61 |
| 1936 | 140 | 112 | 112 | 59 |
| 1937 | 140 | 112 | 115 | 58 |
| 1938 | 141 | 112 | 119 | 57 |

* adjusted for party levies and other deductions

Source: G. Bry, *Wages in Germany 1871–1945* (Princeton University Press, 1960), pp. 264, 331, 362.

marginal wage costs were reduced to encourage re-employment. Subsidies were made available to employers in selected sectors, particularly agriculture, reducing wage costs still further.[55] The expansion of national income and output was faster than the expansion of earnings during the 1930s; and profits took a larger share of industrial income after 1933 than before.[56]

To ensure that the work-force did not exert its own pressure on wages the trade unions and traditional wage-bargaining procedures were removed and were replaced with a state-directed system of Labour Trustees who negotiated pay and conditions, setting minimum rates and suppressing any increase in wage levels. Strikes and industrial action were outlawed, and improvements made in the placement procedures of Labour Exchanges to avoid local labour shortages exerting pressure on wage levels. It is difficult to say with certainty how much effect wage costs had on industry's willingness to re-employ, but it was clearly of some significance since industry blamed its poor performance during the recession on excessive wage costs. But German industry did not get all the benefits that low wages might have brought. In the long term low wages should have generated higher export growth but it failed to do so because of the overvalued mark and controlled trade. Lower costs and prices should have boosted home demand as well, but high taxes and compulsory levies and contributions, and the deliberate suppression of consumer demand in favour of government capital projects and rearmament, kept the level of retail trade well below that of the late 1920s.[57]

Increased government intervention went hand-in-hand with a large increase in the amount of government demand and investment, some of it directly to stimulate employment, some of it indirectly so. The increased expenditure brought with it a significant increase in public sector employment in government services. The administration employed 648,000 in 1925 but 1,039,000 in 1939, and total government employment increased from 10.6 per cent to 12.9 per cent of the labour force. The number of local government employees rose from 544,000 in 1934 to 741,000 in 1938, an increase of 36 per cent in four years.[58] The Nazi Party also increased its employment during the 1930s, setting up its own extensive bureaucratic apparatus. By February 1934 the Party had 373,000 functionaries and another 644,000 part-timers, excluding the SA and SS which had officials of their own.[59] Between them both government and party contributed very substantially to expanded employment after 1933.

The increases in government expenditure, investment and debt are set out in Table 7. In real terms expenditure rose 50 per cent between 1929 and 1934, rising from 15.7 per cent of GNP to 22.9 per cent over the same period,[60] funded by regular budget deficits covered by short-term loans. Public investment was considerably greater in total than private investment between 1932 and 1936. Private firms either lacked the capital resources to embark on new investment programmes, or utilised existing capacity built before 1929, but which had not been fully used during the recession. Private industrial share issues on the German stock exchange amounted to a mere 19 million RM between 1932 and 1935; but public loans totalled 2,030 millions.[61] The state deliberately controlled the issue of new private funds, in order to channel investment into labour-intensive sectors like road-building, or to encourage private investment in civil engineering and house-building.

Two areas of public investment were of particular importance in relation to employment. The first was civil engineering, and particularly road-building; the second was rearmament. Investment in roads, both local and national, totalled more than 3.5 billion RM from 1933 to 1936, of which 800 millions were spent in 1933 and 1,200 millions in 1934.[62] Most of this expenditure was on the ordinary roads, and not on the *Autobahnen*, the new motorways authorised in 1933, which did not become a significant element until 1935. By the end of 1934 210,000 were employed directly on road-building sites, with a further 180,000 engaged in secondary activities (planning, haulage, supply, etc.).[63] Work was also carried out on the railways and the canal network, bridges and public buildings. The effect of all these projects on the wider economy was immediate. Cement

TABLE 7

GOVERNMENT EXPENDITURE, REVENUE, INVESTMENT AND DEBT IN GERMANY 1932/3–38/9 (BILL. RM)

| | Government Revenue | Total Public Revenue | Reich Expendit. | Total Public Expendit.• | Rearmament | Communications | Total Reich Debt | Public Investment• |
|---|---|---|---|---|---|---|---|---|
| 1928/9 | 9.0 | 14.0 | 13.0 | 23.2 | 0.7 | 2.6 | – | 6.6 |
| 1932/3 | 6.6 | 11.5 | 9.2 | 17.1 | 0.7 | 0.8 | 12.3 | 2.2 |
| 1933/4 | 6.8 | 12.1 | 8.9 | 18.4 | 1.6 | 1.3 | 13.9 | 2.5 |
| 1934/5 | 8.2 | 13.3 | 12.6 | 21.6 | 3.? | 1.8 | 15.9 | 4.6 |
| 1935/6 | 9.6 | 14.7 | 14.1 | 21.9 | 5.5 | 2.1 | 20.1 | 6.4 |
| 1936/7 | 11.4 | 16.9 | 17.3 | 23.6 | 10.3 | 2.4 | 25.8 | 8.1 |
| 1937/8 | 13.9 | 19.6 | 21.4 | 26.9 | 10.9 | 2.7 | 31.2 | 8.4 |
| 1938/9 | 17.7 | – | 32.9 | 37.1 | 17.2 | 3.8 | 41.7 | 10.3 |

• calendar years 1928–38

*Source:* C. W. Guillebaud, *The Economic Recovery of Germany 1933–1938* (London, 1939), p. 281; S. Andic, J. Veverka, 'The Growth of Government Expenditure in Germany since the Unification', *Finanzarchiv*, Vol. 23 (1964), p. 245; R. Erbe, *Die nationalsozialistische Wirtschaftspolitik 1933–1939 im Lichte der modernen Theorie* (Zürich, 1958), pp. 22–3, 54–8; S. Lurie, *Private Investment in a Controlled Economy: Germany 1933–1939* (Columbia University Press, 1947), p. 36.

production doubled between 1932 and 1934. The index of sales of the major supply industries stood at 18.0 (1928 = 100) in January 1933, but reached 59 by September and 85.7 the following June.[64]

Military expenditure was on the whole less significant than civil engineering in the early stages of the recovery. Only part of the military budget went on facilities and armaments, or investment in the arms industry, the rest on wages and running costs. Total military expenditure, including the secret 'Mefo' rearmament bills, was 4.8 billion RM from 1933 to 1935, the bulk of it falling in 1934−35. Of this total only about 600 million RM was spent in 1933 and 1934 on military investment, and 1.9 billion in 1935.[65] Rearmament thus began to have a serious effect on employment levels at the point when the civil-engineering and work-creation programmes began to peter out in late 1934. This pattern can be illustrated by looking at the armaments industry itself. Employment in the aircraft industry as a whole was 5,000 in April 1933, 12,000 by October, and then rose sharply to 45,000 by October 1934, and reached 135,000 by April 1936, when it was larger than the German car industry.[66] As orders for aircraft expanded, firms began to pump their own funds into the industry and to plough back profits, so that by 1936 public investment in the aircraft industry was matched by high levels of private investment too. In 1936 the assets of the industry totalled more than one billion marks, with almost half from private sources.[67] It was the same story at Krupp, the major supplier of guns, army equipment and armour plate. Employment in October 1932 in the Essen works was 26,000; by October 1933 this had risen only to 34,000; but by October 1934 the figure was 51,000, and a year later 76,000.[68]

Of course it is not possible to tell how much of this expanded employment was re-employment. Because the bulk of the work-force in the armaments sectors was skilled it may well be that workers were attracted from jobs in other sectors of the economy, helping to create the bottlenecks in certain kinds of skilled labour already evident by 1936. There was no shortage of unskilled or semi-skilled labour, but this was less attractive to the arms manufacturers. The most labour-intensive part of rearmament consisted of the rebuilding of military facilities, barracks, airfields, fortifications, and these became a major employer of labour from 1935 onwards when the work-creation programmes were over (although some of these programmes themselves were specifically for military projects). Rearmament as a whole attracted significant quantities of labour only after the upswing was under way, and then contributed substantially to sustaining it. It is important to remember that not all rearmament expenditure by any means went directly into industry and productive employment. Military expenditure is not the same thing as expenditure on armaments. In 1936 army expenditure on weapons was only 7.6 per cent of the total army budget. In terms of employment it was the large increase in the physical size of the armed forces in 1935 that made the greatest difference. The large capital projects − the Four-Year Plan industries, the synthetics programme, the Westwall − all came later in the 1930s.[69]

Although government expenditure and investment assumed great importance for the economy from 1933 onwards, it was the government's intention to stimulate private activity as well through selective policies directed at particular industries. According to Reinhardt, Hitler wanted to 'overcome the acknowledged lack of purchasing power and incentive and in this way to increase the demand for labour and reduce unemployment'.[70] Kurt Schmitt, Minister of Economics from July 1933 to September 1934, and Schacht who succeeded him, both hoped that the public efforts to stimulate the recovery would encourage what Schmitt called the 'natural upswing and natural upwards development' in the economy. Schmitt told an audience of economic experts in September 1933: 'The government however is now clear about this, that artificial job creation cannot be kept going in the long run, but that it must be solved through a genuine private economic revival of the whole economy, and that only then is a permanent elimination or reduction of the economic crisis produced'.[71] To stimulate these effects the government chose to target particular sectors: house construction, agriculture and the motor industry. These areas were chosen because of their strategic significance for the economy, and their considerable re-employment potential. The government had no intention of stimulating all industries equally and indiscriminately, and while its policies helped certain key industries, they also had the effect of restricting others, notably the major consumer industries.

House construction was helped by a system of subsidies to house-owners initiated by von Papen in September 1932 and expanded during 1933. The scheme paid out some 667 million RM in loans and 332 millions in direct subsidies on the basis that the owners provide 50 per cent of the cost of house conversion or renovation and 80 per cent of the cost of smaller house repairs out of their own pockets. It was estimated that an additional 2.9 billion RM was spent by the owners themselves. House-building and repair doubled between 1932 and 1934, increasing twice as quickly as other forms of construction.[72] Details on the building industry are set out in Table 8. Employment in construction rose from an exceptional trough in 1932, rising faster than all other sectors except agriculture. There were 914,425 building workers and labourers registered unemployed in January 1933, but only 430,787 by October. By June 1934 almost 75 per cent of building workers unemployed in March 1933 were back at work.[73]

The motor industry was helped by a series of tax concessions on private and business purchases which dragged the industry out of the recession faster than any other manufacturing sector. Production of all vehicles was cut by two-thirds between 1929 and 1932, but by 1935 exceeded peak output in 1929. Moreover, there was a switch from motor-cycle sales to car sales as cars became cheaper during the recession, so that the previous peak of car production in 1928 was exceeded by 47 per cent in 1934 and over 100 per cent in 1935 (see Table 8). The boost in vehicle sales, many of which went to business purchasers and farmers, expanded employment rapidly, reaching the 1928 peak in 1934 and substantially exceeding it in 1935. The spin-off effects of a rapid increase in motorisation were also very great, since approximately the same numbers were employed in the components

## TABLE 8
### STATISTICS ON HOUSE CONSTRUCTION AND THE MOTOR INDUSTRY 1928–38

| | Number of Dwellings | | Housing Invest. (Bill. RM) | Motor-vehicle Output | Motor Industry Employment |
|---|---|---|---|---|---|
| | New | Renovated | | | |
| 1928 | 306,825 | 23,617 | 2.82 | 295,929 | 83,751 |
| 1929 | 315,703 | 23,099 | 2.87 | 335,553 | 76,441 |
| 1930 | 307,933 | 22,327 | 2.44 | 189,599 | 54,153 |
| 1931 | 231,342 | 20,359 | 1.19 | 129,424 | 46,134 |
| 1932 | 131,160 | 27,961 | 0.76 | 100,639 | 34,392 |
| 1933 | 132,870 | 69,243 | 0.87 | 158,894 | 51,036 |
| 1934 | 190,257 | 129,182 | 1.35 | 274,684 | 80,8'9 |
| 1935 | 213,227 | 50,593 | 1.56 | 366,072 | 100,9?7 |
| 1936 | 282,466 | 49,904 | – | 449,224 | 110,14? |
| 1937 | 309,345 | 31,447 | – | 491,2?4 | 12?,??2 |
| 1938 | 276,276 | 29,250 | – | 530,73?* | 140,746 |

* Includes Austria

Source: R. J. Overy, 'Cars, Roads and Economic Recovery in Germany 1932–1938', *Economic History Review*, 2nd Series, Vol. 28 (1975). p. 483; *Wirtschaft und Statistik*, Vol. 17 (1937), pp. 494–8.

industries as in the industry itself.[74] If there is a single industrial sector that helped to drag the German industrial economy out of recession in 1933–34, the motor industry has perhaps the best claim. Its rapid growth owed something to the government policies for agriculture too, which stimulated rural demand by cutting interest rates and debt charges, lowering taxes for farmers and raising prices, and granting concessions for new investment. Rural motorisation increased more rapidly than in cities, reflecting the general improvement in rural demand for industrial goods.

There was also selective help for particular regions as well as for individual industries. This help took the form of locating work-creation projects and other major public works in the more economically backward, primarily agrarian regions. From 1936 onwards a central board was set up to authorise the placing of government contracts in depressed areas. The government also encouraged the re-location of industry, partly to move it away from the danger of bombing, into central and southern Germany. The increase in the labour force in these areas was almost double the national average between 1933 and 1938.[75] The result of these initiatives was that unemployment declined in all major regions at a more or less equal pace between 1933 and 1937, falling furthest in central Germany and East Prussia and the least in Silesia and Saxony.[76] The pattern of regional employment and unemployment is set out in Table 9.

TABLE 9

EMPLOYMENT AND UNEMPLOYMENT IN THE GERMAN REGIONS 1933–37 ('000s)

| Region | Unemployment (end June) | | | | | Employment (end June) | | | | |
|---|---|---|---|---|---|---|---|---|---|---|
| | 1933 | 1934 | 1935 | 1936 | 1937 | 1933 | 1934 | 1935 | 1936 | 1937 |
| East Prussia | 76 | 14 | 7 | 4 | 4 | 453 | 535 | 543 | 562 | 576 |
| Silesia | 366 | 195 | 171 | 138 | 58 | 962 | 1122 | 1134 | 1156 | 1233 |
| Brandenburg | 752 | 406 | 249 | 175 | 96 | 1805 | 2104 | 2265 | 2371 | 2557 |
| Pommern | 86 | 24 | 23 | 12 | 7 | 418 | 509 | 484 | 510 | 529 |
| Nordmark | 338 | 192 | 127 | 95 | 53 | 867 | 1003 | 1102 | 1174 | 1242 |
| Lower Saxony | 272 | 112 | 67 | 29 | 8 | 391 | 1086 | 1134 | 1238 | 1316 |
| Westphalia | 390 | 196 | 157 | 114 | 46 | 1093 | 1298 | 1365 | 1462 | 1584 |
| Rhineland | 667 | 393 | 373 | 276 | 151 | 1499 | 1754 | 1837 | 2152 | 2335 |
| Hessen | 280 | 143 | 125 | 87 | 45 | 693 | 849 | 865 | 932 | 1006 |
| Central Ger | 337 | 170 | 95 | 54 | 21 | 1179 | 1412 | 1534 | 1633 | 1759 |
| Saxony | 595 | 321 | 265 | 199 | 97 | 1314 | 1551 | 1592 | 1676 | 1811 |
| Bavaria | 394 | 199 | 140 | 94 | 37 | 1395 | 1640 | 1724 | 1832 | 1950 |
| S W Germany | 254 | 116 | 78 | 48 | 26 | 1104 | 1300 | 1349 | 1425 | 1520 |

*Source: Wirtschaft und Statistik*, Vol. 17 (1937), p. 47.

It is clear from this discussion that no one policy or single sector can explain the recovery of employment during the period in question. Government policies have to be considered as a whole, as a 'package' of employment-creating devices designed to sustain the autonomous upswing of the business cycle. It is possible, however, to demonstrate that the exceptional speed with which employment expanded owed something not just to the general help given to the business revival through cuts in the marginal cost of capital and labour, but to the selective policies aimed at specific sectors, civil engineering, motorisation, agriculture and house construction. Table 10 shows the decline in unemployment in individual sectors between 1933 and 1934. The figures reflect government priorities for heavy industry, agriculture and building. Help for the motor industry and for furnishings, through the marriage loan, are reflected in the statistics for metallurgy, textiles and woodworking. Re-employment was slower among the unskilled (despite the work-creation projects) and among white-collar and transport workers. But there were no sectors where there was not significant re-employment during the first eighteen months of the recovery.

TABLE 10
UNEMPLOYMENT IN THE GERMAN ECONOMY 1933–34

| Sector | March 31 1933 | Unemployed on<br>March 31 1934 | June 30 1934 | June 1934 as % of 1933 |
|---|---|---|---|---|
| Agriculture | 238,305 | 66,144 | 53,333 | 22.4 |
| Mining | 168,224 | 106,168 | 100,246 | 59.6 |
| Stone | 177,556 | 67,111 | 57,081 | 32.1 |
| Metallurgy | 886,086 | 417,287 | 342,548 | 38.6 |
| Chemicals | 23,106 | 14,268 | 12,460 | 54.0 |
| Textiles | 190,167 | 85,184 | 70,814 | 37.2 |
| Clothing | 206,915 | 100,661 | 97,018 | 46.8 |
| Paper | 49,867 | 27,446 | 24,260 | 50.0 |
| Leather | 50,394 | 24,382 | 21,497 | 42.6 |
| Woodworking | 276,962 | 121,151 | 102,590 | 37.0 |
| Building | 493,260 | 107,172 | 139,421 | 28.2 |
| Transport | 339,554 | 210,670 | 184,855 | 54.4 |
| Commerce | 427,455 | 293,178 | 254,316 | 59.5 |
| Unskilled Labourers | 1,220,138 | 669,735 | 624,651 | 51.2 |

Source: F. Baerwald, op. cit., p. 621.

V

The rapid reduction of unemployment and the even more rapid expansion of employment had important consequences after 1933. Because of wage controls and substitute employment there remained large areas of poverty in Germany during the 1930s. Living standards in general were deliberately suppressed through wage controls and high taxes to prevent the threat of inflation or high demand for imports, but also to encourage re-employment with cheap labour. For those working on the work-creation schemes, road-building, Labour Service, *Landhilfe*, etc., there was either no cash pay at all, or nominal payment set in many cases below the level of unemployment relief. This left 1.5 to 2 million workers, mainly men, on incomes no better than they were getting when unemployed, and a great many more on the low wage rates of the recession period. The effect of this long-term experience of low income produced growing dissatisfaction and evidence of labour unrest during 1934 and 1935 and was only prevented from developing into a serious problem by increases in hours and earnings in the rearmament boom, and more ruthless policing of the work-force.[77] Low living standards was the consequence of rapid re-employment in what was still a relatively weak economy, in which consumption was deliberately restrained to release resources for war preparation and large capital projects.

The 'employment' priority of the government after 1933 also had a damaging effect on the productive performance of the economy. Much of the employment was either in labour-intensive sectors or was diverted from manufacturing industry, where it might have been used more productively, into administration, services or the military. Productivity growth was therefore poor during the 1930s and the multiplier effect of the new employment more muted than it might have been.[78] Firms were not encouraged to rationalise more because capital was scarce and labour cheap; and they operated for much of the time in what was effectively a closed economy or with guaranteed government contracts so that they were not faced with the usual market pressures to operate at optimum efficiency. This in turn had an unintended long-term effect on Germany's rearmament programme. Under the employment schemes too many workers were pushed into unskilled or semi-skilled sectors and labour mobility, particularly from countryside to town, was restricted. The pool of new apprentices fell during the 1930s, creating greater pressure on skilled labour reserves when rearmament was stepped up from 1935, and requiring extensive re-training schemes later in the decade. The work-force became locked into employment patterns which then had to be broken down again with the switch to large-scale war preparations, with great difficulty. In the face of low wages and high taxes many German workers preferred not to acquire new skills but to increase household income by expanding the number of wage-earners per household. Where upward labour mobility did occur it was into the state and party bureaucracies, where it was lost to rearmament until Speer's efforts to re-deploy white-collar workers back into industry later in the war. Industry remained slow to rationalise or redirect labour right up to 1939/40, so that the problem of skilled labour shortages carried over into the war when renewed efforts were made to transfer labour rapidly into war industries.[79]

What the government did demonstrate was the political will to reduce unemployment rapidly through state interventionist policies, and its ability to profit from the changed political circumstances that it introduced after 1933. These policies were not the 'Keynesian' recipe for stimulating private consumption and trade, but amounted to setting up a closed economy with strict controls over the capital market, prices, wages, imports and exports. High levels of government expenditure and investment and selective industrial policies soaked up much of the unemployed, although at the price of low productivity growth, declining competitiveness and pressures on the balance of payments; at the price, too, of low living standards, a poor bargaining position for labour, and the militarisation of young workers through compulsory labour services. The government's immediate priority was not, however, balanced economic growth for high living standards, but rapid economic growth to serve military ends. Overcoming unemployment was seen as an essential political precondition, rather than an economic necessity, for embarking on large-scale re-militarisation and an active foreign policy. The irony was that less rigorous controls over consumption and less frantic efforts to achieve re-employment quickly after 1933 might well have produced a larger manufacturing base and a workforce more able to cope with the demands of industrialised warfare after 1939.

*King's College, London*

NOTES

The author is grateful to Professor H. James for his helpful comments on an earlier draft of this article.

1. *Dokumente der deutschen Politik* (Berlin, 1935), Vol. 1, p. 209, Führerrede vor dem Generalrat der Wirtschaft, 20 Jan. 1933.
2. Christie Papers, Churchill College, Cambridge, 180/1/1, Christie to Yencken, 21 Sept. 1930 on interviews with leading Nazis; 180/1/4, Notes of a talk with Göring, '1932'.
3. Graf Schwerin von Krosigk, 'Aufgaben der Finanzpolitik', *Der deutsche Volkswirt*, Vol. 8 (1934), pp. 586–7; F. Reinhardt, *Die Arbeitsschlacht der Regierung* (Berlin, 1933), pp. 7–11.
4. K. H. Minuth (ed.), *Akten der Reichskanzler: Regierung Hitler 1933–1938* (Boppard a. R, 1983), Vol. 1, p. 632, doc. 180, Reichsstatthalterkonferenz, 6 Juli 1933.
5. K. I. Wiggs, *Unemployment in Germany since the War* (London, 1935), pp. 183–4.
6. F. Baerwald, 'How Germany Reduced Unemployment', *American Economic Review*, Vol. 24 (1934), pp. 618–19. In 1910 48 per cent of the population was aged 20–60. In 1925 the figure was 54 per cent.
7. M. Thibert, 'The Economic Depression and the Employment of Women', Part I, *International Labour Review*, Vol. 27 (1933), pp. 449–54.
8. D. Petzina and W. Abelshauser, 'Zum Problem der relativen Stagnation der deutschen Wirtschaft in den zwanziger Jahren' in H. Mommsen, D. Petzina and B. Weisbrod (eds.), *Industrielles System und politische Entwicklung in der Weimarer Republik* (Düsseldorf,

1974), pp. 60–74. See too D. Petzina, 'The Extent and Causes of Unemployment in the Weimar Republic' in P. Stachura (ed.), *Unemployment and the Great Depression in Weimar Germany* (London, 1986), especially pp. 33–4, 40–42. In this article Petzina modifies his earlier arguments on stagnation by looking at the structural problems and market rigidities which gave rise to it. He places particular emphasis on the low investment ratio.

9. Royal Institute of International Affairs, *Unemployment: An International Problem* (Oxford, 1935), pp. 126, 259–64; Wiggs, op. cit., pp. 186–7; G. Bry, *Wages in Germany 1871–1945* (Princeton, NJ, 1960), pp. 22, 362. For a different view on wage rates see J. von Kruedener, 'Die Überforderung der Weimarer Republik als Sozialstaat', *Geschichte und Gesellschaft*, Vol. 11 (1985), pp. 358–76, who argues that wages and welfare contributions taken together were too high for the economy in the late 1920s and early 1930s, in an environment of sluggish growth and a declining world economy.

10. Wiggs, op. cit., p. 35.

11. Thibert, op. cit., pp. 454, 458; J. Grünfeld, 'Rationalisation and the Employment and Wages of Women in Germany', *International Labour Review*, Vol. 29 (1934), pp. 605–32.

12. 'Die öffentliche Fürsorge im Deutschen Reich', *Wirtschaft und Statistik*, Vol. 16 (1936), pp. 82–6. On the government in the crisis see K. Borchardt, 'Zwangslagen und Handelsspielräume in der grossen Wirtschaftskrise der frühen dreissiger Jahre', *Jahrbuch der Bayerischen Akademie der Wissenschaften* (Sonderdruck, 1979), pp. 1–24; W. Jochmann, 'Brünings Deflationspolitik und der Untergang der Weimarer Republik' in D. Stegmann, B.-J. Wendt, P.-C. Witt (eds.), *Industrielle Gesellschaft und politische System* (Bonn, 1978), pp. 97–112.

13. F.-W. Henning, 'Die zeitliche Einordnung der Überwindung der Weltwirtschaftskrise in Deutschland' in H. Winkel (ed.) *Währungs- und Finanzpolitik der Zwischenkriegszeit* (Berlin, 1973), pp. 135–73.

14. H. James, *The Reichsbank and Public Finance in Germany 1924–1933* (Frankfurt am Main, 1985), pp. 326–31.

15. RIIA, op. cit., p. 69.

16. *Statistisches Jahrbuch für das Deutsche Reich, 1939/40* (Berlin, 1940), p. 189.

17. *Wirtschaft und Statistik*, Vol. 16 (1936), pp. 82–7; E. B. Mittelman, 'The German Use of Unemployment Insurance Funds for Work Purposes', *Journal of Political Economy*, Vol. 46 (1938), pp. 529–30.

18. F. Petrick, 'Eine Untersuchung zur Beseitigung der Arbeitslosigkeit unter der deutschen Jugend in den Jahren 1933 bis 1935', *Jahrbuch für Wirtschaftsgeschichte*, 1967, Part I, p. 290. Unemployment among under 25's fell by 61.5 per cent between June 1933 and June 1934 against 46.7 per cent for the population as a whole.

19. By 1938 consumer production was only seven per cent above the level of 1928 (offset by a seven per cent increase in population over the same period), but capital goods were 135 per cent above. See the discussion in O. Nathan, M. Fried, *The Nazi Economic System* (London, 1944), pp. 351–2.

20. H. Köhler, *Arbeitsdienst in Deutschland* (Berlin, 1967), pp. 243–67.

21. Christie Papers, 180/1/1, interviews with leading Nazis, 21 Sept. 1930.

22. *Dokumente der deutschen Politik* (Berlin, 1936), Vol. 2, doc. 77, Rede des Staatssekretär Hierl, 20 June 1934: Vol. 3, p. 249, Reichsarbeitsdienstgesetz, 26 June 1935; W. Benz, 'Vom freiwilligen Arbeitsdienst zur Arbeitsdienstpflicht', *Vierteljahresheft für Zeitgeschichte*, Vol. 16 (1968), pp. 317–46.

23. F. Wunderlich, *Farm Labor in Germany 1810–1945* (Princeton, NJ, 1961), pp. 310–12.

24. Ibid., pp. 313–14.

25. Calculated from 'Die deutsche Arbeitsdienst', *Wirtschaft und Statistik*, Vol. 16 (1936), p. 136. Land reclamation claimed 53 per cent of all hours worked on Labour Service in 1935.

26. Wunderlich, op. cit., pp. 321–2.

27. *Wirtschaft und Statistik*, loc. cit., p. 137; T. Mason, 'Women in Germany, 1925–1940: Family, Welfare and Work', *History Workshop*, Nos. 1, 2 (1976).

28. *Dokumente der deutschen Politik*, Vol. 2, p. 172, Rede des Staatssekretärs im RFM Reinhardt, 20 Jan. 1934.

29. Ibid., Vol. 1, pp. 198–200, Gesetz zur Verminderung der Arbeitslosigkeit vom 1 June 1933.
30. Ibid., p. 199; Vol. 2, Reinhardt speech, p. 172; Petrick, op. cit., p. 291; *Akten der Reichskanzler* (see note 4), Vol. II, pp. 1188–9, doc. 318, Begründung zum Entwurf eines Gesetzes zur Änderung des Gesetzes über Förderung der Eheschliessungen, 20 March 1934. The average value of the loans declined from 730 RM in August 1933 to 560 RM in February 1934.
31. J. Stephenson, *Women in Nazi Society* (London, 1975), pp. 79–87.
32. Thibert, op. cit., p. 451.
33. 'Die Frauenarbeit in der Industrie 1933 bis 1936', *Wirtschaft und Statistik*, Vol. 16 (1936), pp. 779–80; *Statistisches Jahrbuch, 1938* (Berlin, 1939), p. 379.
34. Ibid., 1937, p. 23; D. Petzina, 'Die Mobilisierung deutsche Arbeitskräfte vor und während des Zweiten Weltkrieges', *Vierteljahreshefte für Zeitgeschichte*, Vol. 18 (1970), pp. 455–6.
35. Wunderlich, op. cit., pp. 329–31.
36. Ibid., p. 312.
37. Petrick, op. cit., p. 290.
38. H. Vollweiler, 'The Mobilisation of Labour Reserves in Germany', Part I, *International Labour Review*, Vol. 38 (1938), pp. 448–9.
39. W. Röpke, 'Trends in German Business Cycle Policy', *Economic Journal*, Vol. 43 (1933); O. Donner, 'Voraussetzungen und Konsequenzen öffentlicher Arbeitsbeschaffung', *Der deutsche Volkswirt*, Vol. 7 (1932/3), pp. 1221–2.
40. Mittelman, op. cit., p. 530; O. Weigert, 'The Development of Unemployment Relief in Germany', Part I, *International Labour Review*, Vol. 28 (1933), pp. 169–72.
41. Bundesarchiv, Koblenz, BA R2/18701, Reichsarbeitsministerium, 'Beitrag zur Denkschrift über die Arbeitsbeschaffungsmassnahmen', pp. 1–14; L. Grebler, 'Work-Creation Policy in Germany 1932–1935', Part I, *International Labour Review*, Vol. 35 (1937), pp. 331–8; *Der deutsche Volkswirt*, Vol. 8 (1933/4), pp. 529–31; K. E. Poole, *German Financial Policies, 1932–1939* (Cambridge, MA, 1939), pp. 94–100; M. Schneider, 'The Development of State Work Creation Policy in Germany 1930–1933' in Stachura, op. cit., pp. 173–80.
42. *Der deutsche Volkswirt*, Vol. 8 (1933/4), pp. 529–31. The other financial institutions involved were the Deutsche Siedlungsbank, Rentenbankkreditanstalt, and the Bau- und Bodenbank.
43. Grebler, op. cit., Part II, pp. 513–14; 'Die Entwicklung des Arbeitsmarktes', *Der deutsche Volkswirt*, Vol. 8 (1933/4), p. 1280.
44. 'The Reduction of the Working Week in Germany', *International Labour Review*, Vol. 29 (1933), pp. 774–9.
45. *Der deutsche Volkswirt*, Vol. 7 (1932/3), pp. 1019–20. In his speech at the Reichsbank on 17 April Schacht warned against over-optimistic expectations from work-creation.
46. Ibid., Vol. 8 (1933/4), p. 530; Grebler, op. cit., Part II, pp. 505–13. For a general discussion of the effects of work-creation see C. Bresciani Turroni, 'The "Multiplier" in Practice: Some Results of Recent German Experience', *Review of Economic Statistics*, Vol. 20 (1938), pp. 76–87.
47. M. Wolffsohn, *Industrie und Handwerk im Konflikt mit staatlicher Wirtschaftspolitik?* (Berlin, 1977), p. 113. On the state of communal finances see Poole, op. cit., pp. 13–16.
48. Wolffsohn, op. cit., p. 103.
49. *Der deutsche Volkswirt*, Vol. 7 (1932/3), p. 1020.
50. Wolffsohn, op. cit., pp. 108–9; L. Zumpe, *Wirtschaft und Staat in Deutschland 1933 bis 1945* (Berlin, 1980), pp. 64–5.
51. *Der deutsche Volkswirt*, Vol. 7 (1932/3), p. 1019.
52. *Akten der Reichskanzlei*, Vol. 1, p. 632, doc. 180, Reichsstatthalterkonferenz vom 6 Juli 1933.
53. H. Schacht, *76 Jahre meines Lebens* (Bad Wörishofen, 1953), pp. 399–400.
54. K. Mandelbaum, 'An Experiment in Full Employment: Controls in the German Economy 1933–38' in Oxford University Institute of Statistics, *The Economics of Full Employment* (Oxford, 1944), pp. 183–93.
55. Bry, op. cit., pp. 235, 262–4; C. W. Guillebaud, *The Economic Recovery of Germany 1933–1938* (London, 1939), pp. 187–92.

56. G. Stolper, *The German Economy 1870 to the Present* (London, 1967), pp. 150–51; Guillebaud, op. cit., pp. 183–5.
57. *Statistisches Jahrbuch 1938*, p. 632.
58. J. P. Cullity, 'The Growth of Governmental Employment in Germany 1882–1950', *Zeitschrift für die gesamte Staatswissenschaft*, Vol. 123 (1967), pp. 202–4; figures on local government employment are calculated from *Statistisches Jahrbuch 1935*, p. 453 and 1940, pp. 528–9.
59. D. Orlow, *The History of the Nazi Party 1933–1945* (Newton Abbot, 1973), pp. 72–3. According to Bresciani Turroni, op. cit., p. 81, new administrative organisations set up after 1933 created 400,000 new jobs by 1937.
60. S. Andic and J. Veverka, 'The Growth of Government Expenditure in Germany', *Finanzarchiv*, Vol. 25 (1964), p. 245.
61. Poole, op. cit., p. 166; see too R. Erbe, *Die nationalsozialistische Wirtschaftspolitik im Lichte der modernen Theorie* (Zürich, 1958), pp. 67, 108; S. Lurie, *Private Investment in a Controlled Economy: Germany 1933–1939* (New York, 1947), pp. 21–4.
62. R. J. Overy, 'Cars, Roads and Economic Recovery in Germany 1932–38', *Economic History Review*, 2nd Series, Vol. 28 (1975), p. 483.
63. R. J. Overy, 'Transportation and Rearmament in the Third Reich', *Historical Journal*, Vol. 16 (1973), p. 399.
64. Overy, 'Cars', p. 474.
65. B. H. Klein, *Germany's Economic Preparations for War* (Harvard University Press, 1959), p. 14; Overy, 'Cars', pp. 476–7; L. Graf Schwerin von Krosigk, *Staatsbankrott* (Göttingen, 1974), pp. 230–31.
66. E. Homze, *Arming the Luftwaffe* (Lincoln, NE, 1976), p. 184.
67. National Archives, Washington, DC, T 177, Roll 32, frames 3720914–23, Statistisches Reichsamt, *Die Flugzeugindustrie 1933–1936*, Feb. 1938.
68. Foreign Office Library, London, Krupp Archives, Betriebsberichte, 1933/4, 1934/5; Jahresberichte und Bilanzen, 1934/5–1940/1 (I am grateful to Dr J. Fox for permission to use these papers).
69. On the army budget see BA R2/5156/C Haushalt des Reichskriegsministeriums für das Rechnungsjahr 1937 (Heer). An example of this problem can be found in H. James, *The German Slump: Politics and Economics 1924–1936* (Oxford, 1986), p. 383, where he talks of 'armaments expenditure' where he means 'military expenditure', the largest single item of which was the wage bill.
70. *Dokumente der deutschen Politik*, Vol. 1, p. 201.
71. Ibid., p. 205, Rede des Reichswirtschaftsminister Schmitt, 13 July 1933; *Akten der Reichskanzler*, Vol. 2, p. 754, doc. 213, Erste Sitzung des Generalrats der Wirtschaft, 2 Sept. 1933. On the private 'boom' in consumer spending produced by these policies in 1933–34 see James, *German Slump*, pp. 414–15.
72. *Wirtschaft und Statistik*, Vol. 16 (1936), pp. 788–9; Grebler, op. cit., Part I, p. 336; Poole, op. cit., pp. 188–97.
73. BA R2/18701, Deutsche Bau- und Bodenbank AG, 'Die Entwicklung der deutschen Bauwirtschaft und die Arbeitsbeschaffung im Jahre 1933'.
74. Overy, 'Cars', p. 478.
75. Mandelbaum, op. cit., p. 197.
76. 'Die deutsche Wirtschaftsgebiete im Wiederaufbau der Volkswirtschaft', *Wirtschaft und Statistik*, Vol. 17 (1937), pp. 46–51.
77. T. Mason, *Sozialpolitik im Dritten Reich* (Opladen, 1977), pp. 147–61; I. Kershaw, *Popular Opinion and Political Dissent in the Third Reich* (Oxford, 1983), pp. 82–95, 120–32.
78. Bresciani Turroni, op. cit., pp. 83–8; Erbe, op. cit., pp. 162–3.
79. Guillebaud, op. cit., p. 190 on the number of earners per household, which increased from an average of 1.6 in 1933 to 1.8 in 1936. On labour problems see Mason, *Sozialpolitik*, pp. 216–28, 271–82; Petzina, 'Mobilisierung', pp. 443–55. On the effects on rearmament see BA R7/2229, Economics Ministry memorandum by General von Hanneken, 'Richtlinien für die Gestaltung der Fertigung in der Eisen- und Metallverarbeitenden Industrie'. 'The conquest of unemployment', von Hanneken claimed, 'was directly opposed to rationalisation'.

# VICKERS' BALKAN CONSCIENCE: ASPECTS OF ANGLO-ROMANIAN ARMAMENTS 1918–39

By R. P. T. DAVENPORT-HINES*

Buna tara, rea tocmeala,
Hat'o'n cour de randoneala.
(A good country, badly run,
Don't get entangled, it's no fun.)

(Romanian proverb)

The purposes of this article are threefold. The first is simply to describe the business conditions, baffling politics and social complexity that confronted British manufacturers trying to win contracts and sell products in Romania between the two world wars. The second aim is to illuminate the attempts immediately after 1918 to develop the markets for heavy British industry in Eastern Europe. These efforts, which had largely petered out by 1924, originated from the 'trade warriors' movement of 1915–19 in which leading protectionist manufacturers, such as Hugo Hirst of General Electric, Sir Vincent Caillard of Vickers, Sir Edward Manville of Birmingham Small Arms, Dudley Docker of Metropolitan Carriage & Wagon Co. or Sir James Kemnal of Babcock & Wilcox, urged that British industry should consolidate itself to smash German interests in the anticipated post-war battle for the world's export markets.[1] Eastern Europe, with oil-rich Romania foremost, was one of the battlefields that British industrialists chose for the confrontation.[2] Hard on the Armistice, in January 1919, the Federation of British Industries, whose president was Caillard and which since 1916 had been pre-eminent in organising manufacturers for the post-war export clash with Germany, sent a special mission to the Paris Peace Conference to cultivate the Romanian delegates and discuss large-scale Anglo-Romanian development projects. It was the FBI's misfortune that one of the key members of their mission, Captain Harold Duncan, superficially impeccable as an old Etonian and former confidential secretary at the Imperial Ottoman Bank, was in reality a ruffian who in the 1920s pursued a blackmailing lawsuit against Sir Allan Smith of the Engineering Employers Federation and two Cabinet ministers, Sir Arthur Steel-Maitland and Sir Philip Cunliffe-Lister.[3] Partly because of Duncan's eccentricities, and despite a visit to Bucharest by Major Kennard of the FBI in July 1919, their Romanian overtures were nugatory; but they demonstrated British heavy industry's earnest hopes in the Balkans in the post-war reconstruction period. This essay concentrates on Vickers' experience in Romania, and its third and final aim is to show that their involvement with the Copşa-Miča & Cugir arsenal (properly called Uzinele Metalurgice din Copşa-Miča şi Cugir Societate Anonimă, and hereafter CMC) had transcending importance for their overseas armaments policy in the inter-war period.

In the quarter-century before 1914 Vickers and other armaments companies, both British and foreign, were not only major exporters of naval and military weaponry of all classes, but also exported armaments expertise. In Italy, Spain, Japan, Turkey and Russia, Vickers built arsenals in collaboration with foreign governments,[4] and when war erupted in 1914 they were examining similar proposals for Rio de Janeiro and Shanghai. With joint participation in finance and management, Vickers' national arsenal schemes potentially rendered major benefits to the developing powers by way of technical education, and consolation to Vickers by way of profit. With the exception of Spain, however, none of these projects had existed long enough before the outbreak of world war for the participants to receive their anticipated rewards; the developing powers were neither competent nor self-sufficient in armaments manufacture, nor had Vickers received solid returns on their investments. The convulsion of war transformed their array of arsenals: their links with those in Russia and Turkey were severed by revolution and hostilities, while in Japan and Italy, nationalist and mountingly hostile governments froze Vickers out in the 1920s. Vickers' prolonged cash crisis in the 1920s, and the failure of their London management to control Japan Steel or Vickers–Terni, together with the increasing self-reliance of their foreign partners, contributed to this overseas retreat; but so, too, did their defeats in Eastern Europe, which are scarcely mentioned by their official historian.[5]

In October 1918, during the month Churchill watched 'a drizzle of empires falling through the air', Sir Basil Zaharoff of Vickers adumbrated the company's new policy on foreign arsenals. The forthcoming peace conference, he predicted,

> will create some half a dozen new autonomous and independent States ... the first thing that these new States will do will be to arm ... both for land and sea. We should be prepared, in conjunction with Banks and financiers, to send representatives to their countries the moment they are free, and to offer them their first public loan, out of which we will of course be paid for the armament they will order from us. Although the Big Powers may insist upon these States not arming, nothing can prevent their arming, as they will claim it is for policing their own nation.[6]

Vickers turned to the new states, formed on the edge of the dead Habsburg, Hohenzollern and Romanov empires, with arsenal projects. If they were smaller than the Imperial Powers armed by Vickers before 1914, they had a similar need to strengthen their national identity and expertise in high-technology armaments manufacture. While the French firm of Schneider-Creusot bought Czechoslovakia's Skoda works in 1919, Vickers sought similar ventures in Poland, Estonia, Yugoslavia and Romania. Their participation in the Starachowice mining and metallurgical company (1920), in the Reval dockyards and workshops (1921) and in the Sartid Company (1922) are all significant and interesting stories: but Vickers' connection with the Reşiţa and Copşa-Miča companies was of prime importance. Whereas the Polish venture was the almost exclusive responsibility of Count Leon Ostrorog and his son Stanislaus (Zaharoff's son-in-law), and Reval was largely handled by an official called Emile Cohn, during the 1920s and early 1930s almost every Vickers director of importance journeyed to Romania to cope with the crises in their investment there. Douglas Vickers, Sir Noel Birch, Sir George Buckham, Sir Charles Craven, Sir Trevor Dawson, Sir James Reid Young and others went at different times to Bucharest. The Romanian experience was the most influential on Vickers' foreign policy in 1918–36: its frustrations represented for them the illimitable trouble that arose from foreign arsenals and encouraged them to reduce or liquidate in the early 1930s the overseas investments made in the Edwardian period.

An early impression of Romanian business potential was sent in 1919 by Admiral Sir Charles Ottley of Armstrong Whitworth to the Director of Naval Intelligence:

> I have been here for the past 3 weeks on Armstrongs business ... I regard it as most important that [the Romanian] Navy should be trained and moulded *not* by France, or by Italy or by the U.S.A. but by England. The future wealth and prosperity of Roumania is assured, she is the one Balkan state which gives signs of future stability, and her geographical position and long frontage upon the Danube are assets of real value. Galatz and Braila must tend more and more to be the great entrepots of the fluvial transportation system – though once France or another power gets indirect control of these ... then goodbye to British commercial success in this area ... the League of Nations *may* wish to preclude any sort of naval development here. But, so long as France keeps a naval attaché here, there will be intrigues for the appointment of a French Naval Commission. No impartial and sane individual could hesitate for an instant between such a French Naval Commission, and a British Naval Commission, so far as the future efficiency of the Roumanian Navy is concerned. The thing simply can't be argued. This wretched little town of Bucharest already owes half its ills (and they are many) to the ridiculous endeavours which France has made to impose Parisian culture upon an essentially primitive ... civilization. I knew the French Navy pretty well 15 years ago ... and the seeds of syndicalism sown by that egregious ass Pelletan have blossomed today into something like Bolshevism under the tricolour.[7]

The D.N.I. minuted on this and similar intelligence reports, 'Apart from her natural resources and the commercial importance of the Danube, Roumania is the backdoor into Russia, whose recovery may not be so

long delayed as is commonly thought',[8] and strongly recommended sending a naval mission. This theme of the possible resurgence and reopening
of Russia was echoed in contemporary comment by Vickers and their
overseas business informants. The projected naval mission was linked
with a British offer of a minesweeping force to clear the dangerous stretch
of Black Sea off Romania.

The 'rushed' British commitment to send both the mission and minesweepers was made by Commander Diggle, the Naval Attaché, in a panic
at 'French and Italian counter-influence and intrigue'. He reported on 22
December 1919,

> The King, the Premier and the Minister of War told me at separate
> interviews that they especially welcomed the prospect of a British
> Naval Mission as the 'thin end of the wedge' to the introduction of
> British ... influence ... the matter has now gone too far to be
> wrecked by either French or Italian counter influences; also, it
> seems improbable ... that the Opposition in the Chamber, headed
> by M. Bratiano, would try to throw out a Naval Defence Act purely
> to obtain a party advantage.[9]

Four days later he wrote plaintively,

> The Minister of Marine, supported by the Minister of War, had
> three times put forward to the Cabinet ... a scheme for the accept-
> ance of British assistance, but not French, based on the ... Admir-
> alty offers. On each occasion – and I was shown the papers myself –
> the Cabinet signed it, but it was vetoed, first by Mr Bratiano, and
> then by his nominee, General Vaitiano, the Premier in the Cabinet
> of Generals put in power by Mr Bratiano when he himself resigned.
> This action was not taken on the merits of the scheme, but simply
> owing to Mr Bratiano's objection to any form of British assistance
> *per se*. It was pointed out to him ... but entirely ignored, that to
> leave the waters unswept ran the risk of very high insurance rates:
> even so, his antipathy to everything British overbore their
> arguments.[10]

This was all the more exasperating because the obstructive Brătianu, as
Prime Minister three months earlier, had assured Diggle 'that if a naval
mission were asked for, it would undoubtedly be to Britain that the first
application should be made, and promised his cordial support whether
"in" or "out" of office'.[11] This Romanian technique of rushing nego-
tiators into premature agreements which were then disavowed was one
which Douglas Vickers was to meet in 1925. At this time, French, Italian
and other foreign trade with Romania was done by rail, whereas British
trade was waterborne with British companies carrying 80 per cent of
Romanian waterborne trade, justifying Diggle's suspicion that foreign
interests were prolonging unsatisfactory conditions to hamper British
trade and increase their own. When he warned the King and Cabinet that
the Romanian coasts were so dangerous as to resemble a state of block-

ade, they confounded the proposed British minesweeping expedition by purchasing four French minesweepers. Nevertheless, in February 1920, a British officer was appointed to head the first of several naval missions to Romania, and was soon scornfully reporting 'that the greatest difficulty I have to contend with is the unbounded optimism and cocksureness which permeates all Officers ... they have no conception of the high degree of technical training required for the satisfactory maintenance of modern vessels'.[12] For example, the Romanians confidently broached buying six M-class destroyers from the British Admiralty, although there were only four engineer officers in Romania, none of whom had experience of turbines or oil-fuel boilers.

British attempts to supply Romanian aviation requirements were even more telling. In February 1921 the hangars at Jassy blew down in a storm, destroying 44 newly-delivered French aircraft stored inside: Colonel Rojinksky, Director of the Air Force, wished for French replacements, but his subordinate, Colonel Popovici, favoured British planes (De Havilland 9 Bristol fighters, Avros and Sopwiths).[13] This opportunity was seized by an Englishman called Wright, of Nasmyth, Wilson & Co. of Manchester, who represented a British syndicate seeking to take over Romania's railway workshops. Wright's railway negotiations were dragging, and as a diversion he tried 'to cut out the French' from an aeroplane contract in which they were seeking £2,000 per machine. Wright offered £1,500, and after returning home 'thoroughly disgusted' with the railway concession, he passed the business to Sydney Taylor, Bucharest correspondent of the *Daily News* and agent of the British Westinghouse Electrical Co. Taylor extracted from General Raschano, the Minister of War, so a British attaché recounted,

> *a practical promise* that the papers in connection with the business, which were actually in Raschano's hands last week, would be signed within 24 hours of their interview. Of course, they were not signed, as is the habit in this country, and I was asked if I would give the business a little shove.
>
> I had previously kept myself out of it, because I thought it very much better that a business firm should deal direct with the Roumanians without any official backing [for] *the Roumanians always imagine that in every business there is some political influence at the back of it, and they cannot understand an ordinary firm doing ordinary business in an ordinary way.*[14]

In August 1921 Taylor signed a contract with the Ministry of War for the supply of sixty aeroplanes costing £79,800 and spare parts sufficient to put together some 40 more machines worth £40,950 – a total of £120,750. The contract provided that after an initial payment of £15,750, the Romanians would issue, in September 1921, Treasury bonds for sterling amounts maturing at intervals until September 1922. These bonds were to bear seven per cent from date of issue, and article 5 of the contract stipulated that the Romanian Government would be liable immediately for the whole amount of the bonds if the partial payments were not punctually made.[15]

These machines were supplied by the Aircraft Disposals Co. (ADC) from the post-war surpluses of the Air Ministry and Ministry of Munitions, but after more than a year only 12 aircraft had been received in Bucharest (and only two unpacked): although ADC had received Treasury bills for a total of £105,000 due on fixed dates, none of them had been met, and all were renewed.[16] The Romanians next proposed that instead of the payments in sterling provided in the contract, ADC should accept four per cent bonds of a Conversion Loan. The Company replied that these latter bonds were valueless: 'the largest supplier of Aeroplanes in the world' complained that 'in all our transactions with other Governments of the world, we have not yet met a similar case, and we have been in the habit of dealing with Governments without any such preoccupation as is necessary in dealing with individuals'.[17] They do not appear to have obtained a satisfactory settlement.

Meanwhile, in 1923, Armstrongs' young agent in Greece, Henry Drummond-Wolff, had so vigorously espoused the Royalist cause against the Venezelists that his life was threatened, and he was forced to flee to Romania. There he rapidly became an intimate of Crown Prince Carol (whose wife was a Greek princess of the family which Wolff had lately been supporting in Athens), and set about securing for Armstrongs contracts for a tunnel on the new Braşov-Buzău line, and orders for aircraft.[18] Prince Carol was Inspector General of the Romanian Air Force, and soon intimated his wish to buy 250 aeroplanes and to inaugurate national aircraft construction 'consistent with the doctrines of "Romania for the Romanians"' at the Astra works at Arad, with Armstrongs as technical advisers.[19] In this proposal the British Minister saw 'traces of the all-clutching hand of Monsieur Vintila Brătianu, the Minister of Finance' who had land where the factory would probably be sited, and investments in the Astra Company.[20] However, rather than aggravate what the Crown Prince called the 'beastly jealousy' of the French, the Romanians asked both the French and British Governments to nominate companies suitable to undertake such contracts, the Prince reserving his preference in favour of Armstrongs.[21] The Air Ministry in London enthusiastically advised

> that the supply of machines and concentration of aeroplane factories by British firms in the small states of South East Europe ... should be given every support and encouragement ... in the event of war foreign countries using British aircraft can be controlled as regards supply of equipment and spares ... If a British firm such as Armstrong Whitworth is not selected France will certainly secure the work and the present occasion affords a good opportunity, which may not recur, of getting a footing for the British aircraft trade in this part of the world ... the Air Council do not consider that small countries, such as Roumania, are in a financial position to create large air forces.[22]

In the event, the factory was not built in co-operation with British capital or technical advisers, for instead, in 1925, the Industrie Aeronautique Roumaine aeroplane factory (IAR) was established at Braşov by the Romanian Government in conjunction with the French makers, Blériot and Dietrich-Lorraine. They were enabled to oust Armstrongs from the business by the death at Coventry in February 1925 of the Romanian's 'dipsomaniac' test pilot who crashed one of Armstrongs' Siskin machines while 'very drunk during the trial flight'. The recriminations that followed this fiasco led Rojinsky into a libellous press campaign against Drummond-Wolff; in the upshot the Romanians took the Siskin engines, but refused to accept the machines for which they had already contracted, 'and Armstrongs just managed to scrape out without a loss'.[23] These business misadventures of Armstrongs, following the breach at French instigation of ADC's apparently iron-clad contract, and twenty years of xenophobic attacks on foreign oil interests in Romania, were notorious. In the circumstances, Vickers' participation with the Reşiţa Company in a scheme to erect a national arsenal was unguarded. The risk which they obviously took in Romania was a measure of the straitened overseas markets from which Vickers was suffering.

The Austro-Hungarian State Railway owned Uzinele de Fier şi Domeniile din Reşiţa Societate Anonmiă (known as Reşiţa), comprising steelworks, coal-mines, vineyards and other property, including 250,000 acres of forest in Transylvania. By the union of Transylvania with Romania proclaimed in November 1918, the Banat, in which Reşiţa lay, was transferred from Hungary to Romania, which had been without steelworks before the war. The Romanian Government disliked their only steelworks being owned by an ex-enemy foreign company, and so nationalised it, whilst the Austro-Hungarian Railways sold part of their holding to the Romanians. Wishing to introduce another interest which might secure good management, the Railways offered 30,000 shares to Vickers. By May 1922, Vickers held 30 per cent of Reşiţa's shares, worth £94,941, and intended selling artillery and industrial products from Reşiţa, following 'a policy which they had successfully adopted in Spain' and elsewhere. They regarded Romania as 'of very considerable importance in the future in view of its large population and great potential wealth ... likely to be a large customer for artillery material in view of the ever present menace on its Russian frontier'.[24] Reşiţa was one of the largest industrial employers in Romania: it employed 16,500 workers by 1928, and although the workforce fell to 40 per cent of this figure in the crisis year of 1932, it recovered to 13,500 by 1935. This was in a period when, according to the Romanian census of 1930, only 7.2 per cent of the national workforce were engaged in industry. As late as 1938, only 30.8 per cent of national income derived from industry.

In August 1922, after the Yugoslav Government intimated that they wished to found, with government and private capital, factories for arming the Yugoslav army, Vickers took 15,000 shares worth 10,000 dinars each in Reşiţa's Yugoslav subsidiary, Société Serbe Minière et

TABLE 1

DIVIDEND AND TECHNICAL FEES RECEIVED BY VICKERS FROM REŞIŢA 1922–8

| Year | % dividend received | Dividend | Technical fees in connection with Armaments, less expenses |
|---|---|---|---|
| 1922 | 20 | £2,000 | – |
| 1923 | 30 | £3,526 | – |
| 1924 | 20 | £3,888 | – |
| 1925 | 30 | £2,750 | – |
| 1926 | 12 | £9,711 | £2,476 |
| 1927 | 12 | £9,562 | £2,299 |
| 1928 | – | – | £1,430 |
| Total | | £31,437 | £6,205 |

*Note:* Vickers originally bought 50,000 shares of lei 500 each, costing £94,941. In 1925 they received a bonus issue of 100,000 shares of lei 500 each. Taking the market price of 31 December 1928 at 820 lei to £1, the value of these 150,000 shares was £160,061.

*Source:* Douglas Vickers Papers (note of 9 March 1929).

Industrielle (Sartid). Both the Österreichische Credit-Anstalt für Handel und Gewerbe, of Vienna, and the Austro-Hungarian State Railways also took holdings of this size.[25] As early as 1920, Hofrat Adalbert Veith, the Hungarian-born industrialist running Reşiţa, had entered discussions with the government coalition headed by the Romanian war hero, Marshal Averescu of the People's Party, supported by Tache Ionescu's Democratic Unionist Party and Goga's National Party of Transylvania. They wished to erect a national arsenal, and with Ionesco's lead a syndicate was formed to study the project's feasibility. Ionescu insisted that Schneider-Creusot should head the syndicate, which was joined by the Steyr Company (rifle plant), Manfred Weiss Company (small arms ammunition), the Romanian railway carriage works Astra of Arad, and Nobels. It was envisaged that these companies would together take a half participation in the proposed factory, with the Minister of War 30 per cent and Romanian banks the remaining 20 per cent.

In connection with this scheme, in 1921–2, Vickers were asked to submit proposals for organising Romanian arsenals, and a director, Colonel W. C. Symon, visited the country with assistants and submitted a scheme to the Government.[27] He was assisted by the company's Bucharest agent, Edward D. Madge, obstetrician to Queen Marie: apart from piloting her family into the world, he had no other engineering qualifications, but his Royal influence was thought valuable to Vickers. Negotiations did not produce definite orders owing to lack of financial support and to the secession in December 1921 of Ionescu from the Averescu Cabinet which then collapsed.[28] Zaharoff visited Bucharest in October 1922 and made an important contact in Prince Barbu Stirbey (1872–1946), Administrator of the Royal Domains and 'the most enigmatic figure in Romania ... a curious mixture of the grand seigneur and man of business'. Stirbey had received the German armistice with Romania in

1918, and, by virtue of his connections by marriage, enjoyed a unique position mediating between the Liberal Party and the Court. He was briefly Prime Minister in 1927, but his opposition to King Carol led to exile in Switzerland and a suspected attempt to poison him with chocolates in 1931, although he returned to Romania to influence the transition of 1945.[29] In January 1922 a Liberal government led by Ion Brătianu took office, ruling (with an interruption in 1926–7) until November 1928. Douglas Vickers told Veith in July 1923 that Vintila Brătianu, brother of the Prime Minister, had suggested that a small works for the repairing and reconstructing of field guns might be built at Braşov, and reported a suggestion by the Minister of Industry and Commerce, Tancred Constantinescu,[30] that Vickers send engineers to Romania. Douglas Vickers himself visited Bucharest in October 1923, and on his return reported Veith as saying that both the Prime Minister and Brătianu's brother-in-law, Prince Stirbey, favoured establishing a national arms factory. But he warned

> that, in view of our recent experiences with the Roumanian Ministry, it would be necessary to tie up that Government very much more strictly than had been proposed in the same position as we are, in as far as they have a large quantity of unused plant which they would transfer to the Company to be formed.
>
> Our participation would also be in the form of machinery and technical assistance.
>
> The Government and Banks would participate for cash .... In the original scheme Schneiders occupied our place, and a Mr Castiglione was in for aircraft instead of the Astra Works, Arad, a wagon and carriage works which acts in alliance with Resita ...
>
> It would be a condition that the Government guarantee to place orders to a certain sum every year with the Company to be formed, and if they failed in that they could be bound to buy up the Company for cash.[31]

In June 1924 Vickers were approached by the French company Dietrich-Lorraine, which had been asked to help the manufacture of aircraft engines in Romania, and inquired whether Vickers would collaborate in the project. Vickers already supplied steel for motor-car engines to Dietrich-Lorraine, and in June 1924 met its managing director, Nicaise, in Paris. Dietrich-Lorraine had previously supplied aero-engines to Romania, and Douglas Vickers clearly listed the principles for co-operation which his company required:

> In the first place, we think that the cost of the buildings and general plant should be provided by banks or select associations within Roumania. A certain proportion of capital should be given us in return for our assistance in organisation, for the right to use our present designs and models, and for our future technical assistance and the benefit of experimental work on new types which we are

both continually carrying on at home and which form as large a proportion as manufacturing our specialities. A percentage of the output should be given in consideration of this.

In the second place, we should ask that the new organisation should not be required to manufacture everything from the start; it should build up its experience gradually and, in the meantime, rely upon us for the supply of parts to be assembled into the complete machines.

In the third place, the Government should give guarantees of orders to keep the works employed for a certain period, and failing that, should pay such a sum that would carry the expenses which are unavoidable when works are nearly ... closed down. The works that are contemplated would have only one customer, so that some provision of this sort is necessary.

In the fourth place, we ought to insist upon complete technical control of the works. The Government will, no doubt, try to impose Roumanian management, which, in view of the want of experienced ... Roumanian engineers would probably be fatal ...

These conditions should be obtained from any Government for such a project. In Roumania, caution is particularly necessary, the Government being heavily in debt to their home manufacturers, and having on several occasions treated foreign capital very badly.[32]

Behind these schemes moved Sir Basil Zaharoff. In February 1924 Prince and Princess Stirbey stayed as his guests at Monte Carlo, and Zaharoff described Romanian hopes:

The Ministry want to become by degrees independent of foreign countries regarding their armament, and they intend ... to have in Roumania factories producing guns of various calibres with their mountings and ammunition, explosives and general accoutrements.

The idea of the Roumanian Government is to utilize Resita to a certain extent, but not to a great extent, and their present intention is to apply to England and also to France with a view to appropriate works being constructed .... These works would be in various parts of the kingdom, as far as possible from a probable enemy frontier, and in location near to coal and iron mines, with water power if possible.

The idea is that it would be wise to have the support of English and French institutions and capital, and that the English group should establish itself in one part of the country and the French in another.

The capital necessary would be provided in the following proportions, viz 40% by the Roumanian Government in cash or materials, 15% by the Roumanian public, and 45% by the English and French concerns ... the Roumanian Government intend buying immediately 250 aeroplanes, for which they would pay cash, and I may say here that this cash in foreign currencies is being found by the method I invented two years ago, in taxes on material exported from Roumania, these taxes payable in the monies of the country to which the material is shipped. This material consists principally of wheat, maize, barley, beans, timber and petroleum.

In addition to the 250 Aeroplanes which would be paid for in cash, 250 more would be bought if facilities were given for payment or if a commencement of manufacture of aeroplanes could be made in Roumania, and touching these aeroplanes, I think we ought to follow them up very closely, even to undertaking to make 250 or more in Roumania, the principal being a good price for those to be delivered against cash and a better price for those to be delivered on credit or made in the country.

I told the Prince that although the whole thing came to a big order ... that it could be carried out by beginning on a smaller scale, and a thorough entente between the Roumanian Government and the English and French groups, and I added that *my experience for many years past was that whenever any of our money had gone abroad, we did not easily see it again*, and consequently that very sure arrangements would have to be made for a proper return for the expenditure, and an assurance of its being amortized within a given period.

I also said that it would take three or four years to establish the factories and at least two years to educate local labour and ... it would be necessary for the Government to pay interest from the very beginning on the capital as and when expended by the foreign firms.

I further said that influence should be brought to bear on the Bratiano brothers for them to have more confidence in Mr Veith, who would be exceedingly useful in the whole transaction, and without whose assistance the government might be running risks ... I told Prince Stirbey that a few years before the war we had created the Sociedad ... which had by degrees become the largest industry in Spain, manufacturing everything from a battleship down to a field gun, and that it would be ... encouraging to the Roumanians if their Government would send a small commission to Spain to study the whole question from A to Z on the spot.[33]

Zaharoff also discussed with Stirbey a proposal by Lord Thomson ot Cardington, then Minister of Air in the Labour Government and lover of Stirbey's cousin Princess Bibesco, to circumvent the British Government policy of excluding weaponry from the provisions of the Trade Facilities Act of 1921;[34] but Douglas Vickers replied that Thomson's suggestion was impossible, because the Romanians had already been too indiscreet about the deal.[35] In an internal memorandum, Douglas Vickers commented, 'I cannot imagine any experienced firm' willing to accept the terms brought by Stirbey, 'I would advise strongly against *any direct* financial participation in a *national* armament factory, which would be based on conditions remaining unchanged for many years'.[36] During the summer of 1924 it seemed that the Arad works would be chosen for adaptation into a national arsenal jointly by Dietrich-Lorraine and Armstrongs (Drummond-Wolff, Veith wrote, had an 'almost magnetic influence exercised over the Crown Prince').[37] This did not occur, and in October 1924 Tancred Constantinescu, Minister of Commerce, wrote in longhand to Veith, proposing that Vickers and Reşiţa take an interest in the proposed Copşa factory for guns and ammunition (adding 'Skoda et Creuzot désirent aussi à participer'), and that Reşiţa and Steyr join to manufacture machine-guns and rifles at Cugir.[38] Douglas Vickers reacted sceptically, believing

> that it would be greatly to the advantage of the Government, and would certainly suit Reşiţa and Vickers better, if the comparatively small requirements of Roumania were dealt with at Reşiţa, with Vickers' help. The cost of the additional equipment would be much less than that of a new factory, and the yearly expenses also on a much smaller scale.
>
> The Roumanian Government are now talking of the erection of gun factories, rifle factories, explosives and aeroplane factories all at once. The total expenditure required . . . would tax the finances of a richer country than Roumania.[39]

Veith replied that Steyr was no longer interested in erecting a Romanian arsenal, as it had sold most of its surplus machinery and lacked competent staff to run such a factory. Moreover, the Government would not manufacture arms at Reşiţa because it was too near the frontier and the local population was 'not purely Roumanian'.[40] Sir George Buckham of Vickers arrived in Bucharest on 12 December to give Veith technical advice in negotiations with Constantinescu.[41] Although Vickers did not know that the Romanians were simultaneously discussing with the French the establishment of a munitions factory under private control to undertake *inter alia* chemical warfare research,[42] they were alarmed that Buckham's visit coincided with one by Maglici of the Czech-based but French-controlled armaments firm of Skoda, who propounded a rival scheme. Just as Diggle's scheme for a naval mission in 1919 was signed in a rush to pre-empt foreign rivals, so Douglas Vickers now hastened to sign a convention at Paris on 29 January 1925 with Veith (for Reşiţa) and Constantinescu (for the Romanian Government).[43] Such alacrity was an error: as Otto Niemeyer of the Treasury wrote of Romania, 'The more eagerness we display the less likelihood of doing satisfactory business'.[44]

This Paris Convention provided for the establishment of two factories in Romania: one at Copşa-Miča and the other at Cugir. The former was to be equipped for manufacturing commercial products and guns up to a calibre of 305 mm, shells for the same, and tanks. Cugir was to produce rifles, machine-guns and automatic rifles. The annual capacity of the two factories working sixteen hours a day was stipulated at 500 guns and accessories, 100,000 rifles, 500 machine-guns and 2,000,000 shells with fuses. The Romanian Government provided land at Copşa-Mică and Cugir for the factories together with certain existing buildings and power plant. Reşiţa and Vickers were to provide installations for manufacturing artillery and munitions, with Vickers also assisting in training Romanian personnel. The three participants were allotted shares in the company to be formed, and Vickers also received 75,000,000 lei in cash. 300,000,000 lei was allocated for erecting buildings and installing plant, to be raised by public subscription or supplied by the Government. The new company was constituted for a period of forty years: for the first ten years, the Government guaranteed a dividend of seven per cent on the shares representing the material contributions of Vickers and Reşiţa, and guaranteed a dividend of six per cent for the remaining thirty years. The guaranteed dividend did not release the undertaking from its obligation to work its installations for peace products. For the duration of the agreement the Government undertook to grant it orders for armaments, artillery and ammunition, provided that the price quoted did not exceed outside competitors by five per cent. Until the time when the two factories were functioning, the State agreed to grant orders to Reşiţa in collaboration with Vickers.[45] At the same time Constantinescu also handed a letter to Reşiţa and Vickers undertaking that the Government representatives on the Board of the new company would pay £6,000 to Vickers and Reşiţa for preliminary and technical expenses. Douglas Vickers sent a summary of the agreement to Sir Vincent Caillard, who was staying with Zaharoff in Monte Carlo:

> Machines that have not been used will be put in at present day prices; machines that have been used will be put in good working order and offered at a certain reduced price. Experience of putting similar machines into order indicates that half the cash payment would be more than sufficient to enable this to be done, so that we would be left in the end with £30,000 in cash and shares for the balance on which the Roumanian Government guarantees 7%. You may of course think that Roumanian shares, even with that guarantee, are not of much value, but the surplus machinery, after all, brings nothing in to us, and is losing its value year by year; it also takes room and has to be protected at some cost.
>
> Constantinescu said, somewhat naturally, that he could not put into the contract that Vickers should have the orders of war material pending the creation of the works, but they will go to Resita at reasonable prices and Resita will be allowed to place with us what they cannot make themselves.
>
> The works will not be constructed to material of our design, but we shall be sufficiently well-placed to see that we get more than a fighting chance.
>
> Constantinescu said that he had power to sign and engage the Government, but hedged a little ... it is recognized both by Stirbey and Veith that Vintila Bratianu is the only real authority ...

Constantinescu is also asking for three or four coast submarines, the Roumanians being uneasy about the return of Wrangel's ships to the Soviet. He seemed not to be frightened at the price of £135,000 each and indicated that they might pay for those and take two more if we could give easy terms ...

Constantinescu is a person of some ability and good intentions, but very easily turned.[46]

Vickers, then, were using Romania to export their depreciated surplus capacity left after the First World War. CMC gave a chance of off-loading superannuated and obsolete machine tools, dating from the great munitions expansion of 1915–18, for which Vickers had no use in their post-war programme of diversified peace products. Vickers were financially straitened (passing their ordinary dividends in 1920 and 1923–6), so the promise of recovering some of the cost of their expensive and useless armaments machinery held overpowering allurement. Under the Paris Convention, Vickers were to supply CMC with machinery worth £320,000, inclusive of £130,000 profit, and by March 1929 all but £57,000 of this equipment had been delivered (with £15,000 of reconditioning work also still outstanding). When Douglas Vickers signed the Paris Convention, the consideration of £320,000 for depreciated surplus capacity was probably more important than any other in his company's Romanian strategy.

Caillard replied to him on 29 January from the Hotel de Paris at Monte Carlo, which Zaharoff owned:

We both think the terms you indicate are quite favourable to Vickers, since the cash payment initially runs us against any risk ... the shares in a Roumanian Company – even one in which the Government is a large shareholder and guarantees a dividend of 7% – are not particularly valuable in sterling; but they bring value in other ways – and after all, the natural resources of the country are great, it won't always be badly governed, one may hope.[47]

It is noteworthy that the Paris Convention was signed before any details of capital subscription or legal constitution of the proposed company had been determined, and that Douglas Vickers had repeatedly emphasised that his company was solely interested in providing technical assistance and machinery, not cash, in Romania. It also coincided, in 1925, with the final and official formation at Braşov of the Romanian aeronautical works, Intreprinderile Aeronautice Române (IAR), with the technical collaboration of the French manufacturers, Blériot and Dietrich-Lorraine.

Only a few weeks before, in December 1924, the Blackburn Aeroplane Co. had signed a comparable agreement with the Greek Government to run an aviation factory at Phaleron. The politicians insisted that to obtain the Chamber of Deputies' ratification of the agreement they could only guarantee minimum annual output worth £25,000, but gave informal promises that output would be worth nearer £100,000 per annum. Needless to say, this was not forthcoming, and with annual output dropping from £71,075 (June 1926) to £20,193 (June 1928), Blackburn lost £55,000 in five years. They had difficulty in obtaining payment or technical cooperation from the Greeks, and after interminable wrangles had to renegotiate the agreement.[48]

These were the normal perils for an armaments company involved with a Balkan government suffering from constant paucity of capital for investment and credit, pressure of heavy foreign indebtedness and venal, inexperienced procurement officers. But in Romania there were political and strategic forces that increased Vickers' difficulties. As both Armstrong and Vickers had appreciated in 1919, Romania held an important position in the *cordon sanitaire* around the Soviet Union, but Britain had no place in Romanian political and military strategy. From 1921 Romania was partner with Yugoslavia and Czechoslovakia in the Little Entente, a political alliance with less successful economic overtones, originally directed against Hungary, but from 1927 equally antagonistic to Mussolini's Italy. Also in 1921 Romania entered an alliance with Poland against Soviet Russia, which treaty was renewed in 1926 and 1931. Moreover, between 1924 and 1927, France signed treaties with the individual members of the Little Entente, to whom she also made large financial loans conditioned by political factors. The French-Romanian treaty of 'peace, understanding and friendship', signed in June 1926, while not committing French military assistance against Russia, bound France indirectly to help Romania through the Polish alliance. In these arrangements, Britain held little part: the Balkans and Eastern Europe were unimportant to imperial defence thinking in the 1920s, and British lending was seldom decided by political motives. Teichova has noted that the Czechoslovakian steel industry (with its close affiliations to French capital) intensified its drive into Romania from 1925, after the confirmation of the Czech-French alliance by treaty (1924) and the emergence of Czechoslovakia in a leading role in the Little Entente. Almost at the time that Vickers joined Reşiţa in the Copşa-Mică enterprise, Czechoslovakia's three largest steel companies (the Mining & Metallurgic Company; Vítkovice Mining & Foundry Works; and Prague Iron Company) extracted an agreement from Reşiţa, whereby the latter 'relinquished any claims to exports from Romania and agreed to guarantee to Czechoslovak exporters a third of the Romanian market for iron and steel and rolled materials'.[49] Although only 14.2 per cent of Romania's imports in 1927 came from Czechoslovakia, her military, political and economic orientation was towards the Little Entente and France, to the detriment of British industrial competition generally, and armaments in particular.

The Constitution of the Copşa-Mică & Cugir Company was published in Bucharest on 1 April 1925.[50] Its most salient feature vested all managerial power in an executive committee which was independent of the board of directors, and to which Vickers applied in vain for representation. Vickers' first nominee directors of CMC were Buckham and Baron

Jean Stirçea, Master of Ceremonies at King Ferdinand's Court; in practice, Vickers' interests were watched by Captain E. G. Boxshall, the English son-in-law of Prince Stirbey. Boxshall, whom it was judged politically inexpedient to put on CMC's board, was the son of the British Vice-Consul in Bucharest (who died in 1918) and had seen intelligence service in the Balkans during the First World War. He was regarded in the inter-war period by Vickers as possibly their most shrewd, energetic, alert and reliable foreign representative: in the Second World War he was an officer with the Special Operations Executive, becoming in 1959 Foreign Office adviser on releasing information on wartime espionage.[51] CMC's capital issue in April 1925 failed after concerted press criticism which Boxshall attributed to Skoda (who had been refused an opportunity to participate in March). In the summer of 1925, CMC made another capital issue, but Vickers were foiled when they attempted to increase their holding. As Veith recounted,

> The Commission which ... had to distribute the shares out of our last issue, has – in an utterly incomprehensible way – distributed them in such a manner as to absolutely ignore the subscription of 30,000 shares by Messrs. Vickers ... it is not we who had to suffer most of all at the hands of the Government. Perhaps you may have the occasion one of these days to speak to some of the gentlemen of the Nobel Group. They have had an even more bitter experience with the Roumanian Government.[52]

Later in 1925 a Valuation Commission was appointed in accordance with the Paris Convention to value the contributions of the three parties, and practised consistently 'stupid obstruction', presumably at Skoda's instigation, when inspecting Vickers' machinery sent from Erith.[53] Throughout, the Romanians flouted the two main provisions of the Paris Convention by placing arms contracts with Skoda and by failing to pay, or delaying for years, CMC's guaranteed dividends.

Difficulties were increased by the General Manager of CMC, General Lucescu, and his deputy, Cioc, who disregarded all technical advice offered by Vickers' engineer in Romania, Blackburn.[54] Cioc in particular gave specifications and designs which would far have exceeded the 300 million lei indicated by the Paris Convention as CMC's capital. The difficulties of technical advice were aggravated by the failure of the War Office to decide on types to be adopted: for instance, in April 1926, Vickers were asked to lay out the rifle plant so that it might produce at any time Russian 7.62 mm rifles, Austrian 8 mm rifles, or French Lebel 8 mm rifles. Matters were aggravated by a strike at Reşiţa from March to May 1926, during which Cioc and other managers, who had nothing else to do, planned an expansion of the plant which would have cost 1,500 million lei at minimum. Under this scheme, the Copşa-Miča complex alone would have been the largest arms factory in Europe (dependent for orders, it will be remembered, on the Romanian Government exclusively). These grandiose schemes were all the more remarkable because, although the plans for the Cugir works had been completed in September 1925, building work (the responsibility of the Government under the Paris Convention) did not, through lack of funds, begin until 1926 or near completion until the summer of 1927.[55] In May 1927, Boxshall was nominated a Director of CMC by Vickers, and the report which he rendered showed CMC as financially precarious. 90 million lei had been subscribed by the public, and a further 65 million lei provided by the Government, towards CMC's capital. From this total of 155 million lei, Vickers had received 75 million lei for machinery supplied in accordance with the Paris Convention, but only 3 million lei otherwise remained. The necessary land for the Copşa-Mică site had not yet been expropriated, let alone building planned. (CMC's arms orders to Vickers are shown in Table 2.)

TABLE 2

ARMAMENT ORDERS PLACED IN ENGLAND BY CMC AND SALES EXPENSES 1925-8

| Year | Arms orders placed in England | Sales expenses | Profit and Loss |
|------|------|------|------|
|  | £ | £ | £ |
| 1925 | 43,916 | 1,330 | + 42,586 |
| 1926 | 710 | 3,511 (1) | − 2,801 |
| 1927 | 21,971 | 4,040 (2) | + 17,931 |
| 1928 | 2,068 | 3,167 (3) | − 1,099 |
| Total | £68,665 | £12,048 | + £56,617 |

(1) includes £2,240 for upkeep of Bucharest office
(2) includes £1,258 for upkeep of Bucharest office
(3) includes £1,300 for upkeep of Bucharest office

*Note:* Sales expenses were apparently the only costs charged to these contracts.
*Source:* Douglas Vickers Papers (Note of 9 March 1929).

Skoda began intrigues for admission to CMC alongside Vickers, both in Romania and in London through the British and Allied Investments Corporation which handled their general business in Britain and with whom Vickers also had business relations.[56] Whilst Vickers showed interest in combining in Romania with the French steelmakers Chatillon-Commentry, they were keen to avoid participation with Skoda, foreseeing inevitable clashes of interest. Meanwhile, following the signature of a secret military protocol between France and Romania in June 1926, the French began sending arms to Romania.[57] The sudden death in November 1927 of Ion Brătianu, and the advent of a weaker Liberal government led by his brother Vintila, led Tancred Constantinescu to modify his support for Reşiţa. Douglas Vickers conceded in January 1928:

> that Government pressure or the possibility of effective competition from Skoda may make it desirable to bring them in .... Apart from the possible conflict of interest between Vickers and Skoda inside the Company ... there is another serious objection to their

being allowed in ... there is little prospect of Government orders sufficient to keep the works fully occupied, even on the scale on which they are now being built. If Skoda is to bring a large quantity of further machinery in, the maintenance and amortization of charges will rise and it will be all the more difficult for the Company to make a profit. This would of course be met by Skoda paying cash only for their participation.[58]

He feared however that Constantinescu would favour the more ambitious programme.

After talks in the first half of 1928, two Vickers' directors of CMC, Douglas Vickers and Sir Noel Birch, agreed to admit Skoda on the same terms as Vickers, supplying machinery paid for in preference shares. Skoda stipulated that if their share allotment did not equal those held by Vickers, they would be entitled to subscribe in cash for shares bringing their holding up to equality, and Vickers added a proviso that they were not obliged to provide further machinery. A condition of this agreement between Skoda and CMC was the concurrence of all existing shareholders, which was obtained from all interested parties, except the Romanian Government who for political reasons prevented the ratification of the agreement.[59] In the autumn of 1928 the Cugir works closed entirely owing to lack of funds, while machines supplied by Vickers from England decayed at Constanţa port as there was not money to transport them. In October 1928, Bettany of Vickers' Armaments Contract Department visited both factory sites. The most 'urgent necessity' at Cugir he found was the provision of a new 'Power Plant giving an output of say 1,000 KW, as the existing supply ... frequently fails entirely ... due to insufficiency of water to drive the turbines'. He found other faults at Copşa-Miča's site: 'Insufficiency of ground owned by the War Office requiring expensive appropriations of arable land held by the peasants' and 'lack of housing accommodation for the workpeople ... will prove a heavy burden that must of necessity fall upon either the Company or the State thereby absorbing funds that are required for the enterprises'. The site was 'adjacent to the main line of Railway, and thus exposing War time preparations to travellers from every part of Europe appears ... unwise', and as water was found at a depth of four feet, it would be exceedingly difficult and expensive to construct foundations for heavy machinery.[60] Even granted that Buckham was a gun designer, and not a surveyor, it is extraordinary that he did not notice these disadvantages during his visit of December 1924. Any ordnance survey map would show that Cugir is surrounded by thick forests in a steep valley which is at no point more than a mile wide: the factory was situated at the narrowest point, at the conjunction of the rivers Mare and Mir. This view was confirmed by a confidential report prepared by Skoda for the Romanian Government.[61] Skoda judged Cugir

absolutely without interest as far as the equipping of the Army is concerned. Many of the existing shops are very old and absolutely useless for rational manufacture .... The electric furnace, recently installed, but without a rolling mill, is of no value ... it is too small ... and is not equipped with the auxiliary installations necessary .... The Works do not possess the elementary installations, such as water mains, drains, central heating, telephones etc. It is also so situated as to make extension impossible. The water-power available is insufficient.

The factory had been ready to supply small arms since 1927, but had received no Government orders, and the consequent capital starvation meant that no work could begin. The stubborn mindlessness of Romanian officialdom which this represented reached its nadir in 1931 when Romanian summer time was first introduced: all official clocks were put backwards instead of forwards, and rather than bureaucracy admit its mistake, the country had to tolerate months of 'Extraordinary Romanian Summer Time'.[62]

New political and economic considerations now emerged to worsen Vickers' position. The constant Anglo-French competition, which had been fundamental to the armaments rivalry in Romania, was complicated by increasing German penetration, and by a crisis in Romanian credit after 1928. During the course of the 1920s Romania's external indebtedness had become more acute. By 1930 foreign capital invested in Romania was estimated at £200 million, and external indebtedness at £157 million, or 78 per cent of total foreign capital employed. 91 per cent of the total public debt was external (almost the highest proportion in the world), and by December 1935 Romania had defaulted on all interest due on foreign dollar bonds (viz. $10.9 million). Detailed figures are unavailable, but direct foreign participation in Romania's joint stock capital (industry and banks), despite the Liberal slogan of 'Romania for the Romanians', amounted to 75 per cent or 80 per cent of total equity in the country (mostly invested in oil and heavy industry).[63] The currency depreciated, with one pound sterling worth 225 lei in 1921 but 816.5 lei in 1931. Romanian credit dried up after 1928, and Skoda's supplies of armaments to Romania were credit-financed by Skoda's export agency which accepted Romanian agricultural products in payment for munitions, and sold them on the world market. As world depression deepened, Romania's trade with France and Britain fell, and the former was forced into increasingly bilateral trade with Germany, in which Nazi arms deliveries were taken in exchange for agricultural produce. The economic crisis of 1929–33, and the trade drive of Hitler's Germany after 1933, were new forces working against Vickers in Romania, and were further attacks on their resolve to stay in the country. Although they were accustomed to export armaments on deferred payment terms, it was one of Vickers' most bitter and recurrent complaints to the British Government in the inter-war period that they suffered a major international disadvantage because, under the Trade Facilities Act of 1921, the Government's Export Credit Guarantees were prohibited from applying to munitions (though the prohibition did not extend to aircraft, or their parts). Vickers harked on this exemption in public and private; the Army Council wanted it repealed; and in April 1931 the President of the Board of Trade in the Labour Government made fruitless enquiries, with Cabinet sanction, whether Baring or other merchant bankers would furnish assistance to private armourers equivalent to the 1921 Act. The British Government was not itself willing to face electoral obloquy by providing credit guarantees to 'merchants of death', while privately conceding that such guarantees were necessary to maintain industrial preparedness for war. The French Government were less hypocritical and inconsistent, and for example in 1931 guaranteed to the Sauter Harle Company some 70 per cent of all payments due from Romania on naval mines (whether made in France or Romania), and provided Sauter Harle with facilities to take payment from Romania over seven years.[64]

At the start of 1929 CMC and Vickers agreed to modify their Paris Agreement. Tancred Constantinescu's letter of 29 January 1925 had promised Vickers and Reşiţa for their technical assistance percentages of 2.25 per cent, and five per cent and seven per cent in quarterly terms, on the value of machinery delivered, payable 'au fur et à mesure des progrès de l'installation', but only the 2.25 per cent became applicable as no machines were installed in buildings which remained uncompleted.[65] Since Vickers' technical advice was anyhow disregarded, they agreed in February to terminate all technical responsibility and forego the percentages of remuneration to which they had contractural rights. By June 1929 the factory was about to close, but Iuliu Maniu's National Peasant Government supplied small funds to enable its continuance, and the new Minister of Industry and Commerce, Virgil Madgearu, replaced the management. The following extracts from the Auditor's Report (9 June 1931) to CMC's directors gives some picture of the management:

> We could not find anywhere an exact ruling as to who is entitled to engage personnel. Thus both the engaging and discharging of personnel is done without observing any rules or regulations ... each chief of section engages workmen independently, so that it often happens that one section discharges workmen which might be required by another ... no rule or regulations exist regarding the competence of each employee to incur expenses .... Each functionary spends and disposes without knowing up to what limits he is allowed to go. Orders for the incurring of expenditure and investments were given mostly verbally and were carried out without ... a general co-ordination plan ... we found installed in the large workshops destined for the production of rifles and machine guns two new sections not included in the general manufacturing plan ... for the manufacture of projectiles and the repair of gun carriages. Expensive installations were made in connection with these which cannot be written off in connection with the present orders, and to which orders one must have to renounce in case that

... an order should be placed with the Company for those materials for which the workshops were originally intended ... a large number of repaired machines stored ... [without] even the elementary precaution taken of greasing the exposed parts, which, therefore, have again commenced to rust .... Large quantities of furniture were manufactured to order without distinction whether if bought on the open market they would have been cheaper. This furniture has not been entered into any inventory, as none exists.

The auditors recommended amortizations of about two million lei to be added to the net loss for 1930, noting that the heading 'investments' included (at initial purchasing value) such material as penholders, stamp-pads, rubber stamps and swivel chairs.[66] Douglas Vickers complained:

that the conditions are very bad into which the works have been allowed to drift by the incompetent Roumanian Management introduced for political reasons .... They seem to have no conception of a proper organisation .... I should like the first step to be the removal of Popescu [General Manager], but they are afraid to do it because they feel that if the present Government went out and the Liberals came in again, Popescu would at once be put onto them again, which would make matters worse than ever.[67]

Vickers' expenses and credits in Romania as of March 1929 are shown in Table 1. After this partial disengagement as technical advisers to CMC, Vickers remained involved in Romanian business through Reşiţa and Boxshall. In 1930–1, they discussed with Skoda's chairman, Dr Karel Loewenstein, selling their entire interest in CMC to the Czechs. In February 1931 Skoda sought a further option on the shares up to 30 April 1931 at 30 per cent of the nominal value (about 150 lei per share) and offering 30 per cent on the face value on the Bills of Exchange held by Vickers covering commissions for plans etc. (worth about £12,825) and 30 per cent in cash on the 481 machines still undelivered to Cugir.[68] These proposals were declined by Vickers, but became public property in Bucharest, where one newspaper explained Skoda's thinking:

Supposing the Anschluss idea would materialise and that in consequence Austria, in spite of the opposition encountered in France and the little Entente, would be linked to Germany – a mere glance on the map of Europe will show that the situation of Czechoslovakia in the case of an eventual war with Germany would be completely unsafe and the first shock it would have to support would be precisely at Pilsen ... the geographic situation of Czechoslovakia imposes upon it the duty of seeking, in peace time, another site for its second armament factory which should be protected against any possible surprise from a German attack.[69]

The collapse of Romanian credit in 1931 affected Reşiţa immediately and acutely, since the Credit Anstalt Bank of Vienna was its main creditor, whilst the Romanian Government was its preponderating debtor. Reşiţa's share price fell from a high of 809 lei in 1929 to 402 lei in 1930, 205 lei in June 1931 and 130 lei in 1932, while the value of Romanian industrial production fell by 43.6 per cent over 1929–32. Vickers then requested the Foreign Office that the British Minister in Bucharest should 'make the most vigorous protest possible against the way in which we have been treated', obtain payment of the interest on the preference shares and 'insist upon our moral right to the first refusal of other Armament orders, particularly those at present under negotiation'.[70] Douglas Vickers and Reid Young visited Bucharest in November 1931 and received assurances from both the Ministers of Finance and War about the payment of arrears and future orders to CMC, but no support materialised. On the contrary, arms orders continued to be placed abroad during 1930–1, mainly with Skoda. Exact figures are hard to establish, and even those in the *League of Nations' Armaments Yearbooks* are manifestly incomplete and inconsistent. *Epoca* explained, 'from the Copşa-Miča Cugir Co. with a State Commissar it is difficult to take commissions, without those having to appear in the books; but from Skoda's, whose books are as far as Pilsen, this operation is secure and bears no risks'.[71] In May 1932, excluding advances on account of capital made by the Credit Industriel of Romania at the request of the Government, 129,547,011 lei was due to CMC from the Government, and the Minister of War (who in February 1932 had taken control over the State's interest from the Minister of Commerce) sought its liquidation. He asserted that in the event of liquidation, CMC's buildings and machinery would revert to the State and could not be sold to benefit creditors. An action for the bankruptcy of the company began in July 1932, but was postponed until September, CMC having indicated that it would cite the Government as co-defendants in these proceedings, as the Government's failures had led to the action.

On 31 August, Vickers withdrew from their bankers' deposit their CMC shares, and refused to participate in the Extraordinary Meeting of Shareholders of September 6 voting on the Accounts and Bankruptcy proceedings. They were convinced that it was pointless to participate until the Romanian Government had acknowledged their liabilities.[72] Neilson, Deputy Chairman, also repeated Vickers' request for Foreign Office support.[73] From this time, the British only sought release by CMC from the liability of supplying further machinery (worth £58,481) lying at Sheffield, Erith and Crayford; the discharge of CMC bills amounting to £20,639 for technical aid; and the payment of guaranteed dividends for 1928, 1930 and 1931. Boxshall soon obtained the Minister of Finance's approval in principle for the issue to CMC of Treasury Bonds worth 126,000,000 lei to cover the Government's debt to CMC. He considered Vickers and Reşiţa were fortunate to get Treasury Bonds for both the dividend arrears and 'for the outstanding fee for technical assistance which I had begun to consider a very problematical claim'.[74]

Vickers' final disengagement from CMC was facilitated by Max Auşnit (1888–1957). An enterprising Jewish entrepreneur, he was a resourceful and plucky Anglophile who exerted himself on behalf of Vickers *qua* British, against Skoda *qua* Czech. Indeed it is likely that Auşnit inspired the fateful false report by the Romanian Minister in London of 17 March 1939 that Germany had issued an ultimatum to Romania which so heavily influenced the British guarantee to Poland later in that month.[75] In 1930 Oscar Pollak, Director General of Credit Anstalt, drew up a buying and selling syndicate in Reşiţa shares which was agreed in 1931. The Romanian Credit Bank, the Românească Bank, the Chrissoveloni Bank and the Titan-Nădrag-Călan Metallurgical Company (formed 1924; hereafter TNC) held together 225,000 Reşiţa shares (60 per cent of syndicate), Vickers 50,000 shares (13.3 per cent) and the Austro-Hungarian State Railroad Company 100,000 shares (26.6 per cent). The number of shares in the syndicate was fixed at 375,000, sufficient to secure the majority at any General Meeting, and the proportion of 60 per cent Romanian to 40 per cent foreign was framed to satisfy xenophobes that control remained Romanian. But in fact it was understood that the Romanian Credit Bank and TNC would vote with Vickers, for TNC was controlled by Max Auşnit (who became Reşiţa's Managing Director in 1931) and his brother. Credit Anstalt in Vienna, which controlled the Austro-Hungarian State Railway, was also interested in the Romanian Credit Bank; whilst Max Auşnit shortly afterwards also joined the board of the Chrissoveloni Bank. Douglas Vickers wrote of the Reşiţa share syndicate, 'The union of those who stand for good management is most desirable'.[76]

TABLE 3

VALUE OF LONDON OFFICE ARMAMENTS CONTRACTS
AND AGENCY EXPENSES OF VICKERS IN ROMANIA 1925–34

| Year | Value of contracts received | Total expenses |
|---|---|---|
| | £ | £ |
| 1925 | 92,882 | 1,331 |
| 1926 | 710 | 1,272 |
| 1927 | 321,971 | 2,783 |
| 1928 | 2,068 | 3,047 |
| 1929 | 2,989 | 1,286 |
| 1930 | 1,891 | 1,236 |
| 1931 | 1,205 | 820 |
| 1932 | 15 | 1,087 |
| 1933 | 412 | 833 |
| 1934 | 720 | 1,096 |
| Total | 424,863 | 14,791 |

*Source:* Vickers Papers.

In May 1934 Auşnit concluded an agreement between Vickers and Reşiţa expiring in 1939, whereby Reşiţa paid Vickers two per cent on net value of all artillery and ammunition which Vickers supplied to the Romanian Government during the period of the agreement. A further agreement, to which CMC consented, was signed in June 1936: Reşiţa released Vickers from all liabilities and obligations connected with CMC, and indemnified them against all claims. Both arrangements operated in conjunction with an understanding of April 1934 when 6,106,714 lei, representing Vickers' past expenses in technical assistance to CMC was put in a special Vickers-Armstrong account in the Reşiţa Books, where it remained without interest for one year. Part of this money was transferred to an interest-bearing account in May 1935, and in November 1936 this account was cleared by the direct transfer to Vickers of about four million lei. It is unclear from indecipherable microfilms whether Vickers withdrew the residual three million lei held in their account by Reşiţa after November 1936, but it would seem that the bulk remained with Reşiţa bearing interest.[77] Auşnit also formed in Monaco in January 1934 the Cie. Européenne et Participations Industrielles (CEPI) in which Vickers received 5,960 shares worth 1,000 French francs each in exchange for their holding of shares valued at £73,100 in the Reşiţa Share Syndicate. 'Douglas Vickers was very enamoured' at the idea of moving the assets to a country free of currency restrictions and political danger, but this transaction was the brainchild of the Auşnit brothers, 'the Continental wide boys'.[78] At this period Auşnit enjoyed the favour of King Carol and influence with the Court camarilla, by virtue of his friendship

TABLE 4

YIELD OF VICKERS' HOLDING IN CIE. EUROPÉENNE ET PARTICIPATIONS
INDUSTRIELLES (CEPI) OF MONACO, 1934–9

| Year | Value of holding in million French francs | Percentage Dividend % |
|------|--------------------------------------------|------------------------|
| 1934 | 5.96 | 3 |
| 1935 | 5.96 | 3 |
| 1936 | 5.96 | 4 |
| 1937 | 5.96 | 3 |
| 1938 | ? | 3 |
| 1939 | ? | 6 |

*Source:* Vickers Papers.

with the royal mistress, Magda Lupescu. However, his position was steadily undermined in the later 1930s by a rival industrialist, Malaxa, whose rise as a Court favourite was based on the prevailing anti-semitism, and by the political ascendancy of such quasi-fascist groups as the Iron Guard, the All For the Fatherland League, the National Christian Party and (from February 1938) King Carol's totalitarian Government of

National Union. The rise and fall of Auşnit, and the machinations of Malaxa, were personal dramas which highlighted the Royal favouritism and piquant relations between big business and courtiers which were the facts of life for Romania's ruling class. Auşnit's relations with Vickers seem to have been used to complete his downfall. In September 1937 Vickers agreed with Auşnit to sell him their holding of 5,960 shares in CEPI for £49,294. This purchase appears to have been made in monthly instalments of £1,900 and, after Auşnit's resignation from Reşiţa had been forced by Malaxa and fellow anti-semites in 1939, he was sentenced by a politically biased and racially-bigoted Romanian court, on charges of fraud, instigation to commit forgeries and currency laws breaches, to six years imprisonment, four years loss of civil rights, 30,000 lei damages and costs and an order to repay Reşiţa sums amounting to about 90 million lei, or £76,000. (Auşnit, who evaded an Iron Guard death squad by hiding in a barrel, escaped from Romania in a stolen German bomber in 1944, and after an interval in Monte Carlo became a zip manufacturer in New York).[79]

Vickers at Copşa-Miča was not the only British experience of Romanian methods of financing and planning defence installations. In September 1929 the British Minister at Bucharest interviewed the Minister of Finance, Popovici, who in 'nebulous and ... fatuous' fashion spoke at

> length about a proposed naval base at Constanţa for which he wanted British Technical and, I need to add, financial support. He said that he had spoken both to Mr Henderson [Foreign Secretary] and to Mr Graham [President of the Board of Trade] at the Hague who had ... given the project their entire blessing ... I feared that His Excellency could not have been wholly truthful ... I enquired what his Excellency thought the scheme was likely to cost. He said he supposed a biggish sum – say 8 Milliards of lei. I then asked how he proposed to find the money. He said by a loan, preferably 'entre état et état', which I suppose meant, if anything, Great Britain ... I asked if he had any details which I could submit to my Government. He said no, but that ... experts must come, and as quickly as possible, to Bucarest.[80]

As a result of these discussions, Admiral R. G. H. Henderson, a gunnery officer with flying expertise, visited Romania, reporting:

> There is really not much to talk about, although the Roumanians apparently find a devil of a lot .... They regard themselves as the buffer state of Europe against Russia and Bulgaria, and consider that the Great Powers should be interested in this question ... [for] their own welfare ... if they get the powers to agree that they are going to be the saviours of Europe against USSR, then there should be less difficulty in floating a respectable loan.
> Lake Tasaul, some 20 miles north of Constanţa, would make a magnificent harbour, and the hills surrounding it make it easy to

> defend . . . . To make this lake into a purely naval base is a ridiculous suggestion, and they would never be able to float a loan for it, but if side by side the lake could be developed into a really good commercial harbour, then there are prospects.

Henderson envisaged a canal link from the lake to the Danube ('a splendid Hindenburg line') and concluded 'that in twenty years time, greater Roumania will require a Liverpool'.[81]

Henderson returned to London in June 1930, but shortly afterwards a French naval mission went to Bucharest.[82] Following Henderson's report, the British contractors, Sir Alexander Gibb & Partners, made proposals for developing Lake Tasaul, although the Foreign Office warned against their incurring any expenses.[83] Nevertheless, a cruiser squadron visited Romania in the autumn of 1932 to sustain British naval influence, and the narrative of its commanding flag officer vividly evokes the Romanian Services' and Ministerial mentality.[84] The Romanians dismissed the Gibbs proposals in favour of the rival scheme advanced by an Ulster MP, W. John Stewart. In 1930 he had entered an ambitious roads project, which neither he nor the Romanian Government proved able to finance, and by 1932 was trying to recoup damages of £430,000. He conceived a scheme, of such tortuous complexity as to attract Romanian officialdom, to be compensated for his roadbuilding losses with the Lake Tasaul development.[85] The Romanian Naval Attaché and Minister in London both badgered Whitehall for strategic and financial support, so that the DNI justly minuted 'These people are all intriguers and seem unable to believe that we say what we mean'.[86] The correspondence about the Tasaul base reveals the vaunting tenor of Romanian administration, its inefficiency, trivial enmity and petulance between departments and, above all, the desperate and simple conviction that if the British were persuaded to make any initial commitment, then sooner or later, they would also yield capital.

All these characteristics are reflected in the history of CMC, whose misadventures were the product of Romania's industrial and economic backwardness. The country's crushing shortage of capital and burden of foreign indebtedness determined much of CMC's development, and were one aspect of this backwardness; but other aspects were social or cultural. Whatever the artistic or religious heritage of Romania, it had little business or engineering tradition in any sense that was recognisable in England, and the incomprehension between the Admiralty or Vickers in London and their counterparts in Bucharest was a genuine barrier, and not always a factitious contrivance of Romanian officials to extract bribes. However insistent was Douglas Vickers that his company would not participate for cash, men like Tancred Constantinescu simply disbelieved him. The British, despite Boxshall, do not seem to have understood the Romanians to the extent that the French or Czechs did, while one British diplomat detected in Romanian officialdom 'a constitutional distaste for straightforward British financial methods, which are neither understood nor admitted by devotees of the *pot-de-vin* system, such as Messrs Constantinescu'.[87] Vickers, of course, made specific mistakes themselves. Though Douglas Vickers showed proper caution of Romanian business mentality,[88] he allowed Constantinescu to hustle him into the Paris Convention by the appearance of a Skoda representative during Buckham's visit to Bucharest. It was fatal to sign before the Romanians had published CMC's constitution, with its management board from which Vickers were excluded, and which was independent of CMC's supervisory board on which Vickers had three nominees. Moreover, a guarantee of orders from the Minister of Commerce and Industry was otiose since the Minister of War was responsible for procurement; yet despite previous experience of foreign arsenal projects, in Russia and Japan particularly, Douglas Vickers seemed surprised and defenceless when CMC refused his company's technical advice so obdurately and when the Romanians breached their contract flagitiously. Though Stirbey told the British Minister at Bucharest in 1929 that he thought Vickers had been 'supine',[89] it is hard to know what more the British could have done as self-protection. It indicates Vickers' desperation to be rid of depreciated surplus plant and to win foreign orders, that they chanced the Romanian risk, and they were always at a grave political and economic disadvantage. They had no place in the Little Entente, nor in Romania's alliances with Poland and France, and the Romanian avidity for foreign capital, which the French supplied for political considerations, was never met by the British Government, nor by tame bankers acting in concert with Whitehall and private manufacturers. Relative judgments (whether moral or practical) of the French and British attitudes towards financial loans, or the provision of political credit, have no place in this essay: but there can be no doubt that there was a difference, and that in the immediate term, Vickers and other British business interests suffered. They were bound to lose. 'When political considerations are involved in any degree,' Douglas Vickers wrote, 'the French always seem ready to find money at a price'.[90] This was the antithesis of British policy towards Balkan investment. CMC was the last venture of its sort by Vickers in Europe, though it was less than twenty years later than their Spanish Sociedad, with its similar combination of artillery with industrial work. World conditions were incomparably transformed, and Britain's position, both in the world economy and as an international power, was altogether more precarious; so, too, were the fortunes and self-confidence of Vickers, a company whose performance and strategy has always closely reflected British social and political trends.

Auden and MacNeice in their 'Last Will and Testament' bequeathed to Vickers:

> The Balkan conscience and the sleepless night we think
> The inevitable disease of their dangerous trade.

Vickers had Balkan conscience, sleepless nights and dangerous trade, but in each sense contrary to the images conjured by radical poets.

*Business History Unit*
*London School of Economics*

NOTES

*The author wishes to thank Mr H.E. Scrope of Vickers Ltd for permission to consult the archive on which this article is based, and Clive Trebilcock, of Pembroke College, Cambridge, Joanna Innes, of Somerville College, Oxford, and Alice Teichova, of the University of East Anglia, for valuable criticism of earlier drafts. Other references have been supplied by Luciano Segreto of Firenze.

1. The activities of the trade warriors are discussed at length in my forthcoming biography of Dudley Docker (Cambridge University Press).
2. See generally Maurice Pearton, *Oil and the Romanian State* (Oxford, 1971); C.N. Jordan, *The Rumanian Methane Gas Industry* (New York, 1955); D. Mitrany, 'German Penetration in Romania', *Quarterly Review*, Vol. 226 (1916), pp. 387-410; H. Charles Woods, 'Roumania after the war', *Contemporary Review*, Vol. 119 (1921), pp. 162-9.
3. John A. Cross, *Lord Swinton* (Oxford, 1983), p. 17; House of Lords Record Office, papers of Sir Patrick Hannon; Scottish Record Office, Edinburgh, papers of Sir Arthur Steel-Maitland; Churchill College, Cambridge, papers of Sir Philip Cunliffe-Lister. In July 1919 Romania was visited by Major Kennard of the FBI. See *Documents of British Foreign Policy* (hereafter DBFP), 1st series, Vol. 6 (London, 1956), p. 88.
4. On this subject see Clive Trebilcock, 'British Armaments and European Industrialisation 1890–1914', *Economic History Review*, 26 (1973), pp. 364-79; G.G. Jones and R.C. Trebilcock, 'Russian Industry and British Business 1910–1930: Oil and Armaments', *Journal of European Economic History*, 11 (1982), pp. 61-103; Edward R. Goldstein, 'Vickers Ltd and the Tsarist Regime', *Slavonic and East European Review*, 58 (1980), pp. 561-71.
5. J.D. Scott, *Vickers* (London, 1962), pp. 148-49; cf. R.P.T. Davenport-Hines, 'The British Armaments Industry during Disarmament 1918–36' (Cambridge PhD, 1979), pp. 266-340.
6. Martin Gilbert, *Winston Churchill*, 4 (London, 1975), p. 158; Sir Basil Zaharoff to John T. Coffin, 31 October 1918, Vickers file 450.
7. Adm. Sir Charles Ottley, Athenic Palace Hotel, Bucharest, to Sir Hugh Sinclair, DNI, 20 September 1919, PRO Adm 116/1899. For a favourable appraisal of Romanian national potential in October 1919, by Frank Rattigan, British Chargé d'Affaires in Bucharest, see DBFP, 1st series, Vol. 6 (London, 1956), p. 280. A detailed and optimistic survey of Romanian commercial prospects by a special visiting commission from the Midland Bank is in *Midland Bank Review*, September 1920. A more cautious analysis is the Report on Economic Conditions in Rumania (April 1921) by Alexander Adams, Commercial Secretary at Bucharest (HMSO 1921).
8. Sir Hugh Sinclair, minute of 1 October 1919, PRO Adm 116/1899. For a brilliant account of the Romanian military mind, see Norman Stone, *The Eastern Front 1914–1917* (London, 1975), pp. 264-81. In 1916, 'among the first prescriptions, on mobilisation, was a decree that only officers above the rank of major had the right to use make-up' (pp. 264-5); 'to make the Romanian army fight a modern war was asking a donkey to perform a minuet' (p. 277).
9. Commander Neston W. Diggle to Sinclair, 22 December 1919, PRO Adm 116/1899. Earlier in 1919 the Romanians had asked to be supplied with 12 squadrons of British aircraft, but the British Treasury had effectively blocked the deal, which was apparently secured instead by France: see DBFP, 1st series, Vol. 6, pp. 96-7.
10. Diggle to Sinclair, 26 December 1919, PRO Adm 116/1899.

11. Diggle to W. F. A. Rattigan, 9 September 1919, PRO Adm 116/1899.
12. Capt. Humphrey W. Bowring to Rattigan, 30 April 1920, PRO Adm 116/1899. The Directorate of Naval Intelligence did not succeed until 2 September 1922 in extracting from the Romanian Government back-pay of £3,781 owed to Bowring and his assistant. Minute of C. O. Cochrane, 23 September 1922, PRO Adm 1/8584/52. On British involvement in Danubian navigation at this time, see my forthcoming entry on Arthur Grenfell in *Dictionary of Business Biography* and speech of Sir Frederick Lewis, *Financial Times* 19 December 1921.
13. Report of Francis J. Duncan, British Military Attaché in Bucharest, 17 February 1921, PRO Air 5/274.
14. Duncan to Gen. Sir William Thwaites, 21 March 1921, PRO Air 5/274. Emphasis added.
15. Despatch 467 of Eugene Millington-Drake to Lord Curzon, 16 August 1921, PRO Air 5/274.
16. Despatch 414 of Millington-Drake to Lord Balfour, 27 July 1922. Despatch 45 of Duncan to Sir Herbert Dering, 23 October 1922. PRO Air 5/274. On the Aircraft Disposal Co., see Robin Higham, *Armed Forces in Peacetime* (London, 1962), p. 202, and my entry on Godfrey Isaacs in forthcoming *Dictionary of Business Biography*.
17. Lt. Col. John Barrett-Lennard, joint managing direct of Aircraft Disposal Company, to President of Council of Ministers in Romania, 2 November 1922, PRO Air 5/274.
18. Despatch 585 of Dering to Curzon, 2 October 1923, PRO Air 5/274. For a hostile account of Drummond-Wolff's character, see C. H. Bateman to S. D. Waley, 14 June 1926, PRO FO 371/11418. He was Unionist MP for Basingstoke 1934–5, and later founded (in association with Sir Arthur Bryant) Union and Reconstruction, an imperialist pressure group dissolved in May 1940. See Microfilm 11 of J. O. P. Bland collection, Thomas Fisher Library, Toronto University.
19. Lt. Col. Stephen S. Butler, Military Attaché, report of his audience that day with the Crown Prince, 5 January 1924, PRO Air 5/274. Barbara Cartland's biography *The Scandalous Life of King Carol* (London, 1957), does justice to its subject. See also Lord Vansittart, *The Mist Procession* (London, 1958), pp. 410-11, where Romania is described as 'the most miserable country in Europe'.
20. Despatch 10 of Sir Herbert Dering, 5 January 1924, PRO FO 371/9978.
21. Report by Lt. Col. S. S. Butler, op. cit. and Despatch 14 of Sir H. Dering, op. cit., Air 5/274.
22. Air Ministry to Foreign Office, 29 January 1924; Douglas Vickers memorandum on Romanian request for tenders on 250 aeroplanes (cash payment) and 500 aeroplanes (payment over 3 years), 16 February 1924, Microfilm R284.
23. Veith to D. Vickers, 9 July 1924; Boxshall to D. Vickers, 10 March 1925, Microfilm R284; C. H. Bateman to S. D. Waley, 14 June 1926, PRO FO 371/11418; C. H. Bateman, minute of 3 February 1927, PRO FO 371/12229; for the death of Major Stefan Sanatescu, see *Times*, 19 February 1925.
24. Unsigned memorandum, 'The Copsa-Mica Company', 27 August 1928, sent with covering letter 30 August 1928 to J. Frater Taylor, Microfilm R286. The Reşiţa accounts from 1921 are on Vickers Microfilm G197. See also memoranda in PRO FO 371/13695. The exact chronology of Vickers' involvement with Reşiţa is unclear. Constantin Giurescu, *Chronological History of Romania* (Bucharest, 1974), p. 289, states that British and Romanian capital formed Reşiţa in June 1920.
25. Note on increase of capital of Sartid to 50 million dinars; Serbische Berg und Hutten-industrie to Luterbacher, 21 August 1923, Microfilm R284; Douglas Vickers to Veith, 13 June 1922; Douglas Vickers to James Reid-Young, 12 December 1932, Microfilm R190.
26. Hofrat Adalbert Veith to Douglas Vickers, 4 December 1923, Microfilm R284. On Tache Ionesco, see *Times* obituary 22 June 1922.
27. Symon 'was astonished to find the disorder and chaos which reigned everywhere in munitions depots ... shells of every type, high explosive and others, were left lying about in a very dangerous fashion ... the types of munitions and guns possessed by the Romanians were innumerable, British, German, Hungarian, Russian and others';

Symon saw several unopened cases of Lewis guns supplied by Vickers. Despatch 569 of Sir Herbert Dering (Bucharest), 19 October 1921, PRO FO 371/6232.

28. Symons' visit is mentioned in Microfilm X247; Veith to D. Vickers, 4 December 1923, op. cit. For background, see International Reference Library [i.e. John Clark], *Politics and Political Parties in Romania* (London, 1936), and Joseph C. Roucek, *Contemporary Roumania and Her Problems* (London, 1923).

29. Sir Ronald Greg, 1929, PRO FO 371/13704; Report on leading personalities in Romania (1936), PRO FO 371/20427; PRO FO 371/13695; *New York Times*, 25 March 1946; *Documents of British Foreign Policy*, 1st series, Vol. 6 (London, 1956), pp. 149, 434, 467; Sir Robert Bruce Lockhart, *Guns before Butter* (London, 1938), p. 185.

30. Director General of Ammunitions 1916–18. Sometime Director General of Romanian Railroads, thereafter General Secretary of the Ministry of Industry and Commerce, before being appointed Minister of Industry and Commerce by I. I. C. Brătianu.

31. Memorandum by Douglas Vickers, 14 December 1923, Microfilm R284. Camillo and Enrico Castiglione, mentioned in this letter, were two Italian associates of the German industrialist, Hugo Stinnes, and had bought control of several Austro-Hungarian Motor Car Companies (Puch; Austro-Daimler; Austro-Fiat; Hungarian MAG; Deffag). They failed in a similar attempt on Steyr in 1922. Their London agency was the Alpine Motor Co. The Castigliones had later interests in central European aircraft sales, and were principal shareholders in the Astra railway carriage and aircraft works by February 1924. At this time they were regarded as the richest *nouveaux riches* in post-war inflationary Vienna. In the early 1920s they made a huge fortune by currency speculation, much of which they however lost after Poincaré stabilised the franc. Although British officials referred to the Castigliones disparagingly as Jews, they were in fact Christian. They returned to Italy in the late 1920s, where they remained important businessmen. Archivio Centrale dello Stato, Rome, Carte Perrone, B2, fasc. 18; Colonel Francis W. Gossett, Inter-Allied Control Mission in Budapest, report of June 1922, PRO FO 371/7558; V. Castronovo, *Giovanni Agnelli: La Fiat del 1899 al 1945* (Turin, 1977), pp. 206-9, 220-1; information from John Pearson.

32. Vickers to Nicaise, 19 June 1924, Microfilm R284.

33. Sir Basil Zaharoff to Vickers, 14 February 1924, R284. Emphasis added.

34. Zaharoff to Vickers, letter 16 February 1924, R284. Emphasis in original. Stirbey's wife was the pro-German sister of his cousin Prince Georges Bibesco, whose wife was the mistress (and eventual biographer) of Lord Thomson of Cardington.

35. Vickers to Zaharoff, 20 February 1924, R284.

36. Memorandum 16 February 1924, R284. My emphasis.

37. Veith to Vickers, 9 July 1924, R284.

38. Veith to Vickers, 28 October 1924, R284.

39. Vickers to Veith, 19 November 1924, R284.

40. Veith to Vickers, 28 November 1924, R284.

41. Vickers to Veith, 29 December 1924, R284.

42. Fifth Report of Chemical Warfare Committee (March 1925), p. 29, PRO WO 33/1078.

43. On Skoda, see Alice Teichova, *An Economic Background to Munich* (Cambridge, 1974), pp. 167-97 and *passim*; Davenport-Hines, pp. 275-8; Despatch 878 of Lord D'Abernon (Berlin), 12 November 1922, and report on a visit to the Skoda works at Pilsen by Sir Thomas Montgomery-Cuninghame, 6 December 1922, PRO FO 371/7388.

44. Sir Otto Niemeyer to Sir Frederick Leith-Ross, 28 December 1925, PRO FO 371/11418. For some 'dishonest and impossible' proposals involving Titulescu, the Romanian Finance Minister, see Leith-Ross, memorandum of meeting of 28 January 1926, in PRO T 188/297.

45. A printed text in French and Romanian of the Paris Convention is in Douglas Vickers papers.

46. D. Vickers to Sir Vincent Caillard, 26 January 1925, R286.

47. Caillard to D. Vickers, 29 January 1925, R286.

48. Blackburn Aeroplane Co., memorandum on Greek agreement, December 1929, PRO FO 371/13662.

49. Teichova, op. cit., p. 146; see generally John O. Crane, *The Little Entente* (New York, 1931).
50. Printed copy of the Constitution is in Douglas Vickers Papers. It was reported in *Times*, 6 and 18 February 1925.
51. D. Vickers to Sir Trevor Dawson, 6 December 1926, Microfilm R286; Dawson to Sir Herbert Lawrence, 17 May 1928, Microfilm R321; *Daily Mail*, 25 July 1979. On the return of Carol from exile in 1930 and his deposition of his son Mihai from the Romanian throne, Prince Stirbey fell from favour, resigned from the chairmanship of Reşiţa and was succeeded by Baron Stircea as liaison between the Royal Court and the Cabinet.
52. Veith to D. Vickers, 3 August 1925, R284. See also D. Vickers to Veith, 17 March 1925; Veith to D. Vickers, 25 March 1925; Boxshall to D. Vickers, 5 April 1925; Boxshall to Oliver Vickers, 8 April 1925, R284.
53. Vickers to Veith, 26 March 1926, R284. The Evaluation Commission completed their inspection of Vickers' machines in England on 5 September 1925, but delayed submitting their valuation until March 1926.
54. This of course had been the complaint in 1920 of Captain Bowring cited in note 12. It was a recurrent difficulty met by Vickers in all their foreign arsenal projects. 'Although the Roumanians admittedly do not understand anything at all about ... relining, they insist upon altering the specifications sent out by Messrs Vickers, which are naturally based upon a long experience'. Boxshall to D. Vickers, 4 December 1924, R284. See also F. Blackburn, memorandum of visit to Cotroceni to inspect machines stores there, 12 March 1925, R284.
55. Blackburn to Sir George Buckham, 18 May 1927, Douglas Vickers Papers.
56. Veith to D. Vickers, 25 March 1925; D. Vickers to Veith, 17 March 1925, R284.
57. Anthony P. Adamthwaite, *France and the Coming of the Second World War 1936–39* (London, 1977), p. 24.
58. Memorandum by D. Vickers, 26 January 1928, R286. See also D. Vickers to Veith, 26 January 1928; draft convention between Skoda and CMC, May (?) 1928; Vickers to Boxshall, 8 June and 12 July 1928, Vickers to Tancred Constantinescu, 10 July 1928, R286. Constantinescu to D. Vickers, 17 January 1928, Microfilm X247.
59. Boxshall to D. Vickers, letter 4 June 1927 (Douglas Vickers Papers) reported a rival scheme submitted by the son of General Coanda, Prime Minister *ad interim* in 1927, which had met political favour, and which fronted for a German group which sent out Prince Reuss und Klein, formerly Governor of Kamerun. Boxshall told the British Minister in Bucharest that if the Government attempted to break any provision of the Paris Agreement, Vickers would request the Foreign Office to take up the matter, and expected prolonged disruption from this new influence. See *Flight*, 9 June 1927, p. 385, for an account of the recent Bulgarian Government contract with the Aero Co. of Prague for the construction of a joint aircraft factory at Kazanlik.
60. Memorandum, 27 January 1930. Douglas Vickers Papers.
61. Dated 3 July 1920. A complete copy, now partially indecipherable, was obtained for Vickers and is in Microfilm X247.
62. Narrative of Rear Admiral Bertram Watson (1932), para. 81, PRO Adm 116/2914.
63. Royal Institute of International Affairs, *The Problem of International Investment* (London, 1937), pp. 223-5; Teichova, op. cit., p. 23 and *passim*. These figures prompted one authority to write 'There is no country which has been the cause of greater disillusionment and bitterness to the British investor or exporter than Rumania, and the writer ... feels in duty bound to counsel total abstinence from participation in Rumanian enterprises'. George C. Logio, *Rumania* (Manchester, 1932), p. 115.
64. Davenport-Hines, pp. 290-1 and *passim*; Sir Archibald Montgomery-Massingberd to Lord Hailsham, April 1933, PRO WO 33/3338; Boxshall to Vickers, 9 April 1931, Microfilm R213.
65. Boxshall to D. Vickers, 4 June 1927, Douglas Vickers Papers.
66. Translation of copy in Douglas Vickers Papers.
67. D. Vickers to Sir Bernhard H. Binder, 21 May 1930, Douglas Vickers Papers.

68. H. E. Carter to J. B. Neilson, 20 February 1931, Douglas Vickers Papers. Neilson answered Carter's letter by telephone and discussions seem to have been mostly verbal.
69. *Epoca*, 3 March 1931. Translated typescript in Douglas Vickers Papers.
70. Logio, op. cit., p. 101; James Reid Young to Foreign Office, 27 August 1931, Douglas Vickers Papers. The value of the principal shareholdings in CMC at this time in lei were Romanian government, 178,635,000; Vickers, 164,117,500; Reşiţa, 10,000,000; others, 91,415,000. Total, 444,177,500. Microfilm X247.
71. *Epoca*, 20 February 1931. Typed transcript in Douglas Vickers Papers. On the bribery scandal of 1933 involving Skoda's Romanian agent, Zeletsky, see Philip Noel-Baker, *The Private Manufacture of Armaments* (London, 1936), pp. 159-61, 167-9.
72. Reid-Young to Boxshall, 31 August 1932, Douglas Vickers Papers.
73. Neilson to Foreign Office, 10 August 1932, Douglas Vickers Papers.
74. Boxshall to Vickers-Armstrong, 7 September 1932, Douglas Vickers Papers.
75. Simon Newman, *March 1939: the British Guarantee to Poland* (Oxford, 1976), p. 117; Boxshall to F. C. Yapp, 19 April 1933, Microfilm R213. Born in Galati, Auşnit was educated at the Academy for High Commercial Studies and Exportation in Vienna. In Independent Senator of the Chamber of Commerce and Industry in Galati district in 1929 and 1932–3, he became President of the General Association of the Industrialists of the Banat, and Vice-President of the General Union of Industrialists of Romania (UGIR). By 1936 he was Administrator Delegate of Reşiţa and of the United Iron-works Titan-Nădrag-Călan, and Vice-President of the Romanian Telephone Co., Lujani Sugar Factory and the Chrissoveloni Bank.
76. Memorandum 2 January 1931, Douglas Vickers Papers. Logio, op. cit., p. 101, citing *Epoca* of 24 October 1930, states that in the last financial year, Reşiţa directors received 83 million lei in remuneration, compared to 86 million lei distributed to shareholders. Prince Barbu Stirbey was said to draw over 10 million lei per annum from Reşiţa. The Chrissoveloni Bank, here mentioned, was particularly interested in hydro-electrical development, and was supported by the Nieder-Oesterreichische Eskompto Gesell-schaft of Vienna, the Banque de Bruxelles, Hambros of London and Harriman of New York. The Romaneasca bank (formed 1911) was identified with the Liberal Party, played a leading role in the coal and metallurgical industries, and had other holdings in lumber and petroleum.
77. Memorandum of 13 July 1937, Microfilm R21; memorandum on CEPI Monaco agree-ment of 10 February 1934, Microfilm R319; D. Vickers to Sir Mark Webster Jenkinson, 6 October 1933, Microfilm R332.
78. Memorandum of V. Pritchett to J. D. Scott, 21 July 1959. Vickers Historical Record, file 352.
79. Boxshall to Sir Frederick Yapp, 18 September 1939; *Volkischer Brobechter*, 22 August 1939, Microfilm R213; *Times*, 16 March 1940 and 30 January 1941; *New York Times*, 19 January 1957. On the attempts of Auşnit and Boxshall to raise capital to develop Romanian natural gas and to erect a carbon-black factory, see Sir Frederick Leith-Ross to MacGowan, 13 December 1938, PRO T 188/297. Mr H. E. Scrope recalls that when he joined Vickers in 1947, Auşnit and Sir James Reid Young were in the midst of lengthy correspondence settling CEPI's affairs, which was concluded in Auşnit's favour.
80. Despatch 335 from Sir Robert Greg (Bucharest), 20 September 1929, PRO Adm 116/2710.
81. Sir Reginald Henderson to Sir Barry Domvile, DNI, 28 April 1930. On Henderson's exemplary character, see despatch 200 of Sir Michael Palairet (Bucharest), 27 June 1930, PRO Adm 116/2710.
82. Despatch 200 from Sir Michael Palairet (Bucharest), 27 June 1930, PRO Adm 116/2710.
83. Memorandum of Robin Alers-Hankey of Foreign Office, 1 September 1932, PRO Adm 116/2933.
84. Rear Admiral Bertram Watson, Narrative of Romanian visit (September to October 1932), PRO Adm 116/2933.

85. E.H. Carr to Capt. R.M. Spraggett, 23 March 1934, PRO Adm 116/2933.
86. 5 March 1933, PRO Adm 116/2933.
87. Despatch 101 of Frank Rattigan, 9 July 1919, quoted DBFP, 1st series, Vol.6 (1956), p.61.
88. In many respects the best account of Romanian business methods and backwardness is the portrait of the financier Henri Léon and his Romanian associates in Christina Stead's magnificent novel, *The House of All Nations* (London, 1938 and 1966), based on her first-hand experience of speculative secondary banking in the 1930s and engrossing for business historians.
89. Sir Robert Greg to Sir Orme Sargent, 12 February 1929, PRO FO 371/13695.
90. Douglas Vickers to Stirbey, 19 June 1930, Douglas Vickers Papers.

# LOMBARD STREET ON THE RIVIERA: THE BRITISH CLEARING BANKS AND EUROPE 1900-1960*

By GEOFFREY JONES

I

The aversion of British business to the Continent between the late nineteenth century and at least the 1960s is well-documented, and to some notorious. British business interests preferred to invest in the Empire and the Americas.[1] A variety of reasons have been suggested as explanations for this preference, but the basic point was that British businessmen either could, or thought they could, secure higher profits in those areas than in Europe. There have been no general studies to show why this was so.[2] This article represents an exploratory exercise in filling this gap by offering a case study of the experience of the British clearing banks when they invested in Europe. During the first half of the twentieth century all but one of the 'Big Five' clearing banks attempted to extend their branch network to the Continent. Although these banks comprised one of the strongest sectors of the British economy, these Continental investments met with very little success.[3]

The pre-history of the involvement of British financial institutions with Europe stretched back for several centuries. Many merchant banks had traditional links with Continental countries. Joint stock banks had begun to take an interest in the late 1850s and the 1860s. This period saw the formation of a number of Anglo-European banks. The record of most of these banks was dismal. British banks in France, Spain, Italy and Germany were floated, and promptly sank. A partial exception was the Anglo-Austrian Bank, which failed as a deposit bank but managed to survive by turning itself into a typical European mobilier bank.[4]

During the second half of the nineteenth century a new feature was an influx of Continental banks to London. At first these were in effect merchant banks, but later in the century leading commercial banks also came. In 1879, the Dresdner Bank, Credit Lyonnais, the Comptoir National d'Escompte and other leading Continental banks followed. These banks were attracted by London's pre-eminent position in world finance, and particularly by the dominant role of sterling in the financing of international commerce. A contemporary estimated that there were 13 'first class' foreign banks with offices in London in 1898: by 1911 the number had grown to 26.[5] These banks soon secured a strong hold on the currency exchange business, which had previously been monopolised by the London merchant bankers. It was this aspect of the activities of the foreign banks which prompted a response from the British banks.

The first response came from the Midland Bank, which perceived a threat to its 'correspondent' business. From the 1830s, and perhaps earlier, various

British and foreign banks had entered into agreements whereby the British bank could draw on their foreign 'correspondents', up to an agreed limit, when operating overseas. The foreign banks were granted the same facilities in London. One of the leading correspondent bankers was the City Bank, whose customers included a large number of merchant houses engaged in foreign trade. In 1898 the City Bank merged with the Midland Bank, and this, combined with the transfer of Midland's Head Office from Birmingham to London in 1891, led Midland to emerge as a major 'correspondent' bank. A Foreign Banks Department, dealing with the correspondent banks' business, was established in 1902. Since the Midland Bank held its correspondents' accounts in sterling, and all transactions in those accounts were carried out in sterling, easy and reliable access to foreign exchange was essential to this business. Therefore in order to avoid dependence on the foreign banks for foreign exchange, the Midland Bank in 1905 decided to open a foreign exchange department.[6]

This development was regarded by many, including the Bank of England, as highly unorthodox.[7] Within a few years, however, two of the other clearing banks embarked on the far more unorthodox step of taking the battle against the foreign banks into their opponents' territory. In 1911 Lloyds purchased Armstrong and Co. of Paris, formerly agents of important English banks. This bank was established as a foreign subsidiary of the Bank under the name of Lloyds Bank (France) Ltd. The Bank, the General Secretary later observed, 'was established mainly for the purpose of dealing with English-speaking people'.[8] To emphasise the point the Bank proudly proclaimed — in English — that it was 'A British Bank conducted on British lines'. In September 1913 the London County and Westminster Bank joined Lloyds in France by establishing a subsidiary in Paris. This was also conceived as a British bank for British clients in France. Nevertheless, the Westminster Bank was determined to make an impact in the French capital. The Bank purchased the property of a bank in liquidation in the Place Vendome, 'in the heart of the Parisian fashion and jewellery world'.[9]

These moves by Lloyds and the London County and Westminster Bank aroused even more public comment than the Midland Bank's foreign exchange department. Fears were expressed in the banking journals that the Continental branches of British banks might lock up British deposits in long-term loans abroad, or lead the banks to abandon their 'safe' banking traditions, or make London more vulnerable to foreign banking crises.[10] These issues were still being debated when the First World War broke out.

## II

The next few years saw a substantial expansion of the activities of the British clearing banks on the Continent. Four factors encouraged this development. Firstly, the presence of large numbers of British troops on the Continent offered an immediate and attractive market for British deposit banks. Secondly, the expulsion of German banks from Allied cities led to gaps in banking facilities which the British banks could fill.

A third factor was that the British banks were led to believe by their representatives in foreign countries and by foreign bankers that there existed a considerable demand for their services. In 1911, a representative of the Banque Française told the Chairman of the Midland Bank, Sir Edward Holden, that 'the French Banks were now desirous that English banks should go to Paris'.[11] The Midland Bank's representative in Petrograd in 1917 reported that it was 'more certain every day that we are very much in request'.[12] In the early 1920s Barclays' representative in Italy informed his Head Office that there was 'little doubt that a British Bank would be heartily welcomed in Rome'.[13] It was unfortunate that all these representations were very imprecise about *why* the British banks would be welcome in Paris, Petrograd and Rome. These invitations were strangely reminiscent of the joint stock bank's branch extension policies of the 1830s and 1840s. In that period a petition from an assortment of local dignataries was often taken as sufficient grounds to establish a branch office. This policy of expansion-by-invitation, based on the belief that a branch might survive on a few prestigious private accounts, had proved to be the downfall of some early banks.

A fourth influence on the clearing banks was the Government and the Bank of England. During the War there was anxious debate over what was widely felt to be the unfavourable comparison between the industrial and commercial activities of British banks with those of the great German investment banks.[14] In 1916 the President of the Board of Trade, Walter Runciman, urged British banks to be 'a little more venturesome'.[15] Later in that year an expert Committee chaired by Lord Faringdon recommended the formation of a British Trade Bank. This bank was to assist in the financing of British overseas trade, and also to operate a foreign exchange department. 'If industry is to be extended', the Committee reported, 'it is essential that British products should be pushed, and manufacturers, merchants and banks must combine to push them'.[16] The resulting British Trade Corporation, however, did little 'pushing' and soon expired. A related venture lasted longer, but was to end more disastrously. This was the British Italian Corporation, which was formed in July 1916 by a group of 23 British banks, including the Lloyds, National Provincial and the Westminster Banks. It was supported by a State subsidy of £50,000 per annum for the first ten years, to be repaid without interest out of any profits over 5 per cent. The aim was to be 'the development of the economic relations between the British Empire and Italy'.[17]

The clearing banks were informally encouraged by the authorities to expand their branch network to the Continent. In 1917 the Government suggested to the Westminster Bank that it should open in Spain with the aim of challenging the commercial supremacy of Germany in that country.[18] A Barclays official in Italy in 1924 reported that 'the British Embassy has been urging the entry of a British bank for considerable time past'.[19]

The banks, with business booming, the Government encouraging, and the Continentals welcoming, rapidly expanded their European investments. Lloyds briefly transferred its branch to Bordeaux after the outbreak of War, but after the Battle of the Marne returned to Paris. By the end of 1915 it had moved to new premises in the Place de l'Opera, 'possibly the most prominent site in any European capital'.[20] The business grew rapidly. In 1917 the National Provincial Bank decided to acquire a half share in the bank. The new company was named the Lloyds Bank (France) and National Provincial Bank (France) Ltd. By the end of 1917 the Bank had branches in Paris, Biarritz and Bordeaux, Le Havre, Marseilles and Nice. In 1919 and 1920 branches were opened in Belgium in Brussels and Antwerp, in Germany in Cologne, and in Switzerland in Zurich and Geneva. In 1921 new French branches were opened in Cannes, Roubaix and St Jean de Luz. By that year the Bank, with a capital of £480,000, had a staff of 1,073 employed in France.

The Westminster Foreign Bank followed a similar pattern of expansion. New branches were opened at Bordeaux and Madrid in 1917, Barcelona in 1918, Bilbao, Antwerp, Brussels, Lyon, Marseilles and Nantes in 1919, and Valencia in 1920. By the following year the staff numbered 1,660.[21]

Barclays followed Lloyds, National Provincial and Westminster into Europe after the end of the War. Barclays' association with France originated in the activities of Cox & Co., the Army Agents. Cox & Co. followed the British Expeditionary Force to France in 1914. In 1915 a separate company, Cox & Co. (France) Ltd., was incorporated, to which the London and South Western Bank soon subscribed half the share capital. In January 1918 the London and South Western Bank merged with London and Provincial Bank, and in the following October this new combination merged with Barclays. By then Cox & Co. had branches in Paris, Boulogne, Le Havre, Rouen, Marseilles, Lyons and Amiens. During 1919 branches were opened in Cologne and Algiers, during 1920 in Nice, Menton and Cannes, and during 1921 in Monte Carlo. In 1922 the business was completely taken over by Barclays, which formed Barclays Bank (Overseas), renamed Barclays Bank (France) in 1926. Barclays also acquired half the share capital in the Banque de Commerce of Antwerp.[22]

The motives of Barclays in these years were ambitious, even perhaps grandiose. The Chairman, F.C. Goodenough, shared some of the philosophy of the Faringdon Committee. In August 1917 he wrote of the 'coming struggle for the markets of the world'. Bankers, Goodenough argued, were to play a key role in this struggle, providing 'not only, or even principally, financial help, but rather the hearty co-operation of the Banker in discovering fresh outlets for the manufacturer's wares'. If this was to be achieved, Goodenough concluded, it was essential 'that the Bank should have not only what is usually termed a "Correspondent" in the principal centres, but rather a Branch or the nearest approach to a Branch that can be arranged'.[23]

The expansion of Lloyds and National Provincial, Barclays and Westminster on the Continent was both rapid and ambitious. By the early 1920s, however, it began to dawn on the Parent Banks in London that perhaps it had all been rather too rapid and ambitious. After the end of the War the Westminster Bank, which had undergone the greatest expansion, began to take stock of its Continental investment, and its officials did not like what they saw. In 1919 Charles Lidbury, a tough young Bank Inspector who was later to become first superintendent of Foreign Branches and subsequently Chief General Manager of the Westminster Bank for 17 years, conducted an inspection of the Paris branch. His highly critical report outlined the adverse consequences of the Bank's rapid, but ill-planned, expansion on the Continent.[24] The other banks experienced similar problems. Large staffs and expensive premises had been purchased, but the lack of knowledge of local banking and financial conditions, and the lack of guidance from Head Office, was soon leading to a worrying failure to earn profits and a growing number of bad debts. By the early 1920s the Board of the Lloyds and National Provincial Foreign Bank were also concerned about the performance of their Continental branches. In 1921, in an attempt to improve the quality of the Managers, the Board decided that 'an endeavour be made to find a number of young Public School men for service in the Bank'.[25] They proved of little help. In 1922 the Zurich branch was closed, and it was decided that the Bank would not expand into any country where it was not already represented. There was, however, no Lidbury-type scourge on the Bank, with the result that the organisational and personnel legacy of the early years was left to hang over the Bank until it nearly ruined it in the early 1930s.

The Midland Bank was the only member of the 'Big Five' clearing banks which had stood apart from the extension of branch banking to the Continent during the War. This was at first more by accident than design. Holden, the Chairman, called publicly in 1914 and in 1917, for the British Government to assist British bankers in securing the lifting of the alleged legal and fiscal discrimination against British bankers in France, Spain, Italy and other countries.[26] The implication was that the Midland Bank would have been interested in going to those countries if it could be assured of fair treatment.

It was perhaps providential for the Midland Bank that the two European countries it was most interested in, Russia and Spain, offered the least hospitable conditions for an expansion of the Midland's branch banking. Before 1914 Midland had built up a valuable business in municipal loans in Russia. In 1913 one of the clerks at the Foreign Exchange Department was sent to work at a Bank in St Petersburg (soon to be renamed Petrograd), and in 1917 it was decided to acquire property in that city for an agency.[27] Holden, however, was never convinced of the wisdom of this step, and he was exceptionally cautious after the February 1917 revolution. In May the Midland Bank's representative in Russia reported that Lenin, 'the pro-German provocateur and down-with-everything sort of gentleman', had disappeared from Petrograd.[28] Holden, however, rightly perceived that Lenin would not remain hidden for long, and no branch was opened in Russia. Spain seemed almost as unwelcoming as Russia in 1917, and it took a Midland representative in Madrid barely a month to decide that the Bank should not interest itself in that country.[29] Midland got nearest to opening a Continental branch in Paris, but again providence took a hand. In 1917 the Midland Bank tried to buy Lloyds Bank's old property in Paris. When Lloyds discovered the identity of the would-be purchaser — 'the greatest rival of the Lloyds Bank' — they refused to sell. This episode brought to a discouraging end Midland's schemes to enter Continental branch banking.[30]

A virtue was soon made of this abstinence from Europe. The Midland Bank began to emphasise the advantages, both to the bank and the British economy, of concentrating on the 'correspondent' business. When Holden gave evidence to the Standing Committee on Bank Amalgamation in January 1918 he spoke against the Joint Stock Banks opening branches in foreign countries, 'with the exception perhaps of France'. Instead he suggested that British industry could best be helped by 'cultivating a connection with foreign bankers themselves'. 'By adopting these methods', Holden continued, 'we retain the use of our own Deposits to further our own industries instead of sending them abroad to develop the industries of other countries to compete against our own'.[31]

Holden, however, did not share the insularity and parochialism of many businessmen of this era. He was probably more concerned with Continental affairs than any of the other chairmen of the joint stock banks. In his speeches he repeatedly made comparisons between the British, French and German economies, and he berated the parochialism of some of the financial institutions in London. 'Any view of the financial situation which is confined to local occurrences in Lombard Street', Holden observed in 1914, 'is worse than useless, owing to the growing international character of the world's money markets'.[32]

In 1918 the correspondent business of the Midland was greatly reinforced by the merger with the London Joint Stock Bank. This was perhaps the most experienced of all the banks in overseas business, possessing by the time of the merger 70 foreign agencies and total acceptances of over £2.5 million.[33] After Holden's death it became the orthodoxy in the Midland Bank that the correspondent business was infinitely preferable — and more profitable — than foreign branch banking. The growing number of European banks which banked with the Midland was ascribed to the fact that the Bank had, as the new Chairman put it in 1921, 'refrained from competing with our foreign friends in their own country'.[34] This view was probably well-founded. Both Lloyds and National Provincial lost French and Belgian business when their Continental subsidiary was established.[35]

III

The years from the early 1920s to the outbreak of the Second World War proved traumatic for all three of the subsidiaries of the British clearing banks on the Continent. Beginning with a trade depression and ending with the Nazi occupation of most of Europe, the two decades proceeded through inflation, deflation and depression. The British banks, still suffering from the legacy of their ill-planned and over-ambitious origins, did not fare well against these general economic trends, sinking badly in the troughs and failing to take advantage of any remaining opportunities.

The original reasons for the Banks' European role evaporated one by one in this period. The British Army finally withdrew from the Continent in 1925 when the Cologne garrison was evacuated. The foreigners proved far less welcoming than had been supposed. Moreover, the banks began to meet official hostility, rather than support, for their Continental ventures. From the early 1920s the Bank of England sought to discourage the clearing banks from operating in foreign countries. The banks' commitments in South America and Africa received most attention. In 1925 the formation by the merger of three overseas banks of Barclays Bank (Dominion, Colonial and Overseas) was followed by a Bank of England decision to close down the accounts of the overseas banks controlled by the clearing banks. The Bank of England refused to open an account for Barclays (D.C.O.) right up to the Second World War. This policy did not prevent Barclays and Lloyds, in particular, from expanding their overseas activities, although it did inconvenience them.[36] The relatively small European operations of the clearing banks attracted only marginal hostility from the Bank of England. In the late 1920s, however, the Bank was forcefully reminded of the dangers of Continental entanglements by a crisis affecting its own part-creation in Italy. The Banca Italo-Britannica, which was wholly owned by the British Italian Corporation, had been allowed to go its own way during the 1920s with very little control from its British owners. 'Irregularities' occurred in the Bank after 1926, and three years later it was hit by a series of large losses. It was discovered that £2 million was required immediately to save the Bank. The Bank of England was obliged to put up £250,000, which it did on condition that three clearing banks who were among the shareholders put up the remaining sum. In 1930 the bank was sold off to the American Blair-Giannini group, with total losses to its British shareholders of £3 million. The Bank of England eventually wrote off its £250,000 loan, ,which did not endear the Bank to the Continental adventures of the clearing banks.[37]

The Lloyds and National Provincial Foreign Bank fared worst of the three subsidiaries of the clearing banks in the inter-war period. The Bank was unclear what kind of business it wanted. During the 1920s hopes were still high that there were sufficient British people on the Continent for the Bank to justify itself merely by serving them. During the middle 1920s a string of new branches were opened on the Riviera, in Mentone, Monte Carlo and Le Touquet. A business also developed in the accounts of the continental subsidiaries of British companies, most of whom banked with the parent banks. The foreign bank held the accounts of the Continental subsidiaries of the Anglo-Persian Oil Company, Dunlop, Rolls Royce, Debenhams, Liptons and Schweppes. The Bank was slow in deciding to do business with French and Belgian companies. In November 1918 a proposal that the Bank should advance large sums to Belgian industrial concerns was rejected on the grounds that it 'would not suit the Bank'.[38] It took nearly another decade before the Bank decided that there simply was not enough 'British' business on the Continent to justify its existence, and that it had become seriously involved in local commerce. In 1927 the Board recorded its general opinion 'that it would be better to open up in large commercial towns rather than in seasonal places'.[39] Only exceptional managers, however, had the ability to build a foothold in local business. At Roubaix a dynamic manager did establish a firm base in the local woollen industry, but this was the exception rather than the norm. Most of the branches in the 1920s made significant profits only on exchange dealings. The Monte Carlo branch made money from the casino business. Geneva built up a good profit from the dollar and sterling balances received from the League of Nations, which were let out to other banks.

By the end of the 1920s Lloyds and National Provincial Foreign Bank appeared to have established only a diffuse and rather precarious business. There were fundamental managerial problems, a difficulty which was to affect all the British clearing banks in Europe in the inter-war years. A report on the Paris-based Head Office and General Management in 1931 found 'a general absence of any organised control of the business and policy of the Bank as a whole'.[40] Individual managers and departments went their own way. Lending was not properly supervised. While the total number of accounts in the bank fell from 32,089 to 31,707 and the total number of staff from 1,277 to 1,271 between 1928 and 1930, salaries and allowances increased from £255,728 to £283,172 and 'expenses' from £121,494 to £149,861 over the same period.[41]

After 1928 an increasing number of unwise, and unsecured, advances were made, which had the effect of temporarily boosting the Bank's profits in those years. The onset of the Depression in 1930, however, turned these advances into Bad Debts. On one Paris account the Bank eventually lost £484,000. By January 1931 a further £40,000 had been lost in the Antwerp diamond trade, including £33,400 on one account.[42] The Parent Banks came to their subsidiary's rescue. In 1931 £450,000 of the bad debts were guaranteed by subsidiaries of the Parent banks. A further £450,000 guarantee was given between 1932 and 1935.[43] During 1936 the guarantee was cancelled, and the Parent Banks 'gave' the subsidiary £900,000. Lloyds and National Provincial Foreign Bank was left with a large frozen debt. In June 1935 the proportion of non-revenue producing assets to total deposits had reached 20 per cent.

Table 1 provides a rough indication of the Bank's financial performance in the inter-war years, although these figures do not incorporate the 'special payments' made by the Parent Banks to the foreign subsidiary during the 1930s.

Table 1 :  Lloyds and National Provincial Foreign Bank:
Trading Results 1911-1942 [44]

| Years | Cumulative Profit after all expenses and appropriations | Dividend Paid | Bad Debts (Provision less releases) | Cumulative Profits in Exchange |
|-------|-------|-------|-------|-------|
| | | (£ sterling) | | |
| 1911-14 | 70 | – | 1,600 | – |
| 1915-18 | 11,740 | 15,945 | 43,368 | 22,456 |
| 1919-22 | 67,006 | 75,681 | 128,073 | 837,911 |
| 1923-26 | 56,673 | 75,600 | 63,037 | 1,408,619 |
| 1927-30 | 28,261 | 91,800 | 331,924 | 1,583,448 |
| 1931-34 | 22,515 | – | 325,483 | 1,947,241 |
| 1935-38 | 29,961 | – | (815) | 2,318,667 |
| 1938-42 | 101,153 | – | (839) | 2,439,051 |

Source:  NW 4252.

The cumulative profit figures show that the Bank's fortunes peaked in the early 1920s, and that the performance was extremely bad during the 1930s. Some £637,000 had to be charged to profit and loss as provision for Bad Debts in the years 1930-1936.

In the summer of 1931 London changed the General Management in Paris. Although the new management was rather more conscientious, the business did not prosper, and the Bank survived only because of the continued support of the Parent Banks. By the early 1930s the Riviera business was almost non-existent, and one by one the Riviera branches were closed. Only Monte Carlo stayed reasonably profitable in the thirties, living off the deposits of French and British visitors to the Casino, these visitors' transactions on the British and American Stock Exchanges, and a growing amount of refugee money.

The closing of the Riviera branches was a part of a new strategy devised by the Bank's Chairman, Colin Campbell (of the National Provincial Bank). The aim, Campbell wrote in 1936, 'was to concentrate [the] business in France in as few places as possible and to work in commercial and industrial centres rather than in residential and luxury ones'.[45] This new policy was only a very limited success. The Roubaix branch developed its position in the woollen business of the area, and earned an average of £10,000 per annum between 1928 and 1937. Le Havre developed a large acceptance business in the port's cotton trade, and had connections with the coffee and other produce markets. Antwerp developed rather on the lines of a merchant bank, building a well-spread commercial business. The branch financed the grain, timber, coffee, wool, meat and canned goods trades, and had connections with the Verviens spinning and wool weaving industries. The problems in securing local commercial business, however, were considerable, and only the ablest managers achieved it. Local banks were often intimately connected with local business interests. The Lille branch was faced with interlocking directorates between the local cotton and flax spinning industries and local banks. The Bank almost always found itself at a disadvantage when competing with local banks, 'both as to commercial and local knowledge, and because the type of native business will be second rate and frequently dangerous'.[46] Moreover, strong cartel arrangements between banks in France considerably restricted the freedom of manoeuvre of the Foreign Bank.

Table 2 provides a profile, by nationality, of the sources of deposits of, and the advances made by the Lloyds and National Provincial Foreign Bank by the end of 1937.

Table 2 :  Deposits and Advances of Lloyds and National
Provincial Foreign Bank, by Nationalities, December 1937

(in £ sterling)

| | Deposits | % Total | Advances | % Total |
|---|---|---|---|---|
| British | 2,139,000 | 15.6 | 611,000 | 31.0 |
| French | 5,552,000 | 40.6 | 489,000 | 24.8 |
| American | 1,323,000 | 9.7 | 21,000 | 1.1 |
| Belgian | 1,381,000 | 10.1 | 669,000 | 34.0 |
| Swiss | 479,000 | 3.5 | 1,000 | 0.1 |
| Others | 2,799,000 | 20.5 | 178,000 | 9.0 |
| TOTAL | 13,673,000 | – | 1,969,000 | – |

The greater part of the deposits were in sterling, a fact which was to contribute greatly to the Bank's difficulties in the mid-1930s. By the end of 1937, following a period of declining franc deposits, 12.3 per cent of the Bank's deposits were in French francs, 5.9 per cent in Belgian francs, 5.1 per cent in Swiss francs, 13.6 per cent in US dollars, and almost all the remainder in sterling.[47]

Thus the Bank, although its principal field of activity was France, was in a situation where its French franc deposits were less than one-fifth of the total of its deposits in sterling. The sterling could not be employed for advances, while the francs regularly proved insufficient even for current requirements. Moreover, the franc deposits showed a high volatility, partly because they were held by relatively few people. In December 1937, 22 per cent of the franc deposits were in 24 hands. During one week in May 1936, when the Popular Front Government was formed, some Fcs 35 million (£240,067) were withdrawn. The Bank, by contrast, could not dispose of its sterling deposits, of which less than 9 per cent were lent.[48]

The main profits of the Bank were derived throughout the period from exchange earnings. Table 1 provides an indication of their importance to the earning capacity of the Foreign Bank. The Riviera branches, Paris, Brussels, the London branches of the Bank in the City and Haymarket, were all heavily dependent on exchange earnings. Even at a commercial branch such as Le Havre, exchange earnings contributed 42 per cent of the total working profit in 1936.[49] The difficulty with this situation was that these earnings were highly unpredictable, and varied widely from year to year. The Paris branch, for example, made a total profit in exchange of £677,025 between 1918 and 1933. The mean was £42,314 per annum, the lowest earnings £4,819 in 1919, and the highest £202,330 in 1921.[50] The Bank could never take a level of earnings for granted from one year to the next, and throughout the period the management longed for profitability to be based on 'ordinary' or 'normal' banking business.[51]

In 1935 and 1936 the Bank was badly hit by a crisis of the French franc. The Bank's accounts were always greatly influenced by fluctuations in the rates of exchange, for the simple reason that its capital and reserves were held in sterling. By the early 1930s a general pattern had emerged that the French branches made an overall loss, while the London end of the business made a profit. Every year, when the Profit and Loss account was drawn up in sterling, it was necessary to remit from London profits a sufficient number of francs to liquidate the deficit in the French Profit and Loss account. Fluctuations in the exchange rate made a significant impact on the size of these transactions. In 1931 the rate was 115 francs to the pound. It fell to Fr. 83 in 1935, and then rose to 124 in 1937. These movements affected the Bank's overall 'profitability'. In 1935, for example, the Bank made a loss in francs of Fr. 11,317,000. At the prevailing exchange rate of 75 francs to the pound London had to transmit £151,000 to France. During the same year, total profits in London amounted to £121,000 and branches in other countries earned £15,000, so the net result was a declared 'loss' of £15,000. A lower exchange rate would have transformed this 'loss' into a 'profit'.[52]

During 1935 Lloyds and National Provincial Foreign Bank began to be seriously affected by the growing crisis of the French franc. The 'Poincare franc', established in 1928, came under increasing attack on the exchange markets. From the early 1930s the lack of confidence in the currency led to increasing franc withdrawals as depositors switched to dollars or sterling securities or cash. During 1935 this trickle became a flood. French franc deposits in the Bank fell by 30 per cent during 1935.[53] The Bank, already short of francs and with many of its assets frozen in bad debts, was faced with a liquidity crisis. The Bank was reluctant to buy francs in London and transmit them to France, for if devaluation occurred the francs sent over would have had a smaller sterling value than the sterling resources used to purchase the francs. So the Bank resorted to raising francs on the 'forward' exchange market. As the market was working at a discount of some 6/16 per cent throughout 1935, a heavy loss on each transaction resulted.[54] The Foreign Bank was unable to meet this heavy cost, and at the end of 1935 the Parent Banks were obliged to give it a 'gift' of £150,000.[55] Despite this, the Bank was eventually forced to buy francs outright at rates from Fcs. 75

upward. The situation was not saved until the new Blum government decided to devalue the Franc in September 1936. The 'horrible nightmare', the General Manager wrote, was finally over.[56]

Other nightmares remained. The Bank had been hit, as were all British banks, by the 'Standstill' agreements which had been negotiated in 1931 following the Austrian banking crisis in the May of that year. The first 'Standstill' agreement, signed on 19 August 1931, had aimed at precluding any attempt at the mass withdrawal of deposits and credit facilities from, in particular, Germany. It bound creditors in Britain, France, America and seven other countries to maintain their acceptance, time-deposits and cash advances for a period of six months. The agreement was subsequently renewed every year, becoming an exclusively Anglo-German arrangement. By September 1934 Britain was owed some £34 million.[57] Under the 'Standstill' agreement, Lloyds and National Provincial Foreign Bank was left with a liability of £602,000, Swiss francs 1,112,800, and French francs 12,467,000. Although the interest was paid, the 'disturbing query', as one bank memorandum put it in December 1935, was whether the 'principal amount [was] to be regarded as a doubtful debt'.[58] It was gradually realised that this was one more frozen asset. The Parent Banks once again had to come to the rescue. In 1936 the Parent Banks made a Special Payment of £200,000 to the Contingency Fund as a reserve against losses likely to accrue from the Standstill debt, and a further £250,000 was subscribed to cover losses on the Standstill position.[59]

A further blow came in 1937, when 'irregularities' were discovered at the City Office of the Bank. This was one of the few profit-making branches, but the problem was really that the profits had all stemmed from speculative exchange transactions.[60] The affair at the City Office finally provoked major reforms. The extremely able manager of the Roubaix branch was transferred from Paris to London. The policy of reducing branches, especially in tourist centres, was extended. In 1934 and 1935 the Bank had attempted to persuade the Westminster and Barclays to agree to a rational reduction of the number of branches owned by the three banks in France.[61] After the two other banks had refused to co-operate, Lloyds and National Provincial took unilateral action. Cannes and Nice were closed in July 1938, Biarritz, St Jean and Pau in October 1938.[62] Moreover, in December 1938 it was finally agreed that the phrase 'A British Bank conducted on British lines' should be omitted from the Bank's advertisements.[63]

The Board and its Chairman, Colin Campbell, watched the events of the late 1930s with increasing pessimism. In October 1937, after the revelations of the City Office irregularities, Campbell spoke of his desire to secure 'a gradual curtailment of the business in the hope that a way may be found in a few years' time for getting out altogether'. The Bank, he continued, 'gets no help from any quarter . . . we only get the leavings of business from the commercial community; and we are told quite frankly by the Bank of England that there is no scope for us in France and that we are not wanted there. Under these circumstances it is indeed an uphill fight that we are engaged in.'[64]

By 1939 it was obvious that the Bank had got the worst of the 'uphill fight'. Disaster had followed disaster, and the Bank had only survived through the support of its two Parents. Between 1921 and 1939 Lloyds and National Provincial had received total dividends from their subsidiaries of £203,000. In return, they had paid out during the 1930s £900,000 to cover bad debts in France, £150,000 to cover the 'swap' operations in 1935, and £450,000 to meet the German Standstill debts. For much of the decade, a 1937 report observed, it appeared that 'the Bank was run mainly for the benefit of the staff'. Between 1932 and 1936, while total net profit was a bare £13,000, the total paid out in salaries and allowances was £1,777,000.[65]

The Westminster Foreign and Barclays Banks found themselves equally engaged in an 'uphill fight' during the inter-war years. They too were hit by irregularities, German Standstill, and the crisis over the franc, although in comparison with the Lloyds and National Provincial Foreign Bank their performance seemed almost successful.

The Westminster Foreign Bank came to grief early in its life in Spain. In the immediate post-war period various fiscal measures, such as a tax on the total amounts of foreign banks' nominal capital and reserves, greatly reduced the opportunities of the Bank conducting profitable operations in Spain. Bad management, however, was the main weakness of the Bank. The Bank was soon hit by the same story of bad debts and declining business that had plagued the Lloyds and the National Provincial Foreign Bank. A report in March 1922 discovered that the Barcelona branch had a mere 32 depositors. In Bilbao, the staff costs exceeded the total gross income from all sources. Only the Madrid branch made reasonable profits, although again largely from exchange transactions. As a result of this report it was decided to close all the branches in Spain except Madrid.[66] Madrid itself, however, was hit the following year by agitation by the bank clerks' syndicate. The Westminster Foreign Bank refused to negotiate with the union, and the Madrid branch was also closed. The liquidation of the Madrid branch was finally achieved in March 1924, and the whole Spanish venture written off at a cost of £81,247.[67]

The Bank continued to operate in France and Belgium. The policy was tightly controlled from London; an attempt had been made to control all the French branches from Paris in 1919 but this had been reversed after the Lidbury inspection later in that year. From 1920 all branches were individually accountable to the London management of the Bank. Lidbury's policy was one of extreme 'caution and providence'.[68] The Bank had got off to a spectacularly unsuccessful start. By March 1921 it had accumulated a trading loss of £426,063, and total loss to the Parent had amounted to £965,810.[69] Lidbury was determined that such losses should never recur. Indeed, although he could see no immediate way of the Bank extracting itself from the Continent, for a time he hoped for a merger of all three of the British banks on the Continent. 'Where there is no permanent livelihood for three', he wrote in 1922, 'there may be quite a decent thing for one'.[70]

The great difficulty for the Bank in the inter-war years was that Lidbury's tight conservative control left no room for any expansion of the business.

From the middle of the 1920s the Bank began to experience falling deposits in France. During 1927 one member of the Board argued for a new strategy for the bank, based on the 'development of the commercial side of our business'. This meant that Head Office should not control too closely the local managements and what control it did exercise should be 'judiciously and sympathetically exercised, without carping criticism, and with the recognition of possible differences of method in the examination and appraisement of any proposal entailing risk'.[71] Lidbury's highly conservative policy, however, was maintained, and with hindsight it is clear that this was the right policy. The Westminster Foreign Bank was affected both by Standstill and by the cost of the franc crisis in 1935 and 1936, which it was also forced to meet by 'swapping'.[72] The Bank was also not immune from 'irregularities'. In the early 1930s the Bank lost Frs. 1 million through defalcations at the Paris branch. The Bank, however, was spared the very serious bad debt position and trading losses of the Lloyds and National Provincial Foreign Bank.

Barclays Bank (France) also fared badly, although not as badly as the Lloyds and National Provincial Foreign Bank. During 1921, the last year of Cox and Co.'s (France) existence, the business had made a trading loss of 20.5 million francs.[73] Barclays subsequently experienced more problems than they had anticipated in making the business profitable. Ignorance of local conditions and ill-advised lending led to a growing bad debt problem. By 1925 the Bank was described as experiencing 'hard times'.[74]

During the early 1930s the Bank's fortunes in France fell to their lowest point. 'Conditions in France are very bad and getting worse', a memorandum observed in November 1934. 'In many of its Branches the Bank finds it impossible to make profits, and its reserves are practically exhausted.'[75] Apart from the external problems faced by the other two Banks, Barclays Bank (France) was additionally handicapped by two other problems. The first was that many of the Bank's branches were housed in very lavish premises, with 'more than twice its capital locked up in this way'. The second problem was that by 1934 Barclays Bank (France), for reasons of Group policy, had accumulated investments worth £315,345 in Barclays' loss-making Italian venture and the Banque de Commerce in Antwerp, and the tying up of the Bank's assets in these ventures had an additional depressing effect on its profitability.[76] In 1935 the Board decided on a policy of strict economy measures in levels of staff and salaries.

Barclays Bank (France), however, was a comparative success compared to Barclays' investments in Italy. This was the most bizarre of the Continental schemes of the British banks. In October 1924 Barclays Bank was promised that if it opened in Rome, it would be guaranteed 'within a very short space of time . . . the custom of most important Religious Societies in Rome, including that of the Vatican'.[77] An International Estates Company was planned, which it was hoped would eventually control the Church's finances and 'lay the foundations of an organization which might ultimately develop into a commercial Vatican'.[78] Barclays were to become the bankers of the 'commercial Vatican'.

The Chairman of Barclays, F.C. Goodenough, responded eagerly to this proposal, and plans for a Rome branch proceeded quickly, with the prospect of the rich business to be secured during the 1925 Holy Year acting as a major incentive. £100,000 was spent on buying a building in Rome, and in 1925 a branch of Barclays Bank S.A.I. was opened strategically situated at the foot of the Spanish Steps in the Piazza di Spagna. Barclays' aim, Goodenough wrote to Duncan Balfour, the resident Director in Italy, in February 1925, was 'to carry on a quiet private business, not launching out into commercial business in Italy'.[79]

At first all went well. By March Balfour was able to report to Goodenough that on both 'the religious side and the commercial the Bank is undoubtedly progressing'. Balfour had seen the head of the Augustinians and the Jesuits, and they had promised Barclays some business. He had also had great hopes of large deposits from one order of English nuns, who 'when they go to St Peter's to Mass invariably proceed there in their own private cars, and they live in one of the most magnificent houses in Rome'.[80] At the beginning of 1926 the Vatican itself placed a small deposit at the Bank, and a new branch was soon opened at Genoa.

Unfortunately, this proved to be the high point of Barclays' business. The scheme for a 'commercial Vatican' collapsed. By the end of 1927 problems were arising from unsecured loans and bad debts.[81] During the following year the Bank made a trading loss of £18,000, apart from bad debts, and during 1929 and 1930 losses began to mount. In July 1930 Goodenough complained that these had 'been due chiefly to wrong information in regard to the standing of customers, their reliability and also perhaps, their integrity'.[82] A new conservative lending policy was adopted, but this was too late to prevent further large losses. 'The Bank', Goodenough wrote to Italy in 1934, 'has passed through two phases — the first was one of disaster, and the second, one of liquidation'.[83] By 1934 all Barclays in London hoped was that the Italian bank would become self-supporting. Expenses were cut, loans reduced, and in 1937 the branch at Genoa was closed. The Rome branch lived on small earnings from exchange transactions until the outbreak of war.

Throughout the inter-war period, the Midland Bank watched the subsidiaries of its four United Kingdom rivals floundering in their different ways on the Continent, and adhered strictly to its faith in the 'correspondent' business. On the formation of the Irish Free State in 1924 the Midland Bank disinvested in that country because, in the words of the Chairman, 'it is not the policy of the Midland Bank to own branches in territories outside the United Kingdom'.[84] The correspondent business flourished in these years. Large credits were opened for Continental banks, and for various foreign governments. During the 1920s the Midland Bank established close links with various Soviet banks. In October 1924 the Board agreed that the Russian State Bank could deposit £1 million with the Bank which was to be used to finance trade between Britain and Soviet Russia.[85] In subsequent years other Soviet banks such as the Banque Commerciale et Industrielle de L'URSS, placed deposits with the Midland Bank.[86]

As Table 3 indicates, the Overseas Branch of the Midland Bank saw a considerable expansion in profitability during the inter-war years.

Table3 :  Profitability of Midland Bank Overseas Branch 1918-1937[87]

| Years | Cumulative net profits £'000s |
|---|---|
| 1918-21 | 1,096 |
| 1922-25 | 1,960 |
| 1926-29 | 2,966 |
| 1930-33 | 4,726 |
| 1934-37 | 6,858 |

The business proved particularly lucrative during the 1930s, and between 1931 and 1937 the Overseas Branch's net profits represented 23.1 per cent of the published profits of the Bank. These profits came largely from correspondent banking. In 1939 the Chairman observed that the Bank transacted 'probably the largest share of the overseas business passing through London'.[88]

By 1940 the Midland Bank had even more reason to be grateful that it had avoided direct Continental commitments. As the German armies attacked and occupied France and Belgium, and Fascist Italy entered the war on the side of the Axis, the British staffs of the three banks fled to the nearest seaport and were evacuated back to Britain. It was a tragic, but rather appropriate symbol of their banks' performance on the Continent over the previous two decades.

## IV

During the years of the Occupation, the French and Belgian branches of the three banks were run by locals. Their experience was broadly similar. Until the summer of 1942 they were left with some freedom of manoeuvre. After then the German administration exercised a considerable amount of control over their policy. During this period all three banks earned profits, due, as the Board of the Lloyds and National Provincial Foreign Bank was informed after the Liberation of France, 'to the rates charged to the unsound class of customers who were brought to the Bank at the time'.[89] The local officials of Lloyds and National Provincial Foreign Bank, in particular, emerged from the German occupation unscathed from accusations of collaboration. The Geneva branch of the Bank had remained under the control of London throughout the War, and assisted the Allied war effort by the purchase of German, Italian and French notes for the British Legation, 'to be used by British Secret Service'.[90] Table 1 shows the remarkable recovery in the Banks' profitability once it was stripped of its French and Belgian branches.

The immediate post-war years were ones of great difficulty. The branches of all the banks had been separated from Head Office control for long periods, and this gave rise to serious problems of readjustment. The years after the War were ones of great financial stringency for the Continental countries. Banks became subject to greater control from the State. Post-war legislation in Belgium compelled banks to create a statutory reserve inside the country. This meant that the Lloyds and National Provincial Bank, for example, which before 1939 had no reserves inside Belgium, was obliged to create a reserve equal to 7 per cent of sight and short-term liabilities.[91]

Despite these difficulties, the post-war decade saw an apparent improvement in the fortunes of Lloyds and National Provincial Foreign Bank. Between 1946 and 1951 the total profits of the Bank amounted to £397,364.[92] Yet the structure of the business remained very much as in the pre-war period. Some branches, such as Roubaix and Bordeaux, developed or retained profitable business connections. The business of several other branches, however, remained static. Geneva lived off United Nations accounts, as it had previously lived off League of Nations business. The Lille branch derived 20 per cent of its gross revenue in 1951 from the account of one firm. The tourist trade in the South of France partially recovered, although it was reported in 1951 that Monte Carlo had lost its position as a fashionable resort 'and the summer visitors, although more numerous, are of the "paid holiday" class'.[93]

By the early 1950s one of the shareholders of the Bank, the National Provincial Bank, had had enough. The National Provincial Bank had paid out some £750,000 to the foreign bank, and received a mere £110,250 in dividends.[94] There was little doubt that if National Provincial's original capital and subsequent payments had been invested elsewhere higher returns might have been earned. National Provincial had never felt that it obtained its fair share of whatever benefits did stem from owning the foreign bank. The very name of the Bank led many people to assume that it was a Lloyds venture. A National Provincial manager in 1924 referred to the prevalent feeling that 'apart from a shareholding interest, this Bank does not get a full share of reciprocal business'.[95] In an exchange of letters about the future of the Bank between Colin Campbell and Henry Bell of Lloyds Bank, Campbell observed that there was not much difference between their respective views 'except you suggest that the business abroad attracts a great deal of business to our two home banks, and as far as the NP is concerned we get practically nothing of any consequence'.[96]

In 1954 the National Provincial Bank sold its shareholding in the Foreign Bank to Lloyds, and in 1955 the Bank, under the new name of Lloyds Bank (Foreign) Ltd., became a wholly-owned subsidiary of Lloyds Bank Ltd. Ironically, the departure of National Provincial was followed by an upturn in the Bank's fortunes. This was due, in part, to improved management and especially the work of M.H. Finlinson, who was General Manager between 1956 and 1964. By 1960/61 the gross profit had reached £314,991, which after tax and writing off of exceptional items made a working profit of £132,000. The amount of deposits increased from £23.6 million in 1956 to £47.7 million in 1961, and the amount of advances from £5 million in 1956 to £26.2 million in 1961. Finlinson worked hard to improve the quality of the

Bank's management. 'On the Continent', he wrote in 1961, 'we now have a first class managerial team, average age 48, keen and energetic'. Together with most of British business, the Bank eagerly awaited Britain's entry to the Common Market. 'With Britain's application to join the Common Market', Finlinson observed, 'I do not think it is too much to hope that we shall be able to extend still further our continental banking connections'.[97]

In fact, events took a different course. In 1964 Finlinson was appointed Vice-Chairman with special responsibility for the Bank's development. Under his supervision, the Bank was transformed, during the 1960s, from a small deposit bank operating in four countries to a major international bank. In 1971 Lloyds European interests were merged with the British Bank of London and South America, and the new company became known as Lloyds Bank International in 1974.[98]

The improved fortunes of Lloyds — and the other banks — European operations during the 1960s were closely related to the opportunities provided by the emergence of the Euro-currency markets. These markets were developed by the American banks. As the post-war dollar shortage gave way to a great wash of US dollars by the end of the 1950s, and as markets for such funds began to appear in America and Europe (such as British local authorities), various American banks began to open branches abroad, particularly in London, in order to escape the domestic restrictions which prevented them from directly dealing in such markets. In Britain, government and Bank of England restrictions, and the clearing banks' own cartel, made it difficult for the banks to participate directly in Euro-currency markets. They could, however, participate through their overseas banks or branches. They could offer market rates for deposits and demand market rates for loans in a manner not open to them in domestic banking.

The European banks of Barclays and Westminster Banks followed a broadly similar pattern of development to Lloyds after 1945. Barclays recovered control of its Italian subsidiary in 1945. There was little enthusiasm for continuing the business. A report written in 1947, by the Deputy Chairman of the Bank, A.W. Tuke, held out little prospect of increasing the Bank's business in Italy, unless the Bank resorted to certain devices used by Italian banks to attract capital. 'We must either do as the Romans do', Tuke observed, 'or do without their business. Personally, I prefer the latter'.[99] Barclays, however, were reluctant to shut the whole affair down. There was a feeling that British business might soon expand into Italy, and that Barclays' presence in Rome was 'appreciated by the British Community'.[100] It was hoped that business might look up in 1950, which was a Holy Year. It was argued that Barclays' prestige would suffer if it withdrew from Rome. Above all, there was little point in selling the Bank's only asset, the magnificent building in the Piazza di Spagna, for inconvertible lire.

The position of the Bank, however, got steadily worse. 'From the point of view of Profit and Loss', Tuke reported in April 1948, 'the Bank is again getting into deep water'. The large Head Office staff, and 'the killing cost of maintaining Englishmen in this country at the present time', were major burdens. Tuke could think of no solution for the high costs except the 'very drastic one' of not attempting 'to maintain social contacts on a high level', which he dismissed as unpractical.[101] During 1949 plans were being made for the Holy Year. A Barclays representative long resident in the United States was instructed to proceed to Rome, because the Bank was setting its 'cap at the Americans in connection with the Holy Year'.[102] Holy Year, however, brought a miracle of another kind. Early in 1950 the Banca Commerciale Italiana offered Barclays £110,000 to be paid in sterling in London for its Rome bank. Barclays willingly accepted.

Barclays Bank (France) continued to operate after 1945, although never earning high profits.[103] During the 1960s, however, it was revitalised and the Barclays group expanded elsewhere in Europe. Barclays European Representative opened an office in Zurich in 1961, and ten years later Barclays formed, with a 62½ per cent holding, the Societé Bancaire Barclays (Suisse) S.A. which opened a branch in Geneva. Meanwhile, in 1963 a holding was obtained in the Banque de Bruxelles. The Euro-currency markets again provided the main drive behind this expansion. In 1971 Barclays Bank S.A. became part of Barclays Bank International, which was formed from the old Barclays Bank (D.C.O.).[104]

The Westminster Foreign Bank also remained fairly dormant until the 1960s, when it began to become involved in various consortium banks. Following the merger with the National Provincial Bank in 1968, the new National Westminster Bank used the Westminister Foreign Bank for a policy of aggressive expansion on the Continent and elsewhere.[105]

It was, similarly, not until the 1960s that the Midland Bank's international banking strategy began to change radically. The Midland Bank had experienced a very big expansion in corresponding banking after 1945. By 1949 the Midland Bank was reported to have 16,000 correspondents.[106] The value of foreign exchange transactions handled by the Bank rose from £27 million in 1949 to over £135 million in 1954. Payments made or received on the instruction of overseas banks each year more than doubled between 1952 and 1962 to reach 1.23 million transactions by that year. By the late 1950s, however, the Midland Bank, faced with the growth of the international money markets, was beginning to feel a need for diversification in its international operations. The first product of this new thought came in 1963, when the Bank joined three Continental banks, the Amsterdam-Rotterdam Bank, the Deutsche Bank and the Banque Société Generale de Belgique in an informal agreement to coordinate their banking operations in Europe. This was the beginning of Midland's involvement in a growing number of international partnerships and agreements.[107]

## V

There were, and still are, a number of alternative forms of overseas representation for a bank. The principal alternatives are: the correspondent relationship; participation in consortiums or joint banks with local or international banks; the purchase of foreign subsidiaries and the retention of local autonomy; representative (that is, non-banking) offices; and overseas branches, with a bank operating under its own name for private and corporate customers. Only the Midland Bank, of the 'Big Five' British clearing banks, opted for the first alternative in the period before 1960. There can be no doubt that the Midland's policy proved very lucrative. In contrast, the other clearing banks opted for the fifth alternative, at least so far as their Continental activities were concerned, and this strategem produced at best only mediocre returns. The experience of the three Continental subsidiaries of the clearing banks was remarkably similar. In each case the banks expanded rapidly during the First World War. Their fortunes peaked in the early 1920s and there followed a period of stagnation or decline. The 1930s were extremely difficult for all the banks, and especially for the Lloyds and National Provincial Foreign Bank. The banks were allowed to stay in business during these years largely because of prestige considerations on the part of the Parent Banks. All four Parent Banks paid heavily for any prestige gained. The fifteen years after 1945 were marginally profitable, but totally undramatic. Barclays was glad to sell off its Italian bank, the National Provincial was eager to pull out of its joint venture with Lloyds. It was not until the 1960s that these small Continental ventures emerged as useful bases for their Parent Banks' operations in the new Euro-currency markets. By the 1970s the transformation into international banks was complete, and together with the Midland Bank, these banks were heavily involved in international consortiums and joint banking ventures.

The poor performance of the British banks on the Continent before 1960 cannot be explained entirely by difficult economic and financial conditions. British banks were successful in other parts of the world, even in the inter-war years. Indeed, the achievements of British overseas banks in the Empire and the Americas made the clearing banks' disappointment in their European adventures all the greater. 'I have had a good long experience with commercial business overseas both in my own business in India and as Director of the Chartered Bank operating throughout the East'. Colin Campbell wrote in October 1937, 'but working in the British Empire is easy compared to trying to do so in a foreign country'.[108]

The three banks faced certain specific problems in trying to do business on the Continent. The most obvious problem was the different legal and banking systems and traditions functioning on the Continent, which were made additionally difficult by foreign languages. This all too often led the banks to rely on managerial staff of a quality they would never have considered in Britain. Many of the British staff of Continental subsidiaries do not seem to have been of the highest ability. It is sometimes suggested that the general quality of British bank staff in the inter-war years was not uniformly high. The sudden completion in 1917-18 of the amalgamation process, which reduced the number of leading banks to the Big Five, gave the banks a miscellaneous staff from the various merged banks who may not have been particularly appropriate for the bigger groups into which the smaller banks were absorbed. It is possible that a disproportionate number of the weaker managers were despatched to the Continental branches.[109]

A further problem was managerial control. The three banks possessed different forms of organisation for controlling their Continental subsidiaries, but none of these proved satisfactory. If local managements were given too much freedom, it could, as the Lloyds and National Provincial Foreign Bank discovered, prove almost fatal. On the other hand, too much control from London meant that business could not develop at all. Business conditions were very different from the United Kingdom, and local managers needed sufficient autonomy to adapt their branches to these local conditions. Yet 'local conditions' were sometimes very different from British ones, and this could give rise to unfortunate complications. All three banks experienced staff 'irregularities' during the years in question. In particular, a number of staff were involved in exchange dealings on their own account. To the Parent Banks in London it was outrageous that staff should undertake large exchange speculations, but in countries such as Switzerland where the branches operated such behaviour was the norm, and free from any taint of 'dishonesty'.

The three banks also suffered from a chronic failure to identify their market. They all began with the central idea of serving British people, and British business, on the Continent. By the late 1920s it was obvious that this market was not sufficient, but by then the banks were too well-established in their original moulds to develop an adequate substitute. There was much talk about developing local French and Belgian business, but only exceptional managers were able to secure large amounts of local commercial and industrial custom. Green field investment in competition with local banks is rarely easy, and in this case it was exceptionally difficult because of the bank's origins. Even after Lloyds and National Provincial Foreign Bank had decided to chase local business, the Bank retained a large proportion of high-cost Britishers on its staff — some 44 per cent of the staff in France in 1937 were British — and this made it additionally hard to attract such custom. Significantly, the two more successful banks, Barclays and Westminster Foreign, operated with a far lower proportion of British staff. The upshot was that all three banks ended up with a hodge-podge of expatriate business and low-quality local business, and existed largely off exchange earnings.

In addition to these identifiable problems, British bankers seemed prone to an unusual degree of bad judgement, even eccentricity, whenever they crossed the Channel. The inflated aims and expensive premises acquired during the First World War, which burdened the three banks throughout the inter-war period, is one instance of this, and Barclays' pursuit of Church money is another. Yet these highly optimistic activities were usually underpinned by a lack of faith that profits could *really* be earned on the Continent. Indeed, from the late 1920s there was a lack of faith in Europe itself. 'I have a feeling firmly fixed in my mind', a writer told Colin Campbell in May 1936, 'that some day we may be thankful if our commitments in [France] are on the light side'.[110] This attitude was partly the result of experience, and partly the cause of that experience. Perhaps, as the textbooks say, doing business in the Empire was just *too* easy compared 'to trying to do so in a foreign country'.

An obvious question arises from the story told on the previous pages: how far were the Continental activities of the banks typical of the clearing banks' performance in Britain itself in the inter-war years? Unfortunately, until more is known from internal sources about the history of British banking since 1914, this must remain an idle, but interesting, speculation.

*Business History Unit*
*London School of Economics*

NOTES

\* I would like to thank Barclays Bank International, Lloyds Bank International, Lloyds Bank Limited, the Midland Bank, and the National Westminster bank for permission to consult their archives. Mr Edwin Green, Dr Leslie Hannah and Professor Leslie Pressnell, the archivists of the above banks and an anonymous referee made some very helpful comments on earlier drafts of this article.

1. The Reddaway Report estimated that nearly 70 per cent of British foreign direct investment (excluding oil) was placed in the Commonwealth between 1955 and 1963, 25 per cent in the Americas and 5.1 per cent in Western Europe. W.B. Reddaway, *Effects of UK Direct Investment Overseas*, Interim Report 1966 and Final Report 1968. By contrast, Britain has tended to trade quite extensively with the Continent over the last hundred years, although the period 1930-60 also saw this at a low level.

2. A first attempt to generalise about the overseas investment policies of British multinationals is J. Stopford, 'The origins of British-based Multinational Manufacturing Enterprises', *Business History Review*, 1974. Stopford dates the switch of British companies to the Empire as the inter-war period, and argues that Europe proved unattractive because of its 'highly innovative local firms buttressed by cartels and government policy' combined with 'inflation and unrest'. (p. 327). This is a plausible, but far from empirically proven, generalisation.

3. It is regretable that the official histories of the banks say very little about their Continental activities. See R.S. Sayers, *Lloyds Bank in the History of English Banking* (Oxford, 1951), p. 251; T. Gregory, *The Westminster Bank through a century* (London, 1936), II, pp. 13-4. The subject gets most coverage in A.W. Tuke and R. Gillman, *Barclays Bank Limited* (London, 1972), pp. 56-73.

4. A.S.J. Baster, *The International Banks* (London, 1935), pp. 40-50.

5. W.F. Spalding, 'The establishment and growth of foreign branch banks in London', *Journal of the Institute of Bankers*, November 1911.

6. E. Green, *The Making of a Modern Banking Group* (London, 1979), pp. 66-71.

7. Ibid., p. 72.

8. General Secretary to R.E. Lambton, 3 November 1914, Lloyds Bank Limited Archives (hereafter LBL) File: Lloyds Bank (France) 28 July 1911-31 December 1914.

9. History of the Foreign Bank, n.d., National Westminster Bank Archives (hereafter NW) File: 1494.

10. H.V. Burrell, 'The opening of foreign branches by English Banks', *Journal of the Institute of Bankers*, January 1914.

11. E. Green, op. cit., p. 72.

12. D.A. Miller to E. Holden, 18/31 May 1917, Midland Bank Archives (hereafter MB) File: Petrograd Branch.

13. W.O. Stevenson's Report on his recent visit to Rome, n.d. (?1924), Barclays Bank International Archives (hereafter BBI).

14. H.S. Foxwell, 'The Financing of Industry and Trade', *Economic Journal*, December 1917.

15. A.S.J. Baster, op. cit., p. 193.

16. Report of the Departmental Committee on Financial Facilities for Trade, 31 August 1916, Cmd 8346 (1916).

17. A.S.J. Baster, op. cit., pp. 194-8.
18. Mr Rae: Report on Spanish Branches, 10 March 1922, NW, File: 1642.
19. W.O. Stevenson's Report on his recent visit to Rome (n.d. ?1924), BBI.
20. Notes for Mr Cunnick by Mr Bell, 29 June 1917, NW File: 4243.
21. Mr Rae's Report on the Position and Prospects of the Foreign Business, 15 May 1923, NW, File: 1642.
22. A.W. Tuke and R. Gillman, *Barclays Bank Limited 1926-1969* (London, 1972), pp. 56-8. File: Cox & Co. London and Cox & Co. France Ltd., BBI.
23. Memorandum by F.C. Goodenough, 31 August 1917, BBI, File: Private Papers of F.C. Goodenough.
24. History of the Foreign Bank (n.d.), NW, File: 1494.
25. Lloyds and National Provincial Foreign Bank Board Minute Book, Minute 27 January 1921, Lloyds Bank International Archives (hereafter LBI).
26. Chairman's Report to Annual General Meeting of Midland Bank, 23 January 1914 and 26 January 1917.
27. Midland Bank Board Minutes, 2 February 1917, MB.
28. D.A. Miller to E. Holden, 24/7 May 1917, MB, File: Petrograd Branch.
29. Midland Bank Board Minutes, 2 February 1917 and 16 March 1917, MB.
30. S.B. Murray to E. Molina, 27 April 1917; E. Molina to S.B. Murray, 23 July 1917, MB, File: 30/213-7.
31. Sir Edward Holden's Statement to the Standing Committee on Bank Amalgamations, 12 June 1918, MB.
32. Chairman's Report to Annual General Meeting of Midland Bank, 23 January 1914.
33. E. Green, op. cit., p. 67.
34. Chairman's Report to Annual General Meeting of Midland Bank, 28 January 1921. The new chairman was the Rt. Hon. Reginald Mckenna.
35. C. Jones and H. Barrelet, Report on Investigation Carried out in Paris, 25 April 1938, NW, File: 4246.
36. R.S. Sayers, *The Bank of England 1891-1944*, I (Cambridge 1976), pp. 243-8.
37. Ibid., pp. 259-63.
38. Board Minutes, 28 November 1918, LBI.
39. Ibid., 16 May 1927.
40. Report by F.A. Bease and C.W. Riches, 11 March 1931, NW, File: 4245.
41. Ibid.
42. Board Minutes, LBI.
43. Lloyds and National Provincial Foreign Bank, Report 20 December 1935, NW, File: 4248.
44. The capital of the Bank was £40,000 in 1911. This was raised to £64,000 in 1913, £240,000 in 1914, £480,000 in 1917 and £1.2 million in 1929. The published reserve (there were also other reserves) was £3,011 in 1919. This was raised to £9,257 in 1920, £100,000 in 1921, £150,000 in 1924, £240,000 in 1926 and £250,000 in 1929. It was reduced to £150,000 in 1930, and stayed at that level for the rest of the decade.
45. Colin Campbell to Cecil Jones, 30 July 1936, NW, File: 4244.
46. Report by Mr Riches, 10 December 1935, NW, File: 4247. Report of the Investigation by J. Penny Edwards and Mr W.B. Mayles, 31 March 1938, NW, File: 4251.
47. Report of Investigation by J. Penny Edwards and W.B. Mayles, 31 March 1938, NW, File: 4251. The British total for advances in Table 2 includes £222,000 advanced to French companies under foreign (mainly British) control.
48. Ibid.
49. Ibid.
50. Paris, Profit and Loss figures from 1918, NW, File: 4252.
51. Balance Sheets and AGM Papers, 1923, LBI, Profit and Loss 1946, J.E.H., May 1947, NW, File: 4252.
52. Memorandum on French franc devaluation, 26 October 1936, NW, File: 4244.
53. Report of Investigation by Mr Riches and Mr Stanley, 10 December 1935, NW, File: 4247.
54. Lloyds and National Provincial Foreign Bank Ltd., Report 20 December 1935, NW, File: 4248.
55. Memorandum on Special Payments made by (National Provincial Bank) to L. and N.P., 1943, NW, File: 4252.

56. Cecil Jones to Colin Campbell, 26 September 1936, NW, File: 4244.
57. R.S. Sayers, op. cit., pp. 503-12.
58. Final Report by Mr Riches and Mr Stanley, 10 December 1935, NW, File: 4250.
59. Letter to Mr Cutting, 11 December 1936, NW, File: 4250.
60. Full Inspection: City Office, 18 November 1937, NW, File: 4246.
61. Board Minutes 1934 and 1935, LBI.
62. Committee Meeting, 12 May 1938, NW, File: 4253.
63. Board Minute, 22 December 1938, LBI.
64. Colin Campbell to Alwyn Parker, 25 October 1937, NW, File: 4244.
65. Report of Investigation by Penny Edwards and Mr Mayles, 31 March 1938, NW, File: 4251.
66. Mr Rae, Report on Spanish Branches, 10 March 1922, NW, File: 1642.
67. Historical Notes (n.d.), NW, File: 1494.
68. Hugo Baring to Mr Rae, 4 April 1927, NW, File: 1642.
69. Ibid., Report by Mr Rae and Mr Barthorpe, August and September 1921.
70. Ibid., Mr Lidbury to Mr Rae, 15 August 1922.
71. Ibid., Hugo Baring to Mr Rae, 4 April 1927.
72. 'Secret' Memorandum, 13 June 1936, NW, File: 494.
73. Cox & Co. (France) Ltd., 25 January 1922, BBI, File: Cox & Co. (London) and Cox & Co. (France) Ltd.
74. H.J. Whitaker to F.C. Goodenough, 14 April 1925, BBI, File: Chairman's Overseas Filing-Papers Concerning setting up and ultimate closure of Barclays Italian Subsidiary.
75. Memorandum, 21 November 1934, BBI.
76. Ibid.
77. Mr Szarvasy to Mr Stevenson, 30 October 1924, BBI, File: Chairman's Overseas Filing-Papers Concerning Italian Subsidiary.
78. Ibid.
79. Ibid., Chairman to D. Balfour, 6 February 1925.
80. Ibid., D. Balfour to Chairman, 27 March 1925.
81. Ibid., F.C. Goodenough to D. Balfour, 9 December 1927.
82. Ibid., F.C. Goodenough to D. Balfour, 9 July 1930.
83. Ibid., F.C. Goodenough to D. Balfour, 18 May 1934.
84. E. Green, op. cit., p. 73.
85. Midland Bank Board Minutes, 5 October 1924, MB.
86. Mr Buchanan Diaries, 8 June 1925, MB, File: 30/338.
87. Analysis by Manager of Overseas Branch, June 1938, MB, Overseas Branch Files. The notes attached to this analysis explained that these figures allowed for all bad debts incurred, 'with one exception only: the Austrian Creditanstalt account, which involving a long-term liquidation was taken over by Head Office: eventual loss will be under £50,000'.
88. Chairman's Report to Annual General Meeting of Midland Bank, 26 January 1939.
89. Mr Bezos to Mr Scatcherd, 6 November 1944, NW, File: 4252.
90. Ibid., Report on position of the Bank in Switzerland, 29 October 1945.
91. Ibid., Memorandum on Capital in Belgium, March 1950.
92. Ibid., Memorandum, 15 July 1954.
93. Ibid., Inspection Report on Monte Carlo, January-March 1951.
94. Ibid., Memorandum, 23 June 1952.
95. J.P. Edwards to General Manager in Paris, 6 October 1925, NW, File: 4243. The letter does not appear to have been sent.
96. Colin Campbell to Henry Bell, 27 December 1934, NW, File: 4252.
97. Report by General Manager, 8 November 1961, LBI.
98. D.F. Channon, *British Banking Strategy and the International Challenge* (London, 1977), p. 132.
99. A.W. Tuke's report on Profit and Loss Figures for 1947 and 1948, BBI, File: Chairman's Overseas Filing-Papers Concerning Italian Subsidiary.
100. Ibid.
101. Ibid., Memorandum, 13 April 1948.
102. Ibid., A.W. Tuke to G.E. Meek, 29 June 1949.
103. A.W. Tuke and R. Gillman, op. cit., p. 106.

104. D.F. Channon, op. cit., p. 129.
105. Ibid., p. 132.
106. H. Thackstone, 'Work of the Foreign Branch of a Commercial Bank', in Institute of Bankers, *Current Financial Problems and the City of London* (London, 1949), p. 122.
107. E. Green, op. cit., *passim.*
108. Colin Campbell to Alwyn Parker, 25 October 1937, NW, File: 4244. For the performance of the specialist overseas banks in other parts of the world, see Sir Julian Crossley and John Blandford, *The DCO Story* (London, 1975); D.M. Joslin, *A Century of Banking in Latin America* (Oxford, 1963); and Sir Compton MacKenzie, *Realms of Silver: one hundred years of banking in the East* (London, 1954).
109. I owe this point to Professor Pressnell. The taking back of men who had fought in the First World War, and who were not necessarily suited to continue in their old ruts of jobs, may further have reduced staff competence.
110. Mr G.F. Abell to Colin Campbell, 1 May 1936, NW, File: 4245.

# FAMILY FIRMS AND MANAGERIAL CAPITALISM: THE CASE OF THE INTERNATIONAL MOTOR INDUSTRY

## By ROY CHURCH

'Family firm' is an expression which is commonly employed yet rarely defined. It is a label which has been applied to various kinds of owner-managed firms ranging from personal enterprises, in which owner control is dominant and where the owner is also chief executive, to entrepreneurial organisations: typically, owner-controlled firms which are staffed by managers and where the owners are essentially *rentiers,* lacking either time or inclination to manage. Three characteristics determine the points of focus for discussions of the family firm, although they are not necessarily related: family generations, family ownership, and family management.[1] In the motor industry, which had barely emerged by the beginning of the twentieth century, yet the economics of which required sizeable production units, even in Europe by the early 1920s, there is little scope for discussion of the significance of inheritance in relation to business and managerial development. Among the major mass producers of motor cars with which we shall be concerned, survival of family ownership and management for a period longer than a single generation was exceptional; for this reason family ownership and management will be regarded merely as a special case of owner management, in which the effective locus of control can be identified with a group of proprietorial interests.

Much of the discussion of ownership and control, principally among economists and sociologists, has been bedevilled by disagreement on the criteria for classifying corporate control. For while majority shareholding confers ownership it is not clear how small a percentage of total votes held by an individual or a clearly defined group has been necessary in order to secure minority control, although this might fall short of actual effective control. A recent review of the literature on ownership and control concluded that only a case by case approach could reveal a perpetuation of control by an individual, group, or family which did not possess substantial share ownership.[2] The classification employed in this article, therefore, depends upon behavioural, as much as upon financial, criteria, for the simple dichotomy of owner-control or control by professional manager is both deceptively inadequate and unsatisfactory for the purpose of establishing both the form and the degree to which family influence has persisted among the world's producers of motor cars, and to assess the effects it has had upon performance.

The separation of ownership from control was accompanied by the development of forms of owner-managed firms which may be categorised as follows: those in which owner-managers worked with minimal hierarchies, equivalent to the 'personal enterprises' defined by Sargant Florence; those characterised by extensive hierarchies, defined by Sargant Florence as entrepreneurial enterprises; and enterprises which were managerially supervised, in which external directors continued to own a controlling share of the stock and participated regularly in board and committee meetings. This represents another variant of owner-management, differing in the degree to which a contrast was to be found with the manager-managed firms, in which managers exercised control over the selection of board members – in accordance with the definitions adopted by Berle and Means.[3] Managerial enterprises were typically large with diversified stock ownership, in which full-time salaried managers took decisions at all levels while the owners, possessing neither the time nor commitment to exercise authority, concerned themselves more with dividends than with the operation of their company.[4] As effective competition in national and international markets required an increasing size of enterprise and greater financial resources the traditional form of owner-managed enterprise was gradually transformed, although the overall pattern, in which owner-managers continued to play a role, persisted. Hitherto, in societies where business relations depended upon trust and reciprocity and where information and personal communications were critical to success in business conducted before the era of large-scale joint-stock enterprise,[5] the combination of ownership and management within a single institution over several generations had so often enabled the family firm to provide a continuous supply of managerial competence and capital. After the industrial revolution the social, economic, and cultural environment of Europe, but especially of the United States, provided a climate which became less congenial to the family firm of the traditional type. By the First World War the large firm possessing extensive managerial hierarchies was becoming commonplace in the US, whereas in Europe personal and entrepreneurial enterprises, owner-managed firms with minimal hierarchies, were to retain their dominance at least until the second half of the twentieth century.[6]

The significance of the transformation from personal and entrepreneurial to managerial organisations depends, of course, upon perceived discrepancies between the goals and behaviour of owner-managers and those of the 'professional' managers. In a major comparative study of British and American firms published in 1953[7] Sargant Florence listed the defects commonly associated with business leadership in companies where ownership and managerial control were either in the hands of an entrepreneur who had grown with his own business or in which the hereditary, dynastic, or aristocratic type of entrepreneur was in command (the archetypal family firm). Sargant Florence reckoned that such business leaders typically soon became resistant to large-scale innovation, that they were averse to co-operation with other companies, and characteristically that both types showed caution with respect to reinvestment. Furthermore, the dynastic leader could be assumed to possess a lower profit maximising drive than any other category of business leader. Later, Carter and

Williams stressed in particular the retarding effect upon growth of the fear within family firms of losing control through the infusion of external finance.[8] From the historian's standpoint, Kindleberger exhibited agnosticism regarding the restraining influence of family firms upon French industrial performance.[9] Having underlined the systematisation and professionalisation of capital management allied to the specialisation of other economic functions as distinguishing features of managerial capitalism, Alfred D. Chandler, Jr. has since stressed the inhibiting influences of personal and entrepreneurial enterprise which was slower to be replaced by managerial enterprise in the UK by some 50 years.[10]

Hannah has been specific in citing the history of the British motor industry between the wars as an example of the role of major owner-managed firms: 'It is difficult to resist the conclusion that in many companies the family vested interest inhibited change which could have been desirable'.[11] In the German context, Tilly remarked that entrepreneurial enterprise remained characteristic of large-scale industry, which 'may have been a severe hindrance to the development of concentrated and multi-divisional enterprise on the American model',[12] while Kocka minimises the difference in motivation between German owner-entrepreneurs and their salaried counterparts; he regards independent owner-managers as having been more concerned with non-economic matters, such as family consideration. For this reason he detects a more intense 'striving for expansion' among those unencumbered by ownership.[13] The overview of European industrial development by Landes implies a similar relationship between ownership and managerial policies.[14] By contrast, Laux, whose research concentrated upon the French motor industry before 1914, rejected the hypothesis that family firms seriously retarded progress in the business sector.[15] Most recently as a general proposition Payne contrasted the positive contribution to economic growth of *small* family business with that of the large public company retaining elements of family control which, based on a review of the British experience since 1918, he concluded, 'may retard economic growth'.[16]

Most of the observations we have referred to are thus consistent with the notion that by comparison with managerial enterprises, the ceiling on performance of family and owner-managed firms, particularly in the corporate sector, has been inferior. In examining the significance of owner-management in the mass production motor car industry we shall identify the chronology of and reasons for its decline, and consider the history and performance of the European and American survivors which, to a greater or lesser degree, retained some of the characteristics of owner-management – even of the family firm – until the second half of the twentieth century.

I

Resembling the pioneering phase of motor production in Europe, family firms were among the first to enter upon the manufacture of luxury motor cars for an upper class clientele. A recent history of the automotive revolution in Detroit describes how, in search of profits to stem their increasingly precarious social and political power, the old families of the Midwest had plunged headlong into the new industry, providing initial finance and a tradition of business enterprise. In 1905 old family companies produced more than half the national vehicle output, a share which by 1910 had fallen to only three per cent, the family firms having sold out to the manufacturers of cars based on interchangeable parts, a consequence of the introduction of mass production methods. At this point many of the old families chose to dispose of their investments in vehicle production completely, rather than change their image and incur greater risks by making lower priced cars, but more importantly, preferring to withdraw from the trade completely rather than lose control of their family firms.[17] Henceforth, successful automobile manufacture demanded mass production and distribution; that, in turn, meant bringing in technical experts, professional managers and additional capital – all of which undermined the traditional prerogatives of the old family stockholders. Even among the early established pioneering firms financial dependence upon financiers doomed the founding engineer-entrepreneurs to progressively diminishing control.[18]

Thus, even before the First World War the American automobile industry had passed beyond the phase when relatively small family firms and owner-managements were characteristic. By the late 1920s even the newcomer owner-managed firms founded by the first generation automotive entrepreneurs proved incapable of challenging the 'big three', two of whom were widely regarded as typical of the new managerial organisations, General Motors and the Chrysler Corporation. The Chrysler Corporation was formed in 1924 from the bankrupt Maxwell Motor Car Co. whose history began in 1903. Owned by a succession of financial institutions, the Chrysler Corporation was none the less managed by Walter Chrysler from its foundation in 1908 until his retirement in 1935. Under his command Chrysler acquired the Dodge Motor Co. in 1927 and established a position among the 'big three' shortly after.[19]

Formed in 1908, the General Motors Corporation is often regarded as the corporate apotheosis of bureaucratic enterprise which, socially neutral and anonymous, came to epitomise the antithesis of the typical family, owner-managed firm. Yet, from the Du Pont reorganisation of GM after 1920 until the US government required GM's owners, the Du Pont Co., to relinquish ownership in the late 1950s, the affairs of GM were closely supervised by the Du Pont family. The Du Pont Co. was in turn controlled by the Christiana Securities Co. which was owned by the Du Pont family, some of whom were active members of the important supervisory committees of the board, the compensation and finance committees. This was the mechanism by which the transformation of GM, although administered through relatively extensive managerial hierarchies, was achieved.[20] Such a pattern in which external directors continued to possess a controlling share in the company, regularly participated in board and committee meetings, and exercised managerial supervision was the GM model which, though a special case in the precise structure and organisational detail of the form it took, none the less became more common as the size and financial demands of automobile enterprise rendered family succession increasingly problematical.

Ford carried, and carries still, the banner of family enterprise. That company's chequered history between and since the two world wars may be regarded as a direct consequence of the inhibiting influence of family ownership-control and management,[21] although by contrast General Motors' successful reorganisation and performance owed much to the influence and involvement of the Du Pont family.[22] After the withdrawal of Du Pont from General Motors in the late 1950s, Ford demonstrated the ability of a family firm to reach very large size, to be managed successfully, and to survive continuing competition from its most powerful American rival. Ford continued as an owner-managed firm with extensive managerial hierarchies, in which a third-generation Ford inherited control and leadership in the classic mould of family business. It was he who secured a transfusion of bureaucratic expertise from General Motors, thereby harnessing managerial skills as an instrument of radical modernisation of the Ford Motor Co., lifting it for a period after the Second World War from third to second place among the world's largest motor manufacturers.[23]

In Europe, despite the early advantage through the initial design and construction of cars, the existence of a less favourable middle-income market potential combined with a much slower advance of production methods and commercial development provided a more congenial financial environment for the engineer entrepreneurs, which tax and tariff protection perpetuated until after the Second World War. The willingness of some existing family firms to venture risk capital in markets unreceptive to mass-produced vehicles also favoured dominance in the industry by owner-managers. Both in France and Britain the early years of the industry saw company promotions of the kind which characterised the American experience, and in all three countries the newly created firms which succeeded in this industry began with a modest investment, usually obtained by the founders from their savings, from family, friends, or individual investors.[24] Of those European firms which survived the difficulties produced by the First World War and the highly competitive period which followed, all were owner-managed firms and most were managed by founder-owners.

The Renault Co. originated in the imaginative skills of Louis Renault and the commercial flair of his brother, Marcel, sons of a successful clothing manufacturer. Initial financial backing from the family, followed by early success, enabled Louis Renault to assume sole ownership by 1908. Reinvested profits and personal financial backing perpetuated absolute control and the exercise of managerial authority until his death in 1944.[25] In the case of Peugeot the substantial family resources in metal working provided the initial capital for the car-making venture undertaken by Les Fils de Peugeot Freres, although it was to be Armand Peugeot's separately formed enterprise specialising in car production which was to set the pace until financial difficulties began to threaten its future. When the head of Les Fils de Peugeot Freres died in 1907 the two firms merged, Armand consolidating family dominance.. Subsequent expansion of Automobiles et Cycles Peugeot occurred on the basis of family resources, supplemented by banking finance, but the family remained in control and continued to manage the company after Armand's death in 1915.[26]

In Germany the family sewing machine and bicycle factory of Opel provided the basis for car manufacture which began shortly after 1900;[27] management by the Opel brothers continued so long as the family was in control. This came to an end in 1929 when General Motors secured ownership in the public issue of that year. The British firms which pioneered large-scale manufacture during the inter-war years were the Austin Motor Co. and Morris Motors. External finance from personal backers, to Herbert Austin from a steel manufacturer, to W.R. Morris from an aristocrat, provided the initial foundations for the major British firms, although by 1914 Austin owned more than 50 per cent of the public company and W.R. Morris was sole owner of his firm, which did not offer shares to the public until 1936; even then the founder retained three-quarters of the ordinary stock.[28] There are resemblances between the financial origins of Morris Motors and Fabbrica Italiana d'Automobili Torino (FIAT), which when formed as a joint-stock company in 1899 was financed by two aristocrats, although the commercial affairs were in the hands of the company secretary, Giovanni Agnelli. Six years later Agnelli formed the R.I.B. ballbearing machine concern, which before long became a holding company possessing a controlling interest in Fiat. Managerial control remained in Agnelli's hands and later Fiat came under the direction of the third-generation Agnelli family.[29] Finally, Citroen, the shortest-lived of the major European companies with owner-manager characteristics, was established in 1914 by André Citroen, whose first business venture was transformed from gear cutting to munitions manufacture during the First World War. Citroen reconverted the plant for car production and, although loan capital was necessary to sustain the firm in the short run, commercial success earned profits sufficient to enable him to repay debts by 1924 and to reorganise the company in which henceforth he held 60 per cent of the stock as the self-styled 'administrateur unique'.[30]

## II

When the First World War ended, trends in innovation, output, growth, product development and price competition were similar in kind in Europe to those which had occurred in the United States before the war, and it was the introduction of American-style assembly line plants and the competition from American-owned subsidiaries which brought about increasing industrial concentration in the 1920s and 1930s. In Britain, France, and Germany the largest three producers accounted for more than 70 per cent of national car production by the mid-1930s, while in Italy Fiat alone exceeded that figure.[31] Industrial concentration deriving from the introduction of volume car production and price competition forced firms to invest heavily in plant and machinery in order to survive. This was the phase corresponding to that which had occurred in the United States before the First World War, during which the European managers faced an intensifying challenge to independence and survival.

Success and survival of the owner-managed companies before 1945 was due principally to commercial policies and, critically, the ability to withstand fluctuations in trade which in the downswings forced out firms lacking the strongest financial foundation. Thus, it was in order to survive a financial crisis that Opel accepted an overture from General Motors which, having obtained a majority shareholding in the public issue of 1928, appointed I.J. Reuter, general manager of the Olds division of General Motors, as Opel's managing director.[32] As for Citroen, financial difficulties had been a feature of the company's history since the beginning, and in the 1920s a French banking syndicate had reorganised the firm's finances, temporarily removing from André Citroen the sole managerial control and placing it in the hands of a Board of directors elected by preference and ordinary shareholders.[33] By the 1930s André Citroen had regained control from the Banque Lazard, only to founder in the aftermath of the Great Depression. In 1934 Michelin, a major creditor and a long-established soundly financed family firm, took over 66 per cent of the Citroen stock from the liquidator.[34]

Sir Herbert Austin was compelled to relinquish absolute control of his company as a result of the financial crisis of 1920–21, when considerable limitation of his personal executive power and the establishment of a Board committee of management was the price he had to pay to his creditors, notably the Midland Bank.[35] Attempts first to forge links with Ford and in 1924 to sell equity to General Motors were frustrated, in the latter instance in part by his co-directors who opposed an American solution to Austin's lingering financial difficulties. None the less, until his death in 1941 the founder retained his majority common stock shareholding. The dispersal of ownership of the Nuffield organisation began in 1936, although when merger with Austin occurred in 1952 Lord Nuffield was still the major, if not the majority, shareholder. It is interesting to note that just as Austin had been opposed, for similar reasons, by co-directors in 1924, Lord Nuffield also encountered opposition from his board in 1952. Retirement and the survival of the company he had founded were the reasons why he agreed to the merger to form BMC, to strengthen resistance against American competition.[36]

It was an extraordinary coincidence that neither of the two British leaders could perpetuate their companies in a second generation. Lord Nuffield's marriage was childless, while Lord Austin's son, groomed for succession, was killed on the western front in 1915. In Europe, only at Peugeot, where all six sons of Jules, Robert and Pierre followed their fathers on to the boards of the various Peugeot companies, were second- and third-generation family involved in management and control.[37] Agnelli directed Fiat until his death in 1945 when Vittorio Valetta, an experienced Fiat manager then aged 62, presided over an interregnum. Valetta died in 1966, whereupon two of Agnelli's grandsons, Giovanni and Umberto, resumed managerial dominance for the family.[38] Louis Renault's son was too young to be given responsibility before the company was nationalised in 1944, but a nephew by marriage, François Lehideux, who joined SAUR in 1931, had acted as an important aide to Renault during the 1930s.[39]

While the owner-managers of the motor industry until the Second World War were professional in the sense that they participated in top-level decision-making on a more or less full-time basis, they lacked the professional training which has been suggested as one possible criterion for identifying professionalism in management. Detailed information on this matter is difficult to discover and does not permit unequivocal generalisations. It is clear, however, that only in two instances did the founder acquire a formal professional training of any kind; Austin and Citroen were both qualified engineers. Armand and Robert Peugeot probably received training in the family firm as did the Opel brothers, although Carl Opel was dispatched to England to learn the skills of bicycle manufacture. Louis Renault has been described as a natural mechanic who learned by experience as a designer in an engineering works before launching his own enterprise; Henry Ford I and W.R. Morris were mechanics of sorts, both finding difficulty in reading a blueprint. Giovanni Agnelli's education was at military academy, followed by a career in the army. He was a self-taught mechanic who, on leaving the army, transformed his hobby, tinkering with cycles and engines, into a business venture, culminating in the formation of Fiat.[40] Three of the founding entrepreneurs, Henry Ford I, W.R. Morris and Herbert Austin, experienced early business failure.

The histories of Austin, Fiat, Ford and Morris reveal that while senior professional managers were appointed (at Austin by the company's creditors), the owner-managers themselves retained ultimate power, although somewhat less in Austin's case. They also suggest that, except in the case of Fiat, senior executives from outside the family were able to affect the company's history by exercising independent initiative only in the context of organisational anarchy. Non-family influence was present, despite company policy, and did not represent responsible delegation of managerial power. At Renault, family management underpinned family ownership, and in the 1930s the ageing Louis Renault extended managerial responsibility to a nephew by marriage.[41] Nationalisation ended family participation at Renault in 1945 and within only a few years after the Second World War ended, owner-managed motor producers in Europe had almost completely disappeared, the exceptions being Peugeot and, after an interlude between 1945 and 1966, Fiat, which together remained almost as archetypes of the traditional family firm.

We have excluded the Japanese experience from our review until now because the concept of the family firm translates uneasily into the Japanese business system in which, for the purpose of establishing an indigenous automobile industry, government intervention precipitated trust formation of the 'Japanese Incorporated' type.[42] When this strategy failed, the initiative in the establishment of an indigenous motor industry was seized in the 1930s by two of the younger Zaibatsu, Nissan and Toyoda. The former was a new Zaibatsu in which the leading figure, Yoshisuke Aikawa, found it necessary to finance a merger of his castings and components plant with the Dat car-making firm by forming a public company. The other major firm was Toyota which, while launching the car manufacturing enterprise simultaneously with Nissan, retained its character as an old established local Zaibatsu for which diversification from textiles to textile machinery, financing growth from internal resources, had proved a successful strategy.[43] No fewer than 11 members of the Toyoda family were active directors, vice-presidents, and presidents of the various companies owned by the family between 1920 and the 1970s, although family ownership of the Toyota Motor Co. ended with the financial crisis of 1949. Control passed to the banks, notably the Bank of Japan, and was followed by reorganisation, the establishment of an additional separate motor sales company, and the appointment as President of one of Toyota's sales managers, formerly with G.M.(Japan). At the same time, however, Kiichiro Toyoda, the founder, continued as President of the manufacturing organisation, although he and his board of directors resigned in the course of a labour dispute resulting from a reduction in the workforce in 1950. His successors were Taizo Ishida, hitherto for many years President of the Toyoda Automatic Loom Works, and Fukio Nakagawa of the Teikoku Bank, who it was intended should make way for Kiichiro Toyoda's reinstatement after the repercussions of the labour troubles of 1950 had disappeared. He died, however, in 1952 and cousin Eiji Toyoda succeeded as President.[44] In the mid-1970s both President and Vice-President of Toyota were Toyodas, while Tatsuro Toyoda was director of Toyota Motor Sales Co. Thus, despite the ownership of less than five per cent of share capital the family continues to influence major policy decisions in the management of Japan's largest and most profitable motor company, although these have been much affected, too, by the intervention of the Ministry of International Trade and Industry.[45]

We have charted the chronology of the decline of the family firm and owner-managers in the motor industry, and have identified financial factors as having been critical in their demise. This was the case in the history of the industry in the United States; while Citroen's bankruptcy, Opel's merger with G.M., and Austin's retreat from absolute control are each explained in these terms, too. A combination of the logic of American competition and the absence of heirs eventually brought Austin and Morris together to form B.M.C., the forerunners of British Leyland which, comparable with Renault's transformation to state enterprise, was a political decision. Those business leaders who succeeded in retaining ownership and control until the Second World War pursued conservative financial policies and tended to avoid the capital market.

With the exception of General Motors the growth of large firms in the motor industry before the 1950s occurred as a result of internal expansion rather than by merger, a process which proved favourable to the survival of family influence – although in none of these was family control and influence appreciably greater than that of the Du Ponts in the affairs of General Motors.[46] Since the Second World War financial difficulties, problems of succession and state intervention have hastened the transition between the old family partnership and the managerial bureaucratic enterprise. Chandler attributes Pierre Du Pont's success in transforming General Motors into a modern corporation in part to 'training, lineage, and personality'. These gave him managerial skills, commitment to making a career in the family firm and access to a pool of capital and favourable credit rating.[47]

III

Did the owner-management structure of firms, and in particular family-controlled influence, significantly affect behaviour and performance? For clues to what we might expect we may refer to the findings of economists based on research into the recent history of business organisation. Monsen and Downs have suggested that owner-controlled firms have been less averse to taking risky decisions than organisations described as managerial enterprises.[48] If we regard product policy as the test of risk aversion no clear picture emerges. During the decade prior to the Second World War the American manufacturers combined independent innovation with considerable price competition, whereas both in Britain and France, where owner-controlled enterprises were dominant, manufacturers competed by product differentiation and duplication of models, a policy designed to minimise risk.[49] Yet in all three countries in the 1930s imaginative model design and aggressive marketing saw the resounding, albeit temporary, success of Chrysler in the US, of Rootes and Standard in the UK, and of Citroen, followed by the Fiat-backed Simca, in France. Irrespective of control type, the large motor companies lost ground to the smaller risk-embracing firms reinvigorated by new management.[50] Other recent empirical studies of the relationship between ownership, control, and performance in large corporations, mainly in the period since 1950, suggest caution before concluding that the weakness in management identifiable in the owner-managers of the twentieth century were peculiar to owner-managed firms in general and to family firms in particular.

Reviewing numerous studies of the performance of large owner-manager controlled firms in the US, Kania and McKean concluded that returns on equity indicated both types of firms to have performed equally well and poorly in regard to profit realisation; that there was little support for the hypothesis that managers and owner-managers were motivated towards different goals, and that both sought to maximise owner welfare.[51] Other research on large UK enterprises suggested that owner-controlled firms tend to secure higher rates of profit on average than management-controlled firms and exhibit higher growth rates; although on a different sample another researcher found the difference between mean values of profits and growth rates for owner and managerially controlled firms were not statistically significant.[52] More recently, a study of large French firms by Jacquemin and de Ghellink found that profitability is not directly influenced by the type and control of the firm; however, the positive effect of the firm's size is significantly higher in the case of familial control as compared with non-familial control.[53] Family firms, it is suggested, seemed to be able to limit the internal bureaucratic inefficiencies linked with large size and to safeguard more profitable capital use. Non-family firms, however, achieved higher profitability as size increased. Their conclusion was that only a combination of size and divergent goals causes deviations from profit maximisation; when ownership and management were combined large size has a systematically better impact upon profitability than when separate.

Taken together, these most recent studies offer little support to the views commonly held by the economists and historians quoted earlier concerning the characteristics of behaviour and performance of family and owner-managed firms. And in so far as motivation and policy of such firms have been found to be similar, in some respects more positive compared with managerial organisations, the justification for attributing to the family and owner-managed firms the inhibiting influences absent in others is considerably diminished. In the United States and in Europe in the period before the 1960s when protected markets differed with respect to geography, taxation, income levels and distribution, and socio-cultural characteristics, factors other than family control or management are seen to have exercised greater influences on the performance of firms. Our review of the rise of the owner-managers before 1939 underlines the inventive and innovative contribution from both new and old established family firms. An informed American assessment of the state of three major European motor manufacturers in 1927, Citroen, Morris and Opel, included favourable remarks upon their productive equipment and commercial practices,[54] and A.P. Sloan made it clear at the time of the merger that in Opel, General Motors was acquiring very much more than a dying European duck.[55]

Historians have condemned W.R. Morris for refusing to merge with Austin in 1924, citing this as a case where the personal preference of the owner-manager seriously inhibited the development of the British motor industry. Such an argument depends upon the counterfactual assumption regarding the effectiveness of Morris's managerial skills, for he would have been chief executive in such a merger.[56] The Nuffield organisation was more profitable than its major British rivals, but at the same time between 1929 and 1939 the production of cars as a percentage of the Big Six fell from 51 per cent to 27 per cent. Overy makes the point that the firm encountered managerial problems in the early 1930s and after 1945, but that they are explicable in terms of a rate of growth which was too fast rather than a failure to grow at all, hardly the qualification to manage the reorganisation which the merger mooted in 1924 would have required. Austin, by contrast, had been prepared to merge with Morris, or with Ford or General Motors, yet it was his professional manager-directors appointed by Austin's creditors in 1921 who, anxious to maintain independence, resisted the proposal and rejected G.M.'s bid in 1924. For, while in terms of voting concentration the Austin Motor Co. was a personal enterprise, in fact Sir Herbert was a prisoner of his debenture holders and of the Bank. While we may not be able to explain the motives of his colleagues, Austin's attitude is clearly inexplicable without reference to the death of his only son and heir in 1915, which thus removed one of the principal driving forces typically regarded as fundamental to the aims and *raison d'être* of family enterprise. Lord Nuffield, on the other hand, also lacked an heir, yet refused to merge with Austin until after the latter's death and his own imminent retirement. Thereafter, the merger proved to be an alliance only in financial terms, while the failure to integrate and rationalise the two constituent organisations occurred even though the owner-managers and their families had long relinquished ownership, control and managerial participation.[57]

Henry Ford's attitude to his son was bizarre, denying Edsel Ford, by all accounts a worthy successor, participation in top-level decision-making. The ageing and eccentric Henry Ford hung on until Edsel's death, whereupon illness and family pressure precipitated Henry II's assumption of power, by which time the company's fortunes had slumped.[58] At Fiat a long hiatus occurred between the founder Agnelli's leadership and his grandsons' resumption of family power, when Jan Agnelli became the leading figure in the family-owned firm; but in the interim the chairman was internally recruited from Fiat's managers.[59] There has been little detailed evidence on training for succession in these firms before the Second World War, although the impression is of minimal preparation, based on experience within the family firm. Yet Ford, Peugeot, and Fiat survived the 1930s with second- or third-generation connections by ownership and management continuing to influence the course of industrial change in competition with the managerial firms and the corporate personalities which guided their fortunes. Thus, while owner-managed firms could be seriously affected one way or another by idiosyncratic decision, since that time owner-managing families have shown imagination either by widening the sources of management recruitment or by ensuring adequate preparation of family heirs for involvement in top-level decision-making. In each of the post-war generation of the Agnelli, Ford, Peugeot and Toyota families are to be found graduates, mostly from Harvard, in engineering or business.

Since the late 1950s Ford has struggled to retain just less than a quarter of the US market, compared with an average of 45 per cent held by G.M. In Europe Ford led G.M. in production and profitability, and both of the American subsidiaries showed superior profit records over the indigenous volume car manufacturers. Among all European car-makers Peugeot was the leading producer in the 1970s, followed by Fiat; and with the exception of Volkswagen, Peugeot, followed by Fiat, was the most profitable.[60] In 1979 approximately 40 per cent of the vehicles produced by the world's largest ten motor manufacturers came from firms in which entrepreneurial families played a major managerial role.[61] Family enterprise, bureaucratised as in the case of Ford, or of the traditional variety as at Peugeot and Fiat, demonstrates the continuing ability of the family influence to thrive, though more successfully, hitherto, in the more traditional European markets for motor cars where, until the 1950s, the scale of financial commitments required for effective national and international competition rendered the retreat, though not defeat, of family dominance inevitable. Finally, unlike the dynasties of Europe which are protected by majority shareholdings, or that of the US where a significant minority control has buttressed the Ford family's managerial authority, the continuing influence of the Toyoda dynasty depends, it seems, entirely upon non-financial considerations. Such variation between countries and firms suggests that in the motor industry there has been no simple automatic correlation between type of control, managerial style and performance. Increasingly the survival of owner-managed firms came to depend upon large-scale capital investment, organisation and professional management skills and training suited to a large modern co-operation; these were the principal considerations which in the motor industry led to the retreat of families from control as well as from management.

The persistence of a business elite, whether originating in founder families or within the corporate structure long after an economic justification has disappeared, is of intrinsic interest and testifies to the resilience, despite some discontinuities, of those remaining entrepreneurial families, three of which possess business histories pre-dating the motor car by several generations. However, the convergence of structure and behavioural characteristics of the family manager and owner-managed firm, varying in the extent of hierarchical control, points to its lack of analytical and explanatory significance. Our evidence from the international motor industry suggests that even in very large firms it would be unwarranted to infer either strengths or weaknesses in performance from the mere fact of family ownership or management.

*University of East Anglia, Norwich*

## NOTES

A shorter version of this article was presented as a paper to the Eighth International Economic History Congress, Budapest, 1982; Section B9, 'From Family Firm to Professional Management: Structure and Performance of Business Enterprise'. I am grateful for the comments of those who participated in the discussion or who offered observations on an earlier draft.

1. See the discussion in Theo Nicholas, *Ownership Control and Ideology* (1969), pp.19–21; Robert J. Larner, *Management Control and the Large Corporation* (New York, 1970), pp.63–6; C.S. Beed, 'The Separation of Ownership from Control', *Journal of Economic Studies,* Vol.I (1966), pp.29–46; Philip H. Burch Jr., *The Managerial Revolution Reassessed* (Lexington, MA, 1972), pp.5–19; P. Sargant Florence, *The Logic of British and American Industry* (1953), Ch.V.

2. S. Nyman and A. Silberston, 'The Ownership and Control of Industry', *Oxford Economic Papers*, N.S. Vol.30 (1978), pp.74-8. See also M. Useem, 'Corporations and the Corporate Elite', *Annual Review of Sociology*, Vol.6 (1980), pp.41-69; A. Francis, 'Families, Firms and Finance Capital: The Development of U.K. Industrial Firms with Particular Reference to their Ownership and Control', *Sociology*, Vol.14 (1980), pp.1-26; M. Zeitlin, 'Corporate Ownership and Control: The Large Corporation and the Capitalist Class', *American Journal of Sociology*, Vol.79 (1974), pp.1073-115.

3. A.A. Berle and G.C. Means, *The Modern Corporation and Private Property* (New York, 1937), pp.84-90.

4. Alfred D. Chandler, *The Visible Hand. The Managerial Revolution in American Business* (London, 1979), pp.8-10.

5. N.H. Leff, 'Industrial Organisation and Entrepreneurship in the Developing Countries: The Economic Group', *Economic Development and Cultural Change*, Vol.26 (1978), pp.331-52; J. Kocka, 'Family and Bureaucracy in German Industrial Management, 1815-1914', *Business History Review*, Vol.45 (1971), pp.133-56.

6. Alfred D. Chandler Jr., 'The Development of Modern Management Structure in the U.S. and U.K.', in Leslie Hannah (ed.), *Management Strategy and Business Development* (London, 1976), p.28; A. Jacquemin and E. de Ghellinck, 'Familial Control, Size and Performance in the Largest French Firms', *European Economic Review*, Vol.13 (1980).

7. Sargant Florence, op. cit., pp.295, 303-4, 320.

8. C.F. Carter and B.R. Williams, *Investment in Innovation* (London, 1958), p.40.

9. Charles P. Kindleberger, *Economic Growth in France and Britain, 1850-1950* (Cambridge, MA, 1964), pp.124-7.

10. Alfred D. Chandler Jr., 'The Growth of the Transnational Industrial Firm in the U.S. and the U.K.; A Comparative Analysis', *Economic History Review*, Vol.33 (1980), pp.402-6.

11. Hannah, *Management Strategy and Business Development*, pp.12, 195-6.

12. Richard Tilly, 'The Growth of Large Scale Enterprise in Germany since the mid 19th Century', in H.D. Daems and H. Van der Wee (eds.), *The Rise of Managerial Capitalism* (Louvain, 1974), p.156.

13. Jurgen Kocka, 'Entrepreneurs and Managers in German Industrialisation', *The Cambridge Economic History of Europe*, Vol.VII, Part 1 (Cambridge, 1978), pp.580-81.

14. David S. Landes, *The Unbound Prometheus. Technological Change and Industrial Development in Western Europe from 1750 to the Present* (Cambridge, 1969), pp.527-8.

15. James M. Laux, *In First Gear. The French Automobile Industry to 1914* (Liverpool, 1976), p.200.

16. However, Payne admitted that this might be a weak hypothesis, referring to Hannah's speculation that variability of performance between firms of contrasting structure might undermine such a conclusion. Peter L. Payne, 'Family Business in Britain: An Historical and Analytical Survey', in Akio Okochi and Shigeaki Yasuoka (eds.), *Family Business in the Era of Industrial Growth* (Tokyo, 1984), p.197; Leslie Hannah, 'Visible and Invisible Hands in Great Britain', in A.D. Chandler and H. Daems (eds.), *Managerial Hierarchies* (Cambridge, MA, 1980), p.55.

17. For an overall analysis of the rise of the American industry, see R.D. Kennedy, *The Automobile Industry* (New York, 1941), Chs.3 and 4; John B. Rae, *The American Automobile* (Chicago, 1969), Chs.1-4. An analysis focusing upon the social aspects of business enterprise is to be found in Donald F. Davis, 'The Social Determinants of Success in the American Industry before 1929', an unpublished paper presented at the Colloque International on 'L'incidence de l'environment exterieur sur l'industrie automobile mondiale', Breau sans Nappe, 1981.

18. Donald F. Davis, loc. cit.

19. Rae, op. cit., pp.100-1.

20. Alfred D. Chandler Jr. and Stephen Salsbury, *Pierre S. Du Pont and the Making of the Modern Corporation* (New York, 1971), pp.564-6, 572, 580-87.

21. Allan Nevins and Frank Ernest Hill, *Ford, Decline and Rebirth 1933-62* (New York, 1963), Chs.I-XII; Harold Livesay, 'Entrepreneurial Persistence through the Bureaucratic Age', *Business History Review*, Vol.LI (1977), pp.431-44.

22. Chandler and Salsbury, *Pierre S. Du Pont*, p.598.

23. Kennedy, op. cit., pp.18–36; Harold Livesay, op. cit., pp.431–43.
24. Donald F. Davis, loc. cit., S.B. Saul, 'The Motor Industry in Britain to 1914', *Business History*. Vol.V (1962), p.31; Laux, op. cit., pp.200–1.
25. P. Fridenson, *Histoire des Usines Renault;* Vol. 1 (Paris, 1972), pp.60, 124.
26. R. Sedillot, *Peugeot: de la crinoline à la 404* (Paris, 1960), pp.58–78.
27. H. Hauser, *Opel. Eindeutches Tor zur Welt* (Frankfurt, 1937), pp.99, 104, 110, 119.
28. Roy Church, *Herbert Austin. The British Motor Industry to 1941* (London, 1979), pp.175–6; P.W.S. Andrews and Elizabeth Brunner, *The Life of Lord Nuffield* (Oxford, 1955), p.66–7, 89–90, 209–11, 214.
29. Franco Arnatori, 'Entrepreneurial Typology in the History of Industrial Italy 1880–1960: A Review Article', *Business History Review*, Vol.LIV (1980), No.3, pp.372–4; Arnolda Mondadori (ed.), *Fiat, A Fifty Year Record* (Turin, 1951), pp.37, 75.
30. H.H. Kelly, 'Development of the Citroen Company', *U.S. Commerce Reports,* 18 July 1927, p.136.
31. George Maxcy and Aubrey Silbertson, *The Motor Industry* (London, 1959), pp.115–21; Fridenson, op. cit., p.181; Hauser, op. cit., p.186; Gerald Bloomfield, *The World Automotive Industry* (North Pomfret, VT), p.299.
32. Alfred P. Sloan Jr., *My Life with General Motors* (Garden City, NY, 1967), p.351.
33. *U.S. Commerce Report,* 18 July 1927.
34. John Sheahan, 'Government Competition and the Performance of the French Automobile Industry', *Journal of Industrial Economics,* Vol.8 (1959–60), p.450.
35. Church, *Herbert Austin,* pp.64–5.
36. R.J. Overy, *William Morris, Viscount Nuffield* (London, 1976), p.98; Graham Turner, *The Leyland Papers* (London, 1971), pp.95–9.
37. Sedillot, op. cit., p.130.
38. Bloomfield, op. cit., p.300.
39. Fridenson, op. cit., pp.124, 283.
40. Valerio Castronovo, *Giovanni Agnelli* (Turin, 1971), Chs.1 and 2.
41. Fridenson, op. cit., p.283.
42. Masaru Udagawa and Seishi Nakamura, 'Japanese Business and Government in the Inter-war Period', *Government and Business* (Tokyo, 1980), pp.93–6.
43. Shotaro Kamiya, *My Life with Toyota* (Tokyo, 1976), pp.31–41, 49–55, 100–1.
44. Ibid.
45. I am grateful to Professor Koichi Shimokawa for this information. See also Masaru Udagawa, 'Historical Development of the Japanese Automobile Industry 1917–1971: Business and Government', presented to the Colloque International, 'Incidence de l'environment exterieur sur l'industrie automobile mondiale', Breau sans Nappe, 1981.
46. Chandler and Salsbury, *Pierre S. Du Pont,* pp.593–7.
47. Ibid., pp.599–600.
48. K.J. Monsen and A. Downs, 'The Behaviour of the Large Managerial Firm', *Journal of Political Economy,* Vol.73 (1965), pp.231–4.
49. Maxcy and Silbertson, op. cit., pp.140–41; Sheahan, loc.cit., pp.202–3.
50. Roy Church and Michael Miller, 'The Big Three: Competition, Management and Marketing in the British Motor Industry 1922–1939' in Barry Supple (ed.), *Essays in British Business History* (Cambridge, 1977), pp.108–83.
51. John J. Kania and John R. McKean, 'Ownership, Control and the Contemporary Corporation: A General Behaviour Analysis', *Kyklos,* Vol.29 (1976), pp.272–87.
52. H.K. Radice, 'Control Type, Profitability and Growth in Large Firms: An Empirical Study', *Economic Journal,* Vol.81 (1971), pp.547–62; P. Holl, 'Effect of Control Type on the Performance of the Firm in the UK', *Journal of Industrial Economics,* Vol.23, No.4 (1974–5), pp.257–71.
53. Alexis Jacquemin and Elizabeth de Ghellink, 'Familial Control, Size and Performance in the Largest French Firms', *European Economic Review,* Vol.13 (1980), p.35.
54. Carl Hicks and G. D. Babcock, 'The Automobile Situation in the World and Europe in 1927', a typescript report to the President of the Dodge Motor Corporation, Detroit Public Library, 1927; H.H. Kelly, 'Automotive Products; Distribution of American

Automotive Products in Europe', *United States Bureau of Foreign and Domestic Commerce* (1928).

55. Sloan, op. cit., pp.349–50.
56. Church, op. cit., pp.103, 142; Overy, op. cit., p.124.
57. K. Cowling, *Mergers and Economic Performance* (Cambridge, 1980), Ch. 6, 'Engineering'.
58. Allan Nevins and Frank Ernest Hill, *Ford, Decline and Rebirth 1933*–1962 (New York, 1962), pp.228, 248–51.
59. In 1980 the Agnelli family owned 80 per cent of the capital. I am grateful to Signor G. Sapelli for this information.
60. For comparisons see the relevant tables in Krish Bhasker, *The Future of the World Motor Industry* (London, 1980), pp.93, 105, 162, 165, 220, 230.
61. Jean Pierre Bardan, Jean Jacques Chanaron, Patrick Fridenson, James M. Laux, *The Automobile Revolution. The Impact of an Industry* (Chapel Hill, 1982), Table 9.5.

For Product Safety Concerns and Information please contact our EU
representative  GPSR@taylorandfrancis.com
Taylor & Francis Verlag GmbH, Kaufingerstraße 24, 80331 München, Germany

www.ingramcontent.com/pod-product-compliance
Ingram Content Group UK Ltd.
Pitfield, Milton Keynes, MK11 3LW, UK
UKHW042200240425
457818UK00005B/28